MASTERING
LOTUS NOTES
AND DOMINO R5
PREMIUM EDITION

MASTERING™
LOTUS® NOTES®
AND DOMINO™ R5
PREMIUM EDITION

Scot Haberman
Andrew Falciani
Matt Riggsby

SYBEX®

San Francisco • Paris • Düsseldorf • Soest • London

Associate Publishers: Guy Hart-Davis, Amy Romanoff
Contracts and Licensing Manager: Kristine O'Callaghan
Acquisitions & Developmental Editor: Maureen Adams
Editors: Judy Flynn, Raquel Baker
Project Editor: Ed Copony
Technical Editors: Stacey Grandbois, Heather Urtheil
Book Designers: Patrick Dintino, Catalin Dulfu,
Franz Baumhackl
Graphic Illustrator: Tony Jonick
Electronic Publishing Specialists: Franz Baumhackl,
Grey Magauran
Project Team Leaders: Teresa Trego, Shannon Murphy
Proofreaders: Susan Berge, Patrick J. Peterson
Indexer: Ted Laux
Companion CD: Ginger Warner, Kara Schwartz
Cover Designer: Design Site
Cover Illustrator/Photographer: Jack D. Myers,
Design Site

Library of Congress Card Number: 99-69362
ISBN: 0-7821-2635-9

Manufactured in the United States of America

10 9 8 7 6 5 4 3 2 1

ACKNOWLEDGMENTS

We would like to thank all of the members of the Sybex staff for their help in producing *Mastering Lotus Notes R5*, from which this book was derived. Writing a book is quite a complicated process, one that involves many individuals. We would like to thank the acquisitions and developmental editor, Maureen Adams, and the project editor, Ed Copony. A big thanks goes to our editor, Judy Flynn. She did an outstanding job of editing the manuscript thoroughly and quickly. We would also like to thank Stacey Grandbois, technical editor; Franz Baumhackl, desktop publisher; Tony Jonick and Jerry Williams, graphic artists; Teresa Trego, project team leader; Susan Berge, proofreader; and Ginger Warner, who created the companion CD.

Many thanks to author Matt Riggsby, who was a tremendous help by writing Chapters 5, 6, 22, and 23–28.

Scot and Andrew would also like to extend their gratitude to their employer, Electronic Data Systems. The work experience we gained at EDS gave us the knowledge necessary to complete this endeavor.

Scot would like to thank his wife, Kim; daughter, Sydney; and friends who gave him the incentive and drive necessary to make this book a success. Without their encouragement, he would have never made it.

Andrew would like to thank his wife, Lenora; and sons, Andrew and Alexander, for all of their support and encouragement during this project.

For the premium edition, Matt thanks, in no particular order, Maureen Adams for getting him involved in this project in the first place; the authors of the original edition, Scot Haberman and Andrew Falciani for many useful suggestions and advice, as well as for Chapter 29; Thom Dyson for a series of business decisions ultimately leading to him being qualified to work on this book; Raquel Baker for ably editing the new material; Heather Urtheil for an exquisite job of technical editing; and Grey Magauran, Shannon Murphy, and Patrick J. Peterson for making sure that the material before you is both legible and has all the proper spelling.

CONTENTS AT A GLANCE

TABLE OF CONTENTS

PART II • MASTERING THE BASICS

PART IV • CONFIGURING NOTES 5

13 Setting Up Notes as a Domino Client — 379

14 Setting Up Notes as an Internet Client — 399

PART V • BEYOND THE CLIENT: UTILIZING DOMINO DESIGNER

15 Introducing Domino Designer — 409

APPENDICES

INTRODUCTION

Folks today need a tool to help manage the information inundating them on a daily basis. Notes Release 5 is that tool. It's the first integrated mail client to provide a rich environment for bringing together all of the types of electronic information you encounter from the widest array of sources. Whether it's e-mail from your personal Internet account or your company's internal infrastructure, Web pages from the Internet or your company's intranet, or collaborative workflow applications running on Domino servers, Notes Release 5 handles it all. And Release 5 presents all of this information in a common interface, making it easier for you to complete your work without the technology getting in the way.

Release 5 combines core functionality that allows you to manage your contacts, e-mail, schedule, and tasks with Internet support for browsing, messaging, directory services, and collaboration (Usenet support) to provide a powerful yet easy-to-use environment for managing all of your information. This is in addition to being the client side for the broadest, most scalable architecture ever for developing and deploying collaborative applications. Whether you are using Notes alone to access Internet-based information or using it in a global enterprise to interact with Domino-based applications, Release 5 is built to support your requirements for a powerful, integrated information-management client.

Target Audience for This Book

Mastering Lotus Notes and Domino R5 Premium Edition adds more than 250 pages of advanced material to the best-selling *Mastering Lotus Notes R5*. This edition builds on the fundamentals of how Notes works to teach you more about how to build your own Notes applications, guiding you from conception to deployment. We wrote *Mastering Lotus Notes and Domino R5 Premium Edition* for the beginning to intermediate Notes end-user. Whether you are new to Notes or upgrading to R5, this book will get you up and running with Notes mail, scheduling and calendaring, database functions, and beyond. We included a glimpse into the Domino Developer for those users who want to ramp up their skills and become power users by developing their own Notes and Web applications. We also included information on how to integrate Notes with a Personal Data Assistant (PDA) and how to design forms, views, and applications for your PDA.

What's New in Notes R5

Significant changes have been made for Notes R5. This release marks the complete separation of the client (Notes client), the server (Domino server), and the designer (Domino Designer). This book will provide in-depth discussions of all the improvements for both the Notes client and the Domino Designer products.

The Notes Client

The Notes client is totally redesigned in its look and in its functionality. Here are some of the most important improvements in the Notes client:

- A browser-oriented user interface
- Internet client capabilities
- Enhanced mail and calendaring
- The Welcome page
- Bookmarks
- Personal information management
- Flexible Web access
- Search enhancements
- Mobile client enhancements
- Personal Digital Assistant (PDA) support

Domino Designer

Release 5 also includes significant enhancements for Domino Designer:

- Bookmarks
- Tabbed windows
- New design elements
- What-You-See-Is-What-You-Get (WYSIWYG) HTML editor
- A new interface for developers
- Easy integration with enterprise data
- Industry standards support
- Multi-client support
- Multilingual application support

Because the Release 5 product line has been completely revamped, it is difficult to list all the features in one place. You'll find in-depth discussions of all of the new features and capabilities throughout this book. Chapter 1 contains a brief overview of new features in the section, "What's New in Notes 5."

How This Book Is Organized

This book is organized into six parts, making it easy for you to find the information you need.

Part I: Introducing Notes 5

Part I introduces Notes and how best to use the Notes client. It covers in detail the newly designed user interface and how you can be more productive using the Notes client as your source for both personal and enterprise information. It also covers the basic features of Notes, such as databases, views, and documents, along with Notes core functionality of managing personal information.

Chapter 1: What Is Lotus Notes?

Chapter 1 provides an overview of the Notes client—what it is and how it can be used as an effective personal information management tool. There is also a section that covers many of the new features that are specific to the Notes client.

Chapter 2: Getting Familiar with Notes

Chapter 2 covers the new client user interface—everything from the Welcome page and the application window to using the integrated Notes Help facility.

Chapter 3: Working with Notes Databases

In Chapter 3, you'll find an explanation of the basics Notes database concepts. We'll discuss the relationship between the three main Notes document types and how to use forms and views to interact with the Notes data.

Chapter 4: Introducing the Core Databases

Chapter 4 introduces the four basic databases included within any good personal information manager: the address book, mail, calendaring and scheduling, and the Task Center (or To Do lists). You'll learn how to add Contacts to your Personal Address Book, send and receive e-mail, create appointments and other calendar entries, and take control of your tasks.

Part II: Mastering the Basics

Part II gives you an in-depth look at the basic yet powerful functions included within the Notes client. It describes how to better use Notes mail, calendaring and scheduling, collaboration, and workflow.

Chapter 5: Communicating with Notes Mail

Chapter 5 explains how to use Notes mail as an Internet mail client and as an enterprise mail client. The topics include using the Address dialog box, organizing your mail, and creating special types of mail messages. This chapter also includes sections on the Out of Office feature and Notes Minder.

Chapter 6: Calendaring and Scheduling

Chapter 6 will show you how to better understand and use the calendaring and scheduling features of Notes, as both a stand-alone client and in the enterprise environment. You'll learn how to navigate the calendar, set calendar preferences, create calendar entries, and use your calendar to work with others.

Chapter 7: Using Other Notes Databases

Chapter 7 shows you how to use the personal journal, discussion, and Document Library databases. It includes instructions for keeping a personal journal, using discussions to collaborate with coworkers, and managing a Document Library.

Chapter 8: Searching for Information

Chapter 8 covers the four most common ways to search for information within Notes. You can search for text in documents and for documents in views. You can also search a Domino domain or the Internet.

Part III: Advanced Use of Notes 5

Part III introduces some of the more advanced features of the Notes client. Although they are not difficult to master, they require a bit more understanding of the inner workings of the Notes client, Domino servers, and communications.

Chapter 9: Working with Notes Away from the Office

In Chapter 9, you'll learn how to use Notes to work with your information remotely. You don't need to be connected to a Domino server to take advantage of powerful Notes features. This chapter also includes sections on working with database replicas and connecting to Domino servers through dial-up communications.

Chapter 10: Harnessing the Power of the Internet

Chapter 10 explains how you can take full advantage of the Internet for enhancing your Notes client. This chapter shows how the Notes client has been based on Internet standards and how these standards can help you unleash the power woven throughout the Notes client product.

Chapter 11: Integrating Notes with Other Applications

Chapter 11 demonstrates how you can import and export information to and from your Notes client. The information you need is not always accessible from within Notes, so there are quite a few options that allow you to move information freely, such as attaching files, using the Windows Clipboard, and using the Notes mail migration tools.

Chapter 12: Securing Your Data

Chapter 12 covers the security standards inherent in Notes and Domino. Since its inception, the security model behind Notes has been extremely sophisticated, and this chapter will explain what this means to you and how to implement a security policy to help protect your data.

Part IV: Configuring Notes 5

The chapters in Part IV focus on the flexibility of the Notes client. Depending on your situation, you can use the Notes client to access a Domino server (typically in a corporate environment) or as an Internet client (typically at home). As an end user, you can set up and configure a Notes client to access both your work server and the Internet for the best of both worlds.

Chapter 13: Setting Up Notes as a Domino Client

Chapter 13 explains the various preferences and settings that can be changed so you can use Notes to connect to a Domino server. It also covers the bookmarks and subscriptions databases and how to use the log database to troubleshoot problems.

Chapter 14: Setting Up Notes as an Internet Client

In Chapter 14, you'll learn how to change the preferences and settings so you can use Notes to connect to the Internet. It includes a description of Internet-only user preferences and Internet-only Personal Address Book settings.

Part V: Beyond the Client: Utilizing Domino Designer

Part V introduces you to the development side of Notes: using the Domino Designer development tool to develop Notes and Web applications and recognizing the various design elements that make up a Notes database. This section includes chapters that demonstrate how to incorporate automation into your applications and how to use the LotusScript programming language.

Chapter 15: Introducing Domino Designer

Chapter 15 examines the various components of the integrated development environment (IDE) that a developer uses when creating an application. It also shows you how to navigate the Domino Designer development environment.

Chapter 16: Creating Your First Database

Chapter 16 explains how to create your first database and the various database options that can affect the performance of a Notes application. It includes tutorials on the different ways you can create a database and information to help you keep your databases secure.

Chapter 17: Understanding the Formula Language

Chapter 17 shows you how to use formulas in the various design elements. It explains what a formula is, the different types of formulas, where they can be used, and the different editors incorporated into the IDE for manipulating the formula code.

Chapter 18: Using Forms to Collect Data

Chapter 18 introduces you to Notes forms and how to create them. It also explains the properties of a form and the basic elements that can be used on a form.

Chapter 19: Advanced Form Design

Chapter 19 details the more advanced design elements that can be used on a form (such as subforms, sections, and layout regions) and how they can differ when used in a Notes application versus a Web application. You'll also learn how to use Actions and hotspots and add graphics to your forms.

Chapter 20: Using Views and Folders

Chapter 20 covers views: the elements that make up a view, how to create a view, and view options. This chapter also explains the differences between folders and views and how to use Navigators with views for a more graphical user interface.

Chapter 21: Outlines, Pages, and Framesets

Chapter 21 covers the newest design elements (outlines, pages, and framesets) for creating robust applications for both a Notes client and for the Web.

Chapter 22: Using Agents to Automate Processes

Chapter 22 explains how to incorporate automation into your Notes applications. It covers Agents: what they are, how to create them, and establishing permissions and security for them.

Chapter 23: Language Extensions

Chapter 23 explains the fundamentals of using the object-oriented programming language LotusScript. You'll learn where you can use LotusScript, the basic structure of a LotusScript program, how to comment and debug your scripts, and how to use LotusScript classes to access and manipulate familiar Notes database objects.

Part VI: Developing Databases

Part VI goes beyond pre-built databases and individual design elements and into the realm of application design. This section addresses how to make applications functional, navigable, stable, and secure while incorporating advanced features and using more advanced programming techniques.

Chapter 24: Developing Applications

Chapter 24 considers a number of issues surrounding developing Notes databases, including appropriate applications for Notes and difficulties posed by developing for different environments. This chapter also discusses constructing error-resistant and secure applications.

Chapter 25: Tips, Tricks, and Good Ideas

Chapter 25 is about moving data between people, between formats, and between platforms. It discusses ways of structuring workflow and using data from other applications, including text, OLE-capable applications, and relational databases. It also deals with some advanced LotusScript techniques and how to modify existing databases.

Chapter 26: Web-Enabling Your Applications

Chapter 26 shows you how to take databases to the Web, including how to combine Notes design elements with HTML, incorporate JavaScript into Notes-generated documents, use Agents to process Web input, and search Web content with Domino's powerful search tools.

Chapter 27: An Example Notes Application: Help Desk

Chapter 27 discusses the first of two sample applications: a help desk incident tracking system. It describes the intended goals of the application and explains how the database was constructed to achieve those goals, element by element.

Chapter 28: Another Example Notes Application: The Research Island Web Site

Chapter 28 discusses the second sample application, a Web site for publicizing the results of an ongoing research project. This is a more complex application, incorporating more elaborate Web features and automatic data-maintenance tools.

Chapter 29: Integrating Your PDA with Notes R5

Chapter 29 explains how to create a Notes application that can be placed on your PalmPilot with the help of the PylonPro software. We create a sample application and explain some of the benefits and drawbacks to using a PDA for synchronizing your Notes data.

Appendix A: Installing Lotus Notes 5

Appendix A includes step-by-step instructions for installing the Notes client and Domino Designer on your computer. It covers both upgrading from a previous release and installing from scratch.

Appendix B: Predefined Notes Fields

Appendix B lists some of the not-so-obvious fields that can be used in your Notes applications.

What's on the CD

The companion CD for this book contains a set of programs and files from all three of the authors, including the complete applications presented in Chapters 27 and 28, and various third-party companies. You may want to copy the files to your computer's hard drive so that you can modify them as you learn the material. The authors have included sample databases to use with the examples in the text and various products that you can use to create and manage Domino-based Web sites and to enhance Lotus Notes databases.

Conventions Used in This Book

This book uses a number of conventions to present information in as readable a manner as possible. Tips, Notes, and Warnings, shown here, appear from time to time in the text to call attention to specific highlights.

 TIP   This is a Tip. Tips contain specific product information.

 NOTE   This is a Note. Notes contain important side discussions.

 WARNING   This is a Warning. Warnings call attention to bugs, design omissions, and other trouble spots.

This book takes advantage of several font styles. **Bold font** in text indicates something that the user types. A `monospaced font` is used for code; output; URLs; commands; functions; classes; conditions; values; parameters; and file, folder, and directory names.

Chapters 24 through 29 use a continuation arrow symbol (➡) to show code that is continued on the same line. The code appears on separate lines in the book due to space constraints.

Summary

Notes has been completely redesigned with Release R5. Notes is still an extremely powerful groupware package, but it has been combined with the power and flexibility of the Internet. Combine these capabilities with the Domino server, and you have an extremely powerful tool for both corporate and personal communication and information. As we will demonstrate throughout the book, the list of tasks that can be performed with Notes is virtually endless. With Release 5, Notes is the best solution for an integrated management client.

PART I

Introducing Notes 5

CHAPTER 1

What Is Lotus Notes?

otes is a powerful, integrated information management client. It can help you manage your e-mail, Contacts, schedule, and tasks, and it can act as an Internet client. With Release 5, you can browse Internet or intranet Web sites while connected to the network or retrieve previously browsed information offline. You can search for Contacts in LDAP-based directories on the Internet or your company's intranet. Release 5 can integrate your POP and IMAP mail accounts into a single, universal Inbox. It will even allow you to participate in Usenet discussions on the Internet, online and offline. And Notes does all of this through a consistent, integrated interface.

Lotus Notes is also the client-side software of the Lotus Notes/Domino family of products that provide you with the most complete solution for effectively communicating and collaborating among teams, groups, and entire enterprises. It can be used within environments that include Domino servers or within environments entirely based on Internet-related services, such as Hypertext Transfer Protocol (HTTP)/Hypertext Markup Language (HTML), Light Directory Access Protocol (LDAP), Post Office Protocol version 3 (POP3)/Internet Message Access Protocol (IMAP)/Simple Mail Transfer Protocol (SMTP), Network News Transfer Protocol (NNTP), and so on.

Uses of Notes

Notes can be used in a variety of personal and business situations. You can use Notes with your Internet Service Provider (ISP) account to communicate with family and friends or to access the full range of Web-based information. As a tool for those involved with small businesses, Notes can be used with an ISP account to communicate with colleagues or customers, keep up with changes affecting the industry, research business opportunities, and stay competitive. Combined with Domino, Notes can unleash the full potential of teams, departments, and entire enterprises.

The Core Functionality of Notes

No matter how you plan to use Notes, either as an Internet client or a Domino client, you can start out by recording your personal information. Notes includes core functionality that lets you manage your personal information as follows:

- Store contact information
- Manage your schedule using the built-in calendar
- Take control of your tasks by entering items in the To Do list
- Keep a personal journal

Contact information is stored and managed using the Notes's built-in Personal Address Book. You can think of this as your electronic Rolodex. Notes enables you to store a wide variety of information about each Contact, including phone numbers, addresses, e-mail addresses, and so on. By recording your Contact information in Notes, you eliminate the need for paper address books.

Notes includes a calendar for you to keep track of your schedule. You can enter appointments, anniversaries, reminders, and events just as you can on a paper calendar. The calendar is also used for group scheduling if you are participating in a Domino-based collaboration environment.

There is even a personal To Do list in Notes. It contains personal task entries that can include, for example, priorities, status, and start/due dates. Your To Do list also contains group To Do items assigned to you if you are participating in a Domino-based collaboration environment.

Also, Notes includes a personal journal that can be used to store other information. If Notes is used in conjunction with a 3Com PalmPilot or IBM WorkPad personal digital assistant (PDA), your personal journal is synchronized with your PDA's memo pad application. This makes the personal journal a convenient place to store information you may need when you're away from your desk, such as a travel itinerary, notes for a meeting, or directions.

Notes as an Internet Information Client

If you plan to use Notes as an Internet client, you'll have the following added capability:

- You can receive e-mail from one or more POP/IMAP mail accounts and send mail to any SMTP server.
- You can access LDAP-based directories, such as Bigfoot and Four11, to search for people.
- You can participate in Usenet-based discussions.
- You can browse Internet or intranet Web sites.

As a full-featured messaging client, Notes can be configured to retrieve POP mail and copy it to your local mail database. It can be configured to retrieve IMAP mail and copy it to your local mail database, access IMAP mail accounts online, and even replicate a copy of an IMAP mail account to a locally stored database for offline use. Notes can be configured to send outbound messages directly to an SMTP server. For message content, Notes supports a wide range of standards, including Multipurpose Internet Mail Extension (MIME), Secure Multipurpose Internet Mail Extension (S/MIME), HTML, and X.509 certificates.

Whether you are using Notes to access the Internet or an intranet, you can use LDAP directories to search for people or to address e-mail. On the Internet, you can configure Notes to access popular directories, such as Bigfoot and Four11. On an intranet, you can use Notes to access your corporate directory, assuming it has been made available through LDAP.

Notes can be configured as a newsreader too. This means that you can participate in Internet-based Usenet discussions in the same familiar interface you use with your e-mail. Also, Notes allows you to replicate newsgroups to a local database so you can interact offline or use Notes's powerful full-text search capabilities.

For browsing, Notes provides two integrated solutions. First, Notes includes a native browser. This native browser supports HTML 4 standards and can be used to access most sites. Second, Notes provides integrated browser services using the Microsoft Internet Explorer OLE object. You get the all the features of Internet Explorer within the Notes interface and with Notes's capability to store pages for offline use, forward pages that are formatted exactly as they are in the browser, and so on.

Notes as a Domino Client

In addition to all of the personal information management and Internet client capabilities mentioned, Notes is also the value-added client for Domino server environments. Domino servers can be used exclusively to provide messaging and application services to Internet clients, such as browsers, POP/IMAP mail clients, or newsreaders. This is a great way to provide capabilities to a wide range of client environments. The downside is that you are limiting the functionality to what these Internet clients can support. To go beyond that, you can use the Notes client to add the following functionality:

- The ability to use Domino as your mail server

- The ability to use Domino for group scheduling

- The ability to replicate databases to your computer and work disconnected with full application functionality

- A greater range of application security, including encryption to the field level

- Full-text searching on all locally stored information

- The ability to read all major file formats using built-in file viewer technology

- Data integration and management services, such as import/export and Open Database Connectivity (ODBC)

- Integration with non-TCP/IP network environments

- Presentation of all information in a consistent, easy-to-use manner

You can even use Notes in conjunction with hosted Domino environments and receive all of the benefits mentioned. Lotus has teamed with service organizations, such as EDS, to offer shared or hosted Domino services. Shared Domino services enable organizations to take advantage of all the capabilities of Domino without the burden of deploying and managing the infrastructure. This extends the sophisticated capabilities of Domino to a broader range of organizations.

Flexible Configuration

In addition, Notes is installed on your computer in a way that enables you to start using it for one purpose and easily change the configuration as your needs change. For example, you could start out using Notes exclusively as an Internet client. If you later encounter a situation that requires access to a Domino server, all that's required is a simple change in configuration. You would not be required to reinstall Notes.

Notes can maintain multiple configurations, and these configurations are based on location. This means that you can use Notes with one configuration while you're in the office and another when you work from home, all on the same machine. With this feature, you can use Notes for a variety of purposes.

What's New in Notes 5?

Release 5 represents a significant advance in capabilities for Notes. This release marks the first full separation of client, server, and development environments. These are introduced in Release 5 as Notes, Domino (the Domino Family of Servers), and Domino Designer. Notes is the client environment, Domino is the server, and Domino Designer is the development environment for creating applications that run in the client and the server. Lotus began this separation in 4.6, but Release 5 makes it technically feasible to deploy Notes and Domino independently. For the client, this means operating in environments that do not include Domino servers. And for Domino, it means providing a rich application environment for browsers. Included in this section is an overview of some of the most significant improvements in Notes, including:

- Internet client capabilities
- Browser-oriented user interface
- Enhanced mail and calendaring
- Search enhancements
- Mobile client enhancements

Release 5 also includes significant enhancements for Domino and Domino Designer. Domino is outside the scope of this book, but some of the most significant areas of improvement include the following:

- Full support for Internet-based mail protocol, security, and content standards
- Web application server enhancements
- Server reliability, availability, and scalability
- Simplified administration and more flexibility in administration options

For Domino Designer, the highlights are as follows:

- New design elements
- A new interface for developers
- Easy integration with enterprise data
- Industry standards support
- Multiclient support
- Multilingual application support

For an introduction to Domino Designer and a complete overview of what's new in Release 5, see Chapter 15, "Introducing Domino Designer."

Internet Client Capabilities

As previously mentioned, Notes Release 5 is able to operate in environments with no Domino infrastructure. This enables organizations with infrastructures based on Internet standards to use Notes as a full-featured mail client, Web browser, and newsreader. What makes this possible is Release 5's support of Internet protocols and content standards. The following protocols are supported in Release 5:

- HTTP (Web browsing)
- POP3, IMAP4, and SMTP (mail)
- LDAP v3 (directory)
- NNTP (discussion)

The following content standards are supported:

- HTML
- MIME, S/MIME
- X.509 certificates
- Java

- JavaScript
- Native image formats

In addition to support for these protocols and content standards, Release 5 includes improvements to ensure that Notes is the premier Internet client on the market, including:

Windows Dialup Networking (DUN) integration   Windows Dialup Networking (DUN) integration has been enhanced to provide automatic dialing of ISP connections for Internet-based information. Previous releases included DUN integration to connect to Domino servers on remote networks. This enhancement extends this functionality to non-Domino environments.

Native editor enhancements   Native editor enhancements—including enhanced tables and native HTML editing—make Notes a great content authoring platform.

Browser-Oriented User Interface

Release 5 also includes a completely redesigned user interface. This new interface is based on a browser metaphor, making the client easier to use for individuals familiar with Web browsers. Release 5 also includes usability improvements over previous versions.

As part of the browser-oriented interface, Release 5 introduces *bookmarks* as the main navigation tool. Bookmarks are links to databases, views, documents, or Web pages (URLs) and are organized in folders. You can bookmark the information that is most important to you regardless of its source. Frequently accessed bookmarks and high-level folders of other bookmarks are displayed on the *Bookmark bar*. You can arrange the Bookmark bar and its associated folders however you like, allowing you to personalize the Notes interface. An example of the Bookmark is shown in the left margin.

Another key aspect of the Release 5 user interface is the *Navigation bar*. The Navigation bar contains buttons for navigating around Notes and Web pages. The buttons are similar to those found on Web browsers; they include the following:

- Forward
- Backward
- Stop
- Refresh
- Search
- Open URL

Because these buttons operate like the buttons found on Web browsers, navigating around Notes is easier than ever. Here is an example of the Navigation bar.

Task buttons, which are introduced in Release 5, replace the Window menu for switching between tasks within the Notes window. They represent a big improvement in usability. Task buttons cut down on mouse movement and mouse clicks, which makes Notes much easier to use. Also, the process for closing tasks is significantly improved, you can simply select the *X* on the right side of any task button. You no longer have to open a task's window to close it. Here is an example of what the Release 5 task buttons look like.

Another major improvement in the Notes user interface is the introduction of the *Welcome page*. The Welcome page is a single-page overview of the information most critical to you. It can be customized to meet your needs. You can include sections for your Inbox, calendar, and To Do list, making your personal information available in a simple, concise interface. You can also include sections for important Web pages. Most importantly, you can include a section for your database *subscriptions*. Database subscriptions are another new feature of Release 5; you can set filters on Notes databases to alert you to the information that is most important to you. Database subscriptions sift through information for you, freeing you to *act* upon the information instead of having to *find* it.

One helpful aspect of the Welcome page is that you can create multiple versions. You can have one that is a personal view, which may include your Inbox, calendar, To Do list, and subscriptions. You can have another that includes multiple Web pages, each displayed in a separate frame. There are many possibilities. An example of a Welcome page is shown in Figure 1.1.

Enhanced Mail and Calendaring

The Release 5 mail database has been enhanced to provide a Web-oriented user interface, as has the rest of Notes. To start, it is now based on a frame interface. There are framesets for each of the of three main functions, including mail, calendar, and To Do. Figure 1.2 shows the new Release 5 mail database interface.

FIGURE 1.1

The Welcome page

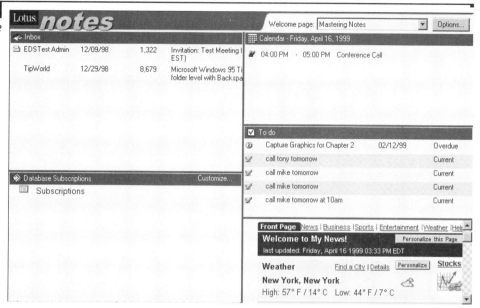

FIGURE 1.2

The Release 5 mail database

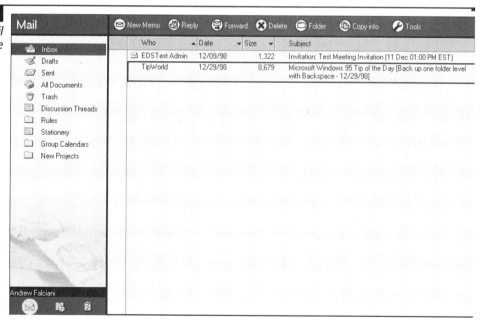

The main message form interface also uses frames. In this case, a stationary frame at the top of the form separates the addressing information from the body. This way, you don't have to scroll through page after page of addressing information looking for a message. Here is an example of the new mail message interface.

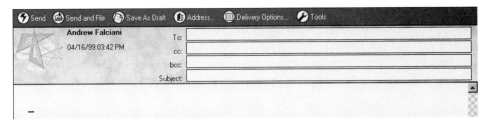

The following sections highlight some of the other new mail and calendaring features of Release 5.

Automatic Spell Checking   When automatic spell checking is enabled, you don't have to remember to spell-check messages before sending them. Notes will start the spell checker automatically.

Sending Messages as HTML   HTML is now supported in messages you send. This allows you to share information in a rich format that most Internet mail clients can understand. Of course, you can always send messages as plain text if necessary.

Mail Signature Files   You can now use mail signature files. You can set your default signature to an external file or text that you type into Notes. When the appropriate option is enabled, Notes will automatically append your selected signature file to all new messages you create.

Notes Minder   Notes Minder is a new tool provided with Release 5 for monitoring Notes mail without running the full client. It inserts itself into the Windows 95/98/NT system tray and notifies you when new messages arrive. You can even launch Notes from here.

Type-Down Addressing   Type-down addressing has been added and can be used in the To field of messages you create or in the Select Address dialog box. As with previous versions, Notes supports type-ahead addressing. As you type addresses in the To field, Notes auto-completes the entry with names it finds in your Personal Address Book or the mail server's Domino Directory. With type-down addressing, you can now use the up and down arrow keys to cycle through similar addresses.

Mail Rules   Mail rules are automated tasks placed on your mail database that can be used to filter messages before you actually see them. These tasks run on the Domino server, which provides processing without user intervention.

Calendar Printing   Calendar printing has been improved to include support for popular output formats. There are four styles to choose from; Daily, Weekly, Monthly, and Calendar List. Notes also includes a *Print Preview* capability that is helpful for displaying calendar output before sending the output to your printer, but is not limited to this one area. Print Preview can be used when printing any information in Notes.

Group Calendar Documents   Group calendar documents have been added, and they allow you to view multiple users' schedules at one time. Because you can save these documents, group calendars are a great way to check the schedules of team members you work with most frequently.

Invitation Form Enhancements   Invitation form enhancements include FYI invitees, optional or required invitees, invitation delivery options, and so on. They provide you with more control over your meeting invitations and more flexible group-scheduling capabilities.

Resource Management   Resource management enhancements include access restrictions to resources, resource ownership, and booking resources across domains, to name a few. These enhancements give you more control over how resources are scheduled.

Holiday Sets   Support for adding holiday sets to your calendar provides a mechanism for making sure everyone is using the same information. Once the Domino domain administrator adds a holiday set to the Domino Directory, you can use the Import Holidays function to add the set to your calendar.

Search Enhancements

Information is only valuable if you can find it when you need it. Release 5 improves on Notes's built-in search capabilities. A few of these improvements are described in the following sections.

Search Button   A Search button has been included on the Navigation bar so you can quickly access the many search capabilities of Notes. From this new interface, you can perform the following:

- Search the current view or document.
- Access the Domain Search interface.
- Access the database search interface.
- Search for Contacts.
- Access any Web-based search engine.

New Search Engine   A new search engine has been incorporated into Release 5. Lotus has replaced the Verity engine with the Global Text Retriever engine from IBM for even more powerful built-in search capabilities.

Domain Search   If you are using Notes in an environment that includes Domino Release 5, you can take advantage of a new capability called Domain Search. It provides searching across databases and file systems. Once a database owner marks a database as being included in Domain Search, information about that database is stored in the Domain Catalog. Domain Search then uses this information to perform its search. For Notes, there is a direct interface to the Domain Search feature, which makes it easy to access this new functionality.

Content Map   If you are using Notes in an environment that includes Domino Release 5, you can take advantage of another new capability called Content Maps. This feature enables document categorization across databases. Domino's Content Map is stored in the Domain Catalog and provides a structure (taxonomy) in which to classify documents. In Notes, you can browse this structure as you would browse a Web-based search site, such as Yahoo!. Notes also includes a new interface for categorizing documents according to the structure.

Database Search   A database search feature has been added to Notes, as well. From either the Search button or the Bookmark bar, you can now initiate a search for databases in the Domain Catalog. Because you can search for keywords from the database title, you no longer have to go browsing through endless directories on the Domino server to find the database you're looking for. Also, you don't need to know where databases are located to find them using the database search. The Domain Catalog is shared by all servers in a domain, so the database search returns all databases in the domain regardless of which server they are on.

Mobile Client Enhancements

Notes has always been a powerful mobile client, for both mail and collaborative applications. Built-in field-level replication provided the mechanism for working with mail and Notes databases offline, enabling individuals to take information on the road and work from any location. Built-in dial-up communications support provided the mechanism for connecting back to the server to replicate databases and deliver mail, enabling individuals to stay synchronized from just about anywhere. Release 5 builds on this strong tradition.

Mobile Directory Catalog   Domino includes a new capability called the Directory Catalog that consolidates person, group, mail-in database, and resource entries for one or more Domino domains into a single, lightweight database. When prepared for mobile users, it is called the Mobile Directory Catalog. This compressed, lightweight directory enables mobile users to look up people and address mail while working offline.

Mobile Internet Client   Release 5 extends the Notes mobile client model to Internet-based information. Along with its ability to replicate Notes databases from Domino servers, Notes can also replicate IMAP-based mail and NNTP-based discussions to your workstation for offline use. In addition, locally stored IMAP-based mail and NNTP-based discussions can be full-text indexed for powerful searches. Also, Release 5 includes support for offline browsing, making it easy to locate information even when you are working offline.

ISP Connection Support   Notes has included integration with dial-up access software, such as Windows Dialup Networking (DUN), for connecting to Domino servers. Release 5 extends this support to ISPs. With this new capability, Notes can be configured to automatically dial your ISP account to access your IMAP or POP mail, replicate NNTP-based discussions, or perform LDAP queries. This is just another example of Notes providing services normally associated with Internet client software.

Summary

In this chapter, we provided an overview of what Lotus Notes is and how it can be used. We also introduced Lotus Domino Designer and highlighted some of the new features of Release 5. In the next chapter, we'll begin to explore the basic features of the software. We'll introduce you to navigating in and customizing the Welcome page. We'll also discuss the elements of the Notes application window, personalizing Notes with bookmarks, and using Notes Help.

CHAPTER **2**

Getting Familiar with Notes

FEATURING:

N ow that you have an understanding of what Lotus Notes is all about, it's time to explore the basics of using the software. Whether you are a new user or an existing user of a previous release, this chapter will quickly familiarize you with the built-in features of Notes.

One of the most dramatic improvements in Lotus Notes 5 is the new user interface. As you will see in this chapter, the new interface is very task oriented. Functions are presented to you according to the tasks you need to perform (for example, creating an electronic mail message or viewing your calendar). Another aspect of the new user interface is that functions are presented in a manner consistent with popular Web browsers, such as Netscape Navigator or Microsoft Internet Explorer. This makes it easier for you to become productive with the software more quickly, and it underscores the other major improvement incorporated in this release, integration with Internet technologies. As you will see throughout this book, Lotus Notes 5 is the one application that can help you cope in this age of information overload.

Starting Your Day in the Welcome Page

The first place you'll notice changes to the user interface is in the new Welcome page, which is displayed immediately upon starting Lotus Notes. The Welcome page replaces the Workspace page as the default starting point for Notes. The default Welcome page, as shown in Figure 2.1, allows you to perform many common Notes functions, including reading your electronic mail (e-mail), creating new e-mail messages, viewing your calendar, creating new appointments, viewing your To Do items, creating new To Do items, and reviewing information about Release 5. You can even create you own customized Welcome pages with what Notes refers to as styles. The default Welcome page's style is called Basics.

 NOTE The Workspace page, which has been the main interface for Notes since its inception, is still available for those who need to ease into major interface changes. Select the Bookmark bar icon labeled Databases. When it opens, select the bookmark called Workspace. Before going back to the old Workspace page, give bookmarks a try. We think you'll find that they provide a more convenient way to navigate Notes, and they are not too difficult to learn.

FIGURE 2.1

The default Lotus
Notes Welcome page

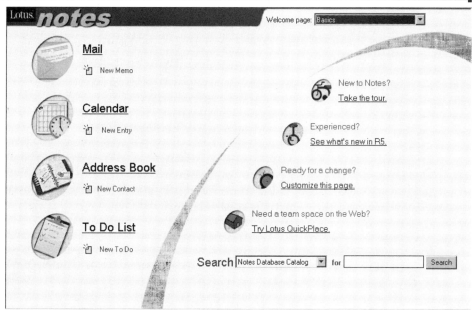

When Notes is launched, you will most likely be asked to enter your password in
the Enter Password dialog box, which is shown here.

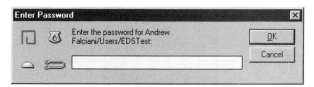

This is generally true if you are using Notes in a corporate environment in conjunction with Lotus Domino servers. If so, just type in the password provided by your Notes/
Domino administration group and press Enter.

As you can see, the Basics style Welcome page is a task-oriented starting point for
accessing the most commonly used features of Lotus Notes. To get a feel for how Release 5
behaves more like a Web browser, just move your mouse over items within the Basics
style Welcome page. Do you notice how the look of each item changes as you move the
mouse over it? This is similar to browsing sites on the World Wide Web. Also, the mouse
pointer changes to an icon representing a hand when you move it over elements on
the page that represent links to other pages, just like browsing the Web.

To show how you can begin to use the features of Notes right from the Basics style Welcome page, let's view your electronic mail Inbox:

1. Move the mouse so it hovers over the image of a letter with the caption Mail on the upper left side of the Basics style Welcome page.

2. When the letter appears to lift off the screen, click the left mouse button.

A screen similar to the one in Figure 2.2 appears. When it does, just press the Escape key to return to the Welcome page.

FIGURE 2.2

The mail Inbox

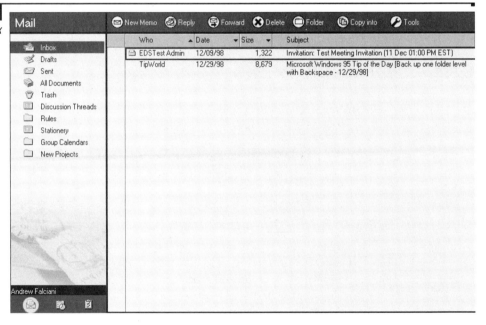

Notes ships with two styles in addition to the Basics style previously mentioned: Headlines with AOL My News and Lotus Notes & Domino News. Both are formatted with two frames displaying your Inbox and calendar and one frame for a Web page.

The Web page displayed in the Headlines with AOL My News style is the news-oriented site that Lotus and America Online have created specifically for Notes customers. The Web page displayed in the Lotus Notes &Domino News style is from Lotus's Notes.net site. As you can see in Figure 2.3, the My News Web page can be personalized.

FIGURE 2.3

The Headlines with AOL My News style Welcome page

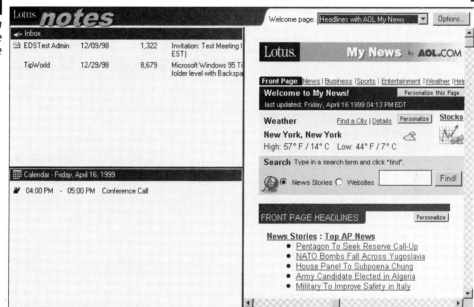

Sections of the Welcome page

You can also use the Welcome page as your personal home page by creating a custom style and including the sections you want. Configured properly, the Welcome page is a single-screen snapshot of your most important information. The sections you can add to your customized Welcome page are:

- Database subscriptions
- Calendar
- Inbox
- To Do list
- Web page

- Quick Links
- Search
- Basic tasks

As shown in Figure 2.4, Welcome page styles can include up to five frames to display sections.

FIGURE 2.4

*A five-frame
Welcome page*

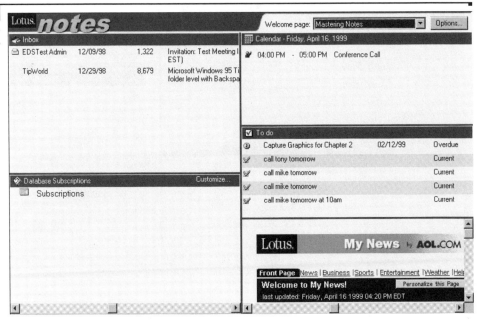

Database Subscriptions   Database subscriptions are another new capability in Notes 5. They allow you to monitor Notes databases for documents that might be of interest. Database subscriptions are similar to the Responder utility made available by Lotus as an unsupported download for previous versions of Notes. For example, you can create a subscription to monitor your mail database for messages containing the term *New Business* or to monitor a particular Notes database for documents containing the word *Java*. From the Database Subscriptions area of your Welcome page, you can see a listing of the matching documents and open them if you wish. Creating and modifying subscriptions is discussed later in this chapter. If you include a Database Subscription section in your custom Welcome page, it will look similar to this.

Web Page   Web pages can be displayed in a section of a Welcome page. You can determine which Web page to use; the Web page can provide a great starting point for browsing the Internet or referencing information on your company's intranet. It also demonstrates how Notes integrates Internet capabilities to provide you with a seamless environment for accessing and managing information. Customizing this section will be discussed later in this chapter. If you include a Web page section in your custom Welcome page, it will look similar to this.

Calendar   Your calendar can also be displayed in a section of a Welcome page. This is a great tool for quickly seeing appointments scheduled for the current day. As you point your mouse over individual appointments, Notes will change the mouse pointer to an icon representing a hand and will highlight the appointment by drawing a box around it. To select an appointment, you only need to click on it once. To close the appointment and return to the Welcome page, press the Escape key or select the *X* on the right side of the appointment window's task button. You can open your calendar by selecting the calendar icon or the word *Calendar* in the bar at the top of the Calendar section; close it by pressing the Escape key or by selecting the *X* on the right side of the Calendar window's task button. If you include a Calendar section in your custom Welcome page, it will look similar to this.

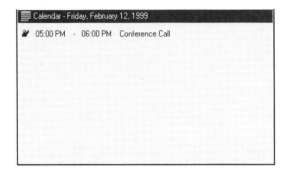

Inbox   Your Inbox can be included in a section of a Welcome page too. This enables you to quickly see a listing of e-mail messages sent to you. Messages appearing in red text are ones you have not read yet (unread), whereas those appearing in black letters are messages you have already read. You can open the messages listed as well as open your mail database. As it does with the calendar, Notes will change the mouse pointer to an icon representing a hand and will highlight an individual message by drawing a box around it as you point your mouse over it. To select a message, you only need to click on it once. To close the message and return to the Welcome page, press the Escape key or select the *X* on the right side of the message window's task button. You can open your Inbox by selecting the Inbox icon or the word *Inbox* in the bar at the top of the Inbox section; close it by pressing the Escape key or by selecting the *X* on the right side of the Inbox window's task button. If you include an Inbox section in your custom Welcome page, it will look similar to this.

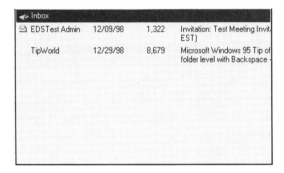

To Do List   Your To Do list can be included in another section of a Welcome page. The To Do section provides a convenient way to see a listing of your current tasks. You can open To Do items listed as well as your entire To Do list. As it does with the calendar, Notes will change the mouse pointer to an icon representing a hand and will highlight To Do items by drawing a box around them. To select a To Do item, you only need to click on it once. To close the To Do item and return to the Welcome page, press the Escape key or select the *X* on the right side of the To Do item window's task button. You can open your To Do list by selecting the check box icon or the words *To Do* in the bar at the top of the To Do section; close it by pressing the Escape key or by selecting the *X* on the right side of the To Do List window's task button. If you include a To Do section in your custom Welcome page, it will look similar to this.

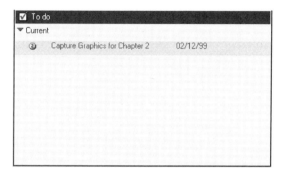

Quick Links   Quick Links can be included in a section of a Welcome page to provide you with a set of convenient links to Internet-based resources, such as Web pages. You can customize these links to suit your needs. If you include a Quick Links section in your custom Welcome page, it will look similar to this.

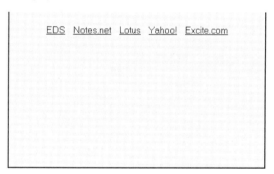

Search   A Search section can be included in a Welcome page to provide a quick way to search for databases in a Domino catalog or for information from popular Internet search engines. A wide variety of search sites are available, including:

- Yahoo!
- Excite

- AltaVista
- Lycos
- Search.com
- HotBot
- Northern Light
- Snap
- Deja News
- AltaVista Usenet

If you include a Search section in your custom Welcome page, it will look similar to this.

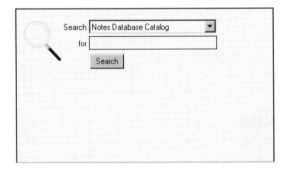

Basic Tasks   The Basic Tasks section includes links to your Inbox, calendar, address book, and To Do list. It is formatted just like the Basics style Welcome page, only the images are smaller so you can include it in a small frame on the screen. If you include the Basic Tasks section in your custom Welcome page, it will look similar to this.

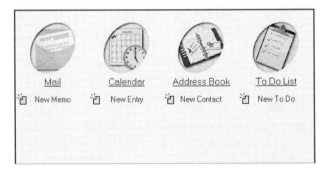

Creating and Customizing Welcome Page Styles

The Welcome page is intended to be a personal starting point for you. As such, it contains styles that are *user customizable*. We use the term *user customizable* because most of the functionality provided by Notes is customizable, but it usually requires a person who is familiar with Lotus Notes/Domino programming techniques and has the appropriate authority. Welcome page styles can be created and customized by you, the end user. You can individualize Welcome page styles by choosing which sections to include and how they are displayed. For example, you may want to display your Inbox, calendar, and To Do list along with your database subscriptions and your company's Web page. Let's use this example to experiment with customizing Welcome page styles:

1. Open your Welcome page by selecting the task button on the left side of the screen labeled Welcome.

2. Select the Welcome page style field's drop-down box arrow to display the style choices currently available.

3. Select the last choice, Create New Page. The New Page dialog box (shown here) appears.

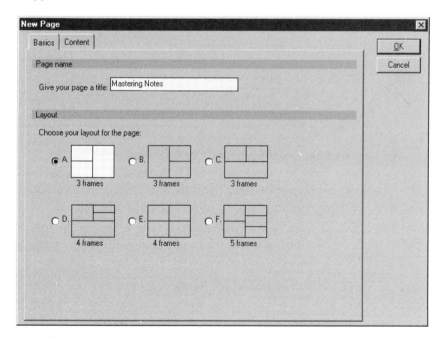

4. Click in the Give Your Page a Title field and type **Mastering Notes**.

5. In the Basics tab, select the layout labeled F (5 frames).

6. Select the Content tab at the top of the dialog box. The upper left frame is highlighted and labeled Inbox. We will leave this frame as it is.

7. In the Select a Frame section at the top of the dialog box, select the lower left frame, which should be labeled Calendar.

8. In the Frame Content section at the bottom of the dialog box, select Database Subscriptions.

9. Go back to the Select a Frame section at the top of the dialog box and select the upper right frame, which should be labeled Web Page.

10. In the Frame Content section at the bottom of the dialog box, select Calendar.

11. Go back to the Select a Frame section at the top of the dialog box and select the middle right frame, which should be labeled Basic Tasks.

12. In the Frame Content section at the bottom of the dialog box, select To Do List.

13. Go back to the Select a Frame section at the top of the dialog box and select the bottom right frame, which should be labeled To Do List.

14. In the Frame Content section at the bottom of the dialog box, select Search.

15. Click the OK button at the top of the New Page dialog box.

The Welcome page will be refreshed and your new style will be displayed.

 NOTE You can modify existing Welcome page styles in this same manner. Just click the Options button to the right of the Welcome page style field. The Welcome Page Options dialog box will display, allowing you to change the current style's configuration.

In addition to setting preferences to determine the Welcome page style's frame layout and content, you can modify the size of the frames displayed on the screen. You may want to enlarge the Database Subscriptions frame so that more information is visible without scrolling. To do so, just follow these steps:

1. Point your mouse over the black line separating the Inbox and Database Subscription frames until the mouse pointer turns into a horizontal or vertical bar with arrows.

2. Click and drag with your mouse so the bar moves down to the desired location.

The Welcome Page as Your Home Page

The Welcome page is also the default home page for Lotus Notes. As such, it is automatically loaded when you run Notes. Also, the task button associated with the Welcome page cannot be closed. If you would rather have another database as the starting point for your environment, Notes gives you this option. To change your home page—to your mail database, for example—do the following:

1. Right-click the mail icon on the Bookmark bar so the following context menu appears.

2. Choose Set Bookmark as Home Page from the menu. The Set Home Page dialog box appears, confirming your request to change the home page.

3. Click the OK button to confirm the change.

You'll notice that the task button for the Welcome page, labeled Welcome, disappears and your mail database's task button changes so there is no *X* on the right side. You can use this feature to set any bookmark as your home page in Notes.

 NOTE To change your home page back to the Welcome page, click the Bookmark button labeled Favorite Bookmarks, right-click the icon labeled Welcome, and follow the procedure outlined in this section.

Creating Subscriptions to Monitor Databases

The Welcome page is also the main interface for a new capability in Release 5 called database subscriptions. As previously mentioned, database subscriptions are monitors that you can establish to keep current with the information that is most important to you. Once a subscription is created, Notes will check the target database on a specific schedule for documents matching the criteria you establish.

Subscriptions represent a great way to individualize Welcome page styles and have Notes work for you. You can create a database subscription that monitors your mail database for messages from a particular person or for messages containing a certain string in the subject line. You can also create database subscriptions on discussion databases in which you participate. This way, Notes informs you of responses to postings you may have entered or of new postings on a particular topic.

Let's create a database subscription on your mail database to monitor high-priority messages. The steps are as follows:

1. Open your mail database by selecting the Mail link on the Bookmark bar on the left side of the screen (top icon).

2. Choose Create ➤ Subscription. A Mail Subscription form is displayed.

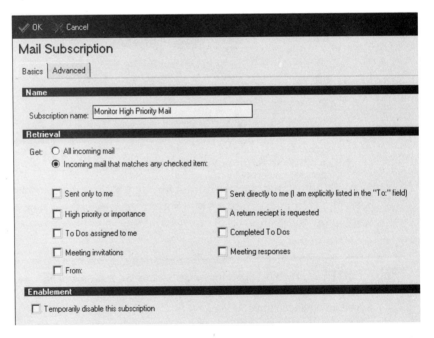

3. Clear any existing text and type **Monitor High Priority Mail** in the Subscription Name field.

4. In the Retrieval section, select the Incoming Mail That Matches Any Checked Item radio button. A set of check boxes will be displayed.

5. Select the High Priority or Importance check box.

6. Click the OK button at the top of the database subscription form.

To see the database subscription you just created, close your mail database by pressing Escape. Click the bookmark button labeled Favorite Bookmarks and click the Database Subscriptions button. In your Database Subscriptions page, you will see a new entry titled Monitor High Priority Mail. If you select any of the document titles listed under a particular database subscription in the left frame, Notes will display a preview of the document's contents in the right frame.

The Database Subscription form used in this example is formatted specifically for the Release 5 mail database. Databases that do not have a specialized Database Subscription form will use the default Database Subscription form, shown here.

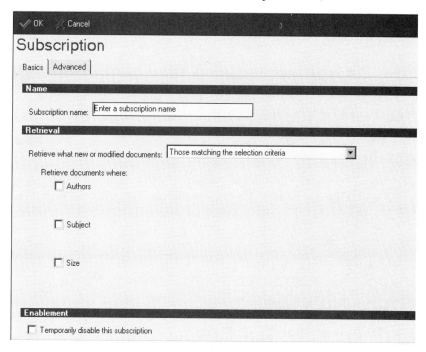

 NOTE The Database Subscription section of custom Welcome page styles is similar to the Database page, except it only displays document titles. It also provides a quick way to access the Database page. Just click the Database Subscriptions button in the section's title bar and the Database page will be displayed.

To manage existing database subscriptions, click the Customize button on the right side of the Database Subscription page. The Subscription Options page opens (similar to the one shown here).

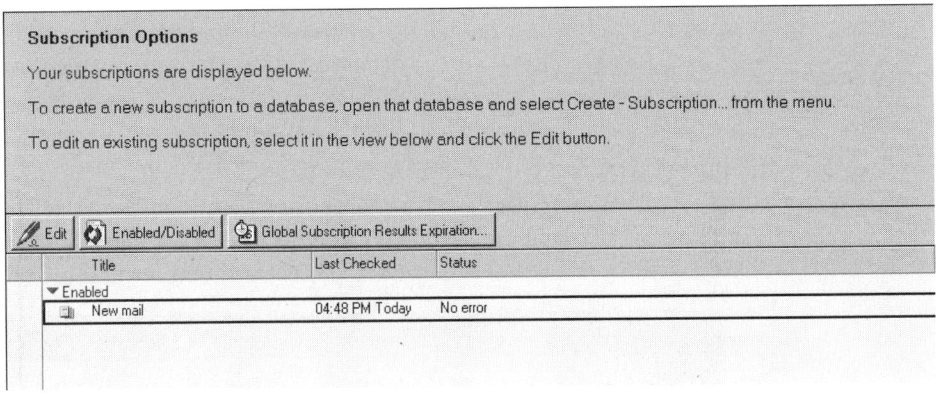

Subscription Options

Your subscriptions are displayed below.

To create a new subscription to a database, open that database and select Create - Subscription... from the menu.

To edit an existing subscription, select it in the view below and click the Edit button.

✎ Edit	⟳ Enabled/Disabled	⟳ Global Subscription Results Expiration...

Title	Last Checked	Status
▼ Enabled		
☐ New mail	04:48 PM Today	No error

From the Subscription Options page, you can edit existing database subscriptions by clicking the Edit button. This lets you change parameters, such as:

- The subscription's name
- What documents to monitor
- The criteria for retrieving documents

You can enable and disable subscriptions by clicking the Enabled/Disabled button. This is a good way to temporarily disable a subscription without losing its definition. To delete a subscription, follow these steps:

1. Select the subscription you would like to delete.
2. Press Delete to mark the subscription document for deletion.
3. Press F9 to permanently delete the subscription.

The Application Window

Before going too much further into the actual functionality provided by Notes, it is important to understand how the application is presented on the screen. When Notes is launched, it creates a window on your screen. This is known as the *application window*. The application window is made up of a number of elements. This section will explain what the major elements of the Notes application window are and how they are used.

PART

I

Introducing Notes 5

The application window is designed to be familiar to users of the platform on which it is running. As shown in Figure 2.5, the Microsoft Windows version of Lotus Notes has the familiar Windows-style interface. At the top of the screen is a title bar, which includes the name of the application and the active task. On the left side of the title bar, there is an icon that allows the user to control the application.

On the right, there are controls for minimizing, maximizing/restoring, and closing the application. On the left side below the title bar, there is a set of menu options that should be familiar to most Windows users. The remainder of the application window is specific to Lotus Notes and is detailed in the next section.

FIGURE 2.5

The Notes application window

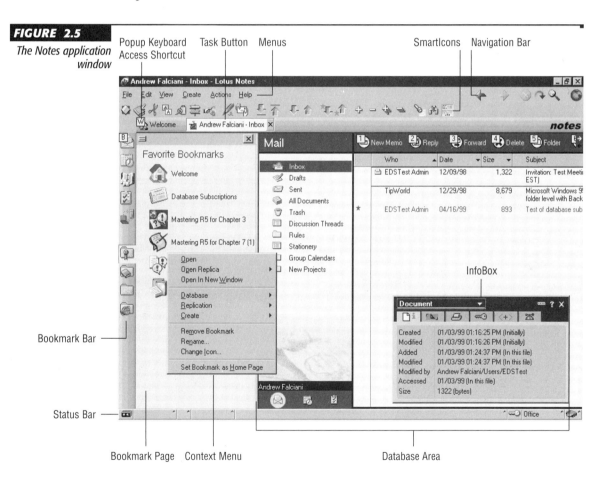

Understanding the Basic Elements of the Notes Application Window

Everything you do with Notes requires you to be familiar with the basic elements of the application window. It is how you interact with Notes and how Notes presents itself to you.

The menus should be familiar if you are accustomed to graphical applications; they represent the traditional method for choosing actions to perform within Notes. The Navigation bar, SmartIcons, task buttons, status bar, context menus, and pop-up keyboard access shortcuts are Notes-specific elements and are explained in the following sections.

Navigation Bar The Navigation bar is new to Notes 5 and allows you navigate in Notes as you would in a Web browser. The buttons are shown in Figure 2.6.

NOTE If you hover your mouse over any one of these buttons, you will see a pop-up box with a short explanation of the button appear. This is called Balloon Help and is available throughout the Notes application window.

The Go Back button takes you to the page or task you were previously viewing. The Go Forward button takes you to the page or task you were on prior to clicking the Go Back button. Each button has two components that can be selected with the mouse individually. The left side is used to navigate in sequential order. The right side is used to select from a recent history list.

The keyboard equivalent for the Go Back button is Alt+left arrow, and Alt+right arrow is the keyboard equivalent for the Go Forward button.

The Stop button interrupts the current process, and its keyboard equivalent is Ctrl+Break. The Refresh button refreshes the current page or view, and its keyboard equivalent is F9.

The Search button has two components that can be selected with the mouse individually. Selecting the button on the left side (see margin) will enable the Search bar on the current view if a Notes database is active.

If a Web page is active when the left side of the Search button is selected, the Find Text in Document dialog box (shown here) will be displayed.

Selecting the drop-down arrow on the right side will bring up a Context menu with a set of search options appropriate for the active page.

The Open URL button toggles the display of a drop-down box directly below the Navigation bar.

You can enter addresses of both Internet-based and Domino-based resources. Internet-based resources, such as Web pages or newsgroup articles, are addressed by using URLs as you normally would in your favorite browser. Domino-based documents are represented with a URL syntax beginning with `Notes://`. You can type in a URL or select from the list of previously entered URLs by selecting the drop-down arrow on the right side.

After you select a URL or type one and press Enter, Notes will navigate to the URL you requested and close the drop-down box. If you prefer to keep the drop-down box open, you can "pin" the drop-down box to the screen as follows:

1. Look at the upper left corner of the drop-down box for the pin icon.

2. Select the pin icon so that it changes to a pin that appears to be pushed into the screen.

The drop-down box will be moved to a location directly below the SmartIcons and run across the entire length of the application window.

SmartIcons   SmartIcons are shortcuts to functions normally selected from menus. There are two sets of SmartIcons, Universal and Context. The Universal icons are available at all times while Notes is active. The Context icons are only available in the appropriate context. For example, there is a set of view navigation Context icons that are only available when a Notes database view is the active task. Use SmartIcons to quickly navigate around a view or to access frequently used editing tools, such as tools used for:

• Formatting text style (bold, italics)

• Aligning text

- Spell-checking

- Working with attachments

SmartIcons are not enabled by default when Notes is installed on your computer. To enable SmartIcons, follow these steps:

1. Select File ➤ Preferences ➤ SmartIcons and the SmartIcons Settings dialog box shown here appears.

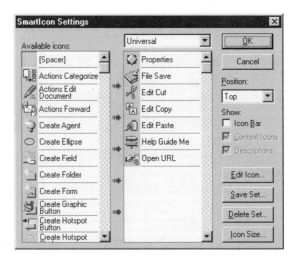

2. On the right side of the dialog box in the Show area, select the Icon Bar check box.

3. If desired, change the position where the SmartIcons will be displayed in the application window. The default is at the top of the application window.

The SmartIcon bar will be displayed at the top of the application window directly below the menus.

Task Buttons　Task buttons are tabs located below the menus and SmartIcons that represent active tasks within Notes. They replace the Window menu from previous versions of Notes. Task buttons allow you to easily navigate between tasks and quickly close active tasks. The active task's task button is always highlighted and includes an *X* on the right side, as shown here.

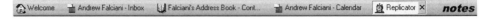

The *X* on the right side is used to quickly close the active task. When you hover your mouse over the task button of a nonactive task, the button is highlighted and the *X* becomes visible. This allows you to quickly close nonactive tasks. Task buttons can also be used to create bookmarks. You can select a task button with the mouse and drag it to the Bookmark bar or one of your Bookmark pages. This is explained further in the section on bookmarks later in this chapter.

The Status Bar The status bar is the bottommost area of the application window. As shown in Figure 2.7, it has eight separate sections that provide you with information and allow you to access frequently used functions. The status bar allows you to perform the following tasks:

- See if Notes is accessing a local network (a lightning bolt appears) or a remote network/server (a modem appears)
- Change the font, point size, or style of the text currently selected if you are editing a rich text field
- See a list of recently displayed system messages
- Quickly identify your access level to the active database
- Switch location or edit the current Location document, which changes your Notes configuration information
- Quickly access common mail functions, such as creating a mail message, opening your mail, and sending outgoing messages

FIGURE 2.7

The status bar

Context Menus Context menus are menus that appear when you right-click your mouse inside the Notes application window. They are not new to Notes 5, but their use has been expanded significantly in this release. These menus include choices that are relevant to the area of the application window that your mouse was pointing to when you right-clicked it. For example, the following context menu will be displayed when you right-click any bookmark.

Context menus are a convenient means of accessing functions within Notes. Because they display a limited set of menu choices, they focus your attention on functions most likely required for the task you are performing. For example, using the context menu associated with the Bookmark page is a great way to quickly open a replica of a database. It also provides quick access to the Database, Replica, and Create menus.

Pop-Up Keyboard Access Shortcuts   Pop-up keyboard access shortcuts are new to Notes 5 and are represented as highlighted letters and numbers in the Notes application window. When the Alt key is pressed, these highlighted letters and numbers appear as small pop-up boxes that are similar to Balloon Help. Pop-up keyboard access shortcuts allow you to quickly perform navigation and task actions that would normally require the use of your mouse. The benefit, especially to those with good keyboard skills, is that you do not have to constantly switch back and forth between the keyboard and mouse when trying to accomplish common tasks. As shown here, the Create New Memo task actions are one keystroke away when you use pop-up keyboard access shortcuts.

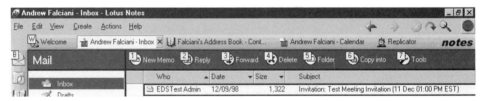

 NOTE Pop-up keyboard access shortcuts are a visual representation of keyboard shortcuts that existed in previous releases, with enhancements for the Bookmark bar and task buttons.

The Properties InfoBox   The Properties InfoBox is a special dialog box that allows you to access a Notes element's properties. Many elements in Notes—such as databases, documents, and forms—have properties. Although not all the elements have the same properties, they all use a Properties InfoBox to access them. You are probably familiar with a similar type of properties dialog box from other products. The Properties InfoBox is a bit different in that it can be left open while you work. Why is that different? When the Properties InfoBox is left open, it reflects the properties of the element that you are currently working on. When you change from one element to another element, the Properties InfoBox reflects the properties of the new element. It also reflects changes without requiring you to click an OK or Done button. Changes to the property settings are made as soon as you click somewhere else in the Properties InfoBox.

The easiest way to open a Properties InfoBox is to first select or highlight the item whose properties you would like to view. To view the properties of your mail database, perform the following steps:

    1. Open your mail database by selecting the Mail link on the Bookmark bar on the left side of the screen (top icon).

2. Choose File ➤ Database Properties. The Properties InfoBox is displayed, showing the database properties for your mail database, as shown in Figure 2.8.

PART

I

Introducing Notes 5

FIGURE 2.8

A Properties InfoBox showing database properties

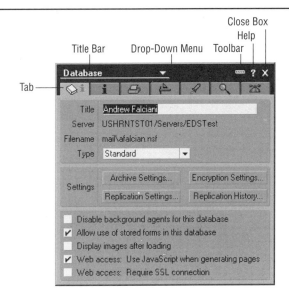

You will use the Properties InfoBox to perform many common functions, including:

- Obtaining information about a database
- Performing maintenance tasks on a database, such as compacting and archiving
- Setting print settings for a database or document
- Manipulating text settings

Also, you'll use many of the properties available in the Properties InfoBox when you are designing Notes databases. Refer to Chapter 15, "Introducing Domino Designer," for more information on how the Properties InfoBox is used while designing Notes databases.

Navigating around the Properties InfoBox is fairly easy. Try some of these methods just to get comfortable:

- To switch to a different property page, click a tab.
- To move the Properties InfoBox, drag it by its title bar.
- To float the Properties InfoBox as a toolbar, click the toolbar icon.
- To get help for the element or options, click the question mark icon.
- To close the box, click the close icon.

Bookmarks   Bookmarks are the new way to get around inside Notes. The graphic in the margin shows the default Bookmark bar.

Bookmarks are detailed in "Personalizing Notes with Bookmarks."

The Database Area   The Database area is the heart of the Notes application window. It is the area where Notes databases are presented to you. The following shows the Database area with the mail database opened to the Inbox view.

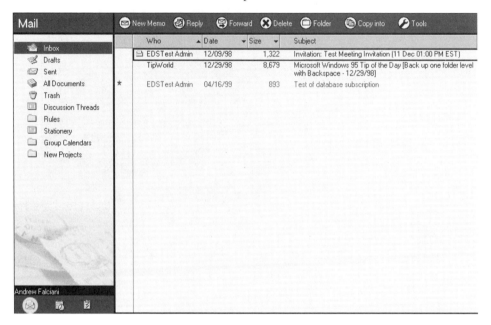

Please refer to Chapter 3, "Working with Notes Databases," for a complete discussion of Notes databases and how you work with them.

Personalizing Notes with Bookmarks

Bookmarks are new to Notes 5 and represent another dramatic improvement to the Notes user interface. If you have used previous releases of Notes, bookmarks essentially replace the Notes Workspace that has been the main interface since Notes 1. As the name implies, Notes's bookmarks are similar to Favorites in Microsoft Internet Explorer and bookmarks in Netscape Navigator. They represent links to Notes objects as well as to Internet-based objects that can be referenced by using a URL. Bookmarks are much more powerful than the old Workspace icons because you can bookmark much more than just databases. You can, for example, bookmark the following:

- Views
- Documents
- Blank forms

- Web pages
- Newsgroups

There are two visual elements to bookmarks: the Bookmark bar and the Bookmark page. The Bookmark bar is located on the left side of the application window in a vertical column and the Bookmark page is displayed directly to the right of the Bookmark bar, as shown in Figure 2.9.

FIGURE 2.9

The Bookmark bar and the Bookmark page

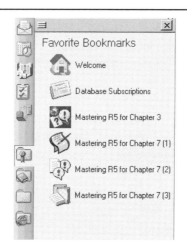

The Bookmark bar is stationary. It remains on the left side of the application window regardless of which task is active in Notes. The Bookmark page expands and collapses to display the contents of folders placed on the Bookmark bar. If you prefer to keep the Bookmark page expanded, you can "pin" it as follows:

1. Select one of the Bookmark bar folder icons to expand it.

2. Select the page menu icon at the upper left corner of the Bookmark page.

3. Choose the Pin Bookmark on Screen menu option.

The Database area will be adjusted to display the entire active task and the Bookmark page will now remain expanded. To manually close the Bookmark page, select the *X* on the upper right side of the Bookmark page. To have the Bookmark bar expand and collapse again, just repeat the preceding procedure. While the Bookmark bar is pinned, you'll notice a check mark next to the Pin Bookmark on Screen menu selection labeled.

The default Bookmark bar contains two sets of links. The top section consists of links that directly access frequently used tasks, such as your mail and calendar. The bottom section contains links to folders of other bookmarks. The default folders include Favorite

Bookmarks, Databases, and More Bookmarks. In addition, you will see a folder for your Microsoft Internet Explorer and Netscape Navigator bookmarks if Notes detects that these applications are installed during setup.

 NOTE Although the most obvious impact of bookmarks in Notes is the new user interface, there is an equally important architectural change as well. Bookmarks are stored in a Notes database, unlike the old Workspace page. This means that you can use the replication facilities built in to Notes and Domino to keep your bookmarks on multiple computers. Also, organizations using Domino can create bookmark databases that are maintained centrally, thus reducing management costs.

How Can I Create Bookmarks?

You can use the Open Database dialog box to create bookmarks, or you can use drag-and-drop techniques. Generally, you'll want to use the Open Database dialog box if you need to bookmark a particular database. Otherwise, you'll use drag-and-drop techniques.

Creating Bookmarks to Databases It's easy to create bookmark using the Open Database dialog box. First, you'll need to know where the database is stored (locally or on a Domino server) and in which directory it is located on the target computer. As you can see in the Open Database dialog box shown here, there is a drop-down list, labeled Server, for selecting the server where the database resides.

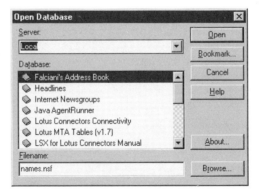

In the Server drop-down list, Local represents your local computer. When Local is selected, the list of databases includes those stored locally on your computer. If you select the drop-down arrow on the right side of the field, a list of servers is displayed. The servers displayed are a combination of those you have previously browsed and those to which you have predefined connections. The Database list box lets you select from a list of databases on the selected server. It also displays folders on the selected server where databases might be stored. The Filename field allows you to enter a file name directly.

 NOTE In the Open Database dialog box, the list of databases available on a given target server is relative to the `Data` directory of the server. When Local is selected, the list of databases displayed is relative to the `Data` directory of your local Notes environment, which by default is `C:\Lotus\Notes\Data`.

The Open button opens the database or folder currently selected in the Database list box or typed into the Filename field. You can also open a database or folder listed in the Database list box by double-clicking its name. If you choose to open a database, the Open Database dialog box will disappear and the selected database will be displayed in the application window. If you choose to open a folder, the contents of that folder will be displayed in the Database list box, and the last entry will be an icon of an arrow pointing upward.

If you double-click the icon or highlight it and click the Open button, Notes will display the contents of the folder up one level in the folder hierarchy.

The Browse button allows you to browse your file system for Notes databases located outside your local Notes `Data` directory. This is handy if you are trying to open a database that you have downloaded from an Internet site or some other external source to a folder/directory on your computer. It is also used to open database templates because the Open Database dialog box only displays database files. Database templates are an advanced topic and discussed further in Chapter 16, "Creating Your First Database." When you click the Browse button, a File Open dialog box appears, allowing you to choose a file from your local computer's file system. Here is an example of the File Open dialog box.

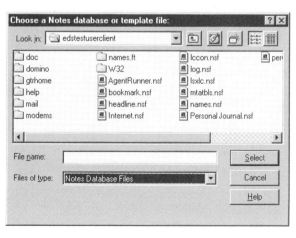

To use the Open Database dialog box to bookmark databases, follow these steps:

1. Select File ➤ Database ➤ Open or press Ctrl+O to open the Open Database dialog box.

2. Navigate to the database you would like to bookmark. For this example, use Local as the server and select your address book. The Open Database dialog box should look something like this.

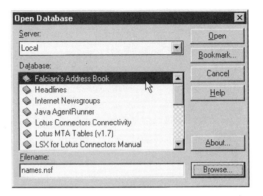

3. Click the Bookmark button. The Add Bookmark dialog box appears.

4. Select the Databases folder. The Databases folder will be highlighted as follows.

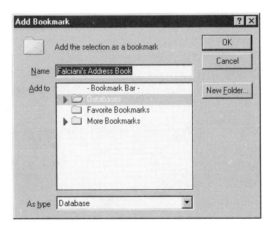

5. Click the OK button to create the bookmark.

The Add Bookmark dialog box closes and the Open Database dialog box redisplays. Just click the Cancel button to close the Open Database dialog box. To see if your bookmark was created, select the Databases folder on the Bookmark bar. The new bookmark should show up in the list.

 NOTE You can also create new bookmark folders by clicking the New Folder button in the Add Bookmark dialog box. New bookmark folders are created in the folder highlighted in the Add To field.

Creating Bookmarks to Notes Documents   It's easy to create bookmarks using drag-and-drop techniques. With a database open, just point to a particular document and drag and drop it on a bookmark folder icon on the Bookmark bar. You can place the link directly on the Bookmark bar by dropping it between existing icons.

Creating Bookmarks to Blank Forms, Views, and Web Pages   You can create bookmarks to blank forms, views, and Web pages by dragging and dropping their task buttons to the Bookmark bar. With the item you would like bookmarked open, just point to the task button and drag and drop it onto a bookmark folder icon on the Bookmark bar. You can place the link directly on the Bookmark bar by dropping it between existing icons.

How Can Bookmarks Be Modified?

Once bookmarks have been added to the Bookmark bar or Bookmark page, they can also be modified. This is useful for changing the name displayed for the bookmark or changing the icon associated with a particular bookmark. Bookmarks can also be rearranged on a Bookmark page or moved to other pages. Of course, bookmarks can be deleted when they are no longer needed.

Moving Bookmarks   It's easy to move bookmarks by using drag-and-drop techniques. You can drag and drop existing bookmarks to a new location on the current Bookmark page. As you drag a bookmark around the Bookmark page, an indicator that shows you where the bookmark will be located after you drop it is displayed. If you drag a bookmark to the Bookmark bar, you can drop it directly on the bar or you can drop it on a folder icon. If you hover over a folder icon, the Bookmark page will open, allowing you to drop the bookmark in a particular location of the folder.

Renaming Bookmarks   You can rename a bookmark by right-clicking it and selecting Rename from the context menu. A Rename dialog box will be presented, allowing you to change the name of the bookmark.

Changing a Bookmark's Icon You can also use the context menus to change a bookmark's icon. You can right-click a bookmark and select Change Icon to display the Insert Image Resource dialog box. From this dialog box, you can select alternate icons to use for the selected bookmark.

Removing Bookmarks Removing bookmarks is another function that is performed by using context menus. Just right-click a bookmark and select Remove Bookmark from the context menu. A warning dialog box like this one appears.

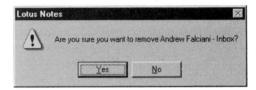

Click the Yes button to delete the bookmark or the No button to skip the delete.

How Can I Organize Bookmark Folders?

Notes is installed with a set of folders for organizing bookmarks. The top level of the hierarchy includes the following folders:

- Favorite Bookmarks
- Databases
- More Bookmarks
- Navigator/Internet Explorer Links

You can add high-level folders, which will show up directly on the Bookmark bar, and you can add subfolders under existing folders. With this capability, you can use bookmarks to personalize your Notes environment.

Adding Bookmark Folders Follow these steps to add bookmark folders:

1. Right-click any of the folder icons on the Bookmark bar. A context menu like the one shown here appears.

2. Select Create New Folder to display the Create Folder dialog box.

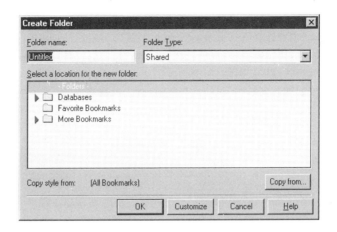

3. Type a name for the new folder in the Folder Name field.

4. To have a folder created on the Bookmark bar, select the special entry labeled – Folders – in the Select a Location field. To create a subfolder, navigate to the location in the Select a Location field where you would like the folder created.

5. Click the OK button to create the folder.

The bookmark folder will show up in the location you selected. Folders can also be renamed and removed from the same context menu.

How Are Bookmarks for Replicas Presented?

In previous releases of Notes, you could display the server name on the Workspace page's database icon. This gave you an indication of the server on which the database was located, including the local workstation. If you had selected the option to stack icons on the old Workspace page, you would have seen a small arrow button on the upper right side of the icon. This arrow was used to select which replica of the database would be opened. With bookmarks, the interaction is slightly different. As you move your mouse over bookmarks, you will notice that the server where that database or Notes object resides is displayed in the system message area of the status bar. If you select the bookmark, it will open from that location.

 NOTE The term *replica* is used to denote special copies of Notes databases that reside on different Domino servers. Replicas are special copies because Notes/Domino can keep them synchronized with the built-in replication facility. Replicas are also very important when you use Notes remotely, such as when you travel or work from home. For an introduction to Notes databases, see Chapter 3, "Working with Notes Databases." For more information on using local replicas of Notes databases, see Chapter 9, "Working with Notes Away from the Office."

Bookmarks operate in a manner similar to the manner in which stacked icons operate. That is, a bookmark represents a link to a database regardless of the location of that database. Selecting a bookmark will open the replica last accessed. If you would like to open a different replica, located on a different server, just follow these steps:

1. Navigate to the bookmark of the database you are trying to open.

2. Right-click on the bookmark. A context menu like this one appears.

3. Select Open Replica from the context menu.

4. Select the server of the replica you would like to open.

The database, or other Notes object, will be opened from the server you choose. This server will also be used the next time you select the bookmark. In the Open Replica submenu, you may have noticed the choice labeled Manage List. Selecting Manage List will bring up a dialog box similar to this.

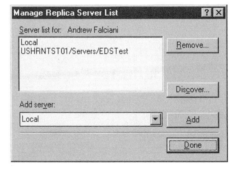

The Manage Replica Server List dialog box enables you to add additional servers where replicas of this database might reside. In previous versions, you had to open each replica to have it added to your stacked icons.

 TIP You can change which replica a bookmark points to without opening the actual database. Just hold down Shift when you choose the server from the Open Replica menu.

Getting Help

Help is always a keystroke away in Notes. Just press F1 and Notes will open a new application window with the help database displayed. The help database is your online document for Notes. It looks similar to this.

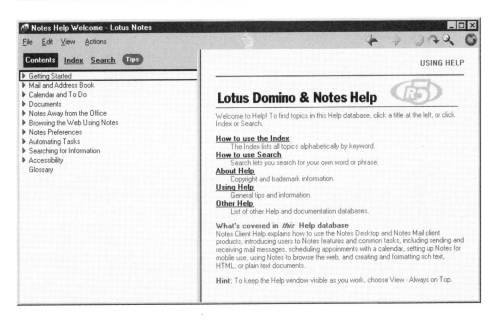

As you can see, the help database is presented in two frames. The left side displays topics and the right shows the content. There are three main views:

- Content
- Index
- Search

These views can be accessed by selecting the appropriate link at the top of the left frame.

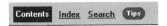

The Content view displays the help information by topic (as a book is organized by chapters). This view makes it easy to read help information by area of interest. When you first start using Notes, you may want to read through the help information this way or print it from this view. Some of the high-level areas of interest include Getting

Started, Mail and Address Book, and Notes as an Internet Client. Topics that have subtopics will have an inverted triangle icon to the left of them.

Clicking this triangle icon will expand the subtopics underneath the main topic. Clicking the triangle again will collapse them. Each subtopic may also have subtopics, creating an outline-type hierarchy. To display the contents of a particular topic, just click on its title. A page will be displayed on the right side. If the page is longer than the frame, a scroll bar will appear on the right side, enabling you to scroll down the page. Pages can also have links to other pages. Links are displayed as blue, underlined text. When you move your mouse over the link, the cursor changes to a hand icon.

Just click the link to go to the page it represents. This is very similar to browsing Web pages. You can also use the Go Back, Go Forward, and Stop buttons shown in the Navigation bar to navigate between pages you have viewed.

TIP The left side of the Help window displays a view, but there is no view selection area displayed. This is the area where you would normally select multiple documents if you wanted to print more than one at a time. To select multiple documents in this view, just click on the title of the document you want to select and press the space bar. Notes will display the view selection area and will indicate that the document has been selected by showing a check mark icon. You can select other documents by clicking in the view selection area. You can also choose Edit ➤ Select All to display the view selection area and have all Help documents selected. Choose Edit ➤ Deselect All to undo this.

The Index view is similar to the index of a book. This view displays the help information in alphabetical order by word or phrase. The view is useful when you know the topic you are looking for. Like the Contents view, the Index view displays an outline-type hierarchy. Each word or phrase has an inverted triangle to the left indicating that there are either additional words/phrases or topics underneath. One difference between this and the Contents view is that no content will be displayed on the right when you click on the hierarchy of words and phrases. You must click on the title of a topic to display the contents of that topic. Navigation is the same as it is in the Contents view.

TIP The Quick Search feature of Notes can be used in the Index view to navigate to specific words or phrases with minimal effort. Just start typing the first few letters of the word or phrase you would like to find. The Starts With dialog box is displayed with the characters you've typed. Click the OK button and Notes will navigate to the first word or phrase in the view starting with the characters you've typed.

The Search view displays all of the topics contained within the help database sorted by title. This view is not organized like the Contents or Index views. There is no hierarchy and the topics are not categorized. Also, this view includes the Search bar at the top of the left frame. Because Help is contained in a Notes database, it can be searched by using the powerful, built-in full-text index features of Notes. You can use the Search bar to initiate a search through all topics in the help database:

1. Enter a word or phrase in the Search For field
2. Click the Search button.

Notes will display topics that include the word or phrase you entered. The contents displayed in the right frame will include highlights on the words or phrases you were searching for. The Search bar can also be used to form complex queries. For more information on using the Search bar, see Chapter 8, "Searching for Information." You can use the Quick Search feature of Notes in this view too.

Bookmarking Help Topics

You can bookmark Help documents to make it easy to find topics of interest later. This is helpful for topics you may refer to over and over. Maybe you don't work with tables all the time and would like to have easy access to the help topic without having to go find it. Follow these steps to bookmark a help topic:

1. Right-click the topic and choose Bookmark from the context menu.
2. In the Add Bookmark dialog box, select an existing bookmark folder in the Add To field or click the New Folder button to create a new one.
3. Click the OK button.

A bookmark to the topic will be placed in the bookmark folder you selected.

Summary

You are now familiar with some of the basic aspects of Lotus Notes. The new Welcome page provides you with a single place to access your mail, calendar, and To Do list. The Welcome page can also be customized to provide you with a single-page view of the information that is most important to you. The Welcome page can also provide the interface for database subscriptions, which monitor databases according to criteria that you define. We explored the Notes application window and identified the screen elements with which you will interact to manage your information. We also introduced bookmarks and demonstrated their use. The next chapter will introduce concepts of the Notes database. It will define what Notes databases are, how they are presented to you, and how to perform tasks common to all Notes databases.

CHAPTER <u>3</u>

Working with Notes Databases

Unlike other general-purpose communication and information management applications, Notes is really a runtime environment for databases created with the Domino Designer integrated development environment (IDE). In fact, the base functionality of Notes—including Mail, Calendar, To Do lists, Contacts, and so on—is provided through a set of databases included with the software. This is the main reason Notes is so powerful; it can be programmed to help you accomplish a wide range of tasks that involve communication, collaboration, or coordination of unstructured information. In this chapter, we'll explain what Notes databases are, how they are presented visually on the screen, and how to perform actions common to all the various databases.

What Are Notes Databases?

To understand aspects of the Database area, it is important to be familiar with the underlying structure of the Notes database. The Notes database is a self-contained application. It consists of both the structure of the application (called the *design* in Notes parlance) and the data. The design provides the following for a given application:

- User interface
- Logic
- Security settings

The logic includes built-in elements such as *forms*, *views*, and *Agents*. Notes databases can be programmed using multiple languages, including a built-in macro language called the *formula language*, a BASIC-like language called *LotusScript*, and, new to this release, *JavaScript* and *Java*. The security settings define the access rights of individuals, servers, and groups according to the security model built in to Notes databases. See Chapter 17, "Understanding the Formula Language," for more information on using formulas and Chapter 23, "Language Extensions," for more information on using LotusScript and Java when designing Notes databases.

The data contained in a Note database is stored as a set of *documents*. A document is a collection of data elements called *fields*. Fields support many different data types, such as text and numeric. There are three types of documents:

- Main
- Response
- Response to Response

These types of documents are used to create a document hierarchy within databases. This hierarchy, if implemented, provides a native discussion capability for Notes databases. The contents of fields on each document can be different, which is what you would probably expect. What is not immediately obvious is that documents are independent from each other in the database. Each document in a Notes database can actually contain a different set of fields. This is what makes Notes a powerful platform for applications that deal with unstructured information.

At first glance, you might think *fields* and *documents* are similar to *columns* and *rows* in relational databases. In fact, they are very different. Relational databases are repositories for structured information. They contain *tables*, which logically structure data into *rows* and *columns*. Every row in a given table has all of the columns defined in the table. This lends itself to collections of rows that are similar to one another, or structured. Another aspect of relational databases that is very different from Notes databases is how data is manipulated in sets. The user or developer interacts with the relational database by using Structured Query Language (SQL), which is designed for working with sets of rows in tables. There are many other differences, but another important one to note is that relational database servers are designed to manage concurrent access to the sets of rows in the database. Because of this, they are well suited for applications/systems in which many users must modify the same information.

What Applications Should and Should Not Be Developed Using Notes/Domino?

The following types of applications are not generally well suited for Notes:

- Those involving a high degree of concurrent editing of the same data
- Those with highly structured data
- Those with high-volume data requirements

An airline reservation system is a clear example of an application that is not well suited for Notes. Thousands of travel agents will be accessing the system concurrently, trying to book reservations on a finite set of flights. It involves a high degree of concurrent edits and has high-volume data requirements.

On the other hand, a system to manage the process of conducting business travel would be a good application for a Notes database. Consider the following simplified process:

1. The employee completes a form to initiate the travel approval process.
2. The request is either approved or denied and communicated back to the employee.

Continued ▐▶

CONTINUED

3. If approved, the employee contacts the appropriate organization to make the travel arrangements.

4. The reservations are made and communicated back to the employee, along with maps, driving directions, and other relevant information.

5. The employee verifies that the arrangements were made properly.

6. The employee completes the trip.

7. After the trip, the employee initiates the expense-reporting process in a similar fashion.

8. If the travel request is denied, the employee completes the instructions provided with the denied request and resubmits it.

In this example, the travel request is only relevant to a single user at a time. The request is created by the employee and sent to management for approval. The manager acts on the request and it is returned to the employee. Also, the process involves communicating with nonstructured data, maps, and other relevant information along with the itinerary. Process-oriented applications such as this are generally well suited for Notes databases. Notes databases are appropriate for many different types of applications, including:

- Process-oriented (as previously mentioned)
- Broadcast, where common information is widely disseminated to a large audience
- Discussion
- Library
- Mail/messaging

It is important to note that Notes databases can be deployed to Notes clients or to Web browser clients. The Domino server supports either client type. Therefore, Notes databases also make for very powerful Web applications. These Web applications consist of the types of applications previously mentioned as well as many other types, including:

- Communities of interest
- Online publications
- Surveys or information collection

Another major difference between relational databases and Notes databases, until Notes 5, was that relational databases manipulated information using a mechanism called a *transaction*. That's right, Notes 5 includes support for database-level transaction processing. Transactions are essentially units of work performed by a given database management system. A typical transaction includes selecting a record to update, applying the update, and setting an indicator. The transaction is not complete unless all actions included complete successfully. Relational database management systems (RDBMSs) are synonymous with this architecture; they have had this functionality since their inception. Generally, transaction processing is implemented so that distinct functions, such as updating a row in a table, are treated as a single unit and logged to a special file outside the database. In the event that something happens while the function is being performed, the entire transaction is *rolled back,* or undone. The addition of transaction processing to Notes 5 is significant. It enhances the Notes architecture by providing better reliability, online maintenance for 24/7 operations, and greatly improved performance characteristics.

NOTE In Notes 5, the software defines transactions. Predefined functions will be treated as transactions if this feature is enabled. A future release will allow the developer to define transactions for specific application requirements, such as in relational database management systems.

You'll use *forms* for your main interaction with documents. A Notes form is a palette that includes prompts and field interface objects that provide you with a means for entering information. They are an electronic version of paper forms. Once you fill in the fields on the form and execute the Save function, a document will be created in the database. To see that document in the future, you will most likely view it through a form. Depending on the application, you may view the document by using the form through which it was created or by using a completely different form. Forms, in this respect, are like *masks* through which documents are displayed and edited.

To demonstrate, think about a piece of paper that has had holes cut out of it, like the one in Figure 3.1. Then, take that piece of paper (the mask) and place it over a paper document that has some information on it, as shown in Figure 3.2.

As you can see, some of the information on the document is displayed through the holes and some is hidden by the mask. The information is still part of the document, it is just not visible through the mask in front of it. Keep this in mind as you use Notes. Understanding the relationship between documents and forms will help you better utilize Notes. Also, it will help you develop more powerful Notes databases.

By now, you might be asking where these databases are stored. Notes databases can be stored either locally (on your workstation where Notes is running) or on a Domino server. Locally stored Notes databases are only available to you, whereas Notes databases stored on a Domino server can be shared with anyone who has the appropriate network connectivity and authority. In fact, the same database can be stored on a Domino server *and* on your local computer. Notes databases on a Domino server can be accessed from workstations running the Notes client and from workstations merely running a Web browser. Again, this is a powerful capability. You can develop a Notes database and have other people participate even if they don't have Lotus Notes on their computer.

FIGURE 3.1

An illustration of a mask

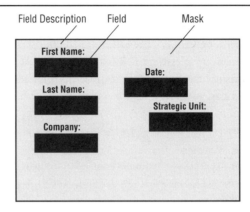

FIGURE 3.2

An illustration of a mask over a data sheet

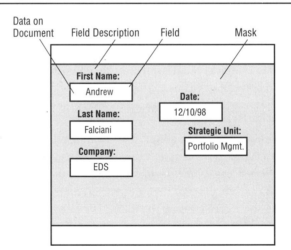

If a Notes database can be stored locally and on a Domino server, how can the two copies be kept synchronized? The answer is a facility built in to Notes and Domino called *replication*. Let's say that a database is stored on a Domino server. You create a special copy—called a *replica*—of this database on your local computer. Then, you initiate the process of replication between your computer and the Domino server, and the two databases are updated with information that has been added to or changed in both copies. There are many aspects to replication, but one in particular stands out. Replication encompasses all aspects of a Notes database, including data and design. This means that Notes databases have a built-in mechanism for deploying application changes to the end users, even remote users who work away from the office. This is one of the most important aspects of Notes and Domino.

This is just an overview of the Notes database. It is meant to introduce you to the basic concepts of databases, documents, fields, and forms. It's important that you understand these concepts because they are fundamental to all aspects of Lotus Notes. As you can see, the Notes database is different from traditional applications and databases. It is a container for both the design and the data. Its data is stored as documents, which can be independent from each other as well as from the form in which they were created. Also, Notes databases can be stored locally on your computer or shared through a Domino server and kept synchronized through the built-in capability of replication.

For more information on replication, see Chapter 9, "Working with Notes Away from the Office." Also, refer to Chapter 15, "Introducing Domino Designer," for a more complete discussion of the Notes database architecture and design elements.

The Database Area

When you open a database or run a specific task in Notes, it will be displayed in the Database area of the application window. This is where most of your interaction with Notes will occur. All elements of the application window are designed to support your use of databases. What is displayed in the Database area will vary, but the two main interfaces of all Notes databases are views and forms. Views provide the means by which you work with sets of documents in the database, whereas forms enable you to manipulate individual documents.

Navigating Around Views

Generally, you will open a database and then work on tasks within it. When you open a database, you will be presented with the view interface, which consists of three main panes:

- Navigation
- View
- Preview

Each database and each view within a given database can present these panes differently. The capability to present the view interface differently in each database makes Notes fairly unique. Again, this is where Notes is different than other integrated clients, offering e-mail integrated with personal information management and Web access. Notes is a runtime environment. It is shipped with a set of built-in databases, but it can be further extended by creating new databases. Figure 3.3 shows the example database, Mastering R5 for Chapter 3, using the default view interface. Notes databases can also be designed to present views using a frameset interface. In this case, the database developer chooses the number of panes and how they are formatted.

 NOTE A runtime environment is a software program designed to run other software programs. Lotus Notes is designed to run Notes databases developed with Lotus Domino Designer.

FIGURE 3.3

Database area with the default view interface

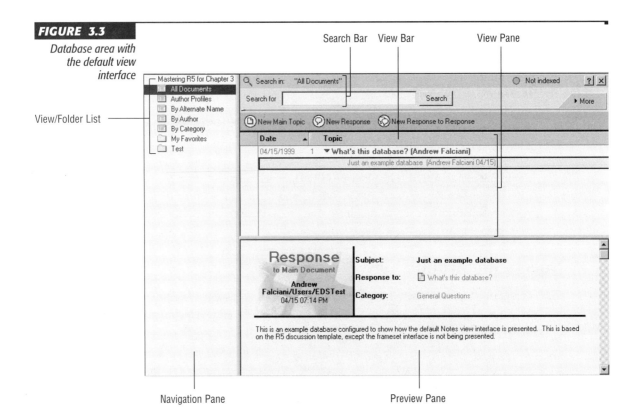

The Navigation Pane

The Navigation pane generally contains objects that guide you to various aspects of the application. This pane can be designed so that its appearance and function is similar to a Web page, or it can use the native navigation capabilities of Notes, which is called the *view/folder list*. You can click the views and folders in the view/folder list to change what is displayed in the View pane. An example view/folder list is shown here.

In some databases, the Navigation pane takes up the entire Database area. These are generally databases that use the Navigation pane to provide links to other databases or tasks within Notes. An example of this type of database is the Welcome page.

The View Pane

The View pane displays the contents of views and folders. Views and folders are your main interface for seeing collections of documents in the database. They are similar to printed reports. Both show summary information from each document as a row (organized into one or more columns) in the view or folder. Also, the rows can be categorized, or grouped, by a shared value. Shown here, discussion topics are grouped by category in the By Category view.

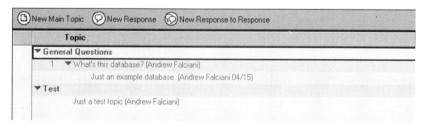

The View pane is normally located in the upper right side of the Database area and consists of four distinct elements:

- The Search bar
- The View Action bar
- View icons
- The View Content area

The Search Bar   The Search bar can be toggled on or off by selecting the Search button in the Navigation bar icon or by selecting View ➤ Search Bar. When it is toggled on, the Search bar is collapsed and shows only the basic options. Here is an example of the collapsed Search bar.

Selecting the More button on the lower right side expands the Search bar to show all available options, as shown here.

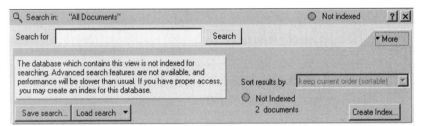

Across the top is an indicator that tells you whether or not the database is indexed. The indicator's setting is based on whether or not the database currently has a full-text index created. A full-text index improves the performance of searches performed on Notes databases and adds functionality—such as searching attachments in Notes documents—but it requires additional disk space. At the bottom of the expanded Search bar is a button to create the full-text index if one does not already exist. The following shows the expanded Search bar on a database that has a full-text index created.

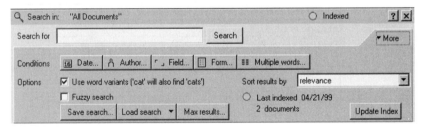

As you can see, there are many options available to you for searching Notes databases. You can specify various sets of conditions, use certain options, and even save searches for future use by you or your colleagues. See Chapter 8, "Searching for Information," for more on full-text indexes and searching.

The View Action Bar   The View Action bar is specific to each view in each database and contains buttons that enable you to perform application-specific functions. For example, the View Action bar associated with the Inbox folder of the mail database enables you to perform common functions associated with reading your e-mail, such as:

- Create a new memo.
- Reply to the message selected in the view.
- Forward the message selected in the view to another mail user.
- Delete the currently selected message.
- Move the currently selected message to another folder or remove it from the Inbox.
- Copy into another document in your mail database.
- Access mail database tools.

The Inbox View Action bar is shown here.

Buttons on the View Action bar can execute a function directly or display a menu of functions from which to choose. For example, the Tools button on the mail database's Inbox folder displays this mini menu of tools.

When the View Action bar has too many buttons to fit on the screen, two arrows are displayed on the far-right side of the View Action bar.

You can use these arrows to shift the View Action bar left and right to access buttons that don't fit on the screen.

View Icons   View icons run along the left side of the View pane and indicate the status of a document in the view:

- Selected for an action (check mark)
- Marked for deletion (trash can)
- Unread (asterisk)
- Involved in a replication conflict (diamond)

The View Content Area   The View Content area makes up the remainder of the View pane and consists of rows and columns in which selected data from documents is displayed. As mentioned earlier, the documents included in the view are determined by the View Selection formula. The columns included in the view determine the actual data displayed. Each column has its own formula and properties that can be modified by the developer. See Chapter 20, "Using Views and Folders," for more information on designing views. At the top of each column, there is a header area. If small up or down arrows like those shown here are displayed in a column's header area, you can click the column header to sort the view by that column.

If the column header has horizontal bars separating it from other columns, you can click and drag the horizontal bar to resize the column.

Options in the view definition determine whether or not these features are enabled.

TIP Use the Quick Search feature of the Notes view by clicking in the View pane to make sure it has focus and typing characters on the keyboard. A Starts With dialog box will be displayed. Type the first few characters of the document you are trying to find. If the view is categorized, you will be positioned at the category matching the characters you typed. If it's not, you will be positioned at the first document containing the characters typed in the view's first column.

The Preview Pane

The Preview pane allows you to view a document's contents without opening a separate task window within Notes. You enable the Preview pane by choosing View ➤ Document Preview ➤ Show Preview. This is a toggle, so choosing it a second time disables the Preview pane. By default, the Preview pane is positioned across the bottom half of the Database area. It can also be positioned on the lower right side or the entire right side. You can change the location of the Preview pane like this:

1. Choose View ➤ Document Preview ➤ Arrange Preview. The Preview Pane dialog box appears.

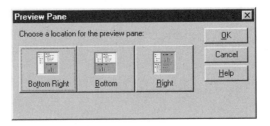

2. Click the button for the location you would like to choose.

3. Click the OK button.

The Preview pane will be repositioned to the location you chose. An example Preview pane is shown here.

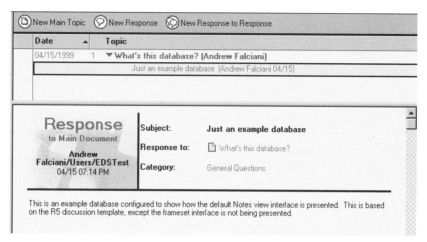

Displaying a document in the Preview pane is similar to opening a document in View mode, which is discussed in the next section. There are some differences to be aware of:

- Menu choices are not the same (click in the Preview pane before selecting menus).

- Certain form actions may or may not be available in Preview mode.

NOTE The menu choices for the Preview pane will not appear when you are using databases that have a frameset interface. If the database developer included a frame for previewing documents, it can be displayed by dragging the bar at the bottom of the view frame. Also, you cannot change its location; this is determined by the frameset designed by the database developer.

Framesets

Framesets are new to Release 5 and present a Notes database in manner similar to the manner in which many Web sites present information, by using *frames*. Frames are used to divide the Database area into separate panes in almost any manner the database developer chooses. Instead of the default set of three panes, the Database area can be divided into more or less panes as needed. The mail database is a good example of a database that uses framesets. As you can see in Figure 3.4, the left side of the Database area is made up of three frames. The first is just a title, the second displays the view/folder list, and the third provides links to other framesets in the database. The right side of the Database area is made up of two frames. The top frame displays the view and the bottom frame displays a preview of the document selected in the view.

Displaying Documents through Forms

Views display summary information about documents in a row/column structure. To display the contents of a document, Notes uses forms. Forms are also used to create new documents and modify existing ones. Again, the form design will vary from database to database, but it will always have two elements, the Form Action bar and the Form Content area, as shown in Figure 3.5.

The Form Action Bar   The Form Action bar is similar to the View Action bar in that it contains buttons for functions that you will most likely want to perform. The buttons contained on the Form Action bar are specific to each form and defined by the database developer. Each form you open will have different sets of Action buttons. Like view Action buttons, these may also contain a menu of functions that can be selected.

The Form Content Area   The Form Content area makes up the remainder of the form interface and is where data from the document is displayed through fields on the form. The content area is defined by the database developer and can include a wide variety of elements.

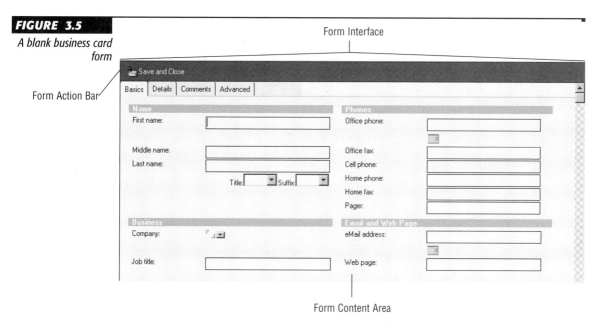

FIGURE 3.5

A blank business card form

Form Interface

Form Action Bar

Form Content Area

 NOTE When a document is opened, the form interface is displayed in the Database area over the view interface. The view interface remains open and can be accessed anytime by selecting its associated task button.

When a document is first selected from a view, it is generally displayed through a form in View mode. This means that data contained in the document is displayed through fields on the form but cannot be edited. To illustrate this, let's open a document in your personal address book. To open the LocalDomainServers group document in your address book, follow these steps:

1. Open your address book by selecting the address book icon on the Bookmark bar (fifth from the top by default).

2. Select the Groups view in the Navigation pane.

3. Double-click the row in the view that shows LocalDomainServers.

The LocalDomainServers group document will be displayed in View mode using the Group form. Press Escape to close this document. While in View mode, you will be limited in what you can do with documents. Unless a database is designed to do otherwise, View mode allows you to perform the following tasks:

- Search for information on the current page (select the Search button or menu option).
- Preview the current document's parent (if it is a Response document).
- Launch or preview any document links on the page.
- Launch, view, or see properties of attachments on the current page.
- Switch to Edit mode.

You can scroll through the form by using the Page Up/Page Down keys or by manipulating the scroll bar on the right side of the Form area. This is similar to other Windows applications.

You can use the following methods to search for information on the current page:

- Click the Search button in the Navigation bar.
- Select Edit ➢ Find/Replace.

The Find Text in Document dialog box will be displayed, allowing you to enter a text string to find. Click the Find Next button to perform the search. The string you are searching for will be highlighted in the Form area. You can also select the Options button and further customize your search. Doclinks and attachments are items that can be entered into fields on a document and are discussed in the next section.

Working in Notes Databases

Now that you have a general understanding of the elements in a Notes database, it's time to explore basic actions you will perform regularly.

Opening Databases

First, you need to open the database in which you need to work. There are a number of ways to open databases in Notes. The following methods are some of the more common:

- Select a link from your Bookmark bar.
- Select a link from one of your Bookmark pages.
- Select File ➢ Database ➢ Open (or press Ctrl+O).
- Select a link embedded in a Notes document.

If you use the Database Open dialog box, you will need to know where the database is stored (locally or on a Domino server) and in which directory it is located on the target computer. As you can see in the Open Database dialog box shown below, there is a drop-down list, labeled Server, for selecting the server where the database resides.

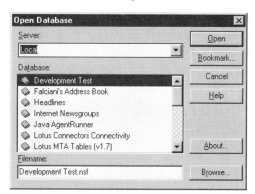

In the Server drop-down list, Local represents your local computer. When Local is selected, the list of databases represents those stored locally on your computer. If you select the drop-down arrow on the right side of the field, a list of servers is displayed. The servers displayed are a combination of those you have previously browsed and those to which you have predefined connections. The Database field is a list box that lets you select from a list of databases on the selected server. It also displays folders on the selected server where databases might be stored. The Filename field allows you to enter a filename directly.

NOTE In the Open Database dialog box, the list of databases available on a given target server is relative to the server's Data directory. When Local is selected, the list of databases displayed is relative to the Data directory of your local Notes environment, which by default is C:\Lotus\Notes\Data.

The Open button opens the database or folder currently selected in the Database list box or typed into the Filename field. You can also double-click a database or folder name listed in the Database list box to open it. If you choose to open a database, the Open Database dialog box will disappear and the selected database will be displayed in the application window. If you choose to open a folder, the contents of that folder will be displayed in the Database list box. When a folder is open, the last entry in the Database list box will be an icon of an up arrow.

If you double-click this icon or highlight it and click the Open button, Notes will display the contents of the folder up one level in the folder hierarchy.

The Bookmark button will allow you to create a bookmark to the database selected in the Database list box or typed into the Filename field. See Chapter 2, "Getting Familiar with Notes," for more information on creating and using bookmarks.

The Cancel button closes the Open Database dialog box without opening a database. All bookmarks created while the Open Database dialog box was active will remain.

The About button displays the About document for the selected database. The About document is created by the developer of the database and normally displays high-level information regarding the purpose and scope of the database. After viewing the About document, click the Close button to return to the Open Database dialog box. Here is an example of an About document.

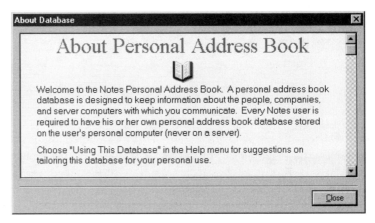

The Browse button allows you to browse your file system for Notes databases located outside your local Notes Data directory. This is handy if you are trying to open a database that you have downloaded from an Internet site or some other external source to a folder/directory on your computer. It is also used to open database templates because the Open Database dialog box only displays database files. Database templates are an advanced topic and discussed further in Chapter 16, "Creating Your First Database." When the Browse button is selected, a File Open dialog box displays, allowing you to choose a file from your local computer's file system. Here is an example of the File Open dialog box.

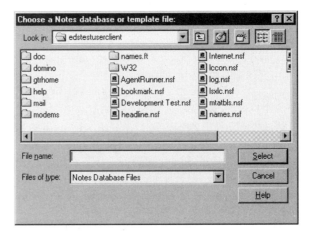

To close a database, just press Escape or click the *X* on the right side of the database's task button.

Working in Views

Once a database is opened, you are most likely to be presented with a view. A view is the main interface to a database and is generally designed to show you summary information about documents in the database. This summary information is displayed in a row/column format, where each document is represented as a row. From the view, you are able to perform many common actions on documents, such as:

- Opening and closing documents
- Deleting documents
- Organizing documents into folders
- Working with sets of documents

Opening and Closing Documents

As previously mentioned, a view displays summary information about documents in a database. This is great if you are trying to find a document or if you are only interested in seeing the summary information. If you want to see or edit the contents of a document, you need to open it through a form. Normally, you will open documents from the view interface. Follow these steps to open an existing Group document in your address book:

1. Open your address book by selecting the address book icon on the Bookmark bar (fifth from the top by default).
2. Select the Groups view from the view/folder list in the Navigation pane.
3. Select a row in the View Content area representing the document you wish to open. For this example, select the row displaying LocalDominoServers.
4. Either press Enter or double-click its row.

The document will be displayed through a form in a new task window. To close the form, either press Escape or click the *X* to the right of the form's task button.

You can also close forms and other task windows by double-clicking the right mouse button. To enable this feature, follow these steps:

1. Select File ➢ Preferences ➢ User Preferences to open the User Preferences dialog box.
2. Select the Basics icon on the left side (this is the default choice).
3. In the Additional options box, scroll up until you see the choice called Right Double-Click Closes Window.

4. Click to the left of this choice to enable it. A check mark-icon appears to the left of it.

5. Click OK.

A warning message dialog box, like the one shown below, appears with the text "Some preferences will not take effect until next time the program is started." This is normal.

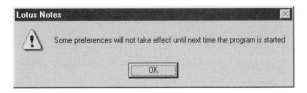

 NOTE The Right Double-Click Closes Window option will not take effect until you exit and restart Notes.

Deleting Documents

Another common action you will perform from the view interface is deleting documents from the database. Follow these steps to delete a document:

1. Select a row in the View Content area representing the document you wish to delete.

2. Either press Delete or select Edit ➢ Clear.

A trash can icon is displayed in the view icon area next to the deleted document. At this point, the document is not actually deleted from the database. If you close the database or press F9 to refresh the view, a message box like the one shown here appears with a message asking if you wish to delete the selected documents from the database.

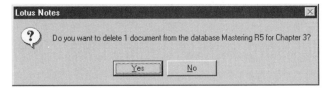

Select the Yes button to permanently delete the documents. If you are refreshing the view, selecting No leaves the documents marked for deletion. If you are closing the database, selecting No removes the deletion mark and closes the database. Upon reentry, the documents are no longer marked for deletion.

NOTE Release 5 introduces a new feature, called soft delete, which allows you to undelete documents. Soft deletes are enabled on a database-by-database basis and are turned off by default. See Chapter 16, "Creating Your First Database," for more information on enabling the Allow Soft Deletions option on databases you create.

Organizing Documents into Folders

Folders enable you to organize documents in an ad hoc manner. Folders can be personal, which allows you to individualize a Notes database. They can also be shared, which allows a group of people to manipulate the organization of documents in a Notes database. One common use for folders is organizing e-mail. You can create folders in your mail database and then file messages in them for future reference. As shown here, you can add folders to your mail file to suit your individual needs.

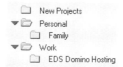

Folders can easily be added to just about any Notes database, but you must have the appropriate authority. Because you should have the authority to create folders in your mail database, we will use it to demonstrate how to create a folder. To create a folder called Projects in your mail database, follow these steps:

1. Open your mail database by selecting the Mail icon from the Bookmark bar.

2. Select Create ➣ Folder. A Create Folder dialog box similar to the one shown here appears.

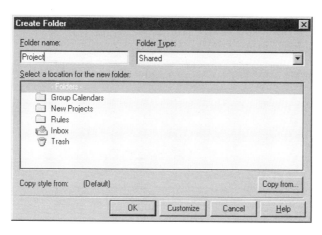

3. Enter a name for the folder in the Folder Name field. For this example, enter **Projects**.

4. Do not change anything in the other fields. By default, the new folder will be created at the top level of the view/folder hierarchy, and its design will be copied from the view/folder listed in the Copy Style From field. For more information on designing folders, see Chapter 20, "Using Views and Folders."

The `Projects` folder will be displayed at the top level of the view/folder hierarchy, and its design will be based on the All Documents view. Folders can also be easily renamed, redesigned, moved, and deleted. To rename the `Projects` folder created in the preceding example to New Projects, follow these steps:

1. Select the `Projects` folder in the Navigation pane.

2. Select Actions ➢ Folder Options ➢ Rename. A Rename dialog box will be displayed.

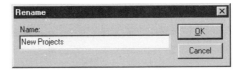

3. Type the new name for the folder in the Name field. In this example, type **New Projects**.

4. Click the OK button.

The `Projects` folder will now be displayed as `New Projects`. The process of moving a folder to another location in the view/folder hierarchy is also fairly simple. It enables you to organize your folders any way you want, even after they have been created. To move the `New Projects` folder under your Inbox, follow these steps:

1. Select the `New Projects` folder in the Navigation pane.

2. Select Actions ➢ Folder Options ➢ Move. A Move dialog box appears.

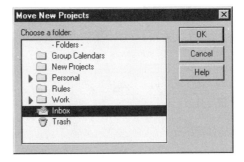

3. Select Inbox in the Choose a Folder field.

4. Click the OK button.

The New Projects folder will now be displayed underneath the Inbox view. To move it back to the top level of the view/folder hierarchy, perform the preceding steps without selecting anything in the Choose a Folder field. Folders can easily be removed when they are no longer needed. To remove the New Projects folder, follow these steps:

1. Select the New Projects folder in the Navigation pane.

2. Select Actions ➤ Folder Options ➤ Delete Folder. A warning dialog box appears with a message that this delete action cannot be undone. This is normal. The warning box will look similar to the one shown here.

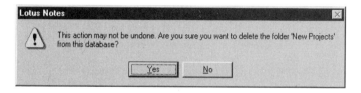

3. Click the Yes button to delete the folder.

The New Projects folder will no longer be displayed in the view/folder list. You can also redesign a folder after it has been created. You can access the folder design screen by selecting Actions ➤ Folder Options ➤ Design after selecting a folder. Folder design is an advanced topic and discussed further in Chapter 20.

NOTE If you remove a folder, the documents contained within it will not be removed, but the pointers to those documents will be deleted. Pointers are explained later in this section.

Folders are visually very similar to views. In fact, they are displayed alongside views in the database's view/folder list, which is generally displayed on the left side of the Database area. Views are shown with a report icon to the left of them and folders are shown with a file folder icon.

Just as views do, folders display documents in rows and columns, and the rows can be grouped by data values contained within documents. The main difference between views and folders is that views show documents meeting specific criteria, whereas folders show documents based on pointers that can be added and removed. The criteria by which documents are displayed in views is called the View Selection formula. It is defined when the view is created or modified by the developer using Domino Designer. In contrast, documents are displayed in folders if the folder contains a pointer to them. You can add document pointers to folders in a number of ways, including:

- Using the Actions menu
- Using a View Action button (if one exists)
- Direct manipulation using drag-and-drop

 NOTE The examples in this chapter will use the Mastering R5 for Chapter 3 Example database (masterr5c03.nsf) provided on the CD accompanying this book.

Using the Actions Menu   The most straightforward way to add document pointers to folders is to use the Actions menu. If a View Action button exists, it will operate the same way. Let's experiment by using the Chapter 3 Example database from the CD. Follow these steps to create a folder called Important Topics:

1. Open the Mastering R5 for Chapter 3 Example database (masterr5c03.nsf). It is in the Masterr5 directory within your Notes Data directory.
2. Select Create ➣ Folder.
3. Enter **Important Topics** into the Folder Name field.
4. Click the OK button.

The Mastering R5 for Chapter 3 Example database has some documents in the All Documents view. We'll use these documents to experiment with adding documents to folders. To add a document to the Important Topics folder, follow these steps:

1. Select the All Documents view.
2. Select a document in the View pane.
3. Choose Action ➣ Move to Folder. A Move to Folder dialog box similar to this one appears.

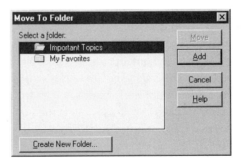

4. Select the `Important Topics` folder from the Select a Folder field.

5. Click the Add button.

You won't see an indication that the document was added unless you select the `Important Topics` folder. If you perform this same procedure from inside a folder, you will notice that the Move to Folder dialog box has an additional button available, the Move button. This button is available because documents in folders represent pointers that can be moved or removed from the folder, whereas views show the actual documents, which can only be removed if the Selection formula is modified.

Direct Manipulation Using Drag-and-Drop   Another way to add documents to folders or move them from one folder to another is to use drag-and-drop to manipulate them directly. Again, the document will not be removed from the view after this action is performed. To move documents from one folder to another folder, just select and drag the document from the folder to a folder icon in the Navigation pane. If you hold down the Ctrl key and then perform this action, the document will be added to the new folder without being removed.

 WARNING Deleting a document from a folder deletes it from the database. If you would like to keep a document but remove it from a given folder, select the document in the folder and choose Action ≻ Remove from Folder.

Views and folders are design elements in a database. As such, they can be modified to suit your needs. You can use views and folders to display information in a variety of ways depending on the task you need to perform. To modify the structure of views or folders, you need to understand how to use Domino Designer to develop applications. Some changes may be simple, but other changes may be very complex. Either way, a basic understanding of how databases are developed is important before starting. Please refer to Chapter 20, for more information on creating and modifying views and folders.

 NOTE Domino Designer 5 must be installed on your computer before you can create or modify design elements, such as views.

Working with Sets of Documents

Sometimes it's helpful to work on more than one document at a time. You can quickly delete, print, categorize, file in folders, mark read/unread, export to a file, and run

Agents against sets of selected documents. To select and deselect documents, you can use one of the following methods:

- Select the row of the document you wish to select or deselect and press the spacebar.
- Click the View Icon area next to the documents you wish to select or deselect.
- Click and drag in the View Icon area to select or deselect multiple, adjacent documents.
- Choose Edit ➤ Select All or Edit ➤ Deselect All to select or deselect all documents in the view.

Selected documents will have a check mark next to them in the View Icon area.

Using Forms to Create and Modify Documents

As discussed earlier in this chapter, you can use forms to create, modify, and display documents. Opening an existing document displays the contents of the document through its associated form. When the contents are displayed through the form but not available for changes, the form is in View mode. Many databases open documents to View mode by default. When the contents are displayed through the form and available for changes, the form is in Edit mode. When a new document is created, a blank form is opened in Edit mode. The main difference between the two modes is that you can make changes to the document only when it is in Edit mode.

Like their paper counterpart, forms in Notes are a collection of fields and field descriptions. Field descriptions provide a simple cue that helps you identify what information should be entered into a particular field. In the field shown here, the word *To* is a field description that tells you that the area next to it is for entering the name or names of recipients for this mail message.

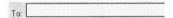

Field descriptions are generally text elements, like the word *To* in the preceding example. These text elements can also be formatted by:

- Font
- Size
- Style
- Color

Forms can also contain more complex field description elements, such as:

- Objects
- Pictures
- Tables
- Sections
- Hotspots
- Java applets

Fields are represented either by distinct blocked-off areas of the screen or by a set of brackets on the screen. They are areas on the screen that accept your input; that is, where you would type information or select from a set of choices. When you enter a field, the cursor will be visible, signifying your position in the field. As you type, the cursor will change position as it does in other Windows applications. There are many types of fields that can be presented on forms in Notes, including:

Text	Combobox
Date/time	Rich text
Number	Authors
Dialog list	Names
Checkbox	Readers
Radio button	Password
Listbox	Formula

As a user, you only need to know that fields on a form accept your input and can include many types of information. Field descriptions provide you with cues that help identify what information should be entered into a particular field. If you are designing forms, see Chapter 18, "Using Forms to Collect Data," and Chapter 19, "Advanced Form Design," for a complete explanation of fields and how they can be used.

Creating New Documents

Most of the tasks you will perform in Notes—such as adding Contacts to your Personal Address Book, sending e-mail to an associate, and managing appointments in your calendar—involve creating documents. The basic process for creating documents is as follows:

1. Open a blank form.

2. Fill in the appropriate information.

3. Execute the Save function.

4. Close the form if necessary.

Generally, opening a blank form involves opening a database and selecting the appropriate form from the Create menu. In the case of common tasks, such as adding Contacts, you can also create bookmarks to blank forms as shortcuts. For instructions on how to add blank forms as bookmarks, see Chapter 2.

 TIP The Create menu also includes a special Mail submenu for documents created within your mail database, such as memos (mail messages), replies, tasks, and calendar entries. The Create ➢ Mail menu is available at all times within Notes so you can quickly access these forms.

To demonstrate how new documents are created in Notes, let's create a new memo in your mail database. Follow these steps to create a new memo:

1. Open your mail database by selecting the Mail icon from the Bookmark bar.

2. Open the Drafts view by selecting Drafts in the Navigation pane.

3. Select Create ➢ Memo or click the New Memo button on the View Action bar.

A blank memo form, like the one shown in Figure 3.6, opens in Edit mode. You can tell the form has been opened in Edit mode because fields are available for entering information and the cursor is positioned in the first field.

FIGURE 3.6

A blank memo form

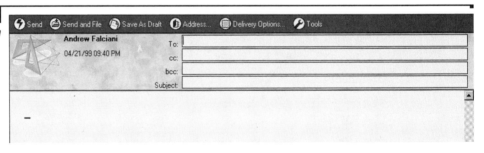

How you fill in the appropriate information on a blank form depends on how the form was designed. It involves navigating around the fields on the form and entering data in the proper places. To navigate around fields on a form, you can use the Tab and Shift+Tab keys or the mouse. Tab and Shift+Tab work like they do in other Windows applications until you encounter a rich text field. Because rich text fields can store formatted text, as well as many other types of data, Tab and Shift+Tab are interpreted as part of the text and not used to navigate fields. To navigate out of a rich text field, use the mouse to select another field. When you use the Tab+Shift keys, your cursor will move from field to field based on the tab order defined by the form's designer. If you use the mouse, you can select any field on the screen in any order you choose. To fill in the blank memo form previously opened, follow these steps:

1. Press Tab to move your cursor to the Subject field, the blank space next to the word *Subject*.

2. Type **Test of creating new document** in the Subject field.

There are a few different ways to save a new document:

- Select File ➢ Save.
- Click the Save button on the Form Action bar if one exists.
- Press Escape and select the Save option in the dialog box that appears.
- Perform an action that causes form logic to save the document if the form is designed this way.

Pressing Escape and selecting the appropriate Save option will also close the form. To close the form yourself after saving the document, press Escape or click the *X* to the right of the form's task button. To save the document we just created and close the form, click the Save as Draft button on the Form Action bar. The form will be closed and you will be returned to the Drafts view, which should contain the document you just created.

Modifying Existing Documents

Editing documents is similar to creating new ones, except some of the fields may already have information in them when you open the form. There are a number of ways to open a document for editing:

- Select a document in a view and then click the Edit button on the View Action bar if one exists.
- Open the document and click the Edit button on the Form Action bar if one exists.
- Open a document and double-click anywhere in the Form Content area.
- Select a document in a view and press Ctrl+E.

TIP To toggle between View mode and Edit mode, press Ctrl+E on your keyboard or double-click inside the Form Content area.

Of course, a form could be designed to automatically open documents in Edit mode. If this is the case, all you would have to do to edit a document would be to open it. Then, you can navigate around the form as if the document was just being created. After making whatever changes are necessary to the document, you can save it and close the form.

Document Features

When you are viewing documents through forms, you can enable and disable a number of available document features. The following options are available while the form is in View mode:

- Show Page Breaks
- Show Pass-Thru HTML
- Show HTML Source

Show Page Breaks   Show Page Breaks can be toggled on and off. When it's enabled, a horizontal line will be drawn across the form where page breaks will occur if the document is printed. This is handy if you are trying to format text within a document so the document will paginate properly. You can toggle the Show Page Breaks option on and off by selecting View ➤ Show ➤ Page Breaks. A check mark will appear to the left of the selection when the option is enabled.

 NOTE To insert page breaks in a rich text field, position your cursor where you want the page break and choose Create ➤ Page Break.

Show Pass-Thru HTML   Show Pass-Thru HTML can also be toggled on and off. This option will display or hide text formatted as Pass-Thru HTML in the document. Text formatted as Pass-Thru HTML is generally used for designing forms. You can toggle the Show Pass-Thru option on and off by selecting View ➤ Show ➤ Pass-Thru HTML. A check mark will appear to the left of the selection when the option is enabled.

Show HTML Source   Show HTML Source is only activated when the form displayed contains HTML data, such as a Web page that you are viewing through the native Notes browser or the integrated Internet Explorer browser supported by Notes. This function is similar to the View ➤ Source menu option common to Web browsers. To view the HTML source of a Web page, follow these steps:

1. Make sure you have a Web page open as a form in Notes.

2. Select View ➤ Show ➤ HTML Source.

A new form will open within Notes displaying a page with the HTML source code of the Web page you were viewing. In other browsers, the HTML source is displayed as plain text. In Notes, however, the HTML is actually formatted with tags highlighted in different colors.

In addition, the following document features are available when the form is in Edit mode:

- Show Field Help
- Show Hidden Characters
- Show Hidden From Notes
- Show Java Applets Running

Show Field Help   Show Field Help can be toggled on and off. When it's enabled, Notes displays the field help associated with fields on the form. Field help is a feature supported by Notes forms that enables a form designer to include text for each field to help the user fill in the proper information. The field help text is displayed in the system message area of the status bar if it is available and the Show Field Help option has been enabled. To toggle the Show Field Help option on and off, select View ➤ Show ➤ Field Help. A check mark will appear to the left of the selection when the option is enabled.

Show Hidden Characters   Show Hidden Characters can be toggled on and off. When it's enabled, Notes displays hidden characters contained within the document. Hidden characters include paragraph marks, tabs, and other formatting characters. To toggle the Show Hidden Characters option on and off, select View ➤ Show ➤ Hidden Characters. A check mark will appear to the left of the selection when the option is enabled.

Show Hidden From Notes   Show Hidden From Notes can be toggled on and off. When it's enabled, Notes displays elements that the designer of the form has designated as hidden to the Notes client. Choosing whether or not elements are hidden from the Notes client is a design topic and is covered in Chapter 18. To toggle the Show Hidden From Notes option on and off, select View ➤ Show ➤ Hidden From Notes. A check mark will appear to the left of the selection when the option is enabled.

Show Java Applets Running   Show Java Applets Running can be toggled on and off. When it's enabled, Notes displays Java applets currently running in the form. Java applets are software components generally associated with Web-based applications. Release 5 supports the execution of Java applets within the client. Java applets represent a sophisticated way to execute software on client computers and are outside the scope of this book. To toggle the Show Java Applets option on and off, select View ➢ Show ➢ Java Applets. A check mark will appear to the left of the selection when the option is enabled.

Entering Information into Fields

As previously mentioned, information is entered into Notes databases via fields on forms. These are called *editable* fields. Editable fields allow you to enter information. Other fields, such as computed or computed for display fields, are used to show information and do not allow data entry. Each editable field type (discussed in the following sections) can be presented differently, and each allows you to enter certain information.

Text Fields   Text fields are used to collect free-form, textual information, such as subjects for an e-mail message or a short description for a discussion topic. Text fields are very common. They can be presented in a number of different ways on the form and in two different styles. The first style should be familiar to anyone who has used Notes in the past. The text field is marked with brackets on the left and right sides, similar to the following.

Text (Bracket):

For Release 5, Notes also supports text fields that use the native interface of the operating system (the second style). In Windows, an OS-style field is similar to the following.

Text (Native OS)

Date/Time Fields   Date/time fields are used to collect date-type information. The Notes database designer can customize the display and edit format, but the actual data is stored as a special numeric value. This makes it possible to perform calculations on dates stored in Notes databases. Storing date/time data as a special numeric value is also very efficient because it takes less space than data stored as text.

Just like text fields, date/time fields can be presented a number of different ways on the form and in two different styles. With the first style, the field is marked with brackets on the left and right sides just like the text field. For Release 5, Notes also supports OS-style date/time fields similar to this.

OS-style date/time fields will generally have a calendar icon to the right of the field. The calendar icon will present a calendar interface for selecting dates.

Date/time fields accept values from 01/01/0001 to 12/31/9999. You will not be allowed to enter information if it's not a valid date or time value. They can also be programmed to require 4-digit years. If a date/time field is not programmed to require 4-digit years, Notes will interpret the information you enter. If the year is entered as a 2-digit number from 50 to 99, it will be entered as a year in the 20th century (1950 to 1999). If the year is entered as a 2-digit number from 00 to 49, it will be entered as a year in the 21st century (2000 to 2049).

Number Fields   Number fields are used to collect numeric information, including currency. They can be presented a number of different ways on the form and in two different styles. With the first style, the field is marked with brackets on the left and right sides just like the text field. For Release 5, Notes also supports OS-style number fields, shown here.

Dialog List, Listbox, Combobox, Checkbox, and Radio Button Fields   Dialog list, listbox, combobox, checkbox, and radio button fields are used to collect information from predefined sets of choices called *keywords*. Like text fields, they are also common fields. They are used to make sure information entered is kept consistent. For example, you may have a database to keep track of products, and each product includes a value for the category field. If you made this a text field and let users enter values, there would probably be many variations of the same category. It would be much better to make it a dialog list or listbox field.

With dialog list fields, the keywords are presented through a dialog box, as shown here.

If dialog list fields are designed to allow multiple values, you will be able to choose multiple keywords. Selected keywords will have a check mark. If dialog list fields are designed to accept new values, you will be able to type new keywords into the dialog box. Dialog list fields may also be designed to present the Directories dialog box, the Access Control List dialog box, or a View dialog box. The Directories dialog box is used to choose names instead of keywords, and the Access Control List dialog box is used to choose names from the database's Access Control List (ACL). The View dialog box is used to display choices based on a view from a database.

Listbox fields present the keywords in a framed element in the Form Content area with arrows on the right side for scrolling through the choices. If listbox fields are designed to allow multiple values, you will be able to choose multiple keywords. Selected keywords will have a check mark. Listbox fields cannot be designed to accept new values.

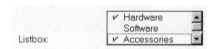

Combobox fields present the keywords in a drop-down element in the Form Content area. Combobox fields cannot be designed to allow multiple values or to accept new values.

Checkbox fields present the keywords as a set of check-box elements in the Form Content area. If checkbox fields are designed to accept multiple values, you can select multiple check boxes. Checkbox fields cannot be designed to accept new values.

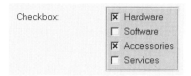

Radio button fields present the keywords as a set of radio button elements in the Form Content area. Radio button fields cannot be designed to allow multiple values or to accept new values.

Rich Text Fields   The rich text field is powerful features of Notes. These fields are like containers for storing many different types of information. See the next section for more information on entering information into rich text fields.

The other field types—names, authors, readers, password, and formula—are used to accommodate special requirements of certain applications. More information on these fields types and the ones briefly mentioned here can be found in Chapter 18, "Using Forms to Collect Data," and Chapter 19, "Advanced Form Design."

Working with Rich Text Fields

Rich text fields contain formatted text and also act as a container for objects, attachments, pictures, tables, and other elements. They enable you to include data from a variety of sources in Notes documents. You can scan a document or picture and copy and paste it into a rich text field. You can work with objects from other Windows applications directly inside them; for example, you can create a Word document inside a rich text field. Files from your computer can also be attached to rich text fields. Attachments can then be viewed or detached. Rich text fields also provide a rich set of native formatting options for text created within them. You can tell you are in a rich text field if the font, point size, and style areas of the status bar display values are accessible.

Adding Formatted Text

It's easy to use rich text fields to create documents that have formatted text. You just type the information into the rich text field, use the mouse to highlight the area to be formatted, and then choose the desired formatting options. The following formatting options are among those available to you in rich text fields:

- Font
- Point size
- Style (italic, bold, underline, strikethrough)
- Effects (shadow, emboss, extrude, superscript, subscript)
- Color
- Paragraph alignment
- Paragraph margins
- List type (bullet, number, check mark, circle, square)

 TIP Use the check mark list type to create lists in Notes rich text fields that can have items checked or unchecked. It can be used to show which items have been completed or items that need emphasis.

Formatting options can be selected from the menu, the context menu, and the Properties InfoBox. When your cursor is inside a rich text field, a Text Properties menu similar to the following appears in the menu bar.

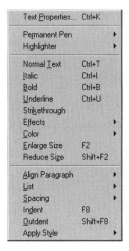

If you right-click highlighted text in a rich text field, a context menu similar to the one below will be displayed.

As you can see, the context menu provides you with some of the more common formatting options. You can also open the Text Properties InfoBox (shown here open to the Font tab) from this context menu by selecting Text Properties.

The first three tabs—Font, Paragraph Alignment, and Paragraph Margins—allow you to modify the most common options, such as:

- Font
- Size
- Style
- Color
- Paragraph alignment
- List style
- Paragraph spacing
- Margins
- Tab stops
- Pagination

The fourth tab, Paragraph Hide-When, allows you to selectively hide paragraphs. Hiding paragraphs is a technique used most often when designing forms. See Chapter 18 for more information. The last tab, Paragraph Style, allows you to create and modify named styles based on the current paragraph's formatting options. Paragraph styles can then be applied to other paragraphs, simplifying formatting.

When you work in rich text fields, Notes can also display a ruler across the top of the Form area. The ruler can be used to modify the left margin, the paragraph indent, and tab stops. To display the ruler, follow these steps:

1. Make sure you are in a rich text field.

2. Select View ➤ Ruler. The ruler, shown below, appears at the top of the Form area.

To practice using rich text fields, let's create a new mail message in your mail database. Here's how:

1. Open your mail database by selecting the Mail icon from the Bookmark bar.

2. Create a new mail message (document) by clicking the New Memo button on the View Action bar or by selecting Create ➤ Memo.

3. Press Tab to move your cursor to the Body field, the blank area underneath the mail header information.

4. Type **Testing the features of rich text fields** in the Body field.

5. Highlight the text you just typed and play with formatting by selecting options from the Text menu or by using the Text Properties InfoBox as previously mentioned.

To close the form, press Escape or click the *X* to the right of the form's task button. A dialog box with save options will be presented, like this one.

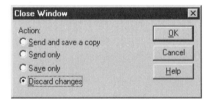

Because we were just testing features of rich text fields and don't need to save this document, select Discard Changes and then click the OK button.

 TIP If you select the Properties InfoBox toolbar icon while editing a rich text field, the Text Properties InfoBox will minimize itself to show a set of common formatting icons. You can use it to quickly change the formatting of text without constantly going back to the menus.

You can also copy and paste formatted text into a rich text field. If you copy information from an application that supports rich text data (such as Microsoft Word) to the Windows Clipboard, it can be pasted into a Notes rich text field with its associated formatting. To see how this works, just follow these steps:

1. Create a memo document in your mail database as explained in the preceding example.

2. In Word (or another application that can copy rich text to the Clipboard), high-light some text and select Edit ➤ Copy.

3. Go back to Notes and make sure your cursor is positioned in the Body field, the blank area underneath the mail header information.

4. Select Edit ➤ Paste Special. The Paste Special dialog box appears.

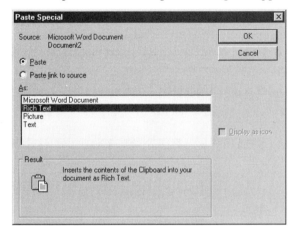

5. Select the Paste radio button, select Rich Text from the As field, and then click the OK button.

The text you copied to the Clipboard from Word should be displayed in the Notes rich text field. The text itself is editable within the rich text field, just as if it were typed directly into the field. To close the form, press Escape or click the *X* to the right of the form's task button. In the Close Window dialog box, select Discard Changes and then click the OK button.

Inserting OLE Objects

OLE, or object linking and embedding, is a protocol built into Windows that enables applications to share data. It was Microsoft's first foray into component software archi-tectures and the precursor to programmatic interfaces such as ActiveX, COM/DCOM, and now, Distributed InterNetwork Architecture. OLE objects can be inserted into rich text fields, making Notes a powerful OLE container application. Notes can control OLE objects programmatically, but it also provides the interfaces required to let you link and embed objects into rich text fields. See Chapter 11 for more information on using object linking and embedding in Notes.

Attaching Files

Rich text fields can also contain attachments, or computer files from other programs (for example, word processor documents, spreadsheets, images, etc.). You can insert attachments anywhere in the rich text field. Just position your cursor where you want the attachment inserted and select File ➢ Attach. A dialog box will be displayed that allows you to choose a file from your computer's disk drive. See Chapter 11 for more information on attaching file in Notes.

Adding Pictures

You can copy and paste graphic images into rich text fields as well as import graphic files. This is useful for discussions in which a picture would help express an idea better than text alone. Pictures can also be included in e-mail.

The Create Picture menu is used to import graphic files into rich text fields. To import a graphic file, follow these steps:

1. Make sure you are in a rich text field.

2. Select Create ➢ Picture. An Import dialog box like the following appears.

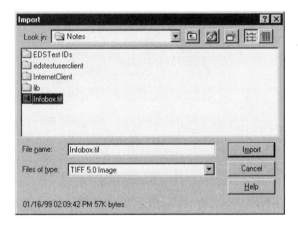

3. Using this dialog box, you can navigate around your computer's file system to locate the graphic file to import into the current rich text field. The dialog box will only display files of the type selected.

4. Once you have chosen a graphic file to import, click the Import button.

The image will be displayed in the rich text field. You can also copy and paste graphics into rich text fields. To do so, follow these steps:

1. Make sure you are in a rich text field.

2. Launch the application containing the image you would like to copy and paste into Notes.

3. Select the image and copy it to the Windows Clipboard by choosing Edit ➢ Copy (the Edit menu exists in most Windows applications).

4. Go back to Notes and select Edit ➢ Paste.

The image will be displayed in the rich text field. To manipulate the image inside the rich text field, use the Picture Properties InfoBox. To display the Picture Properties InfoBox, use one of the following methods:

- Right-click the image and select Picture Properties from the context menu.
- Click on the image and select Picture ➤ Picture Properties.

The Picture Properties InfoBox allows you to do the following:

- Determine how text should wrap around the image.
- Change the image's scaling.
- Add a caption to the image.
- Add hotspots to the image.
- Add a border to the image.

Creating Tables

You can create tables in rich text fields to structure text. Tables present information as a series of rows and columns. Each cell can contain rich text elements such as formatted text, pictures, and so on. Cells can also contain other tables. Notes supports different types of tables including:

- Standard
- Tabbed
- Interval
- Dynamic

Generally, you will create standard tables when you are creating documents. The other table types are primarily used for designing forms and are discussed in Chapter 19. Follow these steps to create a standard table:

1. Make sure you are in a rich text field.

2. Select Create ➤ Table. The Create Table dialog box (shown here) appears.

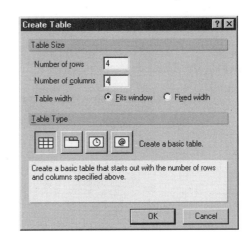

3. Select the standard table icon (the first icon on the left in the Type area).

4. Enter the number of rows and columns to include in the table.

5. Click the OK button.

A table like the one shown here will be displayed with the number of rows and columns you selected.

You can navigate between cells using the Tab key and the arrow keys. You can also use the mouse to position your cursor directly in a cell. Once the cursor is inside a cell, you can add formatted text and other rich text elements as needed. This is a great way to structure information within a Notes document. A table can have formatted text in one cell, a picture in another, an attachment in a third, and any number of other rich text elements in the remaining cells. You can also create another table in a cell. To create a table within a table, follow these steps:

1. Navigate to a cell within an existing table.

2. Select Create ➤ Table. The Create Table dialog box appears.

3. Select the standard table icon (the first icon on the left in the Type area).

4. Enter the number of rows and columns to include in the table.

5. Click the OK button.

Inside the cell where your cursor was positioned, a table will be displayed with the number of rows and columns selected. Here's an example of a table with many rich text elements included.

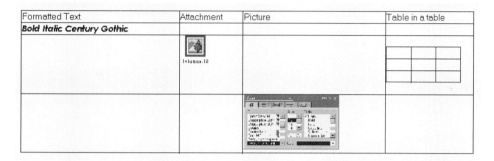

Formatted Text	Attachment	Picture	Table in a table
Bold Italic Century Gothic			
	Infobox.lil		

Once a table has been created, you can modify its formatting properties, including:

- Cell spacing
- Table border style
- Cell border style
- Row and column color/style
- Cell color
- Cell image
- Margins

Formatting properties are modified by selecting options on the Table Properties InfoBox. To display the Table Properties InfoBox, follow these steps:

1. Navigate to a cell within an existing table.

2. Select Table ➤ Table Properties. The Table Properties InfoBox will be opened and the Table Layout tab (shown here) will be displayed.

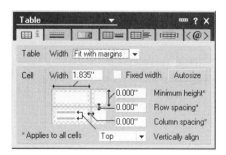

If you select the Properties InfoBox Toolbar button with the Table Properties InfoBox displayed, the Properties InfoBox will be reduced to a toolbar.

The Table toolbar provides a set of buttons that allow you to change the table in a number of ways:

- Modify cell color
- Add and remove borders
- Add and remove columns
- Add and remove rows

Also, from inside an existing table, a Table menu like the following will be visible.

From the Table menu, you can open the Table Properties InfoBox to the Table Layout tab (as previously discussed), add rows and columns, merge cells, and size the table automatically. As you can see, using tables is a powerful way to structure information within Notes documents.

Inserting Links

Another powerful feature of rich text fields is that they can contain *links*, or pointers to other elements in Notes. Links can be created from the following Notes elements:

- Databases
- Views
- Documents
- Anchors

You can insert a link to direct another person to a specific Notes object. For example, you can mail someone a link to a database or a specific document in a database. This is a great way to share information that exists in a Notes database. Links are often used in workflow applications to alert users when they need to act on information. Links are represented as small icons inside the rich text field. These icons are shown in Table 3.1.

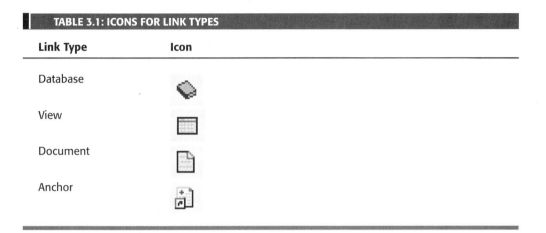

TABLE 3.1: ICONS FOR LINK TYPES

Link Type	Icon
Database	
View	
Document	
Anchor	

To insert a link, open the Notes object to which you would like to link, copy the link to the Clipboard, and paste the link into the target rich text field. To demonstrate, let's create a database link to your address book and insert it into a mail message:

1. Open your address book database by selecting the address book icon from the Bookmark bar.

2. Select Edit ➢ Copy As Link ➢ Database Link.

3. Open your mail database by selecting the Mail icon from the Bookmark bar.

4. Create a new mail message by clicking the New Memo button on the View Action bar or by selecting Create ➢ Memo.

5. Navigate to the Body field, the blank area underneath the mail header information.

6. Select Edit ➢ Paste.

A database link will appear in the rich text field. If you click the database link, your address book will open.

Other Rich Text Elements

So far, we have explored formatted text, objects, attachments, pictures, tables, and links and how they are used within rich text fields. These are the most common elements you'll work with in rich text fields as you create Notes documents. Notes allows you to create a number of other elements (although they are generally associated with designing forms), including:

Hotspots   Text or graphic elements that pop up text, link to Notes objects, perform actions, or link to URLs.

Sections   Elements that enable you to collapse paragraphs to single lines within rich text fields. They can be used to condense large amounts of information contained within documents.

Java applets   Software components that can be written to perform specific functions within a database.

Embedded elements   Notes database design elements that can be embedded in rich text fields.

See Chapter 19, "Advanced Form Design," for more information on these elements.

Checking Your Spelling

Because much of what you do in Notes involves creating documents—either personal documents such as e-mail or shared documents such as those in discussion databases—the need to check spelling is critical. Fortunately, Notes includes an integrated spell checker. This tool enables you to check the spelling of individual words as well as the spelling in entire documents. It checks for misspelled words using the main dictionary and a secondary, customizable user dictionary. The default main dictionary for the North American version of Notes is English (United States) and is stored in a file (us.dic) in your Notes Data directory. The customizable user dictionary is stored in a separate file (user.dic) in your Notes Data directory.

Spell-Checking a Document

To spell-check an entire document, follow these steps:

1. Open the document you would like to spell-check and switch to Edit mode (Ctrl+E).

2. Select Edit ➤ Check Spelling. The Spell Check dialog box (shown here) will be displayed.

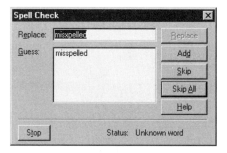

There are several things you can do from within the Spell Check dialog box:

- Fix the misspelled word by typing a replacement word or selecting a replacement from the list of possible guesses that Notes displays and then clicking the Replace button.

- Add the word to your customizable user dictionary by clicking the Add button.
- Skip the misspelled word by clicking the Skip button or skip all occurrences of the misspelled word by clicking the Skip All button.

Spell-Checking Selected Text

To spell-check selected text, follow these steps:

1. Open the document containing the text you would like to spell-check and switch to Edit mode (Ctrl+E).

2. Select the text you would like to spell-check.

3. Select Edit ➢ Check Spelling. If the selected text has any misspellings, the Spell Check dialog box will be displayed. If there are no misspellings, a message box will be displayed indicating that no misspellings were found, as shown here.

Managing Your User Dictionary

We have demonstrated how words can be added to your customizable user dictionary, but what if you accidentally added a word or you just want to see what words are included? Fortunately, Notes includes a mechanism for viewing and changing the contents of your custom dictionary. Follow these steps to access this tool:

1. Select File ➢ Preferences ➢ User Preferences.

2. Click the Basics button (square) in the upper left corner of the User Preferences dialog box.

3. Click the User Dictionary button. The User Spell Dictionary dialog box will be displayed.

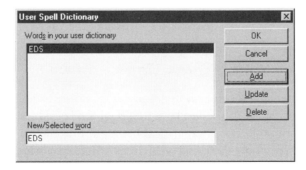

From the User Spell Dictionary dialog box, you can do the following:

- Add new words by typing the word in the field at the bottom of the dialog box and clicking the Add button.
- Update words by selecting the word to be changed, typing the new word in the field at the bottom of the dialog box, and clicking the Update button.
- Delete words by selecting the word to be removed and clicking the Delete button.

When you are finished, click the OK button.

Changing Your Main Dictionary

As we mentioned earlier, the default dictionary for the North American version of Notes is English (United States). If you would like to change the main dictionary Notes uses and you have a version of Notes that has installed alternate dictionaries, just follow these steps:

1. Select File ➤ Preferences ➤ User Preferences.

2. Click the International button (square) on the left side of the User Preferences dialog box.

3. Click the Change button to the left of the Spelling Dictionary prompt (third Change button from the top). The Spell Checking Options dialog box will be displayed.

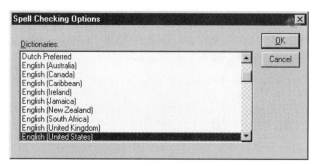

4. Select the dictionary to which you want to change and click the OK button.

Printing Your Information

Working with your information electronically is flexible and convenient, but there are times when you just have to have it printed. Notes provides two main capabilities relative to printed output: document printing and view printing. In this section, we will introduce these two capabilities. Before discussing how to print documents and views, we will introduce the mechanisms Notes uses to control all printing.

Page Setup

Notes provides a set of page setup options to allow you to control how it formats output on the printed page. These options are set using the Page Setup dialog box (shown below). You display the Page Setup dialog box by selecting File ➢ Page Setup.

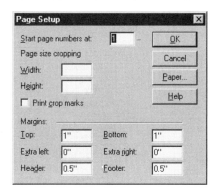

The Start Page Numbers At field allows you to define a starting number for page numbers included in headers and footers. The default is one. If headers or footers include a page number, this value will be used to initialize the page counter.

The Page Size Cropping fields allow you to define how much of the paper will be used to print the output. Notes uses the values you enter for Width and Height to determine the area of the page used. This area is relative to the upper left corner of the page. The Print Crop Marks check box allows you to choose whether Notes will print a border on the page representing the cropping values. This is useful when you are sending output to a professional print service.

The Margins fields allow you to set default margins for the printed output. The values for Top, Bottom, Header, and Footer are relative to the edge of the paper. When documents are printed, the Extra Left and Extra Right fields define how much space will be added to the form's left and right margins. Left and right margins can also be set on individual paragraphs using the Paragraph Margins tab in the Text Properties InfoBox.

To accept the page setup values you have entered and close the Page Setup dialog box, click the OK button. To close the dialog box without saving your changes, click the Cancel button.

Defining Headers and Footers

Headers and footers can be set by database or by individual document. The database header and footer are useful when printing views and to use as a default when documents do not have their own header and footer values. Database headers and footers are set in the Printing tab in the Database Properties InfoBox (shown here).

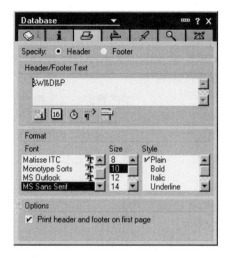

At the top, there are two radio buttons. When the Header radio button is selected, all values entered pertain to the header. When the Footer radio button is selected, all values entered pertain to the footer. As its name suggests, the Print Header and Footer on First Page check box at the bottom allows you to choose whether or not headers and footers are printed on the first page.

The field directly below the radio buttons is where you enter the value for the header or footer. It can be a combination of typed text and special codes. The special codes include:

- Page number
- Date
- Time
- Tab
- Database title

The special codes help you create a more dynamic header or footer for your output. They are entered by clicking their corresponding button directly below the header/footer entry field. Most of the time, these special codes are used in conjunction with text that describes the value that will be printed (e.g., enter **Page:** directly preceding the special code for Page number). The special code for Tabs enables you to create sections in the header or footer. For example, you can create a footer with the database title on the left, date in the middle, and page number on the right as follows:

1. Open you mail database or another database for which you would like to set header and footer properties.

2. Open the Database Properties InfoBox by selecting File ➢ Database ➢ Properties.

3. Select the Printing tab.

4. Select the Footer radio button.

5. Click in the header/footer entry field directly below the radio buttons. Your cursor will be blinking in the upper left corner of the field. The buttons for the special codes are directly below the header/footer entry field. They are, from left to right, Print Page, Print Date, Print Time, Print Tab, and Print Title.

6. Click the Print Title button. &W will be entered into the field.

7. Click the Print Tab button. A vertical bar (|) will be inserted to the right of the &W.

8. Click the Print Date button. A &D will be inserted to the right of the vertical bar.

9. Click the Print Tab button. A vertical bar will be inserted to the right of the &D.

10. Click in the header/footer entry field to the right of the vertical bar.

11. Type **Page** and click the Print Page button. A &P will be inserted to the right of the vertical bar.

The next time you print views or documents from this database, the footer will be printed. To clear the footer, just highlight and delete the text entered into the header/footer entry field. To set the font, size, and style of header and footer text, use the settings on the Printing tab in the Database Properties InfoBox.

This same mechanism is used to define document-specific headers and footers too. The only difference is the Properties InfoBox in which they are set. Database header and footer settings are defined on the Printing tab of the Database Properties InfoBox. For document-level headers and footers, you'll use the Printing tab on the Document Properties InfoBox. Access this Properties InfoBox by following these steps:

1. Open the database for which you would like to set document-level header and footer properties.

2. Select the document by clicking its row in the view.

3. Open the Document Properties InfoBox by selecting File ➤ Document Properties.

4. Select the Printing tab.

As you can see, the Printing tab is the same as the one in the Database Properties InfoBox. Each document in a Notes database can have its own header and footer settings. If established, these document-specific settings override the database header and footer settings.

Printing Views

The ability to print views in Notes is quite convenient. It is a quick way to get a listing of documents in a database. You can use this feature to print a Contact list from your Personal Address Book. If you participate in a tracking database, you can print views of active issues before a meeting. By expanding or collapsing categories beforehand, you can even print customized lists of documents. To print views, just follow these steps:

1. Open the database for which you would like to print a view.

2. Highlight the view by clicking in the View pane.

3. Select File ➢ Print. The Print dialog box will be displayed.

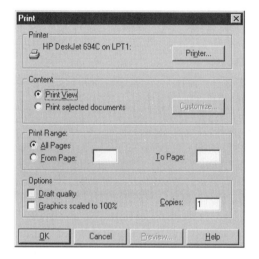

4. In the Content section, select the Print View radio button.

5. Enter the number of copies to print in the Copies field.

6. Click the OK button.

Notes will print the view in a manner that is similar to the way it appears on the screen. Because views contain summary information about collections of documents, the printed view is like a summary report. One thing to keep in mind though is that Notes is not a report-writer application. For more sophisticated reporting, you can have a report-writer application, such as Microsoft Access, access a Notes database using a technology called *NotesSQL*. NotesSQL makes Notes databases appear in Windows as ODBC data sources. For more information on NotesSQL, see Chapter 11, "Integrating Notes with Other Applications."

The view will be printed on the current Windows printer device. To change the Windows printer device before printing, click the Printer button while the Print dialog box is displayed. The Print Setup dialog box will be displayed. Select the printer device you want Notes to use from the list and click the OK button.

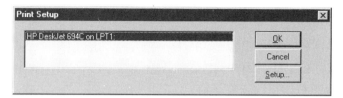

If you want to change the settings for that device, remain in the Print Setup dialog box and click the Setup button. The printer device's Setup dialog box will appear, allowing you to change settings. Click the OK button on the printer device's Setup dialog box to return to the Print Setup dialog box. Click the OK button in the Print Setup dialog box to accept your changes and return to the Print dialog box.

NOTE For Calendar views, Release 5 includes special print formatting capabilities. On the Print dialog box, there will be an additional field labeled Print that will allow you to choose a style for your output. The styles include Daily, Weekly, Monthly, and Calendar List. For more information about printing your calendar, see Chapter 6, "Calendaring and Scheduling in Notes."

Printing Documents

When you need a hard copy of the contents of individual documents, you'll want to print the document. You can print e-mail messages that you might need while you are away from your computer or documents from a discussion database. Whatever the reason, Notes allows you to easily print documents in your Notes databases. To print one or more documents in a database, just follow these steps:

1. Open the database for which you would like to print document(s).

2. Select one or more documents in the view. If you select multiple documents in the view, each will have a check-mark icon the View Icon area.

3. Select File ➤ Print. The Print dialog box will be displayed.

4. In the Content section, select the Print Selected Documents radio button.

5. Enter the number of copies to print in the Copies field.

6. Click the OK button.

Notes will print each document through its associated form. If the view from which you selected the document(s) has a View Selection formula, it will be used to determine which form is used to print the documents. More information on View Selection formulas can be found in Chapter 20. You can also override the form selected in the Print dialog box. To override the form used to print documents, follow these steps:

1. Open the database for which you would like to print document(s).

2. Select one or more documents in the view. If you select multiple documents in the view, each will have a check-mark icon the View Icon area.

3. Select File ➤ Print. The Print dialog box will be displayed.

4. In the Content section, select the Print Selected Documents radio button.

5. Click the Customize button. The Print Selected Documents Options dialog box will be displayed.

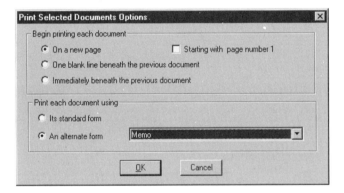

6. In the Print Each Document Using section, select the An Alternate Form radio button.

7. In the drop-down box, select the form you would like to use to print each document.

8. Click the OK button to return to the Print dialog box.

9. Enter the number of copies to print in the Copies field.

10. Click the OK button.

This time Notes prints each document, but it uses the form you selected to format the output. This is a powerful capability. You can use it to format documents just about any way you want. When you are developing solutions, you can use one form to accept input and another to print. It is just one of the ways in which Notes separates content from structure.

When printing multiple documents, you can also customize how Notes separates the printed documents. By default, Notes prints each document on a separate page. You can instruct Notes to separate each printed document with a blank line or to print each adjacent document with no separation. These options can be set in the Print Selected Documents Options dialog box.

You can also print the active document (the document currently displayed in the Notes application window). In this case, the Print dialog box does not allow you to customize the output. Instead, you can choose to print all of the pages of the document or selected pages. The document is printed through its associated form.

In addition, Notes supports print preview. This allows you to review what you are printing before sending it to the printer device. To preview one or more documents, just print as described earlier and click the Preview button in the Print dialog box when it is displayed.

Printing Attachments

Notes can also print the contents of attachments that can be displayed with the built-in file viewer. This is a quick way to print information contained within attachments without having to open the file using the native application. It is also helpful when you don't have the application in which the attachment was created installed on your computer. To print the contents of an attachment, follow these steps:

1. Open the document containing the attachment you would like to print.

2. Scroll to the place in the document where the attachment's icon is displayed.

3. Right-click the attachment's icon and select View from the context menu. The file viewer task window will be opened with the contents of the attachment displayed.

4. Select File ➢ Print. The Print dialog box will be displayed. It will appear slightly different (as shown below) from previous instances. You can choose the printer device by selecting a choice from the Name drop-down box and you can change the printer device's settings by clicking the Properties button.

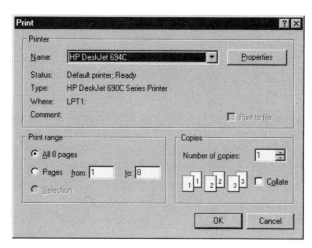

5. Select the print range and number of copies.

6. Click the OK button. Notes prints the contents of the attachment.

 WARNING Although Notes can print the content of attachments, it is a limited capability. If you are trying to optimize the quality of the output, it is better to use the native application instead of the attachment printing capability of Notes. The attachment printing capability of Notes will not format the output exactly the same as the native application software will.

Summary

You're now familiar with what Notes databases are, how they are presented in the Notes application window, and how to perform common tasks within them. Everything we explained in this chapter will be used throughout Notes (and the book). In fact, you may want to refer back to this chapter as you progress through the rest of the book. In the next chapter, we'll introduce you to the Notes core databases that provide the basic Notes functionality, such as e-mail, Contact management, and calendaring and scheduling.

CHAPTER 4

Introducing the Core Databases

FEATURING:

Notes is a runtime environment for databases created with the Domino Designer integrated development environment (IDE). Some organizations may have custom databases developed especially for them, such as a skills inventory database for a consulting firm or a suggestion box database for a Web site. Notes also includes databases to provide the basic functionality of the product, such as e-mail, Contact management, and calendaring and scheduling. We refer to these as the *core databases*. In this chapter, we'll introduce you to some of the most common tasks performed using the core databases.

 NOTE To get the most out of this chapter, you should have a working knowledge of the Notes application window and the elements contained within it, such as menus, universal navigation buttons, the Bookmark bar/page, and the Database area. Please refer to Chapter 2, "Getting Familiar with Notes," and Chapter 3, "Working with Notes Databases," if you need more information on these topics.

Adding Contacts to Your Personal Address Book

The first core database we'll discuss is the Personal Address Book. You'll want to become familiar with this database because it is an important part of Notes. It is the place where you will store all of your personal contact information as well as certain information about the configuration of Notes.

Importance of the Personal Address Book

The Personal Address Book serves a number of purposes. First, it is your place to keep track of personal Contacts. These can include business associates, friends, family members, or whoever else you decide to include. For each Contact, you can enter a wide variety of information, including:

- Name
- Company and title
- Phone numbers (up to six different numbers)
- E-mail address, Web page address, and mail certificates
- Business and home addresses
- Spouse, children, and birthday

- Rich text (comments, pictures, etc.)
- Categories

With your personal Contact information stored electronically in this database, you can take advantage of Notes to find information such as phone numbers or addresses. You can use Notes to print your Contact information or to synchronize with your handheld device (PalmPilot/WorkPad or Windows CE device). You can integrate this information with other applications by importing and exporting data or by using NotesSQL, an add-on utility that makes Notes databases appear as Open Database Connectivity (ODBC) data sources to other Windows applications. For more information on synchronizing Notes-based information with handheld devices, see Chapter 9, "Working with Notes Away from the Office." For more information on integrating Notes-based information with other applications, see Chapter 11, "Integrating Notes with Other Applications."

The Personal Address Book database is also used for addressing e-mail messages. When sending an e-mail message to someone, you can either type in their e-mail address or select it from a directory. One of the directories from which you can select e-mail addresses is your Personal Address Book. If you make sure to enter your important Contacts into your Personal Address Book database, you won't have to remember their e-mail addresses. Also, you'll be able to address e-mail messages when you are disconnected from network-based directory servers, either your company's Domino server or Internet-based directory servers such as Bigfoot or Four11. Finally, your Personal Address Book can contain personal distribution groups so you can use a single address to e-mail multiple people. This is convenient when you e-mail groups of people regularly, such as colleagues working on a project or close family members. For more information on using directory servers to address e-mail messages, see Chapter 5, "Communicating with Notes Mail."

Group entries in the Personal Address Book also play a role in securing databases during replication. When the Notes client replicates with a Domino server, the Domino server must be given the appropriate authority to access databases stored locally on the client computer. This authority can be provided by adding the Domino server's name to the database's Access Control List, but it is more commonly provided by adding the Domino server to a group and adding the group to the database's Access Control List. For more information regarding replication, see Chapter 9.

Finally, the Personal Address Book plays an important role in configuring Notes. Along with Contact and Group documents, the Personal Address Book also contains documents for accounts, connections, locations, and so on. These documents control how Notes accesses Internet-based services, connects to Domino servers and dial-up networks, and maintains configuration information. For more information on configuring Notes, see Chapter 13, "Setting Up Notes as a Domino Client" and Chapter 14, "Setting Up Notes as an Internet Client."

Navigating Your Personal Address Book

To become comfortable with the capabilities of your Personal Address Book, we'll start by showing you how to open the database and navigate around the various views.

Opening Your Personal Address Book

There are a number of ways to open your Personal Address Book database (your own comfort level will determine which method you choose):

- Select the address book icon from the Bookmark bar.
- Select Open Address Book from the default Welcome page (or custom Welcome pages that include the Basic Tasks section).
- Select File ➢ Database ➢ Open (or press Ctrl+O), type **names.nsf** in the File-name field, and click Open.

You will notice that the Release 5 Personal Address Book has a frameset interface, as shown in Figure 4.1. The left side consists of three frames:

- A top frame that displays a description of the window
- A middle frame that displays a Navigation pane for address book or configuration settings
- A bottom frame with icons for switching between the two Navigation panes

FIGURE 4.1

The Personal Address Book

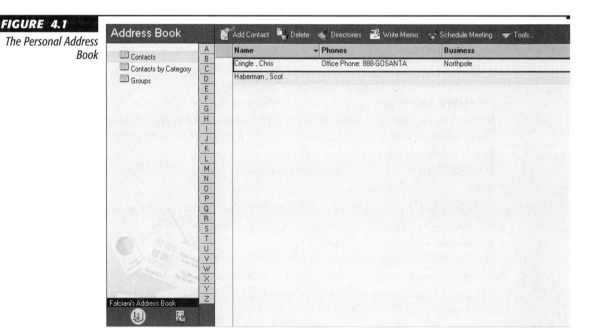

Also, the address book Navigation pane contains a Rolodex-style interface for selecting entries by the first letter of a person's last name. The frame on the right side contains the View pane.

 NOTE The Rolodex-style interface on the address book Navigation pane is tied to the Contacts view. If you have the Contacts by Category view or the Groups view displayed and you select one of the letters on the Rolodex interface, Notes will switch back to the Contacts view.

Try switching between the two Navigation panes by selecting the icons in the lower left frame. The icon on the left will switch to the Address Book pane, and the icon on the right will switch to the Configuration Settings pane.

 TIP Notes provides a quick way to navigate address book entries through its Quick Search feature. Just click in the View pane to make sure it has focus and type the first few characters of a person's last name. A Starts With dialog box will be displayed with the characters you typed. Press Enter and you will be positioned at the first entry containing the characters you typed. If the Quick Search feature is used in the Contacts by Category view, you will be positioned at the first category matching the characters you typed.

 NOTE The Personal Address Book frameset interface does not support folders. If you have existing folders in your Personal Address Book or if you want to create folders, you can use the default view/folder list interface to display them. To use the default view/folder interface, change the When Opened in the Notes Client field to Restore as Last Viewed by User on the Launch tab of the Database Properties InfoBox. Then, close your Personal Address Book database. Right-click the address book icon on the Bookmark bar and select Database ➢ Go To. In the Go To dialog box, select a view or folder and click the OK button. Create a bookmark to avoid having to use the Go To dialog box to open the database each time.

Using the Address Book Views

With the address book Navigation pane active, you will have three views available to you for navigating around Contact and group entries:

- Contacts
- Contacts by Category
- Groups

The first two are for viewing Contacts and the last is for viewing group entries. The Contacts view displays all Contacts by last name or by company name if the last name is not entered. The Contacts by Category view displays all Contact entries categorized. If you enter values in the Category field on each Contact document, this view can be used to quickly locate entries. As you can see, the Action bar for the Contacts view provides easy access to common tasks.

The Add Contact and Delete buttons are self-explanatory. The Directories button will display the Directories dialog box. This dialog box provides a quick method for finding Contacts in all address books and directories configured within Notes (see Chapter 5 for more information on directories). The Write Memo button creates a new e-mail document with the e-mail address of the selected Contact or Contacts already entered into the To field. The Schedule Meeting button creates a new meeting-type calendar entry with the Invite field filled in with the e-mail address of the selected Contact or Contacts.

You can click the Tools button to display a menu with several options. The Tools ➤ Create Group option creates a new Group document with the names of the selected Contact or Contacts already entered into the Members field. The Tools ➤ Categorize option brings up the Categorize dialog box, which is discussed in the next paragraph. The Tools ➤ Visit Web Page option brings up Notes's configured browser to display the Contact's Web page (see Chapter 10, "Harnessing the Power of the Internet," for more information on browsing the Web with Notes). The Tools ➤ Preferences option brings up the Personal Address Book Preferences document, allowing you to set configuration information for the Personal Address Book.

The Contacts by Category view's Action bar provides access to the same functions as well as an additional button for categorizing Contact documents. This feature enables you to quickly categorize one or more Contact entries without having to open each document. To categorize Contacts, follow these steps:

1. Select the Contact or Contacts you want to categorize. If multiple entries are selected, each should have a check mark displayed in the view icon area.

2. Click the Categorize button or select Actions ➤ Categorize. The Categorize dialog box will be displayed.

3. Select one or more categories from the Categories list or enter one or more new categories in the New Categories field. To enter multiple new categories, separate each entry with a comma.

4. Click the OK button. The Contacts you previously selected will be displayed under the appropriate categories.

 NOTE Documents with fields that can contain multiple entries will be displayed in categorized views multiple times. It is the same document; it just shows up multiple times in the view. Because Contact documents contain a Category field that can have multiple values, they can show up multiple times in the Contacts by Category view.

The Groups view displays all Group documents contained within your Personal Address Book. As mentioned earlier, group entries are used to create mail distribution lists and also for providing security during replication. By default, you will have two group entries: LocalDomainServers and OtherDomainServers. These are generally used to provide security and can be ignored unless you are configuring Notes to replicate with a Domino server. As you can see here, the Action bar for the Groups view provides easy access to common tasks.

The Add Group button creates a new Group document for you to fill out. The Add Mailing List button does the same thing except it preselects a group type of Mail Only. The Edit Group and Delete Group buttons are self-explanatory.

NOTE Selecting Delete Group will mark all selected Group documents for deletion. They will not actually be permanently deleted until you close your Personal Address Book or refresh the Groups view.

The Write Memo and Schedule Meeting buttons are similar to the ones on the Contacts View Action bar except the selected group or groups will be entered into the To and Invite fields. The Tools button brings up the Personal Address Book Preferences document, allowing you to set configuration information for the Personal Address Book.

Creating Contacts

You can either create new Contact entries in your Personal Address Book database or import Contacts from another source. For information on importing and exporting information into Notes, see Chapter 11. Also, Lotus is providing tools to migrate from popular e-mail applications. Visit Lotus's SmartMove Web site (`www.lotus.com/migration`) for more information on these tools and migration tools from third-party software developers. As for creating new Contact entries, it is as easy as creating a new Contact document and filling in the fields. With your Personal Address Book open, you can create a new Contact document in the following two ways:

- Select Create ➤ Contact.
- Click the Add Contact button on the View Action bar of the Contacts and Contacts by Category views.

You can also create Contacts from the default Welcome page or any custom Welcome pages that include the Basic Tasks section. Whichever way you decide to create a new Contact document, a blank Contact form will be displayed, as shown in Figure 4.2.

 TIP You can bookmark blank forms to make it easy to create new documents without having to open the database first. In fact, there is a default bookmark folder for just this purpose called Create. This is a real convenience for Contacts because you will be adding them all the time. With your blank Contact form open, select and drag the blank Contact form's task button to the Create folder on your Bookmark bar (or any other location on the Bookmark bar). Then select the New Contact icon from the Create folder on the Bookmark bar anytime you need to create a new Contact.

FIGURE 4.2

A blank Contact form

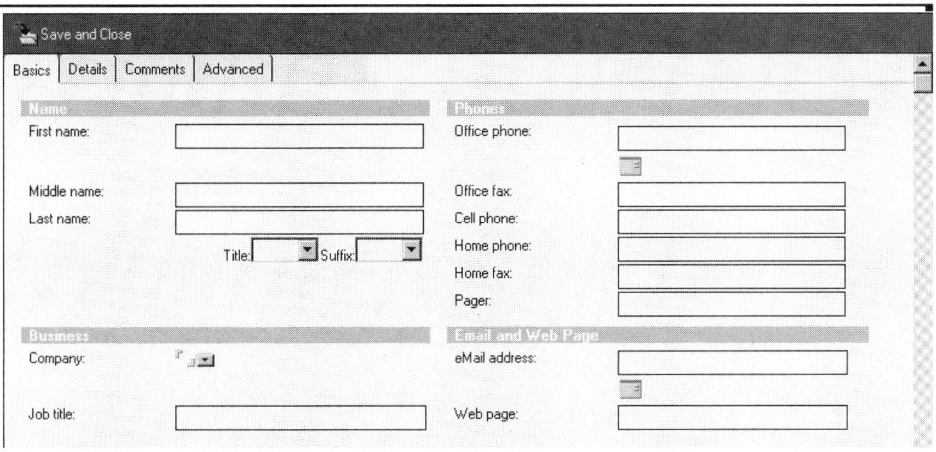

At the top of the Database area, you will see one button on the Form Action bar labeled Save and Close. After you are finished entering the information for your Contact, you can click this button to save the new entry in your Personal Address Book. Below the Save and Close button you will notice a series of tabs labeled as follows:

- Basics
- Details
- Comments
- Advanced

The Basics tab is selected by default when the blank Contact form is displayed and contains fields for information most likely to be filled in for your Contacts. This includes the following:

- Name, title, and suffix
- Company name and job title
- Phones numbers (up to six)
- E-mail address and Web page address

In the Basics section, you can complete only the fields you need. Just enter a last name or a company name and Notes will let you save the Contact entry. The First Name, Middle Name, and Last Name fields are text fields that let you enter what you want. The Title and Suffix fields only allow you to choose from the predefined list. The phone fields let you store up to six numbers per Contact. You can even customize the labels associated with each Contact by selecting the button above the phone fields. This way, you can store any combination of phone numbers required. For example, you may have a Contact with two office phones (and you don't need to know your Contact's home phone number). To change the phone number fields' labels for this Contact, follow these steps:

1. Click the button above the phone fields. A Phones dialog box will be displayed.

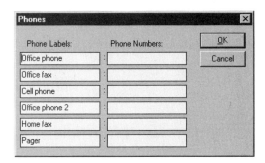

2. Tab down to the fourth phone number field label. It is labeled Home Phone by default.

3. Change the label to Office phone 2 and enter the number.

4. Click the OK button to accept the change. In the Phones section, the prompt next to the fourth phone number field will now be labeled Office Phone 2, as shown next.

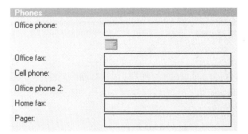

In the e-mail address field, you can either type an address directly in the field or you can select the button next to it. Selecting the button next to the e-mail address field brings up the Mail Address Assistant dialog box.

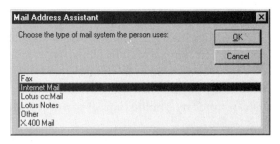

From the Mail Address Assistant dialog box, you can select the target mail system of the Contact from the following choices:

- Fax
- Internet Mail
- Lotus cc:Mail
- Lotus Notes
- Other
- X.400

Each choice has an associated dialog box that assists you in entering the required information.

 NOTE Today, most Contacts that you will store in your Personal Address Book will have Internet mail addresses. These are normally formatted as name@domainname (e.g., smith@acme.com). With the other mail address types, it is assumed you are using Notes in a Domino-based environment.

 TIP You can also enter Internet mail addresses using the following format: "friendly name" <name@domainname> (e.g., "John Smith" <smith@acme.com>). This is helpful when the Internet mail address does not include your Contact's name or when multiple people share an address.

If the Contact you are entering has a Web page, you can enter the URL of the page in the Web page field. This way, you can use the Tools ➤ Visit Web Page button on the Contacts and Contacts by Category views to easily navigate to the Contact's Web page.

 TIP You can enter the Web page address using either the full URL (e.g., http://www.eds.com/) or an abbreviated URL (e.g., www.eds.com).

The Details tab contains fields for the following information:

- Business address, department, manager's name, and assistant's name
- Home address, spouse, and children
- Birthday

PART

I

Introducing Notes 5

For business and home address, you can either type the address lines directly in the field on the form or you can select the button to the right of the field and enter the information in the Address dialog box (the Business Address dialog box is shown here).

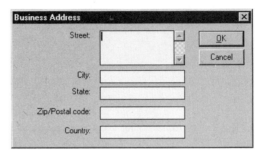

All of the other fields, except Birthday, are just text fields that allow you to enter whatever information you need. The Birthday field allows you to enter a month and day for the Contact's birthday in the format MM/DD. You can also use the Date Picker to select a month and day. If you enter a value for year, it will be stripped off before the document is saved.

The Comments tab contains one rich text field that you can use to store other information, such as:

- Formatted text
- Tables
- Pictures
- Objects
- URLs
- Attached files

The Advanced tab contains fields used in addressing e-mail messages as well as fields used for organizing Contacts, including:

- Full User Name
- Mail Domain
- Short Name
- Internet Certificate
- Internet Certificate Issuers
- Certified Public Key
- Flat Name Key
- Categories
- Logo

The name and certificate fields are used for e-mail and will be explained as necessary in Chapter 5. The Categories field is used to organize Contacts. You can type values directly in the field or use the Categorize feature (which was discussed earlier in this chapter). The Logo field determines which background is displayed when this particular Contact document is displayed.

Example Contact: Person   In this example, we will create a Contact entry for a person by performing the following steps:

1. Open your Personal Address Book database.

2. Click the Add Contact button on the View Action bar of the Contacts view.

3. In the First Name field, type **John**.

4. Tab to the Last Name field and type **Smith**.

5. Tab to the Company field and type **EDS**.

6. Tab to the Office Phone field and type **111-555-1212**.

7. Tab to the Email Address field and type **"John Smith" <smith@acme.com>**.

8. Tab to the Web Page field and type **www.eds.com**.

9. Select the X to the right of the task button to close the Contact form without saving the document.

Example Contact: Company   In this example, we will create a Contact entry for a company by performing the following steps:

1. Open your Personal Address Book database.

2. Click the Add Contact button on the View Action bar of the Contacts view.

3. Tab to the Company field and type **EDS**.

4. Tab to the Office Phone field and type **111-555-1212**.

5. Tab to the Web Page field and type **www.eds.com**.

6. Select the X to the right of the task button to close the Contact form without saving the document.

Creating Groups

Group documents in your Personal Address Book are used as mail distribution lists and as Access Control Lists. As mail distribution lists, they are a convenient way to address mail to a group of people. As Access Control Lists, group entries are used to control security when databases are replicated with Domino servers.

Creating new group entries is similar to creating Contacts. Again, it is as easy as creating a new Group document and filling in the fields. With your Personal Address Book open, you can create a new Group document in the following two ways:

- Select Create ➤ Group.
- Click the Add Group or Add Mailing List button on the View Action bar of the Groups view.

Whichever way you decide to create a new Group document, a blank group form will be displayed (see Figure 4.3).

FIGURE 4.3

A blank group form

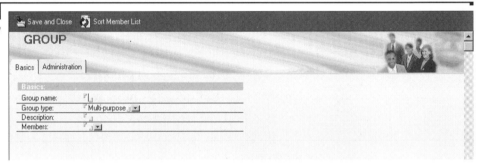

If you use the Add Mailing List button to open the form, the Group Type field will default to Mail Only. This means that the group entry will only be used for mail distribution lists. At the top of the Database area, you will see two buttons on the Form Action bar. The first, labeled Save and Close, can be selected to save the new entry in your Personal Address Book. The second, labeled Sort Member List, will sort the entries typed in the Members field. Below that you will notice two tabs labeled as follows:

- Basics
- Administration

The Basics tab is selected by default when the blank group form is displayed. It contains fields for information most likely to be filled in for your group entries. This includes:

- Group Name
- Group Type
- Description
- Members

You must enter a group name and type. The group name should be something short but descriptive. For example, you could create a group named Family to use as a mail distribution list for family members. The type can be set to Mail Only if the group entry is only to be used as a mail distribution list. If it will also be used for replication security, you can set it to Multi-Purpose. The Description field is optional, but it should be used to further describe the purpose of the group. The Members field is where you enter the names of the people you want listed in the group. The names can be separated by commas or entered on their own line. When the Group document is saved, the entries will be formatted so each entry is on its own line.

Example Group   In this example, we will create a group entry by performing the following steps:

1. Open your Personal Address Book database.

2. Click the Add Mailing List button on the View Action bar of the Groups view.

3. In the Group Name field, type **Family**.

4. Tab to the Description field and type **Family Mailing List**.

5. Tab to the Members field and type **Joe Smith, Edward Jones, John Edwards**.

6. Click the Sort Member List button. You will notice that the three names are reformatted to display on their own lines and they are sorted (as simple strings).

7. Select the *X* to the right of the task button to close the group form without saving the document.

Sending and Receiving E-mail

One of the most common uses of Notes is sending and receiving e-mail. E-mail is the most basic form of electronic collaboration. In the past, this meant connecting Notes clients to a Domino server environment. The Notes client provided the user interface and the Domino servers provided the back-end services for routing and delivery of messages. If necessary, the Domino server environment was connected to other, external environments to provide routing and delivery of messages to foreign mail systems.

Starting with Release 4.6, Notes also included facilities for connecting directly to the Internet for message routing and delivery. But because the Notes client was still designed to be part of an overall Domino environment, users' access to an Internet mail account in addition to their Domino mail was limited. With Release 5, Notes truly becomes a universal mail client, enabling the user to access any and all mail from one spot. Notes can now receive mail from multiple accounts into one mail database, and these accounts can be either Post Office Protocol version 3 (POP3) or Internet Message Access Protocol version 4 (IMAP4) mail service providers. Notes can also be configured to send mail to multiple Simple Mail Transfer Protocol (SMTP) mail servers, choosing the appropriate destination based on location. This section is intended to introduce you to the mail database and some of its capabilities. For a more complete explanation of mail and messaging in Notes, see Chapter 5.

Opening Your Mail Database

As with all databases in Release 5, the mail database can be opened in a variety of ways:

- Select the Mail icon from the Bookmark bar.
- Select Open Mail from the default Welcome page (or custom Welcome pages that include the Basic Tasks section).
- Click the Mail button on the status bar and then select Open Mail from the list.
- Select File ➤ Database ➤ Open (or press Ctrl+O), select your mail server or Local if you use a local copy, select the appropriate database from the list, and click Open.

You'll notice that the Release 5 mail database has a frameset interface, as shown in Figure 4.4.

The left side consists of three frames, which include:

- A top frame that displays a description of the window
- A middle frame that displays a Navigation pane for Mail, Calendar, and To Do lists
- A bottom frame with icons for switching between the three Navigation panes

FIGURE 4.4

The mail database

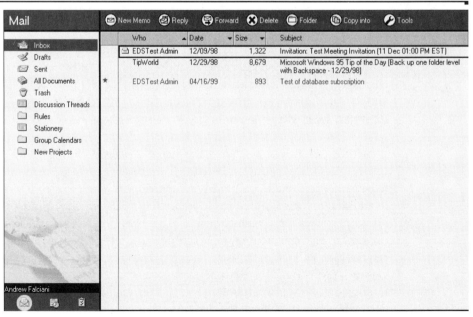

Also, the calendar Navigation pane contains a Date Picker for quickly navigating to specific dates. The right frame contains the View pane. Try switching between the three Navigation panes by selecting the icons in the lower left frame.

The icon on the left will switch to the Mail pane. The icon in the middle will switch to the Calendar pane. And the icon to the right will switch to the To Do pane. These icons will also open each pane as a new task if they are not already open. That way, you can quickly access each function by selecting the appropriate task button. For now, we will focus on the Mail pane. The Mail pane (see Figure 4.4) has a set of special views listed at the top:

Inbox Displays all new messages that are received in your mail database. For this reason, you will focus most of your attention here.

Drafts Displays messages you have drafted but have not yet sent.

Sent Displays all messages that have been sent (assuming you have preferences set to keep a copy of sent mail).

All Documents Displays all documents in your mail database. Keep in mind that Calendar and To Do documents will also be displayed in this view because they are also stored in your mail database.

Trash Displays all messages that have been marked for deletion but have not yet been removed from your mail database.

The Mail pane also includes other views, such as Discussion Threads and Stationery, which are part of the standard mail database design. Your personal folders are also available in the Mail pane, allowing you to organize mail messages as needed. Again, see Chapter 5 for more information on navigating around your mail database.

Unread Marks

Your mail database includes a feature called unread marks, which provide you with a visual cue that indicates when new messages have been added to your database (or when messages you have previously read are modified). Notes also supports unread marks in other databases, such as discussions and document libraries. Unread marks are great tool for identifying documents that require your attention. Unread documents are typically displayed in red with an asterisk in the View Icon area, although this can be customized in each database. Documents that have been viewed by you will be shown in black with no asterisk. You can even instruct Notes to mark documents read after they have been displayed in the Preview pane. To do so, select File ➢ Preferences ➢ User Preferences and look for the option titled Mark Documents Read When Opened in Preview Pane in the

Additional Options field. Databases can also be designed without support for unread marks, but this is generally reserved for databases that will not be viewed by end users directly. See Chapter 20 for more information on setting design properties that affect the management of unread marks.

Notes includes a number of options for managing unread marks. These options are useful when you want to mark all or selected documents in a database as read (or unread). For example, you would mark all documents in a discussion database as read when you first begin participating and are comfortable that you have viewed documents that are pertinent. From that point forward, all new or modified documents will be displayed as unread, making it easier to keep up with input from the other participants. To manage unread marks, select Edit ➤ Unread Marks. This will display a menu of choices, including:

- Mark Selected Read
- Mark All Read
- Mark Selected Unread
- Mark All Unread
- Scan Unread
- Scan Preferred

If multiple documents in the view are selected (displayed with a check mark in the View Icon area), the Mark Selected Read and Unread choices will change the unread mark for all of the selected documents. If not, the unread mark for the currently highlighted document in the view will be changed. Scan Unread will scan the current view for the first unread document and then display it if one is found. Scan Preferred brings up a dialog box for choosing a set of preferred databases and scanning through them one after the other. Scan Preferred can be used to check for unread messages in the databases you access most frequently. You can even instruct Notes to initiate the Scan Preferred process at startup. Just click the Choose Preferred button and select the Start Scanner at Notes Startup check box in the Scan Unread Preferred Setup dialog box.

 TIP While in a view of a database supporting unread marks, you can use the F4 key to navigate between unread documents. You can also use the Insert key to toggle the unread mark for the currently highlighted document.

Creating a Mail Message

To send e-mail to someone, you must first compose the message. This is accomplished by creating a new message document and filling in the fields (as you did with Contacts and groups earlier in this chapter). With your mail database open, you can create a new message document in the following two ways:

- Select Create ➣ Memo.
- Click the New Memo button on the View Action bar of the Inbox, Drafts, Sent, and All Documents views.

You can also create new messages from the default Welcome page or any custom Welcome pages that include the Basic Tasks section. In addition, the following methods can be used to create new messages, regardless of which database you happen to have open:

- Open the Create bookmark folder and select New Memo.
- Select Create ➣ Mail ➣ Memo.
- Click the Mail button on the status bar and then select Create Memo from the list.

New messages can also be created by forwarding existing mail messages, copying existing messages into new messages, and using stationery. Whichever way you decide to create a new mail message document, a blank message form will be displayed (see Figure 4.5).

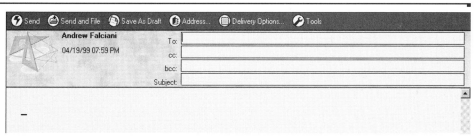

FIGURE 4.5

A blank mail message form

At the top of the Database area, you'll see a set of buttons in the Form Action bar:

Send   Sends the message once you have finished composing it.

Send and File   Similar to the Send button except it also presents a dialog box that allows you to save the message in a specific folder after sending it.

Save As Draft   Saves the message contents without sending it. This is useful for saving messages that you are not ready to send. Just save it as a draft and it will be available when you are ready to finish composing it.

Address   Presents the Select Addresses dialog box, which is used to select e-mail addresses from your Personal Address Book, Domino directories, and Internet directories.

Delivery Options   Presents a dialog box that enables you to set different options for this message, including security, workflow, and delivery settings.

Tools   The Tools button has two options. Tools ➤ Insert Signature inserts your predefined e-mail signature (or another that you choose) as text in the body of the current message. This is text that is usually appended to the bottom of the message and contains your name, phone number, and e-mail address; it is not your written signature or an electronic signature. Tools ➤ Save as Stationery allows you to create e-mail message templates. These templates can then be used to create new messages later.

The message form itself is fairly simple. It consists of the following fields:

- To
- Cc
- Bcc
- Subject
- Body

The To field is where you enter the e-mail addresses of the people to which you would like to send this message. If multiple recipients are included, separate each one with a comma. If it is configured in your Location document, the recipient field supports a type-ahead feature. This means that Notes will use the letters you type in the field to look up possible matching entries in your Personal Address Book or other Domino directories. Type-ahead is supported in the To, Cc, and Bcc fields.

The Cc field is where you enter recipients who should receive the message as a carbon copy. There is no difference between the message and the carbon copy; the Cc field just indicates that the cc recipients were not the main target for the message. This is useful for keeping people informed about a topic. The Bcc (or blind carbon copy) field is similar to the Cc field except the other recipients don't see the Bcc list. This way, the To and Cc recipients don't know that the message was sent to the people on the Bcc list. The Subject field is for entering a short description of the purpose of the message. It is not required, but you should always try to include one. It's easier for people who receive a large quantity of e-mail to sort through messages when they all have subjects entered. The Body field is where you include the actual content of the message. Because the Body field is a rich text field, it can contain a wide variety of information, for example:

- A short memo that you type
- An attached file from your computer
- Information copied and pasted from another program (e.g., spreadsheet, document, etc.)
- Pictures or graphic images
- Other objects

Example E-mail Message   To get a feel for composing mail messages, try creating a test message as described here:

1. Open your mail database. One of the easiest ways is to select the Mail icon from the Bookmark bar.

2. From the Inbox view, click the New Memo button on the View Action bar. A blank mail message form will be displayed.

3. Type your Internet mail address in the To field. Your Internet mail address should be formatted as name@domain (e.g., johnsmith@companyname.com). You can also click the Address button on the Form Action bar to display the Select Address dialog box. The Select Address dialog box can be used to choose an address from your Personal Address Book, Domino directories, or other Internet-based directories (e.g., Bigfoot, Four11, etc.).

4. Tab to the Subject field and enter **Test Message**.

5. Tab to the body of the message and type a short message. You are now ready to send the message.

Sending a Mail Message

Once Notes is set up properly, sending a mail message is simply a matter of clicking the Send button on the mail message form after you have finished composing a message. What happens after that depends on how Notes is configured. Notes can be configured to send messages directly to the Internet or to a Domino server. If you are using Notes at home or in a business environment that does not include Domino servers, you will configure Notes to send messages directly to the Internet. You can accomplish this by modifying your Location document.

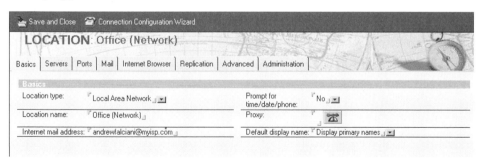

Location documents are stored in your Personal Address Book. You can access them as follows:

1. Open your Personal Address Book.

2. Select the configuration settings Navigation pane.

3. Select the Locations view.

They define many aspects of the Notes configuration, including:

- Network Connectivity
- Mail
- Internet Browser
- Replication

Location documents are an important part of Notes (see Chapter 13 and Chapter 14 for more information).

If you configure Notes (in the Location document) to send mail directly to the Internet, you will also need to set up an Account document for your outbound SMTP mail server.

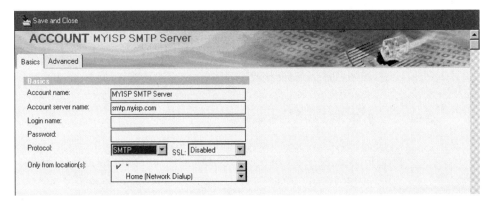

Like Location documents, Account documents are stored in your Personal Address Book. You can access them as follows:

1. Open your Personal Address Book.
2. Select the configuration settings Navigation pane.
3. Select the Accounts view.

They define what Internet-based services Notes can access. These include:

- Post Office Protocol (POP) mail accounts
- Internet Message Access Protocol (IMAP) mail accounts
- Lightweight Directory Access Protocol (LDAP) directories
- Network News Transfer Protocol (NNTP) newsgroups
- Simple Mail Transfer Protocol (SMTP) servers

Account documents are an important part of Notes (see Chapter 14 for more information).

If you are using Notes to access your Internet Service Provider (ISP) mail account, the SMTP server will be provided by your ISP. The name of the SMTP server will be formatted as smtp.*ISPname*.com (e.g., smtp.myisp.com). Check with your ISP for the name of its outbound SMTP server. If you are using Notes to access your company's mail system (and it is not a Domino-based environment), the information technology (IT) group should be able to provide you with the name of the outbound SMTP server. Also, you will need to make sure the Internet Mail Address field in the Basics section of the Location document is set to your Internet mail address. Again, this is either obtained from your ISP or your company's IT group.

Assuming you are sending the message to someone's Internet mail address, Notes will prompt you to choose a format for the message. You can choose from one of the following formats:

- HTML
- Plain Text
- HTML and Plain Text

HTML formats the message as a Hypertext Markup Language stream, which many mail clients are now beginning to support. Plain Text formats the message as ASCII text, or text with no formatting. HTML and Plain Text formats the message as unformatted text but also attaches a second copy in an HTML file. What you choose depends on who is receiving it. If you know the person can read messages formatted as HTML, you should choose HTML because it is the richest way to send the message. Plain Text is the safest because all mail systems can read unformatted text. If you do not know whether or not the recipients can read HTML messages, you can send it in both formats, HTML and Plain Text. You can also set a preference so Notes will not prompt you each time you send an Internet mail message. To change your preference for Internet mail format, follow these steps:

1. Select File ➤ Preferences ➤ User Preferences ➤ Mail and News.

2. Select a choice from the Internet Mail Format field drop-down box.

3. Click the OK button.

If you configure Notes to send mail to a Domino server (in the Location document), you won't need an Account document. The Domino server will interpret the mail address you enter to determine how to deliver the message. If your Domino server is connected to the Internet and configured to route Internet mail, it will also deliver messages addressed to Internet mail users. What you will need is the name of your Domino mail server and domain. The Domino mail server name must be entered in the Home/Mail Server field in the Servers section of the Location document. The domain name must be entered in the Notes Mail Domain field in the Mail section of the Location document. All of this information should be provided by your company's IT group.

In addition to telling Notes how to process outbound messages, you must tell it how to connect to the appropriate outbound message server. If your computer is connected to your company's network and you are connecting to your company's Domino or SMTP servers (which are also on this network), the Location document contains enough information for Notes to make the connection. This is also true if your home computer is connected directly to the Internet, usually through a cable modem or other high-speed Internet service. To connect your computer to a remote Domino or SMTP server, Notes uses Connection documents.

Like Location and Account documents, Connection documents are stored in your Personal Address Book. You can access them as follows:

1. Open your Personal Address Book.

2. Select the configuration settings Navigation pane.

3. Select the Connections view.

Connection documents define how Notes connects to Domino servers and Internet dial-up services. Connection documents are an important part of Notes (see Chapters 13 and 14 for more information).

When Notes is configured to send outgoing messages directly to the Internet and you connect to the Internet via a dial-up service, you'll want to create a Network Dialup Connection document with an asterisk specified in the Server Name field (as shown here).

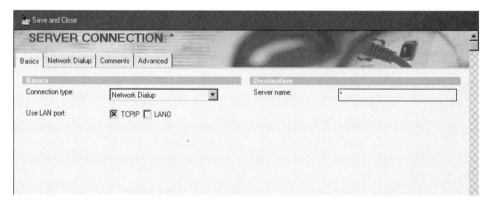

This way, Notes can automatically connect to your dial-up service as needed to deliver mail. Notes can access Internet servers without a Connection document, but you will always need to establish the connection manually before sending e-mail. When Notes is configured to send outgoing messages to Domino and you connect to that Domino server remotely, you must know its connection type, which can be one of the following:

- Notes Direct Dialup or hunt group
- Network Dialup
- Passthru

Notes Direct Dialup and hunt groups are used when your Domino servers are configured with modems. Your computer is then instructed to call the Domino server directly. Passthru is also generally used in these environments, but it allows you to connect to a Domino server through another Domino server. With more and more companies standardizing on Internet technologies, the most common connection type is quickly becoming Network Dialup. As mentioned earlier, the Network Dialup connection is used to connect Notes to Internet servers (e.g., POP, IMAP, SMTP, NNTP, LDAP). It is also used to connect Notes to Domino servers via dial-up networks. Notes uses your computer's remote access software (built in to MacOS and Windows 95/98/ NT) to access your company's dial-up network. This mechanism can be used for Domino servers accessible via a private dial-up network as well as the Internet. When connecting to a Domino server via a Network Dialup connection, enter the name of the Domino server in the Server Name field (as shown next).

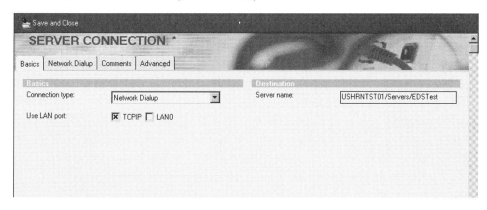

You now have a high-level understanding of how Notes can be used to send mail to Internet-based SMTP servers and Domino servers. Release 5 supports a wide range of features related to e-mail. For more information on Notes mail, see Chapter 5. Also, see Chapter 13 and Chapter 14 for more information on configuring Notes.

Receiving Mail

Again, how you receive mail in Notes depends on how you are using the software. If you use Notes at a company that uses Domino for mail, then your Domino server is generally receiving mail for you. You just open your mail database (located on your Domino mail server), and all new messages will show up in the Inbox view. Other common scenarios include:

• Using Notes at a company that uses Domino for mail, but you access your Domino mail server remotely.

- Using Notes at a company that uses Domino for mail, but you also use Notes to manage your ISP mail account.

- Using Notes at a company that provides standards-based mail services (e.g., POP/IMAP inbound and SMTP outbound), either locally or remotely.

- Using Notes to manage your ISP mail account.

There are many other combinations, but these are the most common. Just as Notes had to be configured to send mail, it must be configured to receive mail too. Again, Location, Account, and Connection documents are used to define the inbound mail servers to which Notes will connect and how Notes will make the connection. For now, we will assume that Notes is configured to use a local mail database and that at least one POP mail account will be polled for new messages. This would be the configuration if you were using Notes to access your ISP mail account. It would also be valid if you were working away from the office with a local replica of your Domino-based mail account and wanted to receive your ISP mail. For more information on configuring Notes, see Chapters 13 and 14.

When you are working with a local copy of your mail database, Notes receives new mail messages by communicating with a server. In the case of Domino-based mail, Notes would communicate with your Domino mail server through a process known as *replication*. Replication is a sophisticated mechanism built in to Notes for keeping multiple copies (or *replicas*) of databases synchronized. For more information on replication, see Chapter 9.

In the case of Internet-based mail, Notes communicates with either a POP server or an IMAP server to receive new mail messages. These are commonly used protocols for mail delivery. POP, or Post Office Protocol, is an offline protocol. This means that client software, such as Notes Release 5, polls the POP server and copies messages to its local data store. Notes copies the messages to your mail database. IMAP, or Internet Message Access Protocol, can be used for both online and offline messaging. IMAP client software, such as Notes Release 5, can interact online with an IMAP server to read messages or post messages to folders. Notes can also treat an IMAP server like a POP server and copy the messages to its local data store instead of interacting online. Notes provides one more capability that most other IMAP clients do not provide, replication. Release 5 allows you to create a replica of an IMAP mail account. That way, you can work offline in a normal Notes database and then synchronize your changes directly back to your IMAP account once you are online again. IMAP is clearly more advanced, but POP is still the most widely accepted form of inbound messaging today. Release 5 can access POP and IMAP servers, providing very comprehensive support for Internet-based mail standards.

NOTE New messages are delivered to your mail database in the background, meaning there is no intervention required on your part. What Notes does not do is refresh the display of your mail database if you happen to have it open when mail is delivered. If the Inbox view has a blue swirl icon in the upper left corner directly below the View Action bar, Notes is indicating that the view needs to be refreshed. Just click the refresh button (one of the universal navigation buttons) or press the F9 key. You will now see the new messages appear.

Notes can also check for new messages in your mail database and notify you when something new arrives by playing a sound or by displaying a dialog box. You can choose the method Notes uses to notify you of new messages by selecting File ➤ Preferences ➤ User Preferences ➤ Mail and News.

Normally, you'll have Notes configured to poll your Internet mail server(s) automatically by establishing a replication schedule. This way, Notes will check for messages in the background while you perform other tasks. If necessary, you can also force Notes to poll your Internet mail server(s). There are a number of ways to do this:

- Click the Retrieve Mail button from the View Action bar of the Inbox, Drafts, and Sent views.
- Click the Mail button on the status bar and then select Receive Mail from the list.
- Open the Replicator page (select the Replicator icon from the Bookmark bar) and click the Send And Receive Mail button.

However you choose to initiate it, Notes will start a background mail retrieval process. This process can be monitored by viewing the Replicator page (again, the fifth icon from the top on the Bookmark bar by default). For more information on using the Replicator page, see Chapter 9.

You now have a high-level understanding of how Notes can be used to receive mail from Internet-based SMTP servers and Domino servers. Release 5 supports a wide range of features related to e-mail. For more information on Notes mail, see Chapter 5.

Creating Appointments and Other Calendar Entries

Also incorporated into the mail database is your personal calendar. It is used to keep track of personal appointments, anniversaries, reminders, and events. Your calendar is also used when you participate in the group scheduling capabilities of the Domino server. Other Domino users can also integrate your calendar with group calendars they create. In this section, we'll introduce you to your Notes calendar and some of its capabilities. For a more complete explanation of calendaring and scheduling in Notes, see Chapter 6.

Opening Your Calendar

Your calendar is stored in your mail database; therefore, you can access it by opening your mail database and selecting the calendar icon in the lower left frame. You can also open your calendar a number of other ways:

- Select the calendar icon from the Bookmark bar.
- Select Open Calendar from the default Welcome page (or custom Welcome pages that include the Basic Tasks section).
- Select the calendar icon in the title bar of the Calendar section (if it is included in your Welcome page).

You will notice that the Release 5 calendar has a frameset interface, as shown in Figure 4.6. The left side consists of three frames:

- A top frame that displays a description of the window
- A middle frame that displays a calendar Navigation pane
- A bottom frame with icons for switching between the three mail database Navigation panes: mail, calendar, and to do

FIGURE 4.6

The calendar

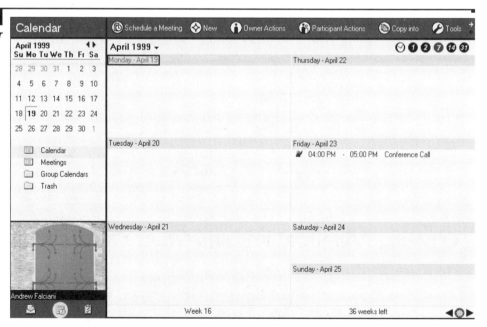

The calendar Navigation pane contains a Date Picker control for quickly navigating to specific dates. Also, the calendar Navigation pane has a set of special views listed in the middle:

Calendar   Displays your personal calendar entries

Meetings   Displays appointment and meeting entries by date

Group Calendars   Displays group calendar entries that you have previously created

Trash   Displays all messages that have been marked for deletion but have not yet been removed from your mail database

The Calendar view (shown in Figure 4.6) is a special type of view that is formatted to look like a paper calendar. It can be modified to display one day, two days, one week, two weeks, and one month. Just select the appropriate view format icon on the upper right side of the View pane. The clock icon on the left side will enable and disable the display of time slots on the view.

On the lower right side of the view is a set of icons for navigating forward or backward in time and for going back to today's entry. The forward and backward icons will navigate time according to the view format. For example, if you are on the one-month format, the icons will navigate forward and backward one month at a time.

The Date Picker control in the calendar Navigation pane can also be used to navigate to other dates. Just select the date in the current month or navigate forward and backward one month at a time by selecting the appropriate icon on the upper right side of the Date Picker control. The calendar entries themselves will be displayed in the boxes representing the days on which they are scheduled. Each type of entry has a specific icon associated with it. For appointments and meetings, the start and end time will also be displayed.

Again, this section is only intended to introduce you to the personal calendar contained within your mail database. See Chapter 6, for more information on navigating around your calendar.

Creating an Appointment

Your personal calendar can be used with or without the group scheduling capabilities of Domino. It is a great place to keep track of appointments. You can also enter anniversaries, reminders, and all-day events in you calendar.

Just as we have seen with mail messages, Contacts, and groups, creating an appointment is as simple as creating a new Calendar document and filling in the fields. With your calendar open, you can create a new Calendar document in the following two ways:

- Select Create ➤ Calendar Entry.
- Click the New ➤ Appointment button on the View Action bar of the Calendar view. This creates a new calendar entry and sets the Entry Type field to Appointment.

You can also create new calendar entries from the default Welcome page or any custom Welcome pages that include the Basic Tasks section. Also, the following methods can be used to create new calendar entries regardless of which database you happen to have open:

- Open the Create bookmark folder and select New Calendar Entry.
- Select Create ➤ Mail ➤ Calendar Entry.

Whichever way you decide to create a new Calendar document, a blank calendar entry form will be displayed (see Figure 4.7).

FIGURE 4.7

A blank appointment form

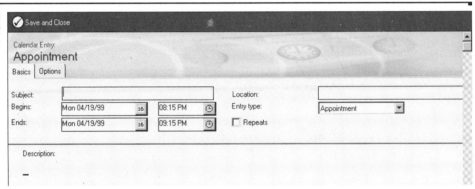

At the top of the Database area, you'll see one button on the Form Action bar labeled Save and Close. After you are finished entering the information for your appointment, you can click this button to save the new entry in your calendar. Right below that you will notice two tabs labeled Basics and Options.

The Basics tab is selected by default when the blank Calendar document is displayed. It contains fields for information most likely to be filled in for your appointments, anniversaries, reminders, and all-day events:

- Subject
- Beginning and ending date/time
- Location
- Entry type

- Repeating entry selector
- Description

In the Basics section, you can complete just the fields you need. Although it is not required, you should always enter a subject so you know what the entry is for when it is displayed in the Calendar view. The beginning and ending date/time fields can be filled in as needed. The Location field is just a text field in which you enter whatever you need (as opposed to predefined sets of conference rooms or other meeting locations). This is handy when you need to enter something such as Joe's cubicle or the cafeteria. The Entry Type field defaults to Appointment, but it can also be set to Anniversary, Reminder, and All Day Event. The Repeat field can be checked or unchecked. If it's checked, a Settings button will appear to the right; it brings up a dialog box for setting repeat options. The Description field is a rich text field and can contain a wide variety of information, including:

- Formatted text
- Tables
- Pictures
- Objects
- URLs
- Attached files

The Options tab contains a set of fields for managing entries, including:

- Pencil In
- Mark Private
- Notify Me
- Categorize

Pencil In keeps the time entered free for others viewing your calendar. Mark Private hides the entry from others, Notify Me allows you to set alarms for entries, and Categorize allows you to select from a predefined set of categories for entries.

Example Appointment   To get a feel for creating calendar entries, try creating a test entry as described in the following steps:

1. Open your calendar. One of the easiest ways is to select the calendar icon from the Bookmark bar.

2. On the Calendar view, select the day for the test entry by clicking the top border of the day's box.

3. Click the New ➤ Appointment button on the View Action bar. A new Calendar document will be displayed with Entry Type set to Appointment.

4. Type **Test Appointment** in the Subject field.

5. Select the Repeat check box. A Repeat Options dialog box will be displayed.

6. Click the OK button to accept the default attribute, which is repeat every day for five days.

7. Click the Save and Close button on the Form Action bar to save this calendar entry.

A new calendar entry will show up in your calendar for today and the next four days. This same process is used to create anniversaries, reminders, and all-day events. The only difference would be the Entry Type value and a few fields on the form. The process for creating meeting entries is similar, except meeting entries are used in conjunction with the group scheduling capabilities of Domino. For more information on group scheduling, see Chapter 6.

Taking Control of Your Tasks

Also incorporated into the mail database is your personal To Do list, which is used to keep track of all your personal tasks. The To Do list is also used to keep track of group tasks assigned to you when you participate in Domino's group scheduling capabilities. In this section, we'll introduce you to your Notes To Do list and some of its capabilities. For a more complete explanation of group tasks in Notes, see Chapter 6.

Opening Your To Do List

Your To Do list is stored in your mail database. Therefore, you can access it by opening your mail database. Just select the check-mark icon in the lower left frame. You can also open your To Do list a number of other ways:

- Select the To Do icon from the Bookmark bar.
- Select Open To Do List from the default Welcome page (or custom Welcome pages that include the Basic Tasks section).
- Select the check-mark icon in the title bar of the To Do list frame (if it is included in your Welcome page).

You will notice that the Release 5 To Do list has a frameset interface, as shown in Figure 4.8.

The left side consists of three frames:

- A top frame that displays a description of the window
- A middle frame that displays a To Do list Navigation pane
- A bottom frame with icons for switching between the three mail database Navigation panes: mail, calendar, and to do list

FIGURE 4.8

The To Do list

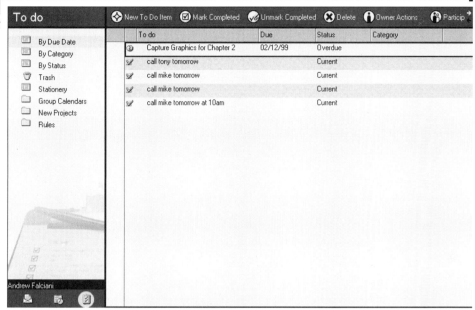

The To Do list Navigation pane contains a set of special views listed at the top, including:

By Due Date   Displays your To Do list entries by their due dates

By Category   Displays your To Do list entries as a categorized list, similar to the Contacts by Category view discussed earlier in this chapter

By Status   Displays your To Do list entries by their current status

Trash   Displays all documents that have been marked for deletion but have not yet been removed from your mail database

The To Do list pane will also include your personal folders, allowing you to organize To Do entries as needed.

Again, this section is only intended to introduce you to the personal To Do list contained within your mail database. See Chapter 6 for more information on navigating around your To Do list.

Creating Personal To Do List Entries

Your personal To Do list can be used with or without the group scheduling capabilities of Domino. It is a great place to keep track of your tasks.

Just as we have seen with mail messages, Contacts, and groups, creating an appointment is as simple as creating a new Calendar document and filling in the fields. With your calendar open, you can create a new Calendar document in the following two ways:

- Select Create ➣ Calendar Entry.
- Click the New ➣ Appointment button from the View Action bar of the Calendar view.

You can also create new calendar entries from the default Welcome page or any custom Welcome pages that include the Basic Tasks section. Also, the following methods can be used to create new calendar entries regardless of which database you happen to have open:

- Open the Create bookmark folder and select New Calendar Entry.
- Select Create ➣ Mail ➣ Calendar Entry.

Whichever way you decide to create a new To Do entry document, a blank To Do form will be displayed (see Figure 4.9).

FIGURE 4.9

A blank To Do form

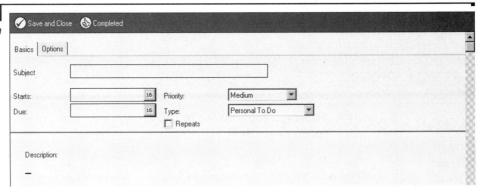

At the top of the Database area, you'll see two buttons on the Form Action bar, labeled as follows:

- Save and Close
- Completed

The Save and Close button can be selected after you are finished entering the information. It will save the To Do entry and close the form. The Completed button will also save the To Do entry and close the form, but it will also mark the To Do item as completed before saving it. Directly below the Form Action bar, you'll notice two tabs labeled Basics and Details.

The Basics tab is selected by default when the blank To Do document is created and contains fields for information most likely to be filled in, including:

- Subject
- Starts and due date/time
- Type
- Priority
- Status
- Repeating entry selector
- Description

In the Basics section, you can complete only the fields you need. Although it is not required, you should always enter a subject so you know what the entry is for when it is displayed in the To Do list views. The Starts and Due date/time fields can be filled in as needed. Type defaults to Personal To Do, but it can also be set to Group To Do. The Priority and Status fields contain predefined choices that you can select to manage your To Do list. The Status field is set to Completed when you select the Completed button on the Form Action bar (or the View Action bar). The Repeat check box can be checked or unchecked. If it's checked, a Settings button will appear to the right; it brings up a dialog box for setting repeat options. The Description field is a rich text field and can contain a wide variety of information, including:

- Formatted text
- Tables
- Pictures
- Objects
- URLs
- Attached files

The Details tab contains a set of fields for managing entries, including:

- Mark Private
- Notify Me
- Categorize

Mark Private hides the entry from others, Notify Me allows you to set alarms for entries, and Categorize allows you to select from a predefined set of categories for entries.

Example To Do   To get a feel for creating calendar entries, try creating a test To Do entry as described here:

   1. Open your To Do list. One of the easiest ways is to select the To Do icon from the Bookmark bar.

2. Click the New To Do Item button on the View Action bar. A new To Do document will be displayed.

3. Type **Test To Do** in the Subject field.

4. Select the calendar icon to the right of the Due field and select the date that is one week from the current date.

5. Change the Status field to Started.

6. Select the Repeat check box. A Repeat Options dialog box will be displayed.

7. Click the OK button to accept the default attribute, which is repeat every day for five days.

8. Click the Save and Close button on the Form Action bar to save this To Do entry.

A new To Do entry will be displayed in your To Do list views. Also, this To Do entry will show up on your calendar today and the next four days. The process for creating Group To Do entries is similar, except it is used in conjunction with the group scheduling capabilities of Domino. For more information on group scheduling, see Chapter 6.

Summary

You now have a good understanding of the basic functionality provided by Notes, such as e-mail, Contact management, and calendaring and scheduling. As mentioned, these functions are provided by core databases included with Notes. In this chapter, we introduced you to some of the most common tasks performed using the core databases, including adding Contacts to your Personal Address Book, sending and receiving e-mail, creating appointments and other calendar entries, and taking control of your tasks.

In the next chapter, we'll discuss additional Notes mail topics, such as setting mail preferences, navigating multiple address books, tracing sent messages, defining mail rules, archiving messages, and using Notes Minder.

PART II

Mastering the Basics

CHAPTER **5**

Communicating with Notes Mail

From its very beginning, the purpose of Notes has been to let people work together more effectively. Notes's first function was to let users share documents. With the release of version 4, Lotus realized that one of the best ways to help people work together was to let them talk to each other, so e-mail was significantly enhanced, thus making Notes a competitive e-mail package. Now, in version 5, Notes e-mail is a powerful, flexible tool for communicating with people in your organization and with others over the Internet. For most users, communication is centered around their mail database. Chapter 4 gave you a quick-and-dirty look at how to use mail. This chapter discusses advanced mail features.

Addressing Mail

There are two ways to address your Notes mail: entering an address by hand or using the Address dialog box. If you know exactly who you're sending mail to, it's probably a little faster just to type in an e-mail address or, if you know that the recipient is in a local address book or Domino directory, a name. However, if you need to search for an address, it's a good idea to use the Address dialog box. With the Address dialog box, you can search local address books, Domino directories, and LDAP servers over the Internet for just about any e-mail address in the world (LAPD stands for Lightweight Directory Access Protocol, an Internet standard for searchable e-mail address directories).

Typing in Addresses

If your Notes client is connected to a mail server with access to the Internet, you can type any valid Internet e-mail address (an address in the format `somename@organization` `.domain`) into the address fields. If you're sending mail to several people, you can put multiple addresses separated by commas in the same line.

If you're sending mail to someone in a Notes address book that you have access to, you can just type in the recipient's name (again, separated by commas if you're sending mail to multiple recipients). If you're sending mail to someone in one of the address books you have access to, Notes can help you out with the type-ahead feature, which automatically completes names in address fields. If you type in a partial name, Notes can search through all the address books it has access to and fill in what it thinks you're trying to type. For example, if you want to send mail to your colleague Chris Peterson, you could just type **Chris** or **Chris Pete**. Notes will look through its directories for names starting with *Chris* and fill in the first one it finds.

Although address type-ahead is faster than using the Address dialog box (described in the next section) to search through directories and can be more accurate than a user typing in an entire name from memory, you should be careful about using it. It's an outstanding feature if you're in a small organization or if you're just using a personal address book. However, a very large organization can have hundreds or even thousands of people in its directories, which can take longer to search through. More important, the more names there are in the directories you have access to, the greater the chance of people having the same or similar names. To return to the preceding example, if you try to send mail to Chris Peterson by typing in **Chris**, Notes might find the name *Chris Petersen* instead. There's a chance of sending personal mail to people you don't know or even, if your organization maintains directories of outside contacts, sending sensitive information to people in other companies.

You can set address type-ahead selectively, using it in some locations (say, while you're on the road and only using your Personal Address Book) but not in others (when you're logged in to a Domino server with access to several different address books). This setting is contained in your Location documents, accessible through your personal address books or File ➤ Mobile ➤ Edit Current Location. If you do use it, always check to make sure that Notes has filled in the right name. Type-ahead is a convenient feature, but it isn't telepathic.

The Address Dialog Box

With a mail message open, press the Address button to bring up the Address dialog box, shown in Figure 5.1. Using the Look In drop-down menu at the top left, you can choose from a broad variety of sources for addresses. The menu is divided into two parts: Address Books and Searchable.

FIGURE 5.1

The Address dialog box. This dialog box is currently set to look in a personal address book.

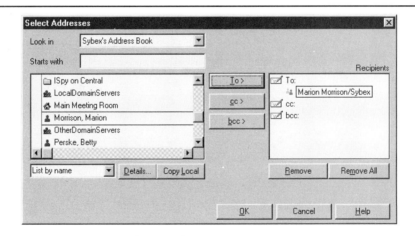

The Address Books section of the Look In menu will provide you with the names of local address books and any directories your Domino server has. This includes your organization's address book, your own Personal Address Book, and any other directories your organization might provide. For example, your Domino administrator may set up a directory of vendors your company regularly buys from or customers you regularly sell to.

To add names from a personal address book or Domino directory to your message, select the desired address book from the Address Books section. The left pane will display a list of people and groups in the address book. The list may include other types of entries with their own special icons, such as servers and physical resources, but the two icons you need to know are the icons for people and groups. People can (or should be able to) receive mail. Most groups can receive mail also, although some groups on Domino servers can be designated as permission groups only rather than mailing lists. Servers and resources can't receive mail, so don't even try sending messages to them.

Domino directories can be very, very large. Depending on the size and hierarchy of your organization, your Domino directories could have thousands of entries. This, of course, can make it hard to find the name you're looking for or at least require you to scroll a long way down the list, but Notes gives you tools for looking up names. If you type in the Starts With field, Notes will jump down to the closest alphabetical fit to what you have typed in.

You can use the List By menu beneath the list pane to categorize the list. By default, the list is uncategorized and sorts by last name (or, for groups, by group name). However, you can have it categorized by Notes name hierarchy (in large organization, users may be divided up among several layers of organizational units), corporate hierarchy (your Domino administrators may assign users to a hierarchy separate from the Notes hierarchy), or by language (which sub-categorizes by the first initial of the person's last name).

If you select a person or group name, you can view the underlying document's contents if you click the Details button to bring up the Details dialog box, shown in Figure 5.2. As you can see, this dialog box displays the contents of the related Person or Group document. It can be useful if you want to check on an address, review the membership of a mailing list, or confirm that the John Smith you're about to send mail to is actually the John Smith you want.

Finally, if you're looking at the contents of an address book other than your Personal Address Book, you can copy any Person or Group document into your Personal Address Book by clicking the Copy Local button. This can be useful for adding the names and addresses of people you want to send mail to while you're disconnected from your Domino server, but use it with caution. Once you copy a document into your own address book, it becomes a completely separate document, not a replica. If the original Person document or the contents of a mailing list change after you copy the document, those changes will not be reflected in your address book unless you go in and make them manually.

PART

II

Mastering the Basics

FIGURE 5.2

The Details dialog box

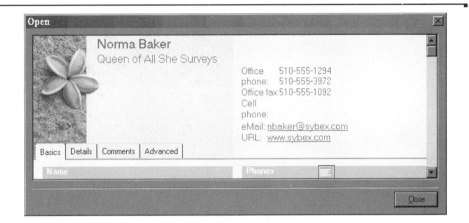

With the Searchable items on the Look In drop-down menu, you have a powerful new tool for searching for addresses outside of your Domino system. The items in the Searchable section are not Domino directories, but rather LDAP directories. You can use Notes to search all of cyberspace in addition to your organization. By default, Notes provides you with connections to some of the biggest publicly available LDAP directories on the Internet, such as Bigfoot, Four11, and Yahoo!. Between them, you'll have access to just about every e-mail address there is. To use Notes's predefined LDAP Connection documents, you must have a connection to the Internet through your computer. However, that's the only connection you'll need. If you're not connected to your home Domino server, you can still do LDAP searches if your computer has a connection to the Internet.

When you choose a Searchable item, Notes gives you a blank For field, as you can see in Figure 5.3. Type a name or a partial name into the For field and click the Search button. Notes will send a request to the remote LDAP server and return the results in the same pane it uses to list names in address books. If you click on a name and click the Details button, Notes brings up the Details dialog box and presents additional information on the name you have selected. Once you've found the address you want, you can use the To, Cc, Bcc, and even Copy Local button as you would for an entry in a Notes address book.

A simple search may not find the address you're looking for. Or, more to the point, it will find so many addresses that you can't find the exact one you're looking for. Remember, with the big LDAP sites that Notes gives you, you're searching globally. Think about how many people there are out there in the world named Mary Jones and Jose Martinez and how many of them have e-mail. However, Notes allows you to narrow the list of search results by performing more detailed searches.

FIGURE 5.3

The Address dialog box, now set to search an LDAP directory

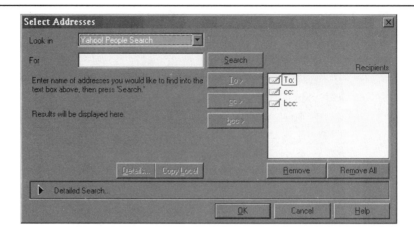

To perform a more detailed search, click the Detailed Search twistie at the bottom of the dialog box. The For field at the top of the dialog will then be grayed out, and a set of fields for more detailed searches will appear at the bottom. You can select a field name (First Name, Street Address, etc.), select an operator (Begins With, Contains, etc.), and fill in data to search for. You can add up to three conditions. You could, for example, search for addresses where the person's first name contains *Rob* (which would include Robby, Robert, Roberta, Robespierre, and so on), his last name is Jones, and he lives in Seattle. Once you have all the conditions in place, click the Search button.

The LDAP servers that appear in the Look In menu are useful for most addresses, but like the Yellow Pages, they can be out-of-date. The big LDAP directory sites are constantly updating their lists of addresses, but there's no central authority over the Internet, so they'll never be completely up-to-date. Your Domino directories are (we hope) kept up-to-date by your Domino administrators, so they'll adequately reflect current e-mail addresses in your organization's Domino system, but they will only reflect Notes users. So what if your organization uses more than just Notes and Domino? A number of large companies use Domino in one department, Exchange in another, other e-mail packages elsewhere. How can you be sure you've got up-to-date addresses for all members of your organization? Or what if you know that there's a useful special-purpose Internet LDAP server out there that you'd love to use?

You don't have to settle for just the list that Notes give you. The items already in your Searchable list are just a few generally useful LDAP sites. You can communicate with as many LDAP servers as you like by setting up Account documents in your Personal Address Book. There are other LDAP directories on the Internet, and many mail-serving programs, including Microsoft Exchange, Netscape Directory, and of course, Domino, can act as LDAP servers as well. You can use Account documents to connect to and search all kinds of address books.

To create an account, open your Personal Address Book and click the tools icon at the bottom of the Navigator in the left-hand pane to get to the Settings Frameset, then go to the Accounts view. Click the New Account button to create a new Account document like the one in Figure 5.4. Fill in a descriptive name for the new server (for example, Shipping Department LDAP Server) and a network address. A fully qualified Internet address, such as `ldap.bigcorporatesite.com`, is necessary for Internet sites, but for sites on an internal corporate network, you can use an IP address (say, 174.121.23.49); you'll probably need to contact the Internet site owner to find out what the right server name is for Internet LDAP servers and contact local administrators for in-house servers. Make sure the Protocol field is set to LDAP and select the locations with which you want to use the Account document. You may, for example, want to be sure you can't try searching an in-house network LDAP server in remote locations. The Account document defaults to using port 389, but if an administrator tells you to use a different port, you can change that on the Advanced tab.

FIGURE 5.4

An Account document

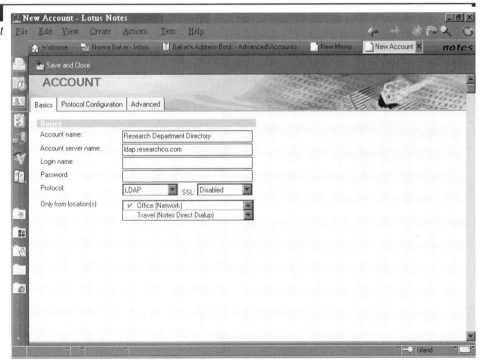

Once you save and close the document, the name you put into the Account Name field will appear in the Searchable section of your Address dialog box's Look In menu (assuming, of course, that you're in one of the locations you have designated for the account).

Whatever method you choose to get a list of addresses, you'll use the same method you always use to get those addresses onto the message. Just select the names and groups one at a time and click the To, Cc, and Bcc buttons as appropriate. The names you have added will appear categorized in the pane on the right. If you add a name by mistake, click on it in the pane on the right and click the Remove button. When you've added everybody you need to the address fields, click the Done button.

Advanced Message Features

In Chapter 4, you got a quick introduction to writing Notes messages, but Notes gives you a broad range of additional features, from elaborate formatting and special message types to integration with word processors. Each option has its uses, but many have drawbacks in certain circumstances, so you should know what you're doing before you use them.

Special Features of the Notes Memo

Notes gives you a large area in which to actually write your message. The message body is a rich text field, which means that you can change fonts (including sizes and colors), insert tables and graphics, and so on. You can even import the contents of some kinds of external files. To import a file, select File ➣ Import, which will bring up a Import dialog box, shown in Figure 5.5. You can navigate through your computer's disks just as you would with a standard Open or Save dialog box. Find the file you want and either double-click it or single-click to select it and click the OK button.

FIGURE 5.5

The Import dialog box

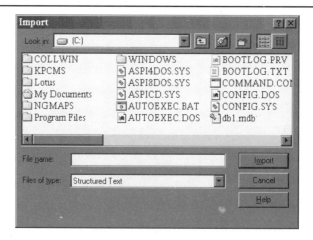

For people used to plain text mail programs, the ability to format messages just as you would in a word processor is an exciting prospect. Nevertheless, try to show a little restraint. There are a few things you should consider before you get too creative with your new abilities:

Font and color limitations   Just as with a word processor document, you have to consider the limitations the people reading it have. If the people you send mail to don't have the fonts you wrote your message with, their computers will have to find a substitute font and your message won't appear quite the way you wrote it. You're safe using common fonts like Times and Helvetica, but you might check with potential recipients before using New Ottoman Hemi-Italic Sans Serif. Notes also gives you 256 text colors to choose from, but they won't appear the way you intended if the recipient has a monitor set to 16 colors.

Size limitations   Users of old versions of Notes will be happy to learn that the 64K size limit for the Body field is gone. There is now a 64K limit on individual paragraphs within the field. You're not likely to hit that limit with most messages; however, be aware that if you work with extremely long messages, your performance can degrade.

Format limitations   Your rich text messages are rich text only inside the bounds of a Domino network. Internet mail protocols can only use a plain-text format. It's possible to have your Internet mail converted to HTML, but not all Internet mail clients can interpret HTML. If they can't, your messages will be difficult to read at best, and at worst, they will be completely illegible. If you use the combined plain text and HTML option, you can be sure that plain-text mail clients can make sense of your messages; HTML-capable clients can approximate your original message, but the messages you send will be twice as large because you're sending the same body twice in a single document.

As you can with any other worthwhile mail client, you can use Notes to send spreadsheets, word processor files, graphics, and any other external file as attachments to your e-mail messages. To attach a file to your document, make sure the insertion point is in the body field and select File ➤ Attach. Just as when you're importing a file, Notes will give you a File Open dialog box that you can use to navigate around your computer and find the file you want. Once you attach the file, an icon will appear in the message to represent the file. Attached files don't count against the 64K limit for the body field (whereas importing the contents of file does).

Special Messages

In addition to plain mail memos and replies, Notes gives you some special message types to work with: the Link Memo, which sends a link to a document, the Phone Message, which sends phone contact information, and the Memo to Database Manager, which sets up a memo to a database's owners. You can also use some word processor programs to edit your messages.

Link Memo

A Link Memo, illustrated in Figure 5.6, gives you a quick method of pointing out a document in any Notes database to another Notes user. To create a Link Memo, select Create ≻ Special ≻ Link Memo. This creates a document which, like a regular memo, has To, Cc, and Bcc fields. However, its body field holds a document link icon. The link is a connection to the currently open or selected Notes document (if there is no open or selected document, the link field will be blank). If you send a Link Memo to another Notes user, he will be able to click the icon to open the document. When sending a Link Memo, be sure that the recipient has permission to read the document. If the recipient does not have permission to open the document or the database it is in, the link will fail.

FIGURE 5.6

A Link Memo

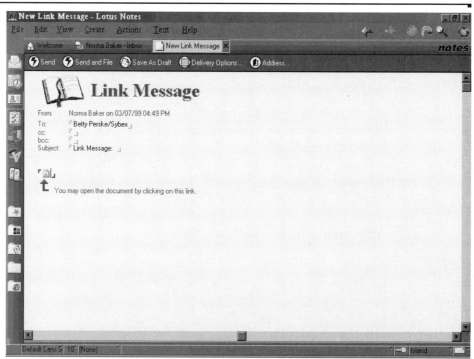

Phone Message

Despite its name, a Phone Message (shown in Figure 5.7) is used for more than just taking down and sending information about phone calls. It can be used for contact information of all kinds, such as visits by delivery people. This can be especially useful for secretaries and administrative assistants. Instead of writing down paper phone messages, you can send them directly to your supervisor's electronic mailbox. To create a Phone Message, select Create ➤ Special ➤ Phone Message. In addition to the standard address fields, it has fields for the caller's name and organization, fields for phone and fax numbers, special-purpose check boxes (letting you mark the message as urgent, request a call back, etc.), and a space for a text message.

FIGURE 5.7

A Phone Message

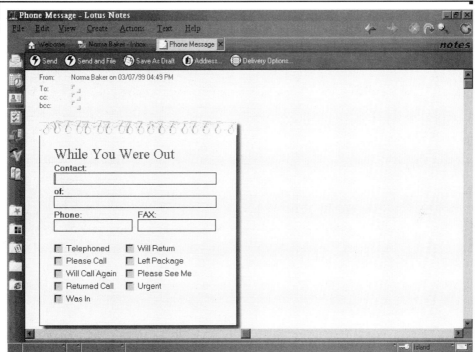

Memo to Database Manager

If a question or problem arises with a database, you may need to communicate with the people who administer it. One method of communicating with a database's "owners" is to create a Memo to Database Manager. To create the memo, select Actions ➤

Send Memo to Database Manager. This will create a regular mail memo addressed to the people and groups with Manager access to the currently open or selected database. Before you use this feature, you should try to make sure the database managers that Notes will give you are actually the people you want to deal with. People with Manager access to a database are not necessarily the ones who approve requests for modifications or otherwise bear responsibility for the database's day-to-day use. Depending on how your organization is structured, MIS personnel may have Manager permission to the databases, but other departments' managers are the ones who actually decide how the database should be used.

Using Word Processors with Notes Mail

Notes's capabilities for writing and formatting text are markedly more versatile than most e-mail packages. Because a message body is a rich text field, you can play with a broad range of fonts, sizes, colors, and other formatting features, but that's not good enough for some people. As versatile as Notes and other rich text editors are, they still don't have the capacities of a full-fledged word processor. So what if you need capabilities that even a standard Notes message won't give you, such as revision marking or footnotes? You've got three choices. You could, if you wanted to invest the effort, hand-tool a Notes message, changing font sizes, colors, and styles to make it look like you could easily produce numbered outlines or drop footnotes into the text—that clearly is the wrong way to go. You might write a document in your favorite word processor and attach it to a Notes message—better, but still clumsy because recipients would have to go through the extra steps of opening your attachment. Or, if you don't want you or your recipients to work that hard, you could just use your favorite word processor within the body of the Notes message itself. Notes supports the use of some popular word processors as message editors.

If you're interested in using a word processor to write your mail, open up your User preferences (File ➢ Preferences ➢ User Preferences, in case you've forgotten) and select the Mail and News tab. Make sure Notes is your mail program (there's a drop-down box at the top of the Preferences dialog box), then look at the Alternate Document Memo menu at the bottom. If the word processor you use is Microsoft Word or Lotus's own Word Pro, you can use it to write messages. Select the word processor you use from the list and click OK.

When you're done, you'll probably notice a new entry on your Create menu: either Word Memo or Word Pro Memo, depending on which word processor you chose (a Microsoft Word Memo is shown in Figure 5.8). Selecting the new menu item will create a new memo with a word processor document as the message body. The memo will retain the Notes message header for the address and subject line as well as your bookmark buttons and tabs for other open documents and databases, but the body of the message will display your word processor's rulers and layout and the word processor's toolbars will appear under the menu bar. Your word processor's menus will mostly replace Notes's menus, although Notes will retain its File menu, and the Help menu will let you choose between two submenus: the Notes Help menu and the word processor's Help menu.

PART

II

Mastering the Basics

FIGURE 5.8

A Word Memo

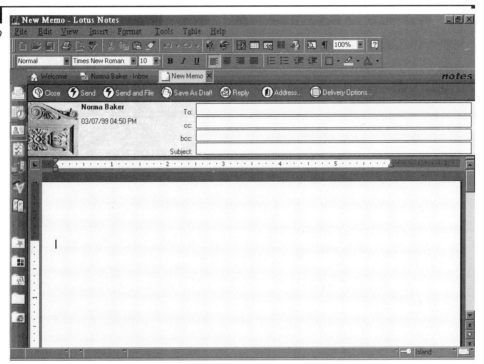

You will be able to use most of your word processor's features: page layout and outline views; customized toolbars; revision tracking; the word processor's native spell checking, table construction, and text formatting features; even most macro-writing features. The features you won't be able to use are file related. For example, you can't save a word processor memo as an external document, although you could copy the contents and paste them into a new document created in your word processor.

At the same time, you can use Notes to store and mail your message. The address fields and addressing features function normally, and you can save your message as a draft if you need to go away and come back to it later.

There are, of course, potential drawbacks to using a word processor as your message editor. You won't be able to use attachments in your word processor messages. After all, you can't attach external files to word processor documents, so you won't be able to attach them to word processor documents that happen to be embedded in Notes documents.

Word processor messages are *much* larger than regular Notes messages. For example, a Word Memo is about 32K bigger than a regular Notes Memo. If you take full advantage of Word's special capabilities, it will only get bigger. Word processor messages take up more room in your mailbox as well as in the recipient's mailbox, and they will correspondingly take longer to send. That won't make much of a difference if you're working on a good in-house network, but it can take a lot longer to send and receive word processor messages over a dial-up modem connection.

Delivery Options

Notes allows you to set a number of options that modify the way a sent message is treated, from encrypting its contents to marking its importance, both to the sender and intermediate mail servers. If you click the Delivery Options button in an open memo, Notes will let you set a number of options, including security, delivery priority, and how your message is encoded. The options you will probably use most often are on the Basics tab.

The Basics Tab

The Basics tab contains options for delivery, security, and mood stamps.

Delivery Options   The options relating to delivery of your mail are as follows:

Importance   This is a marker for the recipient of the mail. You can mark your mail as having High, Middle, or Low importance. Most mail clients, including Notes, have some visible sign of the message's importance, so the recipient will see the significance you place on the message.

Delivery Report   Notes can report on where your messages go. This can be very useful if you're having trouble getting messages to their destination or just want to figure out some things about your network's topology. If you select Only on Failure, you'll get a detailed message tracing the route your message takes if it fails to reach its destination. Confirm Delivery will trace the route your message takes if the message is successfully delivered to its destination. Trace Entire Route will give you a report on the route your message takes regardless of whether or not it reaches its destination.

Delivery Priority   This gives the message a priority that mail servers read. In general, messages marked with high priority are delivered before messages with lower priorities. This can speed up the delivery of your mail, although the precise order in which messages are delivered depends heavily on settings on the mail servers between you and your message's destination.

Return Receipt   If this option is checked, you will receive a message when the recipient opens and reads your message. This option does not work with all mail systems.

Prevent Copying   If this option is checked and the recipient also uses Notes, the recipient will not be able to copy the contents of the message or forward it to others. Although this does not prevent the recipient from, for example, retyping the message or just telling other people about it, it does make it more difficult to inadvertently send sensitive messages to people who shouldn't see them.

Auto Spellcheck   If this option is checked, Notes will automatically check your spelling when you send the message. This can become slightly annoying if you send a lot of short messages using abbreviations, proper names, or other text that a spell checker will flag needlessly, but it can be a lifesaver if you send lots of more normal text.

Security Options   You can set default values for these options in your mail preferences, but override them here:

Sign   If this box is checked, Notes will attach a digital signature to your message. When you open a signed message in Notes, the computer will compare the digital signature with information on a Domino server's address book and tell you whether or not the signature matches the sender's name. If it doesn't, the message may have been tampered with before it got to you.

Encrypt   If this box is checked, Notes will encrypt your message for the recipient. Only you and the recipient will be able to read the message, even if other people get permission to open your mailbox.

Save These Options   If you check this box and click the OK button, the options you have chosen will be sent to your mail profile and become the default options.

PART

II

Mastering the Basics

Limits on Encryption

Notes encryption is excellent for securing data, particularly if the message never leaves the Notes system, but it has its limits. The most important is that encryption will only work within a Notes system. If you attempt to send an encrypted message to an Internet address, Notes will let you know that the message cannot be encrypted and will ask you if it's OK to send an unencrypted copy. You can encrypt yor messages with S/MIME; however, not all mail servers and clients are S/MIME compliant (see Chapter 10 for more details). If you want to protect data sent to Internet addresses, you need to take steps outside of Notes. You could, for example, put the contents of your message into a password-protected document (not a great option; password-protected documents can be broken into by sufficiently determined crackers) or use third-party encryption software such as PGP to encrypt the message contents.

You may also encounter problems sending encrypted mail to some Domino servers. When you encrypt a message, Notes goes to the Domino server and looks up the public key of the person or people the message is addressed to. However, if you're sending mail to a Notes user in a different Notes domain, you may not have access to the other domain's servers and directories. If you want to send encrypted mail to Notes users in a different domain, you'll need to create entries for them in your Personal Address Book, request their public keys, and paste those into the Notes Certifiers fields in the appropriate Contact documents. If the person has a hierarchical ID (all Notes 4.5 and above users, as well as some earlier Notes users), the key will go into the Certified Public Key field. If the user has a flat file ID, the key will go into the Flat Name Key field. If you don't know what kind of ID your correspondent has (and you probably won't), enlist the aid of your Domino administrator.

Mood Stamp   Mood stamps allow you to put a more expressive stamp on your message than the Importance option does. Your options are as follows:

- Personal
- Confidential
- Private
- Thank You
- Good Job
- Flame
- Joke
- FYI

- Question
- Reminder

Each mood stamp has a picture that will appear in both the message and your Inbox. This is another feature that won't translate to non-Notes mail systems.

Advanced Options

The options on the Advanced tab are somewhat more special-purpose options that will make a greater technical difference in how the message is sent.

Workflow Administration   The options in the Workflow Administration section of the Advanced tab let you affect how others interact with your message:

> **Stamp Message with a 'Please Reply by' Date**   You can set a date by which you would like a reply. In addition to letting the recipient know how quickly action must be taken on your message, it will also make the message appear in the recipient's To Do view.

> **Expiration Date**   You can also set a date after which the message becomes obsolete. Aside from being another way of letting the recipient know how much time there is to take action on your mail, archiving formulas can pay attention to expiration dates and immediately move expired documents from your mailbox to an archive.

> **Replies**   You can use this field to set a reply-to address. Although Notes allows you to choose addresses from available address books, you can type in any valid Internet e-mail address instead. This option is useful if you want people to reply to a different address from the one you used to send the message (for example, if you're temporarily sending mail from somebody else's e-mail account but want to get the replies in your own mailbox). Most mail programs will automatically use the reply-to address, if there is one, when they set up a reply.

Internet Message Format   The Internet Message Format section lets you set options governing how the message is treated if it is sent over the Internet:

> **MIME Character Set**   This option refines the character set used for MIME encoding. If you don't know what these settings mean, do not use them.

> **Sending This Notes Document to Other Notes Mail User(s)**   This option lets Notes know that even though your message is leaving your Notes system, it will eventually be read by a Notes user. Checking this option tells Notes to encode the message in such a way that it will appear as much like your original message as possible rather than stripping out most Notes features, as happens with most messages sent to the Internet.

Mail Preferences

Mail options give you considerable control over individual messages, but they need to be set on a message-by-message basis. If you want to have some settings preset for all messages (say, you want to encrypt or spell-check all of your outgoing messages automatically), you need to set your mail preferences. To call up your preferences, you can click the Tools button in your Inbox and select Preferences or select Actions ➤ Tools ➤ Preferences. The Preferences dialog box defaults to the Mail tab, which gives you access to three subtabs: Basics, Letterhead, and Signature. You can also access the Mail Delegation tab, which is the default for the Delegation main tab.

The Basics Tab

The database owner is automatically granted full Manager access to the database. The mailbox's main user should be its owner. If the user's name is not filled in, you can type in a name or click the button to bring up a dialog box from which to choose the name.

If you check the Automatically Check Spelling check box, Notes will check spelling on your mail messages when you send them out.

The Letterhead Tab

Notes gives you the chance to personalize your mail with letterhead. Every mail message you send through the Notes system will have your name and the time you sent the message at the top, but this feature allows you to customize the format. Select items from the menu, and the associated picture will be displayed at the bottom.

The Signature Tab

One of the most requested features of Notes 5 is the mail signature, a small block of text appended to the end of outgoing messages giving identifying information such as a name and address, a standard company disclaimer, or a witty (or, as is often the case, not so witty) quotation. Your signature can go in the signature field, or you can click the File radio button and select a plain-text file holding your signature or even a bitmap graphic file. Although there's nothing in the design to stop you from putting in the complete lyrics to your favorite song or, for that matter, the complete works of Shakespeare, it's polite to limit yourself to four lines of text. If you want your signature to be appended to all of your outgoing messages automatically, you can check the box.

The Mail Delegation Tab

If you would like your assistant or supervisor to be able to read your mail, send it in your name, or otherwise manage it, you can grant that permission if you click the Delegation tab. The Mail Delegation subtab is the default for the Delegation main tab.

There are four levels of delegation, each with its own field: read; read and send mail; read, send mail, and edit documents; and delete documents. Only users who can send mail or send and edit can be granted permission to delete. To grant someone permission, click the button for the appropriate field and add the name from the list. These fields only grant permission to your mail, not your calendar. To learn how to grant permission to your calendar, see Chapter 6, "Calendaring and Scheduling."

Replying To, Forwarding, and Converting Mail

PART

II

Of course, you don't just want to read mail and originate messages. You also want to respond to other people. And, of course, Notes gives you tools to coordinate your mail responses.

Reply

The Reply button on the Inbox and any message gives you four options:

Reply   The Reply option creates a message addressed to the person who sent the message to which you're replying. The subject is Re: plus the subject of the original message (this is a standard practice for the subject lines of responses on the Internet), and the body field is completely blank. If you send a reply to someone within a Notes system, the message they receive will have a document icon next to the message's subject line. That icon is a link to the original document; they can view the message you responded to simply by clicking the link icon. If you and your correspondent use the Reply method, you will be able to backtrack through the entire history of the e-mail conversation simply by clicking reply icons.

Reply with History   The problem with the Reply option is that it doesn't work outside of the Notes system. Internet mail protocols simply don't track messages in a way that allows them to be related to one another. You can, however, use Reply with History. Choosing Reply with History creates a message with the address and subject line set as it is in a reply, but it also brings the entire original message into the body of the reply. You can add your responses before or after the original message text or even insert your responses within the inherited message.

Reply to All   Reply to All creates a message like a Reply, but it addresses the message to everybody the original message was addressed to. The originator's name goes into the To field, and other names go to the Cc field. This is very useful if you're carrying on an e-mail conversation with a group of people, not just one person.

Reply to All with History   This constructs a reply to everybody the original message was sent to, like Reply to All, but also inherits the original message into the message body, like Reply with History.

If you create a reply or reply with history and later decide that you want to send your reply to everybody the original message was addressed to, both reply documents give you a Reply to All button you can use to add the other original addressee names to the reply's address fields.

Once you've created the reply, you can save it as a draft, spell-check it, and otherwise treat it as you would a new memo. However, Notes will keep track of responses even if the subject line changes. If you look at your Discussion Threads view, you'll see any Notes replies you create or receive arranged together, with the original message first followed by its responses. The subject line of each response is indented from the original's. Remember that messages received from the Internet are not connected to other messages in any way that Notes can take advantage of. Although you may reply to Internet mail, any message you receive from the Internet is regarded as the start of a new discussion thread.

Forward

Another way to use one message as the basis of another is to forward it to somebody else. If you click the Forward button, Notes will create a new message containing the contents of an old one, just like a reply with history. It will also inherit the original message's subject line. However, it won't inherit any addresses. Instead, you will need to provide new addresses. A forwarded message is treated as the start of a new discussion thread in the Discussion Threads view.

A common problem that mobile users and multiple users using the same computer have with forwarding mail is that in order to forward, Notes needs to check data in a mail file the current user has access to. The name of the mail file is specified in the current Location document. If you get a permission-related message while trying to forward a message, select File ➤ Mobile ➤ Edit Current Location, click the Mail tab, and check the Mail File field. If the field is blank or doesn't have the location of the mail file, fill it in.

Copy Into

The final method for "recycling" Notes memos is to copy them into new documents. The Copy Into button provides you with three options:

New Memo   The entire contents of the message are inherited into a new mail message, including the addresses and subject. Like a forwarded message, a message created this way is treated as the start of a new discussion thread.

New Calendar Entry   The contents of the message are copied into a new Calendar entry document. This is an excellent way of turning a proposed meeting into an actual meeting. The message body becomes the Details section of the new Calendar entry and the subject becomes its title. If your default Calendar entry is a meeting invitation, the names in the address fields become meeting invitees (the original's To field becomes the list of required invitees, the Cc field becomes the optional invitees, and the Bcc field becomes the FYI list). See Chapter 6 for a full explanation of calendar entries.

New To Do   The subject of the message becomes the title of the new To Do, and its body becomes the Details section. If you make it a Group To Do, the message's To, Cc, and Bcc fields become the To Do's required, optional, and FYI participants.

Documents created with the Copy Into method can be edited just like replies and any other Notes document. The Copy Into method just saves the work you'd have to do constructing new documents by hand.

Organizing Mail

If you do any kind of business with e-mail, you will quickly end up with more old messages than will fit onto a screen. You will also almost certainly want to put together all the messages you get about a particular project, from a particular correspondent, or about a particular topic so you can review the information quickly. In your Notes mailbox, you can organize messages into folders. You can move messages into folders by hand or by using a number of tools. A very powerful tool is the new Rules feature, which you can use to organize your mail as it comes into your mailbox.

Creating and Using Folders

In Chapter 3, you learned about creating and organizing folders. Your mailbox gives you some tools to make it easier to move documents in and out of them. When you mail a message, you can click the Send and File button to put the message you're sending into a folder immediately. If you choose Send and File, Notes will give you the Move to Folder dialog box. Click on the folder you want the message to appear in and click the Move or Add button. If you need to create a new folder, simply click the Create New Folder button and provide a name for the new folder. The message will be placed in that folder immediately.

You can easily move incoming mail as well. Every message has a Move to Folder button. Click the button, choose the folder or create a new one, then click the Add or Move button to place the message in the folder.

Rules

Rules are a feature from one of Lotus's other products, ccMail, a dedicated mail program. However, they were so popular that the idea was picked up for Notes. Rules are essentially Agents (see Chapter 22) that automatically move incoming mail into designated folders. They can also change the importance marking on a mail message and even delete messages. Using rules, you can arrange your mailbox so that mail that fits conditions you give it will appear already in the folders where you want them to end up, and you can even filter out a certain amount of spam, those incredibly annoying e-mail advertisements.

The Rules view gives you tools for creating and editing rules. When you click the New Rule button, you get a dialog box for creating new rules for moving or modifying incoming mail.

Conditions

First, you need to set some conditions. A rule can be told to search a number of fields in incoming mail: the To field, the Cc field, the message body itself, and several others. It can also examine the message's size or where the message comes from. When you have set the condition fields (say, the subject contains the phrase *make money fast*), click the Add button to add it to the list of conditions the rule follows.

You can add a number of conditions to a single rule, connecting them with an AND or OR operator. If you connect conditions with AND, the rule will act on messages for which all of the conditions are true. If you use OR, it will act on messages for which any of the conditions are true. You can also designate additional conditions as exceptions. For example, in Figure 5.9, the conditions will make the rule act on incoming mail that has *Make money fast* in the subject line or that comes from swindle.com. However, the exception means that even if it does have that subject or domain of origin, it won't work on messages from BobSmith (presumably, the person making this rule knows bobsmith@ swindle.com).

If you want to remove a condition, just click on it and click the Remove button. If you want to completely redo the conditions the rule follows, just click Remove All.

FIGURE 5.9

A rule

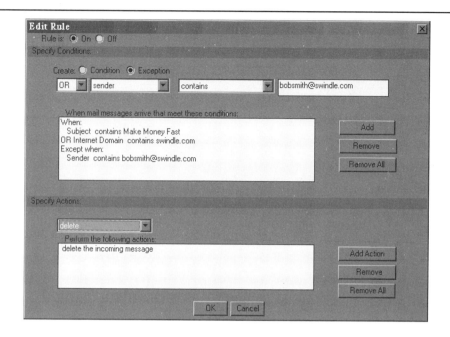

Mastering the Basics

Actions

Once you've decided what your conditions are, you need to tell Notes what to do with the messages it finds. Your choices here are somewhat more limited:

- Add to Folder
- Move to Folder
- Change Importance
- Delete

If you choose the Add to Folder or Move to Folder option, click the Choose Folder button and designate the folder in which you want the message to end up. If you choose Change Importance To, choose the importance you want it to have. Delete has no other options.

When you have selected an action, click the Add button to add the action to the list. As with the conditions, Remove gets rid of a selected action, and Remove All gets rid of all of them. You can add several actions to a rule, and they will be performed in order. You might start with a Move to Folder action to get the document out of your Inbox and then add a set of Add to Folder actions to distribute it around your mailbox.

There's no point in having more than one Move to Folder in a rule because the Move option removes the document from the folder. If you try to move a document into multiple folders, it will only appear in the last folder it was moved into. There's also no reason to set a message's importance more than once because you'll only see the last importance the message is given. Finally, there's no reason to combine Delete with *anything*. If you have a rule that deletes a message, you'll never see it anywhere.

When you're done and ready to put the rule into action, remember to enable it using the radio buttons at the top of the dialog box before you click the OK button. Once you've saved and closed the rule, you can always come back later and disable it or even delete the rule altogether.

Out of Office

The Out of Office feature is an Agent in the Notes mail database that will automatically respond to incoming mail when you're away from the office or wherever it is you use Notes. When you enable Out of Office, people who send you mail in your absence will get a message telling them that their messages have been received but you're away from the office and won't be able to respond until you get back. You can set the contents of the outgoing message, tell Notes how long to send automatic responses, and even list people who should get special responses or no response at all.

To set up the Out of Office feature, you can click the Tools button in your Inbox or select Actions ➤ Tools ➤ Out of Office. This will bring up the Out of Office dialog box, shown in Figure 5.10.

FIGURE 5.10

The Out of Office dialog box

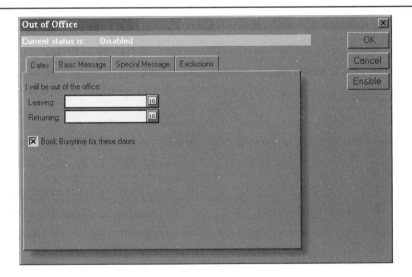

The most important thing to do is to tell Notes when you'll be out of the office. You can do so on the Dates tab by selecting beginning and ending dates—the first date you're out and the first date you're back (*not* the last date you're out). Type dates into the fields or click the calendar icons to bring up a pop-up calendar and click on the appropriate dates. The left and right arrow buttons navigate between months. Checking the Book Busytime for These Dates check box will mark those dates as busy in your Notes calendar. If you check this option, people trying to schedule meetings with you will be able to see that you won't be available (see Chapter 6 for more on Notes calendaring and scheduling).

The Basic Message tab contains information about the default message that will be sent out in response to incoming mail. You can give it any subject line, although it defaults to "*Your name* is out of the office." You can also type in the body of the outgoing message, which defaults to "I will respond to your message when I return." If you're still available by phone or through an alternate e-mail address, you can put those in here.

You may want some people to receive a special message. For example, you may want to tell most people that you're away for a week, but you might want a small group of important clients or colleagues to know how to get in touch with you even though you're away from your regular e-mail address. To set up a special message, click the Special Message tab. As you can on the Basic Message tab, you can set the subject and body text, but it also gives you a field from which to choose the names or Internet addresses of people who get the special message.

Finally, you may not want some people to get anything. To prevent responses to some people or addresses, click the Exclusions tab. If you check the Don't Send Messages to Internet Addresses check box, only people within your Domino network will get out of office messages. People sending mail from outside will not. To prevent specific people from getting responses, fill in their names or Internet e-mail addresses in the Do Not Send an Out of Office Notification to the Following People field. The next field, Do Not Send an Out of Office Notification in Response to Documents Addressed to the Following Groups, will prevent responses based on who the message was sent to (besides you), not who it is from. This option is very useful for users who subscribe to Internet mailing lists. One of the problems with older versions of the Out of Office Agent is that it could flood e-mail discussion groups with out of office messages. Finally, you can fill in phrases in the last field to prevent mail from being sent in response to certain subject lines.

When you're finished filling in the fields, click OK to save your changes or Cancel to reject them. Because you can save your changes without turning the Agent on, you can set up your messages and notification lists well in advance of when you're actually going to be out of the office. When you finally want to turn the Agent on, click the Enable/Disable button. When you return to the office, call up the Out of Office dialog

PART
II

Mastering the Basics

box and click the button again to turn it off. When the Out of Office Agent is active, it will run once a day. The Agent looks through all of the mail that has arrived since the last time it ran. If a sender hasn't been informed that you're out of the office (and isn't on the list of exclusions), the Agent will send the appropriate outgoing message and add his address to the list of people who have been informed. That way, people you're corresponding with will only get a single message letting them know you're gone. If they continue to send you mail, they won't be deluged with messages telling them something they already know.

Archiving

After using your Notes mailbox for a few weeks or months, filing your messages into folders just won't do the trick anymore. Your mailbox will get bigger and bigger, with hundreds or even thousands of messages. Your folders will be packed with messages you never look at anymore, and your searches will get slower and slower as the messages Notes has to look through pile up. Nevertheless, there may be a lot of messages you can't bring yourself to delete because you might need them someday to document the progress of a project or to use for legal purposes. Notes allows you to deal with this dilemma with archiving, letting you put old messages into a copy of the original database. In earlier versions of Notes, you needed special Agents in a database in order to produce an archive version of it, but Notes 5 has made that machinery part of Notes so that you can archive any database you need to (this can be a *very* useful option for large discussion databases).

To archive a database, open it (or select the database icon in your Notes Workspace) and select File ➢ Database ➢ Archive. The first time you select this option, Notes will ask you for some parameters to determine what gets archived.

The Basics tab of the Archive Settings dialog (see Figure 5.11) contains the most basic information Notes needs to archive old documents: which documents should be archived and where should they be archived. Notes allows you to select documents by how long it has been since something has been done with them. You can archive any or all of the documents that have not been read after a given number of days, documents that have not been modified, and documents that have been marked as expired. You could, for example, decide to archive documents that haven't been modified in the past six months, documents that haven't been read in a year, or documents that were marked read more than a day ago. The default location for archiving documents is an `Archive` directory in your local Notes `Data` directory. By default, Notes bases the name of the archive database on the first six letters of the original database's name, with *a_* added to the beginning to show the user that it's an archive database. For example, a database named `maindiscussion.nsf` would produce an archive database named a_maindi.nsf. However, the "initial *a* plus six letters" is only a convenient naming convention. You can rename your archive as you see fit. You can also create the archive in other subdirectories of your Notes Data directory or even on a Domino server (if you have permission to create new databases on the server; check with your Domino administrator).

FIGURE 5.11

The Archive Settings dialog box

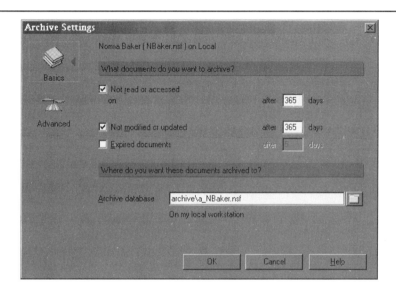

The Advanced tab lets you fine-tune the archiving process. For example, if the database being archived and its corresponding archive are both on a Domino server, you can have the database archived automatically on the server as documents meet the archiving conditions. You also have two options for deleting documents from the database. If you want to keep track of ongoing discussions, check Do Not Delete Documents That Have Responses. With this option checked, original messages won't be removed from your database until all of their responses are ready to be archived as well. You'll be able to follow an exchange of Reply documents all the way back to its origin, even if you haven't actually accessed the original message in a long time. Checking Delete Matching Documents Without Archiving Them is really more a housekeeping setting than an archiving setting. With this option selected, the archiving process will delete documents meeting the archiving conditions without saving them to an archive. Use this option only if you want to periodically remove old documents from the database and aren't worried about never seeing them again.

Once you've set your archiving options, click the OK button. If this is the first time you've archived the database, Notes will create a new database based on the design of the database being archived. Then it will take old documents out of the original database and put them in the archive. This means that documents that appeared in particular views in the original database will appear in those views in the archive, making them easy to find. Users of older versions of Notes will be ecstatic to learn that archived documents will show up in the folders in which they were originally filed as well, a vital feature for finding messages in over-full mail databases.

After the archive database has been set up, you can run the archiving process any time you want by selecting File ➤ Database ➤ Archive. When you do, any documents that have come to meet your archive settings will be archived. If you want to change your archive settings, select File ➤ Database ➤ Database Properties to get the Database Properties InfoBox and click the Archive Settings button on the Basics tab to bring up the Archive Settings dialog box.

Notes Minder

Once you've set your mail preferences, you can have Notes tell you when you get new mail by beeping or popping up a dialog box. You can also have events in your Notes calendar trigger pop-up or audible alarms. In previous versions of Notes, the problem with alarms was that you had to have Notes running for the alerts to come up. The Notes program window could be minimized, but it still had to be open and running in the background.

This was, and still can be, a problem. Many adjectives can be applied to Notes, but *small* is not one of them. All of that power and versatility eats up a hefty chunk of your computer's memory and system resources. That shouldn't be a problem if you're just running Notes and one or two other programs on a fairly new computer, but what if you're using an older computer that just fills the minimum recommended requirements for running the Notes client? Or what if you need to run a word processor, a spreadsheet, *and* a different database program all at the same time? At the very least, having all of those big programs running together will slow everything's performance. At worst, some of those programs won't be well-behaved, rendering your entire system less stable and more likely to crash.

Notes 5 has a solution, letting Notes tell you about your mail and reminding you of your appointments without actually running. The solution is the Notes Minder. The Notes Minder monitors your mailbox for new mail and your calendar for alarms, but it doesn't have any of the other features of the full Notes client. It will alert you to new mail and let you launch Notes when you want to, but without the full Notes client's large memory footprint.

The Notes Minder is installed along with the Notes client and can be launched from the Start menu. When you launch the Notes Minder, it will ask for your Notes password and then sit quietly in memory, leaving an icon in the system tray. The icon indicates the state of your mailbox and the Minder itself. There are four different icons.

The minder is active, but there are no unread messages in your Inbox.

There are unread messages in your Inbox.

The Minder can't find or contact the server.

The Minder is running, but disabled.

PART

II

Now that you've got an icon, what do you do with it? If you move your mouse over the icon, you will be shown the last time the Minder checked your mailbox. If you double-click the icon, you'll jump directly to your mail, Notes will launch, and your Inbox will open. Right-clicking the icon brings up a menu you can use to control the Minder with the following options:

Open Notes   Launches Notes immediately.

Check Now   Checks your mailbox for new mail. The Notes Minder doesn't keep a constant connection open to the Notes server; that would eat up too much memory and processor time. Instead, it checks your mailbox periodically for new messages. Selecting this option tells the Minder to check for mail immediately rather than waiting for the next interval.

View Mail Summary   This option lets you view a summary of new messages without having to launch Notes itself. It brings up a window listing the sender, date, and subject line of every unread message in your Inbox (see Figure 5.12). Using this option, you can see new messages that have arrived and then launch Notes if you decide one of them is important enough to read immediately. Double-clicking on any of the items in the list will immediately launch Notes and open that document.

Properties   This option calls up the dialog box shown in Figure 5.13, which lets you set a number of options for the Notes Minder. You can tell the Minder whether or not to use audible notifications, whether or not it should pop up alerts to Notes messages, and how long it should wait between checks on your mailbox.

Enabled   You can temporarily disable the Minder by unchecking this option.

Exit   Quits the Minder.

FIGURE 5.12

The Mail Summary window

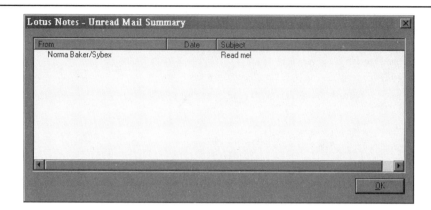

FIGURE 5.13

The Properties dialog box

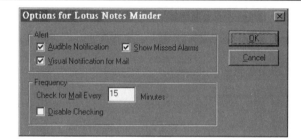

Using Mail Offline

With most of the features discussed in this chapter, it is assumed, or at least implied, that you're connected to some kind of server. However, you'll find that many Notes databases, including your mail, will allow you to work offline, not connected to any servers at all. This is particularly useful for laptop users, who may need to work with their mail while on a plane, on a train, or miles away from the nearest modem or network connection. However, even Notes users with a physical connection to a fast network might find some reason to disconnect from the servers.

The key to working offline is being in Island mode. You can switch to Island mode by selecting File ➤ Mobile ➤ Choose Current Location and selecting Island from the list. Going into Island mode tells Notes that there are no external network connections of any kind, so it shouldn't try to interact with any servers. You may actually have an active network or modem connection, and switching to Island mode won't disconnect your computer from a network. While you're in Island mode, Notes won't try to use that connection, but you and other programs you use still can.

Obviously, there are limitations to working offline. Most important, you can't use any databases that you don't have locally (that is, on your own computer). If you want to work with a database while offline, be sure you have a local replica. See Chapter 9 for more information on replication. You also can't send mail. For mail to go anywhere, it needs to go to a mail server first; if Notes doesn't think it's connected to a server, the mail can't go anywhere.

However, you can still do a lot of work on your mail while offline. You can read existing messages and write new ones. If you have a local copy of your mail database, you can use all of the document-creation and document-editing tools you're used to. Notes even allows you to make *mobile* replicas of Directory Catalogs. The mobile replicas are very compact summaries of the address books that live on the Domino servers, giving you access to your organization's address books in a fraction of the space they usually take up.

You can even send mail... well, sort of. You can go so far as clicking the Send button. As we've already discussed, the mail can't actually go anywhere if Notes doesn't have a server to talk to. It can, though, be stored away for later delivery. If you click the Send button while offline, Notes will create new databases to store the mail in: `mail.box` for Notes mail and `smtp.box` for Internet mail. You can write and "send" as many messages as you want while offline, and they'll all be stored until you make a connection to a mail server. Once connected, you can tell Notes to send the queued mail, actually starting the messages on their way.

Summary

This chapter dealt with some of the complexities of dealing with Notes mail. You can use the Address dialog to search Domino and LDAP servers; you can search for addresses both within and outside of your organization. You can control a number of settings to trace and secure your mail, make many of those settings permanent by setting your mail preferences, sort and control incoming mail with Rules documents, and keep the contents of your mailbox current by archiving old messages. Notes mail allows you to use some external programs as well. Notes allows you to use some word processors to edit mail messages, respond automatically to incoming mail with the Out of Office feature, and even keep track of incoming mail without having Notes running by using the Notes Minder.

The next chapter will go into more detail on the other major part of your Notes mail database: your calendar. The calendar allows you to keep track of your appointments and coordinate meetings with others, integrating your calendar with Notes mail.

CHAPTER **6**

Calendaring and Scheduling

The second major part of your personal mailbox is an appointment calendar. Computer programs that let you keep track of your time are nothing new. What groupware programs like Notes add is the ability to deal not just with your own calendar, but with other people's calendars as well. Unlike the mail portions of the database, which can talk to just about any mail server, you need to be attached to a Domino server if you want your calendar to interact with other calendars, which must in turn be contained by Notes databases as well. There are not, at the moment, widely used standards for dealing with calendaring and scheduling over the Internet or local networks, so anyone who wants group calendar functions needs a proprietary software package. Fortunately, Domino's calendaring and scheduling is very good. Within a Domino network, your calendar can be far more than just a tool to keep track of your appointments. It can be a powerful, flexible tool for organizing groups of people. You can schedule meetings, check on subordinates' free time, and coordinate group actions quickly and easily through your Notes calendar. Chapter 4 introduced you the the Notes Calendar basics, this chapter continues to discuss how to move around your calendar, set up preferences and default values, add entries to your calendar, and use features such as group calendars and meeting invitations to get your calendar to work with others.

Navigating the Calendar

When you open your Calendar, the default is set to list entries within each day in the order they happen without any indication of how much time there is between them. However, if you click the clock icon next to the number buttons, Notes will turn on time slots, displaying an hourly schedule. In addition to being spread out through the days, the time each entry occupies will be shaded, like in Figure 6.1. The up and down arrows in each day are for scrolling up and down through that day's entries. If you're at the beginning of the day, the top arrow is grayed out. Likewise, the bottom arrow is grayed out if you're at the end of the day.

To move to another "page" of your calendar, click one of the arrows in the lower right corner. Clicking the left-pointing arrow moves you back to the previous time period, and clicking the right-pointing arrow moves you to the next time period. Clicking the sun icon between the arrows moves the Calendar view to the current time period and selects the current day. At the bottom of the day, Notes will show how many days, weeks, or months into the year the current view is and how many are left.

You can select a day simply by clicking it. When you create a new calendar entry, the new entry will come up with the day you have selected in its date fields.

FIGURE 6.1

A calendar in the one-week view. Time slots are on.

Calendar Preferences

Before you start keeping track of your time in your calendar, it's a good idea to set up your calendar preferences. You can get to the calendar preferences by selecting Actions ➤ Tools ➤ Preferences or by clicking the Tools button on the calendar button bar and selecting Preferences. This is the same Preferences InfoBox you used to set up your mail preferences back in Chapter 5, but if your calendar is open, it will default to the Calendar tab. Once there, you can select one of the six subtabs.

The Basics Tab

The Basics tab sets up a number of default values for calendar entry documents: the default type of entry, the duration of meetings and appointments, how long in the future to extend anniversaries, and what other views to use to display certain entries. The Conflict Checking section tells Notes whether or not to warn you if you try to

PART

II

Mastering the Basics

schedule a calendar entry at the same time another entry is scheduled. Personal Categories allows you to add categories to a list and make them available for use on calendar entries.

The Freetime Tab

Notes keeps track of free time for every user on a Domino server. The Freetime tab sets the range of times that you are available. After all, most people are available for meetings only during regular business hours. By default, Notes will show you as available from 9:00 A.M. to noon and 1:00 P.M. to 5:00 P.M., Monday through Friday. You can adjust those times to fit your regular work schedule simply by typing in new times and checking and unchecking boxes for different days. For example, you might want to configure your free time so you're available from 9:00 A.M. to 5:00 P.M. (making it easier to schedule lunch meetings), shift some available times to the weekends, or extend your hours on four days but make yourself unavailable on the fifth. If you want to indicate that you will be available during separate periods of time during the day, enter time ranges separated by commas. If you entered **7:00 AM - 10:00 AM, 11:00 AM - 3:00 PM, 5:00 PM - 7:00 PM** for a day, Notes would show that you're available from 7:00 to 10:00 in the morning, 11:00 to 3:00 in the afternoon, and 5:00 to 7:00 in the evening. Calendar entries can block out more of your time.

You can also keep people from reading your free time schedule with this tab. Usually, anybody in the Notes system can read your free time schedule. They can, through their own Notes databases, see when you are available for meetings, although nobody can read your calendar entries unless you specifically grant them access to your mailbox. However, if you don't want everybody in your organization to be able to schedule meetings with you, you can limit the group of people allowed to read your free time schedule by filling in the field at the bottom. Clicking the arrow tab next to the field will bring up an Address dialog box in which you can fill in names from your organization's directory.

The Alarms Tab

Notes can give you audible, visible, and e-mail alarms, but you must enable alarms first. Once alarms are enabled, you can tell Notes to use alarms for some or all types of calendar entries by checking the appropriate boxes and configuring how far in advance to sound the alarms. You might, for example, set the default alarms for appointments and meetings to 10 minutes in advance (giving you enough time to gather important papers) but not use them for anniversaries. You can set alarms for appointments and meeting invitations minutes in advance and other calendar entries and To Do items days in advance. You can also choose the sound for audible alarms from the menu.

Making settings on this tab just enables Notes to use alarms and sets default values. You must also turn on alarms for individual calendar entries.

The Views Tab

In the Views tab, you can set the range of times shown if you decide to view your calendar as a schedule. You might, for instance, only want to see a list of entries between 9:00 A.M. and 5:00 P.M. If there are calendar entries before or after the range of time slots you select, they will appear before and after the time slots, respectively. You can also choose to see the day divided up by hours, half-hour intervals, or 15-minute intervals.

The Autoprocess Tab

You can instruct your mailbox to clean up after some calendar-related tasks for you. If you decided to autoprocess invitations, Notes will automatically accept any invitations you receive if you are free at the time of the meeting. You can also choose to autoprocess only invitations from a particular person or group of people or automatically delegate meeting invitations to somebody else.

If you check Remove Meeting Invitations, invitations will be automatically removed from your Inbox once you respond to them. The invitation is the same document as the calendar event, so if you're in the habit of deleting old messages from your Inbox, it's well worth turning on this option. That way, you won't accidentally delete the calendar entry.

If you check Prevent Event Replies, the e-mail messages that are typically generated by people responding to your invitations will be received but won't appear in your Inbox. They will only appear in your All Documents view.

The To Do Tab

Finally, you can have tasks from your To Do list appear on your calendar as well. If you check the Tasks check box, current tasks will appear on your calendar before the rest of the day's entries.

The Delegation Tab

Some other properties you might want to set are on the Calendar Delegation subtab on the Delegation tab of the Preferences InfoBox. If you want other people to be able to read your calendar, put their names in the Only These People/Groups Can Read My Calendar field. If you want to let everybody in your organization read your calendar, you can click that radio button instead. Permission to read your calendar is *not* the

PART

II

Mastering the Basics

same thing as permission to read your free time schedule. By default, everybody can read your free time schedule (that is, they can see whether or not you're available at any given time), but nobody can read your calendar. Giving someone permission to read your calendar permits him to read the individual calendar documents.

If you want to let somebody else schedule events for you (say, a supervisor or assistant), fill their names in the Only These People/Groups Can Manage My Calendar field. This gives them permission to create new documents in your calendar and edit existing ones. If you want everybody in your organization to be able to manipulate your calendar, click the Everyone Can Manage My Calendar button.

These delegation options only affect your calendar. If you want other people to be able to read your e-mail, use the Mail Delegation tab, which is also a subtab of the Delegation tab of the Preferences InfoBox.

Calendar Entries

In order for your calendar to be of any use, you'll have to fill in some of the blank spaces with calendar entries. There are five different types of calendar entries:

- Appointment
- Meeting invitation
- Reminder
- Anniversary
- Event

Each has its own requirements and special purpose, although they all have some things in common. To create a new calendar entry, you can use one of the following methods:

- Click the New button on the calendar and select the type of entry you want from the menu.
- Click the Schedule a Meeting button on the calendar (it automatically creates a Meeting Invitation document).
- Double-click any day on the calendar.
- Click the Create Calendar Entry button on the Notes Welcome page.

If you accidentally choose the wrong type of event, there's a menu on the right side of the document that will allow you to change its type. Just choose the appropriate name. Performing any of those actions will produce a new calendar entry like the one in Figure 6.2.

FIGURE 6.2

A new Appointment document

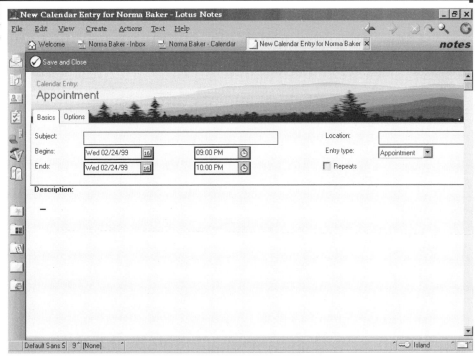

Common Sections

At the top of the calendar entry, you'll see several tabbed sections. All calendar entries have two tabbed sections in common, the Basics and Options tabs, and they all have a Details area, which takes up most of the space on the document. These three parts of a calendar entry work almost identically for all types of entries.

The Basics Tab

The Basics tab contains the entry's important identifying information. Every entry has a Subject field. Its contents will be used as a subject line in the views in which the document appears.

Under the Subject field are the time fields. The different kinds of calendar entries have different time requirements, but they all use the same two tools. You can set the date (available for all calendar entries) by typing it in to the form or by clicking the calendar button next to the field. That will bring up a small pop-up calendar in which you can select the date just by clicking. Likewise, if a time is required (for appointments, meeting invitations, and reminders), you can type in a time or click the time button, which brings up a time-line pop-up. On the time-line pop-up, click and drag the yellow clock icon, or simply click the time you want.

The first field on the right side is the Location field, which you can use to indicate where the event is taking place. You might put the location of a branch office, the name of a convention center, a building address, or just the name of a meeting room. However, if you want to use a meeting room, you might be able to use the Reservation feature, detailed later.

If you want the entry to serve as the basis of an entry for a recurring event, check the Repeats check box to make it a repeating entry. This will bring up the Repeat Options dialog box, shown in Figure 6.3.

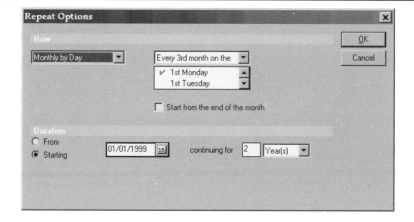

FIGURE 6.3

The Repeat Options dialog box. This entry repeats the first Monday of every quarter for two years, starting January 1, 1999.

Most organizations have regularly scheduled weekly meetings, monthly or quarterly reports, and other recurring events. Notes gives you the ability to schedule repeating events by letting you set up recurrence options for any calendar entry. They can be a little tricky to set up at first because you have a huge number of options to choose from, but with a little practice, you should be able to put them together quickly.

The first thing to decide is how, in general, you want it to repeat. After a given number of days? Every other Tuesday? The fifth day of every month? The first Monday in October? In the first menu in the How section, you can choose Daily, Weekly, Monthly by Date, Monthly by Day, Yearly, or Custom. However, just choosing, say, Weekly doesn't mean that the entry will repeat every week. Rather, it means that the unit of time you choose is the unit of time on which the repeating entry is based. For example, if you choose Daily, you can choose to repeat every day, every other day, every third day, and so on. If you choose Monthly by Day or Monthly by Date, you can repeat every month, every other month, and so on (quarterly meetings are simply held every third month, starting at the beginning of your fiscal year).

The next step, then, is to refine the repeat conditions. The list next to the first Repeat menu (the menu on the right in the How section) allows you make the kind of refinements just discussed. For example, you could have an event repeat every second week, every third month, and so on. Yet another list at the bottom of the dialog box allows you to select a particular day or days within that time period. Your options for refinement are as follows:

Daily   Every *n*th day, from daily to once every 31 days, with an option to skip or move the entry if it happens to occur on a weekend.

Weekly   Every *n*th week, from weekly to every eighth week, plus the day of the week (Sunday through Saturday). You can select multiple days just by clicking them, so you could have a single weekly event (say, an aerobics class) take place every Monday, Wednesday, and Friday.

Monthly by Date   Every *n*th month, from every month to every 12th month, plus the day of the month (first, second, third, etc.). As you can with daily repeating events, you can choose multiple dates (say, every 5th and 18th day), and you have the option to adjust for weekends.

Monthly by Day   Similar to Monthly by Date, except you choose weekdays (first Monday, third Wednesday, etc.) instead of days of the month.

Yearly   Every *n*th year, from annually to once per decade.

Custom   If your event doesn't repeat according to rules, you can fill in your own set of dates.

You can also choose how far in the future to project the event (for a period of time or until a given date) and what to do if the repeating event lands on a weekend. You can have it move to the nearest weekday, the previous Friday, the next Monday, not move at all, or simply not schedule that particular event.

But what if something changes? What if, for example, a regular weekly meeting is moved from 11:00 A.M. to 2:00 P.M.? Fortunately, your existing calendar entries won't become obsolete. If you change the date or time of a repeating entry, Notes will ask you what to do with the related entries, as shown in Figure 6.4. You can make the change apply only to the entry you've edited (say, for a one-time-only time change for a regular meeting), to all related entries (for a permanent change to the regular meeting), to all future entries, or even to all past entries.

PART

II

Mastering the Basics

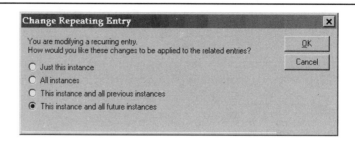

FIGURE 6.4

*The Change Repeating
Entry dialog box*

The Options Tab

The Options tab has four fields, each of which is optional: Pencil In, Mark Private, Notify Me, and Categorize. If you check Pencil In, the appointment will be saved in your calendar, but Notes won't regard the block of time as busy and people trying to schedule meetings with you will see it as free time. A Penciled In appointment essentially functions as a tentative reminder rather than a real time commitment.

Mark Private is useful if you grant other users the ability to read or manage your calendar through the Delegation tab in your preferences but don't want them to be able to read every entry. Any calendar entry marked as private is visible only to the user who created it, but the time it occupies will still be marked as busy in your free time schedule.

If alarms are enabled in your preferences, you can set alarms for individual entries. When you check the Notify Me check box, Notes will bring up a dialog box, shown in Figure 6.5, which will allow you to set alarm options for that calendar entry. Although it takes the default time set in your preferences for that type of entry, you can make the alarm come up any number of minutes, hours, or days before the event, or even after it, presumably to let you know that you're late. When the alarm goes off, it will bring up a dialog box with the message you put in the Description box. If you check the Play Sound check box, you can choose a sound for Notes to play when the alarm goes off (with the appropriate sounds, you can, quite literally, have an alarm with all the bells and whistles). If you check the Send Mail check box, you can have Notes automatically send e-mail reminders as well.

Using the Categorize menu on the Options tab, you can assign a category to your appointment; for example, Phone Calls or Travel. Notes comes with six categories:

- Clients
- Holiday
- Phone Calls
- Projects
- Travel
- Vacation

If those categories aren't enough, you can add more in your calendar preferences.

FIGURE 6.5

*The Alarm Options
dialog box*

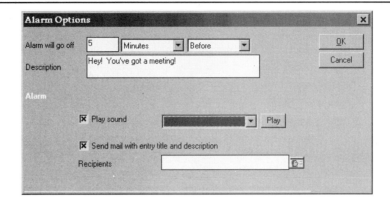

The Details Section

Finally, you can add more information about the appointment in the Details section. This may be a reminder about the topics you want to cover or things to bring with you to a meeting. The Details field is a rich text field, so you can even attach files.

Types of Calendar Entry

Now that you have a general grasp of where things are in calendar entries, we'll discuss the different types. As you probably remember from Chapter 4 and earlier in this chapter, you can choose the kind of calendar entry to create by clicking the New button in the calendar and choosing an option from the menu or by clicking the Schedule a Meeting button to jump directly into creating a meeting invitation. Each of the five types of calendar entries has a specific use and, consequently, somewhat different fields and requirements.

Appointments   An appointment is something that takes up a block of time during which you are not available to other people. You might want to use an appointment for a doctor's appointment, for example, or someone coming in for a job interview. It is *not* something that takes up the time of other people in your organization. An appointment requires two date/time combinations; you must fill in the Begins field and the Ends field. It's entirely possible to have an appointment that spans several days, although multiple-day events are best dealt with through Event documents.

When you're done, click the OK button to save and close the document. The appointment will appear in your calendar under the appropriate day, listing the time, title, and category, if any.

Meeting Invitations   A meeting invitation is a calendar entry that takes up a block of your time and gives you the option to send invitations to others, taking up a block of time in their calendars as well. Meeting invitations are a lot more complex than other calendar entries, so they're dealt with in their own section later in this chapter.

Reminders   Unlike appointments and meeting invitations, reminders don't take up any time. They simply mark a point in time as important; for example, the time to make a brief but important phone call or the time a flight comes in. A reminder requires both a date and a time.

Anniversaries   An anniversary is a calendar entry that marks a particular day as important but does not mark off a specific time during that day. Although an anniversary is, by default, an annual event (good for birthdays, tax due dates, and actual anniversaries), it can be used as a reminder for any event that recurs on a particular day but does not take up any time, such as the day your monthly rent is due. An anniversary only requires a date.

All Day Events   An event is like a meeting invitation or appointment in that it covers a period of time, but it covers a number of days, not a span of hours. An event requires a start date and an end date. It might be anything from a day-long sales conference to Ramadan. An event does not necessarily mark the time as busy. Instead, it simply lets the user know that something is going on during those days.

Holidays

Notes gives you the ability to mark off sets of holidays. Your Domino administrator can assemble a set of documents containing the dates of company or organizational holidays. You can import those holidays to automatically fill in the dates in your calendar. If your Domino administrator builds a set of holidays, select Actions ➢ Calendar Tools ➢ Import Holidays. This will import the data and fill in the dates with Anniversary documents, marking your time as busy.

Editing and Moving Entries

Once you've created a calendar entry, you may need to change it. A doctor's appointment might be delayed, a meeting might be rescheduled for another time, and so on. You can change the contents of a calendar entry at any time by opening it, switching to Edit mode, and making changes just as you would with any other Notes document. However, you have more options for changing times and dates. There are two methods you can use to move most calendar entries: editing and dragging.

Editing the Entry   Open the entry and change the time just as you set the original time, then save and close the document. If you change the date or time, the entry will appear at its new time in the Calendar view immediately.

Dragging   In any of the Calendar views, you can click and drag a calendar entry to a new day. When you do, Notes will ask you to confirm the move. If time slots are on, you can even drag an entry into a specific time slot. Again, Notes will ask you to confirm the time change.

In addition, as you'll see later, you have the option to reschedule meeting invitations.

Copying into New Documents

You can use calendar entries as the basis for other documents. If you click the Copy Into button in the calendar's button bar, you can choose to copy some of the contents of the selected calendar entry into a new memo, calendar entry, or To Do item:

Memo   If you copy into a new memo, the title of the calendar entry becomes the memo's subject and the Details field is inherited into the message body.

Calendar Entry   If you copy into a new calendar entry, all of the attributes of the old calendar entry are copied into a new one except for its duration. The new calendar entry will be of the same type with the same details, participants (if any), and start time as the original, but the new entry's duration will be the default entry duration set in your preferences.

To Do   Copying into a To Do document transfers the original calendar entry's title and details into the fields on the To Do document. However, times are not transferred into the new document.

Once you have created the new document, you can edit it at will without affecting the original.

Meeting Invitations

The meeting invitation is the document that transforms your calendar from a way of keeping track of your time into a major piece of groupware, and it's important and complex enough that it deserves a lot of attention. Like an appointment, a meeting invitation takes up a block of time during which you're not available to other people. However, it also takes up other people's time. This is the type of entry you'll use to call meetings that include people working on a particular project, members of your department, or even everyone in the organization. Setting up a meeting invitation does much more than just put an entry in your calendar. It will send mail to invitees asking them to attend or informing them of the meeting. It can also reserve meeting rooms and other resources for you.

PART
II

Mastering the Basics

A meeting invitation has all the same fields as an appointment, but it adds a new tab to the two you've already seen: Meeting Invitations and Reservations (shown in Figure 6.6). Invitees are people you want to attend the meeting, or at least people who should be informed of it. There are three levels of invitees, each with its own field. You may notice that the invitee fields look suspiciously like the address fields in a mail message:

Required   These are people whose attendance is vital to the meeting. Their invitations will prompt them to accept or decline the invitation.

Cc (Optional)   These people are not necessary for the meeting but might want to attend. The invitation they receive will allow them to add an entry to their calendars, but it won't specifically prompt them.

Bcc (FYI)   People on this list will only receive an informational message letting them know that the meeting is taking place.

You can type names into each field, but clicking on any of the buttons next to the fields will bring up a standard address dialog box, letting you add people to the invitation lists with just a few clicks. People you add to the invitation with the To button will end up in the Required field, people you add with the Cc button go to the Optional field, and people added with the Bcc button go to the FYI field.

FIGURE 6.6

A meeting invitation with the Meeting Invitations and Reservations tab selected. Several invitee names have already been filled in.

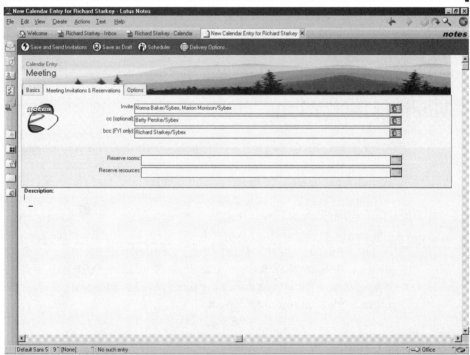

If your Domino administrator has set up Room and Resource documents in the main address book, the Reserve Rooms and Reserve Resources fields will allow you to reserve meeting rooms and other resources for your meeting. Clicking on the buttons next to those fields will bring up an address book dialog box with lists of either rooms or resources, like the one in Figure 6.7.

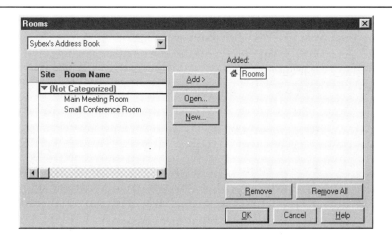

Resources are most likely to include things such as overhead projectors and sound systems for meetings. However, your company may treat laptop computers for trips away from the office, company cars, and other portable pieces of company property as resources in the Domino Directory. If that is the case, you could "check out" a resource for use away from the office by sending an invitation to the resource instead of to people and rooms.

One of the most powerful features of the Notes calendar is in the Tools section. Once you have set a time, selected invitees, and chosen a meeting room and resources (if any), click the Scheduler button on the meeting invitation and select Check All Schedules. If you're connected to a Domino server, this feature will perform the hardest part of scheduling a meeting: finding out whether or not the people you want to attend can make it.

Selecting Check All Schedules will bring up a dialog box like the one in Figure 6.8. The blue blocks of time in a column indicate when the person, room, or resource is busy; the white blocks of time indicate when they're available. The time you've chosen for the meeting will appear as a colored block. The block is red if it overlaps a time when somebody is busy, green if it covers a time when everybody is free. The controls to change the meeting time are a little different from the controls used to set the meeting time. Instead of having separate controls for the start and end time, there is a single combined control for start and end times. Dragging the clock at the top will move the meeting's start time, dragging the clock at the bottom will move the end time, and dragging the box in the middle will move the entire block of time. You can view the free time schedule in several different modes:

All By Invitee This mode gives every person you invite and all the resources you want to reserve their own "time line" column. At the far right (you'll have to scroll if you invite more than a handful of people), there's an aggregate column labeled Everyone. This column is blue where someone is busy and white where everyone is available.

All By Week This mode shows a column for each day in the week containing the day chosen for the meeting. Each column is essentially the Everyone column for that day.

By Can Attend This mode is like the All By Invitee mode, but it only shows those people who can attend the meeting at the chosen time.

By Cannot Attend This mode is like the All By Invitee mode, but it only shows those people who cannot attend the meeting at the chosen time.

By Not Found This mode is like the All By Invitee mode, but it only shows those people for whom free time data cannot be found. This may indicate that the people in question don't have a mail file on the Domino server or that they have not set up free time preferences yet.

FIGURE 6.8

The Free Time dialog box, showing all invitees. As the columns on the right indicate, this is a good time for the meeting.

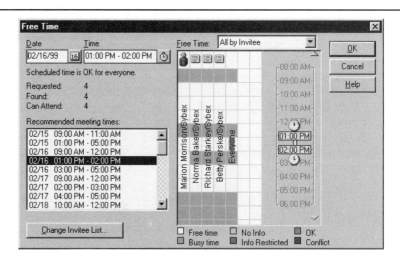

If you've chosen a bad time, you can probably find a good time just by looking for a white spot in the last column, or if you still can't find a good time, Notes will suggest a list of alternative times. You can adjust the meeting time by using the same time-setting tools you used to set the original time or by double-clicking one of the suggested alternate times to move the meeting to that time automatically. If some invitees appear to be busy all the time, they may not have set up their free time profile; you might want to send them a message telling them to check their User preferences.

The Delivery Options button (see Figure 6.6) will bring up a dialog box that will let you select options for the e-mail invitations your Meeting Invitation document will create. In the Delivery Options dialog box, there is a Sign and Encrypt button that will do the same thing as the Sign and Encrypt options for regular e-mail. Typically, you'll receive e-mail from the recipients of the invitation indicating whether they accept or decline. However, checking I Do Not Want to Receive Replies from Participants will prevent automatic e-mail responses. This is useful if you're inviting a large number of people and don't want to be deluged by e-mail, but you won't be able to tell who has responded and who hasn't. Also, invitation recipients can usually delegate an invitation to somebody else or suggest an alternative time if they're not available for the meeting. This dialog box gives you options to prevent those types of responses from being sent to you as well.

Once you've set all the options you want, you can click either Save Only, which will simply save the document, or Send Invitations, which will send out e-mail invitations to the invitees and attempt to reserve the meeting rooms and resources you want.

The ability to quickly and painlessly schedule meetings is one of the first big advantages that new users will notice about working in a Notes system. You can save hours just by eliminating the back-and-forth dialog of scheduling a meeting between perennially busy users. However, the system does rely on users keeping their calendars up-to-date. It's important that you keep track of your time commitments, but you only need to put in entries that will actually prevent you from meeting with other people during a particular block of time. Consider, for example, a progress report that's due on a certain day. Ask yourself whether you really need to be writing between 2:00 and 3:00.

Responding to Invitations

To follow the course of a Meeting Invitation document, we'll need to duck out of your calendar for a while and head to the Inbox. When somebody sends you an invitation, you'll receive it along with the rest of your e-mail. As you can see in Figure 6.9, a meeting invitation in your Inbox will have an "open envelope" icon (if you accept it, the icon will turn into the same "handshake" icon that you're used to seeing in the calendar).

When you open the invitation, it will look a lot like any other calendar entry (see Figure 6.10), but the information fields will be read-only, and you'll have a different set of buttons.

FIGURE 6.9

An Inbox with a lot of invitation activity. The "open envelope" message with the subject "More admin details" is an invitation. The "thumbs up" messages are responses to invitations.

Invitation acceptance

Invitation

FIGURE 6.10

A meeting invitation opened from the Inbox

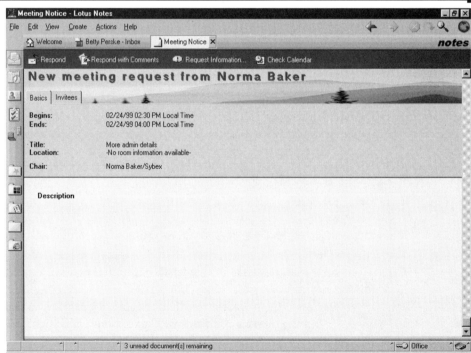

When you receive an invitation, you should take action on it. You have five options under the Respond button:

Accept   This is the option to select if you want to attend the meeting at the time proposed. It will make the meeting invitation appear in your calendar and mark the meeting time as busy. Unless the meeting chair has set an option, you'll also send mail back informing the chair that you will be attending the meeting.

Decline   Choose this option if you don't want to attend the meeting. Be sure to do this *only* if you don't want to go to the meeting and you don't want to be informed of any changes in time or location. If you decline a meeting, you're permanently out of the loop. You won't receive any reschedule notices or meeting confirmations. If it's a meeting that you want to attend (or at least feel obligated to attend) but you can't attend at the scheduled time, choose Propose New Time instead.

Delegate   Use this option if you don't want to or can't attend the meeting but you want somebody you supervise to be there. This option will give you a dialog box that allows you to delegate the invitation to someone else. The person to whom you have delegated will receive an invitation and the chair will receive a notice. Normally, delegating a meeting invitation will take you out of the loop just like Decline will, but if you check the Keep Me Informed check box, you'll continue to receive reschedule notices and other messages the chair sends to invitees.

Propose New Time   If you want to attend the meeting but cannot attend at the chosen time, you can use the Propose New Time option. This option will give you a dialog box with time and date controls to select a new time. The dialog box also lets you check other invitees' free time schedules so you can be sure the time you check isn't bad for other people. When you click the OK button, Notes will send the meeting chair a Change Proposal document. If the chair accepts the time change, all participants will get a reschedule notice. If the chair declines the time change, you'll get a message letting you know.

Tentatively Accept   This option works much like the Accept option, but it will pencil in the invitation, so the time won't be marked as busy in your calendar.

The Respond with Comments button provides you with all of the same options, but in addition to taking the action in question, it will also give you a stripped-down memo form addressed to the meeting chair.

Managing Invitations

Creating a Meeting Invitation document and sending out e-mail invitations is just the first step. Notes provides you with a number of tools to help you monitor responses, reschedule or cancel the meeting, add and remove invitees and responses, and keep in touch with the invitees. Some management functions take care of themselves. For example, if you want to change a meeting time, all you have to do is open the meeting invitation, change the time, and save and close the document (you should, though, use the Reschedule option under Owner Actions; it's a little more elegant and gives you some extra options). If invitations have been sent out, Notes will send reschedule documents to all invitees. Likewise, if you reopen an existing invitation and add invitees or resources to a meeting after the first round of invitations, Notes will invite the new people. However, there are many other management tasks you might want to perform.

Owner Actions

All of the following options are available through the Owner Actions button on the calendar or through the Actions ➤ Owner Actions submenu. To perform an action on any meeting invitation, select the invitation by clicking on it and then choose the menu option you desire.

Tracking Responses   If you haven't selected the meeting option I Do Not Want to Receive Replies from Participants, you'll receive e-mail responses from invitees telling you whether they can make it to the meeting or not. If you select View Participant Status, Notes will show you lists of who has accepted the invitation, who has declined, who has delegated, and so on. It will also show you whether or not the reservations you asked for have been made.

Rescheduling   When you choose the Reschedule option, Notes will bring up a dialog box letting you select new dates and times using the same pop-up calendar and time-line tools you used to set the initial time. Once you set a time, you can use the Scheduler button to make sure all the participants are free. If you check the Include Additional check box, Notes will create a document you can use to add a message to the time change (for example, explaining why you've changed the meeting time). If you click the OK button, reschedule messages will be sent out to all participants and Notes will try to reserve the resources you invited.

Canceling   If you use the Cancel option, Notes will bring up a dialog box to confirm the cancellation. Like a reschedule, you can add a message to the cancellation e-mail, and if you check the Delete All Responses check box, Notes will clear out any e-mail responses you've already received for this meeting. Notes will also cancel any room and resource reservations you have made.

Confirmation   If you select the Confirm option, Notes will send e-mail reminding all participants of the meeting time and place. If you check the Include Additional Comments check box, Notes will allow you to add an additional message to the automatic reminder, perhaps updating the agenda or asking the invitees to bring special materials.

Sending Mail to Participants   If you select the Send Memo to Participants option, Notes will set up a mail message to the meeting participants. This memo will appear in your Discussion Threads view as a response to the Meeting document, but it won't affect the time, place, or participants in the meeting. Although you can discuss such changes in the memo, use one of the other options to actually change the meeting's time, place, and invitees.

Recipient Actions

Formal changes to the meeting as a whole must be made by the meeting's owner, but if you accept an invitation, you may need to change or modify your original response. Notes gives you tools to change your initial response and request changes in the meeting. These options are available through the Participant Actions button on the calendar or the Actions ➤ Participant Actions submenu.

Decline   If you are unable to go to a meeting you have already accepted, you can change your status by choosing the Decline option. Again, be sure to do this only if you don't want to attend the meeting. If you want to attend the meeting but can't attend at the proposed time, use Suggest New Time instead.

Delegate   This option works like the Delegate option on the original invitation. Once you select a person to attend the meeting and click the OK button, Notes will send a response to the meeting chair saying that you have delegated to somebody else and a meeting invitation to the person to whom you are delegating.

Suggest New Time   Again, this option works just like the Suggest New Time option in the original invitation. You'll get a dialog box that lets you choose a new time, and your proposed new time will be sent to the meeting chair for approval.

PART

II

Mastering the Basics

Group Calendars

The Find Free Time feature on meeting invitations is great if you're assembling a group of people for a one-time event, but what if you want to keep track of how a group of people are using their time on a regular basis? And what if you want to see how people you supervise are using their calendars? With earlier versions of Notes, you had to go to extreme lengths to find out when people were free. For example, you could create a bogus invitation and keep it around in your calendar to check free time schedules, and there simply was no way to get quick and easy access to other people's calendars. Notes 5 does away with that with a new kind of document: the group calendar.

A group calendar is a feature that allows you to look at several different calendars simultaneously. This can be a very useful tool for keeping an eye on a department's activities or tentatively planning meeting times. To create a group calendar, go to the Group Calendars view and click the New Group Calendar button. In the dialog box that comes up, shown in Figure 6.11, you can give the calendar a title and add members from the address book. The people you add to a group calendar might include your employees, fellow members of a project team, department heads, or any other set of people you want to keep an eye on. Once you've added everybody to the group calendar, you can either save it or view it immediately.

FIGURE 6.11

*A New Group Calendar
dialog box*

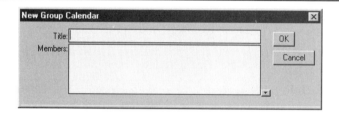

A group calendar, shown in Figure 6.12, will show you the free time schedules of the people you have added. As with the Free Time dialog box you get from a meeting invitation, each person gets their own row, although with a different color scheme. White is busy time, yellow is free, gray is no information (a row will be gray if the person has not set up their calendar preferences yet or if you're looking at days in the past; Notes doesn't keep free time information for the past), and blue indicates that information for that time slot is restricted (if the person's calendar appointment has been marked private). The arrow buttons will move you back and forth through time just as the arrow buttons on your personal calendar do. You can use the Members button to adjust the group of people whose schedules you can view.

By default, the group calendar will show you a 12-hour slice of time for each day shown, starting with the current time. If you click the Options button, you can adjust the amount of time shown and the time of day at which the group calendar starts.

But the group calendar can do more than show you free time schedules. If you click a block of busy time, you'll open the Calendar document that takes up that block of time in the other person's calendar, as shown in Figure 6.13.

FIGURE 6.12

A group calendar

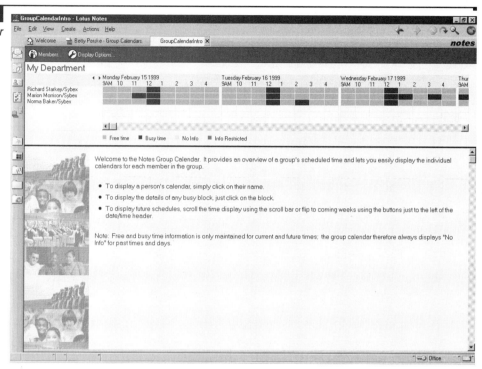

FIGURE 6.13

A group calendar with another user's calendar event open

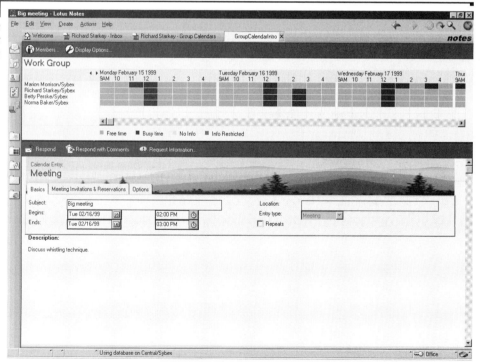

If you click a person's name rather than a block of busy time, Notes will display that person's calendar. Be aware, however, that you can't use a group calendar to view individual events in other people's calendars if you don't already have access to read their calendars. The Group Calendar document only gives you an easy way to get to the data you have permission to read.

Calendar Printing

Earlier versions of Notes were passionately dedicated to the notion of a paperless office. In an ideal Notes system, nobody would ever have to print anything. Invitations would dance around the system and be displayed in Inboxes and calendars, alerts would pop up on screens to alert people to impending meetings and tasks, and users could organize their time just by looking at the screen. And with everything done electronically, there's not much need for elaborate printing features.

Unfortunately, things didn't quite work out that way. Although a paperless office is a nice idea, people really like paper and aren't ready to give it up. They like something they can get their hands on, take notes on, hand out in an off-site meeting, and perhaps use as a bookmark once it's all over. Lotus got the message, and printing features are much improved in Notes 5. And nowhere are the improvements more evident than in calendar printing.

Notes allows you to print your calendar in a number of different ways. You can print out individual calendar Event documents, or you can print your calendar in a calendrical format. When you select File ➤ Print in your calendar, Notes gives you an adjustable range of dates to print and a selection of styles to choose from:

Daily Prints one day per page, defaulting to the current day. Calendar entries are displayed in a schedule format, with a row for each hour.

Weekly Prints one week per page, defaulting to the current week. Calendar entries are displayed in a schedule format.

Monthly Prints one month per page, defaulting to the current month.

Calendar List Prints a list of calendar events for the selected time period.

In addition to the detailed calendars, the Daily, Weekly, and Monthly styles show a compact three-month calendar at the top with the selected date range highlighted.

You can adjust some aspects of the printed calendar by clicking the Options button. You can change the font size by clicking an appropriate radio button in the Fonts section. The Print First Line Only and Wrap Column Data options are mutually exclusive. Selecting the first will make the calendar display a single line of data for each calendar entry. Selecting the second will make the data for each calendar entry wrap so the calendar will show an icon, time, and title. Shrink Column Width to Text will shrink the width of columns if the text of the calendar entries is narrower than the page. Include Weekends (Monthly and Weekly styles only) will show weekends; if the option is unchecked, the calendar will show only weekdays. Finally, Weekly and Daily styles let you select the range of time slots you want to display. Just like your on-screen calendar, you may only care about time slots during the business day, or you may have a more hectic schedule where you'll need to keep appointments in order from dawn to dusk.

To Dos

Notes provides you with one other way to organize your time: To Dos. The To Do view gives you a place to put a list of tasks you need to accomplish; for example, writing a particular report or conducting an annual review. Individual To Do documents are like Event documents in that they have a range of dates associated with them, and some To Do documents (Group To Dos) are like meeting invitations in that one person can create a document that is sent to others to indicate something that they should do as well, but To Dos never occupy any time in your free time schedule. More important, you can change settings in a To Do document to indicate your progress and the priority of the task.

To reach the To Do views, click the check box in the button bar in the lower left corner of your mailbox. This will open the To Do By Due Date view, with the To Do Navigator in the Navigation pane to the left (yes, just like the Mail Navigator appears to the left of your Inbox and the Calendar Navigator appears to the left of the Calendar view). In the To Do Navigator, you can choose between viewing your To Dos by their due date, category, or status; you can also switch to other generic views, such as the Stationery view and the Trash folder. All three To Do views (By Due Date, By Category, and By Status) display the same documents but sort them differently. Buttons for dealing with To Do documents are set across the top of the view, much like they are in your Inbox and Calendar. In fact, the To Do view gives you the same Owner Action and Participant Action buttons the Calendar view gives you.

PART

II

Mastering the Basics

Personal To Dos

There are a number of ways to create a To Do. In addition to copying memos and calendar entries into To Do documents, you can click the New To Do button in the To Do view or click the Add a To Do button on the Welcome page. Taking any of these actions will produce a new personal To Do like the one shown in Figure 6.14.

FIGURE 6.14

A new personal To Do

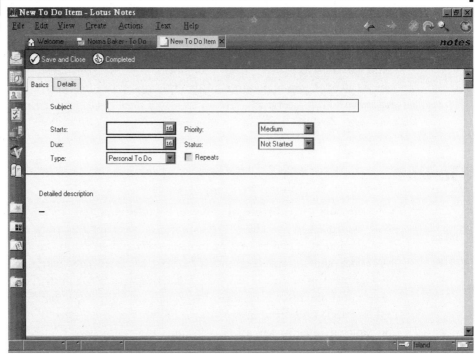

A To Do is similar to a calendar entry in that it has tabbed sections for dates, participants, and other options that are similar to those on a calendar event. A personal To Do has a Basics tab with fields for a title, start and end dates, and repeat options. The To Do also lets you set a priority (high, medium, low, and no priority) and a status (not started, in progress, on hold, and completed). The status of a project can be changed by selecting an option from the menu or set to Completed by clicking the Completed button.

For the other two parts of a To Do, the terminology is a little confusing at first if you're used to calendar entries. The Details section for a To Do is much like the Options section for most calendar entries, with Mark Private, Notify Me, and Categories fields. The Detailed Description field taking up the bottom pane of the To Do is like the Details field of a calendar entry.

Group To Dos

To Dos start as personal To Dos, but you can change them to group To Dos by changing the Type field on the Basics tab from Personal To Do to Group To Do. When you do so, a Participants tab is added. The Participants tab is similar to the Meeting Invitations and Reservations tab on a meeting invitation and includes Assign To (instead of the Invite field), Cc, and Bcc participant fields. Because To Dos don't take up specific times, there are not fields for resource reservations. By filling out the assignment fields, you can send To Dos to other people. Group To Dos send invitations to invitees just as meeting invitations do, and they are maintained using the same tools, but they appear in the To Do view.

To Dos in Views and Calendars

The To Do by Category view categorizes your To Dos according to your progress. There are four categories of To Dos:

Current   The current date is between the task's start and due dates, and the To Do has not been marked as complete yet.

Future   The To Do's start date hasn't been reached yet.

Overdue   The To Do's due date has passed but the To Do has not been marked as complete.

Complete   The To Do has been marked as complete regardless of its start and due dates.

The By Category view will categorize your To Dos by these categories, letting you see at a glance what you need to do.

To Dos also have icons (gold buttons with numbers on them) indicating their priority: 1 is for high priority, 2 is for medium priority, and 3 is for low priority.

Notes keeps you posted on what you need to do by making your To Dos appear in the Calendar view as well as in your To Do views. All To Dos with a past or current start date appear in the calendar on the current day, whereas To Dos with start dates in the future appear on the days when they start. To Dos appear before all calendar events and, if time slots are turned on, will appear before the time slots as well.

Summary

Notes provides you with an appointment calendar that allows you to not only keep track of your own time commitments, but also to coordinate your time with others. Meeting invitations can be used to check on others' free time, invite them to meetings by e-mail, and reserve meeting rooms and other physical resources. Group calendars provide a long-term means of keeping track of other people's individual calendars. To Dos give users a method to construct lists of tasks that aren't bound to specific times. Mail and scheduling are powerful, important functions of Notes, but they're just the beginning. The next chapter will deal with some other kinds of Notes databases you may use, including discussion databases and document libraries.

PART

II

Mastering the Basics

CHAPTER **7**

Using Other Notes Databases

FEATURING:

I n addition to being an integrated client for e-mail, personal and team scheduling, and Web interaction, Notes is a runtime environment for collaborative applications. These applications are represented as databases that have been created using Domino Designer. This is a powerful combination. It makes Notes a single, integrated environment for managing a wide range of information.

As previously discussed, Notes uses a set of core databases to present and manage core functionality, such as e-mail, calendaring and scheduling, and To Do lists. In addition, Notes ships with a set of templates for creating commonly used collaborative applications. In this chapter, we'll explore some of the uses of these databases.

Keeping a Personal Journal

Although not technically a collaborative application, the personal journal is included here because it is a commonly used Notes database. The personal journal is a simple application that is useful for storing free-form personal information or reference information, including:

- Personal notes
- Project notes
- Network information (ISP phone number, TCP/IP addresses, DNS entries)
- Articles
- Book lists
- Gift ideas

 NOTE The Personal Journal database is also used when synchronizing with 3Com PalmPilot handheld devices (including the IBM WorkPad). The PalmPilot Memo List entries are synchronized with Personal Journal database entries, making the PalmPilot Memo List a good place to store free-form information you may need away from the office or away from home.

For this section, we'll use the Mastering R5 for Chapter 7 (1) database from this book's CD-ROM in the examples. It is a customized version of the Release 5 personal journal that includes a Category field on the Journal Entry form and a Categorized Entries view. With the addition of a Category field, this customized journal database matches more closely with the 3Com PalmPilot Memo List structure. You can create your own personal journal from the example journal database or from the Release 5

Personal Journal template. For more information on creating databases, see Chapter 16, "Creating Your First Database."

Opening the Example Journal

Assuming you have installed the example databases from the CD to a directory called `masterr5` in your Notes Data directory, you can open the Mastering R5 for Chapter 7 (1) database as follows:

1. Select File ➤ Database ➤ Open (or press Ctrl+O) to bring up the Open Database dialog box.
2. Keep the Server field set to Local so Notes presents databases from your local Data directory.
3. Scroll down the Database field's list box until you reach the `masterr5` folder.
4. Double-click the `masterr5` folder (or select the folder and then click the Open button).
5. Scroll down the Database field's list box until you see the Mastering R5 for Chapter 7 (1) database.
6. Double-click the database (or select it and then click the Open button).

The database's About document will be displayed. This will happen the first time you open any Notes database. It's the generic About document from the Release 5 Personal Journal template, and it provides a quick overview of the purpose and intent of the generic Personal Journal database. Press Escape to close the About document and display the example journal database.

You'll notice that the Mastering R5 for Chapter 7 (1) database uses the default Notes View/Folder list interface, as shown in Figure 7.1. This is true for the Release 5 Personal Journal template as well.

The Mastering R5 for Chapter 7 (1) database Navigation pane contains two views:

- All Documents
- Categorized Entries

The All Documents view displays your journal entries in the order they were entered. This view shows the title of the Journal entry and the date it was last modified. You can sort the entries by title or by last-modified date by clicking the view column title. The Categorized Entries view is specific to the Mastering R5 for Chapter 7 (1) database; the Release 5 personal journal does not contain this view. The Categorized Entries view displays your journal entries by category. In this view, you cannot sort the entries by title or last-modified date. If you create any folders in your journal database, they will be displayed in the Navigation pane as well.

FIGURE 7.1

The Mastering R5 for Chapter 7 (1) database

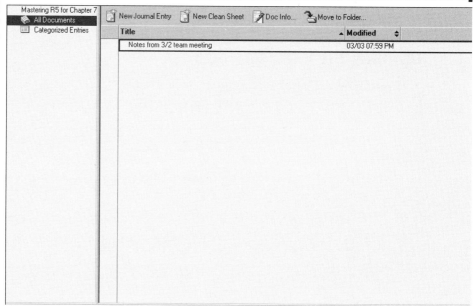

Creating Journal Entries

Just as we have seen with mail messages and Calendar entries, creating a Journal entry is as simple as creating a new Journal document and filling in the fields. With your Mastering R5 for Chapter 7 (1) database open, you can create a new Journal document in the following two ways:

- Select Create ➤ Journal Entry.
- Click the New Journal Entry button on the View Action bar of the All Documents or Categorized Entries view.

However you decide to create a new Journal document, a blank Journal Entry form will be displayed, as shown in Figure 7.2.

FIGURE 7.2

A blank Mastering R5 for Chapter 7 (1) Journal Entry form

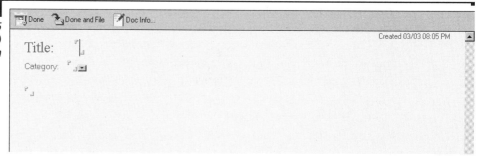

This a customized version of the Journal Entry form found in the Release 5 Personal Journal template. The only difference is the addition of the Category field, which was added to match the 3Com PalmPilot's Memo List structure. At the top of the Database area, you'll see three buttons on the Form Action bar labeled as follows:

Done Saves the Journal entry and closes the form after you are finished entering the information.

Done and File Saves the Journal entry and closes the form. In addition, it will present the Move to Folder dialog box, allowing you to add the Journal entry to a folder.

Doc Info Brings up the Document Info dialog box, which displays information about the Journal entry document and allows you to change the document's title.

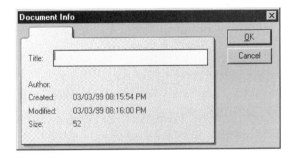

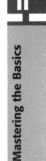

The form content area is fairly plain and includes the following fields (see Figure 7.2):

- Title
- Category
- Body

You can enter a short description of the Journal entry in the Title field. Although it is not required, you should always enter a title to identify the purpose of the Journal entry in views.

The Category field can contain multiple values. If you select the arrow to the right of the field, the Select Keywords dialog box will be displayed, allowing you to select categories or enter new ones. The available category values are compiled from the existing documents in the database. As users enter more documents with different categories, this list expands. You can also add new categories in the New Keywords field. Just separate each value with a comma.

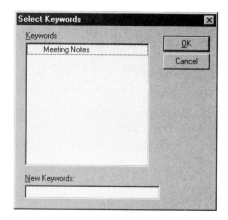

The Body field (the unlabeled field under Category) in the Journal Entry form is a rich text field and can contain a wide variety of information, including formatted text, tables, pictures, objects, and URLs.

Example Journal Entry   To get a feel for creating Journal entries, try creating one by following these steps:

1. Open the Mastering R5 for Chapter 7 (1) database.

2. Click the New Journal Entry button on the View Action bar. A new Journal Entry form will be displayed.

3. Type **Test Journal Entry** in the Title field.

4. Click the arrow to the right of the Category field. The Select Keywords dialog box will be displayed.

5. Tab to the New Keywords field.

6. Enter **Test Category**.

7. Click the OK button to return to the new Journal Entry form.

8. Click the Done button on the Form Action bar to save this Journal entry.

A new Journal entry will be displayed in your Mastering R5 for Chapter 7 (1) database views.

The Mastering R5 for Chapter 7 (1) database includes a second form called New Clean Sheet. The Release 5 Personal Journal template also includes a New Clean Sheet form, but the Mastering R5 for Chapter 7 (1) database contains a customized version that includes a Category field. The Mastering R5 for Chapter 7 (1) database's New Clean Sheet form (shown next) can be used to create Journal entries too. It differs from the new Journal Entry form in that no Title field is displayed.

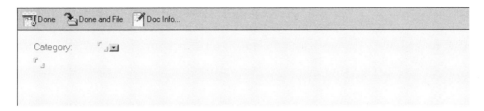

When the Journal entry is saved, the Document Info dialog box is displayed. At this point, you can enter a title. Anytime you edit entries created with the new Clean Sheet form, you will notice that the document is actually displayed using the Journal Entry form. This demonstrates how Notes can create a document using one form and display it later using another form.

Collaborating through Discussions

One of the most common applications for group collaboration is the electronic discussion. Early examples of this were simple, text-based forums in bulletin board systems (BBSs). The Internet has its own version called Usenet (also known as newsgroups). Notes also has its own version, simply referred to as the discussion database. The discussion database has been around since the inception of Notes. It provides an interface for creating new topics and responses to those topics (and responses to responses if needed). It is similar to other electronic discussions; one user posts a questions or other information as a new topic, and other users respond with their input, or even their opinion. The Notes discussion also enables users to categorize topics, mark topics and responses as private, and include rich text. When it's hosted on a Domino server, the Notes discussion can also extend to all users with a Web browser. It is no longer limited to just users who have the Notes client installed.

The discussion database included with Notes is a fairly generic and free-form database, so it can be used for a variety of collaboration situations. Some of its more common uses include the following:

- Forums to discuss technical issues

- A repository for project-related communications

- A tool to brainstorm ideas

The list is endless. For this section, we'll use the Mastering R5 for Chapter 7 (2) database from the CD in the examples. This is just an empty discussion database created from the Release 5 Discussion template. Of course, you can always create your own discussion database from the Release 5 Discussion template. For more information on creating databases, see Chapter 16.

Opening the Example Discussion

Assuming you have installed the example databases from the CD to a directory called `masterr5` in your Notes Data directory, you can open the Mastering R5 for Chapter 7 (2) database as follows:

1. Select File ➤ Database ➤ Open (or press Ctrl+O) to bring up the Open Database dialog box.

2. Keep the Server field set to Local so Notes presents databases from your local Data directory.

3. Scroll down the Database field's list box until you reach the `masterr5` folder.

4. Double-click the `masterr5` folder (or select the folder and then click the Open button).

5. Scroll down the Database field's list box until you see the Mastering R5 for Chapter 7 (2) database.

6. Double-click the database (or select it and then click the Open button).

The database's About document will be displayed. This will happen the first time you open any Notes database. It is the generic About document from the Release 5 Discussion template. It provides a quick overview of the purpose and intent of the generic discussion. When you create your own discussion databases, you should create your own About documents tailored to suit your audience. Click the Click Here to Open This Database hotspot or press Escape to close the About document and display the example discussion database.

You will notice that the Mastering R5 for Chapter 7 (2) database has a frameset interface, as shown in Figure 7.3.

The Release 5 Discussion template has the same frameset interface. The left side consists of three frames:

- A top frame that displays a description of the window
- A middle frame that displays a Navigation pane
- A bottom frame that displays the title of the database

This interface is consistent with the user interface for the core databases discussed in Chapter 4.

FIGURE 7.3

The Mastering R5 for Chapter 7 (2) database frameset

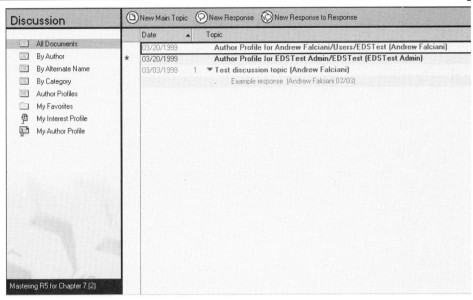

Navigating the Discussion Database

The Navigation pane contains a set of predefined views and folders:

- All Documents
- By Author
- By Alternate Name
- By Category
- Author Profiles
- My Favorites
- My Interest Profile
- My Author Profile

The All Documents and By Category views display discussion topics and their associated responses. The only difference is the order in which the documents are presented. Also, these views display responses as a hierarchy; each response is positioned directly below its parent. The All Documents view displays the documents by the date they were entered, with the latest ones presented at the top of the view.

The By Category view displays the documents categorized by the value(s) entered in the document's Category field. To the left of each Category header is a small arrow that indicates there are documents contained within that category. Selecting this arrow icon will expand the view to show the documents. Selecting it while the view is expanded will collapse the documents under the category header. Within each category, the documents and their responses are displayed in the order they were entered.

The By Author view does not show the documents as a hierarchy. Instead, it lists each document individually, categorized by the author's name. The By Alternate Name view lists the documents by the authors' alternate names.

 TIP Use the Categorize facility while displaying the By Category view to quickly change the Category field value for multiple main topics at one time. Just select the main topic documents you want to categorize and select Action ➤ Categorize. Notes will display the Categorize dialog box, allowing you to choose from existing categories or add new ones.

My Favorites is a folder included in the discussion database. You can use it to keep track of specific documents in the database that you may want to quickly access later. As you can with other folders in Notes, you can drag and drop documents to it or use the Action menus.

 WARNING Remember, If you delete an entry from the My Favorites folder, the actual document will be deleted from the database. If you want to retain the document, select Action ➤ Remove from Folder instead.

The Author Profiles view displays Author Profile documents contained within the database. Author Profile documents are documents created by each author participating in the discussion. They help users determine who is participating in the discussion and what their roles are. You should create an Author Profile document for yourself before participating in a discussion database.

The elements labeled My Author Profile and My Interest Profile are links to special forms in the discussion database. The My Author Profile link will bring up your author profile, which is convenient when the database has many Author Profile documents and you don't want to waste time looking for yours. The My Interest Profile link brings up your interest profile for this database. Interest profiles were used prior to the subscription feature that was introduced in Release 5. You would fill out an interest profile, and assuming you enabled the appropriate Agent, Notes would notify you of changes meeting the criteria you specified. With subscriptions, this is no longer necessary. In fact, there is a mechanism for converting interest profiles to subscriptions if you are upgrading older discussion databases to the Release 5 design.

TIP You can convert existing interest profiles to subscriptions. Select Action ➤ Convert My Interest Profile to a Subscription, enter a name for the subscription in the dialog box presented, and click the OK button. Notes will create a subscription using the criteria specified in your interest profile and will then delete your interest profile.

Creating Discussion Topics

Just as we have demonstrated with mail messages, Calendar entries, and To Do list items, creating discussion topics is as simple as creating a new Main Topic document and filling in the fields. With the discussion database open, you can create a new Main Topic document in the following two ways:

- Select Create ➤ Main Topic.
- Select the New ➤ Main Topic button from the View Action bar of the All Documents, By Author, or By Category view.

For frequently used discussions, you can also create a bookmark to the new Main Topic form so you can create new topics without even opening the database. However you create a new Main Topic document, a blank Main Topic form will be displayed (see Figure 7.4).

FIGURE 7.4

A blank Main Topic form

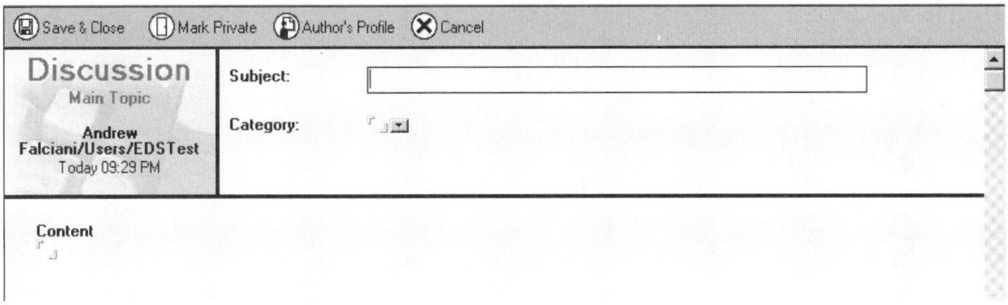

| Save & Close | Mark Private | Author's Profile | Cancel |

Discussion
Main Topic

Andrew
Falciani/Users/EDSTest
Today 09:29 PM

Subject:

Category:

Content

At the top of the database area, you'll see four buttons on the Form Action bar labeled as follows:

Save and Close   Saves the new Main Topic document and closes the form after you are finished entering the information.

Mark Private   Sets a readers field to your username. From that point on, you will be the only one who can access that document. Domino servers will not be able to access it for replication and Domino administrators will not be able to access it either.

Author's Profile Displays a dialog box with the profile of the author of the current document. When you create a new main topic, this button will return your own author profile.

Cancel Closes the form without saving the new Main Topic document.

The form itself is fairly simple and contains the following fields:

- Subject
- Category
- Content

You can complete just the fields you need. Although it is not required, you should always enter a subject so you know what the entry is for when it is displayed in the views. The Category field in the new Main Topic form is similar to the one in the new Journal Entry form (discussed earlier in this chapter). This field can contain multiple values, which you can enter in the field or choose from the Select Keywords dialog box. To display the Select Keywords dialog box, click the arrow button to the right of the Category field. The list in the Select Keywords list box is generated from the current set of discussion topics in the database. You can also add new categories in the New Keywords field. Just separate each value with a comma. The Content field in the new Main Topic form is a rich text field and can contain a wide variety of information, including formatted text, tables, pictures, objects, URLs, and attached files.

Example Main Topic To get a feel for creating new topics, try creating a test entry as described in the following steps:

1. Open the Mastering R5 for Chapter 7 (2) database.

2. Click the New Main Topic button on the View Action bar. A new Main Topic form will be displayed.

3. Type **Test Topic** in the Subject field.

4. Tab to the Category field and select the arrow to the right of the field. The Select Keywords dialog box will be displayed.

5. Tab to the New Keywords field and enter **Category1, Category2, Category3**.

6. Click the OK button. You will be returned to the new Main Topic form.

7. Click the Save and Close button on the Form Action bar to save this main topic.

A new Topic entry will be displayed in the discussion database's views. Notice that the topic we just created appears three times in the By Category view. No, there are not three separate documents. Notes just displays this one document in each of the categories contained in its Category field. In this case, the Category field contains three values.

Creating Discussion Responses

As with Main Topic documents, creating responses is as simple as creating a new Response document and filling in the fields. With the discussion database open, you can create a new Response document in the following two ways:

- Select Create ➤ Response.
- Select the New ➤ Response button from the View Action bar of the All Documents, By Author, or By Category view.

Responses are relative to the main topic to which they refer, so it doesn't make sense to bookmark the new Response form as we did the Main Topic form. However you create a new Response document, a blank Response form will be displayed (see Figure 7.5).

FIGURE 7.5
A blank Response form

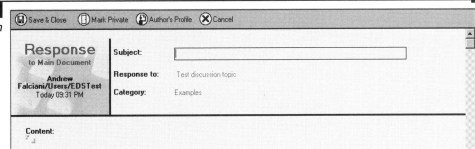

At the top of the database area, you'll see four buttons on the Form Action bar labeled as follows (they function in the same manner as those on the Main Topic form):

Save and Close   Saves the response and closes the form after you are finished entering the information.

Mark Private   Sets a readers field to your username. From that point on, you will be the only one who can access that document. Again, Domino servers will not be able to access it for replication, and Domino administrators will not be able to access it either.

Author's Profile   Displays a dialog box with the profile of the author of the current document. When you create a new Response document, this button will return your own author profile.

Cancel   Closes the form without saving the Response document.

The form itself is fairly simple and contains the following fields:

- Subject
- Content

PART

II

Mastering the Basics

You can complete just the fields you need. Although it is not required, you should always enter a subject so you know what the entry is for when it is displayed in the views. The Content field is a rich text field and can contain a wide variety of information, including formatted text, tables, pictures, objects, URLs, and attached files.

Example Discussion Response   To get a feel for creating new responses, follow these steps:

1. Open the Mastering R5 for Chapter 7 (2) database.

2. Select a main topic to respond to (you can also select any response to the main topic). If you saved the Main Topic document from the previous example, select it in the view.

3. Click the New Response button on the View Action bar. A new Response document will be displayed.

4. Type **Test Response** in the Subject field.

5. Select the Save and Close button on the Form Action bar to save this response.

A new Response entry will be displayed in the discussion database's views. It will be located below the main topic for which it was created and indented slightly to show its place in the hierarchy. A small arrow will be displayed next to the main topic indicating that there are responses. Click the arrow icon to expand the view to show the responses. Click it when the view is expanded to collapse the view.

This method can be used to create Response to Response documents too. The only difference is that Response to Response documents insert themselves in the database's document hierarchy below the document (a Main Topic, a Response, or another Response to Response document) you select when you are creating the new Response to Response document.

Using TeamRoom for Structured Discussions

Release 5 includes another discussion database template called TeamRoom. TeamRoom is similar to the discussion database, but it is more structured and targeted toward project-oriented requirements. There is a setup document for defining the name and purpose of the team and the participants, categories, document types, events, and milestones. There are a large number of predefined views for slicing through the content in a variety of ways. TeamRoom even supports workflow for reviewing documents. It is a very sophisticated template and can be used to effectively bring together teams of people working on projects together. The template is named TeamRoom (5.0) and its filename is `teamrm50.ntf`. To create your own database from an existing template, see Chapter 16. For more information about using the TeamRoom template, see the About document or the Notes Help database.

Managing a Document Library

Another commonly used template is the Document Library template, or Doc Library–Notes & Web (R5.0). This database can be used to store and manage documents for a variety of uses. It can be coupled with a discussion or TeamRoom database to provide a repository for project-oriented documents. It can be used to organize software patches and updates downloaded from various vendor Web sites. It can even be used to store pictures or other objects for fast retrieval.

The Document Library contains topics and responses (which is similar to the discussion database). The topics are the containers for documents stored in the Document Library, and responses are used to provide comments or feedback. The Document Library also enables users to categorize topics and mark topics/responses as private. The Document Library, when hosted on a Domino server, can be extended to all users with a Web browser. It is no longer limited to just users who have the Notes client installed.

The Document Library also incorporates a generic review cycle for documents. When creating new documents, you can choose who should be reviewers and how the process should operate. You can establish serial and parallel review cycles, set time limits for reviewers, and enable notification after each reviewer or after just the final reviewer. The review cycle provides a simple workflow for documents added to the Document Library.

For this section, we'll use the Mastering R5 for Chapter 7 (3) database from the CD in the examples. This is just an empty Document Library database created from the Release 5 Document Library template. Of course, you can always create your own Document Library database. For more information on creating databases, see Chapter 16.

Opening the Example Document Library

Assuming you have installed the example databases from the CD to a directory called masterr5 in your Notes Data directory, you can open the Mastering R5 for Chapter 7 (3) database as follows:

1. Select File ➤ Database ➤ Open (or press Ctrl+O) to bring up the Open Database dialog box.

2. Keep the Server field set to Local so Notes presents databases from your local Data directory.

3. Scroll down the Database field's list box until you reach the masterr5 folder.

4. Double-click the masterr5 folder (or select the folder and then click the Open button).

5. Scroll down the Database field's list box until you see the Mastering R5 for Chapter 7 (3) database.

6. Double-click the database (or select it and then click the Open button).

The database's About document will be displayed. This will happen the first time you open any Notes database. It is the generic About document from the Release 5 Document Library template. It provides a quick overview of the purpose and intent of the generic Document Library. When you create your own Document Library databases, you should create your own About documents tailored to suit your audience. Click the Click Here to Open This Database hotspot or press Escape to close the About document and display the example Document Library database.

You will notice that the Mastering R5 for Chapter 7 (3) database has a frameset interface, as shown in Figure 7.6.

FIGURE 7.6

The Mastering R5 for Chapter 7 (3) database frameset

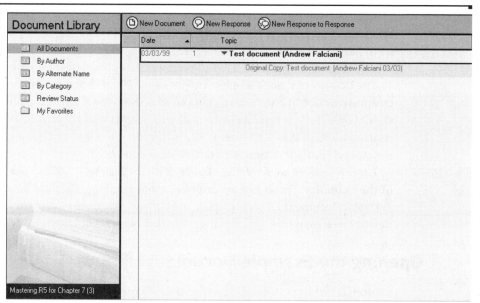

The Release 5 Document Library template also has a frameset interface. The left side consists of three frames:

- A top frame that displays a description of the window
- A middle frame that displays a Navigation pane
- A bottom frame that displays the title of the database

This interface is consistent with the user interface for the core databases discussed in Chapter 4.

Navigating the Document Library Database

The Navigation pane contains a set of predefined views and folders, including:

- All Documents
- By Author
- By Alternate Name
- By Category
- Review Status
- My Favorites

The All Documents, By Category, and Review Status views display documents and their associated responses. The only difference is the order in which the documents are presented. These views also display responses as a hierarchy; each response is positioned directly below its parent. The All Documents view displays the documents by the date they were entered, with the latest ones presented at the top of the view. The By Category view displays the documents categorized by the value(s) entered in the documents' Category field. Just as with the discussion database, a small arrow will be displayed to the left of each Category header indicating that there are documents contained within that category. Within each category, the documents and their responses are displayed in the order they were entered.

PART

II

Mastering the Basics

 TIP Use the Categorize facility when you display the By Category view to quickly change the Category field value for multiple main topics at one time. Just select the main topic documents you want to categorize and then select Action ➤ Categorize. Notes will display the Categorize dialog box, allowing you to choose from existing categories or add new ones.

The Review Status view displays the documents categorized by the document's current review status. Again, a small arrow will be displayed to the left of each Review Status header indicating that there are documents contained within that category. Within each Review Status category, the documents and their responses are displayed in the order they were entered.

The By Author view does not show the documents as a hierarchy. Instead, it lists each document individually, categorized by the author's name. The By Alternate Name view lists the document's authors' alternate names.

My Favorites is a folder included in the Document Library database. You can use it to keep track of specific documents in the database that you may want to quickly access later. As with other folders in Notes, you can drag and drop documents to it or use the Action menus.

WARNING Remember, if you delete entries from the My Favorites folder, the actual document will be deleted from the database. If you want to retain the document, select Action ➤ Remove from Folder instead.

Creating Document Library Entries

Creating Document Library entries is as simple as creating a new document and filling in the fields. With the Document Library database open, you can create a new document in the following two ways:

- Select Create ➤ Document.
- Select the New Document button from the View Action bar of any view.

For frequently used Document Libraries, you can also create a bookmark to the new Document form so you can create new documents without even opening the database. However you create a new document, a blank new Document form will be displayed (see Figure 7.7).

FIGURE 7.7

A blank new Document form

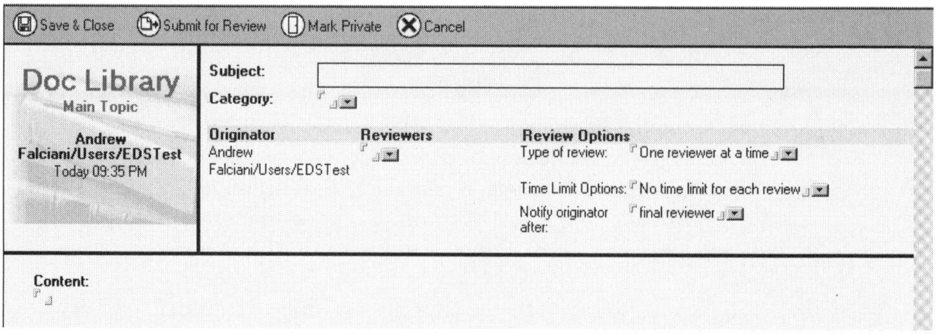

At the top of the database area, you'll see four buttons on the Form Action bar labeled as follows:

Save and Close   Saves the new document and closes the form after you are finished entering the information.

Submit for Review   Initiates the review cycle for this document. See "The Review Cycle" later in this chapter for more information.

Mark Private   Sets a readers field to your username. From that point on, you will be the only one who can access that document. Domino servers will not be able to access it for replication and Domino administrators will not be able to access it either.

Cancel   Closes the form without saving the new document.

The new Document form contains the following fields:

- Subject
- Category
- Content
- Review Options

You can complete just the fields you need. Although it is not required, you should always enter a subject so you know what the entry is for when it is displayed in the views. The Category field in the new Document form is similar to the one in the new Main Topic form (discussed earlier in this chapter). This field can contain multiple values, which you can enter in the field or choose from the Select Keywords dialog box. To display the Select Keywords dialog box, click the arrow button to the right of the Category field. This Keywords list is generated from the current set of Document Library topics in the database. You can also add new categories in the New Keywords field. Just separate each value with a comma. The Content field is a rich text field and can contain a wide variety of information, including formatted text, tables, pictures, objects, URLs, and attached files.

Example New Document   To get a feel for creating new documents, try creating a test entry as described in the following steps:

1. Open the Mastering R5 for Chapter 7 (3) database.
2. Click the New Document button on the View Action bar. The new Document form will be displayed.
3. Type **Test Document** in the Subject field.
4. Tab to the Category field and click the arrow to the right of the field. The Select Keywords dialog box will be displayed.
5. Tab to the New Keywords field and enter **Category1**.
6. Click the OK button. You will be returned to the new Document form.
7. Click the Save and Close button on the Form Action bar to save this document.

A new Document entry will be displayed in the Document Library database's views.

Creating Document Library Responses

Creating responses is as simple as creating a new Response document and filling in the fields. With the Document Library database open, you can create a new Response document in the following two ways:

- Select Create ➤ Response.
- Click the New Response button on the View Action bar in any of the views.

PART

II

Mastering the Basics

Because Response documents are relative to the document to which they refer, it doesn't make sense to bookmark the new Response form as we did the new Document form. However you create a new Response document, a blank Response form will be displayed (see Figure 7.8).

FIGURE 7.8

A blank Response form

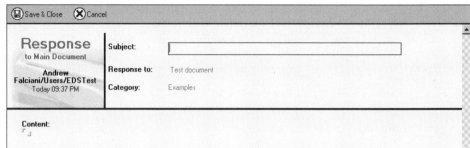

As you can see, the Document Library database's Response form is the same as the discussion database's Response form. See "Creating Discussion Responses" earlier in this chapter for more information on using the Response form.

Example Document Library Response   To get a feel for creating new responses, try creating a test entry:

1. Open the Mastering R5 Chapter 7 Document Library database.

2. Select a document to respond to (you can also select any response to a document). If you saved the document from the preceding example, select it in the view.

3. Click the New Response button on the View Action bar. A new Response document will be displayed.

4. Type **Test Response** in the Subject field.

5. Click the Save and Close button on the Form Action bar to save this response.

A new Response entry will be displayed in the Document Library database's views. It will be located below the document for which it was created and indented slightly to show its place in the hierarchy.

This method can be used to create Response to Response documents too. The only difference is that Response to Response documents insert themselves in the database's document hierarchy below the document you selected when the new Response to Response document was created (which could be a Document, a Response, or another Response to Response document).

The Review Cycle

The Document Library database includes a basic review cycle in the Document form. You can create a document in the Document Library database and have other individuals review and edit it. The review cycle can be serial or parallel. Serial reviews occur when the document is presented to each reviewer one at a time. Parallel reviews occur when the document is presented to all reviewers at the same time. The cycle you should use depends on your needs. If you don't want to wait for any single reviewer, the parallel review may be more appropriate. When you want to be certain that two reviewers don't edit the document at the same time, the serial review may be more appropriate.

On the new Document form, there are special fields that control the review cycle:

- Reviewers
- Review Cycle options (Type of Review, Time Limit options, Notify Originator)

There are also special buttons included on the Document form for controlling the review cycle. When a new document is being created, the Form Action bar will include the Submit for Review button, which you can click after entering the names of the reviewers and the review cycle options. What happens next depends on the type of review cycle you chose. If you chose the review type One Reviewer at a Time, the following will occur:

1. An e-mail message is sent to the first reviewer, and a dialog box appears indicating that this has occurred.

2. Another new document is created for review and the original is saved as a response to the new document. Only the originator can edit the original document saved as a Response document.

3. The first reviewer is listed as the current reviewer.

4. The first reviewer either opens the document to be reviewed by clicking the document link mailed to him or by opening the Document Library database and selecting the appropriate document.

5. The reviewer switches to Edit mode to make changes to the document. At this point, only the current reviewer and the originator have edit capability.

PART

II

Mastering the Basics

6. If the originator edits the document, a Clear Review Cycle button is made available on the Form Action bar. Clicking this button will clear the review cycle.

7. If the reviewer edits the document, a My Review Is Complete button is made available on the Form Action bar. Clicking this button will initiate action that removes the reviewer from the Current Reviewer list, updates the review history maintained on the document, and closes the document. At this point, this particular individual cannot edit the document. Notifications are sent via e-mail as follows:

   • If there are more reviewers, the next reviewer is notified.

   • If the document had the Notify Originator After option set to Each Reviewer, the originator is notified that this review has been completed.

   • If this is the last reviewer, the originator is notified that the review cycle is complete.

8. Notification dialog boxes are displayed indicating which e-mails were sent.

9. The next reviewer is listed as the current reviewer.

This continues until all reviewers have completed their review or the originator clears the review cycle. In either case, the document returns to a state where only the originator can edit it.

If you chose the review type All Reviewers Simultaneously, the following will occur:

1. An e-mail message is sent to all reviewers, and a dialog box appears for each individual indicating that this has occurred.

2. Another new document is created for review, and the original is saved as a response to the new document. Only the originator can edit the original document saved as a Response document.

3. All reviewers are listed as current reviewers.

4. Any of the reviewers can open the document to be reviewed by clicking the document link mailed to them or by opening the Document Library database and selecting the appropriate document.

5. The reviewer switches to Edit mode to make changes to the document. At this point, all current reviewers and the originator have edit capability.

6. If the originator edits the document, a Clear Review Cycle button is made available on the Form Action bar. Clicking this button will clear the review cycle.

7. If the reviewer edits the document, a My Review Is Complete button is made available on the Form Action bar. Clicking this button will initiate action that removes the reviewer from the Current Reviewer list, updates the review history maintained on the document, and closes the document. At this point, this

particular individual cannot edit the document. Notifications are sent via e-mail as follows:

- If the document had the Notify Originator After option set to Each Reviewer, the originator is notified that this review has been completed.

- If this is the last reviewer, the originator is notified that the review cycle is complete.

8. Notification dialog boxes are displayed, indicating which e-mail notifications were sent.

This continues until all reviewers have completed their review or the originator clears the review cycle. In either case, the document returns to a state where only the originator can edit it.

Microsoft Office Document Library Template

Release 5 includes another document library database template called Microsoft Office Library. The Microsoft Office Library database is similar to the Document Library database except it includes additional integration with Microsoft Word, Excel, PowerPoint, and Paint. With it, you can create databases that are repositories for documents generated using these popular applications. This enables you to work with applications with which you are familiar and still take advantage of Notes's ability to manage your data. Like the Document Library discussed earlier, the Microsoft Office Library supports document categorization, public/private documents, and document review cycles. Also, you can take advantage of all the features of Notes because the information is embedded within Notes documents. You can perform the following tasks:

- Organize documents in folders
- Find documents using Notes's built-in full-text search engine
- Archive documents
- Secure documents using Notes's database Access Control Lists
- Work offline with replicated databases

The Microsoft Office Library template includes an additional button on the View Action bar—New MS Office Document. This button includes a menu from which you can choose which type of Microsoft Office document you would like to create. You can also create new documents using the Create ➤ MS Office menu. As the New MS Office Document button does, this menu lets you choose which type of Microsoft Office document you would like to create. When you create a new Microsoft Office document in the Microsoft Office Library template, a Notes form is displayed with only an embedded object for the selected application. There are no other fields displayed on the form. To enter a subject or category for the document, you can click the Properties button on the Form Action bar.

You can enter information in the embedded object the same way you would if the application was running. The difference is that the Notes application window is still active, but the embedded object's menus and tool bars are displayed. The embedded object behaves the same way it does when you create OLE objects in rich text fields, which is explained in Chapter 11, "Integrating Notes with Other Applications."

 NOTE The Microsoft Office Library template is designed for the Notes client only. If you are planning to collaborate with Web browser users (using Domino server), use the Document Library template instead. It is designed to support Web browser users in addition to Notes users.

The template is named Microsoft Office Library (R5.0) and its filename is doc1bm50 .ntf. To create your own Microsoft Office Library database from this template, see Chapter 16, "Creating Your First Database." For more information about using the Microsoft Office Library template, see the template's About document.

Aspects of Notes/Domino Databases

Now that you have a basic understanding of how to participate in Notes discussion databases and store information in Notes Document Library databases, we'll introduce some other important aspects of using Release 5 databases. Although presented here in the context of discussion databases and Document Library databases, these concepts can be applied to all Notes and Domino databases.

Browser Audience

We have demonstrated the use of the discussion database and Document Library from within the Notes client. These databases are also designed to allow Web browser users to participate. When the databases are stored on a Domino server and configured to allow Web browser access, users with a Web browser installed on their computer can create new topics or documents, respond to existing topics or documents, and even participate in review cycles. Most of the functionality is the same, but there are some differences, which are related to the Content field.

The Content field (on the Main Topic, Document, Response, and Response to Response forms) is a rich text field. As such, it can contain a variety of data. (For more information on rich text fields, see Chapter 3, "Working with Notes Databases.") The issue is that Web browsers don't handle rich text fields the way that Notes does. (For more information on how form capabilities map to Web browsers, see Chapter 18, "Using Forms to Collect Data," and Chapter 19, "Advanced Form Design.") For main topics, documents, and responses that only require a simple message, you can type or copy/paste text directly in the Content field. Domino will present the information to Web browser users as it was typed in Notes. Domino will even present formatted text (bold, underline, etc.) properly to Web browsers and allow Web browser users to use a Java applet to format text. This is a powerful feature because Web browser users don't need special software installed on their computer to participate in discussions that include richly formatted information.

If the information comes from an external source, such as a Word document, and is large or needs to retain complex formatting, you should attach it as a file. This way, the Web browser users can save the file to their own computer in its native format. The downside is that all Web browser users need the application software in which the attachment was created installed on their computer.

For this reason, you may want to attach files in universal file formats when possible. The discussion and Document Library database forms are designed to enable Web browser users to attach and detach (save) files. Word format is acceptable because Word is so widely used. There is even a Word file viewer (from Microsoft) for users who don't have Word installed on their computer. If you cannot be sure that all users will have the latest version of the software, save the information in formats supported by older versions. Adobe Acrobat (PDF) is another good format. There is a free viewer available that is widely accepted on the Internet. Of course, HTML can be used in certain circumstances as well.

Because the Content field is a rich text field, these issues apply to any databases that include forms with rich text fields.

Access Rights

When you use the Mastering R5 example databases and they are stored locally on your computer (described earlier in this chapter), you have manager-level access. This means that you have the highest level of access available to Notes databases. When you use other Notes databases from a Domino server (or databases that have Consistent ACL enabled), you will have an access level defined by the owner of the database. This will have an impact on what you can and cannot do in the database. For a complete explanation of database access rights, see Chapter 16. Unless you are the owner of a database, you will most likely have Author access. This means that you can create new topics or respond to existing ones, but you cannot edit (modify) topics or responses created by other users. You can use the Access Level indicator on the status bar to check your access level. With the Mastering R5 for Chapter 7 (2) or Mastering R5 for Chapter 7 (3) database open, perform the following steps to check your access level:

1. Click the Access Level indicator on the status bar. It is the third area from the right. The Groups and Roles dialog box (shown here) will be displayed.

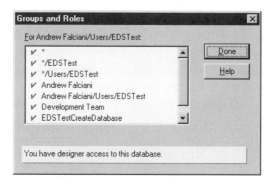

2. In the list box, you'll see check marks next to all groups of which you are a member. Use the scroll bar to navigate up and down in the list box.

3. At the bottom of the dialog box, there will be a sentence describing your access level. In this case, the sentence is "You have designer access to this database."

4. Click the OK button to close the dialog box.

Mail-In Databases

Domino supports a feature called Mail-In databases. With this feature, you can e-mail documents to discussion databases, Document Library databases, or other Notes databases that reside on a Domino server. This is a great way to collect information without a great deal of effort. Whatever you can e-mail can be sent to a Mail-In database. The discussion database is commonly used as a Mail-In database because it has a free-form structure. For example, you can use a discussion database as a Mail-In database for collecting messages from Internet-based list servers. List servers are automated mailers that send messages to individuals who subscribe to them. Usually, they are focused on specific topics, such as technologies, medical conditions, or political interests. There are also many news-oriented list servers. You can use the e-mail address of the Mail-In database to subscribe to list servers. When the message is sent to the Domino server, it delivers the message to the Mail-In database instead of to a mail database. With the information in a discussion database, you can use folders to organize documents or search for information using the built-in full-text search capabilities of Notes and Domino. You can also create a replica of this database on your local computer for offline use.

Archiving

Release 5 includes a built-in archiving facility, which is available to all databases. With it, you can have Notes (or a Domino server) automatically move documents to a separate database based on criteria you establish. This helps minimize the resources needed to support heavily used databases. Moving documents to an archive database frees space in the main database. This makes view indexes and full-text indexes smaller, which in turn helps lower memory and processor utilization. See Chapter 5 for more information on setting up and configuring the archive facility.

Unread Marks

Notes includes a feature called unread marks that is also supported for all databases. Unread marks provide you with a visual cue that indicates when new documents have been added to a database. New documents are typically displayed in red with an asterisk in the View Icon area. See Chapter 4 for more on unread marks.

Compacting Databases

When documents are deleted from Notes databases, the space they had taken is not really freed up. It remains allocated, but not used. This is sometimes referred to as *white space*. On heavily used databases, such as your mail database, this can become a problem over time. Fortunately, there is a way to free up this unused space in your databases. The process is known as *compacting*.

To view the size of a database and how much of that space is unused, select File ➤ Database ➤ Properties and select the Info tab in the Database Properties InfoBox. Click the % Used button to have Notes calculate how much of the space taken by the database is actually being used. Click the Compact button to initiate the process of compacting the database.

PART

II

Mastering the Basics

Summary

In this chapter, we explored three common Notes databases that are used in many situations to help people work better together and share information. The built-in templates provided with Notes and Domino also act as starting points for other databases. You can expand on these database or incorporate features from them into other, new databases. Once you start using Notes databases, you'll want to search for information contained within them, which is covered in the next chapter.

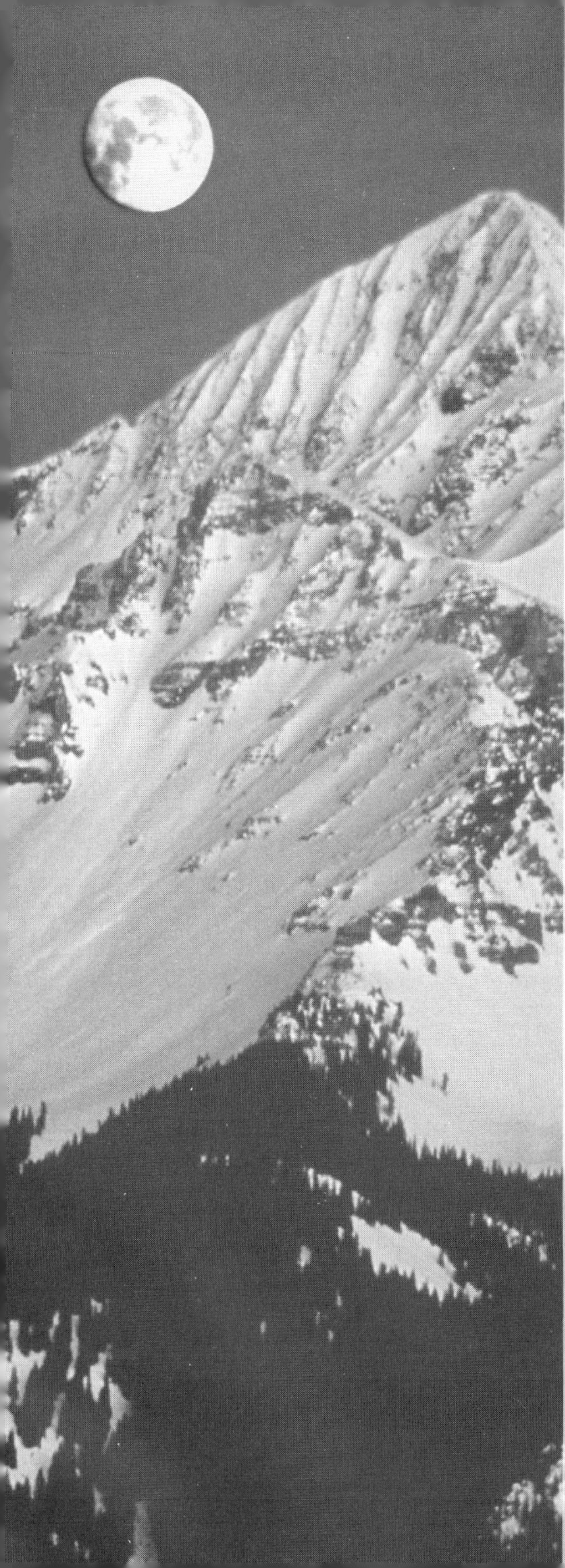

CHAPTER 8

Searching for Information

FEATURING:

nce you start using Notes to communicate via e-mail, organize your personal information, or participate in electronic discussions (and other collaborative applications), you will begin to accumulate a great deal of information in Notes databases. Fortunately, Notes includes powerful search features that enable you to find information stored in its databases. In this chapter, we will explore the search capabilities of Notes.

Searching for Text in Documents

Notes allows you to search for text strings in documents, which is helpful when you're searching through large documents for information. You can also perform search-and-replace on text strings within documents. Notes makes this feature available anytime you are viewing a document (through a form). This is true regardless of the document's source. You can search for text strings within mail messages, To Do list entries, discussion topics, Web pages, newsgroup topics, and anything else that can be represented as a document in Notes.

To search for a text string within a document, follow these steps:

1. Open the document you want to search.

2. Open the Find Text in Document dialog box by selecting Edit ➤ Find/Replace.

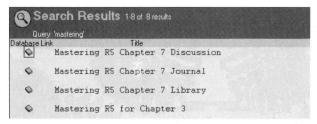

3. Enter the text string you are searching for in the Find field.

4. Click the Find Next button.

If the text string is found, Notes will navigate to the area in the document where it was found and highlight it. You can either click the Find Next button again to find additional occurrences of the text string, or you can click the Close button to close the Find Text in Document dialog box. If the text string is not found, a dialog box will be displayed indicating that it was not found.

When a document is open for viewing, the Find Text in Document dialog box can also be opened in any one of the following ways:

- Click the Search button in the Navigation bar.
- Select Find Text from the Search menu (available by clicking the arrow to the right of the Search icon on the Navigation bar).
- Press Ctrl+F.

The Find Text in Document dialog box has a number of options that enable you to refine your search. To access these options, click on the word *Options* or the expand/collapse indicator to the left of it. The Find Text in Document dialog box will expand to display the available options, which are as follows:

Case Sensitive   Instructs Notes to search for text in which the capitalization matches the exact capitalization of the text you entered. If this option is not enabled, Notes will find all occurrences of the text you entered regardless of capitalization.

Accent Sensitive   Instructs Notes to search for extended or foreign characters only when you enter criteria that includes extended or foreign characters. If the Accent Sensitive option is not enabled, Notes searches for extended or foreign characters even if the criteria only includes regular characters.

Match on Entire Word   Instructs Notes to search for the text you entered with space characters bordering it. If this option is not enabled, Notes searches for the text you entered whether it is bordered by space characters or embedded within other words.

Wrap Around   Instructs Notes to cycle back to the top of the document (or to the bottom of the document if you are searching backward) and continue searching after finding all occurrences of the text you entered. Disabling this option causes Notes to stop searching when it reaches the end of the document.

Find Forwards/Find Backwards   You can choose to search forward or backward in the document by selecting the appropriate option.

You can also enter special characters in the Find Text in Document dialog box by using the Windows Character Map utility or by using a special key sequence. To use the Character Map utility to enter special characters, follow these steps:

1. Run the Windows Character Map utility by selecting Start ➢ Programs ➢ Accessories ➢ Character Map. You can also select Start ➢ Run, enter **charmap**, and click the Open button.

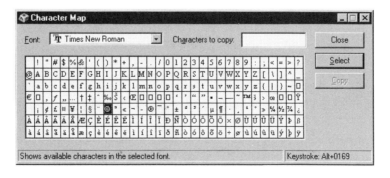

PART

II

Mastering the Basics

2. Select the character you want to enter in the search.

3. Click the Select button and then the Copy button.

4. In the Find Text in Document dialog box, paste the character(s) into the Find field.

To enter special characters using the special key sequence, follow these steps:

1. Find the keystroke number of the special character you want to enter. The Windows Character Map utility displays the keystroke number in the lower right corner.

2. While your cursor is active in the Find field of the Find Text in Document dialog box, press Alt+*keystroke number* using the numeric keypad on your keyboard.

Either way, the special character you entered should display in the Find field of the Find Text in Document dialog box. If not, your default Notes sans serif font probably does not support the special character you entered. Follow this procedure to change your Notes sans serif font:

1. Select File ➤ Preferences ➤ User Preferences to display the User Preferences dialog box.

2. Click the Default Fonts button. The Default Fonts dialog box will be displayed.

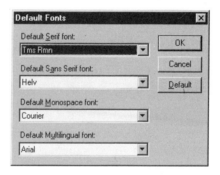

3. Click the Default button to reset your Notes default fonts back to their original values or select an appropriate font from the Default Sans Serif drop-down box.

4. Click the OK button to close the Default Fonts dialog box.

5. Click the OK button to save your changes and close the User Preferences dialog box.

Searching for Documents in Views

As mentioned previously, Notes databases present collections of documents through views and folders. Views and folders can be used to present all documents contained within a database or to present subsets of a database's documents. They display collections of documents in an organized manner. Data from each document is presented in a row/column format, and the rows can be categorized for easier navigation. This is a powerful mechanism for presenting information in a manner that makes it easy to find later.

When you have databases with large numbers of documents, you need additional tools for finding information quickly. Notes's capability to search views is one of these tools. You can search views for documents matching criteria that you choose. The search can be based on simple criteria such as a single word or more sophisticated criteria that includes Boolean logic. You can search views in any database, including:

- Your mail database (to find e-mail messages, calendar entries, or To Do list entries)
- Your Personal Address Book database (to find Contacts or groups)
- Discussion databases (to find topics and responses)
- Document Library databases (to find documents)

The list is endless. You can search any view in any Notes database.

 NOTE When Notes searches views, it only finds documents contained within the view you specify. If you need to search all documents in a database, you can create a view that includes all documents. Otherwise, you'll have to repeat your search in multiple views.

Simple Searches

You can search for a text string contained in any of the fields of any of the documents displayed in a view. We call this a *simple search*. To perform a simple search, follow these steps:

1. Open the database containing the view you want to search.

2. Click the Search button on the Navigation bar. The Search bar will be displayed above the View pane. You can also select View ➤ Search Bar.

3. In the Search For field on the Search bar, enter the text string you are searching for.

4. Click the Search button on the Search bar to the right of the Search For field (or you can press Enter instead of clicking the Search button).

PART

II

Mastering the Basics

Only the documents containing the text string you entered will be displayed in the view. Each will have a check mark to the left of it in the View Icon area. Click the Clear Results button to redisplay all documents in the view. Simple searches are the only way to search a view in a database that has not been full-text indexed. They can also be used on databases that are full-text indexed; in this case, Notes can process the search much quicker and provide a more sophisticated result set.

Full-Text Indexes

Without a full-text index, Notes must search all words in all documents contained within the view. This is a slow process, especially on large databases. In addition, Notes can only return information in the order it found it in the view. To overcome these limitations, you can create a full-text index on any Notes database (as long as you have at least Designer access). This is a feature that makes searching within views faster as well as more sophisticated. When Notes creates a full-text index, it collects all of the data contained in all of the documents and stores it in a separate structure optimized for searching. This separate structure requires additional disk space on your computer (or Domino server), in the range of 20 to 30 percent of the size of the database. With a full-text index, Notes can perform searches faster and provide additional search features, including:

- Searches using operators
- Searches using conditions
- Proximity searches
- Case-sensitive searches
- Fuzzy searches and searches that include word variants
- Search results that are sorted and ranked

These search features are discussed later in this chapter. Also, the full-text index enables Notes to highlight the matches in the documents found. Notes highlights the matches with a green background. While inside the view, you can open the Preview pane to display documents found by the search with the matches highlighted.

With the document displayed in the Preview pane, you can navigate through the matches by clicking the left and right arrow icons next to the Search bar. If you open the document, the matches will still be highlighted. With the document open, you can navigate through the matches using Ctrl+ and Ctrl– (the plus and minus keys on the numeric keypad). The next graphic shows the highlighted matches.

 NOTE Notes will not highlight matches in date or number fields, hidden areas of a form, or attachments.

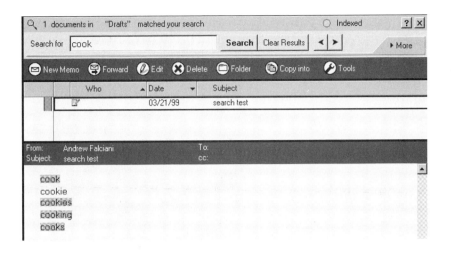

Creating a Full-Text Index

To be able to create a full-text index on a Notes database, you must have at least Designer-level access. For databases (and replicas) stored locally on your computer, you will generally have the appropriate access rights. For databases stored on a Domino server, you may not. For the purpose of our discussion, we will assume you are full-text indexing a local copy (or replica) of your mail database and that you have the appropriate authority.

There are two ways to determine whether or not a database is full-text indexed. The first is to look for the indicator on the right side of the Search bar. It will display a green circle with the word *Indexed* next to it or a red circle with the words *Not Indexed* next to it. To display the Search bar, follow these steps:

1. Open the database containing the view you want to search.

2. Click the Search button on the Navigation bar.

The Search bar will be displayed above the View pane. You can create the full-text index from the Search bar using the following procedure:

1. Click the More button on the right side of the Search bar. The Search bar will expand to include more details. Notice that the expanded Search bar includes a paragraph explaining that the database is not full-text indexed.

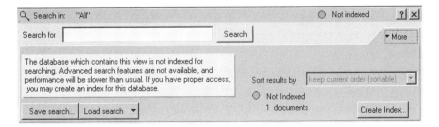

PART

II

Mastering the Basics

Create Index...

2. Click the Create Index button on the lower right side of the expanded Search bar. The Create Full-Text Index dialog box (shown in Figure 8.1) will be displayed.

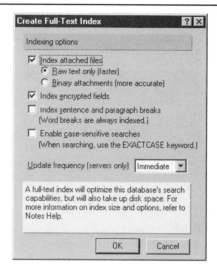

3. Select the options you would like to use by clicking the check boxes. The options are explained later in this section.

4. Click the OK button.

A message is displayed in the message area of the status bar indicating that your request to index the database has been queued locally and that you can search the database when it is complete. When the index has been created, the expanded Search bar will change to include the advanced search features.

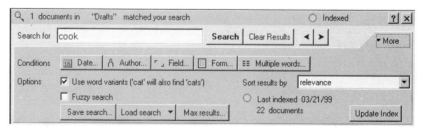

Once the index has been created, Notes automatically keeps it up-to-date. You can also manually update the full-text index. This is useful when you know that documents have been added to the database and the automatic update has not yet taken place. Notice that the Create Index button has been replaced with an Update Index button. You can use this button to force Notes to update the full-text index.

NOTE If the database is stored on a Domino server, the message displayed in the status bar will indicate that your request to index the database is being queued on the server. Also, you will have to close and reopen the database to see the Search bar changed to include the advanced search features.

The second way to determine whether or not a database is full-text indexed is to view the Full Text tab of the Database Properties InfoBox. To display the Full Text tab, follow these steps:

1. Open the database containing the view you want to search.

2. Select Database ➤ Properties. The Database Properties InfoBox will be displayed.

3. Click the Full Text tab (second from the right). For a database that has not been full-text indexed, the Full Text tab will look like Figure 8.2.

FIGURE 8.2

The Full Text tab of Database Properties InfoBox for a database that is not indexed

Notice that most of the InfoBox page is grayed out. Only the Create Index and Delete Index buttons are available. Above the Create Index button, there is a sentence that reads "Database is not full text indexed." You can create the full-text index from the Full Text tab of the Database Properties InfoBox using the following procedure:

1. Click the Create Index button. The Create Full-Text Index dialog box will be displayed.

2. Select the options you would like to use by clicking the check boxes.

3. Click the OK button.

When you use the Properties InfoBox to create a full-text index, the procedure is the same as when you use the Search bar. Like the expanded Search bar, the Full Text tab of the Database Properties InfoBox has an Update button for manually updating the full-text index. In addition, it has a Delete Index button you can use to delete the full-text index. There is also a Count Unindexed Documents button that will display the number of unindexed documents to the right. The full-text index's options are also displayed on the Full Text tab. For databases stored on Domino servers, there is also a drop-down list for selecting the update frequency.

Full-Text Index Options   When creating the full-text index for a database, you can choose from a number of indexing options. The following options are selected in the Create Full-Text Index dialog box (see Figure 8.1):

Index Attached Files   Lets you choose whether or not to index attached files. If you enable this option, searches will return documents that have attachments containing the search string you entered. The sub-option, Raw Text Only, limits the full-text index to searching the ASCII portion of attached files. This makes searches faster, but less accurate.

Index Encrypted Fields   Instructs Notes to include the data from encrypted fields in the full-text index.

Index Sentence and Paragraph Breaks   Determines whether or not Notes stores information required for performing proximity searches using the PARA-GRAPH and SENTENCE operators. See the next section for more information on these operators.

Enable Case-Sensitive Searches   Determines whether or not Notes stores information required for performing case-sensitive searches using the EXACT-CASE operator. See the next section for more information on this operator.

Update Frequency   Determines the frequency at which Domino servers will update this database's full-text index.

Performing Full-Text Searches

Now that you have full-text indexed a database, you can take advantage of the advanced features it provides, including:

- Using operators
- Using conditions
- Using search options
- Sorting search results

Using Operators

Operators are special words and characters that tell Notes how to perform a search. They are used in conjunction with values you are searching for. For example, a search entered as *"value* AND *value"* will find all documents that contain at least one instance of each value. Entering a search criteria of "sales AND january" will find all documents that contain the words *sales* and *january* at least one time. Operators allow you to enter search criteria as you would on a typical Web search engine. Notes even includes operators that enable you to perform proximity searches. You can find documents that contain words in the same paragraph or sentence. There is even an operator that enables you to specify weighting for words found so Notes can rank the result set. Of course, there are wildcard operators in addition to the basic conditional operators such as AND, OR, NOT, = (equal to), < (less than), > (greater than), <= (less than or equal to), and >= (greater than or equal to). Operators are entered directly into the Search bar when you're searching views. Table 8.1 summarizes the available operators and the functionality they provide.

TABLE 8.1: SEARCH OPERATORS

Operator	Description
AND / and / &	AND is used to find all documents that contain all the values or conditions on either side of it.
	Usage: value/condition AND value/condition [AND value/condition…]
	Example: Entering "sales AND january" will find all documents with at least one occurrence of each (the text string "sales" and the text string "january").
	Example: Entering "sales AND FIELD author CONTAINS andrew" will find all documents with at least one occurrence of the text string "sales" in any field where the Author field contains the text string "andrew".
OR / or / | / , (comma) / ACCRUE	OR is used to find all documents that contain any of the values or conditions on either side of it.
	Usage: value/condition OR value/condition [OR value/condition…]
	Example: Entering "sales OR january" will find all documents containing either the text string "sales" or the text string "january".
	Example: Entering "sales OR FIELD author CONTAINS andrew" will find all documents with either the text string "sales" in any field or the Author field containing the text string "andrew".
	Note: ACCRUE is more accurate when sorting results by relevance.

Continued ▶

PART

II

Mastering the Basics

TABLE 8.1: SEARCH OPERATORS (CONTINUED)

Operator	Description
NOT / not / !	NOT is used to reverse the effect of the value or condition.
	Usage: NOT value/condition
	Example: Entering "NOT sales" will find all documents that do not contain the text string "sales".
	Example: Entering "NOT FIELD author CONTAINS andrew" will find all documents where the Author field does not contain the text string "andrew".
	Note: NOT cannot be placed between the =, <, >, <=, >= operators and a date or number value. The following is not valid: FIELD quantity = NOT 100.
FIELD / field / [field name] (in brackets)	FIELD is used to instruct Notes to search a specific field.
	Usage 1: FIELD fieldname CONTAINS search string (for text fields)
	Usage 2: FIELD fieldname *condition operator* value, where *condition operator* is =, <, >, <=, or >= (for date and numeric fields)
	Note: See the row containing =, <, >, <=, >= for examples.
CONTAINS contains =	"CONTAINS" is used with the FIELD operator to instruct Notes to find all documents where the field specified includes the search string following it.
	Usage: CONTAINS search string
	Example: Entering "FIELD author CONTAINS andrew" finds all documents where the Author field contains the text string "andrew".
	Example: Entering "FIELD $file CONTAINS sales" finds all documents where an attachment includes the text string "sales".
	Note: Attachments are stored in a special field called $file even though they appear to be contained in rich text fields (the most common being Body). Use $file when searching for text strings in attachments.
= / < / > / <= / >=	These are condition operators used with the FIELD operator with date and numeric fields. Notes will find all documents matching the expression formed using these condition operators.

Continued ▐▶

TABLE 8.1: SEARCH OPERATORS (CONTINUED)	
Operator	**Description**
	Usage: *condition operator* value, where *condition operator* is =, <, >, <=, or >=
	Example: Entering "FIELD salary > 50000" finds all documents where the Salary field is greater than 50,000.
? / *	These are wildcard characters used in text searches. The ? (question mark) is used to replace one character position in the search string with any possible character. The * (asterisk) is used to replace characters at the beginning or end of the search string with any set of characters.
	? Usage: ?earchstring, Sear?hstring, Searchstrin?
	Example: Entering "?un" finds all documents containing the words *fun*, *run*, *bun*, *sun*, or other three-character strings that end in *un*.
	* Usage: *searchstring, searchstring*, *searchstring*
	Example: Entering "*lam" finds all documents containing the words *lam*, *slam*, *clam*, or other four-character strings that end with the letters *lam*. If you enter "lam*", all documents containing text strings that begin with *lam* will be found (i.e., lamb, lambs, lamp, lamps, etc.). If you enter "*lam*", all documents containing text strings with *lam* anywhere in the string will be found (i.e., clamp).
PARAGRAPH / paragraph	PARAGRAPH is used to find all documents in which the words on either side of the operator are found in the same paragraph and to rank the results by how close the words are to each other.
	Usage: word PARAGRAPH word
	Example: Entering "sales PARAGRAPH january" finds all documents where the word *sales* is in the same paragraph as the word *january*.
	Note: The PARAGRAPH operator requires that the Index Sentence and Paragraph Breaks option be enabled in the database's full-text index.
SENTENCE / sentence	SENTENCE is used to find all documents where the words on either side of the operator are found in the same paragraph and to rank the results by how close the words are to each other.

Continued ▶

PART

II

Mastering the Basics

TABLE 8.1: SEARCH OPERATORS (CONTINUED)	
Operator	**Description**
	Usage: word SENTENCE word
	Example: Entering "sales SENTENCE january" finds all documents in which the word *sales* is in the same sentence as the word *january*.
	Note: The SENTENCE operator requires that the Index Sentence and Paragraph Breaks option be enabled in the database's full-text index.
EXACTCASE / exactcase	EXACTCASE is used to find all documents with text strings matching the exact case of the search string entered.
	Usage: EXACTCASE search string
	Example: Entering "EXACTCASE Sales" finds all documents containing the text string "Sales". Documents containing *sales* or *SALES* are not included.
	Note: The EXACTCASE operator requires that the Make Case Sensitive option be enabled in the database's full-text index.
TERMWEIGHT / termweight	TERMWEIGHT is used to give words a weight or relative importance to each other in the search.
	Usage: TERMWEIGHT number word AND/OR TERMWEIGHT number word [AND/OR TERMWEIGHT number word]
	Example: Entering "TERMWEIGHT 100 sales AND TERMWEIGHT 20 manufacturing" finds all documents containing both *sales* and *manufacturing*, with those containing *sales* ranked above those containing "manufacturing".
" " (quotes)	Placing quotes around operators instructs Notes to treat them as regular words.
	Example: Entering "sales and marketing" finds all documents containing the phrase *sales and marketing*, not all documents containing the individual words *sales* and *marketing*.

 NOTE This discussion is specific to the use of operators when the Notes client is used to search views. When a Web browser is used to search views, operators work somewhat differently. See the Notes Help database for information on using operators when using a Web browser to search views.

Using Conditions

Conditions are used to enter criteria for a full-text search. They can be used alone or they can be used in conjunction with other search criteria to refine full-text searches. They are created by clicking the appropriate button on the expanded Search bar, and they are represented as a token in the Search For field of the Search bar.

Search for | sales date created is after 01/01/99 | Search |

In this example, Notes would find all documents that contain the text string "sales" and were created after January 1, 1999.

NOTE Conditions are only available in the Notes client. They are not available to Web browsers accessing databases on a Domino server.

As mentioned, conditions are created by clicking the appropriate button on the expanded Search bar. The following buttons are present when the Search bar is expanded:

- Date
- Author
- Field
- Form
- Multiple Words
- Fill Out Example Form

Clicking these buttons brings up the Search Builder dialog box, which is used to enter all of the conditions. It changes appearance based on the condition button you click. It will also change appearance if you choose a different condition from the Condition drop-down list box at the top of the dialog box. This is the same as clicking a different condition button on the expanded Search bar form. Each of the variations of the Search Builder dialog box are explained in the following sections.

When you are finished entering conditions in the Search Builder dialog box, click the OK button at the bottom. Notes will add the condition to the Search For field in the Search bar. You can create additional conditions, and they will be appended to the Search For field.

> ⚠️ **TIP** If you want to edit a condition, just double-click the condition token. You can delete conditions by clicking the condition token and pressing Delete.

Entering By Date Conditions   Figure 8.3 shows the Search Builder dialog box with the By Date condition selected. When the By Date condition is selected in the Condition drop-down list box, the Search Builder dialog box includes four fields to enter. The first is a drop-down box that allows you to select Date Created or Date Modified. This determines which field Notes will search. The second field is a drop-down box that allows you to select how Notes will search the date field selected. The third and fourth fields (when they are displayed) are used to enter acceptable date values to be used in the search. The choices and their acceptable values are described in Table 8.2.

FIGURE 8.3

The Search Builder dialog box with the By Date condition selected

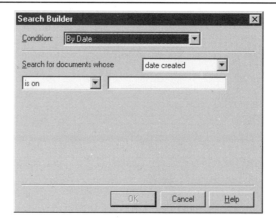

TABLE 8.2: BY DATE SEARCH CHOICES

By Date Search Choice	Acceptable Value
Is On	Valid date (i.e., 3/1/1999)
Is After	Valid date
Is Before	Valid date
Is Not On	Valid date
Is In The Last	Number of days

Continued ▌▶

TABLE 8.2: BY DATE SEARCH CHOICES (CONTINUED)	
By Date Search Choice	**Acceptable Value**
Is In The Next	Number of days
Is Older Than	Number of days
Is After The Next	Number of days
Is Between	Two valid dates
Is Not Between	Two valid dates

Entering By Author Conditions   Figure 8.4 shows the Search Builder dialog box with the By Author condition selected. When the By Author condition is selected in the Condition drop-down list box, the Search Builder dialog box includes two fields to enter. The first is a drop-down box that allows you to select Contains or Does Not Contain. The second field allows you to enter a text string to use in the search. Selecting Contains creates a condition that instructs Notes to find all documents in which the Author field contains the text entered in the second field. Selecting Does Not Contain creates a condition that instructs Notes to find all documents in which the Author field does not contain the text entered in the second field. You can also select names to enter into the second field by clicking the button to the right with the person icon. This displays the Names dialog box (see Figure 8.5), which is used to select names.

PART

II

Mastering the Basics

FIGURE 8.4

The Search Builder dialog box with the By Author condition selected

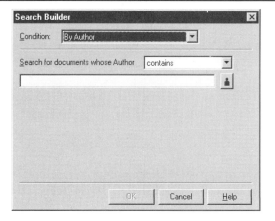

FIGURE 8.5

The Names dialog box

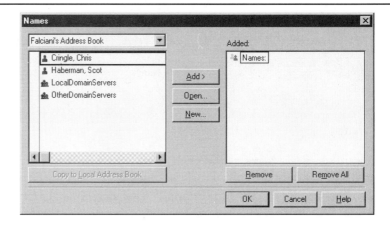

After selecting the names you want included in the condition, just click the OK button. You will be returned to the Search Builder dialog box with the names you selected entered into the second field.

Entering By Field Conditions   Figure 8.6 shows the Search Builder dialog box with the By Field condition selected. When the By Field condition is selected in the Condition drop-down list box, the Search Builder dialog box includes four fields to enter. The first is a drop-down box that allows you to select from the database a field that Notes will use in the search. The second field is a drop-down box that allows you to select how Notes will search the selected field. The third and fourth fields (when they are displayed) are used to enter acceptable values to be used in the search.

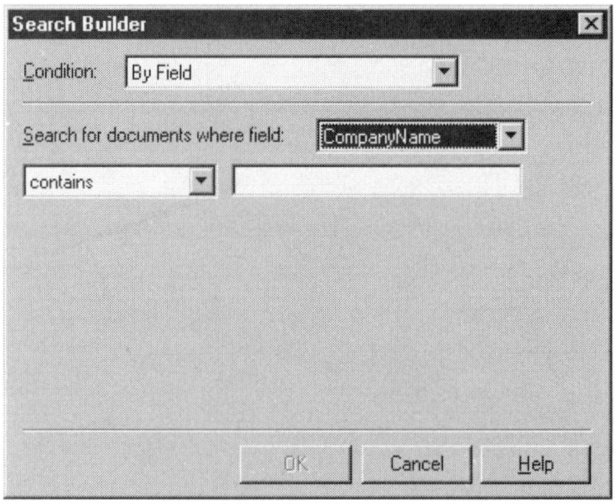

FIGURE 8.6

The Search Builder dialog box with the By Field condition selected

The choices presented in the second drop-down list box change based on the type of field selected. If you select a date field, the choices are the same as those in Table 8.2. If you select a text field, the choices are Contains and Does Not Contain. Selecting Contains creates a condition that instructs Notes to find all documents in which the selected field contains the text entered in the third field. Selecting Does Not Contain creates a condition that instructs Notes to find all documents in which the selected field does not contain the text entered in the third field. You can also select a numeric field; the choices and their acceptable values are described in Table 8.3.

TABLE 8.3: BY FIELD NUMERIC SEARCH CHOICES

By Field Numeric Search Choice	Acceptable Value
Is Equal To	Valid number
Is Greater Than	Valid number
Is Less Than	Valid number
Is Not Equal To	Valid number
Is Between	Two valid numbers
Is Not Between	Two valid numbers

Entering By Form Conditions   Figure 8.7 shows the Search Builder dialog box with the By Form Used condition selected. When the By Form Used condition is selected in the Condition drop-down list box, the Search Builder dialog box includes one field. This field lets you select from a list of form names. Notes will then find all documents in which the form field matches any of the form names selected.

FIGURE 8.7

The Search Builder dialog box with the By Form Used condition selected

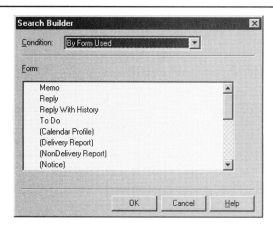

PART II — Mastering the Basics

Entering Multiple Word Conditions   Figure 8.8 shows the Search Builder dialog box with the Words and Phrases condition selected. When the Words and Phrases condition is selected in the Condition drop-down list box, the Search Builder dialog box includes nine fields. The first allows you to choose between searching for any or all of the words or phrases entered in the eight remaining fields. If you choose Any, Notes performs the search as if there is an OR operator between the words or phrases entered. If you choose All, Notes performs the search as if there is an AND operator between the words or phrases entered. See "Using Operators" earlier in this chapter for more information on the OR and AND operators.

FIGURE 8.8

The Search Builder dialog box with the Words and Phrases condition selected

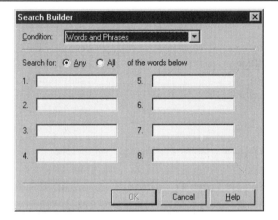

Entering Conditions by Filling Out an Example Form   Figure 8.9 shows the Search Builder dialog box with the By Form condition selected. When the By Form condition is selected in the Condition drop-down list box, the Search Builder dialog box includes one field and a mini-form interface area. The field is a drop-down list box that allows you to select a form name. After selecting a form name, Notes displays that form in the mini-form interface area. You are then able to enter values in the form's fields. These values will be used to search the database. This is a Query by Example interface.

Using Search Options

The search options are available in the expanded Search bar. There are two search options you can enable or disable for your full-text searches. The first, Use Word Variants, instructs Notes to find all documents containing the word entered in the search and variations based on acceptable prefixes and suffixes. For example, you can enter "cook" and Notes will find *cooked*, *cooking*, *cookies*, and *cooker*. The second search option, Fuzzy Search, instructs Notes to find all documents containing words and phrases similar to the search string you entered.

There is also a search option to limit the result set to a specific number of documents. You set this by clicking the Max Results button on the expanded Search bar.

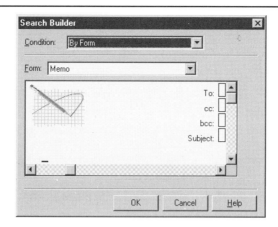

Saving and Reusing Searches   Finally, there are search options for saving and reusing searches. These are available whether or not the database is full-text indexed. They are included in our discussion of full-text index searches because they are usually used to save sophisticated searches, which can only be performed when a database is full-text indexed. To save the current search criteria, follow these steps:

1. Prepare and test the search you want to save.

2. Click the Save Search button. The Save Search dialog box will be displayed.

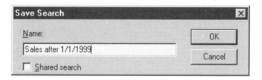

3. Enter a name for your search. To test this feature, just enter **Test Search** in the Name field.

4. Select the Shared Search check box if you would like this search to be available to other users of the database.

5. Click the OK button.

The current search definition, including options and sort order, will be saved. To load a saved search, follow these steps:

1. Click the Load Search button on the expanded Search bar. A menu will be presented, allowing you to delete previously saved searches or load one of the saved searches listed.

2. Select the saved search you would like to load. If you saved one in the previous set of steps, it should be listed.

The search criteria will be changed to the settings previously saved. To delete previously saved searches, follow these steps:

1. Click the Load Search button. A menu will be presented, allowing you to delete previously saved searches or load one of the saved searches listed.

2. Select Delete Saved Search. The Delete Saved Search dialog box will be displayed.

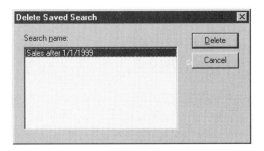

3. Select the search you would like to delete.

4. Click the Delete button.

The dialog box will be closed and the saved search will be deleted.

Sorting Search Results

You can choose how your result set should be sorted from the following options:

Relevance   Instructs Notes to sort the result set by the number of times the search string was found. The documents with the highest number of occurrences are displayed first.

Last Modified   Instructs Notes to sort the result set by the dates the documents were modified. The most recently modified documents are displayed first.

First Modified   Instructs Notes to sort the result set by the dates the documents were modified. Those with the earliest dates are displayed first.

Keep Current Order (Sortable)   Instructs Notes to keep the result set in the order in which the view was already sorted. This is only available when the view supports column sorting.

Show All Documents (Sortable)   Instructs Notes to display all documents in the view; the documents matching the search criteria will be selected. Selected documents are displayed with a check mark in the View Icon area.

TIP The Keep Current Order and Show All Documents options display the result set by selecting the documents matching the search criteria. Selected documents are displayed with a check mark in the View Icon area. For this reason, it is best to use these sort options when searching a calendar-type view.

Searching a Domain

Notes and Domino Release 5 include two new facilities for finding information across database boundaries: Domain Search and the Content Map. These facilities are implemented at the domain level, which means that you can find information from any database (and file system for Domain Search) on any server participating in the same Domino domain. These are powerful additions to the existing view search capability.

Domain Search enables you to perform full-text searches across multiple databases in your Domino domain. Although this sounds complicated, it is relatively easy because these full-text searches are very similar to those performed on views. Domain Search can even search files stored on server-based file systems outside of Domino. This enables you to find information regardless of where it is stored.

The Content Map enables you to categorize documents across databases. It provides a structure (taxonomy) in which you classify documents. You can then browse this structure as you would browse a Web-based search site such as Yahoo!. This provides a powerful mechanism for capturing information about documents. The Content Map becomes a repository for shared knowledge. As more and more documents are added to the Content Map, it becomes more and more useful for finding information quickly.

Performing Domain Searches

The administrator of the Domino domain must enable Domain Search for you to be able to use it. For the purpose of this discussion, we will assume that Domain Search has been enabled. Also, adding databases and file systems to Domain Search is a function most likely performed by the administrator of the Domino domain. Again, we will assume that at least one database and file system definition have been added to the Domain Search.

In Notes, you must have a Catalog/Domain Search server defined in your Location document in order to access Domain Search. The Catalog/Domain Search server is defined on the Servers tab of your Location document. See Chapter 13, "Setting

PART

II

Mastering the Basics

Up Notes as a Domino Client," for more information on configuring the Location document.

You access Domain Search by clicking the arrow to the right of the Search button on the Navigation bar. This displays a Search button menu.

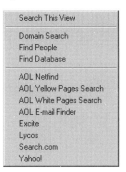

From the Search button menu, select Domain Search. This will bring up the Domain Search form.

The Domain Search form is your interface for performing domain searches. At the top of the form, notice that there are two radio buttons labeled Documents and Databases. By selecting Databases, you can search for databases in the domain matching the criteria you enter. This is the same as selecting Find Database from the Search button menu. If you select Documents, you can search for documents that are contained within the databases and file systems added to Domain Search.

Searching for Databases

To search for databases, select the Databases radio button, enter your criteria in the Title Contains field, and click the Search button on the form. A Search Results form similar to the one shown in Figure 8.10 will be opened to display the results of your search (the options on the form change when the Databases radio button is selected).

Each database with a title meeting the criteria you entered will be displayed as a row on the form. On the left side of each row, there is a database link. Clicking this link will open the database. To close the Search Results form, press Escape or click the X on the right side of the form's task button.

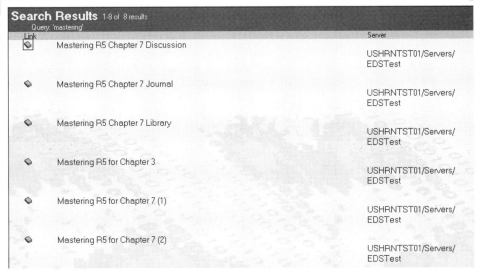

FIGURE 8.10

A Database Search Results form

Searching for Documents

To perform simple searches of documents, select the Documents radio button, enter your criteria in the Containing field, and click the Search button on the form. A Search Results form similar to the one shown in Figure 8.11 will be opened to display the results of your search.

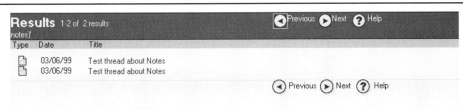

FIGURE 8.11

A Document Search Results form

This time, each document containing the string you entered will be displayed as a row on the form. The title of each document will be formatted as a link. Click the title to open the document. To close the Search Results form, press Escape or click the *X* on the right side of the form's task button.

When the Documents radio button is selected on the Search Form, a number of options are made available to you. You can choose to display the results in a summary fashion or with more details by selecting Terse Results or Detailed Results, respectively. You can also change the sort order of the results by selecting a choice from the Sort By drop-down list box. The Relevance option instructs Notes to sort the results by the

PART

II

Mastering the Basics

number of occurrences of the search string in each document, with documents containing the highest number of occurrences displayed first. The Oldest First option instructs Notes to sort the results by the date the documents were modified, with the documents containing the earliest date displayed first. Newest First is just the opposite, with the documents containing the latest date displayed first. The More tab expands a hidden section on the Domain Search form that contains additional options for creating more advanced domain searches.

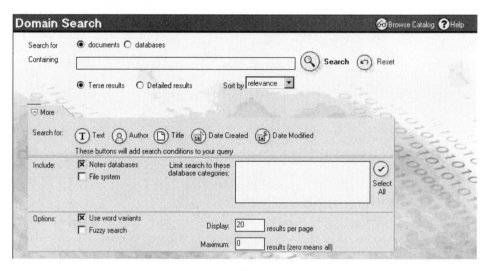

The Search For part of this section is for defining the search criteria. There are five buttons, which add search criteria rows for you to enter additional criteria. You can add up to eight criteria rows. The following shows a row created by clicking the Text button.

The first drop-down box allows you to select an operator; the choices are And, Or, and Not. These work the same way they work for view searches. The second drop-down box allows you to change what to search for. The choices are the same as they are for the Search For buttons and include Text, Author, Title, Date Created, and Date Modified. You can use this option if you clicked the wrong Search For button or if you decide to change what you were searching for. The third drop-down box allows you to choose how the data entered in the fourth field should be used. The choices change based on what you are searching for. When the Search For choice is Text, Author, or

Title, the options are Contains and Does Not Contain. For Date Created and Date Modified, the choices are as follows:

- Is On
- Is After
- Is Before
- Is Between
- Is Not Between
- Is Not On

Entering criteria is very similar to using conditions when searching views, which is explained earlier in this chapter. On the right side of each criteria row is a button with an *X*. If you click the button, that criteria row will be removed.

The Include part of the hidden section contains options for determining the scope of the search. You can use the check boxes labeled Notes Databases and File System to determine whether or not the search should include Notes databases and server-based file systems. If you include Notes databases in the search, you can further limit the categories of databases to include by selecting them in the list box to the right. Figure 8.12 shows a Search Result form generated using a search that included Notes databases and server-based file systems.

FIGURE 8.12

A Document Search Results form with file system documents

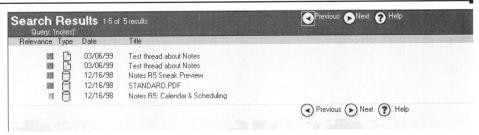

Again, each document meeting your search criteria will be displayed as a row on the form. This time, notice that there are two different icons displayed in the Type column. The database icon indicates that the document resides in a file system, and the page icon indicates that the document resides in a Notes database. As before, the title of each document will be formatted as a link, and clicking the title will open the document. To close the Search Results form, press Escape or click the *X* on the right side of the Search Results form's task button.

The Options part of the hidden section contains search options. The Use Word Variants, Fuzzy Search, and Maximum Results options function the same as they do in a view search (see "Using Search Options" earlier in this chapter). Display Results per Page determines how many documents will be displayed on the Search Result form.

Adding Databases to the Domain Index

If you are the owner of a database that you would like included in domain searches, you may have to add it to the *Domain Index*. The Domain Index is a full-text index maintained on the Domino server for use with Domain Search. This index is created when Domain Search is enabled. It is updated on a schedule defined by the person who configures Domain Search, usually an administrator. You can include a database in the Domain Index by setting the Include in Multi Database Indexing property on the Design tab of the Database Properties InfoBox. To set this property, follow these steps:

1. Open the database that you would like added to the Domain Index.

2. Select File ➤ Database ➤ Properties. The Database Properties InfoBox will be displayed with the Basics tab active.

3. Click the Design tab. The Design tab of the Database Properties InfoBox will look like Figure 8.13.

4. Select the Include in Multi Database Indexing check box.

FIGURE 8.13

*The Design tab of the
Database Properties
InfoBox*

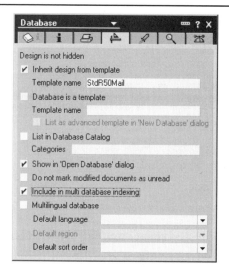

This database will be added to the Domain Index the next time the Domain Index process runs on the Domino server.

NOTE You must have Manager access to set the Include in Multi Database Indexing property. We have assumed that you (the database owner) have the authority to set this property even though many environments require that an administrator set it.

Using the Content Map

Generally, the administrator of the Domino domain will create the taxonomy that will be used to classify documents. This taxonomy is stored in the Domain Catalog. For the purpose of this discussion, we will assume that the default taxonomy has been used. Also, the Domain Catalog is configured to allow all Notes users to add document content by default. Some installations may restrict this, but we will assume that you have the ability to add document content to the Domain Catalog.

As with Domain Search, you must have a Catalog/Domain Search server defined in your Location document in order to work with the Content Map. The Catalog/Domain Search server is defined on the Servers tab of your Location document. See Chapter 13 for more information on configuring the Location document.

As a user, you can browse the Content Map contained in the Domain Catalog and you can post documents to it. The easiest way to browse the Content Map is to bring up the Domain Search form (explained earlier) and click the Browse Catalog button on the upper right side of the form. Follow these steps:

1. Click the arrow to the right of the Search button on the Navigation bar. The Search button menu will appear.

2. Select Domain Search. The Domain Search form will be displayed.

3. Click the Browse Catalog button. The catalog database will be opened and the Content by Category view will be displayed (see Figure 8.14).

FIGURE 8.14

The Content by Category view of the catalog database

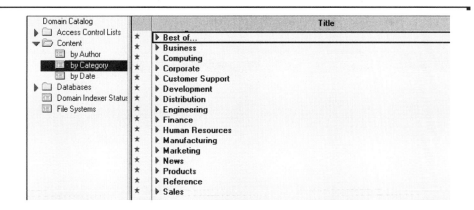

This is a categorized view of content documents. The documents are links to documents in other Notes databases. They are created when you post a document to the domain Content Map. You can navigate around this view as you can others that we have discussed earlier in the book. The taxonomy shown represents the categories entered by users when they posted documents to the Content Map. To view the document represented by the content document, just double-click the title.

The Content Map is not just a random set of links to other documents. First, it is based on a taxonomy (structure) that helps users find information by content. Second, these links are added after someone reviews a piece of information and decides that others may benefit from it. For this reason, the Content Map is really more of a representation of a group's knowledge.

As you can see, the Content Map is of limited value unless it contains content documents. There are a few different ways this can be accomplished:

- Create a Document Content entry directly in the domain catalog.
- Post documents from Notes databases.
- Programmatically add Document Content entries.

We'll limit our discussion to posting documents from Notes databases. When you come across a document that you think would benefit others, you can then go through the process of posting it to the catalog. To post a document to the catalog, follow these steps:

1. Open the database containing the document you want to add to the Content Map.

2. In the view, select the document you want added (or open the document).

3. Select File ➤ Document Properties. The Document Properties InfoBox will be displayed.

4. Select the Meta tab. The InfoBox will look like Figure 8.15.

FIGURE 8.15

The Meta tab of the Document Properties InfoBox

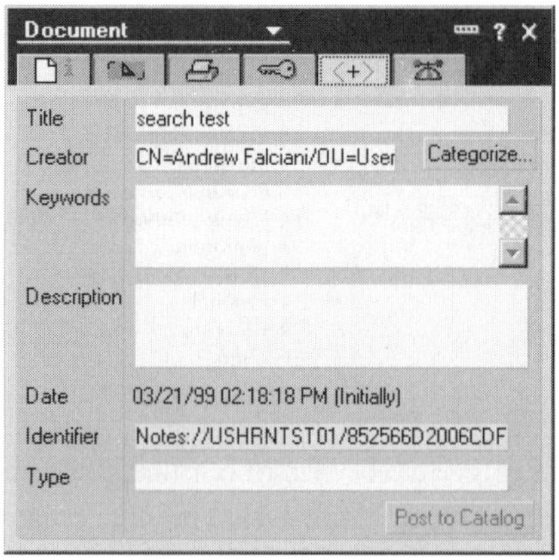

5. Click the Categorize button. The Domain Categorize dialog box will be displayed.

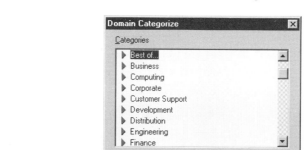

6. Select the category or categories under which you would like this document classified.

7. Click the OK button. The category or categories selected will appear in the Keywords field on the Meta tab of the Document Properties InfoBox.

8. You can optionally add a description and change the other attributes (e.g., Title, Creator, Type).

9. Click the Post to Catalog button. A Document Content entry will be added to the Content Map.

 NOTE You can manually enter categories in the Keywords field. This is a quick way to expand the taxonomy. Keep in mind, though, that this is free-form data entry and mistakes can be propagated to the Content Map.

Searching the Internet

Notes Release 5 includes an interface for searching the Internet from within Notes directly. This is provided by the Web browser capabilities of Notes. You must have Notes configured for Web browsing for the Internet Search feature to work. Web browsing settings are defined on the Internet Browser tab of your Location document. See Chapter 13 and Chapter 14 for more information on configuring the Location document.

You access Internet Search by clicking the arrow to the right of the Search button on the Navigation bar. This displays a Search button menu.

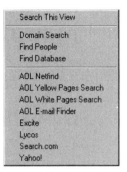

From the Search button menu, select the Internet search site you would like to use. This will bring up the search site's Web page in a new browser form. Just enter your search request as you would if you were using this search site outside of Notes. If your favorite search site is not listed on the Search button menu, you can add it. To do so, follow these steps:

1. Open your search site's Web page by entering the URL in the Open URL box (click the Open URL button on the Navigation bar if the URL box is not already open). The Web page will be opened in a new browser form.

2. Click the browser form's task button and drag it to the More Bookmarks/Internet Search Sites folder.

Notes uses this special folder for defining which search sites are displayed on the Search button menu.

Summary

You now understand how Notes can be used to find information stored in Notes databases. You can find text in individual documents or search for documents in views within specific databases. You can also use Domain Search to find information in databases that are stored on any Domino server in a domain. Domain Search can even be used to find data stored on file systems anywhere in the domain. We have also explained how Notes can be used as an interface for accessing Internet-based search sites. In the next chapter, we'll discuss how Notes can be used as a mobile client.

PART III

Advanced Use
of Notes 5

CHAPTER 9

Working with Notes Away from the Office

FEATURING:

One of the most powerful features of Lotus Notes is that it can operate as a mobile client. Notes provides the same rich application experience whether it is connected to a Domino server or operating in a disconnected, stand-alone mode. It incorporates dial-up communication facilities for seamlessly accessing Domino servers or Internet Service Provider (ISP) accounts. Notes also includes a sophisticated replication capability for keeping local copies of databases synchronized with their counterparts stored on the Domino server. Release 5 even uses the replication capabilities to keep locally stored Internet-based information synchronized—for example, Internet Message Access Protocol (IMAP) mail data and Network News Transfer Protocol (NNTP) discussions. We will explore these features in this chapter.

Working with Database Replicas

Notes can open and interact with Notes databases whether they are stored locally or on a Domino server. This is the key to Notes's ability to work offline (disconnected from a Domino server). No matter where the database is stored, Notes provides you with the same rich application experience.

What are database replicas? The answer is critical to understanding how to work with Notes offline. Well, database replicas are really just special copies of Notes databases. It may sound simple, but that's it. Replicas are copies that contain the same replica ID as the original database. The replica ID is a special code generated when a database is created. You can view the replica ID by opening the Database Properties InfoBox. Follow these steps to view the replica ID of a database:

1. Open the database for which you would like to view the replica ID.
2. Select File ➤ Database ➤ Properties.
3. Click the Info tab.

The replica ID will be listed at the bottom of the Info tab. This is a good troubleshooting tool. You can use the Database Properties InfoBox to verify that two databases have the same replica ID.

One important aspect of database replicas is that they are on a peer level with the original database. Notes and Domino treat the databases the same regardless of which is the original and which is the copy. In fact, they both are referred to as replicas. Replication, the process of synchronizing replicas, does not rely on which database was the original and which was the copy either. Replication depends only on the direction in which it was invoked (send, receive, or both), security, replication settings in each replica, and document changes contained in each replica.

That said, it is also important to note that replicas could contain a subset of the information contained in the original. You can choose to include documents meeting a certain criteria. For example, you could create a replica of a database that tracks sales leads and only includes customers in your region. You could also choose to include only documents added or modified in the last 30 days. If you base the criteria on the form name specified on documents, you can include certain types of documents in a replica. For example, you could create a replica of your mail database that only contains To Do list entries. When you create replicas that contain a subset of the information in a database, the original acts as a master copy of the database.

Creating Database Replicas

Database replicas can be created on Notes workstations or on Domino servers. Because this chapter focuses on using Notes offline, we'll limit our discussion to database replicas created on Notes workstations. Also, we'll assume that the advanced Access Control List (ACL) option, Enforce a Consistent Access Control List Across All Replicas of This Database, has not been enabled. This will allow us to explore the full range of features for database replicas created on Notes workstations. Enabling this option restricts what users can do with locally stored databases replicas, but the restriction it places on users is not very secure. This option is more important in providing support for roles when databases are stored locally on a Notes workstation.

One common scenario in which you would create database replicas is when you use a notebook computer both in the office and away from the office. You can place replicas of key databases on your notebook computer's local disk drive so you can access them when you leave the office (without having to be connected to the Domino server). For example, you can place a replica of your mail database on your notebook computer so you can read messages or compose new ones while you are away from the office. You can also create a replica of an important discussion database so you can read topics others have posted, post new topics, or reply to existing topics, all without being connected to a Domino server. In this scenario, new documents that you create or existing documents that you modify while operating in a disconnected mode are stored locally in your replica copy of the database. When you connect back to the Domino server, these changes are synchronized with the server-based copy of the database through replication. (We will discuss replication in "Using Replication to Keep Databases Synchronized" later in this chapter.) You can also connect to the Domino server through dial-up communications while you're away from the office. (This is also discussed later in this chapter in "Connecting to Domino Servers through Dial-Up Communications.")

Another common scenario for creating database replicas is when you use two computers. For example you may use one computer at work and another at home. In this case, you probably connect to your office Domino server through dial-up communications, which is fairly slow. You could establish realtime access to the databases (which would be like opening them over the network in the office), but access would be sluggish. Alternatively, you could create replicas of key databases on your home computer's local disk drive so you can access them more quickly and without your dial-up communications connection active. Again, we'll discuss accessing Domino servers through dial-up communications later in this chapter.

There are a number of ways to create replicas:

- Create them through the Notes client.
- Use the Domino Administration client.
- Use the Domino Web Administration interface.
- Use LotusScript to create them programmatically.
- Copy the operating system file that represents a database.

 NOTE Copying the operating system file that represents a database is the same as creating a replica in Notes. If you connect to a Domino server's file system over a network—through Windows NT file/print services, for example—you can copy a database file to your computer. We recommend that you don't use this method, however, because you bypass Domino's security. Also, you will most likely be unable to access a Domino server's file system from your computer. Generally, Domino administrators are the only users with the authority to do so.

We'll focus on creating replicas through the Notes client because it is the most common method. You can create a database replica of any database for which you have at least Reader access. To create a database replica, follow these steps:

1. Open the database of which you would like to make a replica.

2. Select File ➢ Replication ➢ New Replica. The New Replica dialog box will be displayed (Figure 9.1).

FIGURE 9.1

The New Replica dialog box

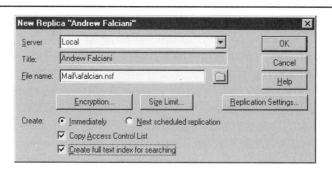

3. Leave the Server field set to Local. This instructs Notes to create the database replica on your computer's disk drive in your Notes Data directory, which is c:\Lotus\Notes\Data by default.

4. Choose a filename for the database replica. The File Name field will default to the filename of the original database. If you want to store the database replica in a subdirectory under your Data directory, either type the name of the subdirectory in the File Name field or click the folder button to the right of the File Name field and select from the list presented in the Choose a Folder dialog box.

5. Select the Immediately radio button so the database replica is created now. If you choose Next Scheduled Replication, creation of the replica will be delayed until the next time your computer replicates with the Domino server on which the original is stored.

6. Select the Copy Access Control List check box. This instructs Notes to copy the original database's ACL to the database replica.

7. Select the Create Full Text Index for Searching check box if you would like Notes to create a full-text index when it creates the replica.

8. Click the OK button.

A replica stub database will be created using the filename specified in the Data directory or the directory you specified. The *replica stub* is an empty Notes database that is unusable until Notes copies the design and data from the original. Because you selected the Immediately radio button, Notes will begin the replication process, in which the original database's design and data will be copied to the replica.

 TIP If you would like to distribute replicas to other users, you can use the replica stub. The replica stub is a small file because it does not yet contain the database design or documents. For this reason, it is easy to attach it to an e-mail message and send it to other users. When users receive the replica stub, they just save the attachment to their Data directory and initiate replication.

The Encryption button will bring up a dialog box you can use to encrypt the database replica. This is a way of securing the local copy so it cannot be accessed without your user ID file. See Chapter 16, "Creating Your First Database," for more information on encrypting local copies of databases.

The Size Limit button brings up a dialog box that lets you set the maximum size for the database replica. This is only valid for Release 4 or lower database file formats. Release 5 no longer uses this maximum. The size of Release 5 databases is only limited by the disk drive on which they are created.

The Replication Settings button brings up the Replication Settings dialog box, which you can use to configure the database replica (see "Replication Settings" later in this chapter).

NOTE You can create non-replica copies of databases too. The design and data are copied, but a new replica ID for the new database is generated. This is valuable in situations where you don't want the new copy to be synchronized with the original database. See Chapter 16, "Creating Your First Database," for more information on creating new databases by copying existing ones.

Opening and Using Replicas

Opening a replica is no different than opening any other database. In fact, it *is* just another database. (For information on opening databases, see Chapter 3, "Working with Notes Databases.") Once you create a replica and Notes copies the original database's design to it, each bookmark that references the original database will now also reference the replica. Bookmarks default to opening the newly created replica unless you specify otherwise. To find out the replica to which a bookmark points, right-click the bookmark and select Open Replica. A menu listing all replicas of the database and an option called Manage List will be displayed. The replica to which the bookmark is currently pointing will have a check mark next to it. Notes will open the replica you select and change the bookmark so it will open by default from now on.

 TIP To change the replica to which a bookmark points without actually opening the replica, just hold down Shift while selecting the replica.

The Manage List selection will bring up a Manage Replica Server List dialog box. You can use it to add and remove replica servers for individual databases. To have Notes query your catalog server's Domain Catalog for replica servers, click the Discover button.

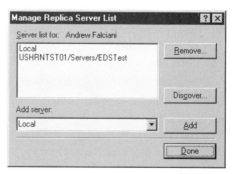

Again, replicas are just Notes databases. You can use them just as you would any other Notes database. You can navigate through views, read and modify existing documents, and create new documents. You can create full-text indexes on replicas so you can perform full-text searches. You can create subscriptions against them and set up archiving just as you can with any other database. The only difference is that replicas are synchronized with other copies. This means that changes you make to a replica stored locally on your computer are propagated to server-based copies of that database. And changes made to server-based copies are propagated to your local replica. It's just like working in the server-based copy except there is a delay between the time when you make changes and the time when others see those changes.

Security of Locally Stored Replicas

As we mentioned earlier, we assumed that the advanced Access Control List (ACL) option, Enforce a Consistent Access Control List Across All Replicas of This Database, was not enabled. This means that you actually have manager-level access to replicas stored locally on your computer. It also means that you can perform actions on these replicas that you would otherwise be unable to perform if the database was accessed from a Domino server. This sounds like a fairly large lapse in security, but don't worry. The replication process will ensure that access levels are observed. It will only allow changes back to the server-based copy that you are authorized to perform. For example, you could change the Access Control List of a locally stored replica because you have Manager access. But if you try to replicate this change back to the server-based copy, the replication process will fail. All other valid changes will be propagated.

With Manager access to locally stored replicas, you also have access to every document stored within those replicas. You could conceivably gain access to information that you would otherwise be unable to access on server-based copies. Again, this sounds like a lapse in security. In this case, there can be lapses in security if information controls are not properly implemented. At first glance, you might be inclined to enable the advanced Access Control List (ACL) option, Enforce a Consistent Access Control List Across All Replicas of This Database. This would provide some degree of security, but this option alone does not secure locally stored replicas. The only way to secure data in Notes databases is to mark them private, encrypt them, or restrict databases that users can access to make replicas.

Marking data private just means using readers fields to restrict who can see what documents. See Chapter 18 for information on using readers fields. Encrypted data is very secure, but it also adds some complexity. See Chapter 16 for more information on creating databases that use encryption. To restrict databases that users can access to make replicas, you have a number of options. One includes creating replicas that contain subsets of a database for specific groups of users. Then you can restrict access to the main (or master) database and the subset replicas on the Domino server so users are forced to use only the subset replica that is appropriate for them. Using readers fields to mark documents private is probably the easiest way to ensure that users have appropriate access to information regardless of where databases reside.

PART

III

Advanced Use of
Notes 5

Using Replication to Keep Databases Synchronized

Notes keeps database replicas synchronized through a process called *replication*. Replication can occur between two Domino servers or between Notes workstations and a Domino server. Because server-to-server replication is a Domino administration function, we won't cover it here. We'll focus instead on replication between a Notes workstation and a Domino server. This type of replication can be initiated in the foreground or background. Background replication is managed by the Notes Replicator, which is a feature that lets you predefine how you want local databases to replicate. Once configured, you can use the Notes Replicator to initiate replication for one or more databases while you work on other Notes tasks. It can even be configured to perform replication on a predefined schedule so your information is kept up-to-date without your intervention. With foreground replication, you can override the Notes Replicator definition and perform one-time replication events. Foreground replication requires that you wait for the process to complete before performing other tasks in Notes.

Replication operates at the document level. During replication, Notes compares the local database with the server-based replica and determines which documents are new, which have been modified, and which have been deleted in each. Then, Notes sends and/or receives document additions, updates, and deletions. When document updates are sent (or received), Notes only copies data from fields whose values have changed. Entire documents are not copied each time a change is made. This is called field-level replication, and it makes Notes replication efficient and fast.

Replication also operates within the security model of Notes and Domino. If you only have Reader access to a server-based replica with which you are replicating, you will only be able to receive new and updated data to your local replica. Changes made to your local replica will not be allowed to propagate to the server-based copy.

 NOTE Replication is independent from the method you use to connect to your Domino server. Replication functions the same way whether you are connected through a local area network (LAN), wide area network (WAN), or remote access service. As long as Notes is configured to connect to a Domino server, you will be able to replicate with it. When using Notes away from the office, you will generally use dial-up communications to replicate with Domino servers. We will discuss connecting Notes to Domino servers via dial-up communications later in this chapter.

Foreground Replication

Foreground replication allows you to perform one-time replication events. This is useful when you want to perform a one-time replication with a different server or with different options. You can choose to send only or receive only. If you choose to receive, you can choose to receive full documents, document summaries, or document summaries with a portion of the document. To initiate foreground replication, follow this procedure:

1. Open a database and select File ➤ Replication ➤ Replicate (or right-click a database bookmark and select Replication ➤ Replicate from the context menu). The Replicate dialog box will be displayed (Figure 9.2).

FIGURE 9.2

The Replication dialog box

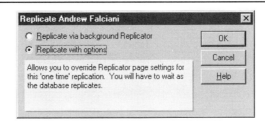

2. Select the Replicate with Options radio button.

3. Click the OK button. The Replicate options dialog box will be displayed (Figure 9.3).

FIGURE 9.3

The Replicate options dialog box

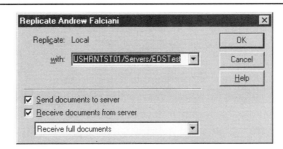

4. Choose a Domino server with which to replicate from the drop-down box. The list is based on which server replicas you have previously used or added to your bookmarks.

5. Select the Send Documents to Server check box, Receive Documents from Server check box, or both.

6. If you're receiving documents, select the receive method you wish to use from the drop-down box below the Receive Documents from Server check box.

7. Click the OK button.

PART

III

Advanced Use of
Notes 5

Notes will display a message box indicating the replication status. When replication completes, the Replication Statistics dialog box will be displayed.

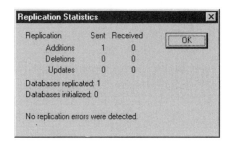

This dialog box shows you how many additions, deletions, and updates were sent and received. It also shows you how many databases were replicated, how many databases were initialized, and whether or not errors occurred during replication. Click the OK button to close it and continue with other Notes tasks. If errors occurred during replication, you can check the Notes log database for more details on the errors. See Chapter 13, "Setting Up Notes as a Domino Client," for more information on the Notes log database.

Background Replication Using the Notes Replicator

The Notes Replicator is a feature that performs a process that executes on your computer when Notes is running to perform background replication. When replication is performed in the background, you don't have to wait for it to complete in order to work on other Notes tasks. You can read your e-mail, manage your To Do list, or participate in a discussion database while background replication is processing. The Notes Replicator also processes e-mail in the background. It pulls e-mail messages from POP3 and IMAP4 mail servers, and it sends Domino and SMTP mail to remote servers. You just configure how you want background replication and e-mail processing to occur and enable a schedule if necessary, and the Notes Replicator will automatically keep your local databases synchronized and your e-mail messages flowing.

Using the Replicator Page to Configure Background Replication   You can configure how you want background replication and e-mail processing to occur by choosing settings on the Replicator page. To bring up the Replicator page, click the Replicator icon. The Replicator page has an Action bar and rows representing replication entries, as shown in Figure 9.4.

Each entry represents a database, an e-mail process, or a special action. The check box located on each Replicator page row determines whether or not the entry is enabled. For replication and e-mail entries, there is also an options button (the button with the arrow) on each row; the arrow indicates replication direction. You can click this button to set replication options for the entry. Special action entries also have options buttons you can click to set options for the special action.

FIGURE 9.4

*An example
Replicator page*

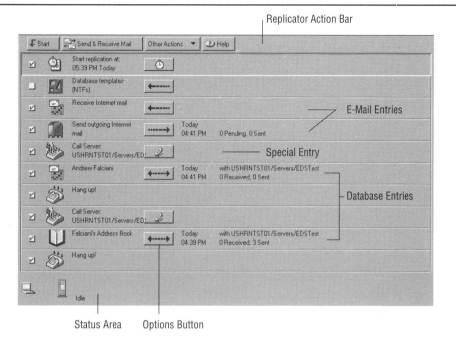

Status Area   Options Button

For database entries, the Replication options dialog box that is presented is the same as the one described for foreground replication. You can set server and send/receive options. The only difference is the server selection drop-down box. In this case, you can select a Domino server or you can select a choice that will enable Notes to try multiple servers. The first choice, Any Available, Try Last Successful First, will instruct Notes to use any server listed but to start by trying the server used in the last successful replication. For each Domino server listed, there will be a corresponding Any Available, Try *Servername* First, which instructs Notes to use any server listed but to start by trying the corresponding Domino server.

The Replication options dialog box presented for send and receive e-mail entries just displays a message stating how that entry sends or receives mail. The configuration of Domino e-mail send entries is performed by modifying the current Location document. The configuration of Internet e-mail send and receive entries is performed by modifying the appropriate Account documents. See Chapter 13, "Setting Up Notes as a Domino Client," and Chapter 14, "Setting Up Notes as an Internet Client," for more information on modifying these documents.

The options button on the Start Replication At row on the Replication page brings up the current Location document so you can click the Replication tab and set a replication schedule. The options button on the Local Free Time Info row brings up the Local Free Time Settings dialog box. See Chapter 6, "Calendaring and Scheduling," for more information on participating in Domino calendaring and scheduling offline. The options button on Call Server entries brings up the Call Server dialog box for

PART

III

**Advanced Use of
Notes 5**

configuring dial-up communication to Domino servers. This is discussed later in this chapter. Hang Up entries have no options button. The options button on the Database Templates row brings up a dialog box that allows you to choose a Domino server with which you want to replicate templates.

If you double-click a database entry, Notes will open the local replica of the associated database. For e-mail send entries, Notes will open the appropriate outbound message storage database. In the case of Domino e-mail send entries, the `mail.box` database will be opened. For Internet e-mail send entries, the `smtp.box` database will be opened. The only special entry that opens a database when double-clicked is the Local Free Time Info entry. Double-clicking this entry opens the `busytime.nsf` database, which contains entries for each person for which you maintain free time information.

 NOTE The Replicator page is related to the current Location document. Any settings you change are saved with the current Location document. This is a powerful feature because you can establish multiple replication configurations and each is specific to a particular Notes configuration.

Manual Background Replication   With the Notes Replicator configuration defined, you can now initiate background replication. Here, we will explore how this is performed manually. Manual background replication is important because it allows you to update a specific database or send/receive e-mail without waiting for the next scheduled event. You can perform the following tasks:

- Initiate all enabled Replicator entries
- Initiate all enabled e-mail send and receive entries
- Replicate all high-priority databases
- Replicate with a specific server
- Replicate a single database
- Send outgoing e-mail

These functions can be performed by clicking the appropriate button (or button menu selection) on the Replicator Action bar shown in Figure 9.4:

Start   Initiates all enabled Replicator entries, including e-mail entries.

Send and Receive Mail   Initiates all enabled e-mail send and receive entries.

Other Actions/Replicate High Priority Databases   Initiates replication for all databases marked as high priority. You can mark a database as high priority by modifying its replication settings.

Other Actions/Replicate with Server   Brings up a dialog box that lets you choose a server with which to replicate. Clicking the OK button in this dialog box initiates replication to the server selected for all enabled Replicator entries.

Other Actions/Replicate Selected Database Initiates replication with the selected Replicator page entry's database.

Other Actions/Send Outgoing Mail Initiates all enabled e-mail send entries.

The Replicator establishes a connection to Domino servers specified in Replicator page entries the same way Notes does when opening server-based databases. It uses the current Location document to determine what connection types are configured. If the server is not available directly, Connection documents visible to the current Location document are used to establish the connection. The current Location document, combined with associated Account documents, is also used to determine how mail send and receive entries are processed.

 TIP Right-clicking an entry will display a context menu that allows you to set options for that entry, initiate replication for the selected entry, access a database's replication settings, access a database's replication history, or set an entry to be high priority.

Scheduled Background Replication With the Notes Replicator configuration defined, you can also initiate background replication on a predetermined schedule. Scheduled background replication is important because it allows you to keep all of your database up-to-date without any manual intervention. It also ensures that your e-mail is received and delivered without any action required by you. In effect, you work as you normally would if you were in the office interacting directly with a Domino server. The Start Replication At entry on the Replicator page shows the status of scheduled replication and whether or not it is enabled. If not, you can click the check box to enable it. You can also modify the schedule from this page. To modify the replication schedule, follow these steps:

1. Select the Start Replication At row's options button. The current Location document will be opened in Edit mode.

2. In this Location document, select the Replication tab at the top. The replication schedule settings will be displayed (Figure 9.5).

3. Select Enabled from the Schedule drop-down box.

4. Configure the schedule as described in the next paragraph.

5. Select Enabled from the High Priority Replication drop-down box if a separate schedule for high-priority databases is desired.

6. Configure the high-priority schedule as described in the next paragraph.

7. Click the Save and Close button on the Location document's Form Action bar.

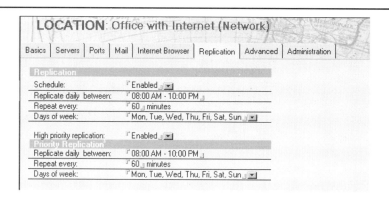

The Location document will be closed and you will be returned to the Replicator page. Background replication will now occur on the schedule you defined. Defining a schedule involves entering values for the following fields:

Replicate Daily Between   Defines the period or periods of time that the Replicator should initiate background replication. It is usually entered as a range (e.g., 6:00 AM - 10:00 PM). You can also enter individual times, which instructs the Replicator to initiate background replication at that time. If you want to replicate continuously, enter a range that covers a 24-hour period (e.g., 6:00 AM - 5:59 AM).

Repeat Every   Defines the repeat interval, in minutes, within the range of times defined in the Replicate Daily Between option. The Replicator will repeat background replication every time this interval of time passes.

Days of Week   Determines which days of the week are included in this schedule.

NOTE   These fields are repeated in the Priority Replication section if you enable high-priority replication.

Finally, Call and Hangup entries can be added to the Replicator page before and after specific entries. This is useful if you replicate with servers that are reachable via different dial-up connections. Without these entries, Notes will automatically call remote servers (that have associated Connection documents) to initiate replication of databases configured on the Replicator page. However, it would not normally disconnect immediately after completing replication for a specific entry. Many times, entries following this one would fail because the connection was still active. Now, you can add a Call entry before one or more Replication entries and a Hangup entry after, and Notes will be able to make successive calls in the same background replication cycle.

Replication Conflicts and Save Conflicts

Replication conflicts occur when multiple people change the same document in different replicas between replication cycles. Notes deals with these situations by designating one of the changed copies as a Main document and making the other a response to it. It determines which document has been modified more times and designates it as the Main document. If both have been modified the same number of times, Notes determines which was saved most recently and designates this as the Main document. The response is marked with a diamond in the View Icon area.

The database designer can choose to enable a property that will allow Notes to merge replication conflicts into a single document. This instructs Notes to determine whether or not the same field was changed in each document, thus causing the conflict. If not, it will merge all changes into a single document. If the same field was changed in both documents, Notes saves the replication conflict as described in the preceding paragraph.

Save conflicts are similar to replication conflicts except they occur when multiple people change the same document in the same database on a Domino server. For save conflicts, Notes designates the first document saved as the Main document. When other users try to save their copy, Notes displays a prompt asking if they would like to save it as a save conflict. If so, the document is saved as a response to the Main document and marked with a diamond in the View Icon area.

When replication conflicts and save conflicts occur, you have two choices:

- Save changes from conflict responses into the Main document and delete all conflict responses.
- Save changes from conflict responses and the Main document into a conflict response, save this conflict response as a Main document, and delete the original Main document and all conflict responses.

You can use copy/paste to save changes from one document to another. Chapter 11, "Integrating Notes with Other Applications," has more information on using copy/paste. To save a conflict response as a Main document, you can follow this procedure:

1. Open the Conflict Response document in Edit mode.

2. Select File ➤ Save.

The Response document will be saved as a Main document. Deleting conflict responses is the same as deleting any other document. See Chapter 3, "Working with Notes Databases," for more information on deleting documents.

Replication Settings

Replication settings determine the characteristics of a database replica. These settings can be used to set up selective replication (or replication of subsets of documents). This is helpful when you need to replicate a large database to your computer's local disk drive, but you don't have space to store the entire database. Selective replication can also be used to limit replication to recently added or modified documents. There is also a priority attribute, which is used in scheduled replication. You can also configure a replica as follows:

- Not send deletes, title/catalog changes, or security changes to other replicas
- Only replicates between specific servers
- Not replicate design elements

Replication settings can be viewed and modified through the Replication Settings dialog box. There are a number of ways to bring up this dialog box:

- Open the database and select File ➤ Replication ➤ Settings.
- Right-click a database bookmark and select Replication ➤ Settings from the context menu.
- Right-click a database entry on the Replicator page and select Replication Settings.

The Replication Settings dialog box includes four buttons on the left side, which represent different categories of replication settings:

- Space Savers
- Send
- Other
- Advanced

Space Savers   When you click the Space Savers button, the Replication Settings dialog box displays the Space Savers settings. The Space Savers section allows you to choose to remove documents that have not been modified in a certain period of time. This is also where you can configure Notes to replicate subsets of documents. You can choose to only replicate documents contained in certain views or folders, and you can choose to define your own criteria using the formula language. See Chapter 17, "Understanding the Formula Language," for more information on formulas.

NOTE   When documents are deleted from a database, Notes retains a delete record for the document. Notes uses this delete record to ensure that the document is removed from all replicas of the database. By default, Notes purges delete records after 30 days (this is called the *purge interval*). If you set a value in the field labeled Remove Documents Not Modified in the Last, the purge interval is one-third the number of days entered. For example, the purge interval is 20 days if you enter 60. Make sure to replicate at least one time during the purge interval to receive deletes made from other replicas.

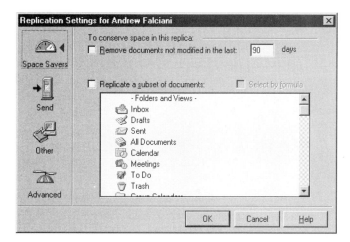

Send   When you click the Send button, the Replication Settings dialog box displays the Send settings. The Send section allows you to choose whether or not to send deletions, title and catalog changes, and security changes to other replicas.

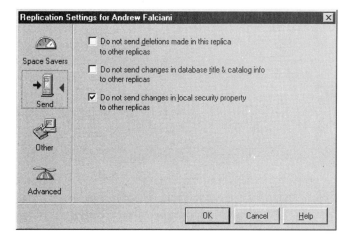

Other   When you click the Other button, the Replication Settings dialog box displays the Other settings. The Other section allows you to temporarily disable replication, set a scheduled replication priority, limit incoming replication by date, and establish a CD publishing date. Temporarily disabling replication is useful when you want to skip replication for a specific database without changing your configuration.

PART

III

Advanced Use of
Notes 5

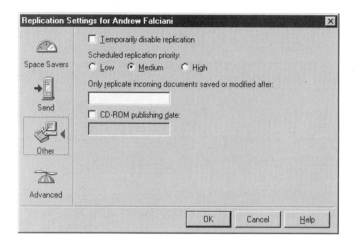

NOTE When you enter a CD-ROM publishing date, Notes only scans for documents created or modified since this date during the first replication. This is helpful when you are using large databases that you receive via CD-ROM.

Advanced   When you click the Advanced button, the Replication Settings dialog box displays the Advanced settings. The Advanced section allows you to choose a specific computer on which this replica will be included in replication. You can also choose a specific server with which this replica should replicate. When this replica is located on a different computer or attempts to replicate with a different server, no replication will occur. You can also configure Notes to replicate subsets of documents in this section; it is a repeat of the settings in the Space Savers section. The check boxes at the bottom allow you to choose specific design elements to replicate. You can also choose individual fields if necessary.

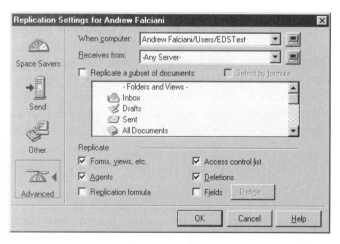

NOTE Replication settings can also be set when the replica is created by clicking the Replication Settings button in the New Replica dialog box.

Replication History

Replication history is maintained in each database. It contains information about previous replication with specific servers. Notes uses this information to determine what documents need to be replicated.

Replication history is viewed through the Replication History dialog box. There are a number of ways to bring up this dialog box:

- Open the database and select File ➤ Replication ➤ History.

- Right-click a database bookmark and select Replication ➤ History from the context menu.

- Right-click a database entry on the Replicator page and select Replication History.

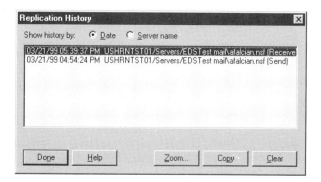

In the Replication History dialog box, you can sort the entries by date or by server. If replication is not properly synchronizing replicas, you can clear the replication history. This forces Notes to reanalyze the documents to determine which ones to include in future replication. You can clear individual history entries or the entire replication history for the database. To clear an individual history entry, perform this procedure:

1. With the Replication History dialog box open, click the Zoom button.

2. Click the Remove button.

Notes will prompt you to verify that you want to remove this history entry. To clear the entire replication history, click the Clear button in the Replication History dialog box. Notes will prompt you to verify that you want to remove the entire replication history for this database.

PART

III

Advanced Use of
Notes 5

Connecting to Domino Servers through Dial-Up Communications

If you use Domino servers at work, you generally access them through a local area network (LAN). This is a communication mechanism that typically connects computers that are physically located in the same building. Most commonly, LANs are based on Ethernet networking technology and provide high-speed access to servers. This technology is referred to as "always on." The connection is never broken. You just configure Notes for the appropriate protocol—that is, Transmission Control Protocol/Internet Protocol (TCP/IP)—and it accesses the Domino server as needed.

You may also connect to Domino servers through your company's wide area network (WAN). WANs typically connect computers that are physically located in different buildings, many times in different geographic areas. A WAN is usually a lower-speed communication mechanism than a LAN is, but it is generally associated with "always on" technologies. Again, you just configure Notes for the appropriate protocol and it accesses the Domino server as needed.

When accessing Domino servers remotely, you are usually forced to use dial-up communication technologies with a modem attached to your computer and normal telephone lines. This includes accessing Domino servers from home, from a client's site, and from a hotel room while you are traveling. The major difference between this type of communications and "always on" communications is that your computer must connect to the network before Notes can access the Domino server. Notes supports two methods for making this connection:

- Notes Direct Dialup
- Network Dialup

Notes Direct Dialup occurs when Notes initiates the process of dialing through your computer's modem directly to a modem attached to the Domino server. Network Dialup occurs when Notes initiates the process of dialing through your computer's modem to a network dial-in server (or ISP) that provides access to the Domino server.

Notes Direct Dialup

Notes Direct Dialup is considered the "legacy" method of remotely connecting to Domino servers. With network dial-up technology included in both Windows (95, 98, and NT) and MacOS and the popularity of network dial-up solutions, the need for Notes Direct Dialup has been reduced somewhat. In addition, Notes Direct Dialup is slightly more complicated when the environment includes multiple Domino servers.

Notes Direct Dialup is a solid solution, but network dial-up solutions can be leveraged for all remote access needs, whereas Notes Direct Dialup can only be used for remote Notes access. With that said, there are a number of areas where Notes Direct Dialup still provides added value, for example:

- Higher security
- Existing infrastructure

Arguably, Notes Direct Dialup is somewhat more secure than network dial-up solutions because the Domino server only accepts calls from Notes clients and all of the inherent security of Domino is applied to the dial-up connection. This may be valuable in environments where network dial-up is not an option. Because Notes Direct Dialup has been an integral part of Notes since its inception, there may be environments that already have properly configured Domino servers. In this case, Notes Direct Dialup may be preferred.

Setting Up Notes Direct Dialup

As previously mentioned, Notes Direct Dialup requires that the target Domino server have at least one modem (and telephone line) installed and be configured to accept dial-in calls. The Domino administrator usually performs the configuration. We will assume that you have this configuration in place. Also, Notes Direct Dialup requires that you have a modem installed on your computer. We will assume that you have properly installed your modem and Windows has assigned port COM2 to the device. If Windows has assigned a different port to your modem, just substitute it in the following example.

In Notes, you need to configure three items:

- The Notes communications port associated with your computer's modem
- The Ports to Use field in the Location document
- A Notes Direct Dialup Connection document that defines how Notes will connect to your Domino server

The first item you need to configure is the Notes communications port. The Notes communications port establishes an association between Notes and the modem installed on your computer. This association allows Notes to "talk" to the attached modem. To enable and set up a Notes communications port, follow these steps:

1. Select File ➣ Preferences ➣ User Preferences. The User Preferences dialog box will be displayed.

2. In the User Preferences dialog box, click the Ports button. The User Preferences dialog box's Ports page will be displayed (see Figure 9.6).

PART

III

Advanced Use of
Notes 5

FIGURE 9.6

*The Ports page in the
User Preferences
dialog box*

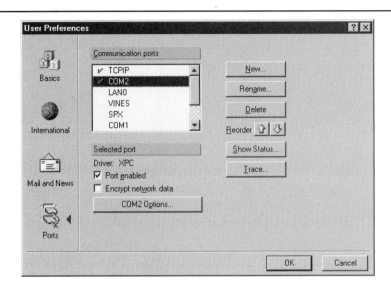

3. By default, a set of port entries (including COM2) will be displayed in the Communication Ports list box. Select the COM2 entry.

4. Select the Port Enabled check box to enable this port.

5. Click the COM2 Options button. The Additional Setup dialog box will be displayed (Figure 9.7).

FIGURE 9.7

*The Additional Setup
dialog box*

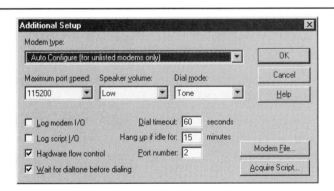

6. Select your modem from the list or select Auto Configure (for Unlisted Modems Only) if your modem is not listed.

7. Select a value from the Maximum Port Speed drop-down box. You can try a value that is twice your modem's speed and then drop to lower speeds if you have problems.

8. Make sure that Port Number matches the Windows port assigned to your modem (without the letters *COM*). In our example, Port Number is set to 2.

9. Change other dialing parameters as required and click the OK button. You will be returned to the User Preferences dialog box's Ports page.

10. Click the OK button to enable the port.

The communications port you enabled (COM2 in our example) will be immediately available for use. There are other options that you can configure in the Additional Setup dialog box. When enabled, Log Modem I/O and Log Script I/O will report activity to your Notes log. These are good debugging tools to use if you are having trouble with Notes Direct Dialup connections. The Modem File button will display the Edit Modem Command File dialog box, in which you can make changes to the modem command file. This file defines how Notes "talks" to your computer's modem. The Acquire Script button will display the Acquire Script dialog box, which allows you to select and optionally edit acquire scripts. Acquire scripts define how Notes "talks" to modems that are available through a communication server, which is a device that provides shared pools of modems over a network. See the Lotus Notes Mobile Survival Kit for more information on modem command files and acquire scripts.

NOTE Lotus maintains a Mobile Survival Kit, which is available from its customer support Web site. This is a database of modem command files and other resources for mobile users. Go to www.support.lotus.com and click on the Downloads link or the Top 10 Files link. The file to download is named msk.exe.

Next, you need to configure the Ports to Use field in your Location document. This field determines which Notes communications ports are actually available to Notes. When you enable a Notes communication port in the User Preferences dialog box as we did in the preceding steps, it is automatically enabled in the current Location document's Ports to Use field. Let's verify that the COM2 port previously enabled has been enabled in the Location document:

1. Select File ➢ Mobile ➢ Edit Current Location. Your current Location document will be opened in Edit mode.

2. Click the Ports tab. The Ports to Use field will be displayed (Figure 9.8).

PART

III

Advanced Use of Notes 5

FIGURE 9.8

FIGURE 9.8

The Location document's Ports tab

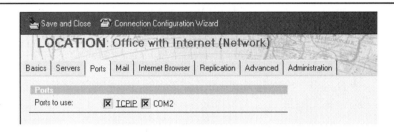

3. Verify that the COM2 check box is checked.

4. Click the Save and Close button on the Form Action bar.

Finally, you need to create a Notes Direct Dialup Connection document that defines how Notes will connect to your Domino server. To create a Notes Direct Dialup Connection document, follow these steps:

1. Select File ➤ Mobile ➤ Server Phone Numbers. Your Personal Address Book will be opened with the Connections view displayed. All existing Connection documents will be listed.

2. Click the Add Connection button on the View Action bar. A blank Connection form will be displayed.

3. Select Notes Direct Dialup from the Connection Type drop-down box. The Basics tab will be displayed by default (Figure 9.9).

FIGURE 9.9

The Notes Direct Dialup Connection Basics tab

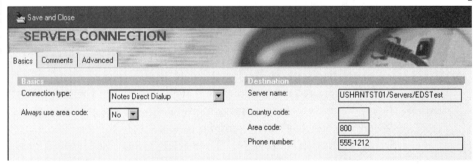

4. Fill in the Server Name, Area Code, and Phone Number fields in the Destination section.

5. Click the Save and Close button on the Form Action bar.

The Notes Direct Dialup Connection document will be created and you will be returned to the Connections view of your Personal Address Book. Notes Direct Dialup

Connection documents can be further customized using the Advanced tab on the Connection form.

The following options are on the Advanced tab:

Only from Location(s)   Defaults to an asterisk, which enables Notes to use this Connection document regardless of your current location. If you would like to restrict a Connection document to specific locations, select them from this list box.

Only for User   Restricts the Connection document to specific users. Enter an asterisk to make this Connection document available to any user who uses Notes from this workstation.

Usage Priority   Used by Notes to determine the order in which it uses Connection documents.

Modem Port(s)   Lets you select the asterisk or individual ports. Selecting the asterisk instructs Notes to use any available port to connect to the server.

Login Script File Name/ Login Script Arguments   Used to define login script information for the connection. The Mobile Survival Kit is a good resource for information about login scripts.

Only to Servers in Domain   Used to restrict the Connection document to a specific domain. Enter an asterisk to allow this Connection document to be used with any domain or enter a domain name.

TIP You can also use the Connection Configuration Wizard to create Connection documents. This wizard is available from the Location form as long as Location Type is set to Notes Direct Dialup or Custom.

Manually Connecting Using Notes Direct Dialup

With Notes Direct Dialup set up, you can connect to the Domino servers manually or automatically. Generally, you connect manually to the Domino server when you need to interact online. For example, you would connect manually to create a replica of a server-based database on your computer's local disk drive. You would also connect manually if you needed to open the server-based copy of a database when you're away from the office. This is possible because Notes operates the same regardless of how you connect to the Domino server. Once the connection has been established, Notes performs as if you were connected through a LAN (albeit much slower). Notes can also connect to Domino servers automatically, in the background, while you work. This is discussed in "Background Replication Using the Notes Replicator" earlier in this chapter. To connect to a Domino server manually using Notes Direct Dialup, follow these steps:

1. Select File ➤ Mobile ➤ Call Server. The Call Server dialog box will be displayed (see Figure 9.10). All servers available through Notes Direct Dialup and Network Dialup Connection documents will be displayed.

FIGURE 9.10

The Call Server dialog box

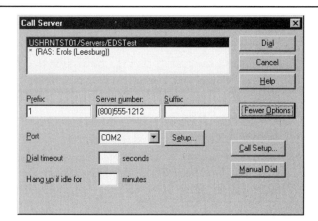

2. Select the server you are calling.

3. Optionally, change connection information in the Call Server dialog box before dialing if necessary. Click the More Options button to view or modify advanced settings. When you do, the dialog box will look like the one in Figure 9.10. The More Options button changes to the Fewer Options button.

4. Click the Dial button.

Notes will initiate dialing through your computer's modem. When the connection has been established, a modem icon will appear in the activity indicator on the status bar. You can open and use server-based databases as if you were connected locally. You can also initiate replication with the server.

Manually Disconnecting the Notes Direct Dialup Connection

By default, Notes will hang up Notes Direct Dialup connections after 15 minutes of inactivity. You can also manually hang up the connection. To do so, perform these steps:

1. Select File ➤ Mobile ➤ Hang Up. The Hang Up dialog box will be displayed with the active dial-up ports listed.

2. Select the appropriate port.

3. Click the Hang Up button.

Network Dialup

Network Dialup allows Notes to use Windows Dialup Networking (DUN) to access Domino servers. If you already have DUN installed on your computer and your Domino servers are accessible through a network dial-up solution (or ISP), this is the easiest way to connect remotely. All configuration related to your computer's modem is taken care of through DUN, not Notes. Notes just needs a properly configured Network Dialup Connection document to access Domino servers through DUN.

Setting Up Network Dialup

Notes Network Dialup only requires that your Domino servers are accessible through a network dial-up solution such as Windows NT Remote Access Server (RAS). In many companies, the information technology group provides this service. Network dial-up can also be provided by an outside service organization. Recently, companies have even begun to use Internet-based virtual private network (VPN) solutions to provide network dial-up services. In Notes, you only need to configure a Network Dialup Connection document that defines how Notes will connect to your Domino server. To create a Network Dialup Connection document, follow these steps:

1. Select File ➤ Mobile ➤ Server Phone Numbers. Your Personal Address Book will be opened with the Connections view displayed. All existing Connection documents will be listed.

2. Click the Add Connection button on the View Action bar. A blank Connection form will be displayed.

3. Select Network Dialup from the Connection Type drop-down box. The Basics tab will be displayed by default (see Figure 9.11).

PART

III

Advanced Use of
Notes 5

FIGURE 9.11

The Network Dialup Connection Basics tab

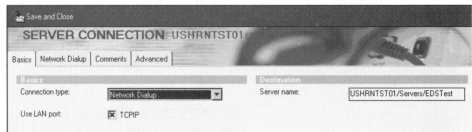

4. Select a port in the Use LAN Port field.

5. Fill in the Server Name field.

6. Click the Network Dialup tab. It will look similar to Figure 9.12.

FIGURE 9.12

The Network Dialup tab

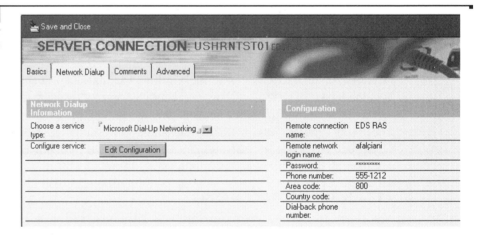

7. Select Microsoft Dial-Up Networking from the Keywords dialog box (click the arrow to the right of the Choose a Service Type field to bring up the Keywords dialog box).

8. Click the Edit Configuration button. The Microsoft Dial-Up Networking dialog box will be displayed (see Figure 9.13).

FIGURE 9.13

The Microsoft Dial-Up Networking dialog box

Microsoft Dial-Up Networking	
Dial-Up Networking name:	EDS RAS
Login name:	afalciani
Password:	*********
Phone number:	555-1212
Area code:	800
Country code:	
Dial-back phone number:	

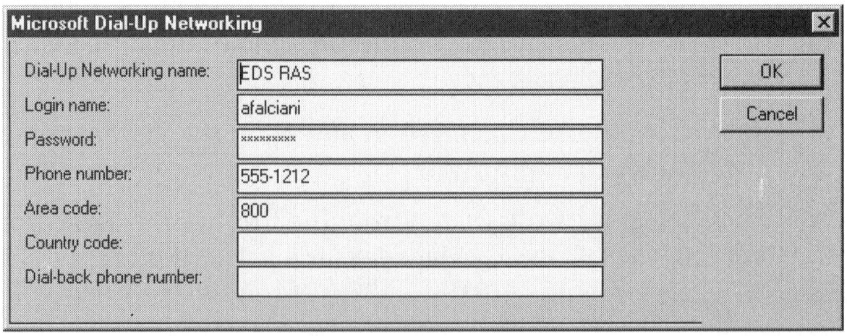

9. Fill in the fields using information from the DUN entry that you would like to use to make the connection. The Dial-Up Networking Name field should be filled in with the Windows DUN entry name.

10. Click the OK button. You will be returned to the Network Dialup Connection document.

11. Click the Save and Close button on the Form Action bar.

The Network Dialup Connection document will be created and you will be returned to the Connections view of your Personal Address Book. Network Dialup Connection documents can be further customized using the Advanced tab on the Connection form.

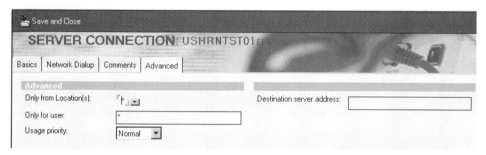

The following fields are on the Advanced tab:

Only from Location(s)   Defaults to an asterisk, which enables Notes to use this Connection document regardless of your current location. If you would like to restrict a Connection document to specific locations, select them from this list box.

Only for User   Restricts the Connection document to specific users. Enter an asterisk to make this Connection document available to any user who uses Notes from this workstation.

Usage Priority   Used by Notes to determine the order in which it uses Connection documents.

 TIP   You can also use the Connection Configuration Wizard to create Connection documents. This wizard is available from the Location form as long as Location Type is set to Network Dialup or Custom. The wizard will even create new Windows DUN entries for you.

Manually Connecting Using Network Dialup

With Network Dialup set up, you can connect to the Domino servers manually or automatically just as you do with Notes Direct Dialup. To use Network Dialup to

PART

III

Advanced Use of
Notes 5

connect to a Domino server manually, select File ➤ Mobile ➤ Call Server and use the procedure discussed for Notes Direct Dialup. One difference is that the Call Server dialog box's More Options button will display a set of advanced options appropriate for DUN connections.

Notes will initiate dialing through your computer's modem. When the connection has been established, a modem icon will appear in the activity indicator on the status bar. Windows will also add a modem icon to the system tray. Just as you can with Notes Direct Dialup, you can open and use server-based databases as if you were connected locally. You can also initiate replication with the server.

Manually Disconnecting the Network Dialup Connection

By default, Notes will hang up Network Dialup inactive connections based on Windows modem settings. You can also manually hang up the connection by selecting File ➤ Mobile ➤ Hang Up and using the procedure previously discussed for Notes Direct Dialup. One difference is that the Hang Up dialog box will only show active DUN connections.

NOTE Notes also supports connectivity options other than dial-up communications. This support is provided by a set of WAN drivers that you can download for free from the Lotus Web site. The WAN drivers include Connect for ISDN, Connect for SNA, and Connect for X.25. Go to www.lotus.com and click the Products link. An expanded list of products will be displayed. Click the Notes WAN Drivers link and follow the instructions provided.

Using Network Dialup to Connect to the Internet

Network Dialup can also be used to establish Internet connections for non-Domino services, including Post Office Protocol version 3 (POP3), Internet Message Access Protocol version 4 (IMAP4), Simple Mail Transfer Protocol (SMTP), Network News Transfer Protocol (NNTP), and Lightweight Directory Access Protocol (LDAP). This feature is the equivalent of an auto-dialer in typical Internet clients. Once it's configured, Notes can automatically dial your ISP account whenever you perform a function that requires Notes to be connected to the Internet. Notes will even dial your ISP account in the background if the Notes Replicator is configured to send or receive Internet e-mail or to replicate newsgroups and IMAP e-mail accounts.

The only difference between a Network Dialup connection configured to access a Domino server and one configured to access Internet services is the Server Name field. As we demonstrated earlier, Network Dialup connections configured to access Domino servers require the Domino server name. If you want to create a Network Dialup connection for use with Internet services, just enter an asterisk in the Server Name field. Notes will use Windows Dialup Networking (DUN) as explained earlier.

Passthru Connections

Notes supports a feature called *Passthru*, which is provided by the Domino server. This feature allows you to connect to one Domino server and use its communications capabilities to connect to another Domino server. One common use of Passthru is in environments where you use Notes Direct Dialup communications to connect directly to Domino servers. After making the connection, you only have access to that one Domino server, so you cannot use databases residing on other Domino servers in your organization. Using Passthru, you can access databases residing on Domino servers other than the one you called. Another common use is for accessing Internet-based Domino servers from within your organization's network infrastructure. At least one of your Domino servers must have either a permanent connection to the Internet or the capability to establish a dial-up connection to the Internet. If this is the case, you can use Passthru to access the internal Domino server and have it connect you to the Internet-based Domino server. We will not go into the details of how Passthru works, only how you use it.

To configure Notes to use a Passthru Domino server, you must create a Passthru Connection document. To do so, follow these steps:

1. Select File ➢ Mobile ➢ Server Phone Numbers. Your Personal Address Book will be opened with the Connections view displayed. All existing Connection documents will be listed.

2. Click the Add Connection button on the View Action bar. A blank Connection form will be displayed.

3. Select Passthru Server from the Connection Type drop-down box. The Basics tab will be displayed by default (Figure 9.14).

FIGURE 9.14

The Basics tab of the Passthru Connection document

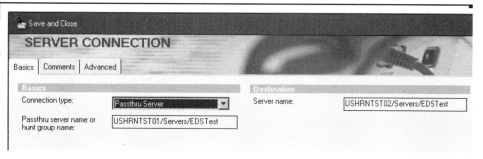

PART

III

Advanced Use of
Notes 5

4. Enter the name of the Passthru Domino server.

5. In the Destination section, enter the name of the Domino server you wish to access via Passthru.

6. Click the Save and Close button on the Form Action bar.

The Passthru Connection document will be created and you will be returned to the Connections view of your Personal Address Book. Passthru Connection documents can be further customized using the Advanced tab on the Connection form, as described in "Setting Up Network Dialup" earlier in this chapter.

Once a Passthru Connection document is created, Notes will automatically connect to the destination Domino server by first connecting to the Passthru Domino server. If the Passthru Domino server is only reachable via dial-up communications, Notes will also establish the dial-up connection.

Using Notes Remotely

Now that you understand how to use replication and the dial-up communication capabilities of Notes, you're ready to work remotely. This means that you can continue to interact with your collaborative applications when you leave the office. Here are some of the more common uses:

- Reading and composing your e-mail
- Staying up-to-date in Notes databases
- Referencing Web pages

Using Your Mail Database Remotely

The ability to read and compose e-mail offline is very powerful. You can search your mail database locally if you need to refer to messages. You can catch up with new e-mail or organize existing messages into folders when it is more convenient. You can even compose new messages as you think of something or respond to existing messages. When you have access to a phone line, you can use dial-up communications to connect to your Domino server and synchronize your changes. To use your mail database remotely, there are certain requirements:

Local replicas   You must create a local replica of your mail database on your computer's local disk drive. You should also create a replica of your organization's Domino Directory or Mobile Domino Directory so you can address messages remotely. Use the information presented earlier in this chapter (see "Creating Database Replicas") to create the replicas of the databases you need to access remotely.

Location document   You must create a Location document (or configure an existing one) to use while working remotely. You must switch to this Location document when running Notes remotely. See Chapter 13, "Setting Up Notes as a Domino Client," for more information on Location documents.

Connection document   You must create a Connection document to use when connecting to your Domino server via dial-up communications. Use the information presented earlier in this chapter to create the appropriate Connection document.

Account Document   If you are using Internet-based e-mail remotely, you must create Account documents to access Internet mail accounts. See Chapter 14, "Setting Up Notes as an Internet Client," for more information on Account documents.

Also, you should understand how Notes processes e-mail, including how it uses your Personal Address Book and locally stored Mobile Domino Directory replicas. See Chapter 5, "Communicating with Notes Mail," for more information on the mail capabilities of Notes.

Using Databases Remotely

Another powerful feature of Notes is that you can work on Notes databases remotely. Let's say that you use a lead-tracking database in the office. You can take a copy of this database with you when you make sales calls. Throughout the day, you can post new information to your local replica. When you get a minute, you can establish dial-up communications with your Domino server and replicate all of your changes. At the same time, you can receive new information posted by colleagues. Of course, you can search through documents in your local replica if you need to refer to information contained within the database. To use a database remotely, there are certain requirements:

Local replica   You must create a local replica of your database on your computer's local disk drive. Use the information presented earlier in this chapter (see "Creating Database Replicas") to create the replicas of the databases you need to access remotely.

Location document   You must create a Location document (or configure an existing one) to use while working remotely. You must switch to this Location document when running Notes remotely. See Chapter 13, "Setting Up Notes as a Domino Client," for more information on Location documents.

Connection document   You must create a Connection document to use when connecting to your Domino server via dial-up communications. Use the information presented earlier in this chapter to create the appropriate Connection document.

Group document   If the database you are using remotely enforces security on all replicas, you may need to add Group documents to your Personal Address Book. If this is the case, your Domino administrator should have the information you need to create these documents. See Chapter 4, "Introducing the Core Databases," for more information on Group documents.

PART

III

Advanced Use of
Notes 5

Referencing Web Pages Offline

If you use Notes to browse the Web, you can also access previously visited Web pages when you're away from the office. You can even search through previously visited Web pages to find information. To access previously visited Web pages, there are again some requirements that must be met:

Location document (for online browsing)   You must create a Location document (or configure an existing one) to use for browsing the Web online using Notes. You can choose to use the native browser built in to Notes or the Notes with Microsoft Internet Explorer feature. This allows you to use Microsoft Internet Explorer's familiar interface and Hypertext Markup Language (HTML) rendering engine and store Web pages in a Notes database for offline use. You must switch to the Location document when you access the Web online via Notes. When you create the Location document, Notes will create your Personal Web Navigator database if it does not already exist. See Chapter 10, "Harnessing the Power of the Internet," for more information on using Notes to browse the Web.

Location document (for offline browsing)   You must create another Location document (or configure an existing one) to use for browsing previously visited Web pages offline using Notes. These pages are stored in your Personal Web Navigator database. You must switch to the Location document when you access this database offline. See Chapter 10 for more information on the Personal Web Navigator database.

Connection document   You must create a Connection document to use when you connect to the Internet remotely to update your Personal Web Navigator database. Use the information presented earlier in this chapter to create the appropriate Connection document.

Summary

You should now have a good understanding of how Notes operates as a mobile client. We discussed Notes replication and dial-up communications support. We even explored some common ways to use Notes remotely. The next chapter will explain how Notes can be used as an Internet client.

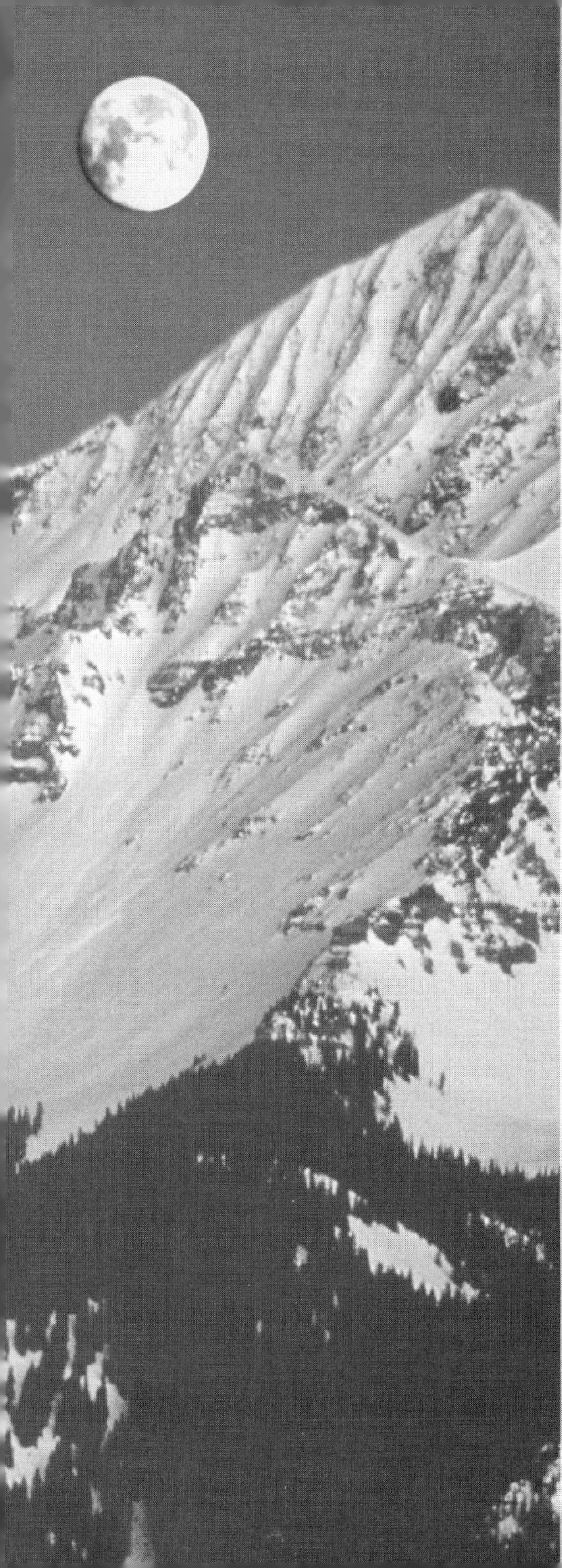

CHAPTER 10

Harnessing the Power of the Internet

FEATURING:

There is no doubt that every major area of technology has been influenced by the Internet over the past couple of years. Lotus Notes is no exception. Release 5 fully integrates Internet support throughout the entire product. This support is not just tacked on either. Notes weaves Internet-based protocols, content standards, and security standards into its proven collaborative computing model. For Web browsing within Notes, you can choose between the built-in native browser or the integrated Microsoft Internet Explorer browser control. Using either of these two browsing modes, you can save Web pages to a database for offline use. If you prefer, you can also just instruct Notes to pass Uniform Resource Locator (URL) requests to a separately running instance of Netscape Navigator or Microsoft Internet Explorer. Notes is also a powerful newsreader application. It can actually replicate entire newsgroups to your computer for offline reading and posting. This model is also supported for Internet Message Access Protocol (IMAP) mail accounts. You can replicate your mail store, including folders, to your computer for offline use.

Notes Support for Internet Standards

The big news in Notes Release 5 is the expanded support for Internet standards. This is important because these standards are the glue that holds the Internet together. They are not perfect, but they enable products from many vendors to interoperate (most of the time). For you, this means being able to use any Web browser to access Web sites. Yes, some sites require that you use specific versions of Microsoft Internet Explorer or Netscape Navigator, but most provide some level of support (text only) regardless of browser type or version. It also means creating content in a format that can be easily read by others. Hypertext Markup Language (HTML) is the formatting language of Web pages. It can also be used as a way to send rich text in e-mail messages and as a way to post rich text messages to newsgroups. Finally, Internet security standards enable you to access Web sites, mail servers, news servers, and so on securely. They also provide support for sending and receiving encrypted mail. In the following sections, we'll explore the Internet standards supported by Notes.

Notes Support for Internet Protocols

Protocols are the mechanisms used to allow computers to communicate with each other and to allow applications to interact with other applications (usually server-based services such as mail, news, Web, etc.). Notes supports the following Internet protocols:

- Transmission Control Protocol/Internet Protocol (TCP/IP)
- Hypertext Transfer Protocol (HTTP)

- Post Office Protocol (POP)
- Internet Message Access Protocol (IMAP)
- Simple Mail Transfer Protocol (SMTP)
- Light Directory Access Protocol (LDAP)
- Network News Transfer Protocol (NNTP)

Transmission Control Protocol/Internet Protocol (TCP/IP)

TCP/IP is the standard communication protocol of the Internet. It is actually a suite of protocols. Most often, TCP/IP is associated with the networking aspects of computer-to-computer communications. We will limit our discussion to that aspect.

Windows provides the actual support for TCP/IP networking. It also provides the interfaces for programs, such as Notes, to access this support. In this respect, Notes is a TCP/IP application. It can be configured to communicate with Domino servers and Internet servers using TCP/IP. For information on configuring Notes to communicate using TCP/IP, see Chapter 13, "Setting Up Notes as a Domino Client."

Hypertext Transfer Protocol (HTTP)

HTTP is the protocol used by Web browsers to access Web servers. Notes supports the use of HTTP in its native Web browser capability. It can also be configured to use HTTP to encapsulate Notes-to-Domino sessions. This is useful for accessing Domino servers through a firewall.

Post Office Protocol (POP)

POP (or POP3) is the common protocol for retrieving e-mail messages from an Internet mail server (POP server). It is considered an offline protocol because it is used to copy messages from the POP server to a local client application for storing, viewing, replying, and so on. Notes supports the use of POP to retrieve messages from POP servers and copy them to your mail database. You can then read, reply to, or delete POP messages as you can any other message.

Internet Message Access Protocol (IMAP)

IMAP (or IMAP4) is another protocol for retrieving e-mail messages from an Internet mail server (IMAP server). It is more sophisticated than POP because it can be used when you're online as well as when you're offline. For use online, it operates in much the same way client/server mail systems such as Microsoft Outlook/Exchange and Notes/Domino operate. The IMAP server contains your message store, or repository. The IMAP client reads and writes to this message store online; messages are not stored locally on your computer. Notes supports this mode by creating a new type of database called a *proxy database*. It looks like your mail database and you interact with it the same way, but no messages are actually stored in it. In addition, there is another option for interacting with IMAP servers that is distinctly a Notes feature. You can create a replica of your IMAP proxy database and work offline. Notes then uses replication to synchronize your local replica with your IMAP server-based message store. Finally, Notes also supports the use of IMAP to retrieve messages from IMAP servers to your mail database; this is similar to POP.

Simple Mail Transfer Protocol (SMTP)

As its name implies, SMTP is the common protocol for sending e-mail messages to Internet mail servers (SMTP servers). Notes supports the use of SMTP to send outbound messages from Notes directly to the Internet. Notes, in conjunction with Domino, has provided users with the ability to use SMTP to send Internet mail for a long time. Direct support for SMTP allows Notes to send Internet mail on its own, without the need for Domino. This, combined with the POP and IMAP support previously discussed, make Notes a stand-alone Internet mail client.

Light Directory Access Protocol (LDAP)

LDAP (LDAP v3) is a common protocol for accessing directories on Internet directory servers (LDAP servers). LDAP directories are used to store contact information for people and groups. They are similar to the Domino Directory in this regard. Some popular LDAP directories are Four11, Bigfoot, and Yahoo!. They contain contact information they get from phone books and other sources as well as from individuals who enter their contact information. You can use Notes to search LDAP directories for a person's e-mail address when you send Internet mail or for other contact information (e.g., phone number, address, etc.) when you are trying to locate someone.

Network News Transfer Protocol (NNTP)

NNTP is the common protocol for Internet-based discussion groups or electronic forums called newsgroups (or Usenet). It is used to read and post messages on news servers (NNTP servers). Newsgroups are similar to bulletin board systems (BBSs), which were popular before widespread use of the Internet. They are a standards-based version of the Notes discussion database. NNTP and IMAP operate in a similar manner; the NNTP server contains a message store, and the NNTP client reads and writes messages to this repository. Notes supports NNTP by using a proxy database as it does with IMAP.

Notes Support for Internet Content Standards

Content standards are predefined or widely accepted methods for storing information. They are defined by international standards organizations or by market presence. Content standards enable an application to read and write data so the data can be easily read and written by other programs. Notes supports the following Internet content standards:

- Hypertext Markup Language (HTML)
- Multipurpose Internet Mail Extension (MIME)
- Java
- JavaScript
- Native Image Formats

Hypertext Markup Language (HTML)

HTML is commonly thought to be a programming language, but in fact it is a formatting language. HTML is the language used to create Web pages, and it is becoming popular for transferring e-mail messages and posting newsgroup topics. Notes supports HTML in a number of ways, including:

- Mail message format
- Newsgroup posting format
- Native browser
- Copy/paste to rich text fields
- Programming (in Domino Designer)

Multipurpose Internet Mail Extension (MIME)

MIME is a method for packaging complex messages. It is used to format data into individual elements (similar to fields) so it can be easily read by other applications. When combined with standard encoding mechanisms (e.g., uuencode and Base64) that can translate binary data into a text format, MIME provides a powerful mechanism for sharing information. Notes supports MIME for sending and receiving Internet mail, for reading and posting newsgroup topics, and in rich text fields exposed to browser users through Domino.

Java

Java is a programming language that creates code that executes in a special Java runtime environment called the Java Virtual Machine (JVM). Java can be considered content in the sense that Java applets (small, stand-alone programs written in Java) can be embedded on Notes forms or in Notes rich text fields. The native browser also supports Java applets on Web pages. All this is made possible because Notes contains an integrated JVM. Also, Domino Designer includes a Java integrated development environment (IDE) for developing and compiling Java programs, and it allows Java programs to be used in developing Notes/Domino applications.

JavaScript

JavaScript is a scripting language primarily used to integrate objects on Web pages. Like Java, JavaScript is content in the sense that the native browser can interpret Web pages containing JavaScript. Domino Designer also allows JavaScript to be used in developing Notes/Domino applications.

Native Image Formats

Images are a major element of Web pages. The formats most commonly used by Web page designers are Graphic Interchange Format (GIF) and Joint Photographic Experts Group (JPEG). Notes stores images based on these formats in their native form in the Notes database.

Support for Internet Security Standards

Security standards are mechanisms for ensuring that information is only accessible to the individual or group of individuals for which it was intended. They can apply to data communications or actual content. Again, these standards are defined by international standards organizations or by market presence. Notes supports the following Internet security standards:

- Secure Sockets Layer (SSL)
- X.509 certificates (Internet certificates)
- Secure Multipurpose Internet Mail Extension (S/MIME)

Secure Sockets Layer (SSL)

SSL is a data communications protocol for TCP/IP. It is used to encrypt network transmission so information is not sent over the Internet in clear text. It is commonly used by Web vendors for securing credit card information entered in Web pages and sent over the Internet. Notes supports SSL in its native Web browser and in its protocol support for POP, IMAP, SMTP, NNTP, and LDAP.

X.509 Certificates (Internet Certificates)

X.509 certificates are part of a standards-based Public Key Infrastructure (PKI), which is a mechanism for ensuring that users are who they say they are. A third-party certifying authority validates the identity of a user and issues that person a key. This key is then used to access the system. It provides a higher degree of security than just a user ID and password provides. Notes supports X.509 certificates for Web browsing and sending/receiving secure e-mail.

Secure Multipurpose Internet Mail Extension (S/MIME)

S/MIME is a standard for sending and receiving secure e-mail. It is used in conjunction with X.509 certificates. Notes supports S/MIME for sending/receiving signed and encrypted Internet e-mail.

Browsing the Web

It's fair to say that Web browsing is commonplace today. Whether for personal or business needs, there are many valuable sites. You can research products and services, or you can purchase them. You can search for information and research topics. You can read news from around the world. Companies even use Web sites internally (intranets) to communicate with employees. Web browsing is becoming an integral part of everyday life. It is for this reason that Notes includes an integrated Web browser.

Notes Integrated Web Browsing

As previously mentioned, there are two choices for browsing from within Notes:

- The native Notes browser
- The Notes browser with Microsoft Internet Explorer

The native Notes browser is fairly robust and supports most features used on common Web sites. It supports HTML 4, Java applets, JavaScript, cookies, ActiveX controls, and plug-ins. The rendering engine runs as a background task, and Web pages are displayed in a form. When you open a Uniform Resource Locator (URL), a task window is opened for the browser form (unless one is already opened) and the page is displayed. Behind the scenes, Notes is using a database called Personal Web Navigator (`perweb.nsf`). This database contains the form used to display Web pages. It also acts as a repository for storing Web pages offline.

You can also use the Notes browser in conjunction with the Microsoft Internet Explorer (IE) browser control. This is a powerful combination. You get the familiar interface and robust rendering engine of IE in addition to the Web-page sharing and offline features of Notes. Browsing with the Notes browser and IE is the same as browsing with the native browser except the form displayed contains the IE browser control as an object. This means that Notes is allowing the IE control to retrieve pages and display them. Other browsing functions, such as forwarding a URL or saving a Web page for offline use, is performed by Notes using special forms and programs in the Personal Web Navigator database.

PART

III

Advanced Use of
Notes 5

If you prefer, you can also just instruct Notes to pass URL requests to a separately running instance of Netscape Navigator, Microsoft Internet Explorer, or other browser application. The difference in this case is that the Personal Web Navigator database is not used and Web pages will not be available for offline use.

Configuring Integrated Browsing

You can configure integrated browsing by setting specific User Preferences, Location document settings, and Personal Web Navigator database options.

Configuring User Preferences

In the User Preferences dialog box, there is an Additional Options list box that contains advanced configuration settings.

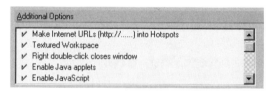

To view or change these settings, select File ➤ Preferences ➤ User Preferences. The User Preferences dialog box will be displayed. A number of the settings have an impact on integrated browsing and fall into two categories:

- Common advanced settings
- Native browser advanced settings

Common Advanced Settings   Common advanced settings affect how Notes operates regardless of which integrated browsing option you have enabled. These include the following:

Make Internet URLs into Hotspots   You can enable this option to instruct Notes to convert URLs listed in rich text fields to links. When this option is enabled, you can click URLs listed in e-mail messages, newsgroup postings, or any other database in Notes.

Make Notes My Default Web Browser   You can enable this option to instruct Windows to use Notes for all URL requests. When it's enabled, you will be able to open Web pages in Notes by entering URLs in the Windows Start ➤ Run box or by selecting shortcuts from your Start ➤ Favorites.

Enable MS Office 97 SendTo to Notes   You can enable this option to instruct Office 97 applications (Word, Excel, PowerPoint, and so on) to use Notes when sending documents to mail recipients.

NOTE If you are using Notes with the IE browser control, you can have Notes synchronize Internet browsing configuration information from the current Location document to your Windows Registry (IE Control Panel settings). This is a great way to maintain multiple browser configurations based on location. To instruct Notes to keep Location document settings synchronized with your IE settings, add the following to your notes.ini file: **SYNCINTERNETSETTINGS=1**. For more information on modifying your notes.ini file, see Chapter 13.

Native Browser Advanced Settings   Native browser advanced settings have an impact on how Notes operates when the native browser is enabled. The settings are as follows:

Enable Java Applets   You can enable this option to instruct Notes to execute Java applets referenced by Web pages. This also has an impact on Java applets contained in Notes documents.

Enable JavaScript   You can enable this option to instruct Notes to execute JavaScript code that it encounters on Web pages. This also has an impact on JavaScript contained in Notes documents.

Enable Java Access from JavaScript   When this option is enabled, Notes will execute Java applets called from JavaScript code that it encounters on Web pages. This also has an impact on Java applets called from JavaScript contained in Notes documents.

Enable JavaScript Error Dialogs   When this option is enabled, Notes will display a dialog box when JavaScript errors are encountered.

Enable Plugins in Notes Browser   When this option is enabled, Notes will support plug-ins.

Enable ActiveX in Notes Browser   When this option is enabled, Notes will support ActiveX controls called from Web pages.

Accept Cookies   When this option is enabled, Notes will support cookies. Cookies are used by Web site designers to save information on your computer.

Configuring the Location Document

On the Internet Browser tab of the Location document, there are two fields for configuring Notes for Web browsing:

Internet Browser   The Internet Browser field provides choices for how you want Notes to process URL requests. You can choose Netscape Navigator, Microsoft Internet Explorer, or Other to instruct Notes to pass URL requests to a separately running instance of the selected browser. In addition, the Other option lets you select the path for the browser's executable file. The Notes and Notes with Internet Explorer options configure Notes for integrated browsing. The Notes option instructs Notes to use its native browser, and the Notes with Internet Explorer option instructs Notes to use the IE browser control.

Retrieve/Open Pages   From the Retrieve/Open Pages field, you can choose how Notes should retrieve Web pages. The From Notes Workstation option instructs Notes to perform page retrieval locally. When this option is chosen, Notes stores retrieved pages in your Personal Web Navigator database. The From InterNotes Server option instructs Notes to pass Web page retrieval requests to a Domino server running the InterNotes task. When this option is chosen, Notes stores retrieved pages in a shared Web Navigator database on the Domino server. We will not cover the Web Navigator here, but you can refer to the Domino Administration Help database for more information on this capability. The No Retrievals option instructs Notes to disable page retrieval.

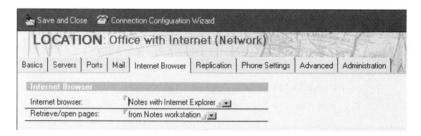

To change the settings on the Internet Browser tab, follow these steps:

1. Select File ➣ Mobile ➣ Edit Current Location, or click the Location indicator button on the status bar and select Edit Current. The current Location document will be opened.

2. Click the Internet Browser tab.

3. Make changes as needed.

4. Click the Advanced tab and then the Web Retriever subtab.

On the Web Retriever subtab, there are four fields for configuring the Notes-based Web Retriever process:

Web Navigator Database   This field contains the name of the Personal Web Navigator database and defaults to `perweb.nsf`. You can use different Personal Web Navigator databases for different Location documents.

Concurrent Retrievers   This field defines the number of threads created by the Web Retriever process running on your computer. A high number will improve performance, but more resources will be required from your computer. The default is 15.

Retriever Log Level   The Web Retriever process can log its activity to your Notes log database. Terse provides minimal logging, Verbose provides more complete logging, and None disables logging altogether.

Update Cache   This field defines how the Web Retriever process maintains its cache of Web pages. If you use the Notes with IE integrated browser mode, the Update Cache setting will correspond to the Windows Internet setting named Check for Newer Versions of Stored Pages. You can check the latter by selecting Start ➤ Settings ➤ Control Panel, selecting the Internet option, and clicking the Settings button in the Temporary Internet Files section of the dialog box.

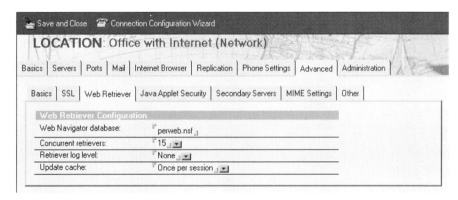

When you are finished configuring the Web Retriever settings, click the Save and Close button on the Form Action bar. The Location document will be closed and your new settings will take effect.

On the Basics tab of the Location document, there is a Proxy field. You can enter a proxy server name and port in this field or click the button to the right of the field to bring up a dialog box to set proxy options. Proxy options are used when you connect to the Internet through a firewall. For more information on setting proxy options, see Chapter 14, "Setting Up Notes as an Internet Client."

Using Integrated Browsing

Again, integrated browsing means that Notes becomes your Internet browser. It can use its own native browsing engine or it can use the Internet Explorer browser control. Either way, a browser form is opened within the Notes application window and you are able to navigate around Web pages as you would in any other browser. You can initiate a browser session within Notes a number of different ways:

Bookmarks   You can bookmark Web pages just as you can any other Notes form; just drag the browser form's task button to the Bookmark bar. Then, you can click a Web page bookmark, and Notes will open a browser form and display the page.

PART

III

Advanced Use of Notes 5

TIP Notes will also automatically display your Internet Explorer Favorites and Navigator bookmarks on the Bookmark bar.

URL link   Notes can present URLs as active links when they are placed on forms or included in rich text fields. This enables you to click links in mail messages, discussion database topics, or any other document in Notes as if it were a Web page. When you click a link, Notes will open a browser form and display the page.

Open URL   You can type URLs directly into the Navigation bar's Address combo box and then press Enter. Notes will open a browser form and retrieve the page represented by the URL you entered.

Internet search   Just click on the Navigator bar's Search button and select a search site. Notes will open a browser form and display the search site you selected.

Welcome page   Web browsing is also incorporated on the Welcome page. You can create a style that includes one or more Web page sections. This can be used to display a news site or portal from which you can launch a browser task.

Personal Web Navigator   You can browse Web pages by opening the Personal Web Navigator database too. This method is used when browsing offline.

Regardless of how integrated browsing is initiated, the operation is the same. A browser form is opened and the requested Web page is displayed. The Navigation bar is used to go back or forward, refresh pages, and stop pages from loading. If you click any Web page bookmarks, click any Web page links, or perform other actions that request Web page retrieval, Notes will display the page in the current browser form.

Because browsing is integrated into a Notes form, it is presented with the normal Notes user interfaces. You can print the active Web page as if it were another document. You can create bookmarks to active Web pages that are just like any other bookmark. As mentioned earlier, to create a bookmark to a Web page, drag the browser form's task button to the Bookmark bar or any bookmark folder.

 NOTE You will not be able to drag the browser form's task button to the Internet Explorer or Netscape Navigator bookmark folders. The bookmarks in these folders can only be used for opening Web pages.

TIP If you are using Notes with IE, you can add the active Web page to your IE Favorites. Just right-click in the browser form and the IE browser object will display its context menu. This menu contains an option for adding the current page to your Favorites.

Along with the normal features associated with Web browsing, Notes provides a few extras. You can forward a Web page as a URL or as a page. When you forward a Web page as a page, the contents of the Web page are copied into a mail message so you can send it to another person or save it for future reference. Because it is stored in its native format in a rich text field, the Web page has the same look and functionality as the actual page on the Web server. Select Actions ➢ Forward to initiate this process. If you have your Personal Web Navigator database configured to save all pages you've visited, you have the option of deleting individual pages. Just select Actions ➢ Delete. If you have it configured to save only pages that you specify, you will have the option of saving the current Web page. This can be done by selecting Actions ➢ Keep Page.

 TIP Release 5 includes an HTML source code viewer that formats the code. To view the source code for the active Web page, select View ➢ Show ➢ HTML Source.

Browsing the Web Securely

You can use integrated browsing to access secure Web sites. With the native Notes browser option enabled, secure access is controlled by Notes. If the Notes with IE option is enabled, secure access is controlled by Internet Explorer. For more information on using IE to browse secure Web sites, see the Microsoft Internet Explorer Help file. The native Notes browser supports SSL for encrypting the HTTP communications, and it supports X.509 certificates (Internet certificates) for accessing secure Web sites. SSL is discussed earlier in this chapter in reference to the NNTP protocol, but it is similar for HTTP. See "Participating in Newsgroups" later in this chapter for more information on configuring SSL. See "Secure Internet Mail" later in this chapter for more information on configuring Internet certificates.

Using the Personal Web Navigator Database

When you configure Notes for integrated browsing, it automatically creates a Personal Web Navigator database for you. As previously mentioned, this database is used as a repository for Web pages that you visit when you're using integrated browsing. The pages can then be viewed offline. Your Personal Web Navigator database also provides two advanced Web browsing features called Web Ahead and Page Minder. Web Ahead is a process that runs on your computer to retrieve Web pages from links that are on pages one or more levels down from the pages you visit. This is helpful when you're browsing offline because many of the Web pages you visit will have links to other pages. Page Minder is a process that runs on your computer to check specific Web pages for changes. If changes are found, it sends either the page or a summary of the page to you via e-mail.

Configuring the Personal Web Navigator Database

The Personal Web Navigator database also contains configuration information. You can set a home page that is opened when you open the Personal Web Navigator database. You can set database size options so that pages are automatically removed based on criteria you define. You can instruct Notes to save all visited pages or just those you specify. We'll discuss a few of the more advanced options. To open the Personal Web Navigator's Internet Options form, follow these steps:

1. Open your Personal Web Navigator database. If it is not already bookmarked, open the database named perweb.nsf. When the database opens, it will open a separate form to display the configured home page.

2. Click the task button for the Personal Web Navigator database.

3. Select Action ➢ Internet Options.

The Internet Options form will be opened. You can use it to configure Web Ahead, Page Minder, and other preferences. The Internet Options form uses a tabbed interface. Each tab contains a specific set of configuration options.

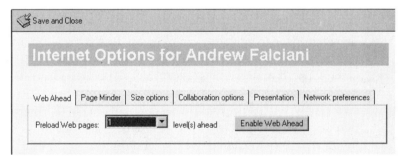

Web Ahead Agent Preferences   You can select the number of levels that Web Ahead should retrieve (up to 4), and you can enable the Web Ahead Agent from this form. To enable the Web Ahead Agent, follow these steps:

1. Click the Web Ahead tab.

2. Click the Enable Web Ahead button. A Choose Server to Run On dialog will be displayed.

3. Select Local and click the OK button. A dialog box instructing you to enable background Agents will be displayed. This is required for Web Ahead to function properly.

4. Click the OK button.

You will be returned to the Internet Options form. The Enable Web Ahead button will be changed to Disable Web Ahead. If you need to enable background Agents, select File ➤ Preferences ➤ User Preferences and select the Enable Scheduled Local Agents check box.

Page Minder Agent Preferences   You can select how often Page Minder should check for updates, whether to send the page or a summary, and the e-mail address that should be used. To enable the Page Minder Agent, click the Page Minder tab and follow these steps:

1. Click the Enable Page Minder button. A Choose Server to Run On dialog will be displayed.

2. Select Local and click the OK button. A dialog box instructing you to enable background Agents will be displayed. This is required for Page Minder to function properly.

3. Click the OK button.

You will be returned to the Internet Options form. The Enable Page Minder button will be changed to Disable Page Minder.

Using Web Ahead

Once Web Ahead is configured and enabled, it will run every half hour. To have Web Ahead retrieve pages from links on Web pages that you have visited, follow this procedure:

1. With the Personal Web Navigator database open, open the All Pages view.

2. Find the page for which you would like Web Ahead to retrieve referenced pages.

3. Copy the page into the Web Bots/Web Ahead folder.

Web Ahead will include this page in its next scheduled retrieval. To remove a page from the Web Ahead schedule, remove it from the Web Bots/Web Ahead folder. Do not delete the page unless you intend to remove it permanently from the database. Instead, select Actions ➤ Remove from Folder.

PART

III

Advanced Use of
Notes 5

NOTE Web Ahead will retrieve Web pages that require name and password authentication as long as you have successfully visited the page online. Notes stores this information in your Personal Web Navigator database, so make sure this database is encrypted if you want to ensure the security of this information. Web Ahead will also function properly through firewalls as long as you have successfully logged in to the firewall in the current Notes session.

Using Page Minder

Once Page Minder is configured and enabled, it will run as defined in the configuration. To have Page Minder check pages for changes, follow this procedure:

1. With the Personal Web Navigator database open, open the All Pages view.

2. Find the page on which you would like Page Minder to check for changes.

3. Copy the page into the Web Bots/Page Minder folder.

Page Minder will include this page in its next scheduled execution. To remove a page from the Page Minder schedule, remove it from the Web Bots/Page Minder folder. Again, do not delete the page unless you intend to remove it permanently from the database. Instead, select Actions ➤ Remove from Folder.

Browsing Pages Offline

Browsing Web pages offline is just a matter of reading documents in your Personal Web Navigator database. The key is to make sure your current Location document is a No Connection Location type. One convenient way to do this is to create a Location document to use while you are not connected to the Internet. By default, Notes creates a Location document with a location name of Island for this purpose. It should also be configured to use the same integrated browser mode your online Location document uses. If you normally use the native Notes browser, configure your Island Location document to use the native Notes browser.

Participating in Newsgroups

Newsgroups are the equivalent of discussion databases in Notes. They allow you to post topics and responses that are just like the topics and responses in the discussion database. There are tens of thousands of public newsgroups in existence and more added every day; this is also known as Usenet. ISPs maintain news servers (or NNTP servers) to host public newsgroups for their customers, and they synchronize their copies with those from other ISPs on a continual basis. All you need is an NNTP client or newsreader application. With Release 5's integrated NNTP support, Notes can be your newsreader.

The way Notes implements NNTP support is fairly unique. Instead of just presenting an entirely different interface in a helper application, Notes presents newsgroups in the form of a Notes database. Because this database is designed like a discussion database, it will already be familiar to you. Under the covers, this database is different than other Notes databases that we have discussed. It is called a proxy database, and it does not actually contain any documents. It retrieves documents from a news server and presents them through views and forms as if they were stored locally.

You can then create a local replica of your newsgroup proxy database, which will allow you to read and post offline. It will also allow you to use the powerful searching capabilities of Notes to find the information you are looking for.

Configuring Notes as Your Newsreader

To configure Notes to be your newsreader application, you only need to create an NNTP Account document in your Personal Address Book. This Account document will define the news server and protocol information that Notes needs to create the proxy database. When you save the Account document, Notes will automatically create the proxy database for you. To create an NNTP Account document, follow these steps:

1. Open your Personal Address Book database (there is an icon on the Bookmark bar for this database).

2. Click the Configuration Settings icon in the lower left frame. The Settings frameset will be displayed with the Accounts view selected (Figure 10.1).

**FIGURE 10.1**

The Personal Address Book Accounts view

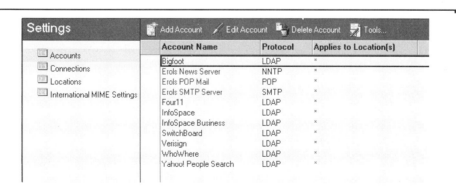

3. Click the Add Account button on the View Action bar. A New Account form will be opened (Figure 10.2).

FIGURE 10.2

A New Account form

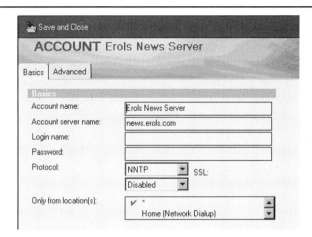

4. Select NNTP from the Protocol drop-down box. This is the protocol used to communicate with the News server.

5. Enter a descriptive name in the Account Name field. This name is used to generate the filename of the proxy database. Because Notes automatically generates this name based on 8.3 file-naming conventions, make sure the beginning characters are descriptive.

6. In the Account Server Name field, enter the name of your news server. Your ISP will provide the server name. If you are configuring Notes to connect to a corporate news server, your organization's internal information systems (IS) group will provide it.

7. Enter a login name and password if they are required by your ISP (or internal IS group).

8. Select Enabled from the SSL drop-down box if you want to encrypt the network communications between your computer and the news server. For some news servers, you must enable SSL. Again, check with your ISP or IS group.

9. Select * (asterisk) from the Only from Location(s) list box to make this Account document available to all locations or select individual locations through which it should be available.

10. Click the Advanced tab if you need to change the TCP/IP port or if you want to disable the use of replication history with this proxy database.

11. Click the Save and Close button on the Form Action bar.

The Account document will be closed. Notes will automatically create a news server proxy database if one does not already exist. A bookmark to the proxy database will also be added to the Databases folder of your Bookmark bar. To open the proxy database, you can either use the bookmark or open the Account document and click the Open Proxy button on the Form Action bar.

Configuring SSL

If you choose to enable SSL, you will also need to configure SSL settings in the SSL subtab of the Advanced tab in the Location document. Notes supports SSL 2 and 3; it can also negotiate the appropriate version with the server. You can set which version Notes will support by selecting the appropriate value from the SSL Protocol Version field. If you select a value that involves SSL 3, you will also need to obtain an Internet cross certificate for the server you wish to access. To obtain an Internet cross certificate, follow these steps:

  1. Select File ➤ Tools ➤ Add Internet Cross Certificate. The Add Internet Cross Certificate dialog box is displayed (Figure 10.3).

FIGURE 10.3

The Add Internet Cross Certificate dialog box

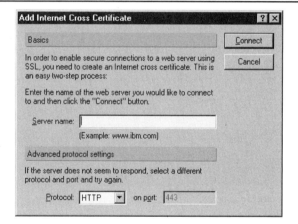

  2. Select the protocol you want to use when you connect to the server.
  3. Enter the name of the server and click the Next button.
  4. If Notes can access the server you enter using the protocol selected, the Issue Cross Certificate dialog box will be displayed (Figure 10.4).
  5. Click the Cross Certify button.

The cross certificate will be added to the Certificates view of your Personal Address Book.

PART

III

Advanced Use of
Notes 5

TIP You can also create Internet cross certificates from existing Internet Certifier documents in your Personal Address Book database (Internet Certifier documents can be found in the Certificates view in the Settings frameset). Just open an Internet Certifier document and select Actions ➣ Create Cross Certificate. When the Create Cross Certificate dialog box is presented, select a certificate to which you want the Internet cross certificate created and click the OK button. When the Issue Cross Certificate dialog box is displayed, click the Cross Certify button.

 NOTE This process will configure SSL for all protocols supported by Notes.

FIGURE 10.4

The Issue Cross Certificate dialog box

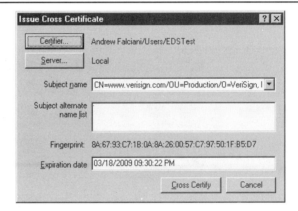

Subscribing to Newsgroups

Once you create an Account document (and associated news server proxy database), you need to subscribe to specific newsgroups provided by your ISP's news server. If you've used a newsreader before, the process should be familiar. To subscribe to newsgroups, follow these steps:

1. Open your news server proxy database. You can either click the appropriate bookmark or open the associated Account document and click the Open Proxy button on the Form Action bar. The news server proxy database will be opened to the Outbox view by default (Figure 10.5).

2. Click the Newsgroups button on the View Action bar. The Newsgroups at *Server-name* dialog box will open (Figure 10.6), and Notes will begin retrieving the list of newsgroups provided by the news server. Be patient. Most ISP's news servers support the full set of public newsgroups, which is currently over 30,000.

FIGURE 10.5

The news server proxy database Outbox view

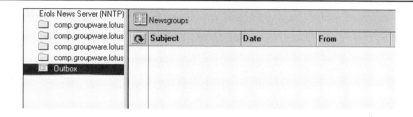

FIGURE 10.6

The Newsgroups at Servername dialog box

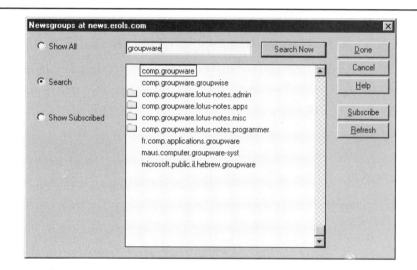

3. Click the Show All radio button to show all newsgroups provided by the news server, or click the Search radio button to search for specific sets of newsgroups based on criteria you enter.

4. Select the newsgroup to which you want to subscribe and click the Subscribe button. A folder icon will be displayed to the left of the newsgroup entry, and the Subscribe button will be replaced with the Unsubscribe button.

5. When you are finished, click the Done button.

You will be returned to the proxy database's Outbox view.

 NOTE The list of newsgroups provided by a news server changes frequently. Click the Refresh button in the Newsgroups at *Servername* dialog box to reload the list of newsgroups provided by the news server.

The Newsgroups at *Servername* dialog box is also used to unsubscribe from newsgroups. To unsubscribe, follow these steps:

1. With the news server proxy database open, click the Newsgroups button to open the Newsgroups at *Servername* dialog box.

2. Click the Show Subscribed button. Only the newsgroups to which you have subscribed will be displayed.

3. Select a newsgroup and click the Unsubscribe button. The folder icon displayed to the left of the newsgroup entry will be removed and the Unsubscribe button will be replaced with the Subscribe button.

4. When you are finished, click the Done button.

You will be returned to the proxy database.

Reading and Posting to Newsgroups

Once you have subscribed to newsgroups provided by your news server, you are ready to read and post entries. Notes displays each newsgroup to which you subscribed as a view. To see the messages in the newsgroup, just click the newsgroup name in the Navigation pane. Notes will display the message summaries previously retrieved from the news server. If the view refresh indicator is displayed, there are additional message summaries to be retrieved. Notes retrieves message summaries in blocks or sets of messages. To retrieve a block of message summaries from the News server, press F9 or click the Refresh button on the Navigation bar. Notes will display a dialog box showing the progress of the retrieve process.

As we said, the view shows message summaries. When you open a message, Notes actually retrieves the full message from the news server and displays it through the form. To open a message, double-click its row in the view. The message will be displayed through the Main Topic form. As you can see, reading and posting to newsgroups is the same as working in any other Notes database.

From the Main Topic form, you can post a response. This is done as follows:

1. Click the Response button. A New Response form will be opened (Figure 10.7).

FIGURE 10.7

A New Response form

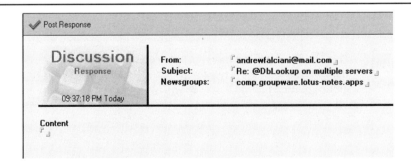

2. Change the default information entered in the From, Subject, and Newsgroups fields if necessary.

3. Enter your response in the Content field.

4. Click the Post Response button on the Form Action bar.

The New Response form will be closed and you will be returned to the original message. Notes immediately sends the new response to the news server.

 NOTE If you want to enter rich content, make sure you enable the option in Notes that allows you to post HTML to newsgroups. This can be done by selecting File ➢ Preferences ➢ User Preferences, clicking the Mail and News button, and selecting one of the HTML options from the Internet News Format drop-down box.

You can post new topics from either an existing topic that you are viewing or the Newsgroup view. To post new topics, follow these steps:

1. Click the New Main Topic button. A New Discussion Topic form will be opened (Figure 10.8).

FIGURE 10.8

A New Discussion Topic form

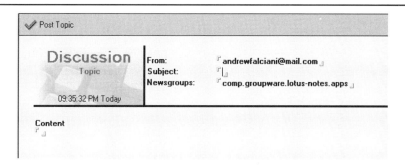

2. Change the default information entered in the From and Newsgroups fields if necessary.

3. Enter a short description in the Subject field.

4. Enter your topic in the Content field.

5. Click the Post Topic button on the Form Action bar.

The New Discussion Topic form will be closed and you will be returned to the message or newsgroup that you were previously viewing. Notes immediately sends the new topic to the news server.

Using Newsgroups Offline

In true Notes fashion, newsgroups can also be replicated to your computer for offline use. This is a great way to speed up interaction if you connect to the Internet via dial-up communications. It also provides additional functionality in that the local newsgroup replica can be full-text indexed for sophisticated searching.

Creating a Replica

The first task is to create a replica of your news server proxy database. The process is the same as it is for creating a replica of any other database. See Chapter 9, "Working with Notes Away from the Office," for more information on creating replicas.

Synchronizing through Replication

After you create a replica of your news server proxy database, an entry is added to the Replicator page for the new replica. This entry is used to control how the Notes Replicator keeps the local replica synchronized with the news server. It is the same as other replication entries in that it can be enabled or disabled and you can set replication options. Double-clicking this entry will also open the local replica just as double-clicking any other entry opens it. The Notes Replicator will synchronize your local replica with the news server in the background, as it does with Domino servers. You can work on other Notes tasks while it is synchronizing, and you can schedule replication.

You can also manually replicate your local replica with the news server in the foreground. Foreground replication is generally used to perform one-time synchronization between scheduled events. This is also the same as foreground replication with Domino servers. For more information on foreground and background replication, see Chapter 9.

 NOTE The only way to search newsgroups in Notes is to create a local replica. You can then create a full-text index and perform sophisticated searches as you can with any other database. See Chapter 8, "Searching for Information," for more information on searching Notes databases.

Sending and Receiving Internet Mail

One of the major reasons people use the Internet is to send and receive mail. It is still the most basic form of electronic collaboration and widely used by all types of users. Notes Release 5 integrates Internet messaging the same way it integrates other Internet services—by wrapping the Notes interface around the appropriate protocols and standards.

Using Notes as an Internet mail client is just a variation of using Notes as a Domino Mail client. For this reason, we will only summarize Notes Internet mail support here. See Chapter 5, "Communicating with Notes Mail," for a more complete discussion of Notes messaging.

Receiving Internet Mail

Notes supports a variety of options for operating with Internet mail servers, including:

- Receiving POP messages into your Notes mail database
- Receiving IMAP messages into your Notes mail database
- Interacting live with an IMAP mail server
- Replicating your IMAP message store to a local Notes database

Notes can also support all of these options simultaneously. This is why Notes Release 5 is categorized as a universal mail client. We'll summarize these capabilities in the following sections.

Receiving POP Messages into Your Notes Mail Database

As previously mentioned, POP is considered an offline protocol. It is used to access a mail server and copy messages to a local data repository. Notes is actually well suited for this type of operation. It includes a variety of communication options, from dial-up to wide area networks (WANs). It also has a sophisticated data repository, the Notes database, that can be full-text searched, replicated, secured, and customized, just to name a few capabilities. Notes provides support for POP mail servers through Account documents in your Personal Address Book. You can create a POP Account document for each POP account you want pulled into your mail database. You can define as many as you need and associate them with Location documents as desired. You can make them available to all Location documents or just a subset. The Account document also includes a choice for leaving messages on the mail server.

When you create a new POP Account document, Notes adds an entry to the Replicator page. This entry is used to control how Notes accesses your POP account on the POP server. Clicking the Send and Receive Mail button on the Replicator page or the Receive Mail button in your mail database will instruct Notes to connect to your POP mail server and retrieve your messages in the background. Mail retrieval will also be initiated if you have background replication scheduled.

IMAP Support

IMAP is more sophisticated than POP. It can be used to provide interactive sessions with the server, or it can be used as an offline protocol. Notes supports both of these scenarios and adds one that is unique to Notes—creating a local replica of your IMAP message store.

PART

III

Advanced Use of
Notes 5

Receiving IMAP Messages into Your Notes Mail Database   When IMAP is used to receive messages into your Notes mail database, it operates the same way POP operates. Notes provides support for offline IMAP through Account documents in your Personal Address Book. You can create an IMAP Offline Account document for each IMAP account you want pulled into your mail database. You can define as many as you need and associate them with Location documents as desired. You can make them available to all Location documents or just a subset.

When you create a new IMAP Offline Account document, Notes adds an entry to the Replicator page just as it does for POP accounts. This entry is used to control how Notes accesses your IMAP account on the IMAP server. Clicking the Send and Receive Mail button on the Replicator page or the Receive Mail button in your mail database will instruct Notes to connect to your IMAP mail server and retrieve your messages in the background. Mail retrieval will also be initiated if you have background replication scheduled.

Interacting Live with an IMAP Mail Server   When IMAP is used interactively, Notes operates in a manner similar to that described for newsgroups. You create an IMAP Online Account document, and Notes creates an IMAP server proxy database. This database is designed like a normal Notes mail database, so using it is very similar to using Notes mail. When you open the IMAP server proxy database, Notes retrieves message summaries from the IMAP server and displays them as documents in a view. If you open one of these documents, Notes retrieves the full message from the server and uses a form to display it. You can then create a reply and Notes will send it through the currently configured outbound mail path, most likely an SMTP mail server. Notes even presents folders from your IMAP account as folders in the IMAP server proxy database.

Replicating Your IMAP Message Store to a Local Notes Database   The process for creating a replica of an IMAP server proxy database is similar to the process for creating a replica of a news server proxy database. This enables you to work interactively offline and adds powerful capabilities (such as full-text searching) to standard IMAP messaging. The first task is to create a replica of your IMAP server proxy database. This is the same as creating a replica of any other database. See Chapter 9 for more information on creating replicas.

After you create a replica of your IMAP server proxy database, an entry is added to the Replicator page for the new replica. This entry is used to control how the Notes Replicator keeps the local replica synchronized with the IMAP server. It is the same as other replication entries in that it can be enabled or disabled and you can set replication options. Double-clicking this entry will also open the local replica. The Notes Replicator will synchronize your local replica with the IMAP server in the background the same way it does with Domino servers. You can work on other Notes tasks while it is synchronizing, and you can schedule replication.

You can also manually replicate your local replica with the IMAP server in the foreground. This is generally used to perform one-time synchronization between scheduled events. This is also the same as foreground replication with Domino servers. For more information on foreground and background replication, see Chapter 9.

Sending Internet Mail

Regardless of how you receive mail, through POP or IMAP, Notes provides two methods for sending outbound mail:

- Direct to the Internet
- Through a Domino server

If you are using Notes in an environment that includes Domino servers, you will most likely send outbound mail through a Domino server. If the Domino server is properly configured, it can be used to send messages to Internet recipients. All you do is enter a properly formatted Internet mail address and Domino will take care of the rest. To configure Notes to send outbound messages through a Domino server, just select Through Domino Server in the Send Outgoing Mail field on the Mail tab of your current Location document.

The Notes client can also be configured to use SMTP to send outbound messages directly to the Internet. This is done by selecting Directly to Internet in the Send Outgoing Mail field on the Mail tab of your current Location document. After this change is saved to your current Location document, Notes will create an smtp.box database in your Notes Data directory. This database is used to queue outbound messages sent directly to the Internet.

In addition, you need to create at least one SMTP Account document in your Personal Address Book database. The document defines the SMTP server to which Notes will send outbound messages. The SMTP Account document is similar to NNTP, POP, and IMAP Account documents in that it can be made available to all Location documents or just those selected. Once you create an SMTP Account document, Notes adds an entry to the Replicator page just as it does for POP and IMAP offline accounts. This entry is used to control how Notes accesses the SMTP server. You can click the Send and Receive Mail button on the Replicator page to instruct Notes to connect to the SMTP server and deliver any messages queued in smtp.box in the background. Notes can also be configured to connect to the SMTP server when the number of messages queued reaches a predefined threshold. Notes also delivers queued mail if you have background replication scheduled.

Using Internet Directories to Address Messages

You can enter Internet mail addresses of recipients directly in the Mail Memo form. This is useful when you know the recipient's Internet mail address or can reference it quickly. You can also add frequently used Internet mail addresses to your Personal Address Book. Notes can even use Contact entries in your Personal Address Book for type-ahead addressing, where Notes translates names as you enter them in the To, Cc,

or Bcc field of the Memo form. If you are using Notes as an Internet mail client, there is another option.

You can access LDAP directories on the Internet to search for Internet mail addresses of people you are trying to contact. Notes provides support for LDAP directories through Account documents in your Personal Address Book. You can create an LDAP Account document for each LDAP directory you want to search for Internet mail addresses. You can define as many as you need and associate them with Location documents as desired. You can make them available to all Location documents or just a subset.

For each new LDAP Account document you create, Notes adds an entry to the Look In drop-down box on the Select Addresses, Directories, and other dialog boxes used to search address books. You just select this entry and enter search criteria as you normally would, and Notes passes the request to the LDAP server. The results of your search are presented in the dialog box as usual. This is a great way to search Internet directories such as Bigfoot, Four11, and Yahoo!.

Secure Internet Mail

Notes supports S/MIME for secure Internet mail. S/MIME uses X.509 certificates (Internet certificates), which make up a system of trusted certificates to ensure the validity of signatures and encryption of messages. The sender and recipient each have a certificate issued by a Certifying Authority (CA), or an organization that can be trusted. This is the same as states issuing driver's licenses. Because people trust the state's system, they trust that licenses issued by the state are valid. Domino can be used as the CA within your company, but third-party CA service providers are commonly used to ensure validity of certificates outside individual organizations. Individual users can also obtain certificates from these third-party CAs. For example, you can obtain a personal certificate from VeriSign. The process is explained at their Web site (`www.verisign.com/client/index.html`), but it basically follows the same procedure as other CAs. The process is as follows:

1. Go to the CA's Web site and request an Internet certificate. If the CA does not have specific instructions for Notes Release 5, follow the process for Netscape Navigator. (If your Notes ID is based on International security, select the low-security option.)

2. Wait for the CA to e-mail you a key or PIN.

3. Open the URL e-mailed back to you from the CA. Copy and paste the key or PIN e-mailed to you where requested. Submit the form.

4. Notes will display a dialog box stating that an Internet certificate is available and asking if you want to install it. Click the Yes button.

5. Check your Notes ID file to verify that the Internet certificate was installed. Select File ➤ Tools ➤ User ID and click the Certificates button. Your new Internet certificate will be listed in the Certificates Issued By field.

NOTE To obtain Internet certificates, Notes must be configured to use its native browser. See "Browsing the Web" earlier in this chapter for more information on configuring Notes this way. Also, you must have a trusted certificate and an Internet cross certificate for the CA from which you would like to obtain an Internet certificate. For information on obtaining a CA's trusted certificate, see the following set of steps. For more information on issuing an Internet cross certificate to a CA's trusted certificate, see "Configuring SSL" earlier in this chapter.

The only way to ensure that a certificate issued by a particular CA is valid is to obtain the CA's trusted certificate, usually the root. Trusted certificates are stored in your Personal Address Book database. The default Personal Address Book database contains a set of trusted certificates for popular CAs. If there is not already an Internet certificate document for the CA you are using to obtain your Internet certificate, you must add one. To add an Internet certificate for a particular CA, follow these steps:

1. Make sure you have configured Notes to use the native Notes browser. This is explained in "Configuring Integrated Browsing" earlier in this chapter.

2. Go to the Web site of the CA for which you would like to obtain the trusted certificate and click the link to the root certificate. If the root certificate is in Raw X.509 BER format or Base64 Encoded format, you will be prompted to install it.

If you choose to install the root certificate, it will be added to your Personal Address Book. You will also be prompted to create an Internet cross certificate to this root certificate. This is similar to manually creating Internet cross certificates, which was discussed in "Configuring SSL" earlier in this chapter.

After you go through the process of requesting and picking up your Internet certificate, it will be added to your Notes ID file with your Notes certificates. See Chapter 12, "Securing Your Data," for more information on your Notes ID file.

 NOTE The process for obtaining Internet certificates is browser dependent. For Certifying Authority Web sites that do not have direct support for Notes Release 5, you must configure the native Notes browser to emulate Netscape Navigator. To do this, add the following to your notes.ini file: **WebUserAgent=Mozilla/4.0 (Windows-NT)**. For more information on modifying your notes.ini file, see Chapter 13.

Sending Secure Internet E-Mail

You must install an Internet certificate in your Notes ID file to send secure Internet e-mail messages. This is explained in the preceding section. To send a signed e-mail message to another Internet e-mail user, just compose a message as you normally would and select the Sign delivery options before sending the message.

To send encrypted e-mail, you must have the recipient's Internet certificate in the Contact entry in your Personal Address Book. With a signed e-mail opened, select Actions ➢ Tools ➢ Add Sender to Address Book to add the sender's Internet certificate to your Personal Address Book. To send encrypted e-mail messages, just select the Encrypt deliver option before sending.

Receiving Secure Internet E-Mail

If you receive an S/MIME signed e-mail message, Notes will recognize the digital signature by displaying signature information in the message area of the status bar when you open the message. If Notes is not already configured to trust the CA of the digital certificate used to sign the message, you will be prompted to create a cross certificate. This is similar to manually creating Internet cross certificates, which was discussed in "Configuring SSL" earlier in this chapter.

Connecting to the Internet

With built-in support for TCP/IP and dial-up communications, Notes has the technology to connect to the Internet. Notes's TCP/IP support is easy to configure. You just enable the TCP/IP communications port in the User Preferences dialog box and configure a Location document to use that port. For more information, see Chapter 13, "Setting Up Notes as a Domino Client."

If you use Notes remotely, you will most likely connect to the Internet through dial-up communications. Notes includes support for Windows Dialup Networking, which is the standard Windows mechanism for using dial-up communications to access the Internet (as well as private networks). For more information on using dial-up communications in Notes, see Chapter 9, "Working with Notes Away from the Office."

You may also connect to the Internet through a firewall. A firewall is a device that sits between two networks—usually an organization's private network and the Internet—and provides secure communications between them. If you use Notes in an environment that uses a firewall to connect to the Internet, just make sure you configure your Location document properly. More information on configuring proxy settings is available in Chapter 14.

Summary

In this chapter, we discussed how Notes provides support for Internet standards. We also detailed how integrated browsing works in Notes Release 5, how you can use Notes as a newsreader, and how Notes sends and receives Internet mail. In the next chapter, we'll discuss how other applications can be integrated with Notes and how Notes can be integrated with other applications.

CHAPTER 11

Integrating Notes with Other Applications

We have demonstrated how Notes can be used to manage your e-mail, calendaring and scheduling, To Do list, Web browsing, and newsgroup interaction. It also has prebuilt templates, including an electronic discussion and a document library, that can be used to share information with colleagues. With all of these capabilities, Notes is a powerful information management tool. As such, you will need to share information with other applications. Here, we'll discuss the Notes features that end users can use to integrate Notes with other applications. Notes also provides programmatic interfaces for more advanced integration; these are introduced in Chapter 23, "Language Extensions."

The Windows Clipboard

The most basic form of application integration that Notes supports is copying and pasting to and from the Windows Clipboard. When you are creating or editing documents, you can copy and paste information from another application to fields on the form. The data that is copied must match the data type of the field in which it is being pasted. For example, you can only paste a number into a numeric field.

You can also copy and paste formatted text into a rich text field. If you copy information from an application that supports rich text data (such as Microsoft Word) to the Windows Clipboard, it can be pasted into a Notes rich text field with its associated formatting. To see how this works, just follow these steps:

1. Create a memo document in your mail database.

2. In Word (or another application that can copy rich text to the Clipboard), highlight some text and select Edit ➤ Copy.

3. Go back to Notes and make sure your cursor is positioned in the Body field.

4. Select Edit ➤ Paste Special. The Paste Special dialog box appears (Figure 11.1).

5. Select the Paste radio button, select Rich Text from the As field, and then click the OK button.

The text you copied to the Clipboard from Word will be displayed in the Notes rich text field. The text itself is editable within the rich text field just as if it were typed directly into the field. To close the form, press Escape or click the *X* to the right of the form's task button. In the Close Window dialog box, select Discard Changes and then click the OK button.

 TIP Notes Release 5 allows you to paste Web pages copied from Microsoft Internet Explorer into rich text fields. This is a great way to save a Web page into a Notes document.

FIGURE 11.1

*The Paste Special
dialog box for a
Word Object*

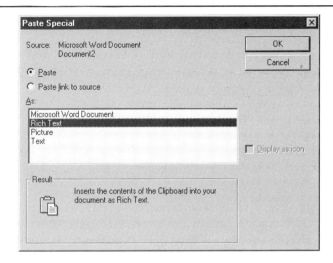

Windows Object Linking and Embedding (OLE)

Windows object linking and embedding (OLE) objects can be inserted into rich text fields (and on forms), making Notes a powerful container application. OLE is a protocol built in to Windows that enables applications to share data. It is an outgrowth of a technology called Dynamic Data Exchange (DDE) that was included in earlier versions of Windows. OLE is also Microsoft's first foray into component software architectures and is the precursor to programmatic interfaces such as ActiveX, Common Object Model/Distributed Common Object Model (COM/DCOM), and now, Distributed InterNetwork Architecture (DNA). Notes can control OLE objects programmatically using LotusScript (see Chapter 23), but it also provides the interfaces required to let end users link and embed objects into rich text fields. You can insert OLE objects into rich text fields two ways:

- Copy and paste from an OLE-enabled application.
- Use the Create menu.

Let's say you want to include a Microsoft Word document in a Notes document because you want to either e-mail it to a colleague or share it with a group by adding it to a discussion. If the Word document already exists, you can either copy and paste it into Notes or use the Create menu.

Copying and Pasting OLE Objects

The easiest way to insert OLE objects into a rich text field is to copy and paste them. Follow these steps to copy and paste a Word object into a rich text field:

1. Create a memo document in your mail database.

PART

III

**Advanced Use of
Notes 5**

2. Within Word, select the text to be inserted into Notes and copy it to the Clipboard.

3. Go back to Notes and make sure your cursor is positioned in the Body field.

4. Select Edit ➢ Paste Special. The Paste Special dialog box appears.

5. Select the Paste radio button, select Microsoft Word Document from the As field, and click the OK button.

The text you highlighted in Word will appear in the Notes rich text field. If you click on the text pasted into Notes, a box will appear around it. This indicates that the text is an object. To close the form, press Escape or click the *X* to the right of the form's task button. In the Close Window dialog box, select Discard Changes and click the OK button.

 NOTE Selecting the Paste Link to Source radio button in the Paste Special dialog box creates a link to the object instead of embedding it into the rich text field. The main difference is that links are kept synchronized and embedded objects are not. Links are also more fragile; anyone opening a document containing a link must have access to the object represented by the link. If you e-mail a message containing a link to a file on your computer, the recipient will most likely be unable to access it because he probably does not have access to your computer's hard drive.

Using the Create Menu to Insert OLE Objects

Another way to insert an OLE object into a rich text field is to use the Create menu. You can insert Word text as follows:

1. Select Create ➢ Object from the Notes menu. A Create Object dialog box appears (Figure 11.2).

2. Select the Object from a File radio button in the Create New section.

3. Either type in the filename of the Word document you want to insert or click the Browse button to explore your computer's disk drive.

4. After filling in the File field, click the OK button.

The text from your Word document will appear in the Notes rich text field. Again, if you click on the text pasted into Notes, a box will appear around it. This indicates that the text is an object.

FIGURE 11.2

The Create Object dialog box

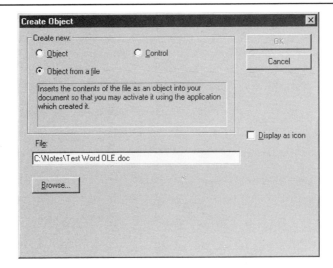

Editing Embedded Objects

You can edit an OLE object embedded in a rich text field. Just double-click the Word object in the rich text field. You'll notice that Notes is still running, but the menus appear to be those of Microsoft Word (see Figure 11.3). This is called in-place editing, and it's part of the OLE specification.

Some of the core applications shipped with Notes use OLE to integrate with popular desktop applications. Notes mail provides the option of using Microsoft Word or Lotus Word Pro. Also, the Document Library for Microsoft Office template uses OLE to integrate Word, Excel, PowerPoint, and Paint with Notes. This particular Notes database never even displays a Notes form; it just launches each application from the view interface and automatically stores the data back to a Notes document.

You can also edit the object by opening it in the application in which it was created. You can right-click the object and select Open from the context menu. If you have the application installed on your computer, it will be launched with the object selected. You will notice that the application that is launched will have a few new options in the File menu. For Microsoft Word, there will be a Close and Return to *Document Title* option (where *Document Title* is the title of the Notes document in which the object is contained) and an Update option. If you select Update, changes made to the object will be saved back to the Notes document. If you select the Close and Return to *Document Title* option, the object will be saved to the Notes document, the application will be closed, and you will be returned to Notes.

PART

III

Advanced Use of
Notes 5

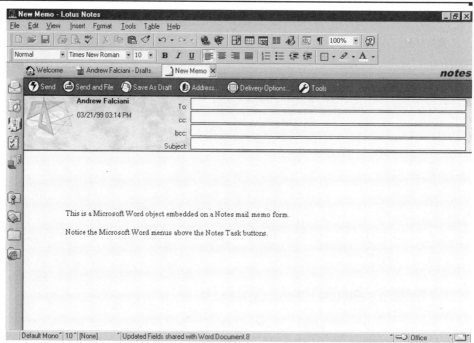

FIGURE 11.3

In-place editing in a Word document

 NOTE The ability to insert OLE objects into Notes documents is a powerful feature, but it can cause some problems when the documents are also being shared with browser-only users through a Domino server. Some browsers are not designed to be OLE containers and may not render the object properly. Even when all of the users have Notes, OLE may not be the best way to store information. It requires that all users have the application that created the object installed locally on their computer.

Notes Import and Export

You can also import and export data to and from Notes. Notes supports two modes of import and export:

- View import/export
- Document import/export

View import allows you to take a set of records from an external data source and create a Notes document for each record. View export is just the opposite. It allows you to take a set of Notes documents displayed in a view and create a set of records that can be used by another application. For example, you may have a Notes-based time entry database that you would like to use. Before you start entering your time, you would like to populate the database with data that you have been keeping in a spreadsheet for the last six months. Assuming that the Notes database contains one document for each time entry, you could use view import to create time entry documents from data stored in your spreadsheet.

Document import allows you to import picture files, word processing documents, and spreadsheet files from popular desktop applications into rich text fields on Notes forms. Document export allows you to export a Notes document that is displayed through a form to either a word processing document or image file.

View Import

View import allows you to create documents in a Notes database from records contained in an external file. Notes can perform view imports from three file formats:

- Lotus 1-2-3 worksheet files
- Structured text files
- Tabular text files

Regardless of the type of file you're importing, you must choose a form to use to create the documents. The form's field definitions are used in defining the fields on the documents. You must also choose to create either Main documents or Response documents from the external data. Optionally, you can choose to calculate fields on the form as documents are created. This option should be selected if you have computed fields on the form.

 NOTE If you choose to create Response documents, they will be created as responses to the currently selected document in the view. If no document is selected, you will not be able to create Response documents.

Lotus 1-2-3 worksheet files are spreadsheet files generated by Lotus 1-2-3 (or other applications that can export to the WK1/WK2/WK3/WK4 format). The rows contained in the 1-2-3 file are translated to documents when imported by Notes. The columns represent the fields on the documents. When importing 1-2-3 files, you can enter a range name to import a subset of the spreadsheet or import the entire spreadsheet. In

Advanced Use of Notes 5

addition, you must choose how fields are defined on the documents created during import. The options are as follows:

- View Defined
- WKS Title Defined
- Format File Defined

View Defined instructs Notes to use the structure of the view to correlate columns from the spreadsheet to fields on the documents created during import. The data in the first column in the 1-2-3 file will be copied to a field defined from the first column of the view, and so on. WKS Title Defined instructs Notes to correlate column titles from the spreadsheet to fields on the documents created during import. Format File Defined instructs Notes to refer to the format defined in an external text file to correlate columns in the spreadsheet to fields on the documents. This file is called a Format file (or COL file because it is created using a .col extension). The following is an example of a Format file:

```
;COL File for BUSNADDR.TXT
;Ignore leading quote
(") : width 1
Company: UNTIL '","'
Department: UNTIL '","'
Last: UNTIL '","'
First: UNTIL '","'
Middle: UNTIL '","'
Title: UNTIL '","'
Phone: UNTIL '","'
FAX: UNTIL '","'
DateActive: UNTIL '","'
Dateinactive: UNTIL '","'
Street1: UNTIL '","'
Street2: UNTIL '","'
City: UNTIL '","'
State: UNTIL '","'
Zip: UNTIL '","'
Notes: UNTIL '","'
```

Structured text files are text files that contain data formatted so that each field from each record is listed with its field name, value, and a carriage return/line feed character. Each record is separated with either a form feed character or some other special character code (chosen when the data was exported). This format is used to export documents from Notes database views. When importing structured text files, Notes uses field names contained in the file to correlate data values to fields on the documents created during import.

Tabular text files are text files that contain data formatted so that each field from each record is listed in the same position on the line and records are separated by a carriage return/line feed. This format is very generic and can be exported from most applications. When importing tabular text files, Notes correlates fields from the tabular text file to columns in the view. If you choose to use a Format file, Notes refers to this file to correlate fields in the import file to fields on the documents.

Again, view import is used to create documents in a Notes database from records contained in an external file. To perform a view import, follow these steps:

1. Open the database in which you would like to perform the view import.

2. Open the view to use for the view import.

3. Select File ➤ Import. The Import dialog box (Figure 11.4) will be displayed.

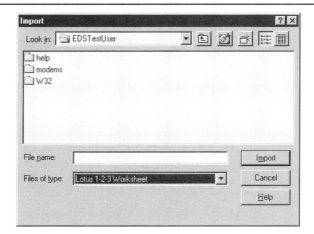

4. Select the type of file you would like to import from the Files of Type drop-down box.

5. Select a file from your computer's file system or enter a filename.

6. Click the Import button. An import settings dialog box specific to the type of file being imported will be displayed. Figure 11.5 shows the import settings dialog box for 1-2-3 worksheet files.

7. Select the appropriate import settings. See the information previously discussed in this section.

8. Click the OK button.

Notes will process the file you selected. A document will be created for each of the records in the external file.

PART

III

Advanced Use of
Notes 5

Worksheet Import Settings dialog box

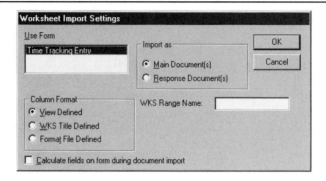

View Export

View export allows you to create an external file containing records for documents selected from a Notes database. Notes can export data to the same formats mentioned in the preceding section:

- Lotus 1-2-3 worksheet files
- Structured text files
- Tabular text files

When performing a view export, Notes creates a record in the output file for each document selected in the view. You can also choose to export all documents. To perform a view export, follow these steps:

1. Open the database in which you would like to perform the view export.

2. Open the view to use for the view export.

3. Select File ➤ Export. The Export dialog box (Figure 11.6) will be displayed.

The Export dialog box

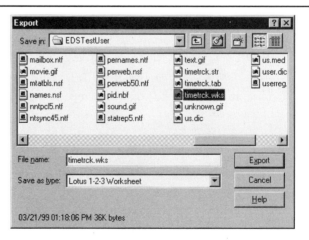

4. Select the type of file you would like to export from the Save as Type drop-down box.

5. Select a file from your computer's file system or enter a filename.

6. Click the Export button. An Export dialog box specific to the type of file being exported will be displayed. Figure 11.7 shows the Export dialog box for 1-2-3 worksheet files.

FIGURE 11.7

The Export dialog box for 1-2-3 worksheet files

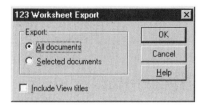

7. Select All Documents or Selected Documents, depending on what you want to export.

8. Select the other options as necessary.

9. Click the OK button.

Notes will process the export. The file created will contain rows for all documents or a row for each of the documents selected.

 NOTE If the export file exists, Notes will prompt you to replace the file or cancel the export. If you are exporting to a tabular text file, you will also be given the choice of appending records to the existing export file.

Document Import

Document import allows you to copy data from an external file to a rich text field on a Notes form. Notes can import a number of file formats into rich text fields:

Ami Pro

ASCII text

Binary with text

BMP image

CGM image

PART

III

Advanced Use of
Notes 5

Excel spreadsheet

GIF image

HTML file

JPEG image

Lotus 1-2-3 worksheet

Lotus PIC

Microsoft Word RTF

PCX image

TIFF 5 image

Word for Windows

WordPerfect 5.*x*

WordPerfect 6/6.1

WordPro 96/97

Importing graphic files is the same as creating pictures in rich text fields. See Chapter 3, "Working with Notes Databases," for more information.

 NOTE When importing graphic files, Notes will only import the first image contained in the file.

When importing word processing files, Notes translates the formatting contained in the document to equivalent rich text field attributes. See the Notes Help file for information on which formatting is translated during import. When importing spreadsheet files, Notes supports named ranges for 1-2-3 and Symphony files. It does not support named ranges for Excel spreadsheets. When importing HTML files, Notes does not copy graphic images into the rich text field. A red square appears where a graphic image is supposed to be placed.

To import an external file into a rich text field on a form, follow these steps:

1. Open the database in which you would like to perform the document import.

2. Open the document containing the rich text field to which you would like the external file imported.

3. If the document is not already in Edit mode, press Ctrl+E or double-click the form.

4. Position your cursor in the rich text field to which you want the file imported.

5. Select File ➤ Import. The Import dialog box will be displayed.

6. Select the type of file you would like to import from the Files of Type drop-down box.

7. Select a file from your computer's file system or enter a filename.

8. Click the Import button.

If a particular file type includes import options, Notes will present a dialog box for selecting options. The file you selected will be imported into the rich text field at the point where the cursor was positioned.

Document Export

Document export allows you to create an external file containing data from a Notes document displayed through a Notes form. Notes can export to a number of file formats:

Ami Pro

ASCII text

CGM image

Microsoft Word RTF

TIFF 5 image

Word for Windows 6

WordPerfect 5.1

WordPerfect 6

WordPerfect 6.1

To export a document to an external file, follow these steps:

1. Open the database that contains the document you want to export.

2. Open the document you want to export.

3. Select File ➤ Export. The Export dialog box will be displayed.

4. Select the type of file you would like to export from the Save as Type drop-down box.

5. Select a file from your computer's file system or enter a filename.

6. Click the Export button.

If a particular file type includes export options, Notes will present a dialog box for selecting options. The document you selected will be exported to an external file.

PART

III

Advanced Use of
Notes 5

Notes Attachments

Another way to include information from other applications in Notes documents is to use file attachments. You can attach any file from your computer's file system, so there are no limitations on which types of data you can share.

Test Word OLE.doc

In a view, a document with an attachment is usually displayed with a paper clip icon. When you open the document, the attachment will be displayed as an icon in the rich text field of the document.

From within the document, you can do the following:

- Attach files
- Obtain information about the attachment
- Detach the attachment
- View the attachment
- Launch the attachment

Attaching Files

Files are attached from within rich text fields. It is simply a matter of choosing the file or files from your computer's file system. To try this, let's create another new memo (document) in your mail database and attach a file as follows:

1. Create a memo document in your mail database.

2. Make sure your cursor is positioned in the Body field, the blank area underneath the mail header information.

3. Select File ➤ Attach. The Create Attachment(s) dialog box appears (Figure 11.8).

FIGURE 11.8

The Create Attachment(s) dialog box

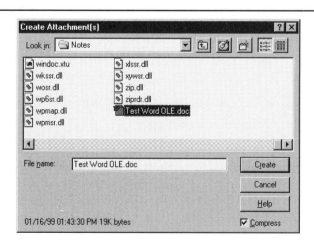

4. Select a file from your computer's file system. Try to select a document or some other data file (such as a Microsoft Word document). Notice that the Compress check box is selected by default.

5. Click the Create button after choosing a file.

An icon representing the file you chose will be displayed. The file will be compressed and attached to the document. To close the form, press Escape or click the *X* to the right of the form's task button. In the Close Window dialog box, select Discard Changes and then click the OK button.

Obtaining Information about Attachments

You can obtain information about attachments by viewing the attachment's properties. This is usually performed to find out the size of the attached file before opening it or saving to your computer's file system. There are a couple of ways to view the attachment's properties:

- Double-click the icon representing the attachment.
- Right-click the icon representing the attachment and select Attachment Properties.

Either way, the Attachment Properties InfoBox will open and display the Info tab (Figure 11.9).

FIGURE 11.9

The Attachment Properties InfoBox

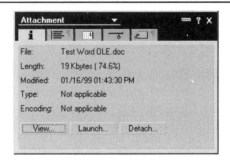

Saving (Detaching) Attachments

Saving (detaching) attachments is another common practice. If you come across a document in a discussion database or if someone mails you a message with an attachment, you may want to save that file to your computer's file system. This is called *detaching*. You can detach files by using one of these methods:

- Right-click the attachment icon and select Detach from the context menu.
- Double-click the attachment and click the Detach button on the Info tab of the Attachment Properties InfoBox.

PART

III

Advanced Use of
Notes 5

A Save Attachment dialog box will be presented, and you can choose the location in which to save the attachment on your computer's file system.

 TIP If a document has multiple attachments and you need to detach all of them, right-click one of the attachment icons and select Detach All from the context menu. In the Save Attachments To dialog box that is presented, select the location to which you would like to save the attachments in your computer's file system.

Viewing Attachments

You can use the built-in viewers to view attachments in Notes. They enable you to quickly preview an attached file without having to load the application in which it was created. This is a great feature when you don't have the application that created an attachment loaded on your computer. To view attachments, you can use either of the following two methods:

- Right-click the attachment's icon and select View from the context menu.
- Double-click the attachment's icon and click the View button on the Info tab of the Attachment Properties InfoBox.

A File Viewer window opens in your Notes application window and the attachment is displayed. With the attachment displayed in the File Viewer window, you can do the following:

- Navigate around the attached file.
- Select rich text from the attached file and copy it to the Clipboard (for pasting into a Notes rich text field or another application).
- Print the information displayed by the file viewer.

When you are finished viewing the attached file, press Escape or click the *X* to the right of the File Viewer window's task button. According to the R5 release notes, the following file formats are supported by the file viewer (this list is for the 32-bit Windows version of Notes):

Ami Pro 3.*x* (.sam)

Lotus WordPro 96/97 (.lwp)

Microsoft Word for Windows 6, 7, 97 (.doc)

Microsoft Word for Macintosh 2, 3

Rich Text Format (.rtf)

Revisable Form Text (.rft)

WordPerfect 5.x, 6.x, 7.x

WordPerfect 8

WordPerfect for Macintosh 2, 3

HTML (.htm)

Text file (.txt)

Executable file (.exe)

Zip file (.zip)

Lotus 1-2-3 3, 4, 5, 6.x (.wk*, .123)

Lotus 1-2-3 97 and 98 (.123)

Lotus 1-2-3 for Macintosh

Lotus 1-2-3 for OS/2 (.wg2)

Microsoft Excel 2.x, 3, 4, 5, 7, 97 (.xls)

AmiDraw (.sdw)

Bitmap (.bmp)

CCITT Group 3 Fax (.tif)

Computer Graphics Metafile (.cgm)

CompuServe (.gif)

JPEG file (.jpeg, .jpg)

Lotus Freelance (.pre, .prz)

Lotus Freelance for OS/2 (.prs)

Lotus PIC (.pic)

Microsoft PowerPoint 4.x, 7, 97 (.ppt)

Paintbrush/DCX (multipage PCX) (.pcx)

PICT and PICT2 Graphics (.pct)

Tagged Image File Format (.tif and .eps)

Windows Metafile Graphic (.wmf)

WordPerfect Graphics (.wpg)

PART

III

Advanced Use of
Notes 5

TIP If you view an attached Zip file, the file viewer will display its contents and let you extract the files contained within it.

WARNING You may get unexpected results when you print files from a viewer. If possible, print files from their native applications.

Launching an Attachment

If you launch an attachment from within Notes, you can load the application in which the attachment was created and open the attached file in one step. This option is useful if you need to modify the attached information. To launch an attachment from within Notes, use one of the following methods:

- Right-click the attachment's icon and select Launch from the context menu.
- Double-click the attachment's icon and click the Launch button on the Info tab of the Attachment Properties InfoBox.

 NOTE Edits made to files launched from attachments are not automatically saved back to the attachment. You must detach the file, make the edits, and then reattach the file.

Notes Mail Migration Tools

Notes and Domino Release 5 include two sets of mail migration tools. These tools enable you to switch from an existing mail system to Notes and/or Domino. There are server-side tools for automatically creating people and group entries based on information from an external directory and end-user tools for migrating user data from an existing mail system to a Notes mail database. These tools are called Domino Upgrade Services (DUS).

The server-side tools are designed to integrate with the Domino Administrator client and are made available to the Domino system administrator in the user registration screen. Domino ships with a predefined set of tools that support major mail and directory systems. Also, third-party developers can create additional tools that become part of DUS. See the Domino Administration Help database or other administration documentation for more information.

The end-user tools are designed to work in conjunction with DUS. Generally, the Domino system administrator would initiate an *upgrade-by-mail* process that would send an upgrade e-mail to end users; the upgrade e-mail will walk them through the migration process. The end-user tools can also be run manually at the Notes client machine. The following tools are packaged as an executable file that you can launch at the command line:

- cc:Mail client migration tools
- Microsoft Mail client migration tools
- Microsoft Exchange/Outlook client migration tools

These tools only migrate archives and personal address books. Some of the other tools are actually Notes databases that you launch by selecting File ≻ Database ≻ Open, including:

- GroupWise 4 client migration tools
- GroupWise 5 client migration tools
- Netscape client migration tools
- Eudora client migration tools
- Calendar client migration tools (supports Organizer 2.x/97, Schedule+ 1.0/7.x, and OnTime)

If you install these migration tools, the associated Notes database will be installed in your Notes Data directory. See the specific database for more information on migrating manually.

 NOTE The end-user tools are not installed by default. You must select Custom when performing the Notes setup. In the Lotus Notes Installation dialog box, select the Migration Tools check box. Click the Change button to select which specific end-user migration tools you wish to install.

As previously mentioned, the end-user migration tools are designed to run in conjunction with the server-side tools in DUS. For more information on running these tools on your own, visit the Lotus SmartMove Web site at www.lotus.com/migration. This is also a good resource for finding migration tools offered by third-party partners, which is important if you are using an existing mail system that is not directly supported by Release 5.

Notes SQL

Another way to integrate Notes with other applications is a technology called Notes SQL, which turns Notes databases into Open Database Connectivity (ODBC) data sources. These data sources are then available to other Windows applications that support ODBC.

PART

III

Advanced Use of
Notes 5

For example, you can perform a mail merge in Microsoft Word by using your Notes Personal Address Book database and Notes SQL. Other Microsoft Office applications support ODBC as well. You use Microsoft Access to read (and modify) Notes databases or use Microsoft Excel to perform analysis. This is a powerful and relatively easy way to integrate other applications with Notes.

To obtain Notes SQL, visit the Lotus Developer Central Web site at `www.lotus-developer.com` and search for "Notes SQL". Look for Notes SQL version 2.05. It is designed to support Notes Release 5 and has many improvements and fixes.

Summary

In this chapter, we explored various methods for integrating Notes and Notes data with other applications. We explained how Notes supports the use of the Windows Clipboard for copying and pasting information and how Notes supports the Windows object linking and embedding (OLE) specification for integrating with other Windows applications. We have demonstrated the import/export and attachment capabilities of Notes. In addition, we introduced the migration facilities bundled with Notes and the Notes SQL technology that can be downloaded from the Lotus Developer Central Web site. In the next chapter, we will explore the security features of Lotus Notes.

CHAPTER 12

Securing Your Data

FEATURING:

Since its inception, Lotus Notes has incorporated sophisticated security capabilities. In large part, early adopters were attracted to Notes because of its security features. What we're referring to is the Public Key Infrastructure (PKI) technology built in to Notes and Domino. This certificate-based PKI solution provides authentication between Notes workstations and Domino servers, secure e-mail with electronic signatures and encryption, database encryption, data encryption for documents or fields, and much more. The Notes/Domino PKI solution ensures secure communication and collaboration across entire enterprises.

The Notes/Domino PKI solution is highly sophisticated. It includes an end-to-end management system for creating certifying entities, creating User IDs (also called Notes ID) with specific certificates, changing the identity of users (e.g., when a person's name changes due to marriage), renewing certificates that expire, and recovering ID files. In this chapter, we'll explain how this technology affects you as a user. See Chapters 16, 18, and 19 for more information on how to incorporate security into databases that you develop. For more information on administering Domino security, see the Domino 5 Administration Help database.

Notes and Domino Release 5 also support X.509 certificates (Internet certificates) for using standards-based PKI solutions to communicate securely. Domino servers can establish secure communications with non-Notes clients, such as Web browsers, and Notes can establish secure communications with Internet servers other than Domino. Notes stores X.509 certificates in your User ID file the same way it stores Notes/Domino certificates. For more information on using X.509 certificates in Notes to communicate securely in standards-based PKI environments (including the Internet), see Chapter 10. For more information on Domino X.509 support, see the Domino 5 Administration Help database.

Understanding User ID Files

Your User ID file is the key to security in Lotus Notes. It contains everything you need to establish a connection to a Domino server. In Release 5, it is also used to store certificates required for secure Internet communications.

What Is a User ID File?

The User ID file is a special file provided to you by your Domino administrator. It tells Domino servers who you are. Your ID contains your name, certificates issued to you, your public/private keys, and secret encryption keys issued to you. It is generally stored in your Notes Data directory, but it can also be stored on removable media such as a disk. Your User ID file is critically important to the operation of Notes.

NOTE In Notes Release 5, your ID file is used for both Domino and Internet security. For information about how your ID file is used for Internet security, see "X.509 Certificates (Internet Certificates)" later in this chapter.

Examining Your ID File

Notes provides a mechanism for examining the contents of your ID file. Because many of the features of Notes depend on security information contained within this file, it is important to understand how to use this tool. You can view, for example, the following information:

- Your name
- ID filename
- ID type (hierarchical or flat)
- Certificates
- Public/private keys
- Secret encryption keys

You can examine your ID as follows:

1. Select File ➢ Tools ➢ User ID. The Enter Password dialog box will be displayed.

2. Type your password and press Enter (or click the OK button). The Basics section of the User ID dialog box will be displayed, (see Figure 12.1).

 NOTE In Notes, passwords are case sensitive. This means that you must type your password exactly as it was typed when it was set. Also, Notes displays multiple *X* characters for every character you type when entering your password. This is a security feature that prevents others from determining how many characters are contained in your password.

The Basics section displays information about your ID file and has buttons for setting and clearing your password. The Certificates section displays information about certificates issued to you and has buttons for managing certificates. The Encryption section displays information about encryption keys contained within your ID and has

PART

III

Advanced Use of
Notes 5

buttons for managing them. The More section has buttons for managing your ID and your public key. To close the User ID dialog box, click the OK button or press Escape.

FIGURE 12.1

The Basics section of the User ID dialog box

 NOTE The Security field identifies whether you are using International or North American security. North American is more secure, but it is subject to United States encryption export regulations. See the Notes Help database for more information.

The Importance of Your Public Key

Your public key is a special code contained within your ID. As the name implies, it is the portion of your unique identity that is shared with others. With your public key, other Notes users can participate in secure Notes/Domino communication with you. For example, other users can send you encrypted messages. These are messages that have been scrambled so that other users, even administrators of the Domino environment, cannot read them. When other users send you encrypted messages, your public key is used to encrypt them. When you receive an encrypted message, Notes is able to decrypt it because your ID contains a private key that can unlock encryption that was performed using your public key. Only your private key can decrypt these messages.

 NOTE Your public key is also used to verify the validity of certificates and cross certificates, which are discussed later this chapter.

Your public key is stored in the Domino Directory and is available to other users in your Domino domain. Colleagues outside of your Domino domain need a copy of your public key in their Personal Address Book database. The easiest method of providing your public key to people outside your Domino domain is through e-mail. To e-mail your public key to someone, perform these steps:

1. Select File ➤ Tools ➤ User ID. The Enter Password dialog box will be displayed.

2. Type your password and press Enter (or click the OK button).

3. Click the More Options button. The More Options section of the User ID dialog box will be displayed, as shown in Figure 12.2.

FIGURE 12.2

The More Options section of the User ID dialog box

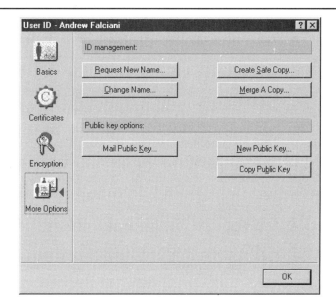

4. Click the Mail Public Key button. The Mail Public Key dialog box will be displayed.

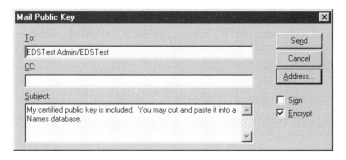

PART

III

Advanced Use of
Notes 5

5. Enter the e-mail address of the person you would like to send your public key to, or click the Address button to select an address from your Personal Address Book or other directory.

6. If necessary, change the text in the Subject field.

7. To send a secure message, select the Sign and Encrypt check boxes.

8. Click the Send button. An e-mail message will be sent to the recipients listed. The body of the message will contain your public key.

9. Click the OK button to close the User ID dialog box.

When the recipients receive the message, they can copy and paste your public key from the e-mail message to their Personal Address Book database. You can also use the Copy Public Key button in the More Options section of the User ID dialog box. This button copies your public key to the Windows Clipboard. You can then paste it into an e-mail message. You can also paste it into a text (ASCII) file that can be copied to a disk and mailed through the postal service.

The New Public Key button in the More Options section of the User ID dialog box is used to create a new set of keys (public and private) for your ID. If you create a new set of keys, your ID file containing these new keys is sent to your Domino administrator. Your Domino administrator recertifies your ID with these new keys and sends you an e-mail with your new certificate and instructions on how to accept it. When you receive the e-mail message, follow the instructions to accept your new certificate into your ID file.

 WARNING Your new certificate replaces your original one. Any previously encrypted data will become inaccessible. Only use this option if your ID has become compromised.

Understanding Certificates

If you think of your ID file as being similar to your driver's license, certificates are like the seal placed on your license from the issuing state. Just as the seal verifies the authenticity of your license and your identity, certificates verify the authenticity of your User ID file and the information it contains (name and public key).

Originally, Notes used a "flat" certificate structure. ID files contained a name and individual certificates that validated that name to specific certifying entities. Validation and authentication between Notes clients and Notes servers (before they were called Domino servers) using flat certificates occurred when their associated ID files contained a certificate in common. Flat certificates were also used to sign and encrypt e-mail and to encrypt documents in databases. Since Release 3, Notes has also supported a more sophisticated "hierarchical" certificate structure. We will only discuss hierarchical certificates here. For more information on using flat certificates in your Notes Release 5 environment, see the Notes 5 Help database and the Domino 5 Administration Help database.

NOTE Validation and authentication is the process performed when a Notes client attempts to connect to a Domino server. It is also used between Domino servers. This process ensures the identity of both participants. It is a two-way process. The server ensures the identity of the client, and the client ensures the identity of the server. The details of the validation and authentication process are outside the scope of the book, but you can find more information about it in the Domino 5 Administration Help database.

With hierarchical certificates, ID files contain a name and a certificate that validates the name to an organizational certifying entity. In addition, they contain a hierarchy of certificates that validate the organizational certifying entity to intermediate organizational certifying entities and ultimately to the root certifier (the certifying entity that validated all organizational certifying entities in the hierarchy). Validation and authentication between Notes clients and Domino servers using hierarchical certificates occurs when their associated ID files contain certificates generated from the same root certifier (meaning that they are in the same hierarchy). If the client and server are in different hierarchies, Notes will attempt to use cross certificates. Cross certificates provide a system of trust between hierarchies.

NOTE Your identity in Notes is your fully qualified name, which includes your full name plus your hierarchy of certifying entities (e.g., Andrew Falciani/Users/EDSTest).

Renewing Certificates

Certificates issued to you have an expiration date. When they expire, they become invalid. This ensures security by requiring that the Domino administrator renew certificates periodically. You can use the User ID dialog box to check the expiration dates for certificates issued to you by following these steps:

1. Select File ➤ Tools ➤ User ID. The Enter Password dialog box will be displayed.
2. Type your password and press Enter (or click the OK button).
3. Click the Certificates button. The Certificates section of the User ID dialog box will be displayed, as shown in Figure 12.3.

PART

III

Advanced Use of
Notes 5

FIGURE 12.3

The Certificates section of the User ID dialog box

4. Select an entry in the Certificate Issued By field. The expiration date of the certificate will be displayed underneath the Certificate Issued To field.

5. Click the OK button to close the User ID dialog box.

Prior to the certificate's expiration date, you will be presented with a dialog box notifying you of the expiring certificate every time you launch Notes. To continue using Notes, you will need to renew the certificate. When you do so, its expiration date is updated. Here's a simple process for updating your certificate:

1. Select File ➣ Tools ➣ User ID. The Enter Password dialog box will be displayed.

2. Type your password and press Enter (or click the OK button).

3. Click the Certificates button. The Certificates section of the User ID dialog box will be displayed.

4. Click the Request Certificate button. The Mail Certificate Request dialog box will be displayed.

5. Enter the e-mail address of the administrator you would like to send your Safe ID to, or click the Address button to select an address from your Personal Address Book or other directory (see the next section for more on Safe IDs).

6. Click the Send button. An e-mail message will be sent to the administrator(s) listed. A secure copy of your ID will be included as an attachment to the message.

7. Click the OK button to close the User ID dialog box.

When the Domino administrator receives this message, he will renew the certificate and send an e-mail message back to you. Upon receiving this message, you need to merge the updated certificate into your ID file by following these steps:

1. Open the e-mail message containing the updated certificate. The subject of the message contains the instructions for merging the updated certificate into your ID file.

2. Select Actions ➤ Accept Certificate. The Enter Password dialog box will be displayed.

3. Type your password and press Enter (or click the OK button).

4. A message stating that the certificate has been inserted into your ID file will be displayed on the status bar.

Requesting Cross Certificates

To successfully validate and authenticate with a Domino server whose ID was created from a different certificate hierarchy than your User ID, cross certificates must be issued. Cross certificates act as a trust mechanism between two certificate hierarchies. The Domino administrator must issue a cross certificate to your ID, to the ID of any organizational certifying entities in your hierarchy, or to the ID of your hierarchy's root certifier. The level at which the Domino administrator issues the cross certificate determines the scope of the access being offered. Issuing the cross certificate to your ID is the most restrictive, and issuing it to your hierarchy's root certifier is the most open. Because issuing cross certificates is a Domino administration function, we will not discuss it in detail here. See the Domino 5 Administration Help database for more information on issuing cross certificates.

As a user or database developer, you will need to know how to request a cross certificate. This will initiate the process by which the Domino administrator will issue the cross certificate for your ID. If the Domino administrator to whom you are making the request is accessible via e-mail, you can request a cross certificate by sending an e-mail message. If not, you can request a certificate by mailing a disk through the postal service. Either way, you will need to create a safe copy of your User ID file. This is called a Safe ID. Safe IDs contain only enough information (including your public key) to enable others to issue cross certificates for your ID. To create a safe copy of your ID and request a cross certificate via e-mail, follow these steps:

1. Select File ➤ Tools ➤ User ID. The Enter Password dialog box will be displayed.

2. Type your password and press Enter (or click the OK button).

3. Click the More Options button. The More Options section of the User ID dialog box will be displayed.

PART

III

Advanced Use of
Notes 5

4. Click the Create Safe Copy button. The Enter Safe Copy ID File Name dialog box will be displayed.

5. Select a location for the Safe ID, enter a filename, and click the Save button.

 NOTE If you cannot send the request via e-mail, save your Safe ID to a disk. Then, skip the remaining steps and mail it to the Domino administrator through the postal service.

6. Click the Certificates button. The Certificates section of the User ID dialog box will be displayed.

7. Click the Request Cross Certificate button. The Choose ID to Be Certified dialog box will be displayed.

8. Select your Safe ID and click the Open button. The Mail Cross Certificate Request dialog box will be displayed.

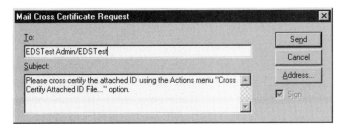

9. Enter the e-mail address of the administrator you would like to send your Safe ID to, or click the Address button to select an address from your Personal Address Book or other directory.

10. Click the Send button. An e-mail message will be sent to the administrator(s) listed. Your Safe ID will be included as an attachment to the message.

11. Click the OK button to close the User ID dialog box.

When the Domino administrator receives your Safe ID, he will issue the cross certificate for your ID.

 NOTE If the Domino administrator has not properly issued the cross certificate, you will receive an error stating that the server does not contain any cross certificates capable of authenticating you.

Accepting Cross Certificates

After a Domino administrator issues a cross certificate to your ID, you will need to accept a cross certificate from the foreign hierarchy. This is required to complete the two-way process of verifying certificates (mentioned earlier in this chapter). When you acccpt a cross certificate, it is stored in your Personal Address Book database. You can view your current cross certificates by opening the Advanced/Certificates view of your Personal Address Book database. Accepting cross certificates is an automatic process that is initiated when any one of the following occurs:

- You attempt to access a Domino server in the foreign hierarchy.
- You read a signed or encrypted message from someone in the foreign hierarchy.
- You open a database signed by a person from a foreign hierarchy.

When the automatic process of accepting cross certificates is initiated, the Create Cross Certificate dialog box will be displayed (see Figure 12.4). Just click the Yes button and Notes will automatically accept the cross certificate.

FIGURE 12.4

The Create Cross Certificate dialog box

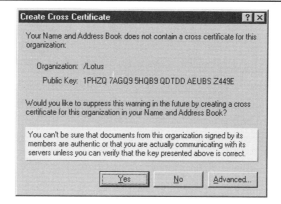

Protecting Your ID File

Your ID file is your key to using Notes. Anyone who gains access to it can impersonate you in the system. For this reason, it is critically important that you protect this file.

Setting a Password on Your ID File

The most important security measure you can implement is a password. This ensures that no one can easily use your ID file if they happen to obtain a copy of it. The Domino administrator chooses the minimum level of password protection required for your ID file when it is created. ID file password protection ranges from no password to very complex password patterns. If you are setting a password for the first time, you will either have no starting password or one established by your administrator. To set the password on your ID file, follow this procedure:

1. Select File ➤ Tools ➤ User ID. If your ID file currently has a password, the Enter Password dialog box will be displayed.

2. If the Enter Password dialog box is displayed, type your password and press Enter (or click the OK button). The Basics section of the User ID dialog box will be displayed.

3. Click the Set Password button. If your ID file currently has a password, the Enter Password dialog box will be displayed again.

4. If the Enter Password dialog box is displayed, type your current password and press Enter (or click the OK button). The Set Password dialog box will be displayed. The dialog box will include a message stating the minimum password requirements.

5. Enter a new password for your ID file and click the OK button (or press Enter). Another Set Password dialog box will be displayed.

 NOTE If you do not enter a password meeting the minimum requirements set by the Domino administrator, a dialog box will be displayed requesting that you enter another password.

6. Enter your new password again and click the OK button (or press Enter). This is intended to verify that you know what password you entered. You will be returned to the User ID dialog box.

7. Click the OK button to close the User ID dialog box.

If your Domino administrator has configured your ID file so no password is required, you will also have the option of clearing the password from your ID file. In the Basics section of the User ID dialog box, click the Clear Password button.

 NOTE This same procedure is used to change your password.

Backing Up Your ID File

Because your User ID file contains a private key that uniquely identifies you, there is no way to re-create it. This is quite different from systems that simply use name and password combinations from a user access list. For this reason, you must take precautions to protect your ID file. Make sure you create a secure backup. In fact, it is good practice to create multiple secure backups just in case one becomes corrupted. We recommend copying your ID file to a disk that you can store in a locked cabinet or room.

WARNING Your User ID contains a public/private key pair that is calculated when the ID is created. It cannot be re-created! If the file becomes damaged, you forget the password, or you lose the file, you will not be able to read data encrypted with that ID.

ID Recovery

Notes and Domino Release 5 include a new ID recovery mechanism. ID recovery requires that the Domino administrator set up ID recovery for your ID file. This adds recovery information to your ID file and creates an encrypted copy in an ID repository database. For more information on setting up ID recovery, see the Domino Release 5 Administration database.

As a user, you will initiate the ID recovery process if you lose your ID, you forget your password, or your ID file becomes damaged. You initiate the ID recovery process by selecting File ➤ Tools ➤ Recover ID and selecting an ID file to recover from the File Open dialog box presented. You will be required to enter a series of passwords provided by your Domino administrator (or administrators). For more information, see the Notes 5 Help database.

WARNING During the recovery process, you will be prompted to enter a new password. If you do not enter a new password, you will need to recover your ID file again.

NOTE Remember to replace all copies of your ID file with the recovered ID file.

PART

III

Advanced Use of
Notes 5

Switching ID Files

When you launch Notes and access a Domino server (or perform any other action that requires your User ID file), Notes opens the most recently used ID file on the workstation. If the most recently used ID file is stored on the computer, Notes will attempt to open it. Notes prompts you for a password if one exists. If the most recently used ID file is stored on a disk or other external media, Notes prompts you to insert the appropriate media or select another ID file. Selecting another ID file is called *switching IDs*. Switching IDs is useful when multiple users share the same computer to use Notes. IDs are also switched when one person has multiple User ID files, such as a Domino administrator who has ID files for each environment she manages. In addition to switching IDs when Notes is first launched, you can switch IDs at any time in your Notes session. To switch IDs, follow these steps:

1. Select File ➤ Tools ➤ Switch ID. All active Notes tasks will be closed, and the Choose ID to Switch To dialog box will be displayed.

2. Select an ID file and click the Open button. Notes will present the Enter Password dialog box if the selected ID file has a password.

3. If the Enter Password dialog box is presented, enter your password and press Enter (or click the OK button).

Notes locks the original User ID file (synonymous with logging out) and activates the selected User ID file. If you switch back to the original User ID file, you will be prompted for a password.

 NOTE You should always lock your ID file when you walk away from your computer. You can do this manually by selecting File ➤ Tools ➤ Lock or by pressing the F5 key. You can also set a time-out that will automatically lock your User ID file after a predetermined period of inactivity. To set a time-out, select File ➤ Preferences ➤ User Preferences and enter the number of minutes in the Lock ID After field.

Changing Your Username

Notes allows you to change your username. When you do so, all of your existing certificates are invalidated, so a name change should only be performed when absolutely necessary. One common event that makes a name change necessary is marriage. Because your existing certificates are invalidated when your name is changed, you will be required to obtain new certificates. Notes and Domino perform this automatically.

You inform your Domino administrator of your new name, the administrator makes the appropriate changes to the Domino Directory, and you are prompted to accept the name change the next time you connect to your home/mail server. You can also use Notes/Domino mail to initiate a name change as follows:

1. Select File ➤ Tools ➤ User ID. The Enter Password dialog box will be displayed.

2. Type your password and press Enter (or click the OK button).

3. Click the More Options button. The More Options section of the User ID dialog box will be displayed.

4. Click the Request New Name button. The Change User Name dialog box will be displayed.

5. Enter your new username and click the OK button. The Mail New Name Request dialog box will be displayed.

6. Enter the e-mail address of the administrator you would like to send your name change request to or click the Address button to select an address from your Personal Address Book or other directory.

7. Click the Send button. An e-mail message will be sent to the administrator(s) listed. Your ID with the new name will be included as an attachment to the message.

8. Click the OK button to close the User ID dialog box.

When the Domino administrator receives your ID with the new name, he will recertify the ID and make the appropriate changes to the Domino Directory. The next time you connect to your home/mail server, you will be prompted to accept the name change into your ID file. If the Domino administrator does not make the appropriate changes to the Domino directory, you can manually accept the name change into your ID as follows:

1. Open the e-mail sent back to you from the Domino administrator.

2. Select Actions ➤ Accept Certificate. The Accept New ID Information dialog box will be displayed.

3. Click the OK button to accept the name change into your ID file.

 NOTE You can also use Safe IDs on a disk to request a name change. See the Notes 5 Help database for more information.

PART

III

Advanced Use of
Notes 5

WARNING Your name is used in database Access Control Lists (ACLs) to provide access to information. In addition to changing your name, the Domino administrator must also ensure that database ACLs contain your new name. Your name must also be changed in any Domino Directory groups to which it was added.

X.509 Certificates (Internet Certificates)

Your User ID is also used to store X.509 certificates (Internet certificates). These certificates are similar to the Notes/Domino certificates discussed earlier. They allow you to trust the Internet server with which you are communicating or the secure Internet e-mail messages you exchange. X.509 certificates are based on accepted standards and are supported by most leading Internet client and server applications. For example, you can use Notes to send a secure e-mail message to a person who is using Netscape Messenger (the Internet mail client application included with Netscape Communicator). These certificates function in a manner similar to the way original Notes flat certificates function. If the client and server (or two servers) have a certificate in common, they allow secure communication to occur. For more information on using X.509 certificates, see Chapter 10, "Harnessing the Power of the Internet."

 WARNING If you use Notes in an Internet-only configuration, you will still have a User ID file. Notes will create your User ID file automatically during the installation process. This ID file will not contain any Domino certificates, but it will be used to store X.509 certificates. There is no way to re-create this file, so making a backup copy is extremely important. See "Backing Up Your ID File" earlier in this chapter for more information.

Securing Databases

Your User ID is used to establish secure communication with Domino servers. This is accomplished by using the validation and authentication process mentioned in "Understanding Certificates" earlier in this chapter. After successfully validating and authenticating, the Domino server will then determine whether or not you are authorized for access based on additional security established by the Domino administrator. Assuming you are authorized to access the server, you will then have to pass database-level security to actually open and use databases.

Access Control Lists

The database Access Control List (ACL) is the Notes/Domino database-level security mechanism. It determines who can access a given database and what level of authority they have been granted. The ACL can also contain database-specific roles that further define the functionality in the database to which the user has access. See Chapter 16, "Creating Your First Database," for more information on defining the ACL for databases that you develop. Also, maintaining the database ACL is generally a Domino administration function. See the Domino 5 Administration Help database for more information.

Notes includes an interface for viewing the database ACL and for modifying it if you have the appropriate authority. To view the ACL of a particular database, follow these steps:

1. Open the database for which you wish to view the ACL.

2. Select File ➤ Database ➤ Access Control. The Access Control List dialog box will be displayed (Figure 12.5).

FIGURE 12.5

The Access Control List dialog box

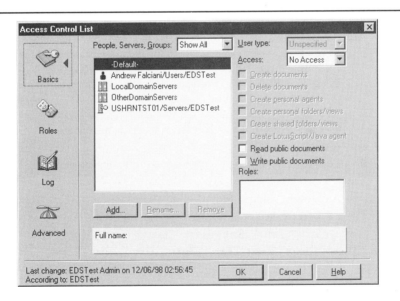

The Access Control List dialog box has four sections: Basics, Roles, Log, and Advanced. The Basics section is where you define which individuals or groups have which level of access to the database. Groups listed in the ACL match group entries in the Domino Directory or your Personal Address Book database if the database is stored locally on your computer. There are seven access levels: Manager, Designer, Edit, Author, Reader,

Depositor, and No Access. You can also choose to add individuals or groups to roles. See Chapter 16 for more information on access levels and roles. The Roles section allows you to add, rename, or delete roles from the ACL. The Log section displays an audit trail of changes made to the ACL. This is useful when you're trying to determine why a change was made to the ACL. The Advanced section includes additional special options. The administration server defines which Domino server will control the Admin Process for the database (see the Domino 5 Administration Help database). The Enforce a Consistent Access Control List Across All Replicas of This Database option instructs Notes to enforce the ACL even when the database is replicated. This is generally used to ensure that roles work properly when databases are run from the local workstation instead of a Domino server. The Maximum Name & Password option defines the maximum access level allowed when this database is used with a Web browser through a Domino server. If this option is set to Editor, you would be restricted to Editor access when using this database with a Web browser even if you have Designer or Manager access.

 NOTE When databases are replicated locally, the ACL is ignored unless the Enforce a Consistent Access Control List Across All Replicas of This Database option is enabled. Contrary to the wording of this option, it does not provide complete security to local replicas. All you have to do to gain access to the database is add a group that has higher authority (such as Manager rights) to your Personal Address Book database and add your name to that group. The only way to ensure security of data locally is to encrypt it.

 You can also use the Access Level indicator on the status bar to check your access level to the current database. This is the third area from the right on the status bar. It will display an icon corresponding to your access level to the current database. The key icon represents Manager access, which is typically the access level you will have to your mail database and other databases where you are the owner. If you click the Access Level Indicator button, the Groups and Roles dialog box will be displayed. There will be a check mark next to all groups to which you belong. Click the Done button to close the Groups and Roles dialog box.

Database Encryption

Database encryption protects a database that is stored locally. It scrambles the database so only the authorized person can gain access. This is generally done to protect databases that you store locally on your computer so others may not access them. Database encryption is useful when you are sharing a computer with multiple users or when you are traveling with your notebook computer (it would protect your information if your notebook computer is stolen). Your User ID is used to perform database encryption. The only way to open an encrypted database is to use the ID with which it was encrypted. The interface for encrypting databases is in the Database Properties InfoBox. See Chapter 16 for more information about how to encrypt databases.

Document Encryption

Document encryption protects individual data elements on documents by scrambling data in specific fields. You can use document encryption to ensure that only appropriate individuals can read certain data in Notes databases. For document encryption to work, at least one field on a form must be designed to support encryption. Fields that support encryption are designated with red brackets instead of the normal brackets. Optionally, a form can be designed to use a default secret encryption key. See Chapter 18, "Using Forms to Collect Data," for more information on designing forms.

Field data can be encrypted with either secret encryption keys or the public keys of specific users. You can encrypt data with public keys when there are only a few individuals who need access (because you have to select each person from the Domino Directory). For more information on public keys, see "The Importance of Your Public Key" earlier in this chapter. Secret encryption keys are keys that you can create and share with other Notes/Domino users. Anyone who has the secret encryption key can access the encrypted data by using that key. These keys require a little effort to set up, but they make it much easier to provide access to larger numbers of people. To manage your secret encryption keys, follow these steps:

1. Select File ➤ Tools ➤ User ID. The Enter Password dialog box will be displayed.

2. Type your password and press Enter (or click the OK button). The User ID dialog box opens to the Basics section.

3. Click the Encryption button. The Encryption section of the User ID dialog box will be displayed, as shown in Figure 12.6.

From this dialog box, you can create new secret encryption keys, delete existing keys, mail keys to other users, and import/export keys to files. If you are just establishing a secure database, you will use this dialog box to create a new secret encryption key. Only one person needs to create the new key. After it is created, that person just mails it to the other people using the Mail Key button or exports it to a file that can be imported by the other users. If you receive any secret encryption keys via e-mail, just open the message and follow the instructions to accept the encryption key. If you have successfully accepted it, the key will appear in your ID file.

FIGURE 12.6

The Encryption section of the User ID dialog box

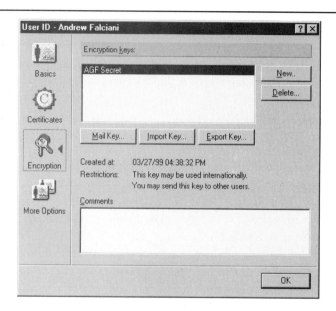

 WARNING Do not delete a secret encryption key from your ID file unless you are absolutely certain that there are no documents requiring this key. You will not be able to access encrypted field data on these documents after deleting the associated secret encryption key.

Field data will be automatically encrypted when you save a document by using a form that has a default secret encryption key and at least one field designed to support encryption. If you do not have the default secret encryption key designated on the form, you will not be able to save the document. Field data must be manually encrypted when the form does not have a default secret encryption key defined. To manually encrypt field data on documents, follow these steps:

1. Open the document for which you would like field data encrypted or select it in a view.

2. Select File ➤ Document Properties. The Document Properties InfoBox will appear.

3. Click the Security tab. The Security tab will be displayed (Figure 12.7).

FIGURE 12.7

*The Security tab of the
Document Properties
InfoBox*

4. Click the check-mark button to the right of the Secret Encryption Key drop-down box. A list of your existing secret encryption keys will be displayed.

5. Select the secret encryption key(s) from the list.

The selected secret encryption key(s) will be used to encrypt the field data. Anyone who opens this document and does not have at least one of the selected secret encrypted keys will be presented with a dialog box informing them that some of the data is not accessible. Data in the fields designed for encryption will also be hidden from these people.

This is also how you encrypt field data with public keys. Just click the Add Public Key button and select the appropriate people from the Domino Directory or your Personal Address Book database. Only those individuals selected (or those possessing one of the selected secret encryption keys) will be able to access the encrypted field data.

 NOTE An individual only needs one of the selected encryption keys (either a secret encryption key or his public key) to access the encrypted field data. Also, all fields designed to support encryption are encrypted using the selected public or secret encryption keys. Users with the appropriate keys will be able to access all encrypted field data on the document.

Mail Encryption

Notes supports encryption of e-mail messages that you send and those that you save in your mail database. When you encrypt e-mail messages that you send to other users, the message can't be read by anyone except the intended recipient. The message is encrypted using the recipient's public key, so only the recipient's User ID can decrypt it. When e-mail messages that you save to your mail database are encrypted, they can't be read by anyone but you. This is true even when someone gains access to your mail database. The Mail and News section of the User Preferences dialog box has options for enabling encryption of all sent and saved messages. You can also encrypt sent messages individually by selecting the Encrypt option in the Delivery Options dialog box when you send an e-mail. See Chapter 5, "Communicating with Notes Mail," for information on how to encrypt sent and saved messages.

 NOTE To encrypt sent e-mail, you must have access to the recipient's public key. If you are sending encrypted Notes/Domino mail, you need the recipient's Notes public key. See "The Importance of Your Public Key" earlier in this chapter for more information on Notes public keys. If you are sending encrypted Internet mail, you need the public key from your recipient's X.509 certificate. See Chapter 10 for more information on X.509 certificates.

Domino also supports encryption of incoming e-mail messages. This feature instructs the Domino server to use your public key to encrypt messages prior to delivering them to your mail database's Inbox. This protects e-mail messages even when another person gains access to your mail database. The Domino administrator can configure the server to encrypt incoming messages for all users, or it can be configured on a per-user basis. If you have requirements for protecting incoming e-mail messages, ask your administrator to enable encryption in your Person document in the Domino Directory.

Specifying Workstation Security

Notes includes a feature called the Execution Control List (ECL) that puts a restriction on what application code is allowed to do within the Notes environment. The ECL is used to restrict Notes formula/LotusScript code, Java applets, and JavaScript code signed by specific users. In many cases, the Domino administrator will establish your workstation's ECL. In some environments, you may not have access to change the ECL. To view your workstation's ECL, follow these steps:

1. Select File ➣ Preferences ➣ User Preferences. The User Preferences dialog box will be displayed.

2. Click the Security Options button. The Workstation Security dialog box will be displayed (Figure 12.8).

*The Workstation
Security dialog box*

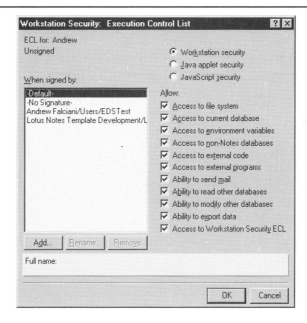

When you select an entry in the When Signed By field, the security options to the right will change to reflect that person's security settings. In addition, the security options that are allowed will change based on the type of security selected. The security types available include Workstation, Java Applet, and JavaScript. The Add, Rename, and Remove buttons allow you to manage names in your ECL. Click the OK button to save changes made to your ECL or click the Cancel button to keep your previous settings.

Summary

In this chapter, we presented an overview of the security system used by Notes. We discussed the purpose of the Notes User ID file and how it is used to establish secure communications. We explored the database security features of Notes and introduced the workstation security features. In the next chapter, we'll discuss the Notes configuration and show you how to set up Notes as a Domino client.

PART

III

Advanced Use of
Notes 5

PART IV

Configuring Notes 5

CHAPTER **13**

Setting Up Notes as a Domino Client

I n the Notes setup process, the Notes program files are copied to your computer's disk drive. The setup process initiates a Configuration Wizard that prompts you for information about your Domino server and Internet server environments. Based on the answers you provide, the Configuration Wizard completes the initial setup of Notes so you are able to use the software. See Appendix A, "Installing Lotus Notes 5," for more information on the installation process. In this chapter and in Chapter 14, "Setting Up Notes as an Internet Client," we'll explain what is involved in configuring Notes and how to change the configuration after the initial installation to meet your changing needs. This chapter focuses on Notes as a Domino client, and Chapter 14 focuses on Notes as an Internet client.

NOTE Because you can configure Notes to access Internet-based resources whether or not it is connected to a Domino server environment, we'll discuss the overall configuration in this chapter. In Chapter 14, we'll explain how to configure Notes in environments that do not include Domino servers.

Setting Preferences

One of the main elements of the Notes configuration is the notes.ini file, which is stored in the Notes program directory by default. It contains settings that define the Notes Data directory, import/export filter parameters, communication port information, and other properties. Normally, you won't need to modify this file directly. Elements inside of Notes are used to manipulate settings contained in this file. For example, you can change the Notes Data directory in the Local Database Folder field of the User Preferences dialog box. The two main interfaces for manipulating settings in the notes.ini file are the User Preferences dialog box and the Location document. The User Preferences dialog box is discussed in the next section, and the Location document is discussed later in this chapter.

If necessary, you can also use a standard text editor such as Windows Notepad to modify the notes.ini file. Again, this is not normally required. Notes makes changes to the file as needed based on changes you make inside the User Preferences dialog box and the Location document. For a complete reference to notes.ini file parameters, see the Notes/Domino Release 5 Administration Help database.

WARNING If you plan to make changes to the notes.ini file directly, make sure you create a backup copy first so you can revert to the saved copy if your changes cause problems in Notes.

NOTE The `notes.ini` file can also be moved to the Notes `Data` directory if you plan to create more than one data directory on the same machine. If you do move the `notes.ini` file, make sure you modify Windows shortcuts to specifically identify where it is located on your computer's disk drive. For example, a shortcut containing a target of `c:\notes\notes .exe =c:\notes\user2\notes.ini` instructs Windows to launch Notes using a `notes.ini` file located in the `c:\notes\user2` directory.

Notes also maintains certain settings in the Windows Registry. These settings define the services that Notes offers to other Windows programs. For example, Notes can insert itself in Windows as the default Web browser so that all Web pages accessed from within Windows will be opened inside of Notes. Again, these settings are manipulated in the User Preferences dialog box and the Location document. You can use the Windows RegEdit utility to modify these settings directly in the Windows Registry, but there is usually no need to do so.

 WARNING If you plan to modify Windows Registry settings directly, make sure you back up your computer's Windows Registry first so you can revert to the saved copy if your changes cause problems in Notes.

Using the User Preferences Dialog Box

One of the key methods of manipulating the Notes configuration is to use the User Preferences dialog box, which contains settings that have an impact on the operation of Notes. Most of the settings affect Notes whether it is being used as a Domino client or an Internet client. For this reason, we'll cover all of the settings in this section. To access the User Preferences dialog box, select File ➢ Preferences ➢ User Preferences. There are four buttons on the left side, which represent different categories of settings:

- Basics
- International
- Mail and News
- Ports

Basics   When you click the Basics button, the User Preferences dialog box displays a set of general settings (see Figure 13.1):

  Display Options   Allows you to choose the icon color scheme and the size of the bookmark icons. You can click the Default Fonts button to modify the default fonts that Notes uses. You can also click the User Dictionary button to

PART

IV

Configuring Notes 5

bring up a dialog box you can use to manage your user dictionary (discussed in Chapter 3, "Working with Notes Databases"). In addition, you can choose how you want Notes to empty the Trash folder in Notes databases.

Startup Options   Allows you to enable processes that run when Notes is launched. The Check Subscriptions option instructs Notes to monitor subscriptions in the background. (See Chapter 2, "Getting Familiar with Notes," for more information on using subscriptions.) The Scan for Unread option instructs Notes to perform the Scan Unread process when Notes is first launched. You can also select Edit ➢ Unread Marks ➢ Scan Unread to perform this process after Notes is already running. The Prompt for Location option tells Notes to prompt you to select a location to use when Notes is launched. If this is not enabled, Notes will use the Location document from the preceding session. Location documents are discussed later in this chapter. The Enable Scheduled Local Agents option tells Notes to execute a background process to run Agents that have been scheduled to run on your computer. The Local Database Folder field allows you to change the Notes Data directory.

Additional Options   Allows you to enable other options that Notes supports. The following options affect how Notes functions as an Internet client and are explained further in Chapter 10, "Harnessing the Power of the Internet":

- Make Internet URLs (http://.....) into Hotspots
- Enable Java Applets
- Enable JavaScript
- Enable Java Access from JavaScript
- Enable Plugins in Notes Browser
- Enable ActiveX in Notes Browser
- Accept Cookies
- Make Notes the Default Web Browser on My System
- Enable MS Office 97 SendTo to Notes

The Retain View Column Sorting option instructs Notes to "remember" your view sorting selections between sessions. Without this option enabled, you would have to sort views each time you launched Notes. The Use Web Palette option instructs Notes to use the color palette supported by Web browsers. This provides a more seamless interface for viewing both Notes databases and Web pages. The other options are self-explanatory. The Security Options button brings up a dialog box that allows you to modify the workstation security settings for the machine you are using to run Notes. See Chapter 12, "Securing Your Data," for more information. The Lock ID After field instructs Notes to clear your password after the amount of time entered in the text box has passed. It is the same as selecting F5 to clear your password manually.

FIGURE 13.1

*The Basics settings in
the User Preferences
dialog box*

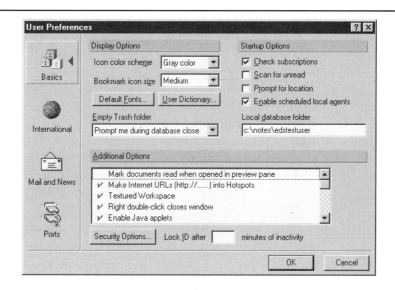

International   When you click the International button, the User Preferences dialog box displays a set of localization settings (see Figure 13.2):

> **General Settings**   Allows you to choose which regional settings Notes should use. The option you choose for Regional Settings determines which localization options will be set in the Override section.
>
> **Override Settings**   Allows you to choose individual overrides to the Regional Settings option you chose.

FIGURE 13.2

*The International
settings in the User
Preferences dialog box*

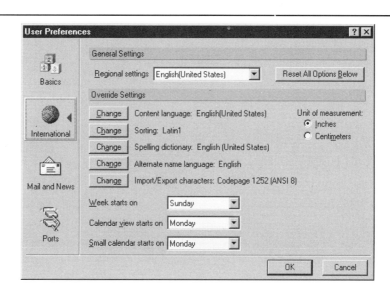

Mail and News   When you click the Mail and News button, the User Preferences dialog box displays a set of mail and newsreader settings (see Figure 13.3). The following summarizes the Mail and News settings (see Chapter 5, "Communicating with Notes Mail," for more information):

Configuration   Allows you to customize the Notes mail and newsreader features. You choose either Lotus Notes or None from the Mail Program drop-down box. None disables mail features and should only be selected if Notes is used exclusively for interacting with Notes databases. In the Local Address Books field, you can include additional Personal Address Book databases or replicas of Domino Directories used for local e-mail addressing. Databases included here are displayed in address dialog boxes and used to resolve addresses when e-mail is sent. The Internet Mail Format, Multilingual Internet Mail, and Internet News Format options determine how messages are formatted when sent via e-mail or posted to newsgroups.

Sending   Allows you to choose whether or not Notes saves sent messages. You can also enable options to sign all sent messages, encrypt all sent messages, and encrypt all saved messages. If you don't select these options, you can still enable these functions on a per-message basis.

Receiving   Includes options that tell Notes how often to check for new mail in your mail database. You can also enable visual and audible notifications. For audible notification, you can choose which sound Notes will play when new messages arrive in your mail database.

FIGURE 13.3

The Mail and News settings in the User Preferences dialog box

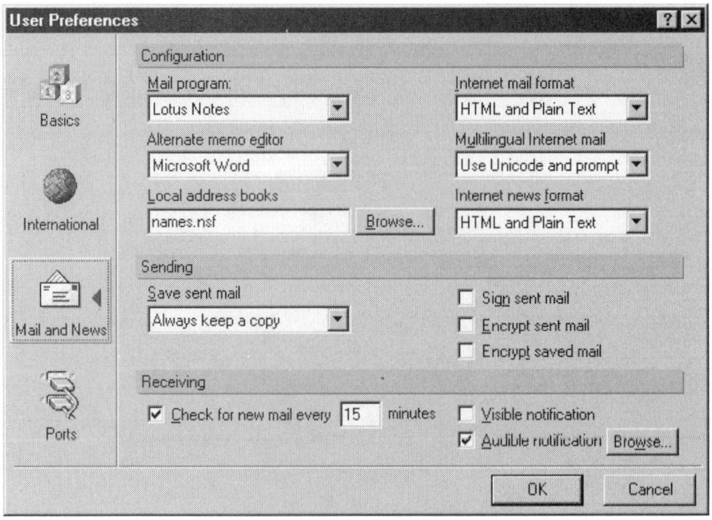

Ports   When you click the Ports button, the User Preferences dialog box displays a set of communication port settings (see Figure 13.4):

Communication Ports   Allows you to add, remove, rename, and reorder communication ports used by Notes. You can also show a port's status and trace connectivity to Domino servers that are available via specific ports. Communication ports enable Notes to communicate across networks to Domino servers and Internet servers. They correlate directly to the communication configuration of your computer. For example, you need to enable a TCP/IP port in order to have Notes use the TCP/IP communications capability of your computer (local or dial-up) to communicate. This is true for all supported protocols, including TCP/IP, Microsoft NetBIOS, Banyan Vines, and Novell SPX. COM ports are used to perform Notes Direct Dialup communications, which is explained in Chapter 9, "Working with Notes Away from the Office."

Selected Port   Displays the driver configured for the selected port. You can choose to enable the selected port and to enable network encryption on the selected port. The Encrypt Network Data option ensures that data transferred across the network is secure and only works between Notes clients and Domino servers. You can also click the Options button to bring up a dialog box for setting driver-specific options for the selected port.

FIGURE 13.4

The Ports settings in the User Preferences dialog box

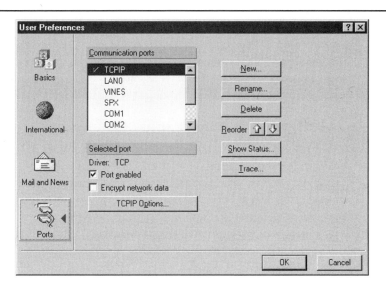

Modifying Personal Address Book Settings

Your Personal Address Book database performs two functions in Notes. First, it provides a repository for you to store information about Contacts and groups. It's not only a good place to keep track of names and addresses, it's also used to address e-mail messages. See Chapter 4, "Introducing the Core Databases," for more information on using your Personal Address Book to manage Contacts and groups. Your Personal Address Book also contains documents that affect the configuration of Notes, including:

- Location
- Connection
- Account

Using Location Documents to Customize Your Notes Environment

Location documents are used to customize your Notes environment. They define how Notes connects to communication networks, processes e-mail, schedules replication, and so on. You can create multiple Location documents in your Personal Address Book database for different configuration scenarios. If you use Notes on a notebook computer, the Location document is a powerful tool for managing your configuration based on the location from which you use Notes. You can create one Location document to use when you are in the office and configure it for local connections to Domino servers, server-based mail, and a proxy for Web access. Then, you could have other Location documents to use at home, in a hotel room while traveling, or even offline when you have no connection to a network.

Switching Location Documents

When you have multiple Location documents, only one can be active at a time. This is called the *current* Location document. The current Location document determines the configuration that Notes is currently using. You can determine which Location document is active by clicking the Location Selector button on the status bar. The name of the current Location document is highlighted in the list. You can also change to a different current Location document. This makes it is easy to maintain multiple configurations and switch to them whenever necessary. To change to a different Location document, follow these steps:

1. Select File ➤ Mobile ➤ Choose Current Location. The Choose Location dialog box will be displayed.

2. Double-click a Location document name in the list or select a Location document name and click the OK button.

Notes will make the Location document you selected the current Location document. Active tasks will not be affected, but all configuration settings in the selected Location document will take effect immediately.

 TIP You can also switch Location documents by clicking the Location Selector button on the status bar and selecting a Location document name from the list presented.

The Location document also affects the Notes Replicator, which is the process that manages background replication between your Notes workstation and Domino servers. Each Location document contains configuration information for each entry on the Replicator page. Therefore, you can set different options, based on the Location document, for each Replicator page entry. You can configure entries to replicate with different servers or to replicate in a specific direction (send/receive) depending on the Location document. This provides you with a great deal of flexibility in configuring background replication. See Chapter 9 for more information on Notes replication.

 TIP The default replica for each bookmark is also stored with Location documents. This means that you can have Notes launch a server-based replica when you're in the office and a local replica when you're using Notes remotely. Of course, you can always change the replica Notes launches by right-clicking a bookmark and selecting Open Replica ➤ *Servername*.

Editing the Location Document

To customize the Notes configuration, you'll need to edit Location documents in addition to modifying the User Preferences covered earlier in this chapter. You can edit the current Location document or other Location documents in your Personal Address Book. Editing the current Location document will affect Notes as it is currently running, whereas editing other Location documents will have no effect unless you make them active. To edit the current Location document, follow these steps:

1. Select File ➤ Preferences ➤ Location Preferences. The current Location document will be opened in Edit mode.

2. Modify configuration settings as necessary.

3. Click the Save and Close button on the Form Action bar.

Notes will save your changes, close the form, and make your changes active immediately. Notes will also save certain settings to your notes.ini file as needed. To open the current Location document in Edit mode, select File ➤ Mobile ➤ Edit Current Location or click the Location Selector button on the status bar and select Edit Current.

 NOTE If you choose any Location type other than No Connection, a Connection Configuration Wizard button will appear on the Form Action bar. Click this button to initiate the Connection Configuration Wizard, which will walk you through the process of creating a Connection document for this Location document. Connection documents are discussed later in this chapter.

To edit Location documents other than the current Location document, follow these steps:

1. Select File ➤ Mobile ➤ Locations. Your Personal Address Book database will open to the Location view. All Location documents available in your Personal Address Book database will be displayed.

2. Select a Location document and click the Edit Location button. The Location document will be opened in Edit mode.

3. Modify configuration settings as necessary.

4. Click the Save and Close button on the Form Action bar.

Notes will save your changes and close the form, but the changes will not be made active because you didn't edit the current Location document.

Configuration Settings in the Location Document

Location documents contain many configuration settings. In this section, we'll summarize them in the order in which they appear on the form. We'll also refer to other parts of this book where configuration settings have been discussed in greater detail.

Basics   The fields on the Basics tab (see Figure 13.5) affect a number of Notes functions:

Location Type   Defines how you are connected to Domino servers or the Internet from this location. The Local Area Network option enables Notes to use network communication services that are configured on your computer (e.g., TCP/IP, NetBIOS, SPX/IPX, etc.). Notes Direct Dialup and Network Dialup enable Notes to use dial-up communications to access Domino servers or the Internet (see Chapter 9 for more information on dial-up communications). The Custom option lets you configure Notes to use both local area network (LAN) and dial-up communications. The No Connection option configures Notes for offline use.

Location Name   Includes a short, descriptive name for the Location document. This name is then referenced when Account and Connection documents are linked to specific Location documents.

Internet Mail Address   Defines the return address to use when you send e-mail to other Internet e-mail users (see Chapter 5 for more information).

Prompt for Time/Date/Phone   Determines whether or not Notes displays the Time and Phone Information dialog box when it is making this Location document active. You can also manually display the dialog box by selecting File ➤ Mobile ➤ Edit Current Time/Phone.

Proxy   Defines proxy servers for Notes to use. You can enter a proxy server name (and port), or you can click the propeller icon to the right of the field to bring up the Proxy Server Configuration dialog box. Proxy server settings affect two areas. First, they have the same effect on Web browsing in Notes that they have on browsing with any other Web browser. Second, you can use these settings to configure Notes to access Domino servers through a proxy server (using HTTP tunneling or SOCKS). For more information on accessing Domino servers through proxy servers, see the article "Playing with Firewalls" in the Iris Today section of the Lotus Notes.net site (www.notes.net).

Default Display Name   Determines whether or not Notes uses alternate display names contained in your ID file. See your Domino administrator for more information about your Notes ID.

FIGURE 13.5

The Location document's Basics tab

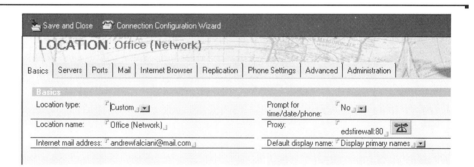

 TIP   If you are using Notes with the IE browser control, you can have Notes synchronize Internet browsing configuration information from the current Location document to your Windows Registry (IE Control Panel settings). This is a great way to maintain multiple browser configurations based on location. To instruct Notes to keep Location document settings synchronized with your IE settings, add the following to your notes.ini file: **SYNCINTERNET-SETTINGS=1**. For more information on modifying your notes.ini file, see "Setting Preferences" earlier in this chapter.

Servers   The following fields, which are on the Servers tab (see Figure 13.6), determine which Domino servers Notes uses for various functions:

Home/Mail Server   The Domino server to which Notes sends messages when it is configured to send outgoing e-mail through a Domino server. It is also the Domino server that Notes will monitor for new mail when it is configured to use a server-based mail database. If no Domino Directory server is defined, this server will also be used to populate address dialog boxes.

Passthru Server   The Domino server that Notes will access for Passthru when it cannot find the Domino server you are trying to access. Passthru is a Domino server function that allows Notes to tunnel through one Domino server to access another. It is typically used in conjunction with dial-up communications for accessing remote Domino servers (see Chapter 9 for more information on using Passthru to access remote Domino servers). It can also be used to securely access Domino servers across the Internet. See your Domino administrator to find out if your Domino environment is configured to support this capability.

Catalog/Domain Search Server   The Domino server that Notes will access when you initiate Domain Search (see Chapter 8 for more information on Domain Search).

Domino Directory Server   The Domino server that Notes will access when determining which Domino Directories to present in its address dialog boxes.

FIGURE 13.6

The Location document's Servers tab

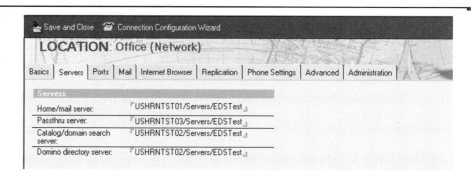

Ports   The fields on the Ports tab (see Figure 13.7) determine which communication ports configured in the User Preferences dialog box will be used by this Location document. All communication ports enabled in the User Preferences dialog box will be displayed as check boxes on this page. You can select the appropriate check boxes to make specific ports available to this Location document. Ports that are not selected will not be used when Notes tries to connect to Domino servers or the Internet.

FIGURE 13.7

*The Location
document's Ports tab*

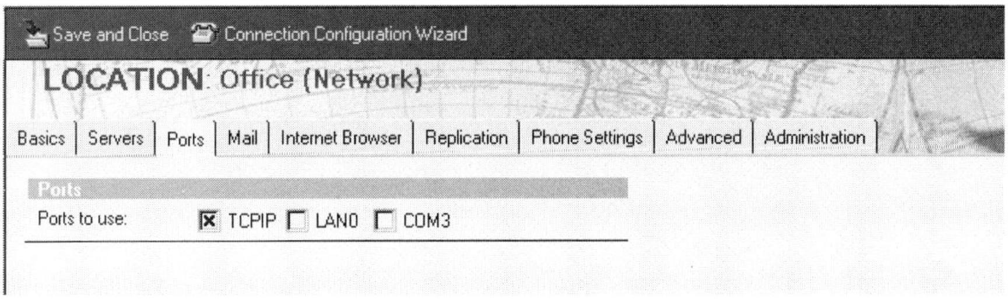

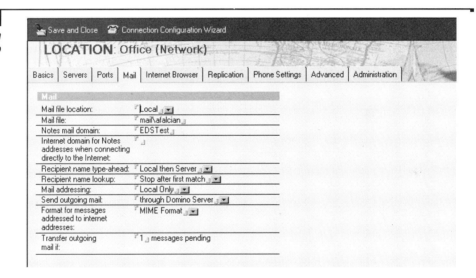

Mail The fields on the Mail tab (see Figure 13.8) compliment the Mail and News settings in the User Preferences dialog box. The main difference is that the Mail and News settings affect Notes e-mail functionality regardless of location.

FIGURE 13.8

*The Location
document's Mail tab*

The following is a summary of the Location document's Mail settings (see Chapter 5 for more information):

Mail File Location Determines where Notes looks to find your mail database. Local instructs Notes to look on your computer, and On Server instructs Notes to look on your mail server (defined on the Servers tab). Notes uses this information for all functions that require a mail database. This includes populating the Create ➤ Mail menu and processing the new mail notifications.

Mail File Used in conjunction with the Mail File Location field. It contains the path and filename of your mail database.

Notes Mail Domain   Defines the Notes/Domino domain name.

Internet Domain for Notes Addresses   Defines the Domain Name System (DNS) domain to use when messages are addressed to Notes mail users and your outgoing mail is set to go directly to the Internet. This is intended to be used when you are replying to messages sent to you from other Domino mail users when you are connected to the Internet (not your Domino server) for outbound mail. It assumes that your Domino server is connected to the Internet using the DNS domain listed in this field.

Recipient Name Type-Ahead   Controls the type-ahead feature. The options are Disabled, Local Only, and Local Then Server. For Location documents configured for using Notes remotely, this field should be set to Disabled or Local Only. Local Then Server is only valid when Notes is used in an environment that includes Domino servers.

Recipient Name Lookup   Determines how Notes processes addresses when sending e-mail. If you choose Exhaustively Check All Address Books and Notes finds duplicate entries, you will be presented with a dialog box from which you can select recipients. This ensures that messages do not go to the wrong recipients.

Mail Addressing   Determines which directories Notes will use for addressing e-mail. Local Only instructs Notes to use only the address books listed in the Local Address Books field in the User Preferences dialog box. Local and Server instructs Notes to use all local address books as well as all Domino Directories configured on your mail or directory server.

Send Outgoing Mail   Determines how Notes will send outgoing messages. Through Domino Server instructs Notes to send all outgoing messages to the Domino server listed as your mail server. Directly to Internet instructs Notes to send all outgoing messages to the SMTP server defined in the active SMTP Account document.

Format for Messages Addressed to Internet Addresses   Defines how the Domino server will format Internet messages. This field is only available when outgoing messages are sent through a Domino server.

Transfer Outgoing Mail If   Determines the number of outgoing messages that can be queued before the Notes Replicator forces a connection to the Domino server or SMTP server. This field is only available when you are using a local mail database.

Internet Browser   The fields on the Internet Browser tab (see Figure 13.9) determine how Notes will process Internet URLs. You can choose to use the integrated Web browser features of Notes or configure Notes to pass URL requests to an external Web browser. See Chapter 10 for more information.

FIGURE 13.9

The Location document's Internet Browser tab

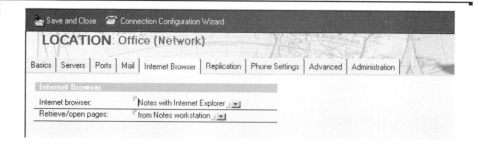

Replication   The fields on the Replication tab (see Figure 13.10) define the background replication schedule for Notes. You can enable or disable scheduled background replication. If you enable it, you can further define the scheduling parameters. See Chapter 9 for more information.

FIGURE 13.10

The Location document's Replication tab

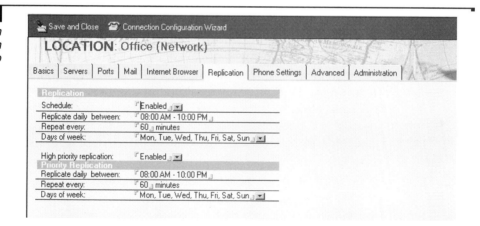

Phone Settings   The fields on the Phone Settings tab (see Figure 13.11) are used when Notes Direct Dialup is used to connect to Domino servers. These settings are similar to the Dialing properties for Windows Dialup Networking. You can define the area code for the location so Notes Direct Dialup can determine whether or not to dial long distance. You can define prefixes for getting an outside line if you are using Notes in an office or hotel room. More information is available from Lotus in their Mobile Survival Kit. See Chapter 9 for more information on how to obtain the Mobile Survival Kit and for more information on Notes Direct Dialup.

Advanced   The fields on the Advanced tab (see Figure 13.12) are further broken down into subtabs. Instead of going into detail about every field, we'll highlight several settings on each tab:

Basics   The fields on the Basics subtab affect a number of areas. The Only for User field defines who can use Notes on this workstation using this Location document. Enter an asterisk in this field to allow any user to use this Location document. The User ID to Switch To field instructs Notes to switch to a specific User ID file whenever you make this location current. The Bookmarks Filename and Subscriptions Filename fields allow you to define specific databases for certain Locations. All of these fields can be useful if you are sharing a Notes workstation with multiple users.

SSL   The fields on the SSL subtab determine how Notes supports Secure Sockets Layer (SSL) communication with Internet servers. See Chapter 10 for more information.

Web Retriever   The fields on the Web Retriever subtab affect integrated Web browsing in Notes. See Chapter 10 for more information.

Java Applet Security   The fields on the Java Applet Security subtab define security aspects of the Java Virtual Machine (JVM) built in to Notes.

Secondary Servers   The fields on the Secondary Servers subtab are used to define Domino servers (and their associated network address) that can be queried to resolve the names of Domino servers with which Notes is having trouble establishing communication. Instead of creating Connection documents (or HOSTS file entries) for every Domino server not listed in DNS, you can enter the name and TCP/IP address of one Domino server here.

MIME Settings   The fields on the MIME Settings subtab define what encoding method Notes uses when formatting Multipurpose Internet Mail Extension (MIME) data.

FIGURE 13.12

The Location document's Advanced tab

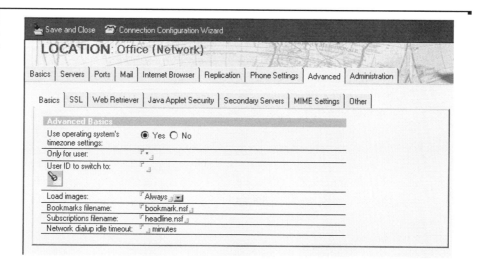

The Relationship between Location Documents and Account/ Connection Documents

The current Location document also determines which Account and Connection documents are active. When you create Account and Connection documents, you select individual locations or the asterisk for all locations in the Only From Locations field. This specifies Location documents to which these Account and Connection documents are made available. If an Account or Connection document doesn't have the current Location document selected, it is ignored. This is a great way to configure different connection methods for a specific Domino server based on the Location document. For example, you could create a Passthru Connection document to use in the office and a Network Dialup Connection document to use from home to access a Domino server connected to the Internet. Account and Connection documents are discussed in the next section. You can also use Location, Account, and Connection documents to configure different connection methods for Internet-based accounts. For example, you could create two Account documents for the same Internet mail account. One could reference the Internet mail server directly, and the other could reference a proxy server through which that mail server is accessible. Then you could associate each Account document to different Location documents that define how you access the Internet.

Setting Up Connections to Remote Domino Servers

Connection documents are also used to customize your Notes environment. They define how Notes connects to specific Domino servers and to the Internet. Generally, they are used to connect to Domino servers that are not directly accessible from your computer. This includes Domino servers that are available through dial-up communications. In Notes Release 5, Connection documents are also used for accessing the Internet through dial-up communications. See Chapter 9 for more information on using Connection documents in conjunction with dial-up communications. Also, see Chapter 9 for information on Passthru Connection documents.

You can also use Connection documents to specify the TCP/IP address of a Domino server that is not listed in your organization's DNS database. DNS is used to associate domain names (e.g., domino1.mycompany.com) with specific TCP/IP addresses. If your Domino server has not been entered into the DNS database, you can either create entries in your computer's HOSTS file or create a Connection document. It may be more useful to create a Connection document because it can be linked to a specific Location document. It is also more visible. You may forget that there are special entries in your computer's HOSTS file, but you will probably remember Connection documents added to your Personal Address Book database.

 NOTE To create a Connection document that identifies the TCP/IP address of a Domino server, follow the procedure outlined for creating dial-up communication Connection documents in Chapter 9. The only difference is that the connection type should be specified as Local Area Network and the Destination Server Address field should contain the TCP/IP address of the Domino server.

Finally, remember that Connection documents are linked to Location documents. This link is established by selecting locations in the Only from Locations field on the Advanced tab of the Connection document. See "The Relationship between Location Documents and Account/Connection Documents" (the preceding section) for more information.

Setting Up Accounts to Access Internet Servers

Account documents determine how Notes accesses Internet servers for mail, news, and directory services. See Chapter 10 for more information on Account documents and how they are used to configure Notes to access Internet-based information.

Other Databases That Affect the Notes Configuration

In this section, we'll mention some of the other databases that have an impact on the operation of Notes. They are as follows:

- Bookmarks
- Subscriptions
- Log

The Purpose of the Bookmarks Database

Although you will not typically modify entries in the bookmarks database directly, it is included here because it is part of the overall configuration of Notes. The bookmarks database contains information about the Bookmark bar, the Bookmark pages, and individual bookmarks that provide the main user interface for Notes. As you manipulate bookmark entries, Notes records the changes in the bookmarks database (see Chapter 2 for more information on using bookmarks). This database is called `bookmark.nsf` by default and resides in the Notes Data directory. You can also create another bookmarks database and change your Location document (in the Bookmarks Filename field on the Basics subtab of the Location document's Advanced tab) so it references this new database. As previously mentioned, this is useful when a single computer is shared by multiple users. It allows you to provide user-specific bookmarks based on location. If you do create a new bookmarks database, make sure you use the Bookmarks template (`bookmark.ntf`).

The bookmarks database also defines the overall layout of the Notes application window. It contains a special frameset that determines what sections are included and how each section is presented. The application window can be customized, but doing so requires an advanced understanding of the Notes software design.

The Purpose of the Subscriptions Database

As with the Bookmarks database, you will not typically modify entries in the subscriptions database directly. The subscriptions database contains entries for each of the subscriptions you create. See Chapter 2 for more information on using subscriptions. This database is called `headline.nsf` by default and resides in the Notes Data directory. You can also create another subscriptions database and change your Location document (in the Subscriptions Filename field on the Basics subtab of the Location document's Advanced tab) so it references this new database. Again, this is useful when a single computer is shared by multiple users. It allows you to provide user-specific subscriptions based on location. If you do create a new subscriptions database, make sure you use the Subscriptions template (`headline.ntf`).

Using the Log Database to Troubleshoot Problems

Notes includes a special database in which it records information about tasks performed. It's called the log database, and it's named `log.nsf` by default. If Notes does not detect the presence of a log database, it creates one automatically at start-up. Again, you will not be modifying anything in this database, but it is a good tool for troubleshooting problems. For example, Notes records information regarding replication activity in the Log database. If you are having problems replicating with a particular Domino server, chances are this database can help. You can read the entries in the Replication Events view to determine if your workstation had trouble connecting to the Domino server or if the Replicator had trouble accessing specific databases because of security problems. Notes also records mail activity in the log database. You can read the entries in the Mail Routing Events view to troubleshoot problems with Notes mail. The entries in the Miscellaneous Events view show general Notes activity.

Summary

In this chapter, we discussed how to configure Notes when you are integrating it into environments that include Domino servers. We summarized the configuration settings available in the User Preferences dialog box and those provided by the Location document. We explained how to change these settings and the impact they have on Notes configuration. We also introduced the bookmarks, subscriptions, and log databases. In the next chapter, we'll explore how these configuration elements are used for integrating Notes into environments that do not include Domino servers.

CHAPTER **14**

Setting Up Notes as an Internet Client

Notes Release 5 is the first version of Notes that can be used without the presence of Domino servers. Release 5 includes a rich set of features that make Notes a powerful Internet client. If you have an Internet account, you can use Notes to send and receive Internet e-mail, interact in newsgroups, and browse the Web. This is in addition to your ability to manage your calendar, To Do list, and other personal information.

As previously mentioned, the Notes setup process copies the Notes program files to your computer's disk drive. It also initiates a Configuration Wizard that prompts you for information about your Domino server environment and your Internet server environment. If you select the option for no Domino server, the Configuration Wizard completes the initial setup of Notes for an Internet-only configuration. See Appendix A, "Installing Lotus Notes 5," for more information on the installation process. In Chapter 13, "Setting Up Notes as a Domino Client," we explain how various options affect the Notes configuration and how to change the configuration after the initial installation to meet your changing needs. In this chapter, we'll focus on the settings that enable you to use Notes in environments that do not include Domino servers.

 NOTE We recommend that you read Chapter 13, "Setting Up Notes as a Domino Client," before reading this chapter. Chapter 13 contains detailed information on the overall configuration of Notes, whereas this chapter just discusses the settings that affect an Internet-only configuration.

Internet-Only Preferences

The notes.ini file is used in the Internet-only configuration the same way it is used when Notes is configured as a Domino client. Also, Notes maintains Windows Registry settings the same way whether or not Domino servers are used. As discussed in Chapter 13, the two main interfaces for manipulating settings are the User Preferences dialog box and the Location document. See Chapter 13 for details on the notes.ini file, the Notes Windows Registry settings, and the options available in the User Preferences dialog box and Location document. In the remainder of this section, we'll discuss User Preferences dialog box options that affect an Internet-only configuration.

User Preferences Dialog Box Options for Internet-Only Configuration

As mentioned, this section includes a discussion of the User Preferences dialog box options that affect an Internet-only configuration. If an option is not mentioned, it is because it functions the same regardless of how Notes is being used. See Chapter 13 for a complete explanation of User Preferences dialog box options. The dialog box includes the following sections:

- Basics
- International
- Mail and News
- Ports

Basics   The following Basics options affect an Internet-only configuration:

Startup Options   Although the subscriptions feature is a Notes/Domino function, the Check Subscriptions option could be selected. Subscriptions can be created for databases stored locally on your Notes workstation, not just for databases stored on Domino servers. See Chapter 2, "Getting Familiar with Notes," for more information on using subscriptions. Because the Personal Web Navigator database uses locally scheduled Agents to perform some of its functions, the Enable Scheduled Local Agents option should be enabled. See Chapter 10, "Harnessing the Power of the Internet," for more information.

Additional Options   In the Additional Options section, you can enable other options that Notes supports. A number of these options have an impact on how Notes functions as an Internet client and are explained further in Chapter 10. They include the following options:

- Make Internet URLs (http://…..) into Hotspots
- Enable Java Applets
- Enable JavaScript
- Enable Java Access from JavaScript
- Enable Plugins in Notes Browser
- Enable ActiveX in Notes Browser
- Accept Cookies
- Make Notes the Default Web Browser on My System
- Enable MS Office 97 SendTo to Notes

The Use Web Palette option instructs Notes to use the color palette supported by Web browsers. This provides a more seamless interface for viewing both Notes databases and Web pages.

International   The options in the International section all function the same regardless of whether or not Domino servers are used.

Mail and News   The options in the Mail and News section all function the same regardless of whether or not Domino servers are used.

Ports   In a configuration where Domino servers are not included in the environment, the only communication port enabled will be the TCP/IP port. This is the communication protocol used for all Internet communications. There would be no reason to have any other ports enabled.

Internet-Only Personal Address Book Settings

This section includes a discussion of the settings in Personal Address Book documents that affect an Internet-only configuration. If a setting is not mentioned, it is because it functions the same regardless of how Notes is being used. See Chapter 13 for a complete explanation of settings contained in Personal Address Book documents. The following documents affect the configuration of Notes:

- Location
- Connection
- Account

Location Document Settings for an Internet-Only Configuration

Location documents are used the same whether or not Domino servers are used. In an Internet-only configuration, they define how Notes connects to the Internet, processes Internet e-mail, schedules replication of newsgroups, and so on. As explained in Chapter 13, you can create multiple Location documents in your Personal Address Book database for different configuration scenarios. See Chapter 13 for information on switching Location documents, Editing Location documents, and linking Account and Connection documents to Location documents.

Basics   The following options on the Basics tab affect an Internet-only configuration:

Location Type   The only difference with the Location Type field is that the Notes Direct Dialup option is not applicable. This option is used exclusively for connecting Notes to Domino servers.

Internet Mail Address   The Internet Mail Address field is required in Internet-only configurations. It is used to define your return address when you send outgoing messages directly to Simple Mail Transfer Protocol (SMTP) servers. This field should have no effect when using Notes in an Internet-only configuration, but it requires a value. Just enter your ISP domain name.

Proxy   This field is used to define proxy servers to use for Web browsing and for accessing Domino servers through firewalls. Because they are used for accessing Domino servers, do not enter values in the HTTP Tunnel and SOCKS fields.

Servers   The entire Servers tab is devoted to identifying Domino servers for the Notes client to use. All of these fields should be left blank.

Ports   TCP/IP should be the only communication port enabled in the User Preferences dialog box. You should also select the TCP/IP port to configure this Location document to connect to the Internet.

Mail   The following options on the Mail tab affect Internet-only configuration:

Mail File Location   Because you will be using Notes without Domino servers, this field should always be set to Local. This instructs Notes to look on your computer for your mail database.

Mail File   This field is used in conjunction with the Mail File Location field. It contains the path and filename of your mail database.

Notes Mail Domain   Because you are not using Notes mail, this field should be left blank.

Internet Domain for Notes Addresses   Because you are not using Notes mail, this field should be left blank.

Recipient Name Type-Ahead   Because you will be using Notes without Domino servers, this field should be set to Disabled or Local Only.

Mail Addressing   Because you will be using Notes without Domino servers, this field should be set to Local Only.

Send Outgoing Mail   Because you will be using Notes without Domino servers, this field should be set to Directly to Internet.

Transfer Outgoing Mail If   Set this field to the number of outgoing messages you want queued before the Notes Replicator forces a connection to the SMTP server.

Internet Browser   The options on the Internet Browser tab work the same way whether or not Domino servers are used. You can choose to use the integrated Web browser features of Notes, or you can configure Notes to pass URL requests to an external Web browser. See Chapter 10 for more information.

Replication   The options on the Replication tab work the same way whether or not Domino servers are used. In an Internet-only configuration, the Replicator receives messages from Post Office Protocol (POP) and Internet Message Access Protocol (IMAP) servers, sends messages to SMTP servers, and manages replication with Network News Transfer Protocol (NNTP) and IMAP servers. You can enable or disable scheduled background replication. If you enable it, you can further define the scheduling parameters. See Chapter 9 for more information.

Phone Settings   The options on the Phone Settings tab are not used because they define settings for Notes Direct Dialup, which is only used to connect to Domino servers directly through dial-up communications. All of these fields should be left blank.

Advanced   The following subtabs of the Advanced tab include options that affect Internet-only configuration:

> **Basics**   The Network Dialup Idle Timeout field can be used to force Notes to hang up Network Dialup connections after a predefined period of inactivity. All other fields function the same whether or not Domino servers are used.

> **SSL**   The fields on the SSL subtab determine how Notes supports Secure Sockets Layer (SSL) communication with Internet servers. This is also true in Internet-only configurations. See Chapter 10 for more information.

> **Web Retriever**   The fields on the Web Retriever subtab affect integrated Web browsing in Notes. This is also true in Internet-only configurations. See Chapter 10 for more information.

> **Java Applet Security**   The fields on the Java Applet Security subtab define security aspects of the Java Virtual Machine (JVM) built in to Notes. This is also true in Internet-only configurations.

> **Secondary Servers**   The fields on the Secondary Servers subtab are only used to access Domino servers. All of these fields should be left blank.

> **MIME Settings**   The fields on the MIME Settings subtab define what encoding method Notes uses when formatting Multipurpose Internet Mail Extension (MIME) data. This is also true in Internet-only configurations.

Setting Up Connections to Remote Domino Servers

Connection documents are used the same way whether or not Domino servers are used. In an Internet-only configuration, they define how Notes connects to the Internet through dial-up communications. If you plan to access the Internet through dial-up communications, you must create a Connection document. See Chapter 9 for more information on using Connection documents to connect to the Internet.

Also, remember that Connection documents are linked to Location documents. This link is established by selecting locations in the Only From Locations field on the Advanced tab of the Connection document. See Chapter 13 for more information on the relationship between Connection and Location documents.

Setting Up Accounts to Access Internet Servers

Account documents are used the same whether or not Domino servers are used. They determine how Notes accesses Internet servers for mail, news, and directory services. In an Internet-only configuration, you must create Account documents for each Internet service you need to access. See Chapter 10 for more information on Account documents and how they are used to configure Notes to access Internet-based information.

Also, remember that Account documents are linked to Location documents. This link is established by selecting locations in the Only From Location(s) field on the Advanced tab of the Account document. See Chapter 13 for more information on the relationship between Account and Location documents.

Summary

In this chapter, we discussed how to configure Notes when integrating it into environments that do not include Domino servers. We summarized User Preferences dialog box options and Location document settings that affect Internet-only configurations. This is the last chapter devoted to exploring the end-user capabilities of Lotus Notes Release 5. The remaining chapters introduce you to Lotus Domino Designer Release 5 and how it is used to create Notes databases that can be used by Notes clients and Web browser clients.

Beyond the Client: Utilizing Domino Designer

CHAPTER 15

Introducing Domino Designer

One of the more drastic changes to Notes R5 is the separation of the Notes client and the development environment known as Domino Designer. For those of you who are new to Notes, this will not come as a big surprise, but for those of you who have been using previous releases, this is a huge change.

In addition to being separated from the Notes client, one of the biggest surprises with Domino Designer is the user interface. As you'll soon see, the interface is task oriented like the Notes client interface. Domino Designer technologies have been integrated with Web technologies, which brings the native Web technologies to the Notes environment and extends the native Domino technologies to the Web environment. You can now write your application once, and it will run both in the Notes client and on the Web. Domino Designer provides you with various design elements that you could previously only use in the Notes client; you can now use them in Web applications too. These design elements have been written as Java applets to provide more robust functionality to the Web browser.

Entering the World of Designer

As mentioned, Domino Designer is now a separate program; it is no longer part of the Notes client. There are three ways you can open Domino Designer:

- Select the Designer icon from the Notes client.
- Launch Designer from an open database in the Notes client.
- Use the Start menu.

To use these options, Domino Designer must be installed when Notes is initially installed. If you do not see any of the following options, review Appendix A, "Installing Lotus Notes 5."

Using the Designer Icon

When you start the Notes client, the Designer icon is located on the vertical Bookmark bar, which is displayed on the left side of the application window. Click the icon to automatically launch Domino Designer. Once it is launched, one of the databases will be automatically opened for you. You will be positioned on the opening splash screen.

NOTE If you don't see the Designer icon in the Bookmark bar, you did not install the Domino Designer program during the installation process. Please review Appendix A, "Installing Lotus Notes 5."

Launching Designer from a Database

To open Domino Designer from an opened database within the Notes client, choose View ➤ Design and Domino Designer will be automatically launched. One nice side effect of using this method is that the database will also be opened in Designer, positioning you in the Design list on the Forms element. The Work pane for all of the forms will also be displayed.

 NOTE If you don't see the menu option for Design within the View menu structure, you may not have installed Designer or you may not have Designer or Manager access to the database.

Using the Start Menu

The final option for launching Domino Designer is to use the icon placed in the Start menu. The placement of the Domino Designer icon depends on how you defined your installation. By default, the program icon will be placed in a program group called Lotus Applications. The title for the Designer icon is Lotus Domino Designer. When you select this option, Designer will be automatically launched and you will be positioned on the splash screen (just as if you clicked the Designer icon from within the Notes client).

 NOTE If you don't see the Designer icon in the Lotus Applications group, you did not install the Domino Designer program during the installation process. Please review Appendix A, "Installing Lotus Notes 5."

Navigating Domino Designer

Throughout the remaining chapters of this book, we'll be referring to the various areas of the Domino Designer user interface. So before we embark on exploring what Designer has to offer, let's first go over the different areas that make up the user interface. To open Domino Designer, just select the Designer icon from the Notes client. Once opened, Domino Designer will look similar to Figure 15.1.

The overall look of Designer is similar to that of the Notes client. Let's take a closer look at the individual elements that make up the general Designer user interface.

FIGURE 15.1

The Domino Designer program interface

Menu Bar

Display Infobox

Tabbed Windows

Bookmark Bar

Preview Icons

Smart Icons

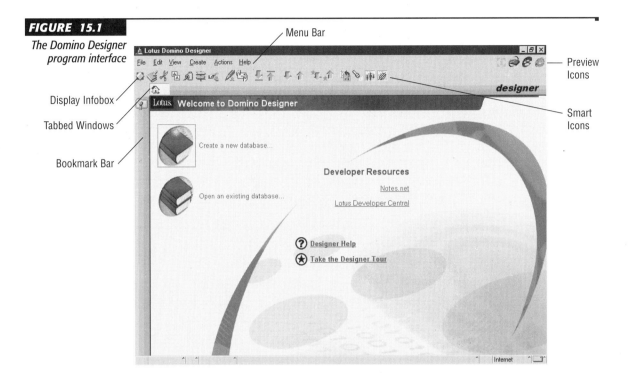

The Designer User Interface

As shown in Figure 15.1, there is a context-sensitive menu bar along the top of the Domino Designer interface. The available options displayed are determined by what actions are available for the active window. In Figure 15.1, only the File, Edit, View, Create, Actions, and Help menus are available. This is not to say that these are the only menus available in Designer, but rather that these are the only options available for the currently active element (the Welcome screen).

NOTE Depending on your preferences, the SmartIcons may or may not display in Domino Designer. This option is configurable; you can change it by choosing File ➤ Preferences ➤ SmartIcon Settings.

To the right of the menu bar (in the upper right corner of the window) are the Properties InfoBox icons and preview icons, or buttons (*icons* and *buttons* are used interchangeably for the Properties InfoBox and preview icons). The Properties InfoBox icon allows you to quickly display the Properties InfoBox for the active design element. The preview icons allow you to quickly preview your design in either the Notes client or a currently installed Web browser (you can also preview via the menu bar). In Figure 15.1, there are three preview icons. The first icon will launch the design element in the Notes client, and the remaining icons will launch the element in the Notes browser or Internet Explorer, respectively.

 NOTE The number of browsers you have installed on your machine will determine the various preview icons that will be displayed.

Vertically aligned along the left side of Designer is the Bookmark bar, which contains a list of icons known as Design bookmark folders. The first icon is reserved for a special folder and is automatically created for you. This is the Recent Databases folder, which will always display the five most recently accessed databases. This list is dynamic in that the oldest database will automatically be rolled off so that only five databases remain in the list. Any remaining icons are completely configurable. To create a new Design bookmark folder, just right-click the Bookmark bar and choose Create New Folder from the pop-up menu. A new folder icon will display in the Bookmark bar. You can change the icon and also rename the folder by right-clicking the actual icon and selecting either the Change Icon or Rename option from the pop-up menu. Each of these folders will contain a bookmark to the actual design of a database.

PART

V

Beyond the Client: Utilizing Domino Designer

 NOTE As soon as you change the design of any element in a database, the database will be added to the Recent Databases folder.

The Tabbed Windows can be seen just below the menu bar (if you have the Smart-Icons turned on, the Tabbed Windows are just below them). Whenever a database or design element is opened, a corresponding Tabbed Window will also be displayed. Tabbed Windows allow you to quickly navigate among open windows on your workspace. When you place your cursor over the button, an *X* that can be used to close the corresponding window will appear.

 NOTE By default, Domino Designer will always have one open Tabbed Window, known as the Home Window. Selecting this tab will always display the Welcome to Domino Designer page, which is shown in Figure 15.1.

TIP You can press Ctrl+Tab to move between the Tabbed Windows. You can also press Alt+W to display a number for each Tabbed Window. Pressing the number will take you to the corresponding window.

The Design and Work Pane

To open the Design pane, click one of the Design bookmark folder icons. The Design pane, shown in Figure 15.2, is a sliding window that displays whenever a Design bookmark folder icon is clicked. You can keep the Design pane open by clicking the icon located in the upper left corner of the pane (this icon is known as a pushpin, hence you are pinning the Design pane open). You can close the Design pane by clicking the *X* in the upper right corner of the pane. If you have not pinned the Design pane open, the Design pane will automatically slide shut when the cursor is removed. The Design pane contains a list of all the databases and templates that have been bookmarked. Each database or template is displayed by its respective application icon, database title, and database path and filename.

TIP If the title of the database is cut off by the Design pane, you can hover the mouse over the application icon and the entire title will be displayed.

The application icon can be selected to expand/contract the Design list, which contains a list of the all the design elements for the database. Once a design element is selected from the Design list, the Work pane will be displayed with all the elements listed.

The Work pane lists everything in the database for the currently selected design element. Don't confuse the Work pane with the work area, which we will examine next. The Work pane is a selection window, as shown in Figure 15.2. To open a specific element from the list, just double-click the entry (you can also right-click the element and choose Edit from the pop-up menu) and the Designer workspace will display.

TIP A quick way to create design elements is to select the Design Action button from the Work pane. Every design element from the Design list has a Design Action button to create a new element.

FIGURE 15.2

The Design pane in
Domino Designer

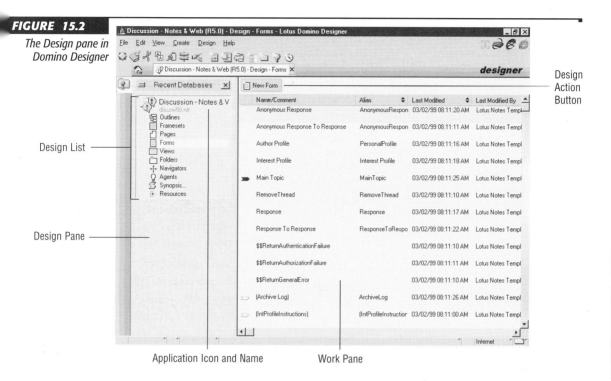

Design List

Design Pane

Design
Action
Button

Application Icon and Name   Work Pane

The Designer Workspace

The Designer workspace is composed of the work area and the programmer's pane
(although the programmer's pane is actually more than one pane). The work area and
programmer's pane can be displayed simultaneously, as shown in Figure 15.3, but you
can also use the pane separator bars to resize either area to your liking. The upper pane
is the work area and the lower pane is the programmer's pane.

When you first open a design element from the Work pane, you will be automatically placed in the work area for that element. In Figure 15.3, a form has been opened
and the work area is displaying the individual design elements that make up the form.
The work area is where the actual design work for an element is done.

The programmer's pane is composed of two parts, the Info list and the script area.
To make matters even more confusing, the Info list contains two tabs, the Objects tab
and the Reference tab.

The Objects Tab   The Objects tab gives you access to any individual design element
and the associated events and attributes for the opened element (the opened element
in Figure 15.3 is the form). You can scroll down through the list and see that each
design element has various events or attributes, which are discussed in more detail in
later chapters. You can navigate through the list by clicking on the + or – signs to
expand or collapse the events and attributes for a design element.

FIGURE 15.3

The Designer
workspace

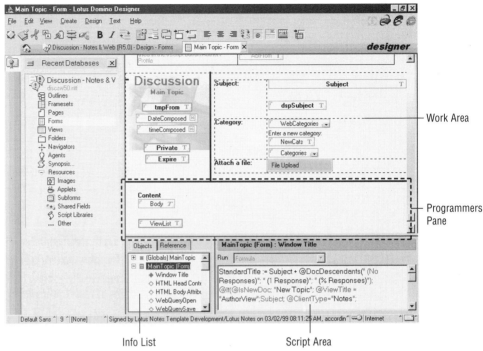

Info List   Script Area

The Reference Tab

The Reference Tab   The Reference tab is a context-sensitive list displaying the information about each programming language recognized in the programmer's pane. From the Reference drop-down list box, select the language you would like information about, and the Reference tab will display a list of events, properties, or methods for that language. You can paste the information from this list directly into the script area. Table 15.1 shows a complete list of information available in the Reference list for each programming language.

TABLE 15.1: PROGRAMMING LANGUAGE AND REFERENCE LIST COMPONENTS

Programming Language	Reference Tab Components
Formula language	Database fields, formula @commands, formula @functions
Java	Core Java, Notes Java
JavaScript	JavaScript objects and functions
LotusScript	Notes: classes, Notes: constants, Notes: subs and functions, Notes: variables, OLE classes

The Reference tab can be extremely handy when you're trying to master a new language. It is also quite an asset for databases that contain a large number of fields. Instead of having to remember all the names, you can just select them from the list of database fields.

The Script Area   The script area is also context sensitive. It will determine the programming language allowed for the element you select from the Objects tab. Unless you've chosen an element that only allows one type of programming language, you can select different programming languages from the drop-down list box (the languages you can choose are listed in Table 15.1). Most of your programming will be performed in the script area. Keeping that in mind, Lotus has put a lot of effort into making the script area more robust for the developer. You can adjust the various attributes from the Design Pane Properties InfoBox, which can be displayed by right-clicking in the script area and choosing Design Pane Properties from the pop-up menu. Depending on the programming language, your code will be displayed in various colors, allowing you to easily identify the constants and the commands. You can also change the font and font size to make it easier to read.

Because we refer to them quite frequently, it's important that you understand the various components of Designer. We recommend that you bookmark these pages for later reference.

Domino Design Elements

To access the database design elements, you need to understand the Design list for each database displayed in the Design pane. Finding most of the design elements is an easy task, but there are a few that are somewhat hidden. The Work pane is also quite a valuable tool for displaying information about each design element. With that in mind, let's go over the design elements with a brief synopsis of each. We'll start from the top of the Design list and make our way down to the last element.

The Outline Design Element

First in the list is the new outline design element. Outlines allow you to visually lay out the design of your application. Using outlines, you can create and manage all types of element links within your database and links to external sources as well. You can use the outline to create a visual map that the end user can use to navigate to the various pieces of your application.

 NOTE   The outline design element can also be used in a Web application as a Java applet.

PART

V

Beyond the Client: Utilizing Domino Designer

If you select the outline design element, the Work pane will open and display all the outlines currently defined for the database (note that all of the elements discussed in the following sections contain the same type of information in the Work pane unless explicitly stated). The Work pane is broken down into six columns, as shown in Figure 15.4. The Name/Comment column displays the common element name and any associated comments that the designer has typed in for the element. The Alias column is exactly that, an alias for the element. This name is typically used internally by the designer when accessing this design element. Because the name can change, programming to the alias name may save you maintenance in the future. The Last Modified and Last Modified By columns show when and who was the last person to change this design element. The last two columns, Notes and Web, tell you whether or not this design element can be displayed in either the Notes client or a Web application.

FIGURE 15.4

The Work pane for the outline design element

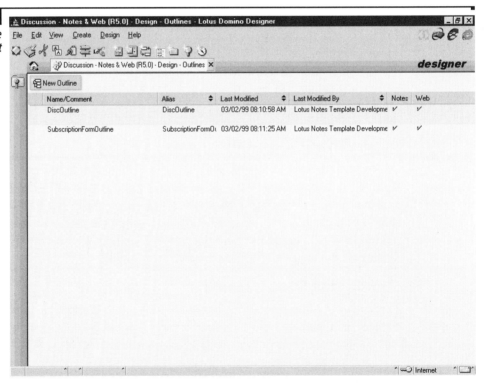

 TIP You should always specify an alias for a design element.

NOTE You'll use the Outline Designer to design your outline element. This editor is automatically used whenever an outline design element is opened.

The Frameset Design Element

Framesets are more commonly known as a Web development tool; they are used to break up a window into sections, or frames. With Notes R5, you can now use framesets in applications that are designed for the Notes client. You can easily create a multipane interface for the user. The panes can be used to access different areas of the application or even different applications or Web sites. Domino Designer includes a Wizard that allows you to quickly generate a frameset without having to write one line of code.

 NOTE You'll use the Frameset Designer to design your frameset element. This editor is automatically used whenever a frameset design element is opened.

The Page Design Element

Pages are again more common in Web development, but they have been integrated into Domino Designer for access from within both the Notes client and Web applications. You can use the Page Designer, which is a What-You-See-Is-What-You-Get (WYSIWYG) HTML authoring tool, to design pages for both environments. This doesn't mean that you can only use HTML. The page design element was primarily designed with the Web developer in mind, but it is flexible enough to be used for Notes client applications as well. Pages are typically used as containers for outlines, Help screens, and embedded views.

 NOTE A page is used for display purposes only. If you would like to capture information as well, you need to use a form.

The Form Design Element

Forms are the most common design element used within a Notes database. A form is used as the basis for entering and viewing document information. If you want a user to enter information, a form must be used (don't confuse this design element with a page).

A form is the most flexible of all the design elements in that it can contain fields, text labels, subforms, layout regions, graphics, tables, objects (such as OLE), file attachments, URLs, links, Action buttons, and background colors and graphics. Other design element can contain some of these things, but a form can contain *all* of them. See Chapters 18 and 19 for detailed discussions of understanding and utilizing forms in applications.

The View Design Element

Views are the second most common design element used within a Notes database. Views are used to list the documents in a database. The designer has total control over what documents—and what information from each document—to list. It is through views that users access documents (they are sometimes accessed through folders).

 NOTE The view design element can also be used in a Web application as a Java applet.

You can sort and group (categorize) documents based on their contents. Typically, you will display information about documents so users can easily identify each one. You can also use views as reports by displaying the important information from each document so the user has no need to actually open the document.

The Folder Design Element

A folder is exactly like a view. The only major difference is that you cannot specify which documents to list in a folder. Documents are copied to a folder, usually from a view, but they can also be programmatically placed into a folder (not, however, from within the folder design element). A folder is usually created as a repository into which the user places documents.

The Navigator Design Element

A Navigator is a graphical design element that allows the user to easily access other database elements, such as views, folders, and documents. Navigators can include graphical buttons and hotspots that, when clicked, execute some action. Navigators can be used as a central home page for when a user first enters a database or as a home page for a Web application. With the addition of new design elements in R5, however, you may find that a Navigator is a bit restrictive.

The Agent Design Element

Agents are used to automate tasks within a Notes database. They can be used to perform a specific task in the database for the user. You can program them to perform tasks as simple as changing a field value and as complex as interacting with external applications.

Agents can run in either the foreground or the background. For Web applications, an Agent is similar to a Common Gateway Interface (CGI) program.

The Work pane for an Agent is slightly different than it is for the previous design elements. There are two additional columns called Trigger and Owner. The Trigger column displays how the Agent is executed (or triggered). This column might display values such as Menu, Scheduled, or Hidden. The Owner column displays the name of the owner of the Agent. For all non-private Agents, the value is Shared. For private Agents, the name of the actual user who created the Agent will be displayed.

The Synopsis Element

The synopsis element is not really a design element; it's a tool that can be used to gather information about all the design elements within the database and generate a report. When you select the synopsis element, the Design Synopsis dialog box, shown in Figure 15.5, is displayed. You can gather information about any combination of design elements. You can also elect to have the report generated to the screen or to a database.

PART

V

Beyond the Client: Utilizing Domino Designer

FIGURE 15.5

The Design Synopsis dialog box

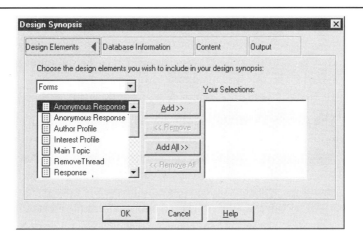

The synopsis is quite flexible in that it allows you to pick and choose the design elements for which you want a report generated and also what you want the report to include. By filtering the data, you can control the length of the report. This is a useful tool for gathering information about the design of a database. It can also be helpful when you're trying to locate information within a database. For example, if you want to see if a field is still being used, you can generate a report containing all the design elements, save it to a database, and then search the database for the particular field.

The Resources Element

The resources element is not really a design element either. It is an element that expands and collapses to expose the following design elements:

- Images
- Applets
- Subforms
- Shared fields
- Script libraries
- Other

The Image Element   New to Notes R5 is the ability to store images as resources in the database (the images placed in a database as an image design element are commonly known as *image resources*). A common problem with previous releases of Notes was the inability to store images in a central location. Now, using an image resource, you can place graphic files (GIF and JPEG) in one common location, and they can be used throughout your application. This will save on maintenance time because you only need to update the image resource in one place. Any references to that image resource will automatically be updated. You can use an image resource on pages, forms, Action buttons, and outline entries and as background images on forms, documents, pages, table cells, and Action buttons.

The Work pane for an image resource does not contain the Notes or Web columns.

The Applet Element   You now have the ability to save Java applets as a shared resource for the database. For large applets, you can also store some of the related files as a shared applet resource. The Resources section is used as a "shared" or common pool. Suppose you have a file that several Java applets use (a set of error messages, for example). This file could change. You have the option of including this file as part of each individual applet. You could also store this file in the shared applet resource. Then, instead of having to change the file in every applet, you only need to go to one place to make the change.

The Work pane for applet resources does not contain the Notes or Web columns. A detailed discussion of Java applets is beyond the scope of this book. The purpose of this discussion is to introduce you to the use of Java applets as elements in Notes databases.

The Subform Element   A subform is a design element that contains fields, text, and so on. The subform can be shared among multiple forms. Although you cannot use a subform by itself, you can insert them into forms to save time on maintenance. For example, if you display the same information as a footer in multiple forms, you can create one subform to replace that information. If that information needs to be changed, you only need to update it in one place, the subform.

 NOTE A subform can contain the same elements as a form.

The Shared Field Element A shared field is another type of shared resource. You can define a field once and share it across multiple forms and subforms. For example, if you want each of your forms to have an authors field called From, just define a shared field called From, set it to an authors field, and insert it into any form or subform within the database.

The Work pane for shared field resources does not contain the Notes or Web columns.

The Script Library Element The script library is a shared resource that allows you to define a set of LotusScript or Java programs that can be used by any element within the database. As with other shared resources, by using a common, shared resource, the time spent on maintaining an application can be reduced.

The Work pane for script library resources does not contain the Notes or the Web columns.

The Other Element Like the resources element previously discussed, the other element is not actually a resource; rather, it is a container for other miscellaneous resources. When you select the other element, the Work pane will expose the following design elements:

Icon An icon that, when selected, brings up the Design Icon dialog box, which allows you to directly edit the current database icon for a database.

The "Using Database" document A document in which you can tell users how to use this application.

The "About Database" document A document in which you can explain the purpose of this application.

The database script A script into which you can enter LotusScript or formula code for events that occur at the database level, such as when the database is opened or closed.

Shared Actions A centralized repository for storing Action buttons. Now you can create an Action button (with all of its attributes) that can be accessed from any form, page, or view within the database.

The Work pane for displaying these elements is a bit different as well. There are only four columns displayed: Name, Defined, Last Modified, and Last Modified By. The

PART

V

Beyond the Client: Uti-
lizing Domino Designer

Defined column is the oddball in the group and, if checked, tells you that something has been defined for that element.

 NOTE The Action bar, which displays the Action button, can also be used in a Web application as a Java applet.

Summary

In this chapter, we discussed the various components that make up the Domino Designer application. We identified and explained the various panes and windows a developer needs to use to create applications for either a Notes or Web environment. Although there are quite a few similarities between the Notes client and Domino Designer, there are also quite a few areas that make Domino Designer distinctly different. Lotus has made every effort to standardize the look and feel of both programs to lower the learning curve.

Those of you who are seasoned Notes programmers will find that the design has changed drastically. Although the changes are quite significant, the overall structure is still intact. The new Designer interface has new capabilities that should improve the environment for rapid application development. Some of the major advantages are that most properties are available via point and click and that the addition of Java applets eases the burden of trying to create both a Notes client and Web application.

In the next chapter, we'll discuss how to begin creating new databases. We'll also cover the basics for database security and the various options that can affect database design and performance.

CHAPTER **16**

Creating
Your First
Database

FEATURING:

Now that you have a basic understanding of navigating around the Domino Designer workspace, it's time to get to the nitty-gritty: creating your first database. In this chapter, we will describe the three different ways you can create a database: from scratch, from an existing template, or by copying an existing database.

Although there is no right or wrong way to create a database, the following sections will help explain when to use each type of database creation method and allow you to decide which method best fits your needs. Whichever method you decide to use, creating a database is the first step in the design process.

This chapter will also cover options for creating databases, database properties in the Properties Info Box, and database security.

Without further ado, let's get cracking.

 NOTE It is a good idea to install the chapter sample databases and templates before proceeding any further. The examples in this chapter will be referring to the Mastering R5 for Chapter 16 database (`MasterR5c16.nsf`) provided on the CD-ROM.

Creating a Database from Scratch

Although it's easy to create a database in Notes, creating one from scratch (which is the default option) is the most difficult of the three options presented. Basically, you start with an empty database and manually create all the elements (forms, pages, views, etc.) that will eventually make up the completed database application. The completed application can be as simple as a few linked pages or as complex as a complete multidatabase Internet site.

To design a database from scratch, first you need to create an empty database. To create a new database using Domino Designer, follow these steps:

1. Choose File ➢ Database ➢ New (or press Ctrl+N). The New Database dialog box (shown in Figure 16.1) appears.

2. From the Server drop-down list, select Local or select or enter a server name:
   - Selecting Local will store the database on your PC's hard drive (you should select this option).
   - Selecting or entering a server name will store the database on that server. This will allow multiple people to work on the same database design.

3. Enter a short descriptive title for the database. For this example, type in **Blank Mastering R5**. This title is very important for identification by your end users. It is used in conjunction with the bookmarks and all subsequent Open Database dialog boxes. Make sure the title is intuitive enough for users to recognize the function of the database.

 TIP The Help file specifies that there is a 32-character limitation for database titles. Testing has revealed that the limitation is actually 96 characters.

4. Enter the filename for the database (note that the default filename will be the title with an .nsf extension). For this example, type **R5Book/Blank_Mastering_R5.nsf**. R5Book will become a subdirectory within the Notes data directory.

 TIP Using spaces in the actual database name may cause you quite a few headaches when you are designing databases for use on the Web. Use underscores in place of spaces.

5. Click the OK button.

FIGURE 16.1

The New Database dialog box

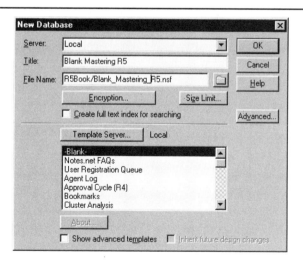

Once you have completed the database creation process, the database will automatically open, displaying the various design elements in the Design pane. Because the database you have just created is empty, the Work pane will not display any design elements. Also, a bookmark for the new database will be placed in the Recent Databases portfolio list in the Design pane. You should also create a bookmark and place it in another portfolio folder (for each application, we usually create one portfolio folder that contains all the databases relating to that application). The Recent Databases portfolio list only contains the bookmarks for the five most recently accessed databases.

TIP To add a bookmark to another portfolio list, simply drag a window tab onto one of the portfolio tabs.

Where Does My Database Get Saved?

When you create a new database, you'll notice that there's a file folder button next to the File Name field. If you click this button, the database file can be saved into a different directory. By default, all new databases are saved to the Notes root `Data` directory. Clicking the file folder button will open the Choose a Folder dialog box. For a local server, this dialog box is nothing more than a directory tree of your hard disk, as shown in Figure 16.2. Selecting a directory and clicking the OK button will prefix the database filename with the drive and directory selected. If you selected or entered a server name, a different dialog box will appear when you click the file folder button. Because most servers do not allow users access to the entire hard disk, the Select Folder dialog box only displays a list of subdirectories contained within the Notes root directory, as shown in Figure 16.3. Selecting a subdirectory and clicking the Select button will still prefix the database filename with the directory, but the directory will be relative to the Notes data directory residing on the server.

FIGURE 16.2

The Choose a Folder dialog box for the Local server

FIGURE 16.3

The Select Folder
dialog box for a Notes
server

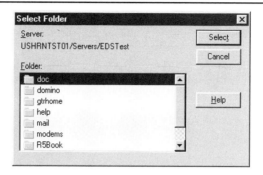

Another shortcut to placing database files into subdirectories is to type in the subdirectory name manually. This will automatically create the subdirectory underneath the
Notes root Data directory whether the server selected is Local or an actual Notes server.
For example, if you type **MyDir\MyDatabase.nsf**, the database MyDatabase.nsf will
be placed into the MyDir subdirectory within the Notes root Data directory.

TIP When you are deleting databases that are contained within a subdirectory on a
server and you remove the last database, the subdirectory will automatically be removed.

Creating a Database from a Template

It's a bit easier to create a database from a template than it is to create one from scratch.
Selecting one of the master templates, which are automatically available when Notes
is installed, will give you a head start on designing your database by offering you many
of the elements you need. For example, the discussion template, Discussion–Notes &
Web (R5.0), is a complete application for both the Notes client and the Web.

The template contains a complete discussion-style database with all the forms, pages,
outlines, views, and so on already written and tested. Once the database is created with
the template, your application is ready to be used.

One nice feature of the Domino Designer is the many templates that have already
been created for you (commonly referred to as master templates). Table 16.1 lists the
most commonly used master templates included with Domino Designer.

TABLE 16.1: THE MASTER TEMPLATES INCLUDED WITH DOMINO DESIGNER

Template Title	Description
Discussion–Notes & Web (R5.0)	An electronic conference room that allows threaded discussions with built-in author profiles and automatic mailing for topics of interest. Designed for both Notes clients and Web browsers.
Doc Library–Notes & Web (R5.0)	General document storage with built-in review workflow (both serial and parallel) and archiving. Designed for both Notes clients and Web browsers.
Microsoft Office Library (R5.0)	Just like the Doc Library template except designed specifically for the Microsoft Office suite; loads the OLE object and sizes it to the window. Designed only for the Notes client.
Personal Journal (R4)	Electronic diary in which a user can write and organize thoughts and ideas. Designed only for the Notes client.
Site Registration 5.0	A sample database showing how to register Web users for a Domino-based application. Designed only for Web browsers.
TeamRoom (5.0)	A database for team collaboration; allows several different types of document communication that represent meetings, discussions, and Action items. Built-in parallel review and archiving. Designed for both the Notes client and Web browsers.

The Site Registration and TeamRoom templates reside on the server and are not installed with Domino Designer.

Although each template may not fulfill all the requirements for your database, it does give you, the designer, a helpful head start. You only need to modify the various design elements to fit your requirements instead of having to code everything over and over again.

To use Domino Designer to create a database from an existing template, follow these steps:

1. Choose File ➢ Database ➢ New (or press Ctrl+N). The New Database dialog box, shown in Figure 16.4, appears.

 TIP Instead of selecting File ➢ Database ➢ New from the menu, you can also press Ctrl+N to display the New Database dialog box.

PART

V

Beyond the Client: Utilizing Domino Designer

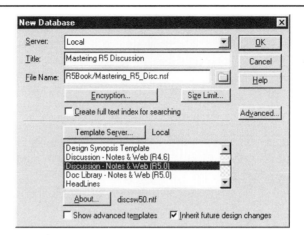

FIGURE 16.4

Selecting a template for a new database

2. From the Server drop-down list, select Local or select or enter a server name:

   • Selecting Local will store the database on your PC's hard drive (you should select this option).

   • Selecting or entering a server name will store the database on that server. This will allow multiple people to work on the same database design.

3. Enter a short descriptive title for the database. For this example, type in **Mastering R5 Discussion**.

4. Enter the filename for the database. For this example, type **R5Book/Mastering_R5_Disc.nsf**. The new database will be saved within the R5Book subdirectory along with the database from the preceding example.

5. Select a template from the list (see Figure 16.4). To display additional templates, do one of the following:

   • Select the Show Advanced Templates option, which will display all the basic and advanced templates for the selected server.

   • Click the Template Server button, which will display the Template Servers dialog box (Figure 16.5) and allow you to select a different server. Once a server is selected, the list of templates that reside only on the selected server will be shown.

 NOTE When a template is selected (except for Blank), the Inherit Future Design Changes option will be enabled automatically.

FIGURE 16.5

Selecting a template server

6. Click the OK button.

Once you have completed the database creation process, the database will automatically open and display the various design elements in the Work pane. Because the database was based on an existing template that already contained quite a few design items (unlike in the preceding example), the Work pane will display all of defined design elements, as shown in Figure 16.6.

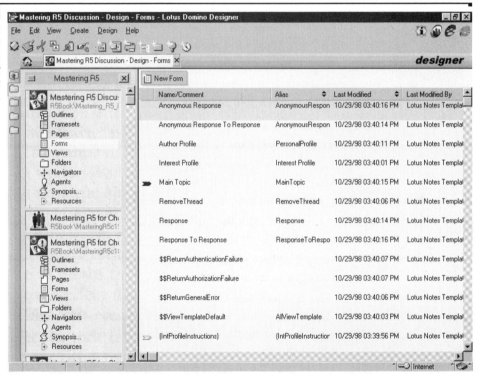

Templates and Databases (NTF and NSF)

Before we go any further, a quick review of a template and database is in order to ensure that there is no confusion about these two types of files. Although they are similar, there are some basic differences.

A template is a file with the .ntf extension, and a database is a file with the .nsf extension. A template is a database skeleton that contains design elements but no documents, whereas a database contains both the design elements and the documents. The confusion arises because both file types are essentially databases. You can create documents and execute design elements within a template just as you would inside a database. So what really distinguishes a template from a database? The difference is a property that is located in the Database Properties Info Box, which will be discussed later in the chapter. Both the template and the database have this property available, and to make things more confusing, you can set this option for both. Keep in mind that the .ntf and .nsf extensions do *not* determine if the file is a template or a database; the property does. Although it may seem like the extension is the determining factor, it isn't. It is a good practice to keep the property set for the appropriate extension, but Notes will not inform you if you have a database (.nsf) property set as a template, nor will it inform you if you have a template (.ntf) set as a database.

Why use a template? This is a good question because both a database and a template seem to be the same. The main reason is that, in a template, all of the design elements can be kept separate from the database. There is an option that allows a database to be either *replaced* or *refreshed* from a template (the refresh can be done manually or automatically on a schedule). If a database is replaced, all the design elements will be blindly copied from a template into the database. This is a powerful option and extreme caution should be used when executing this command. On the other hand, the Refresh option is quite handy. For example, when you decide to refresh a database's design elements, Notes will automatically refresh those elements for you based on a template. You do not need to select a template; this has already been predetermined by you, the designer.

There are quite a few combinations that can be used when you are refreshing a database. The simplest example refreshes all of the design elements. In Figure 16.4, an option called Inherit Future Design Changes is selected. This option sets a database property for the database you are creating so the entire design will always be refreshed from the template. This is a global (or database-wide) setting. In other words, an exact copy of all the template's design elements will be placed into your database. You can also set the Refresh option so that individual design elements are refreshed from a template and other design elements are never refreshed. And you can update different design elements from other templates. This is quite useful when you want to include some design elements from one template and other design elements from another template. As you can see, there is quite a bit of flexibility when using templates.

Continued

CONTINUED

What is the advantage of using a template? Actually, there are quite a few advantages. Anyone can use a template to quickly and easily create a new database. The Mastering R5 Discussion database was created in a few seconds using the template. You will also save design time by using templates. Common Agents or forms that do not require any additional work can be copied from a template. If the common Agent changes, the change can be refreshed to all the databases without any interaction from the designer.

As you can see, a template is an integral part of the application design process. We always use a template for each database when we create an application. We also have a Common or Base template that contains all types of forms, Agents, views, and so on that we seem to use over and over again. Keep in mind that, when a database is refreshed, the Access Control List (ACL) is never changed. The only components that get refreshed are forms, fields, form Actions, event scripts, views, folders, view Actions, Agents, outlines, pages, framesets, Navigators, shared fields, and some of the Database Property selections.

Copying an Existing Database

Finally, you can create a new database by making a new copy of an existing database. This option is usually the preferred choice if you have found an existing application that contains the majority of the functionality you desire. Before copying the database, make sure the designer of the database has not hidden the design elements. This will prevent you from being able to modify any of them. To determine if the design is hidden, open the Database Properties Info Box for the database and select the Design tab. If the design is hidden, you will see the message "No design information available."

To create a database by using Domino Designer and copying from an existing database, follow these steps:

1. Open the Mastering R5 Discussion database you created in the preceding section.

2. Choose File ➤ Database ➤ New Copy. The Copy Database dialog box, shown in Figure 16.7, appears.

NOTE You can also right-click the database's design bookmark icon in the Design pane and choose Database ➤ New Copy.

FIGURE 16.7

The Copy Database
dialog box

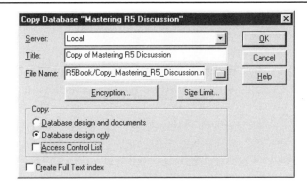

 WARNING When you copy an existing database, only the title of the database is displayed in the title of the Copy Database dialog box. The dialog box doesn't tell you the server from which you are copying.

3. From the Server drop-down list, select Local or select or enter a server name:

   - Selecting Local will store the database on your PC's hard drive.

   - Selecting or entering a server name will store the database on that server. This will allow multiple people to work on the same database design.

4. Enter the title **Copy of Mastering R5 Discussion** for the new database. The default is to use the same title as the original database. To eliminate any possible confusion, the title should be changed.

5. Enter the filename **R5Book/Copy_Mastering_R5_Discussion.nsf** for the new database. By default, the title and filename are filled in with the same title and filename as the database being copied. If you forget to change the filename, the system will respond with an error message, either warning you that the database is in use (for local databases) or asking you to replace the existing databases (for databases on the server).

6. Select the Database Design Only radio button. Because you are attempting to create a new database based on the design, there is no need to copy over all of the data documents as well.

7. Deselect the Access Control List check box. By default, this option is selected and will copy over the current ACL settings, which may render you powerless. Deselecting this option will ensure that you will be placed as the Manager of the database.

8. Leave the Create Full Text Index option blank (you are not copying over any data documents, so there is not much to index anyway).

9. Click the OK button.

Once the database copy process is complete, you may notice that the new database is not automatically opened for you as in the previous examples. The new database is also not in your list of the most recently accessed bookmarks. You will need to manually open the new database and place a bookmark to it in one of your portfolio folders.

Once you open your newly copied database, there really is no difference from the original. All of the design elements are intact, and if they are based on a template, the relationship will still be intact as well. The only big difference is the title and the actual name of the database (assuming that you changed them).

Other Options You Can Choose

Up to this point, you may have noticed that there are quite a number of options for creating databases that were not mentioned. In the previous examples, the defaults were used so you could get comfortable with the entire creation process. Now that you have a better understanding of how databases are created, we can inundate you with the various options, including:

- Local database encryption
- Size limit for a database
- Advanced database options
- About the template

Encrypting a Local Database

Once you begin to get comfortable with Notes and using local copies of the databases, security becomes a major concern. With the advent of notebook computers, data can be replicated from a server and carried around by the user. Because notebooks are a popular item to steal, your corporate data can be carried away by the thief as well. This is where locally encrypting the database comes in handy.

Local database encryption will prevent "prying" eyes from getting at your data. When encryption is enabled, the physical database file is encrypted or scrambled using the public key of the designated ID. This "scrambling" prevents anyone from browsing the data unless they have the corresponding Notes key (the appropriate Notes ID). Keep in mind that this added security does have a price—performance. Because the data needs to be scrambled when it is written and unscrambled when it is read, it will take a bit longer for data to be transferred to and from the file. This is a small price to pay for the added security.

When creating a new database, you will notice that there is an Encryption button on the New Database dialog box (refer to Figure 16.1 or 16.4). To encrypt the Mastering R5 Discussion database, just click the Encryption button and the Encryption dialog box appears (see Figure 16.8).

The Encryption dialog box for the current database

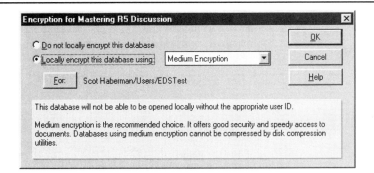

To remove encryption from a database, select the Do Not Locally Encrypt This Database option (this is the default encryption option). To encrypt the database, select the Locally Encrypt This Database Using option. There are three levels of encryption that can be selected for a database. Let's examine each a bit more closely.

 TIP Don't worry if you can't remember the details for each encryption option. A brief description of each selected option displays in the Encryption dialog box.

Simple Encryption   Simple encryption provides some limited security. This type of security will not keep out most hackers, but it will give you the best performance. You can also use disk compression utilities on this type of database.

Medium Encryption   Medium encryption is the best choice for most databases. This type of security is strong enough to give most hackers a lot of trouble but still give you good performance. Keep in mind that you cannot use this type of encryption if you use a disk compression utility.

Strong Encryption   Strong encryption is the highest level of security and will stop almost all hackers from getting at the data. There is a definite performance degradation

PART

V

Beyond the Client: Utilizing Domino Designer

when accessing the data. Keep in mind that you cannot use a disk compression utility with this type of encryption.

 NOTE You can change the encryption on an existing database. To encrypt a local database, choose File ➤ Database ➤ Properties and click the Encryption button on the Basics tab.

 WARNING When you encrypt a database locally, you will notice that there is a For button and a username. This determines the User ID that has access to the locally encrypted database. If you change the user to someone other than yourself, make sure you have a replica copy of the database or you will deny yourself access.

Setting the Database Size Limit

There is no longer a need to specify a size limit for a database. Databases can now be as large as 32GB. The Size Limit button that is displayed when a new database is created (refer to Figure 16.1 or 16.4) is only used for earlier versions of Notes databases for backward compatibility. When the button is clicked, the Size Limit dialog box appears (see Figure 16.9). You can select 1GB, 2GB, 3GB, or 4GB.

FIGURE 16.9

The Size Limit dialog box for a new database

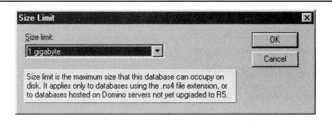

Setting Database Advanced Options

Some other options that are available when you create a new database are listed under the Advanced button (refer to Figure 16.1 or 16.4). These options don't need to be specified only at the time the database is created. You can also access the options from the Database Properties Info Box under the Advanced tab (discussed later in this chapter). Keep in mind that, if you change an option, you may need to compact the database for the setting to take effect.

To display the Advanced Database Options dialog box (shown in Figure 16.10) when you are creating a new database, just click the Advanced button.

FIGURE 16.10

The Advanced Database Options dialog box for a new database

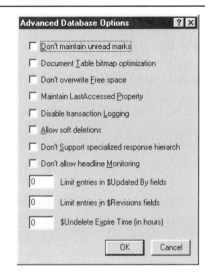

Some of these options may give your databases a significant performance boost, whereas others may actually degrade performance. By default, none of the options are selected. Although some of the options are beyond the scope of this book, the more important options are listed in the following sections.

Don't Maintain Unread Marks   System resources are required to maintain unread marks in a database, which can slow down performance. This option should only be selected for databases in which unread marks on a document are not very useful, such as log files or the Help files. Do not confuse this database option with views that do not display unread marks. If this option is not selected, the overhead required to maintain unread marks is still in effect regardless of what the views options specify. On the flip side, if you aren't getting unread marks for any of your views in a database, you may want to check to see if this option has been selected. In order for this option to take effect, you will need to compact the database.

NOTE   Using the Don't Display Unread Marks option for a view is not the same thing as not maintaining unread marks for a database. Using the view option does not improve database performance.

Maintain LastAccessed Property For every document, there is an internal Last-Accessed field that maintains the date when the document was last modified or read. Selecting this option will change the default behavior so that the internal LastAccessed field will be updated every time a document is read. This increases the amount of I/O for every document read. To view the contents of this internal field, select any document in the database, open the Document Properties Info Box, and select the Info tab. You'll see an Accessed field and the date when the document was last accessed (read or modified, depending on the status of the database option).

 WARNING You must select the Maintain LastAccessed Property option if you use the Database Properties archive tool that deletes documents based on days of inactivity.

Allow Soft Deletions Although this option really doesn't have an effect on performance, it is a nifty tool available to the designer. When documents are deleted, you can now specify that they "stick around" for a while before they are physically deleted from the database. When Allow Soft Deletions is used in conjunction with the $Undelete Expire Time option, you can specify how many hours a deleted document will remain in the database. You can also create a special view that will display the deleted documents. Within the Shared, Contains Deleted Documents view type, mistakenly deleted documents can be retrieved simply and easily. Once the specified number of hours has passed, the documents are permanently deleted from the database. By default, this option is not selected.

 WARNING The Shared, Contains Deleted Documents view will not show the deleted documents unless the Allow Soft Deletions property is selected.

Don't Support Specialized Response Hierarchy You can select this option to achieve another performance improvement. Every document in a database stores information that associates it to a parent or Response document. This information is only used by the @functions @AllChildren and @AllDescendants. These two @functions are commonly used in view selection or replication formulas. If you don't plan to use either of these two commands, select this option. Selecting this option does *not* disable the response hierarchy information in the database, so it will not affect views or replication formulas. If you are creating a view or replication formula that uses @AllChildren or @AllDescendants and it is not working correctly, check the status of this option. By default, this option is not selected.

Don't Allow Headline Monitoring   Using this option will also help performance on your database. Users can set up headline monitoring on a database for any type of information that interests them. Enable this option to prevent the database from being monitored (this can also be set up at the server level). If this option is enabled, users will get the message "Subscriptions are disabled for this database" when they try to set up a subscription. Subscriptions are stored in the Headlines database for a user, which is most likely how this option got its name. By default, this option is not selected.

Limit Entries in $UpdatedBy Fields   Each document contains a hidden field called $UpdatedBy; each time the document is edited, the $UpdatedBy field stores, by default, the name of the user who edited it. After numerous edits, this field can become quite large, consuming disk space and, more importantly, slowing view updates and replication. Use this option to limit the number of entries that are maintained in the $UpdatedBy field. Once the number of entries is reached, the oldest entry is removed to make room for the newest entry. By default, this option is set to 0, signifying no limit to the number of entries stored in the field.

 TIP   Anonymous forms do not have the $UpdatedBy field.

Limit Entries in $Revisions Fields   This option is similar to the Limit Entries in $Updated By Fields option. The only difference is that the $Revisions field tracks the date and time for each document editing session. This field is primarily used by Domino to resolve replication or save conflicts that can occur between two users editing the document. By default, the $Revisions field saves 500 entries, consuming 8 bytes of disk space for each entry. Again, this field can grow, slowing down view updates and replications. Use this field to limit the number of entries that are maintained in the $Revisions field. Once the number of entries is reached, the oldest entry is removed to make room for the newest entry. Also keep in mind that a setting that is too low may increase replication and save conflicts. A suggested limit is 10. By default, this option will store 500 entries. Each entry consumes 8 bytes of disk space.

$Undelete Expire Time (in Hours)   As mentioned previously, this option determines the number of hours the system waits before it deletes the documents pending for deletion. It is used in conjunction with the Allow Soft Deletions option.

The About Button

Although it's not really an option, the About button (refer to Figure 16.1 or 16.4) for database templates is worth mentioning. When you are scrolling through the list of templates (both basic and advanced templates), it's difficult to determine what the template really contains unless the designer gives the template a descriptive title. If you click the About button in the New Database dialog box, the About document for the highlighted template will display. If the designer of the template did a thorough job, the About document should tell you everything that you need to know about the template. As shown in Figure 16.11, the Discussion–Notes & Web (R5.0) template's About document gives a brief overview about what the database does, the recommended ACL settings, and so on.

FIGURE 16.11

A brief overview of the Discussion–Notes & Web (R5.0) template via the About button

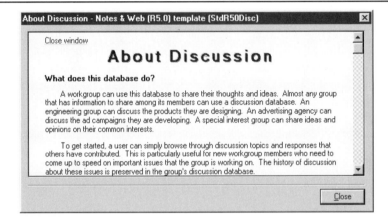

The Database Properties Info Box

Now that you have a basic understanding of the database creation process and the database creation options, it's time to explain how to modify database properties on an existing database. But before we get into more detail about the database properties, we'll explain the concept of Property Info Boxes.

What Is a Properties Info Box?

A Property Info Box is a special dialog box in Notes that gives the user and the designer access to an element's properties. Many element in Notes—such as databases, documents, and forms—have properties. Although not all the elements have the same properties, they all use a Property Info Box to access them. You're probably familiar with a similar type of properties dialog box from other products. The Properties Info Box is a bit different in that it can be left open while you work. Why is that different? When the

Properties Info Box is left open, it reflects the properties of the element that you are currently working on. When you change from one element to another, the Properties Info Box reflects the properties of the new element. The Properties Info Box also reflects changes without requiring that you select an OK or Done button. Changes to the property settings are made as soon as you click somewhere else in the Properties Info Box.

The easiest way to open a Properties Info Box is to first select or highlight the item whose properties you would like to view. Select the Mastering R5 for Chapter 18 database's design icon from the Design pane. To display a Properties Info Box (see Figure 16.12), click the Properties SmartIcon on the SmartIcon bar.

> **NOTE**   You can also open the Properties Info Box by right-clicking on an element (such as a database, document, or form) and choosing the Properties menu item.

FIGURE 16.12

*The Properties Info Box
for a selected design
element*

Tab   Title Bar   Drop-Down Menu   Toolbar   Help   Close Box

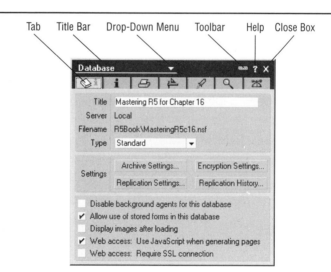

The tabbed pages allow you to choose many different options for the selected element:

- To switch to a different property page, click a tab.
- To move the Properties Info Box, drag it by the title bar.
- To float the dialog box as a toolbar, click the toolbar icon.
- To get help for the element or options, click the question mark icon.
- To close the box, click the close icon.

The Properties Info Box also has a drop-down menu that allows you to select a different element (the element values change depending on the element currently being viewed). Now that you have the basic understanding of what a Properties Info Box contains, let's move on to a working example.

Select the Mastering R5 for Chapter 16 database from the Design pane. Display the Properties Info Box for the database by either clicking the Properties SmartIcon or right-clicking and selecting Database ➤ Properties from the pop-up menu. The drop-down menu for the Properties Info Box should say Database. If this is not the case, select the database again, but this time with the Properties Info Box visible. Remember that the Properties Info Box reflects any changes immediately.

The Basics Tab

The Basics tab (shown in Figure 16.12) displays the general database information. The title of the database can be changed, but note that the server and filename cannot. The database title is the text that is always seen in the Open Database dialog box by the end user. The database title is also the default label when new database bookmarks are created.

Database Type   The database type, which is located in the Type drop-down list box, can be one of the following:

- Standard
- Library
- Personal Journal
- Address Book
- Light Address Book
- Multi DB Search
- Portfolio
- IMAP Server Proxy
- News Server Proxy
- Subscriptions
- Mailbox

Although it is not necessary for you to know the details of each database type, you should realize that a type is used in conjunction with one of the predefined Notes master templates. For example, the Personal Journal database type is automatically assigned to a database created from the Personal Journal template. The Personal Journal type, when applied to a database, will not offer the option of creating shared views, Agents, or folders because it is designed for your personal use. We do not advise changing the database type. The Standard type will fit 99 percent of your needs.

Archive Settings   The Archive Settings button is a bit deceiving. Clicking it brings up the Archive Settings dialog box, which *does* archive documents, but it's also a document deletion tool. When documents are archived, they are removed from the current database, hence the deletion portion of the preceding statement. The Archive Settings dialog box is broken down into two sections (as shown in Figure 16.13): Basics and Advanced. The archive process should be performed regularly to remove inactive documents, which saves space, makes it easier for users to search for information, and improves overall database performance.

FIGURE 16.13

The Basics tab of the Document archiving and deletion tool

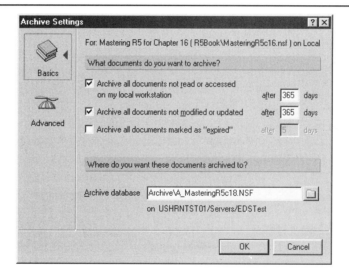

The Basics tab of the Archive Settings dialog box displays the following options (see Figure 16.13):

What Documents Do You Want To Archive?   This section allows you to specify the number of days since the last time a document was read, modified, or updated that should pass before the document is deleted. You can also specify the number of days since a document was marked as Expired. (This only applies to database documents that use an ExpireDate expiration date field. This functionality is built in to some of the Notes master templates, such as the discussion database template.) To determine a document's inactivity, its FileAccessed property must be enabled. This requires that you select the Maintain LastAccessed property in the Advanced Database Options dialog box as described earlier in this chapter (see "Setting Database Advanced Options").

Where Do You Want These Documents Archived To? This section allows you to specify the subdirectory and filename of the archive file. The archive file will contain all of the documents that have been removed from the database (as you can see, the documents are not really deleted, just moved to another database). Selecting the file folder icon next to the Archive Database text box will display the Select Folder dialog box and allow you to select the subdirectory for the archive database.

The Advanced tab displays the following options (see Figure 16.14):

How Do You Want To Archive This Database? This option allows you to decide if you want to archive the database from your workstation or from a server. If you elect to archive the database from your workstation, you can choose which server should house the archive. You can also elect to store the archive on your own workstation. If you elect to archive the database from the server, the archive will automatically reside on that server.

Advanced Archiving Options You can also decide to keep a log of all the archiving activity. You need to supply both a subdirectory and filename. Selecting the file folder icon next to the Log Activity To text box will display the Select Folder dialog box and allow you to select the subdirectory for the logging database. You can also elect not to delete documents that have responses. This will ensure that a parent document is not deleted until all the associated Response documents are deleted, which will eliminate potential *orphaned* documents. An orphaned document is a Response document that does not have a parent. Because most views use the parent-child response hierarchy, a Response document without a parent would never get displayed in the view. The final option allows you to just remove the documents entirely without copying them to the archive database. Be very careful about selecting this option because, once the documents are deleted, you'll need to find a backup copy of the database containing those deleted records to restore them.

Encryption The Encryption button allows you to encrypt local databases to prevent those without the proper Notes ID from accessing the local data. This was covered in detail in "Encrypting a Local Database" earlier in the chapter.

Replication Settings The Replication Settings button allows you to set the various replication options for the database. Clicking this button will display the Replication Settings dialog box, shown in Figure 16.15. You don't have to use the Database Properties Info Box to access the Replication Settings dialog box. This dialog box can also be displayed via the Replication page or by choosing File ➤ Replication ➤ Settings. If you have databases that reside on multiple servers and there seem to be some irregular problems, this is a good place to look to ensure that all the settings are correct.

FIGURE 16.14

The Advanced tab of the Document archiving and deletion tool

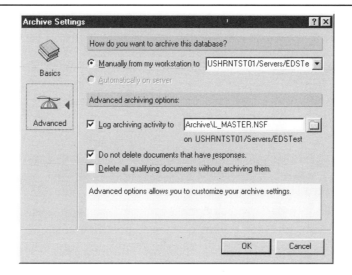

Replication History   Notes maintains a replication history for any database that has been replicated at least once. The replication history is used to determine which documents to include in the next replication. This ensures that only added, modified, or deleted documents are replicated, which saves both time and bandwidth. Figure 16.16 displays a typical example of a replication history. Keep in mind that clearing the replication history will make the next replication take much longer because the servers will have nothing to compare against to determine which documents have been added, modified, or deleted.

FIGURE 16.15

The Replication Settings dialog box

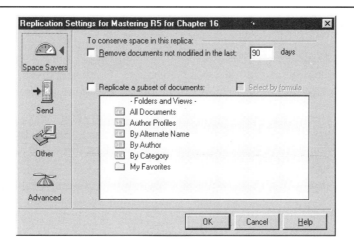

FIGURE 16.16

The replication history tracks the database documents.

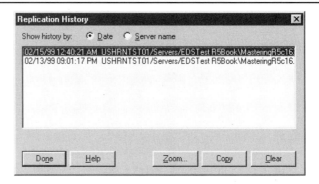

Disable Background Agents for This Database   Selecting the Disable Background Agents for This Database option will prevent automated tasks from executing on or changing any of the database documents. Use this with caution because many users have tasks for moving or copying documents or moving folders.

Allow Use of Stored Forms in This Database   Select the Allow Use of Stored Forms in This Database option to allow documents within the database to store the form along with the actual data. Having the form inside the document ensures that the document will display properly. This feature is typically implemented when documents will be mailed to other databases or mailed to other users and you are not sure if the form will be available. Without the correct form, you have no idea what data will display.

 WARNING   The Allow Use of Stored Forms in This Database option requires a lot of disk space. Every document stores the document data along with a copy of the form.

The final options on the Basics tab only apply to the database when the application will be displayed through a Web browser. Remember that databases can be designed for both the Notes client and a Web browser. Therefore, many of the options are intermixed.

Web Access: Use JavaScript When Generating Pages   This option is *extremely* important, especially when used with databases designed for older versions of Notes. Selecting this option for v4.5 databases could cause unexpected behavior on Actions, buttons, and hotspots. First, we'll clear up one misconception. Deselecting this option does not preclude you, the designer, from using JavaScript in the database. You can code JavaScript wherever you like regardless of the setting of this option. Selecting this option determines how Domino will interpret and render the Web pages for your application. That is all the option does. If you select this option:

- Web documents and Navigators display faster because the hotspot formulas are not evaluated until a user clicks each hotspot.

- You can design forms with multiple buttons.
- Domino will not automatically generate a Submit button.
- You can use additional @commands.

If you deselect this option:

- Hotspot formulas in documents and Navigators are evaluated at display time, slowing down the initial page rendered to the browser.
- Domino will only recognize the first button on a form and automatically convert it to a Submit button (if no buttons are defined, Domino will automatically create one).
- All formulas and commands are evaluated before the page is displayed and any nonsupported @functions or @commands will not be displayed.
- Many of the @commands, such as @Command([FileSave]), are not supported on the Web.

For most Web applications, you'll want to select this option. We use this option just for the @Command([ViewRefreshFields]) command. This allows you to recompute a Web page without actually saving the document. This may not sound like a useful feature, but it saves time and can't be done unless the Use JavaScript When Generating Pages option is set.

PART

V

Beyond the Client: Uti-
lizing Domino Designer

Upgrading Ramifications

The decision to select or not select the Use JavaScript option can have serious consequences on older v4.5 Web applications. As mentioned earlier, selecting this option will change the behavior of formulas and Actions, buttons, and hotspots. It also changes the generation of the URL syntax a bit and could potentially display elements that were hidden in v4.5.

So what can you do? Carefully review every form and Navigator in the application for the following:

- Check all elements for any unsupported @function or @command. They would automatically be hidden in v4.5 but will now be displayed because the commands are evaluated after the Web page is displayed.
- Make sure there is a Submit button defined for the form. With v4.5, the first button was automatically changed to a Submit button, or if no button was defined, v4.5 would create one.

Continued

CONTINUED

- Replace any attachment fields with a file upload control. In R4.5, an attachment field was created by using the `@Command([EditInsertFileAttachment])` command. Because all commands are evaluated after the page is displayed, the attachment field will not be displayed.

- Check any formulas that relied on the `Query_Info` or `Path_Info` CGI variable. The URLs are a bit different with v5. Release v5 uses a modified Post URL and also has the option of using a ! over the ? command separator.

Web Access: Require SSL Connection Secure Sockets Layer (SSL) is a security protocol that protects data by encrypting it as it passes from the client to the server. SSL can be set up at the Web-server level, but this would require that all Web applications be running SSL. This option, when selected, protects all data that uses SSL and resides only within the database. Only select this option when you need a secure connection between the client and the data residing on the Web server because it will affect performance.

The Info Tab

The Info tab (shown in Figure 16.17) provides file-related information about the database, such as the size, time, and date created or modified; the number of documents; and space utilization. The Size field shows the total amount of space the database has allocated, and the Documents field is the total number of data documents for the database. The actual design elements are not counted as documents (even though a design element is a document). Therefore, when you are replicating a database, you may see a much higher number of documents being transferred than this number reflects.

FIGURE 16.17

The Info tab from the Database Properties Info Box

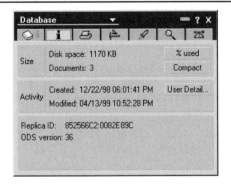

% Used   Clicking the % Used button displays the percentage of white space currently in the database. The number will display to the right of the button. This number is not automatically displayed; you must click the button.

Compact   Click the Compact button to compact the database, which removes the white space. If the % Used number falls below 90%, you may want to compact the database. White space is generally created from deletions in the database, especially if some of the deleted documents contain large attachments. The percentage of white space in the database represented in Figure 16.19 is 6.2% (100–93.8), so a compact should not be performed. If you want to start the compacting process, just click the Compact button, which is conveniently located to the right of the percentage number.

 WARNING   If medium or strong encryption is in use, you cannot compact the database.

Activity   The Activity area displays the time and date the database was created and the last time it was modified.

User Detail   The User Detail button brings up the User Activity dialog box, which is a useful feature for analyzing user reads and writes. As shown in Figure 16.18, an audit trail shows what happens every time a user accesses a document. To begin recording the user activity for the database, you must activate the Record Activity option. Turning the Record Activity option on does not affect the results recorded to the Notes log, but it does require an additional 64K for recording the information. Also, you can select the Activity Is Confidential option. There may be times when you don't want users to be able to see who has been doing what inside the database. Enabling this option prevents those without Manager or Designer access from seeing this dialog box.

PART

V

Beyond the Client: Utilizing Domino Designer

FIGURE 16.18

The User Activity dialog box

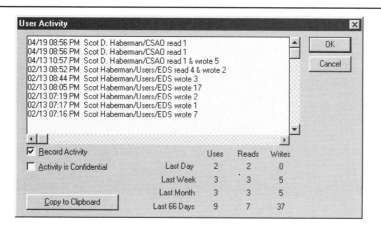

NOTE If you elect to disable the Record Activity option for a database, the Statlog task running on the server will turn it back on.

Replica ID Notes allows you to keep multiple copies, called replicas, of a database on multiple servers and workstations. Each replica has the same replica ID as the original database. The replica ID distinguishes a replica from a copy of a database and allows you to replicate changes between the replica and the original database. Every database has a unique replica ID, which is used to identify it. This ID is also used in many different functions that refer to a database within Notes. The replica ID is displayed on the information tab as a read-only field.

 TIP You may have noticed that the replica ID for a database is rather long and can be an easy target for a typo. To prevent this from happening, use the design synopsis to copy and paste the replica ID into your code. From the Design pane, select the Synopsis option. Click the Database Information tab and select the Replication check box. When the synopsis is displayed, simply highlight the replica ID and copy it to your code.

The Printing Tab

 The Printing tab (see Figure 16.19) is used to specify headers and footers when you print out information from the database. This is the one tab that is exactly the same for many of the Properties Info Boxes (such as those for a document and for a form). From this tab, you can change the header and footer text, the font, the point size, or the style.

FIGURE 16.19

The Printing tab in the Database Properties Info Box

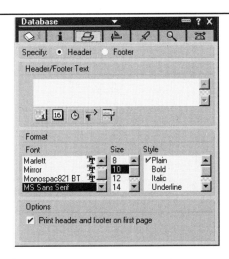

There are actually three types of headers and footers that you can specify when printing data: headers and footers for a document, for a form, and for a database. With that in mind, there is also a type of hierarchy associated with the three different types of headers and footers. Just remember that headers and footers for documents override headers and footers for forms and databases and that form headers and footers override database headers and footers.

It's also a bit of a challenge to format the text placed in the header and footer area. Notes uses a macro or symbol language to represent dynamic information. You don't have to remember the symbols because there are icons that represent them (see Table 16.2).

TABLE 16.2: SYMBOLS AND ICONS FOR HEADERS AND FOOTERS

Symbol	Icon
Print Page (&P)	
Print Date (&D)	
Print Time (&T)	
Print Title (&W)	

PART

V

Beyond the Client: Utilizing Domino Designer

There is also an icon that, when clicked, inserts the vertical bar symbol in the header or footer.

There are three preset tab stops for the header and footer: left, center, and right. Follow these conventions to align the text:

Left-align text   Do not use any Print tabs.

Center text   Place a Print tab on either side of the text to be centered.

Right-align text   Place two Print tabs before the text.

You get the idea. The tabs take a bit of getting used to because they are inserted randomly and not where you place your cursor. The last option, Print Header and Footer on First Page, will, as its name suggests, place the header and footer on the first page. If you deselect this option, they will not be printed on the first page.

The Design Tab

The Design tab is one of the more important tabs for the designer. It allows you to set the properties for the design of the database. As seen in Figure 16.20, you can specify whether a database is a template, inherits from a template, or gets displayed in an Open Database dialog box. Let's step through each option one at a time.

FIGURE 16.20

The Design tab properties

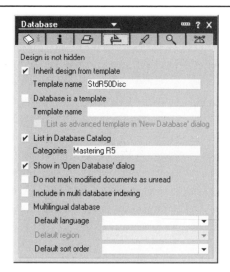

Design Is Not Hidden Although not really an option, this line lets you know whether or not you will have access to the design elements of the database. As mentioned earlier, you can create a copy of a database and "hide" the actual database design. This will allow you to protect your code from accidental changes or from prying eyes. If the design is hidden, you will see the message "No design information available."

How to Hide the Template Design

Before we tell you how to hide the design of the database, we must warn you that, once this process has been completed on a database, there is no way to get the design back. Please make sure that you always have a copy of the design stored someplace in case you need to make a change to it.

Continued

CONTINUED

To hide the design, your entire database design should reside in a template. This template *must* be in the root directory of either your local workstation or the Domino server (the list of templates is only pulled from the root directory, yet when a template is refreshed, it can be anywhere within the data directory structure). With your master copy of the design safely tucked away, you are ready to hide the design.

Assuming that the database already exists, you will need to replace the database design with the design residing in a template. To replace the design, follow these steps:

1. Open your database from your portfolio bookmark folder.
2. Choose File ➢ Database ➢ Replace Design. (You can also right-click on the database design icon in the Design pane and select Database ➢ Replace Design.)
3. From the Replace Database Design dialog box, select the server location of the template by clicking the Template Server button.
4. In the template list, highlight the template that will be used to replace the database design.
5. If you are not sure which template to use, highlight the template and click the About button. The About This Database document will display (this step is optional).
6. If your template is not listed, select the Show Advanced Templates option; the template may have been marked as an advanced template (this step is optional).
7. Select the Hide Formulas and LotusScript option. This is the key to hiding the design.
8. Click the Replace button.
9. A warning message box will display, asking if you really want to do this. Click Yes to proceed or No to abort the replace.
10. A progress dialog box will display and update as each element is replaced. Once the replace is completed, your design is hidden.

To verify that the design of the database is hidden, open the Design tab of the Database Properties Info Box. You should see that no design information is available. If you open the database in Designer, you will see that none of the design elements are visible.

PART

V

Beyond the Client: Utilizing Domino Designer

Inherit Design from Template   This option will be automatically selected if you created a database from a template and selected Inherit Future Design Changes. When a design refresh is initiated, the Inherit Design from Template option tells the database to use the template (whose name is in the Template Name field) to refresh the entire database. The template name is not the actual filename of the template; it's the name you have assigned to the template (this is the next option we will discuss). In this example, the template name is StdR50Disc and the entire database design will be inherited from that template. Make sure design changes are performed in the template, or when the next refresh is initiated, your changes will miraculously disappear.

WARNING You need to be aware that your databases can be automatically refreshed on the server from a template if the Design task is initiated on the server (the Design task is a server-initiated program that will refresh *all* databases from their templates). This can be good and bad. It's positive if you need to refresh a lot of databases and do not wish to do it manually. It's negative if your templates are residing on the same machine as your application and you want to update them manually.

Database Is a Template   Setting this option determines whether the database is a template or not. Please keep in mind that any file can be marked as a template. The extension .nsf or .ntf does not determine whether a file is a template or not; the extension is used for displaying files in dialog boxes such as the Open Database dialog box. If you select this option, the Template Name field will also need to be entered. Type in a name that is somewhat descriptive of the template. This is the name that will be used in the Template Name field for the Inherit Design from Template option. Do not confuse the template name with the database title that is displayed in the template lists (such as in the New Database dialog box or the Replace Design dialog box). The template name is only used for inheritance when design elements are refreshed or replaced. In this example, the database is not a template, so the option is not selected. If the properties for the template that this database uses were displayed, the option would be selected and the template name would be StdR50Disc.

NOTE The Inherit Design from Template and Database Is a Template options are not mutually exclusive. You can select both for a database.

WARNING Notes does not automatically check to see if the template name you type in is already in use. It only checks when a refresh is initiated, and if the name is already in use, an error message will be displayed in the status bar and also written to the Notes log.

List in Database Catalog   There is a special database that resides on the server called the Database Catalog. A task that runs on the server (the Catalog task) can automatically place any database that resides on the server into this catalog. The end user can review the Database Catalog for databases that interest them or use the catalog as a central point for listing all the databases on the server. Selecting this option allows the

Domino server to create a document for the database inside the Database Catalog. You can also use the optional Categories field to group similar databases. For example, all of the sample databases for this book will be under the Mastering R5 category. If you look in the Database Catalog using the Databases by Category view, you'll see a list of all the sample databases grouped under the heading Mastering R5. We advise that you always place your databases in the catalog because there are many views that you will find helpful to you as a designer.

 TIP If you would like to assign a database to multiple categories, just separate each entry with a semicolon (;).

Show in 'Open Database' Dialog   If you find that a database will just not show up in any of the Open Database dialog boxes, this is the option to check. If Show in 'Open Database' Dialog is not selected, the database will never show up in any of the database lists. This does not mean that the database cannot be opened, just that it cannot be seen by the "casual" user. If Notes users know the path and filename of the database, they can type it in the Open Database dialog box and the database will open right up. This option should not be used as a security measure because it is not secure.

Do Not Mark Modified Documents as Unread   Become quite familiar with this command because using it correctly will keep your users quite happy. If you select this option, documents won't be marked as unread even if you modify them. By default, when a document is updated, it is automatically reset back to unread. This way, a user can open a database and scan for all the documents that are new or modified. This technique is an extremely efficient way to make sure you have read all the documents in a database. Imagine your users' surprise if one day they open the database and all the documents are marked as unread! This can easily occur if an Agent is written to update each document and this option is not selected. In some cases, letting the users know that the data in all the documents has changed is beneficial. But if you write an Agent to update hidden data and forget to select this option, your e-mail inbox is going to be quite full of questions and complaints. So keep that in mind the next time you need to write an Agent that could possibly affect a large number of documents.

Include in Multi Database Indexing   The Include in Multi Database Indexing option is used to mark a database for inclusion in the Domain Search. New with Release 5 is a searching scheme called the Domain Search. The Domain Search is a replacement for the 4.6 version called Site Search (although Site Search is still included in Release 5, the functionality will *no* longer be enhanced). The Domain Search allows a user to search for information across all databases that are within the Notes domain. This is an extremely powerful tool, yet it only takes a few seconds to implement. All you need to do is enable the Include in Multi Database Indexing option and your database will be searchable via the Domain Search.

Multilingual Database   This option is used primarily for applications that will have different language versions. This falls outside the scope of this book, but keep in mind that the language and region options work in conjunction with a user's browser. If the user's browser is set to a language and you have a database set to the same language, the Web server will automatically display it to the user.

The Launch Tab

The Launch tab controls what a user will see when your application is opened (launched) in either a Notes client or a Web browser. There is a separate launch option for each as well, as shown in Figure 16.21. This gives you the flexibility of launching one application on a workstation and another application on the Web.

FIGURE 16.21

The Launch tab properties

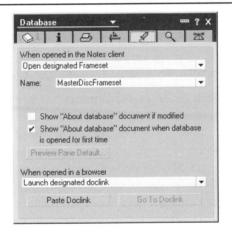

When Opened in the Notes Client   This option will allow you to specify what should happen when the database is opened from the Notes client. In this example, the database will launch a specific frameset, MasterDiscFrameset. There are quite a few launch options available for the Notes client, as can be seen when the drop-down list is selected. Keep in mind that, depending on the launch selection, other fields and options may display. The following list includes all the current Notes launch options available:

Restore as Last Viewed by User   This is usually the default for new databases and will return users to the same place in a database they were when they left the application. You also have the option of selecting whether or not to show the About document for the database if it has been modified and/or to show the About document for each user the first time they open the database (for clarity, in the remaining launch options, we will refer to these options for the About document as the About document options). If you select either of these options, the About document may display first and then the user will be returned to the same place in the database they were when they left the application.

Open "About Database" Document   This option will launch the About document every time the user opens the database. Please keep in mind that many people find this quite annoying.

Open Designated Frameset   If this option is selected, a specific frameset must be selected from the Name list box. The Name list box contains a list of all the framesets currently defined in the database. This is the option that is selected for the current example database. The About document options are also available.

Open Designated Navigator   This option will allow you to select which type of Navigator to display in the Navigation pane of the application. There are three types of Navigators that can be selected (and the About document options are available for all three as well):

Folders   This option displays the standard navigation "tree" style, showing all the views and folders available to the user.

Standard Navigator   This option requires that a Navigator (the graphical kind) be selected from the Name list box that displays all the current Navigator design elements defined to the database.

Page   This option requires that a page be selected from the Name list box that displays all the current Page design elements defined in the database.

Open Designated Navigator in Its Own Window   This option will allow you to select which type of Navigator to use as well, but there are only two selections: Standard Navigator and Page. This option is typically selected when a full-page Navigator will be used as the main portal for the application (such as a home page). The About document options are not available.

Launch First Attachment in "About Database"   This option will automatically launch the first attachment contained within the About document. It is useful when another application will be used as the main portal for the application. The About document options are not available.

Launch First Doclink in "About Database"   This option will send the user to either a database, element, or document (depending on the type of doclink used). It is useful when you would like to send the user to a specific place within your Notes application. The About document options are not available.

Preview Pane Default   If you select the Preview Pane option (View ➤ Document Preview ➤ Show Preview), the document Preview pane will be displayed according to this setting. This option is not available if the Notes launch option is set to Open Designated Frameset.

When Opened in a Browser   This option is exactly the same as the When Opened in the Notes Client option except that it only affects the users accessing the application via a Web browser. Note that the About document settings do not have any bearing for Web users. The following options appear in the When Opened in the Notes Client drop-down list:

Use Notes Launch Option   This option tells Notes to use the same launch option specified for the When Opened in the Notes Client option.

Open "About Database" Document, Open Designated Frameset, and Launch First Doclink in "About Database"   These are the same as the options described for the When Opened in the Notes Client option.

Open Designated Page   This option will allow you to select from a list of Pages that are currently defined in the database.

Open Designated Navigator in Its Own Window   This option will allow you to select from a list of Standard Navigators that are currently defined in the database.

Launch Designated Doclink   This option allows you to paste a doclink to jump to when the database is opened. When you use this option, you'll notice that two new buttons appear underneath the list box: Paste Doclink and Go to Doclink. The doclink to be pasted can be a valid database, an element, or a document. You must first copy the link to the Clipboard (Edit ➤ Copy as Link) or you will receive an error message when the Paste Doclink button is selected. To paste the doclink, click the Paste Doclink button. To test your link, click the Go to Doclink button.

Launch First Document in a View   This can be quite an interesting option. At first glance, it may not seem interesting, but this option can be used to dynamically display a different document each time a user opens the database. It all depends on how often the first document in a view changes. Before passing over this option quickly, make sure that you give it a little thought.

The Full Text Tab

One of Domino's most powerful features is its ability to extract information through the built-in searching facility. Although a full-text index is not required for a user to have the ability to search documents, the lack of one makes searching extremely slow and takes up valuable computer resources. Without a full-text index, the search options available to the user are also limited. You can use the Full Text tab to determine if the database has a full-text index and also to determine what settings were selected when the index was created.

As shown in Figure 16.22, the example database has already been indexed. The Full Text tab shows the date and time the index was last updated and the current amount of space the index has used. Keep in mind that, if the database resides on a Domino server, the index will automatically be kept up-to-date based on the value in the Update Frequency field. Also shown on this tab are the options that were used when the index was created. In the example database, the index included attachments (Index Attachments: On) and word breaks (Index Breaks: Words Only). If the database has not been indexed, you'll see the message "Database is not full text indexed" in place of "Last index time" across the top of the tab.

FIGURE 16.22

The Full Text properties tab for the database

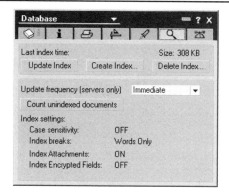

PART

V

Beyond the Client: Uti-
lizing Domino Designer

One last thing to consider when performing full-text indexing on a database is the amount of space that will be required. This is very subjective and depends on the options selected, but it will typically be about 60 to 70 percent of the total database size. With that in mind, let's find out how to index your database.

Create Index   This button starts it all. Clicking this button will display the Create Full-Text Index dialog box, shown in Figure 16.23. From this window, you can select the combination of options that you would like the full-text index to include. Once you make all of your selections for the index, click the OK button and your request will be queued on the server for processing. When the creation process is completed, you can look in the directory that contains the database and see a new directory with the .ft extension. This directory contains all the files that the full-text index uses. Let's take a look at the index options in more detail:

Index Attached Files   One feature of the full-text index is the ability to index attached files. This allows the user to search for text not only in the Notes documents but also in any of the attachments. For example, if the Notes document has an MS Word file or an Adobe Acrobat PDF file attached and the attachment contains the word *testing*, when the user searches for *testing*, the full-text index will find a match and display the document in the results to the user. By default, this option is not selected.

Index Encrypted Fields   This option allows encrypted fields to be placed in the full-text index for searching as well. Selecting this option will compromise encrypted fields. By default, this option is selected.

Index Sentence and Paragraph Breaks   This option allows the user to apply proximity parameters to searches within the text. A *proximity parameter* is a special keyword in the search text that allows two words that are in the same proximity to be found. For example, if you use the search text "car sentence tire," the full-text index will return the document if the words *car* and *tire* are contained in the same sentence. By default, this option is not selected.

Enable Case Sensitive Searches   This option is self-explanatory. The only catch is that users may not know that this option is enabled, which can cause quite a problem because a search on "Car" will not find a match on the text "car." By default, this option is not selected.

Update Frequency   This option applies to databases that reside on the server only. This is described in more detail later in this section.

FIGURE 16.23

*The Create Full-Text
Index dialog box*

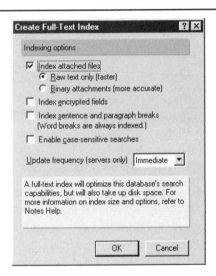

Delete Index   The Delete Index option deletes the current full-text index and removes all the files that the index created. If you need to change any of the index options, make sure you delete the index first and then create the index again.

Update Index   Selecting this option will queue a request to the server to update the full-text index immediately, regardless of the Update Frequency setting. To determine if the index needs to be updated, click the Count Unindexed Documents button to see how many documents are not included in the current index.

Update Frequency   This option determines how often the full-text index will be updated. To determine the frequency, look at the size of the database, how often data is updated, and how soon users will need the information. The process of updating full-text indexing can be quite time consuming and resource intensive. See Table 16.3 for a description of each option and when the updates to the index will occur.

TABLE 16.3: FULL TEXT INDEX FREQUENCY OPTIONS AND TRIGGERS

Frequency Option	Update Trigger
Immediate	As soon as possible after the database is closed
Hourly	Every hour as scheduled by the Chronos server task
Daily	Every night when the Updall server task is executed
Scheduled	As scheduled by a program document for the Updall server task located in the Domino directory (if the program document is not in the Domino directory, the update to the full-text index will not be performed)

The Advanced Tab

Does the Advanced tab sound familiar? Although the options are the same, this is actually a different dialog box than the one displayed by clicking the Advanced button in the Create Database dialog box (the Advanced Database Options dialog box is shown in Figure 16.10). This dialog box is a bit smaller, and everything on the screen has been described earlier in the chapter. We mention this tab to let you know where you can change the advanced options if necessary. If you do decide to change any of the options listed in the dialog box, it is a good idea to compact the database to ensure that the options will take effect.

Protecting the Data Using the ACL

As the designer of the database, it is your responsibility to decide who will have access to what. Don't confuse this responsibility with that of the administrator. You will not maintain the security for the database; you are responsible for *defining* the security. You should work closely with your administrator to determine the security requirements for your database. By defining the database security, you can provide access to the information to some users and deny access to others.

What Is the ACL?

ACL stands for Access Control List. Every database includes an ACL, which is used to control the level of access for users and servers. Although the process of assigning access levels to a user and to a server is the same, the access level for a user restricts the tasks a user can perform, and the access level for a server determines what a server can replicate. When you are determining the security for a database, keep in mind that setting up security for a Notes client is different from setting up security for a Web-based or Internet client. Because the Web-based client does not use the Notes ID as does the Notes client, the Web server is more limited in enforcing the security for the application.

To access the ACL for the example database (shown in Figure 16.24), open the Mastering R5 for Chapter 16 database and choose File ➢ Database ➢ Access Control. In the People, Servers, Groups drop-down list, you can see the default entries that are created each time a new database is created on the server. There is one special group, –Default–, that cannot be removed. This is the default access to the database if a user or server is not listed. If Anonymous is not listed, any users accessing the database from the Web will be granted the –Default– access.

FIGURE 16.24

The Access Control List dialog box

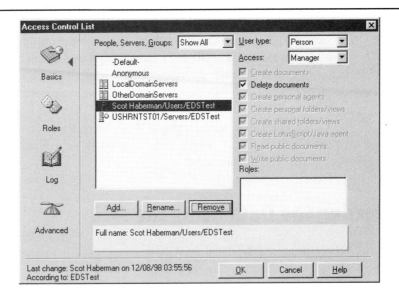

TIP Whenever you create a new template or a database, make sure you assign Manager access to yourself and that you have the ability to delete documents. Failure to do so may render the database useless to you.

Understanding Access Levels

Notes allows you to assign seven different access levels to your database. To assign an access level to a group, server, or person, select the Access drop-down box on the right side of the Access Control List dialog box. The Access levels are as follows (from least to most restrictive):

Manager   Can perform just about any operation within a Notes database. The manager of the database is the only one who can modify the ACL, encrypt the database, modify replication settings, and delete the database. The manager can also perform all the tasks of the lower access levels.

Designer   Can modify all design elements, modify replication formulas, create a full-text index, and perform all the tasks of the lower access levels.

Editor   Can create documents and edit all documents, even if the documents were created by another user.

Author   Can create documents. Can also edit documents, but only those they created. This is solely dependent on the existence of an authors field within the document; the user's name must be in an authors field.

Reader   Can only read documents.

Depositor   Can create documents but can never read them (this is typically used for survey-type applications).

No Access   Can do nothing at all.

To modify the list of servers, people, or groups from the ACL, just use the Add, Rename, or Remove buttons located under the access list.

 WARNING   When creating a Web application, be sure to check the Maximum Internet Name & Password Access option (accessed by clicking the Advanced icon in the Access Control List dialog box). This may save you from many frustrating moments.

Access Privileges

Also note that, for each access level, there are access-level privileges that can be assigned as well. The access privileges give you the flexibility of further refining data access. For example, you could grant users Author access yet not allow them to delete any documents that they created.

The Read Public Documents and Write Public Documents access privileges are a bit different from the others. You will notice that you can select these privileges for the various access levels, which will allow the reading or writing of documents that have been created with a form marked as Available to Public Access Users. You can also mark folders and views as Public Access, making them available as well. Using the Public Access privilege, you can allow those with no access or Depositor access to read and write specific documents.

Roles

One last tool available to you that allows further refinement of the security process is the roles tool. There are no hard and fast rules for using roles. You decide how they would work best for you and your application. You can assign roles to any entity that is defined in the ACL. A typical use for roles is to further refine a specific access level—for example, if you need to differentiate between groups of people that have the same access level.

A good example of using roles is displayed in the Public Name and Address book. Most users are granted Author access. This allows them to maintain their own Person record. But you would also like a specific group of individuals to be able to create groups. If you assign this group the GroupCreator role, the application can differentiate between the two groups of people who both have Author access.

To create a role, open the Access Control List dialog box and select the roles icon, which will display the Roles list box and the Add, Rename, and Remove buttons.

Just enter as many roles as you need (up to 75). Each role name is limited to 15 characters.

NOTE If you decide to reference a role inside your application, remember to add the brackets around the role name.

Summary

In this chapter, you gained a better understanding of how to create a database. You can create a database from scratch, from a template, or by copying over an existing database. We also discussed all the database creation options available. Finally, we went into detail about the database properties and the importance of setting security for your database.

To better understand the various design elements that make up a database application, you should first look at the basic formula language that Notes supports. The next chapter will describe what formulas are, how to create a formula, and where they can be used.

CHAPTER 17

Understanding the Formula Language

FEATURING:

Like most other development environments, Notes has its own internal language for enhancing and automating applications. The formula language is a simple yet powerful language that is used heavily throughout Notes applications. Formulas broaden the flexibility of an application and automate everyday tasks into a few simple commands. Because the language is understood only by the Notes and Domino environments, it is written to take advantage of the internal structure and processes. Formulas are used in all aspects of Notes application design, ranging from simple display fields to complex document processing.

In the examples throughout this chapter, we'll be referring to the Mastering R5 for Chapter 17 database (`MasterR5c17.nsf`) provided on the CD-ROM.

What Is a Formula?

A formula is a series of one or more expressions that comprise one or more constants, variables, operators, keywords, @functions, and @commands. It is different than most structured programming languages—such as COBOL or BASIC—because the formula language does not contain any flow control, type declarations, or data structures. Rather, it is a language of simple macro commands similar to those found in spreadsheet applications such as Lotus 1-2-3. In almost all cases, a formula is expected to either evaluate to some result or perform some sort of action and can be used just about anywhere within Notes.

Figure 17.1 is typical of a formula returning some type of result. This formula can be found by opening the Computed Field Example form and clicking the CurrentDate field. In this example, the formula is only one command, @Now. So how does this return a result? The @Now command will always return a time-date value representing the current date and the current time. By placing this command in a computed field, the current date and time will be displayed to the user. Because the CurrentDate field is a computed field, you need to place the value to be displayed in the Value event (this is much like setting a default value for the field). As you can see, this formula does not perform an action; it just returns some value (in this case, the current date and time).

In Figure 17.2, the formula is a bit different because it can be seen performing an Action. This example can be found in the same form by clicking the Close Document Action button. To view the Action button, choose View ➤ Action Pane and select Close Document. @Command([FileCloseWindow]) will close the document for the user. Because this is an Action command, nothing is returned, but an Action takes place (the closing of the document).

FIGURE 17.1

Setting a formula to
return a result for the
CurrentDate field

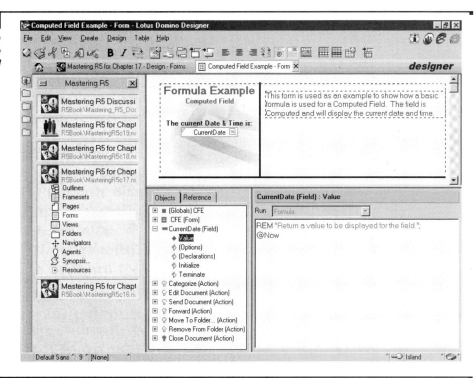

FIGURE 17.2

Setting a formula to
perform an Action

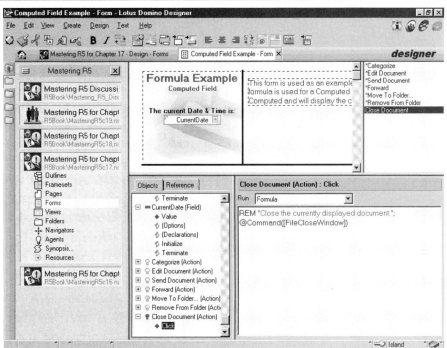

To see the form in action, select the Notes preview icon located in the upper right corner of the screen.

When the icon is clicked, the form will automatically launch in the Notes client. As you can see, the current time and date is automatically displayed. Now click the Close Document button and the document will automatically close.

Anatomy of a Formula

A formula is not just a compilation of statements that are thrown together in some indiscriminate manner. There is a general syntax, a set of basic rules, that must be followed:

Top-down left-right processing   Each statement expression in a formula is executed in sequence, from top to bottom, left to right. No formal conditional-type branching exists for a formula (although some @functions can perform some control logic). For example, if a formula contained the following statements, statement 2 will execute after statement 1 and statement 3 will execute after statement 2:

```
Statement expression 1;
Statement expression 2;
Statement expression 3;
```

Statement separator   If the formula contains multiple statements, a semicolon must separate each statement, for example:

```
FIELD FullName := @UserName;
FIELD FirstName := @Left(FullName;" ");
```

Spaces   The amount of spaces you use in a formula is solely up to you. The only requirement is that a keyword must be bordered by at least one space. In the following two lines, the first statement is as valid as the second one:

```
FIELD temp:="1";
FIELD temp := "1"
```

Case   When a formula is saved, Notes will automatically convert the @functions, @commands, and keywords to their proper case. In general, keywords are in all caps and the @functions and @commands are mixed upper- and lowercase. Any text constants you define will not be altered.

TIP Notes will automatically color-code your formulas based on text expressions, key-words, and @functions/@commands. This makes it easier to read a formula.

A formula is composed from a collection of one or more statements that fall into one or more of the following categories:

- Constants
- Variables
- Operators
- Keywords
- @Functions

Each of these categories will be discussed in the following sections.

Formula Constants

A constant used in formulas is always one of the following three types:

- Text
- Numeric
- Time-date

To declare a constant, just assign a value to a variable. You don't have to worry about case, but remember to use the assignment operator (:=) instead of the equality operator (=). Both of these operators are discussed later in the chapter. An example form, Constant Variable Example, has been set up to give a working example for each type of constant. Each of the following sections will refer to a field contained on that form. To follow along, open the Constant Variable Example form in Designer.

Text Constants

A text constant is composed of any character surrounded by quotation marks. If you need to include quotation marks as part of the constant value, you must use the back-slash followed by the quote. Table 17.1 shows a few examples of constants and their values.

TIP The backslash character (\) is also known as the escape character in Notes. Keep this in mind because it is used quite frequently when formulas are created in Notes.

TABLE 17.1: EXAMPLES OF TEXT CONSTANTS

Constant Declaration	Value of Constant
X := "My Name"	My Name
X := ""My Name""	Generates an error when saving
X := "\"My Name\""	"My Name"
X := "c:\temp"	c:temp
X := "c:\\temp"	c:\temp
X := "12"	12 (this is text, not numeric)

On the example form, the Msg field has been set up using text constants to display a message to the users, as shown in Figure 17.3. In the programmer's pane, select the Objects tab and then select the Value event for the Msg field. If you select the Msg field directly on the form, the Value event will be highlighted by default.

FIGURE 17.3

An example of using a text constant in a formula

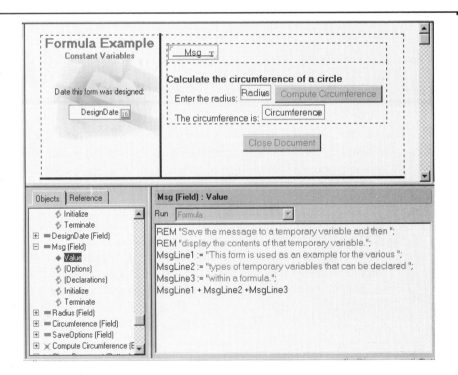

Numeric Constants

A numeric constant is composed of a combination of numbers from 0 to 9 and any other special numeric punctuation (such as the period, scientific notation, negative sign). Table 17.2 shows a few examples of numeric constants and their formats.

TABLE 17.2: EXAMPLES OF NUMERIC CONSTANTS

Constant Declaration	Value of Constant
X := 123	123
X := 12e3	12000
X := 12E3	12000
X := -23	-23
X := -1234.5	-1234.5

On the example form, the Circumference field uses a numeric constant for the value of PI, as shown in Figure 17.4. In the programmer's pane, select the Objects tab and then select the Value event for the Circumference field. If you select the Circumference field on the form directly, the Value event will be highlighted by default.

PART

V

Beyond the Client: Uti-
lizing Domino Designer

FIGURE 17.4

An example of using
a numeric constant in
a formula

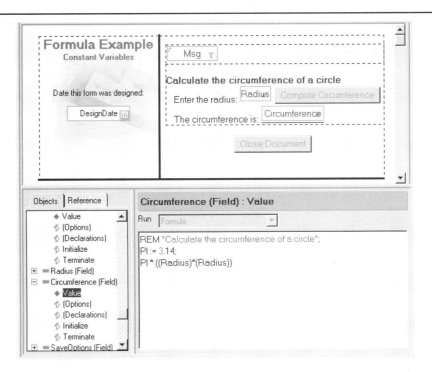

Time-Date Constants

A time-date constant is composed of a date, a time, or a date and a time enclosed in square brackets. For constants containing both the time and date components, it doesn't matter if you specify the time first and then the date or the date first and then the time. You can specify time in a 24-hour format (military time) or a 12-hour format (you must use the A.M./P.M. designation for the 12-hour format). When you enter a date, the year is optional; it will default to the current year. If you decide to specify a year with 2 digits, 50 or above will default to 1900, whereas less than 50 will default to 2000. You can also specify a year with 4 digits. Table 17.3 shows a few examples of time-date constants and their values.

TABLE 17.3: EXAMPLES OF TIME-DATE CONSTANTS

Constant Declaration	Value of Constant
X := [1/1]	1/1/98
X := [1/1/45]	1/1/2045
X := [1/1/55]	1/1/55
X := [05:00]	05:00:00 AM
X := [13:00]	01:00:00 PM
X := [13:00 1/1]	1/1/98 01:00:00 PM
X := [1/1 13:00]	1/1/98 01:00:00 PM
X := [13:00 AM]	Generates an error when saving

 TIP In "true" military time, the time does not include a colon. In Notes, the 24-hour format must contain the colon or the formula will not save.

On the example form, the DesignDate field has been set up using a time-date constant to display the date we actually designed this form, as shown in Figure 17.5. In the programmer's pane, select the Objects tab and then select the Value event for the DesignDate field. If you select the DesignDate field on the form directly, the Value event will be highlighted by default.

To see the form in action, select the Notes preview icon located in the upper right corner of the screen. When the icon is pressed, the form will automatically launch in the Notes client. Notice how the text constant and time-date constant are being displayed. Go ahead and type in a value of 2 for the radius of a circle. Click Compute Circumference, and the form will calculate the circumference, as shown in Figure 17.6. Now click the Close Document button, and the document will automatically close.

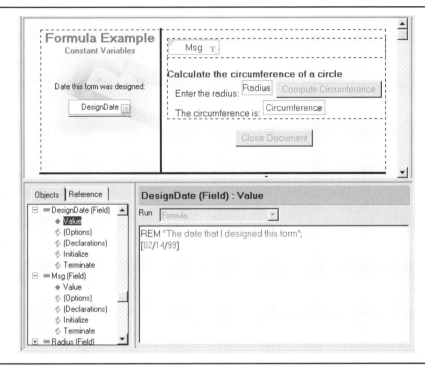

FIGURE 17.5

*An example of using a
time-date constant in a
formula*

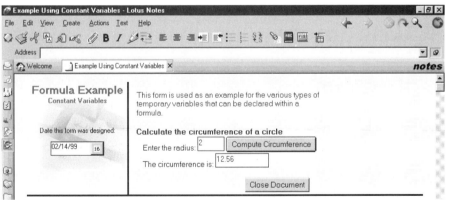

FIGURE 17.6

*Viewing the form in
the Notes client*

Formula Variables

When you use a formula, there are really only two types of variables that you need to
be concerned with. They are temporary variables and field variables.

Temporary Variables

A temporary variable is nothing more than a temporary storage area. It sounds silly,
but the life for this type of variable is no longer than the life of the formula. This type

of variable is usually used for holding values that will only be needed later in the formula.

 WARNING You can assign a value to a temporary variable only once in a formula or you will get the error "Variable already defined." To get around this problem, compound your statements or use a lot of variables.

For example, Figure 17.7 shows a formula in the Value event for the WelcomeMsg field. Open the Formula Variable Example form and click the WelcomeMsg field. In the programmer's pane, select the Objects tab and then select the Value event for the WelcomeMsg field. If you select the WelcomeMsg field directly on the form, the Value event will be highlighted by default. The second line of the formula is using a temporary variable called *WhoAmI*, which is set to the first name of the current user. Following that there are a few other temporary variables being declared. The *MorningMsg*, *AfternoonMsg*, and *EveningMsg* variables are storing some text message values. The *CurrentHour* variable is storing the current hour of the day. All of the variables will be needed only in the @If function on the next line where the code is trying to determine the time of day and display a personalized message to the user. Once the comparison is over, there is no reason to hold the temporary variables any longer.

FIGURE 17.7

The WelcomeMsg Value event uses temporary variables.

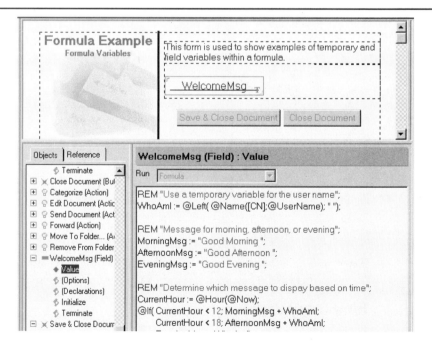

The results of this field can be seen in Figure 17.8. To see the form in action, select the Notes preview icon located in the upper right corner of the screen. When the icon is clicked, the form will automatically launch in the Notes client. Notice how the welcome message reflects the time of day and who the user is. Now click the Close Document button, and the document will automatically close.

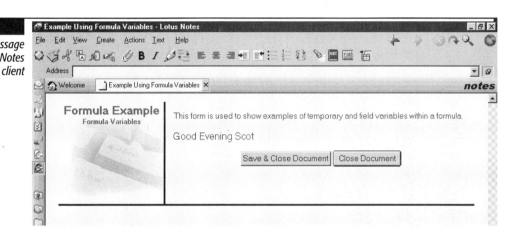

FIGURE 17.8

The welcome message as seen in the Notes client

If for some reason you need to hold a value after the formula has completed, there are a couple of options. You can save the value to the current document and then delete the variable later, but this is not a very clean solution (it uses a field variable, which is discussed next). Another option is to use environment variables. This is not an actual variable type, but it does allow field values to be saved for later use.

Environment Variables

One problem when using formulas is the inability to pass parameters from one formula to another. In most cases, this does not pose a problem, but the need eventually arises. Thankfully, there is a mechanism that allows a developer to save a value from one function and read it from another. This mechanism involves the use of environment variables.

An environment variable has special @functions and keywords available to assist the developer. Each environment variable is written and read from the notes.ini file. Every Notes client must have this file defined. The Domino server has one as well.

Continued ▶

CONTINUED

This seems great, but there is one catch: Which `notes.ini` file is updated, the user workstation file or the server file? This is a very important question. If the formula is in a database that resides on a server and it's a replication formula, scheduled Agent, selection formula, or column formula, it will be stored on the server.

When you use environment variables, prefix the actual name with a $ within the `notes.ini` file. For example, if you set an environment variable called *CompanyName* in your formula, it would show up in the `notes.ini` file as *$CompanyName* (this is more important when you are using LotusScript because it does not prefix variables with $).

Setting and retrieving the variables is easy. To set the value of variable *CompanyName*, use the `@SetEnvironment` @function (although you can also use `@Environment` or the ENVIRONMENT keyword). For example, to set the *CompanyName* variable to EDS, code one of the following lines:

```
@SetEnvironment("CompanyName";"EDS")

ENVIRONMENT CompanyName := "EDS"

@Environment("CompanyName";"EDS")
```

To retrieve the value of a variable, use `@Environment` (yes, it both sets and retrieves values). Here is an example to retrieve the previous value:

```
SCompanyName := @Environment("CompanyName")
```

There are two final points to keep in mind when you use environment variables. First, you can only set and retrieve text values to `notes.ini`. If you want to save a numeric value, you must first convert it to text. Second, when you are done with the environment variable, you can remove it from `notes.ini` by setting the variable to null, as in this example:

```
@SetEnvironment("CompanyName";"")
```

Field Variables

Field variables are used to either retrieve or store a value on the current document. They are used in the same fashion as temporary variables are used except the value will not disappear when the formula terminates; instead, the value will be stored on the current document (assuming you save the document at some point). Keep in mind that you can also use a field variable to create a field on a document. If you store a value to a field variable and the field you create by doing so doesn't exist on the current document, it will be created. To create a field variable, you only need to prefix your variable with the FIELD keyword.

For example, Figure 17.9 shows the formula for the Save and Close Document button of the Formula Variable Example form. Open the Formula Variable Example form, and click the Save and Close Document button. In the programmer's pane, select the Objects tab and then select the Value event for the WelcomeMsg field. If you select the Welcome-Msg field directly on the form, the Value event will be highlighted by default. The first line of the formula is using a field variable by placing the value of 1 into the SaveOptions field. If you look closely at the form, you may notice that a field definition for the SaveOptions field exists at the bottom of the form. In this case, the formula is modifying the field for the current document. The purpose of this formula is to save the document. The default value for the SaveOptions field is 0, which tells Notes to never save the document. Changing this value to 1 will allow the document to be saved. To avoid any confusion, the SaveOptions field is a reserved field in Notes; you'll find more details in Appendix B.

PART

V

Beyond the Client: Utilizing Domino Designer

FIGURE 17.9

Using a field variable in the Save and Close Document button formula

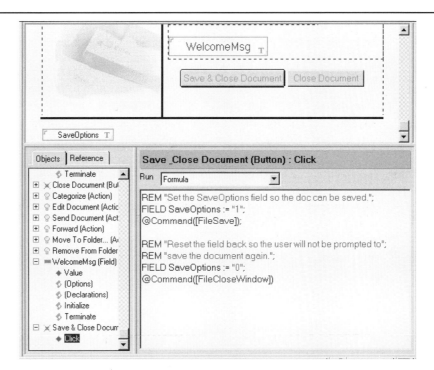

When you access fields on a document, make sure your formula understands what type of field you are using. An error will result if your formula treats the document's numeric field as a text field.

You can access any field on a Notes document regardless of the actual field type with one exception, a rich text field. You can only access the attributes of a rich text field, not the actual contents. Because a rich text field can contain any type of data, including graphics and attachment files, it makes sense that the text contents cannot be retrieved by a formula. For example, assume that you would like to determine if a field called Body exists on the selected document. Using a formula, you cannot read the contents of the Body field, but you can determine if the Body field exists on the document with the `@IsAvailable( "Body" )` statement.

NOTE It is possible to extract text from a rich text field by using the `@Abstract` command. Keep in mind that rich text fields are not actually part of the document until the document is saved, so you can only access modifications to the field if the document is saved and then reopened. Also, a rich text field can contain a large amount of text. A text variable is limited to a size of 15K. If you try to extract text from a rich text field that contains 250K, you'll encounter a few problems.

Forgetting to prefix the variable with the FIELD keyword is another mistake commonly made when creating formulas that access field documents. This is a common mistake because your formula will actually execute properly but will not return the expected results. You see, a variable without the FIELD keyword is nothing more than a temporary variable, which was discussed in the preceding section.

Formula Operators

Operators are used to carry out some type of action within a Notes formula. These actions can include assigning, modifying, and combining values. The following sections include a list of the operators (with an explanation of their precedence) and a discussion of each of the seven categories of operators:

- Arithmetic
- Assignment
- Comparison
- List
- Logical
- Text
- Unary

Operators and Precedence

Table 17.4 lists all the operators in their order of precedence. Those that are grouped together are of equal precedence.

TABLE 17.4: OPERATORS IN ORDER OF PRECEDENCE

Operator	Operation
:=	Assignment (precedence is not applicable)
:	List concatenation
+	Positive
-	Negative
*	Multiplication
**	Permuted multiplication
/	Division
*/	Permuted division
+	Addition
*+	Permuted addition
-	Subtraction
*-	Permuted subtraction
=	Equal
*=	Permuted equal
◇, !=, =!, ✕	Not equal
*◇	Permuted not equal
<	Less than
*<	Permuted less than
>	Greater than
*>	Permuted greater than
<=	Less than or equal
*<=	Permuted less than or equal
>=	Greater than or equal
*>=	Permuted greater than or equal
!	Logical NOT
&	Logical AND
|	Logical OR

Operations occur in the following order:

Parentheses Operations enclosed within parentheses are always evaluated first.

Precedence Operations not enclosed within parentheses are always evaluated based on the values specified in Table 17.4.

Left to right Operations of equal precedence are always evaluated from left to right.

Arithmetic Operators

The arithmetic operators are *, /, +, -, and they perform multiplication, division, addition, and subtraction respectively.

The Assignment Operator

The assignment operator (:=) is responsible for moving the value on the right side of the equation to the left side. The value on the left side of the assignment operator always assumes the type (such as text or numeric) from the right side. Any variable on the left side that is not preceded by the FIELD keyword will be a temporary variable. Do not confuse the equal sign (=) for the assignment operator because it will not work. The equal sign (=) is only used for comparison. For example, the first statement is not the same as the second:

```
MyVar := "Are these the same?"
MyVar = "Are these the same?"
```

This is a common mistake and easy to make. It will not generate a syntax error, but it will cause a lot of hair pulling.

NOTE The most common mistake developers make when they try to use formulas is using the equal sign (=) instead of the assignment operator (:=) when assigning values. It is a common mistake that needs to be emphasized.

Comparison Operators

The comparison operators (=, <>, !=, =!, ><, >, <, <=, >=) are used to compare values of the same type and return either true (1) or false (0).

The List Operator

The list operator (:) allows you to combine values (of the same data type) into a list. A list can be thought of as a type of array if that makes it easier to understand. For example, to build of list of cities into a temporary variable called *Cities*, just do the following:

```
Cities := "Atlanta":"Baltimore":"Seattle"
```

There are also quite a few @functions that are designed just for processing lists. Some functions, such as @Subset and @Replace, are designed specifically for processing lists of data. It is important that you get a full understanding of how formulas and lists work because there are no looping constructs. This is probably the hardest thing for most people to master when they first start using Notes.

Using the *Cities* variable from the previous example, how would you write a formula that returns a list where all the cities are in their proper case? The first thing that comes to mind is to build a for...next loop, but there is no such beast in formulas—remember, no looping constructs. As mentioned, this is a hard concept for structured programmers to handle. Well, the answer is as simple as one command:

```
@Propercase( Cities )
```

That is all that is required. It was somewhat of a trick question because we failed to mention that a list will perform some form of iteration of the elements that it contains. In the preceding example, @Propercase is applied to each element of the list individually, which is pretty snazzy. This can be used by a wide variety of @functions. It may not seem like much, but with a bit of imagination, you can perform some amazing things.

 WARNING When you operate on lists, make sure all negative numbers are enclosed in parentheses or you may not get the result you expect (remember that the list operator has the highest precedence). If a negative is not enclosed in parentheses, the negative is carried through the rest of the list. For example, if ListA := 1:-2:3 were added to ListB := 1:1:1:, the result would be 2:-1:-2, not 2:-1:4.

You can also perform operations on lists. There are two types of operators:

- Pair-wise
- Permuted

Pair-wise operators act on lists just as the name suggests, in pairs. When two lists are processed, the first element of list 1 is paired with the first element of list 2, the second element of list 1 is paired with the second element of list 2, and so on. Pair-wise operators are exactly the same as permuted except pair-wise operators don't have the asterisk (*).

Permuted operators pair each element in one list with each element in the second list. When two lists are processed, the first element of list 1 is paired with each and every element in list 2, the second element of list 1 is paired with each and every element in list 2, and so on.

You may be confused by now, so we'll give you an example of each type performed on the same lists. If you have two numeric lists, 2:4 and 6:8, and you multiply the two lists together using a pair-wise operator, such as 2:4*6:8, the result would be the list 12:32. If you use a permuted operator, such as 2:4**6:8, to multiply the same lists, the result would be the list 12:16:24:32.

Logical Operators

The logical operators (!, &, |) allow you to combine logical values that will return true (1) or false (0). This may sound easy, but it can get quite complicated. Table 17.5 shows you a few examples using all three of the logical operators. Pay special attention to the last three because the OR (|) logical operator behaves a bit differently than you may think.

TABLE 17.5: EXAMPLES OF LOGICAL OPERATORS

Example	Logical Values	Result (True or False)
(1=1) & (1=1)	(True) and (True)	True
! 1=1	Not True	False
1=1 | 1=1	True or True	True
1=2 | 1=1	False or True	True
1=2 | 1=2	False or False	False

The Text Operator and Unary Operators

The text operator (+) allows you to combine two or more text variables. The unary operators (+, -) allow you to specify the sign of a numeric variable.

Formula Keywords

Luckily, there aren't many keywords for formulas that you need to memorize. Table 17.6 lists all the keywords with a description of each. Remember that a keyword is always the first word in a formula statement. They will always be in uppercase because the formula editor automatically converts them when the formula is saved.

TABLE 17.6: FORMULA KEYWORD VALUES AND DESCRIPTIONS

Keyword	Description
DEFAULT	Applies a default value to a field. If the field exists on the current document, the current value of the field is used. If the field does not exist, the field is created with the default value. For example: `DEFAULT MyVar := "Some default value"`
ENVIRONMENT	Assigns a value to an environment variable in the `notes.ini` file. For example: `ENVIRONMENT MyVar := "Some text value"`
FIELD	Assigns a value to a field for the current document. If the field exists on the current document, the contents are replaced. If the field does not exist, the field is created with the value assigned. For example: `FIELD MyVar := "Some value"`
REM	Inserts comments into the formula. For example: `REM "These are my comments"`

Continued ▶

TABLE 17.6: FORMULA KEYWORD VALUES AND DESCRIPTIONS (CONTINUED)	
Keyword	**Description**
SELECT	Determines if the current document is valid for processing in the formula (must return a logical value). For example:

```
SELECT Form = "Main Topic"
```

@Functions

Notes contains hundreds of @functions that are used in a wide variety of ways. Each @function always returns some type of value. When returning a value, the function essentially replaces itself with the value. These functions can be used anywhere within a formula and can also be nested within themselves. For example, the following piece of code is a valid nested formula:

```
FIELD Readers := @Trim( @Unique( From : @UserName ) )
```

Breaking down the formula, you can see that the contents of the From field are being combined with the result of the @Username function to form a text list. The @Unique function then removes any duplicates from the list. The @Trim function then removes any beginning or trailing blanks from each entry in the text list, and the results are stored in the document field called Readers.

The Notes Help files are an invaluable asset in the area of functions. They contain a complete description, the syntax, usage, examples, and the various objects that a function can act upon.

The @Function Syntax

The general format for an @function is as follows:

```
@functionname( argument1; argument2; ....argumentn)
```

An @function always starts with the @ symbol followed by the name of the function. Not all functions require arguments. For those that don't, the parentheses are not required. Parentheses are required for functions that have arguments.

If the @function has multiple arguments, each argument must be separated by a semicolon. Each argument's data type must match that of the @function's description. @Functions may also require special keywords, which are always surrounded by brackets ([ ]) and are *not* placed in quotes as a text literal is. The keyword must match those described in the function's Help description.

NOTE Multiple arguments within an @function are separated with a semicolon (;). Remember too that multiline formulas are separated by a semicolon. And to make matters even more confusing, the semicolon is also used as a separator for values within a multi-value field.

The Various Functions and Commands

@Functions can be commonly grouped or associated based on their intended usage. What you may find even a bit more confusing is that many of the @functions can also have more than one syntax. Identifying and explaining all the various uses and syntax is outside the scope of this book, but we will discuss a few of the more common @functions and how they are applied.

Error @Functions   There are basically five @functions that we would classify as error related. They are most commonly used in fields for user data entry. @Failure() and @Success are typically used within Input Validation formulas. If the data input by the user is incorrect, @Failure() will display an error message to the user and stop the current process of saving the document. @Success is returned from the formula if everything is OK. @IsError() is used to test a field or variable to see if it contains an error. When an error occurs, the contents of the variable are set to @Error. Whether or not you check for an error is completely up to you. If a field contains an error and is left undetected, the field will display @Error to the end user. The last function, @Return(), allows you the option of terminating a formula and returning a value.

String/Text Functions   Notes is a document-based programming language and repository. Keeping that theme in mind, you can imagine that there are quite a few text-oriented functions. Notes has @functions for converting all data types to text, concatenating and comparing text, and locating and extracting strings and substrings of text. The most common function you will probably use is the @Text() function, which will take any data type and convert it to text. For example, @Text(@Document-UniqueID) is commonly used in a view column. Another common text function combination that we use is @Right("00000" + @Trim(field); 5). This will take an ordinary alphanumeric field and return a zero-filled variable (the value of 52 would be transformed to 00052). This may appear uncommon, but for sorting, it becomes a necessity. There are also fields that convert text to numbers or time-date values and fields for manipulating strings, such as @TextToTime, @Replace, and @ReplaceSubstring.

Arithmetic Functions   There are some basic number and mathematical functions as well. @Sum() is an interesting function in that it sums number and number lists (remember lists from earlier in the chapter) and returns the total value. There is also @Round(), @Min(), @Max(), and @Random() for other numeric manipulation. Notes also contains the simple mathematical functions such as @Abs(), @Sign(), @Sin(), and @Tan().

Time-Date Functions   Notes has a multitude of functions for processing the time-date fields and variables. There are functions that are document specific, such as @Created() and @Modified(), and some that are date oriented, such as @Month() and @Year(). One interesting function is @Adjust(), which will allow you to adjust a time-date value (either forward or backward) by years, months, days, hours, minutes, or seconds—quite flexible indeed.

User Functions   Some of the functions are directed solely at identifying the user and the environment. The most common in this area are @Name() and @UserName. @UserName returns the current username (or server name), and @Name() allows you to format the results in many different ways. For example, Scot's @Name() would be CN=Scot Haberman/OU=Users/O=EDSTest—not a very personal hello. To return just Scot Haberman, Scot's common name, use @Name() as in the example @Name([CN]; @UserName).

Database and View Functions   There is also a set of functions designed for accessing information about the current view or database. The most common functions are @DBName and @ViewTitle, which return the database name and view name respectively.

Lookup Functions   Lookup functions are designed for accessing groups of data both inside and outside the current database. The @DBColumn() function will return all the values for a column in a view. @DBLookup() will search for a specific value in a view and, when a match is found, return a specific field or column value. These two functions are commonly used in formulas for dialog box–style fields (such as a list box or check box).

NOTE   Another lookup @function is @DBCommand, which is used by Web applications. For example, if you want to display the next set of documents, you can issue @DBCommand("Domino"; "ViewNextPage"). This command is typically associated with Open Database Connectivity (ODBC) except in this context.

@Command/@PostedCommand Functions   These two commands are a special form of @functions. They are used to emulate menu commands, hence they can only be used in the context of the user interface. Almost every menu command can be mimicked by these commands. There are some "specialty" commands available as well. For example, @Command([Compose];"Formula Variable Example") opens a new Formula Variable Example document. The only difference between the two command functions is when they are executed. @Command is executed immediately, whereas @PostedCommand is executed at the end of the formula regardless of where it is actually located in the formula.

Web Applications and Formulas

When delivering Web applications, you will soon learn that formulas are extremely important. LotusScript will not be rendered to the Web for any of the elements or events on a form. In fact, the only place LotusScript can be used for a Web application is in an Agent (either the WebQuerySave or WebQueryOpen event). On the other hand, most formulas can be understood and translated by the Web browser (assuming that the Use JavaScript option is enabled).

For example, you can use formulas in the Input Translation event, the Input Validation event, Action buttons, and hotspots. One powerful feature is the ability to refresh the fields on the Web form. This gives you the ability to recompute fields based on the values the user typed in. If you have drop-down lists that are based on the value of an input field, they will be recomputed as well.

Now there are limitations as to which formulas you can use on the Web. You will not be able to issue @Prompt() to display a pop-up dialog box, but all the @functions that cannot be used are listed in the Notes Help database. Another not-so-obvious feature of using formulas is using them along with pass-thru HTML. There is no reason you cannot place a field on the form right in the middle of the pass-thru HTML. This field can use formulas to grab and format the data, which will be used by the HTML. This technique is an extremely powerful combination utilizing the power of Notes along with JavaScript or native HTML.

So the next time you need to complete a task in Notes, evaluate the task to determine if it is possible to complete it with a formula. If not, look at some of the other tools available, such as JavaScript, LotusScript, and Java. For more information on the other languages available for Notes programming, refer to Chapter 23, "Language Extensions," or to the upcoming book, *Notes and Domino 5 Developer's Handbook*, by Cate Richard (Sybex, 2000).

Formulas That Expect a Result

Listed in Table 17.7 are the formulas that expect a result and what evaluated result is expected.

TABLE 17.7: FORMULAS EXPECTING A RESULT

Object	Formula Type	Expected Result/ Activated	How to Access
Database	Replication	Evaluates to true (1) or false (0) and is applied to each document in the database. Activated when replication occurs.	Open the database and choose File ≻ Replication ≻ Settings or right-click the database design bookmark icon and choose Replication ≻ Settings. Click the Space Savers icon, shown here. Space Savers Then select the Replicate a Subset of Documents and the Select by Formula options.
View/Folder	Form	Evaluates to the name of a form. Activated when a document is opened from the view.	Open the view/folder and click the Objects tab in the programmer's pane. Expand the View object and select the Form Formula event.
	Selection	Evaluates to true (1) or false (0) and is applied to each document in the view. Activated when the view or folder is opened.	Open the view/folder and click the Objects tab in the programmer's pane. Expand the View object and select the View Selection event. In the script area, select Formula from the drop-down box.
	Column	Evaluates a value to a text string. Activated when the view or folder is opened.	Open the view/folder and click the Objects tab in the programmer's pane. Expand the Column object and select the Column Value event (you can also just click the column header). In the script area, select the Formula radio button.

Continued ▸

TABLE 17.7: FORMULAS EXPECTING A RESULT (CONTINUED)

Object	Formula Type	Expected Result/ Activated	How to Access
	Show Action	Evaluates to true (1) or false (0). Activated when the view or folder is opened.	Open the view/folder and choose View ≻ Action Pane (you can also slide the Action pane slider bar). Double-click the Action to display the Action Properties Info Box and select the Action Hide-When tab.
			Enable the Hide Action If Formula Is True option. Type the formula in the text area or click the Formula Window button.
Form	Window title	Evaluates to a text or numeric value. Activated when a document based on the form is opened.	Open the form and click the Objects tab in the programmer's pane. Expand the Form object and select the Window Title event.
	Section title	Evaluates to a text or numeric value. Activated when a document based on the form is opened.	Open the form and select the section. Choose Section ≻ Section Properties to open the Section Properties Info Box (you can also right-click the section and choose Section Properties). Select the Section Title and Border tab.
			Select the Formula radio button. Type the formula in the text area or click the Formula Window button.
	Section access	Evaluates to a name or list of names. Activated when the section is accessed.	Open the form and select the section. Choose Section ≻ Section Properties to open the Section Properties Info Box (you can also right-click the section and choose Section Properties). Select the Formula tab.
			Type the formula in the text area or click the Formula Window button.

Continued ▌▶

Object	Formula Type	Expected Result/ Activated	How to Access
	TABLE 17.7: FORMULAS EXPECTING A RESULT (CONTINUED)		
	Show Action	Evaluates to true (1) or false (0). Activated when a document based on the form is opened.	Open the form and choose View ➤ Action Pane (you can also slide the Action pane slider bar). Double-click the Action to display the Action Properties Info Box and select the Action Hide-When tab. Enable the Hide Action If Formula Is True option. Type the formula in the text area or click the Formula Window button.
	Insert subform	Evaluates to a text value that is the name of a subform. Activated when a document based on the form is opened.	Open the form and click the Objects tab in the programmer's pane. Expand the Computed Subform object (you can also select the subform directly from the form) and select the Default Value event.
	Hide paragraph	Evaluates to true (1) or false (0). Activated when the text is accessed.	Open the form and place the cursor in the paragraph you want to hide. Choose Text ➤ Text Properties and enable the Hide Paragraph If Formula Is True option. Type the formula in the text area or click the Formula Window button.
	Hotspot formula pop-up	Evaluates to a text value that is displayed in the pop-up box. Activated when the hotspot text is selected.	Open the form and click the Objects tab in the programmer's pane. Expand the Hotspot object (you can also select the hotspot directly from the form) and select the Click event.

Continued ▶

PART

V

Beyond the Client: Utilizing Domino Designer

TABLE 17.7: FORMULAS EXPECTING A RESULT (CONTINUED)

Object	Formula Type	Expected Result/ Activated	How to Access
Field	Default value (editable field)	Evaluates to a text value that is displayed in the pop-up box. Activated when the hotspot text is selected. Evaluates to a value that matches the current field type. Activated when the document is created.	Open the form and click the Objects tab in the programmer's pane. Expand the Field object (you can also select the field directly from the form) and select the Default Value event.
	Input translation (editable field)	Evaluates to a value that matches the current field type. Activated when the document is saved or recalculated.	Open the form and click the Objects tab in the programmer's pane. Expand the Field object (you can also select the field directly from the form) and select the Input Translation event.
	Input validation (editable field)	Evaluates to true (1) or false(0). Activated after the input translation.	Open the form and click the Objects tab in the programmer's pane. Expand the Field object (you can also select the field directly from the form) and select the Input Validation event.
	Value (computed field)	Evaluates to a value that matches the current field type. Activated when the document is created, saved, or recalculated.	Open the form and click the Objects tab in the programmer's pane. Expand the Field object (you can also select the field directly from the form) and select the Value event.
	Dialog list, checkbox, radio button, listbox, or combobox field	Evaluates to a text value or a list of text values. Activated when the field is edited.	Open the form and select the field directly on the form. Choose Design ➤ Field Properties and select the Control tab (you can also right-click the field and select Field Properties). Type the formula in the text area or click the Formula Window button.

Continued ▶

	TABLE 17.7: FORMULAS EXPECTING A RESULT (CONTINUED)		
Object	**Formula Type**	**Expected Result/ Activated**	**How to Access**
Rich Text Field	Section title	Evaluates to a text or numeric value. Activated when a document based on the form is opened.	Enter a rich text field in Edit mode from the Notes client. Select the section and choose Section ≻ Section Properties (you can also right-click on the section and select Section Properties). Select the Section Title and Border tab. Select the Formula radio button. Type the formula in the text area or click the Formula Window button.
	Hide paragraph	Evaluates to true (1) or false (0). Activated when the text is accessed.	Enter a rich text field in Edit mode from the Notes client. Place the cursor in the paragraph to hide and choose Text ≻ Text Properties (you can also right-click on the paragraph and select Text Properties). Select the Paragraph Hide-When tab. Enable the Hide Paragraph If Formula Is True option. Type the formula in the text area or click the Formula Window button.
	Hotspot formula pop-up	Evaluates to a text value that is displayed in the pop-up box. Activated when the hotspot text is selected.	Enter a rich text field in Edit mode in the Notes client. Select the hotspot and choose Hotspot ≻ Edit Hotspot. Click the Objects tab in the programmer's pane. Expand the Hotspot object (you can also select the hotspot directly from the form) and select the Click event.

The formulas that return a result may be as simple as a one-line @function or as complex as a multiline compilation of variables, constants, and @functions. In either case, the final statement of the formula must return a value that the object container understands.

Formulas That Perform an Action

Table 17.8 contains a list of the formulas that expect to perform some type of action.

TABLE 17.8: FORMULAS THAT PERFORM AN ACTION

Object	Formula Type	Expected Result/ Activated	How to Access
Workspace	SmartIcon	Executes when the SmartIcon is selected	Choose File ➢ Preferences ➢ Smart-Icons. Click the Edit Icon button and select an icon from the list to edit. Click the Formula button to display the formula editor.
Database	Agent	Executes on the database when triggered. Will process those documents determined by the selection criteria specified in the UI and the SELECT keyword in the formula.	Open the Agent and click the Objects tab in the programmer's pane. Expand the Agent object and select the Action event. If the Action event is not shown in the event list, make sure Formula is selected from the drop-down list box in the script area.
View/ Folder	Action	Executes on the view when selected. Activated when Actions ➢ Name-ofAction is selected or when the button is clicked.	Open the view/folder and click the Objects tab in the programmer's pane. Select the Action object from the list. From the script area, select Formula from the drop-down list box (you can also select the Click event from the expanded Action object in the Objects tab).
	Event	Executes on the view when triggered. Activated when the event occurs.	Open the view/folder and click the Objects tab in the programmer's pane. Expand the View object and select one of the following events: QueryOpen, PostOpen, RegionDoubleClick, QueryOpenDocument, QueryRecalc, QueryAddtoFolder, QueryPaste, PostPaste, QueryDragDrop, PostDragDrop, QueryClose. In the script area, select Formula from the drop-down list box.

Continued ▶

TABLE 17.8: FORMULAS THAT PERFORM AN ACTION (CONTINUED)			
Object	Formula Type	Expected Result/ Activated	How to Access
Form	Action	Executes on the form when selected. Activated when Actions ➢ Name-ofAction is selected or when the button is clicked.	Open the form and click the Objects tab in the programmer's pane. Select the Action object from the list. In the script area, select Formula from the drop-down list box (you can also select the Click event from the expanded Action object in the Objects tab).
	Event	Executes on the form when triggered. Activated when the event occurs.	Open the view/folder and click the Objects tab in the programmer's pane. Expand the View object and select one of the following events: QueryOpen, PostOpen, QueryModeChange, Post-ModeChange, PostRecalc, QuerySave, PostSave, QueryClose. In the script area, select Formula from the drop-down list box.
	Hotspot button	Executes on the form when selected. Activated when the button is selected.	Open the form and click the Objects tab in the programmer's pane. Select the Button object from the list. In the script area, select Formula from the drop-down list box (you can also select the Click event from the expanded Action object in the Objects tab).
	Hotspot action	Executes on the form when selected. Activated when the hotspot text is selected.	Open the form and click the Objects tab in the programmer's pane. Select the Hotspot object from the list. In the script area, select Formula from the drop-down list box (you can also select the Click event from the expanded Action object in the Objects tab).

Continued

PART

V

Beyond the Client: Uti-
lizing Domino Designer

TABLE 17.8: FORMULAS THAT PERFORM AN ACTION (CONTINUED)

Object	Formula Type	Expected Result/ Activated	How to Access
Standard Navigator	Hotspot	Activated when the user clicks the hotspot.	Open the Navigator and click the Objects tab in the programmer's pane. Select one of the following Hotspot elements from the list: Hotspot Rectangle, Hotspot Polygon, Hotspot Circle, Graphic Button, Button, Text, Rectangle, Rounded Rectangle, Ellipse, Polygon, Polyline. In the script area, select Formula from the drop-down list box (you can also select the Click event from the expanded Action object in the Objects tab).
Layout Region	Hotspot button	Executes on the form when selected. Activated when the button is selected.	Open the form and click the Objects tab in the programmer's pane. Select the Button object from the list. In the script area, select Formula from the drop-down list box (you can also select the Click event from the expanded Action object in the Objects tab).
Rich Text Field	Hotspot button	Executes on the form when selected. Activated when the button is selected.	Enter a rich text field in Edit mode from the Notes client. Select the button and choose Button ➤ Edit Button. In the script area, select Formula from the drop-down list box (you can also select the Click event from the expanded Action object in the Objects tab).
	Hotspot action	Executes on the form when selected. Activated when the hotspot text is selected.	Enter a rich text field in Edit mode from the Notes client. Select the hotspot and choose Hotspot ➤ Edit Hotspot. In the script area, select Formula from the drop-down list box (you can also select the Click event from the expanded Action object in the Objects tab).

These formulas do not necessarily depend on the return of an actual result, but with them, you can manipulate existing objects and execute different commands for various results.

What Is an Event?

Within Notes, every action performed by a user is known as an event. An event can be opening a form, closing a form, clicking a button, or deleting a document. Certain objects within Notes are "event aware," meaning that the object can be programmed to respond to specific events. This is known as *event-driven programming*.

Not all objects within Notes can be programmed to act on events. Each object is only aware of its own events that can occur. For example, the view and the form can both respond to the QueryOpen event, but a form cannot respond to the view's QueryOpen event, nor can the view respond to the form's QueryOpen event. Events may have the same name, but that is all they have in common.

As a programmer, you can use events to alter the default behavior of an object's event. This flexibility allows you to develop applications that are more robust and responsive to the needs of the users. Event-driven programming is not limited to just formulas either (refer to Chapter 23, which discusses LotusScript and JavaScript).

Using the Formula Editors

Now that you have a basic understanding of what a formula is, let's look at a few examples of how to define a formula and how to debug them. Formulas can be defined in many different places in the Notes environment, as described in the previous tables. To make matters a bit more confusing, there are also three different formula editors:

- The Edit Formula window
- The script area formula editor
- The SmartIcon formula editor

Although each editor interprets the formulas exactly the same, they all have different options available to aid in the development process.

The Edit Formula Window

The Edit Formula window is displayed when the Formula Window button is clicked. Typically, this button resides in dialog boxes such as the Paragraph Hide-When tab of a Properties Info Box for an element. Open the Mastering R5 for Chapter 17 example database and select the Formula Editor Example form. Double-click the Editor-Comments field to display the Field Properties Info Box and then select the Paragraph Hide-When tab.

You will see the formula text box (see Figure 17.10). You can type in the formula directly on the dialog box, but the space is rather limited, so for a complex formula, it can be downright confusing.

FIGURE 17.10

Using the formula text box on the Hide-When tab of the Field Properties Info Box for a form

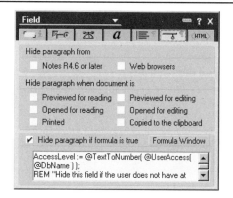

For a bit more room, you can select the Formula Window button to display a larger formula-editing window, as shown in Figure 17.11. The added space will allow you to type in and format your formula for easier reading.

FIGURE 17.11

The Edit Formula dialog box

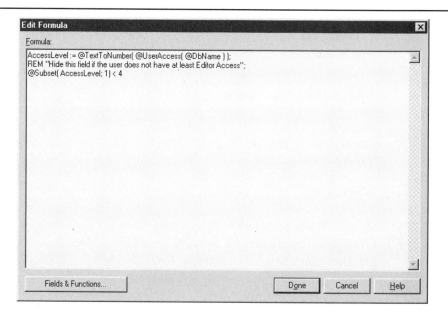

You will also note a Fields and Functions button in the Edit Formula dialog box. This button saves you from having to memorize every @function or database field. Selecting this button will display the Fields and Functions dialog box, shown in Figure 17.12.

FIGURE 17.12

FIGURE 17.12

The Fields and Functions dialog box

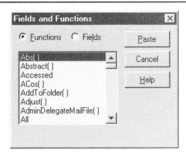

Select the Functions radio button to list all the available @functions. One limitation of this list is the lack of a complete @command listing. The @command is listed as one of the functions, but all the keywords (of which there are many) that are used with the @command function are not on the list. It would be nice to see an additional radio button selection for @commands, but for now, you must type in the keywords yourself.

Select the Fields radio button to list all the current fields that are defined for the database. This is an extremely helpful option; it may help you eliminate many field name typos.

Once you have typed your formula in the Edit Formula window, just click the Done button. If you have made any syntax errors, the Formula Error message box will display, explaining your error. Clicking the OK button will close the Formula Error message box and highlight the line in which the error occurs within the formula. Once the entire formula is correct, the formula editor will close and your code will be displayed in the small formula window, as shown in Figure 17.10. If for any reason you want to cancel your code changes, just click the Cancel button in the Edit Formula window.

The Script Area Formula Editor

The script area editor in the programmer's pane is a bit different than the Edit Formula window in that it is a multipurpose editor. Not only can you define formulas, you may also be able to define LotusScript, define JavaScript, or select a Simple action for an object (these selections are determined by the type of event). Because this chapter only deals with formulas, when we make a reference to the script area, we are assuming that the Formula option has been selected (sometimes this option may be in the form of a radio button or a drop-down list box) in the script area.

Figure 17.13 displays the entire design layout for the Formula Editor Example form. If you look closely at the programmer's pane in the lower left corner, you can see that the Input Translation event has been selected for the UserComments field (also known as a Field object). In the script area, the actual formula is displayed for the Input Translation event of the UserComments field.

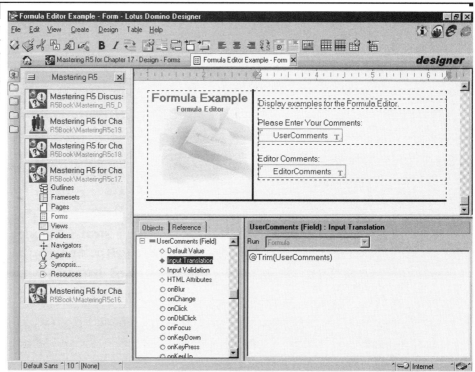

FIGURE 17.13

The programmer's pane of the Designer workspace displaying the Input Translation formula in the script area

One thing in particular to note is that only a formula can be specified for an Input Translation event because the drop-down list of the script area is grayed out. When you use the script area for developing, there are many cases in which only one type of programming is allowed. We mention this to point out how the Reference tab of the programmer's pane is "aware" of the programming language too. Because the Input Translation event can only contain a formula, the Reference tab will only display or make reference to those statements that can be used inside a formula. The Reference tab is data aware. In Figure 17.14, notice that the only valid selections for the Reference tab are database fields, @functions, and @commands.

PART

V

Beyond the Client: Uti-
lizing Domino Designer

FIGURE 17.14

*List box choices for the
Reference tab*

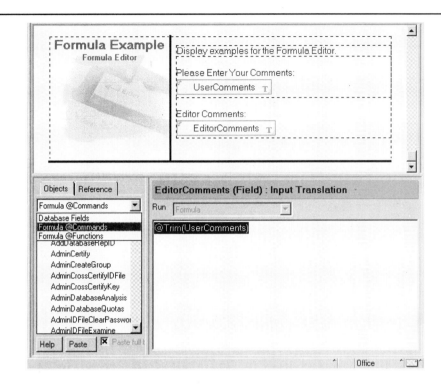

Once you make a selection from the Reference tab's drop-down list box, the list will populate with all the various commands or fields for your selection. If you would like to have the command or field automatically populated into your script, just highlight the command and click the Paste button. The code will be inserted into the script area where you last positioned your cursor in the script code. Once you have completed making all your changes, just click the Accept icon (see margin) to accept the changes. If you make a mistake, do not worry. Just click the Cancel icon to cancel all your changes.

One nice thing about the script area editor is the color syntax. Notice that keywords, functions, errors, and other text are highlighted in various colors as you type. This helps you track down errors and also makes it easier to read. The colors are also configurable. To configure the properties, just right-click in the script area and select Design Pane Properties from the menu. From the Design Pane Properties Info Box, you can define the colors and the size of the text. Change the options to those that fit you best.

NOTE Before you decide to use a formula, check first to see if a Simple action may do the job. Simple actions do not require any programming and are supported for some of the elements. Refer to the script area of the programmer's pane to see if the Simple action is a valid selection for any element in question.

The SmartIcon Formula Editor

The SmartIcon formula editor is used in only one place within all of Notes. We are mentioning it only because it is quite different from the other two. To access the editor, follow these steps:

1. Choose File ➢ Preferences ➢ SmartIcons.

2. Click the Edit Icons button.

3. From the list, select the SmartIcon you want to edit and click the Formula button. The SmartIcons formula editor appears.

4. Type in your formula for the icon or use the Add @Func or Add Command button to paste in your favorite function.

5. To save the formula, click the OK button. If you have typed in an invalid formula command, an error message dialog box will display.

Debugging Formulas

One major flaw to using formulas is the lack of a good debugging tool, which tends to create some rather creative ways to debug a formula. The formula editor will trap any syntax errors for you. The default setting is to highlight the error in red and place the cursor on the line in error. If a runtime error occurs, a cryptic message may display in the Notes client. A Web application may just ignore the code or display an error message page. There are, however, a few tricks available for debugging a formula.

@Prompt   Use the @prompt function as much as you can to debug a formula in the Notes client environment. This @function will allow you to display a pop-up dialog box and display the contents of various fields. For example, if you want to see the contents of a field called MyName, just code @Prompt([OK];"Contents of MyName";MyName), and when the code is executed, a dialog box will appear displaying the contents of the MyName field.

Environment Variables   If displaying a dialog box is out of the question, another alternative is to save the contents of each field in question to the notes.ini file. Use the command @SetEnvironment("WhatIsTheName",MyName) to save the contents of the variable *MyName* to a variable in the notes.ini file called $WhatIsTheName. To see the contents of the variable, just open the notes.ini file.

Document Fields   If neither of the two previous options are acceptable, the last alternative is to save the contents of the variables to a document. For example, suppose you need to run an Agent for a Web application. Displaying a dialog box is not possible because the program is run via the Web. Saving the values to the notes.ini file is not acceptable because the values would be written to the server's notes.ini and not your workstation's. The last alternative is to use the FIELD keyword and save all the temporary variables to the current document. Once you have completed your debugging sessions, either delete the fields from the document or just delete the whole document.

NOTE   Now that you know how to properly debug a formula, we will share an undocumented tip. There is a built-in formula debugger for Notes. It is unsupported and, in some cases, not very stable. It is an extremely helpful tool for debugging formulas. To activate the debugger, hold down the Ctrl and Shift keys simultaneously and choose File ➣ Tools ➣ Debug LotusScript. This should place a check mark next to the Debug LotusScript menu option. However, when you select the option, no fancy debugger will display or start up automatically. The formula debugger will activate when you execute a formula in the Notes client. *The debugger does not work in Designer; you must execute a formula.* Give it a try. It takes a bit of getting used to, but it does work (although not in all situations). Use it at your own risk.

Summary

In this chapter, we covered the various elements that a formula comprises. We also discussed where a formula can be used and how to use the different formula editors. Formulas are an important piece of the Notes application structure and should not be ignored. There are other alternative languages available, but none are as simple or as efficient as the formula language.

In the next chapter, we will discuss how to create document forms and the basic elements that can be placed on a form. We'll cover the document response or parent-child relationship and how a form is used to retrieve and save document data.

CHAPTER **18**

Using Forms to Collect Data

The form is the backbone of the Notes database. It is the structure that is used for inputting and viewing data in all documents you'll work with in Notes. As a developer, you will most likely spend most of your time working with forms because end users will spend most of their time using your forms to interact with the databases.

A form's design, its look and feel, is a subjective issue and therefore not discussed in this chapter. Each developer has his own ideas about what looks good and what doesn't. What this chapter will do is give you a basic understanding of forms, their properties, and how to create them. And throughout the chapter, we'll point out the difference between forms for the Notes client and those for a Web application. Although the gap is closing between the two, there are still quite a few differences you should be aware of.

What Is a Form?

Most people are already comfortable with the concept of a paper form. Some simple examples are a credit card application, a fax cover sheet, and a personal check. Whatever kind of form it is, you are responsible for placing pieces of information in the areas provided. Once you have placed information on a form, you tend to think of it as a document rather than a form. That is exactly what a Notes form is, except it is an electronic document instead of a paper document.

A Notes form provides the areas for the end user to enter information. Of course, the form can be jazzed up to look nice and include helpful text, but the end result is that information is gathered from a form and saved into a Notes document. Figure 18.1 shows an example of the Main Topic form from the Mastering R5 for Chapter 18 example database.

The first time you create a Notes database, you may wonder where to define its fields. This is another difference between Notes databases and other databases. In a Notes database, the form is also used to define the fields for a document. When you create a form, you are defining both the data and the user interface at the same time.

Understanding the Form/Document Relationship

The relationship between a form and a document is a difficult concept to understand. As we stated previously, a form is used to place data on a document. But this is not the only way data can be defined on a document. Remember the FIELD keyword discussed in Chapter 17? In the description it said that if the field exists, the contents of the field would be updated; otherwise a field would be created. That's correct. You can create a new field using a formula.

FIGURE 18.1

The Main Topic
discussion form
example from the
Mastering R5 for
Chapter 18 Database
displayed in the
Notes client

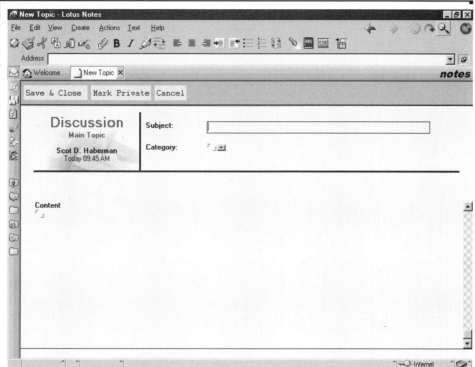

PART

V

Beyond the Client: Uti-
lizing Domino Designer

So how can the data on a document be viewed if the field doesn't exist on the form? This is the tricky part. A form really doesn't have any relationship to the data document. A form is nothing more than a template you use to view the underlying data in the document.

A document stores both the data and the associated field names. The form is then applied to the document and requests to see only certain fields. For example, suppose there are three forms defined for a database. FormA has two fields defined: FieldA1 and FieldA2. FormB has two fields defined: FieldB1 and FieldB2. FormC has four fields defined: FieldA1, FieldA2, FieldB1, and FieldB2.

Now create a document using FormA. Type **A1** in the first field and **A2** in the second field. Save the document. Now open the same document but use FormB (yes, you can use any form to open any document). What would you expect to see in the fields? You won't see anything because there are no FieldB1 or FieldB2 fields with data on the document. The document only contains data for fields FieldA1 and FieldA2. Now type **B1** and **B2** in the fields and save the document. Open the same document one last time but use FormC. All four fields would contain data where each field maps to its respective field name. Refer to Figure 18.2 for a graphical depiction.

FIGURE 18.2

*A form is actually
a template for the
document and
the data.*

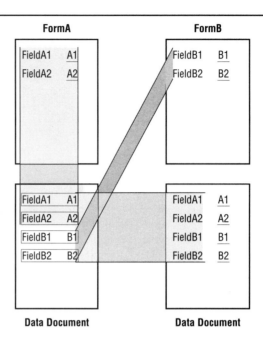

What this example shows is that a data document can contain any number of fields and a form can choose to show any number of fields from a document. This allows you to pick and choose which fields to show a user.

How does Notes know when to pull up which form? There is a set of rules that Notes uses to determine which form to use; they are as follows (in order of priority):

- If a form is stored with the document, that form is used to display the document.

- If a view has a form formula, the formula is used to determine which form to use to display the document.

- The form used to create the document (this value is stored in the internal field called Form) is used to display the document.

- The default form for the database is used to display the document.

You can design various forms for specific processes. For example, you can design one form for the data input and another for reading the document, or you can have one form for printing and another for accessing data from a Web application.

The Document Hierarchy

So far, we've been discussing data documents, which are created when information is saved into fields on a form. Now we'll discuss the document hierarchy. The designer determines the hierarchical type a data document will have when it is created with a form. Just as databases have a specific type (you learned in Chapter 16 that there are database types such as Standard, Library, Journal, etc.), there are also different types of documents. In this case, there are only three:

Document   The high-level document (commonly referred to as the Main document) that cannot respond to any other document type.

Response   Created in response to a Main document. There are special internal fields that keep track of this parent-child relationship. This type of document can inherit data from the Main document. Within a view, the Response document will appear indented under the Main document.

Response to Response   Created in response to a Main, Response, or another Response to Response document. They are similar to Response documents in that there are special internal fields that keep track of the document relationship. Response to Response documents also appear indented under the documents to which they respond.

These types will determine where a document resides within the Notes document hierarchy. One of the most common databases in Notes is the discussion database. A discussion database is very similar to a forum or newsgroup threaded discussion. Someone will post a main question or comment, and others can respond to either the main question or any response while maintaining the relationship between the main question and the responses.

A user will create a main topic, which is of the Document form type (the highest level of documents). Other users can respond to the main topic with a Response document or to a response with a Response to Response document. These types of documents carry special meaning in Notes. Notes realizes the relationship between the documents and maintains that relationship for you. There are many special @functions and view options that take advantage of this special document relationship. Figure 18.3 shows an example of a discussion in the Mastering R5 for Chapter 18 example database.

 WARNING   Be careful of *orphaned* documents. An orphan occurs when a parent document is deleted from a group of related documents. Make sure there are not any child (Response) documents before removing the parent.

FIGURE 18.3

A Discussion view
with the Document,
Response, and
Response to Response
type documents

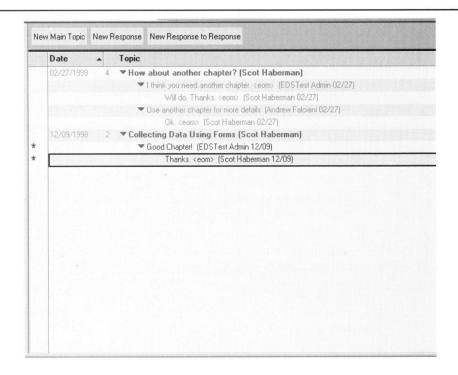

Profile Documents: A Special Type of Document

There is another type of document that has not been mentioned, but it is quite powerful: the Profile document. Profile documents are special because they will never show up in a view, yet they can be accessed anywhere and at any time.

So why use them if they never show in a view? The main reason is to store data about either an application or an individual. For example, it is sometimes a problem to pass data from one Agent to the next (you can use Environment variables, but that has its own set of problems). The answer is to use a Profile document. You can save the data from the first Agent and retrieve it from the second Agent just as if the data were passed to the second Agent. Because you are able to specify a key value for saving and retrieving data, you can ensure that you extract the correct data.

Continued ▮▶

You can also use a Profile document to store data or preferences for an individual. Using the individual's username as the key to the profile, you can store any type of user-specific preferences. This can have a big impact on Web applications. Users can set their preferences, and each time they return, their preferences can be looked up and restored. This eliminates having to use a cookie.

How do you create a Profile document? There are special commands for both formulas and scripts (@functions and LotusScript) that create and modify these documents. If you use these commands, Notes will automatically create the document as a Profile document. No special form is required. Use the same forms you use to create any other type of document (but don't use a form that is a type Response or Response to Response). To demonstrate how easy it is to use a Profile document, we'll show you an example using an @function. Assume that the form to use is called UserData and the field to use is called NickName. Grabbing the contents of the field from a profile for an individual is as easy as writing the following line of code:

```
@GetProfileField("UserData";"NickName";@UserName)
```

If you need to store data or save the state of either an application or an individual's preferences, consider using a Profile document. There is one caveat, however. As mentioned earlier, a view will not display a Profile document. Remember too that they don't get replicated. Keep that in mind if you plan to store information that needs to reside on multiple servers.

Form Design Considerations

One thing we have seen over and over with new Notes developers is that they try to get as much information as possible on one form. It seems that the parent-child relationship is not an easy concept to apply, especially for seasoned programmers who usually use other languages and database management systems. Keep in mind that a Notes form should be modeled after a process. The form should help users, not hinder or confuse them.

As mentioned at the beginning of the chapter, we're not going to discuss how to lay out your form. That is totally up to you. But we will give you a few helpful tips to get you started in the right direction.

First, make sure you get the users involved. Notes is a flexible and dynamic environment. You can design a form quickly and allow your users access for immediate feedback. We cannot stress this enough. The users will decide whether or not to use the system, so it's important to get them involved early. If you make them feel like part of the process, they will accept the change more easily and may actually promote your application.

Try to limit the amount of data on one screen. The last thing a user wants to do is scroll endlessly through a form. There are some tools that can help you accomplish this, but the best defense is to limit the number of fields on one form. For example, instead of creating one form that contains an entire invoice, why not create a parent document for the main information and Response documents for each item on the invoice?

Here are some other tips to keep in mind:

- Lay out your form first. Too many programmers put a form together without a plan. Just as you wouldn't build a house without a blueprint, you shouldn't lay out a form without a plan.

- Use tables to align the elements on a form. You can embed tables within tables, which can give you pinpoint accuracy for presenting your data. In addition, by using tables, you can give your form a slim and clean look.

- Group all the hidden fields together, either at the top or the bottom of the form. Also, make the color of all the hidden fields red so they stand out, and change the point size of the font to something smaller than the default.

- Leave lots of white space to make the form easier to read. Also, use consistent spacing between elements so they don't look like they're scattered all over the form.

- Use a consistent header on all your forms.

Consider whether the form is to be used in a Web application too. The Notes client and Web applications work a bit differently, and there are special design considerations for each. For example, to edit a document from a view in the Notes client, you can right-click the document and select Edit from the menu or open the document and just double-click the form. On a form for a Web application, you must add an Action button that will allow the user to edit the current document.

Designing a Form

A form is the basic interface for viewing and entering information in a database. It can include various fields, text, graphics, and Actions. A form can also be used for both a Notes client and a Web application. Let's see how the entire process starts.

Creating a Form

There are two ways to create a form. You can either copy an existing form or create a new form from scratch.

Copy an Existing Form

When deciding whether to copy an existing form, look for one that closely represents your intended functionality. You don't have to copy a form from the current database only. You can look at other databases and even templates. A good place to begin looking for a form is in the master templates, which are the templates included with Notes.

We'll guide you through the process of making a copy of the Main Topic form. To copy a form from Domino Designer, do the following:

1. Open the Mastering R5 for Chapter 18 database.

2. In the Design pane, select the Forms design element from the Design list (this will display all the forms in the Work pane).

3. In the Work pane, highlight the Main Topic form.

4. Choose Edit ➤ Copy (you can also right-click on the Main Topic form and choose Copy).

5. Open the database that will contain the new form (in our example, we'll make a copy of the form in the same database).

6. With the Forms design element selected from the Design list of the database, choose Edit ➤ Paste (you can also right-click in the Work pane and choose Paste).

This process places a copy of the Main Topic form in the Work pane, as shown in Figure 18.4. The copy is called Copy of Main Topic (because a form of the same name already exists, Notes will automatically add *Copy of* to the beginning of the new form's name). Now you can open the copied form and change it to fit your needs.

FIGURE 18.4

A list of form design elements in the Work pane

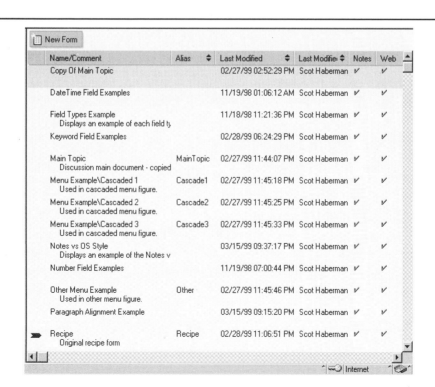

Creating a Form from Scratch

It's just as easy to create a blank form. You'll need to decide which method works best for you. In the beginning, you'll probably create blank forms to learn the basics. As you get more experienced, you'll most likely copy more forms to use as your starting point. To create a new blank form, just follow these steps:

1. Open the Mastering R5 for Chapter 18 database.

2. Choose Create ➢ Design ➢ Form.

A blank form will display in the Work area of the Designer workspace, as shown in Figure 18.5.

FIGURE 18.5

A blank form in the Work area of the Designer workspace

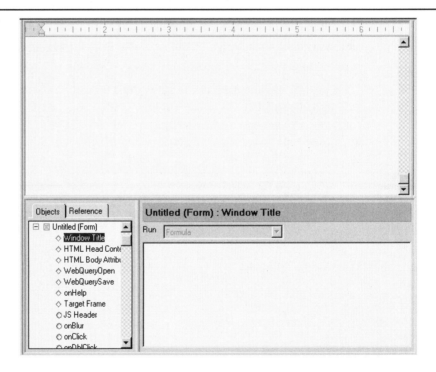

As you can see, the form is entirely blank, which means that you'll need to input everything. This can be quite tedious at times, and copying a form is sometimes a better option. With the blank form still displayed, let's step through some of the highlights of the form properties.

The Form Properties

Just like the database, a form has a set of properties that control its overall behavior. To open the Form Properties InfoBox, choose Design ➤ Form Properties. The InfoBox contains seven tabs: Form Info, Defaults, Launch, Form Background, Header, Printing, and Security. Because the Printing tab is the same as it is in the Database Properties InfoBox, it will be skipped in this section.

The Form Info Tab

The Form Info tab is used to store fundamental information about the form. An example of the Form Info tab is shown in Figure 18.6. The properties are discussed in the following sections.

PART

V

Beyond the Client: Uti-
lizing Domino Designer

FIGURE 18.6

The Form Info tab of the Form Properties InfoBox

Name   When you create a form, you must assign a name to it. For our example, type **Recipe | Recipe** in the Name field. The name of the form is Recipe and the name following the vertical bar (|) is the form's alias (in this case, it is the same name as the form). Sometimes an end user won't like the name you selected for the form. The name of the form will appear in various places in the Notes client (the Create menu, the Search Builder, etc.), and you may have to change it if the users don't like it. To complicate matters, you may have already hard-coded the form name in various places throughout your application. This is where aliases come into play. With an alias, you can assign a name to the form that is separate from the name the user sees. If you rename the form, the alias remains the same. You can reference any design element by either its true name or its alias.

Comment   Although dreaded by most developers, it is a good idea to add some basic comments for every design element. We assure you that it will pay off in the long run. For our example, type **Original recipe form** in the Comment field.

Type   As mentioned previously, there are three document types. This form is a Document as opposed to a Response or Response to Response. When a new document is created, the Recipe document will always be created first (you cannot create a Response or Response to Response document until the Main document is created).

Display   The Include in Menu check box and drop-down list box determine if an option to create the Recipe document will be included in the Create menu in the Notes client. The Include in Search Builder check box determines if the recipe form can be used for entering search criteria when you use the By Form button, which is one of the advanced properties of the search bar. Selecting this option will not have any effect on a Web application.

Versioning   Versioning is a powerful option that allows you to determine if the original, unmodified version of a document should be saved when the document is modified. It is similar to taking a snapshot of the original document, saving the snapshot, and then allowing changes to be made. You can decide if the new version should become a response to the document, if the prior version should become a response to the document, or if the new version should become a sibling document. You can also specify whether versioning is automatic or manual. Selecting this option will not have any effect on a Web application.

Default Database Form   The Default Database Form option designates the form as the default for the database. There may be cases when the form for a document is not available (if someone deleted it, for example). If that happens, the default form is used. You should always specify a default form for a database. For our example, select this option.

Store Form in Document   If the Store Form in Document option is selected, Notes keeps a copy of the form within the document. Not only will the data be stored in the document, but the entire definition for the form will be stored as well. This option makes the form static because the definition is stored in the document. A major drawback to this approach is that changes made to the form will not be reflected in any document created before the form was changed. This option also takes up a lot of space in your database. Each time a document is saved, the form must be saved as well. You should consider using this option when documents will be sent to other users or in databases in which the original form is not available. For our example, do not select this option.

Disable Field Exchange   The Disable Field Exchange option disables Notes Field Exchange (F/X) for the form. F/X allows you to design forms so the field contents of an OLE server application (such as MS Word) will automatically appear in the corresponding fields of a Notes document. Depending on the types of fields involved, changing the contents of a field in Notes may automatically update the field in the OLE application or vice versa. Selecting this option will not have any effect on a Web application. For our example, do not select this option.

Automatically Refresh Fields   The Automatically Refresh Fields option could have a dramatic impact on performance when it is selected for forms that contain a large number of computed fields. This option will force the form to recalculate when each field is exited. It has the same effect as pressing the F9 key or choosing the View ➤ Refresh menu option. This option can be quite helpful on forms that require the user to see how changing various field entries affects other fields. When this option is selected, however, field validation occurs on each field as it is exited, which can sometimes be distracting to users. Selecting this option will not have any effect on a Web application. For our example, do not select this option.

Anonymous Form   When Anonymous Form is selected, the $UpdatedBy field (which usually stores information about who last updated the document) will not be created. Instead, the $Anonymous field will be created with a value of 1 to try to hide the name of the user. You can, however, still capture the name via the @UserName function and store it in a field, hence eliminating the anonymity of the user. Selecting this option does not automatically remove any reference to a user, nor will it have any effect on a Web application. For our example, do not select this option.

PART

V

Beyond the Client: Uti-
lizing Domino Designer

 WARNING   You can also use the User Activity log to determine who an anonymous user is. Just look at the date and time a document was created and compare that to the date, time, and users in the activity log.

Merge Replication Conflicts   A replication conflict occurs when two people on different servers edit the same document. When you select Merge Replication Conflicts, Domino will attempt to merge the replication conflicts when the database is replicated to another server. If the two users happen to change the same fields when they edit the document, the documents will remain "conflicting" and the merge will not be completed because the server doesn't really know which document's field value should override the other. Selecting this option will not have any effect on a Web application. For our example, do not select this option.

What Are Replication and Save Conflicts?

In Notes, multiple users can edit and save the same document in the same database or on multiple replica databases. When this happens, either a replication or a save conflict could occur. When either of these conditions happens, Domino will store one document as the Main document and any other documents as Response documents. Each Response document will be named either Replication Conflict or Save Conflict. Domino keeps track of the date and time a document is edited to determine which document becomes the Main document and which document(s) become Response documents.

A replication conflict occurs when two or more users edit the same document on different replicas. During the next replication, the actual replication conflict will occur. To determine which document will become the Main document and which document will be become a response, Domino follows a few simple rules:

- The document that has been edited the most will become the Main document and all others will become responses.
- If all copies of the documents have been edited the same number of times, the most recently saved document will become the Main document and all others will become responses.
- If one document has been deleted and any other documents have been edited, the deletion will take precedence and all of the documents will be removed (unless the edit took place after the time the document was deleted).

If the Merge Replication Conflicts option is enabled for a form, Domino takes a slightly different approach to resolving the conflicts. If no two identical fields have been edited in any of the documents, Domino will automatically merge all the changes into one document, thus resolving the conflict. The key to remember is that, if the same field has been edited on different replicas, Domino cannot merge the documents because it would be required to decide which change is valid and which change to ignore. As you can see, this can be quite challenging.

On the other hand, a save conflict occurs when two or more users edit the same document on the same server. Which fields the users change does not matter. If this occurs, the first document to be saved becomes the Main document. After that, any of the other users saving the document will be prompted by a dialog box warning them that the document will be saved as a save conflict. If the user chooses to save the document, it will automatically become a response to the Main document.

The Defaults Tab

The Defaults tab defines the overall form defaults when the form is used to either open or close a document. Figure 18.7 shows an example of the Defaults tab of the Form Properties InfoBox.

The Defaults tab of the Form Properties InfoBox

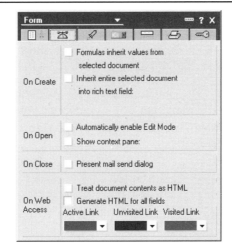

On Create The On Create options only affect a document when it is being created. One nice feature is the ability to "inherit" values from a selected document. Select the Formulas Inherit Values from Selected Documents option to allow a field on a form to inherit the values from the selected document (this can be a document highlighted on a view or the document that is currently open). A small bit of programming using a formula is required for each inheriting field (more about this later in the chapter). The Inherit Entire Selected Document into Rich Text Field option is similar but does not require any programming. When this option is selected, two new drop-down list boxes are displayed. The first will list all of the rich text fields that are on the form. You can select any of them to contain the inherited document. The second allows you to specify how the inherited document will be displayed on the form. You have three options to choose from: as a link, as collapsible rich text, or as regular rich text. The first option just places a link to the inherited document into the rich text field. The second and third options make a copy of the inherited document and place the contents into the rich text field. The main difference between the second and third options is that one will be collapsible. Although you can inherit values from a document for a Web application, you cannot inherit an entire document into a rich text field as a link. For our example, do not select any of the On Create options.

On Open   The On Open options affect the behavior of the document when it is opened. When Automatically Enable Edit Mode is selected, the selected document is opened in Edit mode in both the Notes client and a Web application. If the user has only Read access, the document will open in Edit mode within the Notes client but cannot be saved (the user will get an "authorization failure" message). If the Show Context Pane option is selected, the screen automatically splits in half when the document is opened in the Notes client (this option is not supported on the Web). The upper pane will always show the opened document. The lower pane will display either the parent document (for Response documents) or the document for the first doclink found in the text. For our example, do not select either of these options.

On Close   The On Close option affects the behavior of the document when it is closed. Present Mail Send Dialog is a bit of a misnomer. When a document is closed in the Notes client, the Close Window dialog box displays. This dialog box does not allow users to address mail; it only allows them to send or discard the mail message. It is up to you, the designer, to make sure there is a special field called SendTo that contains the mail addresses. Without this field, the user will get an error message stating that the SendTo field does not exist. This option works a bit differently on the Web. Instead of the Close Window dialog box displaying, an attempt to send the document is automatically made (if the SendTo field is not set up correctly, an error will be generated). This option doesn't actually work every time a document is closed. The function is smart enough to determine if a field has changed or not. The mail message will be sent only if a field has changed. For our example, do not select this option.

On Web Access   As its name implies, this section contains options that apply only to Web applications. When the Treat Document Contents as HTML option is selected, the Domino server knows that all the data on the document is already in HTML and doesn't convert it. This option is helpful for pasting HTML files directly into a Notes database. Generate HTML for All Fields fixes one of the most troublesome problems with the previous release, hidden fields. When this option is selected, an HTML field is generated for every field on the form. Although the fields are hidden, you still have programmatic access to their contents. This is great news for Web developers, but it also increases the size of the HTML document dramatically. The last three options allow the developer to change the default active link, unvisited link, and visited link colors. For our example, do not select any of these options and leave the colors set to the default.

The Launch Tab

In the Launch tab, you can specify that various options "automatically" launch when an event occurs. The Auto Launch options will automatically launch the first attachment, document link, or OLE object in the document when it is opened, depending on which property you select. These options do not work for a Web application. The site to which the URL points will also launch when the document is opened (this option does work on the Web). The remaining Auto Launch options are somewhat dependent on what applications you have defined on your workstation. For example, if you select the Word-Pad Document Auto Launch option and keep all the defaults, an empty WordPad window is presented when the user is creating a new document. After the user creates the document and closes WordPad, the information is saved in the Notes document as well. You can design a form specifically for these options and create a powerful combination of Notes and other software packages. For our example, leave the default setting.

The Form Background Tab

The options on the Form Background tab are for those who don't like the generic white background of the form. The Autoframe options allow you to specify whether or not the form should use frames. If a frameset and frame are selected, the form will always be displayed in the selected frame within the frameset. As shown in Figure 18.8, there are quite a few options available.

PART V
Beyond the Client: Utilizing Domino Designer

FIGURE 18.8

The Form Background tab of the Form Properties InfoBox

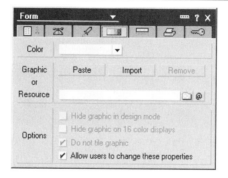

Click the arrow next to the Color drop-down list box to display the Color Picker, from which you can choose a color for the background.

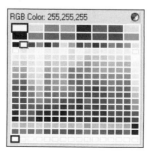

You can also paste or import a custom image by using the buttons in the Graphic or Resource section. To paste an image, you must first copy it to the Clipboard. If you forget to place the image on the Clipboard, a dialog box appears with the message, "Background image must be a bitmap." When importing an image, you'll be presented with the Import dialog box. You can select from BMP, GIF, JPEG, PCX, or TIF image files. If you want to remove your image, just click the Remove button (this button is not selectable unless an image is already present as the background).

 TIP If you want to insert high-quality graphics onto your form, don't use the Paste button because it will decrease the color fidelity. Instead, either import the image or use an image resource. It is also more work to copy an image to the Clipboard and then paste it than it is to just select an image.

You can also select an image from the Insert Image Resource dialog box, as shown in Figure 18.9. These images, which have been saved as image resources (discussed in more detail in Chapter 19) in the database, can be selected from a dialog box and pasted directly on the form. You can also use a formula to dynamically change the background image on a form. Just base the formula on the value of a field, and when the formula is recalculated, the image changes. All of these options work on the Web.

FIGURE 18.9

The Insert Image Resource dialog box

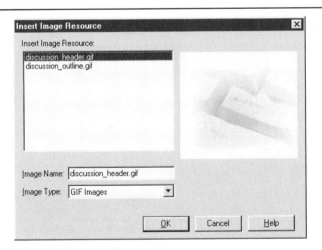

There are also a few selections available to you in the Options section of the Form Background tab. When selected, Hide Graphic in Design Mode allows you to prevent the graphic from being displayed while you are working on the form (it is sometimes distracting to display the graphic while you are trying to lay out the form). You also have the ability to hide the graphic from users whose monitors can only display 16 colors by selecting the Hide Graphic on 16 Color Displays option. With the Do Not Tile Graphic option, you can prevent the image from being tiled across your entire form. The last option, Allow Users to Change These Properties, allows users to override the background properties. For our example, leave the default settings.

The Header Tab

Domino Designer allows you to create a non-scrollable header simulating the look of having two frames within a form. With this option, you can slice the form into sections that may or may not scroll. You can freeze the header so that certain key pieces of information are always visible as a user scrolls through a document. One drawback is that this option is only available for users in the Notes client.

Getting this option to work is a bit tricky. You must select the Add Header to Form check box (see Figure 18.10) to enable the other options on the tab. However, you must first select the text the header should contain, so if you don't have any text or fields on your form, you won't be able to select the Add Header to Form check box (it will be grayed out). This means that you must have at least one line containing either a field or text to select. Once you select the text, the Add Header to Form check box option will be enabled, allowing you to select it. You can also change the height, the scrolling, and how the header separator line will display (the Border option). For a good example of how to use this option, refer to your mail file and the Memo form. For our example, leave the default settings (because we don't yet have any text or fields on our form).

PART

V

Beyond the Client: Utilizing Domino Designer

FIGURE 18.10

The Header tab

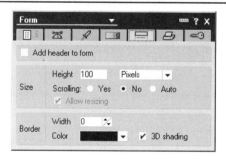

The Security Tab

Security is everywhere in Notes, and the form is no exception. As a designer, you can use the Security tab to decide who can read and create documents. As shown in Figure 18.11, there are two security options for reading and creating documents.

FIGURE 18.11

The Security tab of the Form Properties InfoBox

All Readers and Above   With this option, you can allow or deny Read access for any documents created with this form. By default, the All Readers and Above option is selected, so all users who have Read access (dependent on the database ACL) will be able to read the document. You can override this by deselecting the option, which will open up the list box for selecting individuals, groups, or servers who can read the document. The list box is a duplicate of the current database ACL. If the entry you would like to select doesn't exist in the list, you can click the address book icon, which displays the Names dialog box and allows you to "pick and choose" from the Domino Directory. When a document is created, Notes will automatically insert a readers field called $Readers, which includes all the entries selected from the Security tab. Because the security uses a Readers field, if a user is not listed in the readers field, the document will never display in a view in the Notes client or a Web application (readers fields will be discussed in more detail later).

WARNING   Deselecting the All Readers and Above option only affects documents created after the change. Everyone will still be able to read documents created prior to the change.

All Authors and Above   With the All Authors and Above option, you can decide who can use this form to create documents. By default, this option is selected, so all users who have Create access (dependent on the database ACL) will be allowed to create documents. You can override this by deselecting the option, which works the same as the All Readers and Above option. Users who are denied access to create documents using the form won't be able to create a document from the Create menu. If they try to create a new document via the form, they will see the error message "You have insufficient access to perform this operation." If the user tries to create a document using the form via a Web application, they will see the error message "You are not authorized to perform that operation." Don't get this option confused with author fields. It does not use an author field to prevent document changes; it blocks the user from using this form to create a document.

There are two other options on the Security tab. The Disable Printing/Forwarding/Copying to Clipboard and Available to Public Access Users options are both not selected by default. The Disable Printing/Forwarding/Copying to Clipboard option is not really a *secure* way to prevent users from printing the form, forwarding it, or copying it to the Clipboard. It is more of a convenience for the developer to disable this function; instead of having to mark each element as not printable, for example, the developer can just mark it at a high level.

On the other hand, the Available to Public Access Users option is quite handy and powerful. It works in conjunction with the database ACL and lets you allow those with No Access or Depositor access to view specific documents without having to grant them Reader access to the entire database (you should also grant this access to at least one view or folder). All you need to do to make this work is select the option and create a field on the form called $PublicAccess. Set the value of this field to 1 to grant public access for viewing (set it to 0 to block access to the public users). This works for both the Notes client and Web applications.

Creating a Document

Before continuing with the creation of our form, let's digress for a moment and look at how documents are actually created by a user. Earlier in this chapter, we mentioned allowing a user access to create a document via the Create menu. Although this method is simple, there are quite a few variations for allowing a user to create documents.

Cascading Menus

If you have a number of forms available, it may be a bit overwhelming to the end user if they're listed one after another under the Create menu. To organize the list, you can group related forms so they cascade from a submenu. To create a cascading menu, all you need to do is use the \ operator (commonly referred to as the escape character) in the name of the form. For example, suppose you have created three forms called Cascaded 1, Cascaded 2, and Cascaded 3. To have all three grouped together under the Create menu option, add a group name followed by the \ to the name of each form. In this example, you would name them Menu Example\Cascaded 1, Menu Example\Cascaded 2, and Menu Example\Cascaded 3. Select the Create Menu option from the Include in Menu drop-down list box in the Form Info tab, and all three forms will display in the Notes client as shown in Figure 18.12.

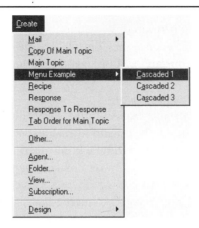

FIGURE 18.12

Grouping common forms on the Create menu

The Other Menu

If the Create menu is beginning to get a bit crowded or confusing, another option is to place some of the less important forms under the Other submenu (refer to Figure 18.12 and you'll see that there is a menu option called Other). When this option is selected in the Notes client, the Other dialog box will display. To place a form on the Other submenu, select the Create-Other Dialog option from the Include in Menu drop-down list box on the Form Info tab.

Web Applications

Because the Create menu option is only available in the Notes client, users must create documents in Web applications differently. First, there is no easy selection on the Form Info tab that will magically display a Create Document option. Every create option must be coded by the designer.

The simplest technique is to create a button, Action, or hotspot that includes the necessary formula, such as `@Command([compose];"Your form name here")`. A good example of this was shown in Figure 18.1. Notice that there is a New Topic Action button that appears in the top of the view. This Action button is located in the actual view itself. Although this type of process is designed for Web applications, it works equally well for the Notes client.

The Design Document Properties InfoBox

We'll discuss one last topic before we proceed further. By now, you probably realize that every element within a Notes database has an associated Properties InfoBox. There is another type of InfoBox that is available for all of the design elements: the Design Document Properties InfoBox. Every element accessible from the work area of the programmer's pane has one. To see this InfoBox in action, follow these steps:

1. Open the Mastering R5 for Chapter 18 database.

2. In the Design pane, select the Forms design element from the Design list (all the forms in the Work pane will display).

3. In the Work pane, highlight the Main Topic form.

4. Choose Design ➤ Design Properties (you can also right-click on the Main Topic form and choose Design Properties).

The Design Document Properties InfoBox consists of four tabs: the Info tab, the Fields tab, the Design tab, and the Document ID's tab.

NOTE There is another very similar InfoBox called Document Properties. It can be accessed by selecting a document from a view and choosing Edit ➤ Properties, pressing Alt+Enter, or right-clicking on the document and selecting Document Properties.

The Info Tab

The Info tab, shown in Figure 18.13, is a "display-only" tab. It displays various dates and times related to the design element; you cannot modify any options. The Created field displays the date and time the design element was initially created. The Modified field displays the date and time the design element was modified in the original file (remember that there could be replicas). The Added field displays the date and time the design element was originally added to this database. The second Modified field displays the date and time the design element was last modified in this database. The Accessed field displays the date on which the design element was last read. The tab also displays the size (in bytes) of the entire design element.

FIGURE 18.13

*The Info tab for a
design element*

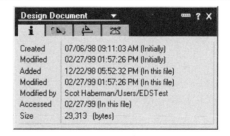

The Fields Tab

The Fields tab contains a list of every field in the design document. The left pane lists all the fields, and the right pane lists the highlighted field's properties, such as field name, data type, length, and so on. The right pane will also show the contents of the highlighted field.

The Design Tab

In Chapter 16, we discussed using a template to create a database. When a database is refreshed (either manually or automatically via the Domino Design task), the template designated for the database will automatically update the design elements. This is great when you only have one template, but sometimes a database uses more than one template, and there may be elements in the database that the various templates should refresh. For this purpose, you can use the Inherit from the Design Template field on the Design tab (see Figure 18.14). For each individual element, you can specify whether the design should be refreshed from a template. This option overrides using the template designated for an entire database, but only for the individual element. For example, if you put something into the Inherit from the Design Template field for, say, a particular form or view in a database that inherits from some other template, that form or view will then inherit from the named template rather than the database template.

FIGURE 18.14

The Design tab for an individual design element

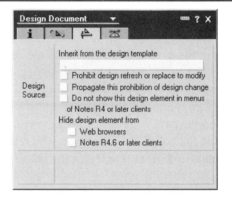

Select the Prohibit Design Refresh or Replace to Modify option to prevent either a refresh or replace from removing or modifying the design element. This feature can be extremely handy when you have modified a design element and want to keep your changes, yet you are also inheriting the database design from a template. Another option that also deals with design elements inheriting changes is Propagate This Prohibition of Design Change. Enabling this option will prevent the Prohibit Design Refresh or Replace to Modify setting from being sent along when a database is refreshed. This option can be quite helpful in very specific situations. For example, suppose you have a template and you don't want any of the design elements to be refreshed or replaced, so you enable the Prohibit Design Refresh or Replace to Modify option. When a database is refreshed from this template, it will also inherit this setting. The problem is that none of the database design elements will ever get refreshed. If you enable the Propagate This

Prohibition of Design Change option, the Prohibit Design Refresh or Replace to Modify option will not be enabled on the database, but it will stay intact on the template.

 WARNING When a design element is copied, the Prohibit Design Element Refresh or Replace to Modify option is automatically enabled unless the design element inherits from a template.

The options in the Hide Design Element From section are quite powerful yet not very evident to the designer. You can choose to hide an element from Web browsers, Notes R4.6 or later clients, or both. This can be important for design elements to which you don't want a particular environment to have access. For example, assume that an application will be accessible from both the Notes client and the Web. For design reasons, a form needs to be specifically designed for each environment. The Notes client version of the form will allow editing, whereas the Web version will only allow viewing. The Notes client form's name is Form Client | MyForm, and the Web form's name is Form Web | MyForm. There are two forms with the same alias, so how will Notes know which to use? This is where hiding the design element comes in handy. For the Form Client, select the Web Browsers option so the Form client cannot be viewed from a Web browser. For the Form Web, select the Notes R4.6 or Later Clients option so the Form Web cannot be viewed from the Notes client. Any document created with the Form Client will store the form alias MyForm internally in the Form field. Because the Form Web also has the alias MyForm, there won't be any problem displaying the document correctly. When creating an application that will be accessed from both the Web and the Notes client, we prefer to create two separate forms and hide them from the appropriate environments. This may duplicate some maintenance, but it allows you to design your form specifically for a particular environment.

The Document ID's Tab

 The Document ID's tab is also a "display-only" tab. It includes the internal identification information for the design document, as shown in Figure 18.15. Remember that everything in a Notes database is a document and design elements are no exception. Therefore, what is described here will also apply to the actual data documents themselves.

FIGURE 18.15

The Document ID's tab

The combination of letters and numbers actually do have some meaning. Contained within the ID section are the following:

Originator ID (OID) Consists of the Originator ID File (*OF* followed by 16 digits), the Originator ID Note (*ON* followed by 16 digits), the Sequence Time (*SD* followed by 16 digits), and the Sequence Number (8 digits following *SN*). The OID identifies a particular revision of a note regardless of the location (remember that documents can reside in multiple replicas).

Universal Note ID (UNID) Consists of the Originator ID File (*OF* followed by 16 digits) and the Originator ID Note (*ON* followed by 16 digits). The UNID identifies all copies of a note regardless of location or time it was modified.

Global Note ID (GNID) Consists of the Database ID (*DB* followed by 16 digits) and the Note ID (*NT* followed by 8 digits). The GNID identifies a specific note in a specific database.

Database ID The database ID, as identified in the GNID, is actually the replica ID for the database.

Note ID (NID) The NID, as identified in the GNID, identifies a note in a database. The NID is the actual file position of the note.

Basic Form Design Elements

An empty form is useless (which is exactly the state of your Recipe form). Without any of the form elements, the user won't be able to interact with the database. Domino Designer has a wide variety of design elements available for the designer to use for both the Notes client and Web applications. In this section, we'll review the more basic, common form design elements. The more advanced design concepts and elements can be found in Chapter 19, "Advanced Form Design."

The Form Events

In Chapter 17, we briefly mentioned some form events when discussing areas in which formulas can be used. In this section, we'll expand a bit further.

To get started, refer back to your empty Recipe form (if the form is not open, select it from the Work pane). When a form is first opened, the Form object is always highlighted in the Objects tab of the programmer's pane, as shown in Figure 18.16. Notice that the Form object is shown by its alias name (remember that our form name and alias name are the same). The type of object is in parentheses next to the name. For our example, it is labeled Recipe (Form). Each object in the Objects tab is expandable by clicking the plus (+) sign. This will reveal all the events available for the selected object.

FIGURE 18.16

*The Form object for
the Recipe form in the
Objects tab*

Each event in the list of events for the object has a symbol next to it. This symbol
has two meanings. First, it can designate what type of programming language was
used to create the event. Second, if the symbol is filled in (used), you know that there
is an Action associated to the corresponding event. If there is not an Action associated
to the event, the symbol is unused. Table 18.1 displays the programming language,
the unused symbol, and the used symbol.

TABLE 18.1: EVENTS SYMBOL LIST

Programming Language	Unused Symbol	Used Symbol
Formula language	◇	◆
Java	◻	◼
JavaScript	◯	◉
LotusScript	⚡	⚡
Simple action(s)	♟	♟

Specifying a Window Title

The Window Title event allows you to decide what should display in the title bar for the form. This works for both Notes client and Web applications. To add a title for the form, follow these steps:

1. Highlight the Window Title event in the Objects tab. This will display the script area in the programmer's pane.

2. Type **@If(@IsNewDoc;"New Recipe";NameOfRecipe)** for the title to be displayed.

With this particular event, you can only use a formula to specify the title. You may notice that the drop-down list box is grayed out. As you will see later, some events allow you to use various types of code. Also, the title displayed for the script area window always reflects the current object, a colon, and then the selected event.

NOTE Pay special attention to the commands you use in the Window Title event if the application is to be used on the Web. Some commands that work in the Notes client don't work on the Web.

The code for the Window Title event looks a bit overwhelming, but it's really not that complicated. The formula first checks to see if the document is new or if the document already exists. For a new document, the title will be New Recipe. For an existing document, the title will display the contents of the NameOfRecipe field, which we will be creating shortly.

Formatting Documents with HTML

There are two specific events that let the designer manipulate some of the HTML generated by the Domino server. Both of these events are recognized regardless of how Treat Document Contents as HTML is set on the Defaults tab of the Form Properties InfoBox. The HTML Head Content event allows you to specify a formula that will modify the <HEAD> tag attributes for a Web page. None of the contents within a <HEAD> tag are actually displayed, but you can specify things such as keywords for search engines. The other event, HTML Body Attributes, allows you to modify the <BODY> tag attributes. These tags can include the different link colors, the form background colors, or margin sizes for the Web page. Both of these events only affect Web applications.

NOTE For developers with previous Notes design experience, the HTML Head Content event can be used to replace the contents of the $$HTMLHead field.

The Web Query Agents

One major drawback to Web applications is that many of the events related to a document are not recognized, most notably, the QueryOpen and QuerySave events (these will be discussed later). This is not because of any fault of the Notes software; it's caused by a major difference in how browsers interact with the server. This limitation brought about a need to trap an event for Web applications just before a document is displayed and just before a document is saved.

Hence, the WebQueryOpen and the WebQuerySave events were created. When displayed, both contain the following command in the script area:

```
@Command([ToolsRunMacro]; "<Your agent goes here>")
```

By replacing the text *Your agent goes here* with the name of your Agent, you can easily access a Web document just before it opens or just before it is saved. The actual semantics of how this is accomplished will be discussed in Chapter 22, which covers Agents specifically. You just need to be aware that it is possible to accomplish either of these tasks by using the two events. These two events only pertain to Web applications because the Notes clients has many more events that are specific to its environment and allow a designer programmatic access to the document.

Giving the Users Help

The HelpRequest event is specifically designed to work in conjunction with the F1 key in the Notes client. When a user presses the F1 key while accessing a document using this form, the HelpRequest event will be checked for access to a specific Help document.

Using the following syntax, you can specify that a specific document in the database be displayed:

```
@Command([OpenHelpDocument]; server : database; viewname; key)
```

Because this event is activated by pressing the F1 key, it doesn't apply to Web applications. To create Help for a Web application, define a button or hotspot and use the @Command([OpenHelpDocument]) function.

 WARNING In the Domino Designer Help file, a search for the HelpRequest event will yield no documents. The Help file refers to this event as onHelpRequest.

 TIP You can also create pages within the database and use the @Command([OpenPage]) command to open them.

PART

V

Beyond the Client: Utilizing Domino Designer

The JavaScript Events

One big improvement with R5 is the ability to run JavaScript in the Notes client (it has always worked with Web applications). With this new ability came the incorporation of JavaScript events in Domino Designer. These new events benefit both the Notes client and Web applications. The new JavaScript events do not replace the LotusScript user interface (UI) events but work alongside them and enhance the capabilities of an application.

Before R5, for a Web application to trap certain events (such as onClick), Java-Script code had to be embedded on forms as pass-thru HTML. Now that these events are exposed in Domino Designer as events, the code can be placed directly into the event. This makes the form not only much cleaner but a lot easier to maintain as well. These events are also extremely beneficial to the Notes client. Many of the new Java-Script events that have been added to Domino Designer could never be trapped in previous versions. This will make it possible to develop more powerful applications. Now you can have a form that has code for both the Notes client and the Web application in one place. Just remember that each of the following events are defined on the form and that each element on a form will also have its own series of JavaScript events.

Table 18.2 lists the JavaScript events, many of which can be closely correlated to a LotusScript UI event. Keep in mind that most of these events work in both the Notes client and Web applications.

TABLE 18.2: THE JAVASCRIPT EVENTS

Event	Description
JS Header	This event is actually a JavaScript placeholder. You can use it to define JavaScript functions and variables that will be used in other places on the form. Now you can type and maintain all of your JavaScript in one place. This may seem a bit trivial, but in previous releases, JavaScript would have a tendency to be scattered and hidden in various elements.
onBlur	Triggered when a window, frame, or frameset loses focus.
onClick	Triggered when the mouse is clicked in the window.
onDblClick	Triggered when the mouse is double-clicked in the window (this event will yield unpredictable results if you also specify an onClick action because the onClick event will always occur before the onDblClick event).
onFocus	Triggered when a window, frame, or frameset receives focus.
onHelp	This event does not ever occur for the window.

Continued ▶

TABLE 18.2: THE JAVASCRIPT EVENTS (CONTINUED)	
Event	**Description**
onKeyDown, onKeyPress, onKeyUp	Triggered when the user depresses a key (onKeyDown), presses or holds down a key (onKeyPress), and releases a key (onKeyUp).
onLoad	Triggered when the window is completely loaded.
onMouseDown, onMouseMove, onMouseOut, onMouseOver, onMouseUp	Triggered when a user depresses the mouse button (onMouseDown), when a user moves the cursor (onMouseMove), when the mouse pointer leaves the client area (onMouseOut), when the mouse pointer moves over the client area from outside the client area (onMouseOver), and when the user releases the mouse button (onMouseUp).
onReset	Triggered when a user resets a form via a Reset button.
onSubmit	Triggered when a document is submitted in Web applications or when a document is saved in the Notes client. This event is similar to the QuerySave event.
onLoad	Triggered after a document is loaded in Web applications or opened in the Notes client. This is a good place to perform any type of initialization for a document. This event is similar to the PostOpen event.
onUnload	Triggered after a document is unloaded in Web applications or closed in the Notes client. This is a good place to perform any type of cleanup for a document. This event is similar to the QueryClose event.

The UI Events

The remaining events on the form are commonly referred to as the LotusScript UI events. This is a bit of a misnomer because you can use formulas or LotusScript in all but four of the events. All of the events are only recognized by the Notes client user interface (UI) and do not apply to Web applications.

Why would you need to know about all these events? They can come in quite handy for an application. A good place to initialize a wizard that would guide a user through a specific set of steps would be from one of these events (such as the PostOpen). Knowing about these events is extremely helpful if you ever need to understand or dissect one of the master templates. Table 18.3 lists the UI events.

TABLE 18.3: THE UI EVENTS	
Event	**Description**
(Options), (Declarations), Initialize, Terminate	These events only recognize LotusScript. The (Options) and (Declarations) events define the options and variables that are global in nature to the form. Once set, all events of the form will recognize these settings. The Initialize event is executed only once when the form is opened. The Terminate event is also executed only once, when the form is closed.
QueryOpen	This event is triggered when a document is opened in the Notes client, but it's triggered before the document is actually opened. You may not be able to access all of the document fields because the document has not been fully initialized.
PostOpen	This event is triggered when a document is opened and fully initialized in the Notes client. All fields are available for querying.
QueryModeChange	This event is triggered before a document is changed to Read or Edit mode in the Notes client.
PostModeChange	This event is triggered after a document is changed to Read or Edit mode in the Notes client.
PostRecalc	This event is triggered after a document has been refreshed in the Notes client. All of the values on the document have been recalculated.
QuerySave	This event is triggered before a document is saved in the Notes client.
PostSave	This event is triggered after a document is saved in the Notes client.
QueryClose	This event is triggered before a document is closed in the Notes client.

 TIP If you need to declare LotusScript variables and functions/subroutines that are global to all elements of a form, use the (Globals) object of the form.

Domino Form Events

Table 18.4 is a quick reference for all the form events, the language you can use, and whether or not they work in the Notes client or the Web.

TABLE 18.4: DOMINO FORM EVENTS

Event	Language	Notes	Web
Window Title	Formula	Yes	Yes
HTML Head Attributes	Formula	No	Yes
HTML Body Attributes	Formula	No	Yes
WebQueryOpen	Formula	No	Yes
WebQuerySave	Formula	No	Yes
HelpRequest	Formula	Yes	No
TargetFrame	Formula	Yes	Yes
JS Header	JavaScript	Yes	Yes
onBlur	JavaScript	No	Yes*
onClick	JavaScript	Yes	Yes
onDblClick	JavaScript	No	Yes**
onFocus	JavaScript	No	Yes
onHelp	JavaScript	No	No
onKeyDown	JavaScript	No	Yes
onKeyPress	JavaScript	No	Yes
onKeyUp	JavaScript	No	Yes
onLoad	JavaScript	Yes	Yes
onMouseDown	JavaScript	No	Yes
onMouseMove	JavaScript	No	Yes
onMouseOut	JavaScript	No	Yes
onMouseOver	JavaScript	No	Yes
onMouseUp	JavaScript	No	Yes
onReset	JavaScript	No	Yes
onSumbit	JavaScript	Yes	Yes
onUnload	JavaScript	Yes	Yes
(Options)	LotusScript	Yes	No
(Declarations)	LotusScript	Yes	No
QueryOpen	LotusScript		
	Formula	Yes	No
PostOpen	LotusScript		
	Formula	Yes	No
QueryModeChange	LotusScript		
	Formula	Yes	No
PostModeChange	LotusScript		
	Formula	Yes	No

Continued ▶

* The event is not being properly interpreted, hence it does not work.

** Yields unpredictable results if you also specify an onClick event.

TABLE 18.4: DOMINO FORM EVENTS (CONTINUED)			
Event	**Language**	**Notes**	**Web**
PostRecalc	LotusScript		
	Formula	Yes	No
QuerySave	LotusScript		
	Formula	Yes	No
PostSave	LotusScript		
	Formula	Yes	No
QueryClose	LotusScript		
	Formula	Yes	No
Initialize	LotusScript	Yes	No
Terminate	LotusScript	Yes	No

* The event is not being properly interpreted, hence it does not work.

** Yields unpredictable results if you also specify an onClick event.

Using Static Text

Also referred to as a label, static text is not actually a field. Placing static text on a form is as simple as typing. Static text is typically used to explain or help a user determine what each field should contain.

Let's start shaping our example Recipe form so it can be more useful for the end user. To add static text to the form, follow these steps:

1. Open the Mastering R5 for Chapter 18 database.

2. In the Design pane, expand the Forms design element in the Design list by clicking the plus (+) sign (this will display all the forms in the Work pane).

3. In the Work pane, open the Recipe form by double-clicking the Recipe form design element.

4. With cursor at the top of the form, type **My Favorite Recipe**, which will be used as a title for the form.

5. On the next line (press the Enter key to move the cursor to the next line), type **Name of Recipe:**.

6. Type the following text, each on a separate line: **Recipe Instructions:**, **Comments:**, **Created By:**, **Created On:**, **Last Updated By:**, and **Last Updated On:**.

When you have finished, your Recipe form should look similar to Figure 18.17. You can see that there is really nothing separating the title and the other static text. We need to make some formatting changes to make the text stand out a bit better. To change the size of the static text, you'll use the Text Properties InfoBox.

FIGURE 18.17

*The Recipe Form
containing static text*

```
My Favorite Recipe
Name of Recipe:
Recipe Instructions:
Comments:
Created By:
Created On:
Last Updated By:
Last Updated On:
```

As with any other InfoBox, the Text Properties InfoBox has various tabs you can use to change the text properties: Font, Paragraph Alignment, Paragraph Margins, Paragraph Hide-When, and Paragraph Styles. We'll discuss each tab individually and also change the text when applicable.

The Font Tab

You can use the Font tab to change text characteristics such as size, color, style, and font type. The fonts you can choose from are the fonts currently installed on your workstation. The only choices for styles are plain, bold, italic, underline, strikethrough, superscript, subscript, shadow, emboss, and extrude. Note that certain combinations can be selected together, whereas others cannot (you cannot have text that is both superscript and subscript). Be careful when choosing fonts for Web applications. If the user doesn't have a font you've chosen on his machine, it will not display properly.

For our Recipe form, let's go ahead and change the font characteristics for the static text:

1. Open the Text Properties InfoBox by choosing Text ➤ Text Properties (you can also right-click the static text and choose Text Properties). Select the Font tab.

2. Highlight the form title, My Favorite Recipe.

3. Choose Arial from the Font list box.

4. Select 18 from the Size list box (you can also type **18** directly in the Size field).

5. Select both the Bold and Shadow options from the Style list box (if you cannot see the Shadow option, scroll down in the list box). A check mark will be displayed next to each option you select.

6. From the Color drop-down list box, select Navy.

7. Leave the remaining text labels as they are (the default font options are Default Sans Serif, 10, Plain, and Black).

The Paragraph Alignment Tab

A paragraph of text can be left justified, right justified, centered, or formatted with equal spacing or no justification. You also have the ability to create hanging indents on the first line of each paragraph. Another handy tool for lists of text is the ability to create list identifiers. There are six choices: None, Bullet, Circle, Checkbox, Square, or Number. Instead of trying to explain how these options differ, we have created a sample form that displays the justification and list identifiers (see Figure 18.18). To see this form in action, open the Mastering R5 for Chapter 18 database in the Notes client and select the Example view. Open the document titled Paragraph Alignment Example.

There are also spacing options available for lines within the paragraph (interline), after the paragraph, and before the paragraph. All of the options on the Paragraph Alignment tab translate quite well in Web applications except the spacing options for within, before, and after a paragraph.

FIGURE 18.18

Text paragraph alignment properties

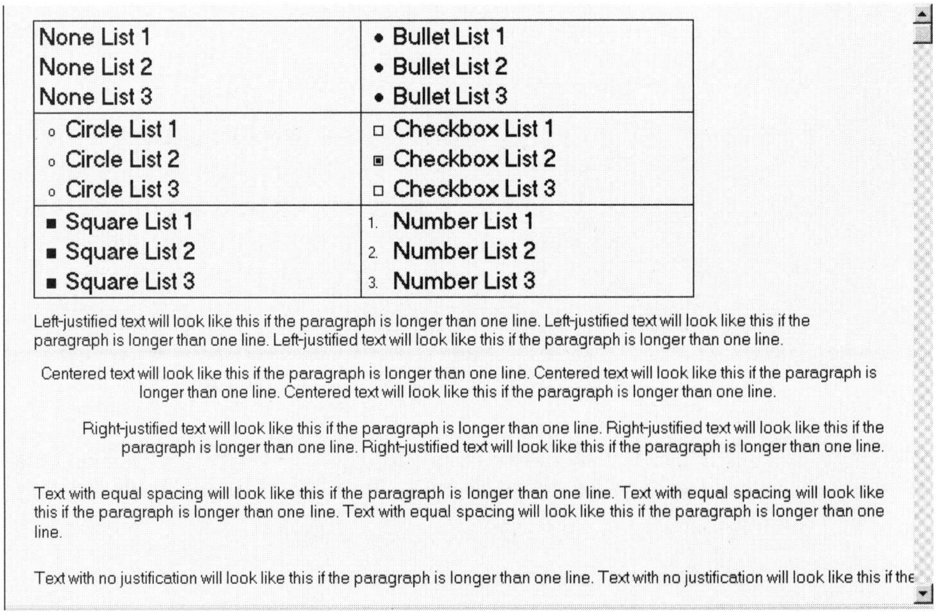

None List 1	• Bullet List 1
None List 2	• Bullet List 2
None List 3	• Bullet List 3
○ Circle List 1	□ Checkbox List 1
○ Circle List 2	▣ Checkbox List 2
○ Circle List 3	□ Checkbox List 3
■ Square List 1	1. Number List 1
■ Square List 2	2. Number List 2
■ Square List 3	3. Number List 3

Left-justified text will look like this if the paragraph is longer than one line. Left-justified text will look like this if the paragraph is longer than one line. Left-justified text will look like this if the paragraph is longer than one line.

Centered text will look like this if the paragraph is longer than one line. Centered text will look like this if the paragraph is longer than one line. Centered text will look like this if the paragraph is longer than one line.

Right-justified text will look like this if the paragraph is longer than one line. Right-justified text will look like this if the paragraph is longer than one line. Right-justified text will look like this if the paragraph is longer than one line.

Text with equal spacing will look like this if the paragraph is longer than one line. Text with equal spacing will look like this if the paragraph is longer than one line. Text with equal spacing will look like this if the paragraph is longer than one line.

Text with no justification will look like this if the paragraph is longer than one line. Text with no justification will look like this if the

To make a few modifications to the paragraph alignment in our Recipe form, follow these steps:

1. Open the Text Properties InfoBox by choosing Text ➤ Text Properties (you can also right-click the static text and choose Text Properties). Select the Paragraph Alignment tab.

2. Place the cursor on the same line as the form title, My Favorite Recipe.

3. Change the alignment of the paragraph to centered by clicking the centered button. Select $1^1/_2$ from the Spacing drop-down list box.

4. Place the cursor on the same line as the *Name of Recipe:* text.

5. Select 1^1/$_2$ from the Spacing drop-down list box.

6. Place your cursor at the beginning of the line that contains the *Comments:* text. Select all the text to the bottom of the form.

7. Select 1^1/$_2$ from the Spacing drop-down list box (because more than one paragraph is selected, this setting will apply to all of them in one shot, saving you a few steps).

The Paragraph Margins Tab

On the Paragraph Margins tab, you can specify both left and right margins for the selected text (in an absolute size in inches or a relative size in percentage). You can also specify various individual tab stops and pagination options. Other than the options for margins, these options do not necessarily work very well in Web applications. For our Recipe form, we'll just use the defaults.

TIP The relative percentage option for margins works extremely well for users who may be using different screen resolutions for your application. Instead of hard-coding a value, you can just specify that the right and left margins have a gap of 5 percent of the screen size.

The Paragraph Hide-When Tab

The Hide-When tab is probably the most widely used tab for most form elements. The Paragraph Hide-When tab will allow you to display or hide text based on quite a number of different options, as shown in Figure 18.19. The Hide Paragraph From section allows you to hide the text from either a Notes client or a Web browser. You can also hide text depending on the mode in which the document is opened (Read, Edit, etc.). Finally, you can use a formula to hide paragraphs. The options on this tab work equally well in both the Notes client and Web applications. For our example, leave the default settings (that is, nothing should be selected).

PART

V

Beyond the Client: Utilizing Domino Designer

FIGURE 18.19

The Paragraph Hide-When tab

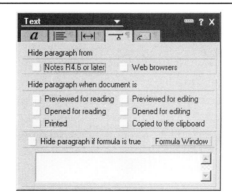

TIP If you always want to hide certain text, such as comments about the design of the form, you can select both the Notes R4.6 or Later and the Web Browsers options. You could also select all the options in the Hide Paragraph When Document Is section. One last alternative is to select the Hide Paragraph if Formula Is True option and type **1** for the formula (1 means True in the formula language).

The Paragraph Styles Tab

Styles allow you to predefine a specific set of text paragraph options and then save them. You can then apply these styles to various selections of text without having to redefine the paragraph options from the Text Properties InfoBox. Depending on which options you have selected for a style, they may or may not render correctly for Web applications. For our Recipe example, just leave the defaults.

When you have finished entering all the static text, your form should look similar to the Recipe form shown in Figure 18.20. Now you need to fill in all the gaps with fields that will allow the user to actually enter and view data for documents.

FIGURE 18.20

The Recipe form with the formatted static text labels

Creating Fields

By now, you should have a pretty good understanding of the properties of a form and how a form processes various user actions. The next step is to add all the components that the user will actually interact with.

Notes has quite a few different fields that you can use on a form. One really handy feature is that each field displays not only the field name but also an icon representing the actual field type. No longer do you have to open the Field Properties InfoBox to determine the field type. This visual representation of the field type is easy to understand and should save you quite a bit of time when you are designing a form. Because our Recipe form doesn't contain each and every type of field, we have created a sample form that displays each field type and its associated icon. To see this form in action, open the Mastering R5 for Chapter 18 database in Designer and select the Field Types Example form, shown in Figure 18.21.

FIGURE 18.21

The Field Types Example form, showing each field type and its icon

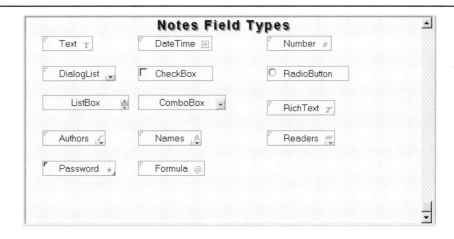

When a field is added to a form, the Field Properties InfoBox will automatically display because it is used to configure all fields. Each field has seven tabs for controlling its behavior:

- Field Info
- Control
- Advanced
- Font
- HTML Tag Attributes
- Paragraph Alignment
- Hide-When

All of the tabs except the Control tab are essentially the same for each type of field. The Control tab will be explained in more detail in "Selecting the Field Type" later in this chapter. Because the Font, Alignment, and Hide-When tabs are basically the same as the Font, Alignment, and Hide-When tabs for static text, we'll discuss only the Field Info, Advanced, and HTML Tag Attributes tabs here.

The Field Info Tab

The Field Info tab allows you to specify the field's name and type. When a new field is created, the default name is always Untitled and the field type is Text and Editable. Just type in a new name to change it. The name must begin with a character, the underscore symbol (_), or the dollar sign ($). The rest of the name can contain the letters *A* through *Z*, the numbers 0 through 9, and the underscore and dollar signs. The name cannot contain any spaces and is limited to 32 characters.

Field Type   To change the field type, select a type from the first drop-down list box (the field types will be described in "Selecting the Field Type" later in this chapter). The second drop-down list box to the right is a bit different. It determines if the field is editable by the user or automatically calculated by the Notes system. There are five different values for this field:

Editable   When a field is marked as Editable on a form, the user can modify its contents. There are also three events you can use to help the user populate the data entry field (the events are listed in the Objects tab of the programmer's pane): Default Value, which provides an initial value (such as the user's name) that the user can change; Input Translation, which modifies the contents of the field after the user is finished to aid in standardization (such as changing a name to the proper case); and Input Validation, which checks the contents of the field to ensure that the data is input correctly and issues an error message if it's not.

Computed   The data is automatically populated in a computed field. Each computed field has a Value event that can be populated by using a formula to supply a value. Computed fields are recalculated when a document is created, refreshed, or saved.

Computed for Display   This is another type of computed field, but it is only recalculated when a document is opened or refreshed. Also, the contents within this field type are never saved to the actual document.

Computed When Composed   This is also a computed field, but it is only calculated once when a document is created. Unlike the Computed for Display field, the contents within this field type are saved to the actual document and are not refreshed. Use this type of field to preserve the information about a document when it is created (such as the author or the data and time the document was created).

Literalize Fields   This field type is only available for the Formula field, which is discussed in more detail in "The Formula Field" later in this chapter.

 WARNING   Because the value for a Computed for Display field is not actually saved to the document, the field will not be visible in a view.

The last two options are Allow Multiple Values and Compute After Validation. If Allow Multiple Values is selected, a field can contain more than one value, and if

Compute After Validation is selected, the value of a computed field is recomputed after all the validation for a form is complete.

Style   You can also select the style for your fields on the Field Info tab. There are two choices available:

Notes Style   When this option is selected and a document is opened in Edit mode, a field marked by brackets will appear on the form. This is how Notes has always marked fields, and until now, developers didn't have a choice. The size of a field is not restricted with this style. As the user types, the field grows. If this option is selected, the Size option on the tab will be grayed out.

Native OS Style   This option is totally new to Notes. It allows you to create an outlined box for a field. You can select the height and width in the Size selection area. You can also decide whether the field box should expand to fill the width of the page. If you would like the field to grow as the user types in data, select the Dynamic height option. The field will expand to display three rows of data at one time. If more data is entered, a scroll bar will appear. For Web applications, this option is ignored.

A picture is worth a thousand words, so we created a sample form to show the differences between the two styles (see Figure 18.22). These choices are not available for the dialog list, checkbox, radio button, listbox, combobox, and rich text field types.

FIGURE 18.22

The various field styles available for a field (shown in the Notes client)

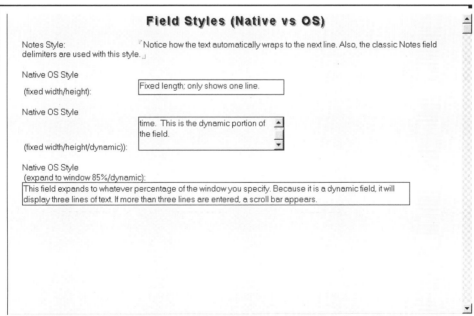

Field Styles (Native vs OS)

Notes Style: "Notice how the text automatically wraps to the next line. Also, the classic Notes field delimiters are used with this style."

Native OS Style
(fixed width/height):   Fixed length; only shows one line.

Native OS Style

                                    time. This is the dynamic portion of the field.

(fixed width/height/dynamic)):

Native OS Style
(expand to window 85%/dynamic):
This field expands to whatever percentage of the window you specify. Because it is a dynamic field, it will display three lines of text. If more than three lines are entered, a scroll bar appears.

You may notice that there is a gap on the tab between the Size and the Tab Key sections. If you select a field type of rich text, the Web Access section will appear. However, this doesn't mean that other fields cannot be accessed via the Web; they all can. The Web Access section is for formatting rich text only. You can specify how the field will be displayed on the Web. With Notes R5, you have the option of using native HTML or a Java applet for editing a rich text field within a Web application. The Java applet is a powerful feature that allows the user to create formatted text using the following properties:

- Bold, italics, underline
- Single-level indent
- Ordered and unordered lists
- Color selection
- Size and font selection
- URL link hotspots

Figure 18.23 displays an example of the Java applet in a Web browser.

FIGURE 18.23

The rich text field Java applet for the Main Topic form as shown in a Web browser

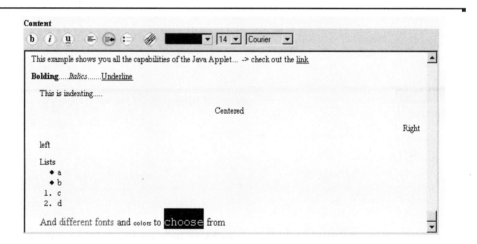

The last selection on the Field Info tab is the tabbing order for the fields and which field will get the default focus when a form is first displayed. We have created a sample form that displays how the tabbing order works. If you open the Tab Order for Main Topic form in Designer, you'll notice little yellow numbers in the upper left corner of the Subject, Categories, and Body fields. These numbers determine the tabbing sequence when a user presses the Tab key. The sequence for this form does not make sense; it was only designed to show you how this option works.

To see the tabbing sequence in action, choose Design ➢ Preview in Notes. The form will display in the Notes client, and the cursor should be placed in the Category field. Press the Tab key. See how it jumped to the Subject field? Now press the Tab key once more. It jumped down to the Content field. The default tabbing sequence is top-down, left-right, but now you can control where the user goes.

The Advanced Tab

The Advanced tab allows you to specify a Help message, multivalue field options, and security options for the text data field, as shown in Figure 18.24. If a Help message has been typed in for the user, the message will display across the bottom of the screen when the user enters the field. For a multivalue field, you have the option of deciding which data delimiters to use when data is input and displayed. Both the Separate Values When User Enters and the Display Separate Values With options allow a space, comma, semicolon, new line, or blank line to be used as a delimiter. The difference between the two selections is that multiple input delimiters can be selected, whereas only one output delimiter can be used. The security option allows you to specify encryption options for the field. Selecting Security Options or entering a Help message have no effect on a Web application.

TIP To display field help for a Web application, display a message in the browsers status bar by placing the JavaScript code `window.status="<your help msg>"` in the onFocus event for the field.

FIGURE 18.24

The Advanced tab for a multivalue text field

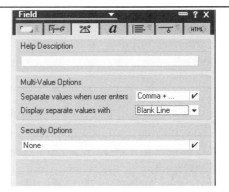

NOTE The field help text message will not be visible to users unless they are in Edit mode and the Field Help option is selected from the View ➢ Show menu.

The HTML Tag Attributes Tab

The HTML Tag Attributes tab allows you to assign various HTML tag values, which are then accessible via JavaScript. The values for these tags only work when the application

PART

V

Beyond the Client: Utilizing Domino Designer

is viewed with a Web browser. If you set these values and view the application in the Notes client, nothing will happen.

Name   With this option, you can assign the name that is used by JavaScript when referencing the field element. By default, any design element that already has a name, such as a field, will be automatically populated and cannot be changed. For design elements that do not have a name, such as an image, you can enter a name to be referenced in the JavaScript code.

ID   With this option, you can assign an ID attribute to an element. If you are familiar with Cascading Style Sheets (CSS), you will understand how to use this field.

Class   With this option, you can classify an object. If you are familiar with Cascading Style Sheets (CSS), you will understand how to use this field.

Style   You can specify a specific style for the object. For example, if you want the text for a field to be blue, type **color:blue** in the Style field.

Title   The Title option allows you to store a prompt for the object.

Other   You can type in additional HTML tab attributes for the object. These attributes must be valid HTML code, such as Size=10 and MaxLength=8. You can also specify these attributes in the HTML Body Attributes event for a field.

Adding Fields to Your Form

Now that we have gone over the basics for a field, let's return to our Recipe form. With the Recipe form open in Designer, we need to add a field for each one of the labels you entered earlier in the chapter (except for the form title, of course). To add fields to the Recipe form, just follow these steps:

1. Place the cursor at the end of the Name of Recipe: label. Press the spacebar once and choose Create ➢ Field (you can also right-click and choose Create Field). This will automatically create a text and editable field called Untitled. The Basics tab should display by default. Change the name of the field by entering **NameOfRecipe** in the Name field. From the Style section, select the Native OS Style. Type **3.00** in the Width field in the Size section.

2. We'll create two more text fields as well. Place your cursor at the end of the Created By: label. Press the spacebar once and choose Create ➢ Field. Change the name of the field to **CreatedBy**. Change the type of field in the second drop-down list box from Editable to Computed When Composed. Because this field is computed, you also need to enter a value for the field to contain. To do so, select the Value event in the Objects tab of the programmer's pane. In the script area, type **@Name([CN];@UserName)**. This will populate the CreatedBy field with the name of user who initially creates this document.

3. To create the next text field, place your cursor at the end of the Last Updated By: label. Press the spacebar once and choose Create ➢ Field. Change the name of the field to **LastUpdatedBy**. Change the type of field in the second drop-down list box from Editable to Computed for Display (we don't need to save this value because it is already saved in the $UpdatedBy field). Again, you will need to add a formula for the Value event. Enter **@Name([CN];@Subset($UpdatedBy;-1))** in the Value event of the script area for the field. The formula will grab the last entry in the $UpdatedBy field and place it in this field (the $UpdatedBy field contains a list of all those who update the document).

4. We now need to add two date/time field types to the form. Place your cursor at the end of the Created On: label. Press the spacebar once and choose Create ➢ Field. Change the name of the field to **CreatedDateTime**. Change the field type to Date/Time in the first Type drop-down list box. In the second drop-down list box, change the field type from Editable to Computed for Display. Add the formula **@Created** to the Value event for the field. This will place the date and time the document was initially created in the CreatedDateTime field.

5. To create the next field, place your cursor at the end of the Last Updated On: label. Press the spacebar once and choose Create ➢ Field. Change the name of the field to **LastUpdatedOn**. Change the field type to Date/Time in the first Type drop-down list box. In the second drop-down list box, change the field type from Editable to Computed for Display. Add the formula **@Modified** to the Value event for the field. This will place the date and time that the document was last modified in the LastUpdatedOn field.

6. The remaining two fields to be added are rich text fields. Place your cursor at the end of the Recipe Instructions: label. Press the Enter key so that your cursor ends up on the line underneath the label. Choose Create ➢ Field. Change the name of the field to **RecipeInstructions**. Change the field type to Rich Text in the first Type drop-down list box. In the Web Access section, select Using Java Applet from the Display drop-down list box. Select the Alignment tab. In the Spacing section, select $1\frac{1}{2}$ from the Below drop-down list box.

7. For the final field, place your cursor at the end of the Comments: label. Press the Enter key so that your cursor ends up on the line underneath the label. Choose Create ➢ Field. Change the name of the field to **Comments**. Change the field type to Rich Text in the first Type drop-down list box. In the Web Access section, select Using Java Applet from the Display drop-down list box

8. Place your cursor back on the same line as the Comments: label. From the Alignment tab, select Single from the Below drop-down list box.

When you have finished adding all your fields, your form should look like the one shown in Figure 18.25. Make sure you save your new form and, if you wish, preview it in the Notes client.

FIGURE 18.25

The Recipe form with fields

Selecting the Field Type

The preceding section explained the common properties available for a field. For each specific field, there are also some uncommon properties, which we'll explain in detail in this section.

When you assign a field to a form, you are defining the type of data a user can save to the document. As we mentioned earlier, the form that contains the fields is nothing more than a *template* for the data. If you use a text field called Birthdate on one form and then use a date/time field called Birthdate on another form, Notes will try to grab the data assigned to the Birthdate field when the document is opened. Depending on which form is used, the user may not get the results they expect. It is up to you, the developer, to ensure that the proper field type is used for each form.

The Text Field

A user can type any letters, numbers, punctuation, and spaces into a text data field. Data that is placed in a text field cannot be formatted by the end user. Whatever you specify as the format will remain constant (in other words, if you specify bold, all the text will be bold). Each text field is also limited to only 15KB of data. Also keep in mind that the properties on some of the InfoBox tabs are dynamic in that the choices may change depending on selections made on other tabs.

With so many options available, it's hard to get a complete understanding how each selection can work. To help visualize the various types of text fields, we have created a sample document that shows the options available for a text field. In the Notes client, open the Text Field Examples document from the Example Views view in the Mastering R5 for Chapter 18 example database. There are two tabs that distinguish between using the Notes style and the Native OS style.

The Control Tab for the Text Field   The text data field only has two options available on the Control tab, as shown in Figure 18.26. These two options, Show Scroll Bars and Allow Multiple Lines, are only available when the Native OS style is selected (a Notes style field will only have one option available, which allows you to enable/disable field delimiters). Both of these options should be selected for ease of use. It is hard to use a multiline field with no scroll bars. None of these options will make any difference for a Web application.

 NOTE   When you select the Notes style field option from the Field Info tab, you will always have the ability to enable/disable field delimiters. A field delimiter surrounds a Notes field with a starting and ending angle bracket, visually depicting the start and end of the field.

FIGURE 18.26

The Control tab for a text field when the Native OS style is selected

The Date/Time Field

The date/time field displays date and/or time information in many different formats. As you can with other fields, you can allow the user to enter the data into a date/time field or allow the field to be computed (to show today's date, for example). Here are some of the various formats that can be used in a date/time field:

- 1/31
- 1/31/98
- 1/31/1998
- Today

- 1/31/1998 11:00 PM

- 11:00 PM

- 11:00:01 PM

To help you visualize the formats for a date/time field, we have again created a sample document that shows the various options available. In the Notes client, open the DateTime Field Examples document from the Example Views view in the Mastering R5 for Chapter 18 example database. The layout for this form is similar to the layout used for the text field example in the preceding section.

The Control Tab for the Date/Time Field   You use the Control tab to format the date/time field. There are an extremely large number of possibilities for formatting the data, as shown in Figure 18.27. Although they're not, the implementations seem endless. One feature in the On Display section of the tab does help you determine the look and feel for your date/time field. The Use Preferences From drop-down list box contains two choices: User's Setting and Custom. The User's Setting option will use the date/time format from the operating system on the user's machine for formatting. Selecting the Custom option will allow you to mix and match how you would like the date/time to display.

FIGURE 18.27

The various formats for a Notes date/time field

Directly beneath the Use Preferences From drop-down list box is the Sample field. This field directly reflects any changes you make to any of the options on the tab. For example, if you disable the Display Time option, the Sample field will change from displaying both the date and time to displaying just the date. This feature will help you quickly narrow down which options look best for your application. Besides all of the date and time formatting options, you can also specify that the year display with four digits and that the month must be displayed with letters instead of numbers. One important aspect to keep in mind when implementing a date/time field is whether to use the Notes style or Native OS style for the field. If the Native OS style is used, either a Date or Time Picker control element (see Figure 18.28) will be displayed next to the field. These tools allow the user to select the value instead of having to type it in. The Date and Time Pickers are not active for Web applications.

FIGURE 18.28

The Date and Time graphical selection tools

PART

V

Beyond the Client: Uti-
lizing Domino Designer

The Number Field

The number field type is typically used for any type of numeric data. The field allows you quite a bit of flexibility in formatting your data; you can use decimal numbers, percentages, scientific display, and currency. Notes can store numbers from $2.225E{-}308$ to $1.798E308$ with 14-digit accuracy.

To see this field type in action, in the Notes client, open the Number Field Examples document from the Example Views in the Mastering R5 for Chapter 18 example database. Four tabs have been set up to display how the decimal, percentage, scientific, and currency numeric fields display.

The Control Tab for the Number Field   The Control tab allows you to select the type of numeric data and the format to apply to the numeric field. As shown in Figure 18.29, the formats allowed are Decimal, Percent, Scientific, and Currency. Based on your selection, options on the tab may be grayed out. You can select the preferences to use for the decimal separator and the thousands separator by selecting either Client or Custom. You can select either a fixed number of decimal places or allow it to vary for all the numeric types except Scientific. You can also use parentheses for negative numbers and a thousands separator (the Scientific format does not use the latter). If you select Currency, you have the option of defining the currency indicator. You can place the indicator before or after the numbers. You also have the option of putting a space between the indicator and the numbers. All of the numeric types render on the Web.

FIGURE 18.29

*The Control tab for the
number field*

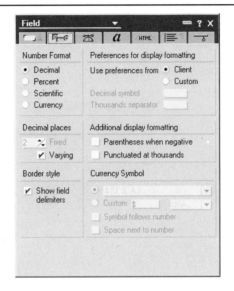

The Keyword Field

Keyword is a pre-Notes R5 term for a special field type that displays a list of choices to the user. With Notes 5, the keyword field is gone and replaced with the actual types of fields available, which are as follows:

- Dialog list
- Checkbox
- Radio button
- Listbox
- Combobox

Each field type presents a text list of values from which the user can select an entry. It is much easier on the user to select from a list rather than having to remember the value and type it in. Displaying a list will also eliminate a lot of potential data entry errors. In some cases, more than one entry can be selected from a keyword field, and sometimes the user can type in a value that is not in the selection list. Please refer to Table 18.5 for a description of each keyword type.

TABLE 18.5: DESCRIPTION OF KEYWORD ENTRIES

Field Type	Description	Add New Values[*]	Multiple Values
Dialog list	Presents a list of choices in a dialog box. The user can display the list by clicking the "helper button" or by pressing the Enter key. To select an entry, the user can either click the entry or press the spacebar. The user can add new values by typing them in the space provided.	Yes	Yes
Checkbox	Presents a list of choices in the check box format. To select an entry, the user can click the entry or press the spacebar.	N/A	Yes
Radio button	Presents a list of choices in the radio button format. To select an entry, the user can click the entry or press the spacebar.	N/A	N/A
Listbox	Presents a list of choices in an expanded list box (shows more than one entry at a time). To select an entry, the user can either click the entry or press the spacebar.	N/A	Yes
Combobox	Presents a drop-down list box. To select an entry, the user can click the entry or scroll through the list until the desired entry is found.	Yes	N/A

* This option does not work as expected when used in Web applications.

One thing all the keyword fields have in common is their ability to display one or more entries. This can be accomplished in various ways, depending on the type of keyword field. There are essentially five different ways to display data in a keyword field (see Table 18.6). The data choice is an option displayed on the Control tab for the keyword field. The field types are dialog list (DL), checkbox (CH), radio button (R), listbox (L), and combobox (C). Depending on the type of field, the choices available may vary.

TABLE 18.6: KEYWORD DATA CHOICES						
Data Choice	**Description**	**DL**	**CH**	**R**	**L**	**C**
Enter Choices (One per Line)	Allows you to enter a fixed number of choices for selection. For example, you can enter Yes and No.	✔	✔	✔	✔	✔
Use Formula for Choices	Allows you to enter a formula to display a list of choices. This option will allow you to create a "dynamic" set of choices and is extremely useful. For example, use @DBColumn to display a list of values from a column in a view. Be careful when using this option because only 64KB of data can be returned from a function.	✔	✔	✔	✔	✔
Use Address Dialog for Choices	This selection displays the Address dialog box to the end user. This is similar to the dialog box that is used for addressing mail. Allows the user to select names and groups for the entry.	✔				✔
Use Access Control List for Choices	This selection displays a dialog box with the Access Control List entries from the current database.	✔				✔
Use View Dialog for Choices	This selection allows you to select a view to be used for the contents of the keyword field. You have the option of selecting which database, view, and column to be used for the data. This will display the entire view in a dialog box but only return the data from the column number you select.	✔				✔

An example form has been set up so you can see exactly how each of these various field types works. In the Notes client, open the Keyword Field Examples document from the Example Views view in the Mastering R5 for Chapter 18 example database.

Next, let's look at the Control tab in which you can select the various options for each field type. Keep in mind that certain options will be grayed out depending on the type of field selected. Also note that you don't have the option of selecting the style for the field. The Notes and Native OS style options are not accessible on the Field Info tab.

NOTE   When keyword fields are used in a Web application, they do not render the same as in the Notes client. A combobox will display just like the dialog list field. One area to keep in mind is allowing values to be added in the list. When displayed on the Web, the field loses all the keyword features and becomes an entry field. There are ways around this nuance. It's difficult to explain, so look at the Main Topic form in the Mastering R5 for Chapter 18 example database and pay close attention to the three category fields. There are two dialog list fields, Webcategories and Categories. The only difference is that the Webcategories field does not allow values to be added to the list. The NewCats field allows new values to be added to the Webcategories field when the form is rendered on the Web. This is a good example to follow if you ever need to allow a user to add new entries to a keyword field in a Web application.

The Control Tab for the Keyword Field   As shown in Figure 18.30, the Control tab allows you to control not only the contents of the keyword field but also its look and feel. From the Display section, you can select whether or not the field will have field delimiters. This section will change for both the checkbox and radio button fields and allow you to select the border style and number of columns to display. The Choices section allows you to decide what data to display to the user. You can select from the choices described in Table 18.6. The Options section allows you to fine-tune the field for the user. From this section, you can allow a user to add entries that aren't in the selection list, display the entry helper button, or refresh the values of the list. Each option is dependent on the field type, so you'll need to play around with them a bit.

The Rich Text Field

The rich text field is very similar to the text field type. The biggest difference is that a rich text field will allow the user to format the data and input just about any type of data, including attachments and graphics. This free-form field is extremely useful because it allows users to type in as much data as they need. There is not a limit on the size of this type of field.

FIGURE 18.30

The Control tab for a dialog list field

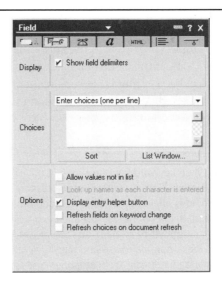

The Control Tab for the Rich Text Field   The options are pretty limited for a rich text field, as shown in Figure 18.31. You can specify whether the field will have delimiters and also whether pressing the Tab key will insert a tab or move the cursor to the next field (some users find inserting the tab annoying and would rather move to the next field). The Store Contents as HTML and MIME option is new to Notes 5. When this option is selected, the data is stored in native HTML or MIME format. In prior releases of Notes, a rich text field was always saved in a rich text format composed of composite data (CD) records. Now with Notes 5, you can select this option and, for example, have the bolded text *Hello World* saved as <B>Hello World</B>.

FIGURE 18.31

The Control tab for a rich text field

The Authors Field

The authors field is used to identify a user, group, or role that has access to edit the document. This field is used in conjunction with the database security (ACL). Just list those individuals who can edit the document in the authors field and grant them Author access to the database. You can name each author individually, within a group, or through an ACL role. In each case, if the person with Author ACL access is not listed in the field, they will not be able to edit the document. For those individuals with Editor access or greater, the authors field does not apply. A sample form has not been set up for this field type because it affects security.

The Control Tab for the Authors Field   The Control tab for the authors field is very similar to the Control tab for the keyword field. The major difference is in the Choices section. You have the option of allowing the user to select from an address book dialog, an ACL dialog, or a view dialog. There is also a choice labeled None, but that forces the user to type in the names, so you should avoid using it unless the authors field is computed. If an authors field has a typo in it, it could block access to the original creator. Also note that, because an authors field can display a dialog box, the rules described for keyword fields also apply when an authors field is rendered for a Web application. A dialog box will render correctly in the Notes client, but it won't in a Web application.

 WARNING   When you use authors fields, it is a good idea to always include the original authors' names or they won't be able to edit the documents they created.

The Names Field

The names field type is similar to the authors field type except a names field has nothing to do with a document's security. One other difference is how the name is displayed. The names field will convert the Notes hierarchical format to a more abbreviated form. For example, if a Notes name is CN=Scot Haberman/OU=Users/O=EDSTest, the names field would render it as Scot Haberman/Users/EDSTest. Other than that, all the options are the same. Why would you use this field type? There may be cases where you want a user to select a name or group of names for the application, but not for security reasons. A good example would be for mailing a document. The user can select whom the document should be sent to.

The Readers Field

A readers field is used to identify a user, group, or role that has access to read the document. This field is also used in conjunction with the database security. List the individuals who can read the contents of the document in the readers field and grant them Reader access to the database. You can name each author individually, within a group, or through an ACL role. In either case, if the person with Reader ACL access is not listed in the field, they will not be able to read the document.

Don't get this field type confused with an authors field. Users who aren't defined in the readers field but have Manager access won't be able to read the document. This is a major difference between the two field types and a source of a lot of confusion. It is very important that you make sure a role or group is always placed into the readers field. There is nothing worse than having Manager access to a database yet not being able to read a document. A sample form has not been set up for this field type because it affects security.

The Password Field

The password field type is used for privacy. Whenever a character is typed into this field, an asterisk will be displayed. Typically, this field type is used for typing in a password.

 WARNING The contents of a password field are not secure. Anyone can use the Document Properties InfoBox to view the contents of the field. If you need the field contents to be secure, encrypt the field.

The Formula Field

The formula field type is specifically for populating a subscription list and is outside the scope of this book. For more information, refer to the Notes Help database.

Using Shared Fields

If you find yourself creating the same field for use on different forms, it may be time to create a shared field. A shared field is a common repository for fields. The field still retains all the events and properties a non-shared field has, but the field definition is located in one place (yet it can be used in many places). Shared fields can be displayed by clicking the Resources item on the Design list. This will expand the Resources item to expose the Shared Fields item. Select the Shared Fields item to display all the current elements (shared fields) in the Work pane.

Continued

The process for creating a shared field from scratch is quite simple:

1. Choose Create ➤ Design ➤ Shared Field.
2. Enter a name for the field.
3. Assign all the field types, properties, and events.
4. Close and save the field.

You can also create a shared field from an existing field definition. If you have a field that would make a good candidate for a shared field, do the following:

1. Open the form in which the field resides.
2. Click the field to be shared.
3. Choose Design ➤ Share This Field.

Once this process has been completed, you'll notice that a dark border appears around the field. The border indicates that the field is actually a shared field. It is a subtle difference that makes it easier to tell which fields are single-use fields and which are shared fields.

Converting a single-use field to a shared field eliminates the need to create a shared field from scratch. To insert an existing single-use field into a shared field, follow these steps:

1. Open the form and place the cursor where you want the field.
2. Choose Create ➤ Insert Shared Field.
3. From the Insert Shared Field dialog box that appears, select the field you want to use from the Insert Shared Field list box (once a shared field has been placed on the form, it will no longer appear in the Insert Shared Field list box).

If you want to convert a shared field back to a single-use field, just do the following:

1. Open the form.
2. Select the shared field.
3. Choose Edit ➤ Cut.
4. Display the list of shared fields for the database. To access the shared fields, expand the Resources object in the Design list and select Shared Field.
5. Highlight the shared field you want to remove in the Work pane and press the Delete key.
6. Switch back to the form and choose Edit ➤ Paste.

Testing Your Form

Once you've created your form, you need to test it. To see the various ways to test a form, open the Recipe form you created in the Mastering R5 for Chapter 18 database. Domino Designer includes a few options called preview icons in the upper right corner of the window. Depending on your workstation configuration, you could have quite a few icons displayed, as shown in Figure 18.32. In this case, we have only IE installed as a browser.

FIGURE 18.32

The preview icons located in the upper right corner of the Designer workspace

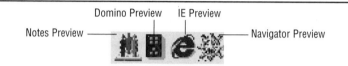

With the Recipe form displayed in Designer, click the Notes preview icon to display the Recipe form within the Notes client environment (see Figure 18.33). You can interact and test the form to see how it looks and performs. You can also test the form in the Notes client by choosing Design ➢ Preview in Notes.

FIGURE 18.33

Testing the Recipe form in the Notes client

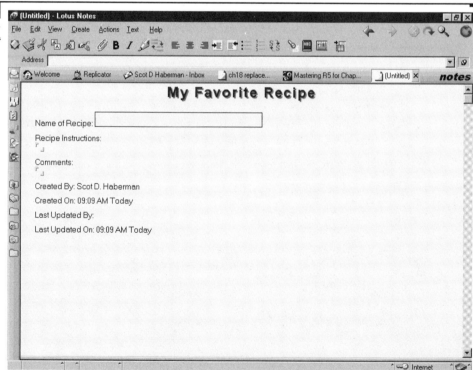

Switch back to Domino Designer, and once there, click the Domino preview icon. This will render the Main Topic document in the Notes browser unless you have configured your Location document to use Notes with Internet Explorer. The remaining IE and Navigator preview icons will render the Main Topic form in Internet Explorer and Navigator, respectively. Figure 18.34 shows the Recipe form displayed in Internet Explorer. You can also test the form in a browser by choosing Design ➤ Preview in Web Browser and selecting the Web browser of your choice.

FIGURE 18.34

Testing the Recipe form in the Internet Explorer browser

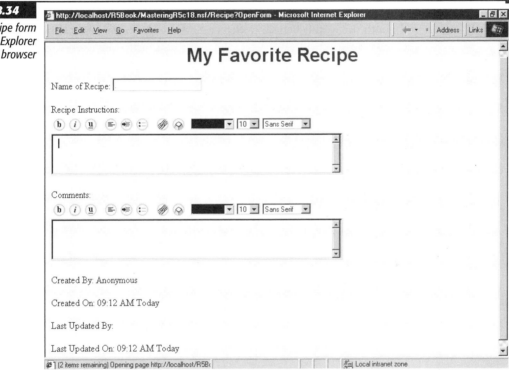

As you can see, testing from Domino Designer is quite easy. You can now render the form in each environment to see how it looks and acts. Because Domino Designer can also act as a Web server, you can do all of your testing for both the Notes client and Web applications from your local workstation.

Summary

In this chapter, you learned how to create a form, which is the interface in which the end users create documents. A form is also used to create the document hierarchy, or parent-child relationship, commonly referred to a Response document. You learned about the form properties and also about all the events that make up a form. These events establish the backbone for developing a powerful Notes application for either the Notes client or the Web. You also learned about the types of data fields and when to use the properties for each field type. Finally, we discussed how to actually test a form in both the Notes client and Web environments. In the next chapter, we'll continue working with forms, but we'll take them a bit further by using more advanced design elements.

CHAPTER 19

Advanced Form Design

Now that you know how to put static text and fields on a form, it's time to get down to the really fun stuff. In the preceding chapter, the forms were pretty straightforward, boring, and not all that friendly. You placed the fields on a form and that was about it. In this chapter, you'll learn how to jazz them up and make them a bit more user friendly.

All of the examples we'll use for this chapter are in the Mastering R5 for Chapter 19 example database. We'll enhance the basic forms you developed in Chapter 18 by using some of the more advanced features, such as subforms, sections, layout regions, tables, Actions, hotspots, and graphics. We'll also explain how using each of these advanced features can affect a Web-based application.

Adding a Subform

In the preceding chapter, you learned what a form is and how it is used. A subform is similar to a form except that it cannot be used by itself. A subform must be embedded within a form to be displayed to the user. This may not sound like an advantage at first, but because the contents of a subform are separate from the form, you can reuse the subform in many different forms (this is similar to using shared fields). Any change you make to the subform will be automatically reflected in every form in which the subform is embedded. This allows you to make changes from a central location, which means less work for you.

Creating a Subform

Creating a subform is similar to creating a regular form. In our Mastering R5 for Chapter 19 database, you'll create a subform that contains an audit trail. The subform will display information about who created the document and when plus who last modified the document and when. To create a blank subform, choose Create ➣ Design ➣ Subform. This will display the Design workspace with a blank form, as shown in Figure 19.1.

The Audit Trail subform will contain fields for username, dates, and times. To add these fields to the newly created subform, perform the following steps:

1. Type **Created By:** on the first line.

2. With the cursor just to the right of the text, choose Create ➣ Design ➣ Field, which displays the Field Properties InfoBox. Type **CreatedBy** in the Name field and make sure Text and Computed When Composed are selected from the drop-down list boxes. Because this is a computed field, in the Value event for the field, type the formula **@Name([CN];@UserName)**, which will store the current username in the field.

3. On the next line, type **Created On:**.

4. With the cursor just to the right of the text, add a field named **CreatedDateTime** and select Date/Time and Computed for Display from the drop-down list boxes. You will also need to select the Control tab.

   Make sure both the Display Date and Display Time options are enabled (you'll want to display both the date and the time). Because this is a computed field, in the Value event for the field, type in the formula **@Created** to display the date and time the document was created.

5. Follow the same steps to type the text **Last Updated By:** and **Last Updated On:** and the fields **LastUpdatedBy** and **LastUpdatedOn**. Text and Computed for Display should be selected for both fields. The Value events for the two fields should be **@Name([CN];@Subset($UpdatedBy;-1))** and **@Modified**, respectively.

6. Save the subform. You'll be prompted for a name. Type in the name **Audit Trail** and click OK. Your form should look similar to the form in Figure 19.2.

FIGURE 19.1

A blank subform ready for designing

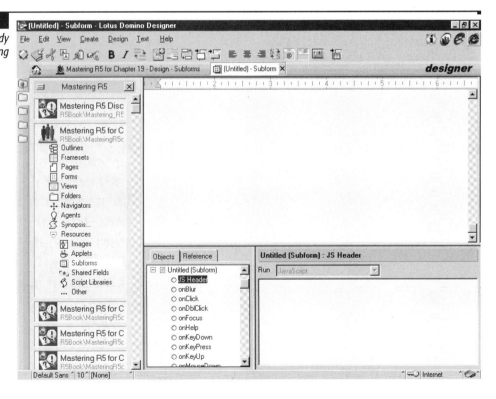

FIGURE 19.2

The Audit Trail subform

Created By:　CreatedBy T

Created On:　CreatedDateTime [16]

Last Updated By:　LastUpdatedBy T

Last Updated On:　LastUpdatedOn [16]

Using the Subform

To use the subform, you must place it on a form, which is easy to do. The only prerequisite is that you must have a form open on which to place the subform. You'll place the Audit Trail subform on both the Recipe and Ingredient forms in the example database.

There are two types of subforms available in Notes:

- Standard
- Computed

The only difference between these two types of subforms is how they are placed on a form. Both subform types are created and act the exact same way both in the Notes client and for a Web-based application.

The Standard Subform

To insert a standard subform on a form, just follow these steps:

1. Open the Recipe form in the Mastering R5 for Chapter 19 example database.

2. Place the cursor at the bottom of the form after the Comments field.

3. Choose Create ➤ Insert Subform. The Insert Subform dialog box appears.

4. Select Audit Trail from the Insert Subform list box (as shown in Figure 19.3) and click the OK button.

FIGURE 19.3

Selecting the Audit Trail subform from the Insert Subform dialog box

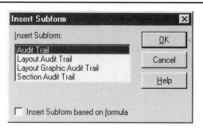

Because you inserted a standard subform, its contents will display within the context of the Recipe form, as shown in Figure 19.4. Although you can see the individual subform fields and labels, you cannot change them within the context of the form. You must open the subform using the Design list in the Design pane. There is, however, a more convenient way to open it; you may notice that, in the script area of the programmer's pane for the selected subform, there is a reminder that you can double-click the subform to edit the contents.

FIGURE 19.4

The Recipe form with a standard subform placed on it

NOTE To open a subform from the Design list, expand the Resources design element and select the Subforms element to display a list of all the current subforms in the work pane.

The Computed Subform

To insert a computed subform on a form, follow these steps:

1. Open the Ingredient form in the Mastering R5 for Chapter 19 example database.

2. Place the cursor at the bottom of the form after the Description field.

3. Choose Create ➤ Insert Subform.

4. Select the Insert Subform Based on Formula option in the Insert Subform dialog box and click the OK button. This will place a Computed Subform marker on the form. Notice that, although the Formula option is enabled, you cannot select a subform from the list.

5. From the Objects tab in the programmer's pane, select the Computed Subform object (you can also select the Computed Subform object directly on the form).

6. Type the formula **"Audit Trail"** in the script area of the programmer's pane, which will evaluate to the name of the subform in the Default Value event, as shown in Figure 19.5.

FIGURE 19.5

Entering a formula to calculate the name of the subform to display

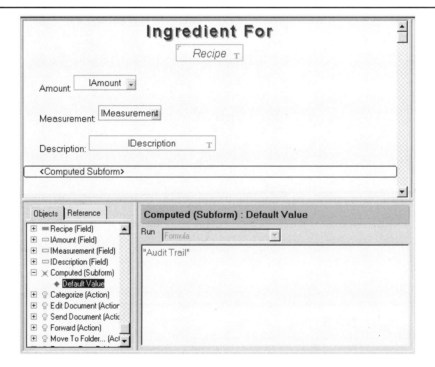

 NOTE "Audit Trail" is not actually a formula (it is a text string), but you can write a complex formula that will evaluate to the name of any subform you wish. Using this idea, you could display different subforms based on the user's name, the time of day, or the security access level.

You will notice that the contents of the subform are not displayed on the form; instead, a box that contains the text *<Computed Subform>* is displayed. You elected to *compute* the name of the subform to use; hence, no subform will display until the form is actually used.

One of the nice features of using the computed subform is the ability to decide at runtime which subform to use. In this example, the Audit Trail subform is always used, but there is no reason you couldn't enter a formula that returns a different subform name based on certain criteria. One drawback to using this type of subform is not being able to actually view the subform contents on the form. If you want to see what the subform contains, you must open it from the Design list of the Design pane (unlike with the standard subform, there is no shortcut to open the computed subform).

The Subform Properties InfoBox

There are a few options that are only enabled and disabled through the Subform Properties InfoBox. To display the Properties InfoBox (see Figure 19.6), you must first open the subform in Domino Designer. Double-click the embedded subform and it will automatically open. To open the Properties InfoBox choose Design ➤ Subform Properties.

PART

V

Beyond the Client: Utilizing Domino Designer

FIGURE 19.6

*The Subform
Properties InfoBox*

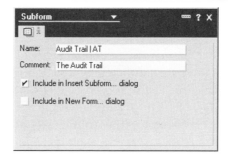

Name   The Name field allows you to change the name of the subform. You can also use an alias; separate the name and the alias using the | separator, such as Audit Trail | AT, as shown in Figure 19.6.

 TIP By using aliases, you are not tied to using the actual name of the design element in your programming code. Referencing design elements by alias is a good practice to get in the habit of performing.

Comment   The Comment field is used for placing a brief description of the design element. There is a Comment field for almost every design element, and it should be used at all times. The comments you place in this field will be displayed in the Work pane of the Designer workspace underneath each element and will give you a quick reference to the function of the design element.

Include in Insert Subform... **Dialog**   When you are trying to insert a subform on a form, you are prompted with a list of subforms via the Insert Subform dialog box (refer to Figure 19.3). If for some reason your subform does not display in this list, the Include in Insert Subform... Dialog option is probably not selected; hence, you cannot select the subform to place it on your form. Enabling this option (the default) will ensure that the subform will always display in the dialog box list.

Include in New Form... **Dialog**   You can also have the Insert Subform dialog box automatically display when you are creating a new form. This option is disabled by default, which will prevent the dialog box from automatically popping up every time you create a new form. When it's enabled, this option can be a bit irritating, so you may want to leave it disabled.

Adding a Section

If you look at our new Recipe and Ingredient forms in the Notes client, you may notice that there are quite a few new fields being displayed. Making the audit trail information available to the user is a nice touch, but it takes away from the actual recipe and ingredient fields and clutters the screen when it's always displayed. All of the fields seem to run together without some type of field separator. In addition, most users don't want to see the audit trail information *all* the time because it really has nothing to do with the actual document contents.

This is where sections come into play. Most designers have a tendency to place a lot of information on one form, which can be quite confusing to the user. A section allows you to group like information together. These groupings can be displayed or hidden based on options selected by you or by the end user. You also have the ability to limit access to these groups of information by assigning security rights.

There are two types of sections that you can define in Notes:

- Standard
- Controlled access

The major difference between these two types of sections is that, with a controlled access section, you have the ability to limit who can access the contents of the section.

Creating a Standard Section

There are two ways a section can be created. Depending on your situation, you can have a selected group of existing fields automatically placed into a new section, or you can create a new section and manually place each field. For our example, we'll have the field automatically placed into the new section.

We mentioned earlier that it would be nice to have the ability to hide the audit trail fields when either the Recipe or Ingredient form is displayed. Using a section, you are going to hide the fields from the end user but also give the end user the ability to see the contents of those fields. To create a section containing all the audit trail fields, follow these steps:

1. Make a copy of the Audit Trail subform by selecting the subform from the Design list and choosing Edit ➣ Copy and then Edit ➣ Paste (you can also right-click on the subform and choose Copy and then right-click and choose Paste).

2. Open the newly created subform called Copy of Audit Trail.

 NOTE When you copy and paste an element, Designer will automatically add *Copy of* to the beginning of the name of the original element (therefore, the name of a copy of the Audit Trail subform will be Copy of Audit Trail). If you were to make yet another copy of the same element, Designer will automatically begin the name with *Another Copy of*. The name of each subsequent copy will also begin with *Another Copy of*.

3. Highlight all the labels and fields on the subform.

4. Choose Create ➣ Section ➣ Standard. All of the labels and fields are immediately placed into a section. Note that the title for the section defaults to the first label that was selected, in this case, Created By:.

5. Choose Design ➣ Subform Properties and change the name to Section Audit Trail. You may also elect to type in some additional comments.

By default, the section is collapsed. To view the contents of the section, click the twistie and all of the labels and fields within the Section will be displayed, as shown in Figure 19.7.

PART

V

Beyond the Client: Uti-
lizing Domino Designer

*The section on the
Section Audit Trail
subform*

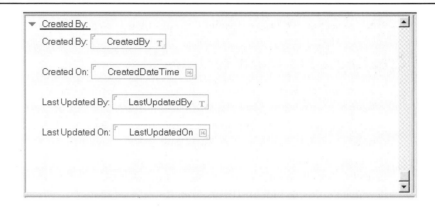

Because you had Notes automatically populate the contents of the section, you may have noticed that it also populated the title for the section. The Created By: title is not very descriptive of the section contents, so you'll need to change it.

Changing the Section Title

You can change the title for a section from the Section Properties InfoBox. To display the Properties InfoBox, click on the section and choose Section ➤ Section Properties. The Section Properties InfoBox, shown in Figure 19.8, appears (you can also right-click on the section and choose Section Properties).

*The Title tab of the
Section Properties
InfoBox and Border*

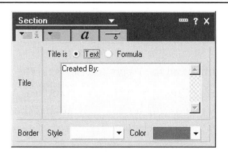

You may notice that the Title and Border tab contains a radio button with which you can choose to either enter a text section title or allow the section title to be generated via a formula. Keep the Text radio button selected (the default), highlight the text in the Title text box, and type **Audit Trail**. Let's also change the current default border style. Select the first entry from the Style drop-down list, which will box the section title. Keep the current color because it stands out a bit from the other parts of the form.

Expanding and Collapsing Sections

When you use sections, you can collapse or hide information from the user. In our example, the entire audit trail is placed into a section. When a Recipe form is viewed in the Notes client, the audit trail information is tucked neatly into a collapsed section, as shown in Figure 19.9. Temporarily hiding the audit trail information makes the screen less cluttered and easier to read.

There are some additional properties for the section that allow you to control how it is presented to the end user. In this example, we want to make sure the section is always collapsed. You have the ability to control the Expand/Collapse Action when a document is previewed, opened for reading or editing, and printed. To set this property, follow these steps:

1. Open the Section Audit Trail subform.

2. Click the section and choose Section ➤ Section Properties to open the Properties InfoBox.

3. Select the Expand/Collapse tab.

4. Select the Auto-Collapse Section option from the Opened for Reading drop-down list, as shown in Figure 19.10.

5. Save the subform.

FIGURE 19.10

The Expand/Collapse tab of the Section Properties InfoBox

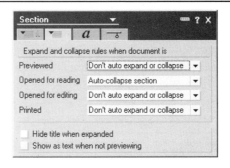

Now when a Recipe document is opened, the audit trail section will always be collapsed, giving a cleaner look to the form. The Auto-Collapse option can also be chosen from any of the other drop-down lists on the Expand/Collapse tab.

Creating a Controlled Access Section

The only real difference between a standard section and a controlled access section is security rights. With a controlled access section, you or the end user can choose who has access to edit particular sections. This feature can be quite useful for a document that many different people or groups are allowed to edit. Using controlled access sections, you can group data based on who will have access to it. In the standard section, we grouped common data together. We can go a step further with the controlled access section by grouping common editable data.

You can create a controlled access section by choosing Create ➤ Section ➤ Controlled Access. Once the controlled access section is created, a new tab called Formula appears in the Section Properties InfoBox. This tab allows you to enter an access formula, as shown in Figure 19.11. In this example, a text list of names is typed in, giving only two people edit access to the section (however, everyone will be able to read the contents of the section).

FIGURE 19.11

The Formula tab of the Section Properties InfoBox

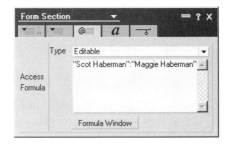

NOTE When you use a controlled access section in a Web application, the security for the section will remain in effect. The end user will not have the ability to double-click the section title to add or remove section editors.

Controlled Access Type

It's critical that you understand the Type option (see Figure 19.11) of a controlled access section. If you select Editable from the drop-down list box, any user with the correct database and document security access can add and remove users from the Controlled Access list. When editing a document, the user only needs to double-click the section title and the Edit Section dialog box will appear (see Figure 19.12).

PART

V

Beyond the Client: Uti-
lizing Domino Designer

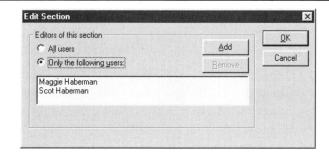

FIGURE 19.12

The Edit Section dialog box, which allows you to add or remove users

If you choose Computed from the Type drop-down list for the controlled access section, the list of users can be calculated via a formula each and every time the document is refreshed. The Computed When Composed option will calculate the list of users only once (when the document is first created). No changes can be made to this type of controlled access section.

Layout Regions

A layout region is a special type of element that can be placed on either a form or a subform. The layout region is a fixed-size design area that allows elements placed in the region to be easily moved around and resized for pixel-perfect placement. In earlier releases of Notes, the layout region would have been categorized as a place to display design elements in ways not possible in regular forms and subforms. With Notes R5, that statement no longer holds true.

To explain, let us digress for a moment. In previous releases of Notes, you were not able to display fields in both the native OS style and the Notes style. You had to display all fields in the Notes style unless you were using a layout region. In addition, you couldn't display either the Date or Time Picker, which allow the user to select a date or select a time. These too were reserved only for layout regions, as was tabbing between fields. Layout regions were also used to size pop-up dialog boxes based on forms. There were quite a few advantages to using a layout region on a form/subform. The gap in functionality between forms and subforms with layout regions and those without is now extremely narrow.

Creating a Layout Region

In this section, you'll create another Audit Trail subform, except in this case, you'll use a layout region to contain the fields. Make a copy of the Audit Trail subform (see step 1 in "Creating a Standard Section" earlier in this chapter). Open the subform you just copied and follow these steps:

1. Place the cursor in the upper left corner of the subform.

2. Choose Create ➤ Layout Region ➤ New Layout Region.

3. Select the layout region (the black rectangle) and choose Design ➤ Layout Properties (or right-click in the layout region and choose Layout Properties) to display the Layout Properties InfoBox, shown in Figure 19.13.

FIGURE 19.13

The Properties InfoBox for the layout region

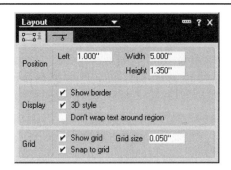

4. Select both the Show Grid and Snap to Grid options. Also make sure that the value in the Grid Size field is 0.050. These options will help align all the design elements within the layout region. You may also elect to enable the 3D Style option. This will give the layout region a dialog-box look (a gray background).

5. With the layout region still selected, choose Create ≻ Layout Region ≻ Text to insert a Control object (a text label in layman's terms) within the layout region. Display the Control Properties InfoBox for the new object by choosing Design ≻ Object Properties (you can also just double-click the object). From the Static Text Info tab, you can enter the text to be displayed for the object. This field will be the title for the layout region, so type **Audit Trail** in the Text field and center the text both horizontally and vertically. Select the Font tab, resize the text to 18, and change the color to dark blue. Next, size the field so that it is centered across the top of the layout region, as shown in Figure 19.14.

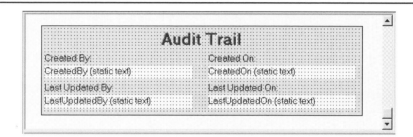

6. The next step is to add the four fields that make up the actual audit trail to the layout region. First, add the text labels to the layout region; arrange them as they appear in Figure 19.14.

7. Add the four fields to the layout region. To add a field, choose Create ≻ Field. To define the properties of each field, you must display the Field Properties InfoBox, which does not display by default. To display the Properties InfoBox, choose Design ≻ Field Properties (you can also double-click the field). Define the properties for each field. Also remember to type the formulas in the Value event for the computed fields. When you are finished, the layout region should be similar to Figure 19.14.

NOTE You cannot cut and paste fields from a non–layout region to a layout region and vice versa.

8. Choose File ≻ Close to save your new subform. You will be presented with a prompt asking if you would like to save the subform. Click the Yes button, enter the name **Layout Audit Trail** in the Lotus Domino Designer dialog box, and click the OK button.

PART

V

Beyond the Client: Uti-
lizing Domino Designer

Adding Graphics to Your Layout Region

You can also add graphics to your layout region. There are two options available: you can add a graphic, and you can create a graphic button. Neither of these options allow you to import a graphic directly or allow the use of the image resources (defined later in this chapter). You must first copy the graphic to the Clipboard. You will need to use some type of graphics program—such as Microsoft Paint or even a Web browser—to display the image. Once you have selected the image and copied it to the Clipboard, it will be automatically pasted into the layout region when you insert a graphic or create a graphic button.

Once a graphic is added, you can move the image anywhere within the layout region. If you would like the graphic to be used as a background for the layout region, you can use the Design ➤ Send to Back command. Follow these steps to create a background graphic:

1. Make a copy of the Layout Audit Trail subform.

2. Open the newly created copy and rename the subform Layout Graphic Audit Trail (to rename the subform, open the Subform Properties InfoBox and enter the subform name in the Name field).

3. Copy the graphic image of your choice to the Clipboard. From the Design pane, expand the Resources item in the Design list, select Image Resources, and find an image called Background.gif. Highlight this element, choose Resource ➤ Export, and select the directory to which you want to export the image. Once the image is imported, open it and copy it to the Clipboard.

4. With the layout region selected, choose Create ➤ Layout Region ➤ Graphic. The image should cover everything in the layout region.

5. Choose Design ➤ Send to Back, and you should have a subform that looks like Figure 19.15.

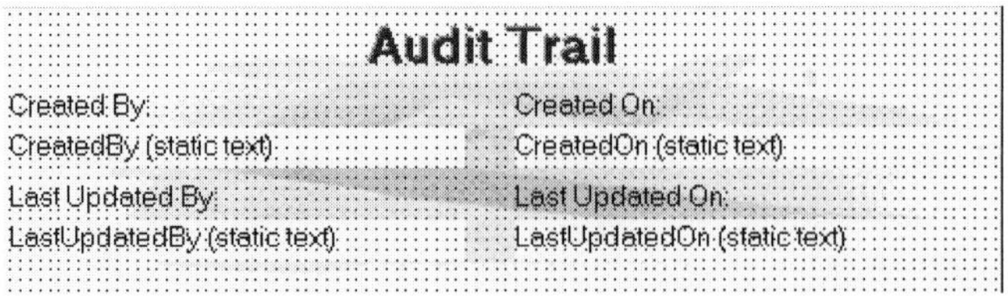

FIGURE 19.15

The Audit Trail subform with a graphical background image in a layout region

Audit Trail

Created By: Created On:
CreatedBy (static text)   CreatedOn (static text)
Last Updated By: Last Updated On:
LastUpdatedBy (static text)   LastUpdatedOn (static text)

The same thing can be accomplished for a graphic button, although you'll probably want to use a smaller image. The name of this element implies a button with an embedded image, but in actuality, a copy of the image is just placed in the layout region. To create a graphic button, follow the steps for creating a graphic but choose Create ➤ Layout Region ➤ Graphic Button to actually place the graphic in the layout region. Once the graphic button has been created, you can program specific events to occur when the button is clicked. The language you decide to program with determines the events that can be programmed.

Advantages and Disadvantages of Layout Regions

You know what a layout region is; now it's time to discuss when and if you should actually use one. The biggest advantage to using a layout region is the ease with which you can place and move fields. With pixel placement, you can arrange the layout in just about any shape. This helps save development time. Although it is easy to move fields around, you still cannot move groups of fields around. The fields must be moved one at a time.

It's also nice to use a background graphic in a layout region. You can insert a graphic anywhere in the layout region and move it around freely. Another nice feature is that a layout region is fixed in size, so once you set everything up the way you like it, it will not be altered or changed when displayed. This will ensure that graphics do not get cut off from dynamic resizing.

The fields also look nice in a layout region. Instead of the typical Notes field delimiters, you can display fields in three-dimensional boxes so your form will look and feel more like a form. Most users are more comfortable with this look than they are with Notes delimiters. When placing fields in the layout region, you may have noticed that you do not have as many choices as you have with fields placed outside a layout region. You cannot chose to display Notes delimited fields in a layout region, and you cannot display the following types of fields:

- Dialog list
- Password
- Formula
- Rich text

You also cannot use the following elements:

- Attachments
- HotSpots
- Links
- OLE objects
- Pop-ups
- Sections
- Tables

Another major limitation is that layout regions will not display over the Web. If you plan to create a Web-based application, refrain from using layout regions.

If you will have a lot of pop-up dialog boxes, layout regions help to create a nice-looking interface. The 3D style is complimentary for this style of dialog box. If you are going to develop a set a "how to" wizards, the layout regions will be extremely helpful.

Tables

Tables have been significantly enhanced for this release of Notes. Many of the limitations imposed in previous releases have been removed. You can do just about anything you want with a table. Tables are typically used in Notes for aligning fields and labels or summarizing data. You can think of a table as a spreadsheet with a set number of rows and columns. You can place anything you want in any row or any column, such as text labels, fields, and even another table.

 TIP You can now nest tables within tables for enhanced control over your form. You can only nest tables up to four deep.

The most common use for tables in Notes is for aligning labels and fields on a form. Because you cannot move labels and fields around a form as you can within a layout region, you need to use a table to impose a definitive starting position and a definitive ending position. Using tables correctly, you can mimic anything you can do in a layout region, but it requires a bit more planning. Placing fields in a table column will also ensure that data stays within the boundaries of the table cell instead of wrapping over the width of the entire form (this only applies to Notes style fields because the OS style fields are fixed in nature).

Types of Tables

Creating a table is a bit more involved than in previous releases. You now have to choose which type of table you would like to create. There are four basic table designs/types allowed in Notes R5: basic, tabbed, animated and programmed. When you create a table, you choose the type via the Create Table dialog box, as shown in Figure 19.16.

FIGURE 19.16

The Create Table
dialog box, where you
select the type of table
to create

Create Table

Table Size

Number of rows   2
Number of columns   2
Table width   ○ Fits window   ● Fixed width

Table Type

Create a basic table.

Create a basic table that starts out with the number of rows
and columns specified above.

OK   Cancel

Basic   The basic table has a typical row and column layout. You define the number of rows and columns to display and a spreadsheet-like grid is created, allowing you to begin entering your information.

Tabbed   The tabbed table is also defined by rows and columns, but each row is translated to a tab. This creates a more intuitive interface that allows groups of fields to be placed underneath a tab and hidden from the user until that tab is selected.

Animated   The animated table is a special type of table that scrolls through each of its rows based on some time interval.

Programmed   The programmed table allows you to display specific rows in a table based on the value of another field. You also have the option of displaying each row with a tab (similar to the tabbed table).

All you need to do is determine the number of rows and columns the table should contain, decide if you want to use a fixed width, and click the OK button. Don't worry if you make a mistake. Once the table is created, all the options can be changed after the fact using the Table Properties InfoBox.

For all the table examples, we will again use the Recipe and Ingredient forms from the Mastering R5 for Chapter 19 example database. We will make a copy of the existing forms and start working from there. This will alleviate the need to create the fields, window title, and so on all over again. Every time the instructions ask you to make a copy of the Recipe and Ingredient forms, just follow these steps:

1. Click the Ingredient form.

2. Press the Ctrl key and click the Recipe form.

3. Choose Edit ➤ Copy and then Edit ➤ Paste (you can also right-click, choose Copy, right-click again, and choose Paste). This will create two new copies called Copy of Ingredient and Copy of Recipe.

Creating a Basic Table

We mentioned earlier that the Recipe form didn't look very good. The fields are staggered, which gives the form an unpolished look. To eliminate this problem, you are going to insert a basic table; each row in the table will contain one of the labels and its corresponding field. You will also create two columns and place the label into one column and the field into another to align them all on the same boundary. This may seem confusing right now, but it will make more sense once the table is laid out.

To add a table to the form, just follow these steps:

1. Create a copy of the Recipe and Ingredient forms.

2. Open the Recipe copy and change the name of the form to Recipe Using Basic Table | RecipeSTable. You can also update the comments in the Table Properties InfoBox to reflect this name change.

3. Place the cursor on the blank line in between the form title and the first label/field.

4. Choose Create ➢ Table. Click the basic table button and make sure the value in the Rows field is 7 and the value in the Columns field is 2. Click the OK button and the table will be inserted on the form.

5. Cut and paste the text labels for each field into the first column of the table. Place them in order, each on a separate row. For example, *Name of Recipe:* should be in row 1, column 1. *Recipe Instructions:* should be in row 2, column 1. Do this for each text label. Keep in mind that the audit trail text labels and fields are actually on a subform. You will need to open the subform and copy the labels and fields directly from there.

6. Cut and paste the fields into the second column of the table, each on the same row as its corresponding text label. For example, the field NameOfRecipe should be on the same row as the text *Name of Recipe:* (but not the same column). When you complete all the fields, the form should look similar to Figure 19.17.

You may look at this form and think that it doesn't look any better than it did before, but we're not yet finished with the table. There are a lot of properties that can be associated to a table from the Table Properties InfoBox, properties that will greatly influence how the table currently looks. Let's take a look at some of these properties. To open the Properties InfoBox for a table, place the cursor inside the table and choose Table ➢ Table Properties (you can also right-click in the table and choose Table Properties).

FIGURE 19.17

The Recipe form with a basic table

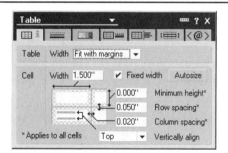

The Table Layout Properties

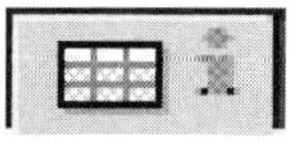

Select the Table Layout tab to customize the size and position of both the table and the cells within the table. You can also position the text within each cell. Once you select the tab, the window shown in Figure 19.18 appears.

FIGURE 19.18

The Table Layout tab in the Table Properties InfoBox allows you to size and position the table and table cells.

The Table Section In the Table section, you can choose how to size your table. There are three possible selections in the Width drop-down box:

> **Fit with Margins** Selecting this option will automatically set the table width so the dimensions will fit *inside* the current size of the window. We prefer this option in most situations because you can maximize the use of screen real estate and you won't have to worry about the user's screen resolution.

Fixed Width   The Fixed Width option allows you to set the size of the table. When you select this option, you will have the option of using the Position drop-down list box to set the table position (Left, Right, and Center).

Fit to Window   If you select the Fit to Window option, the table width will be automatically set so the dimensions will be the *same* as the current size of the window.

The Cell Section   The Cell section of the Table Layout tab allows you to set various properties for the cells within the table. The Width property allows you to set how wide an individual cell should be, which in effect can determine the overall width of the table. This setting only affects the selected cell. If you select either the Fit with Margins or Fit to Window option in the Table section, the Fixed Width check box will display. If you select it, you can have one or more cells that do not resize but remain fixed (even if other cells of the table change as the window size changes). The Auto-size button is a handy feature that will automatically size all the columns of the table according to the text contained within each cell.

The remaining table cell size features—Minimum Height, Row Spacing, and Column Spacing—are self-explanatory. Note, however, the asterisk (*) next to each label. It signifies that a change to any three of these fields will affect *all* cells of the table. This is different from the other cell properties, which change on a cell-by-cell basis.

The last property, Vertically Align, affects the text contained within a cell. You can align the text vertically at the top, center, or bottom of each cell.

Using the Table Layout Properties

With the Recipe form open in the Designer workspace, display the Table Properties InfoBox and click the Table Layout tab. Then follow these steps to use some of the table layout options to clean up our table:

1. From the Table Width drop-down list box, select Fit with Margins.

2. With the cursor placed in the first column of the table, check the Fixed Width check box and adjust the Cell Width value to 1.5 inches. This will ensure that the first column of the table will always be 1.5 inches while the second column expands to fill the window.

 WARNING If you decide to use a fixed-width column, make sure you select the Fixed Width check box before you adjust the cell width. Failure to do so will result in an incorrect cell width setting.

3. Enter **0.050** for the Row Spacing option.

4. Enter **0.020** for the Column Spacing option.

5. Select all the cells in the first column and right-justify the text by choosing Text ➤ Align Paragraph ➤ Right.

6. Select the NameOfRecipe field, display the Field Properties InfoBox, and change from the Native OS style to the Notes style (it will look better in this context).

When you have made the changes, your table should look similar to Figure 19.19. By using a simple table, you have been able to give your form a bit more structure. It's not perfect, but the text labels and fields form a nice even vertical line, which makes it easier for the end user to read the form. This technique works very well for applications that are to be used in the Notes client and also on the Web. Now let's see if we can do something with those grid lines.

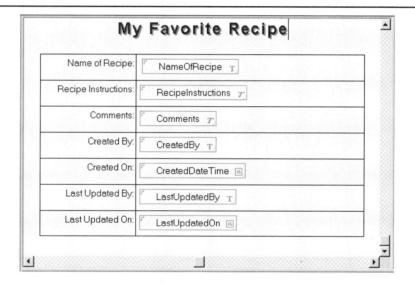

FIGURE 19.19

The Recipe form after the table layout properties are set

The Cell Borders Properties

In the Cell Borders tab, you can select both the border style and the thickness for each cell in the table. Once you select the tab, the window shown in Figure 19.20 appears.

 NOTE Be aware that Web applications cannot display partial cell borders. If one cell has a border, all the cells and the entire table will have borders.

FIGURE 19.20

The Cell Border tab of the Table Properties InfoBox allows you to style and size each cell border.

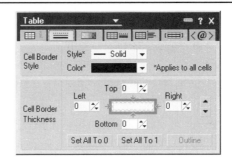

The Cell Border Style Section   The Cell Border Style section allows you to select one of three styles of borders:

Solid   The Solid style is a plain simple line that surrounds the borders of the cell.

Ridge   The Ridge style gives a 3D appearance that simulates a wall being raised off the page.

Groove   The Groove style gives a 3D appearance that simulates a small trench being grooved into the page.

The Color property allows you to select the color for the line around the cells. The Style and Color properties both have an asterisk next to them, which means they affect every cell in the table. Neither variable has an effect on Web applications; the Solid, Ridge, and Groove styles will all produce the same border, and the Color property is totally ignored.

The Cell Border Thickness Section   The Cell Border Thickness section is used to adjust the thickness of the selected border style for an individual cell or group of table cells. You can adjust each border of a cell individually by using the Top, Left, Bottom, and Right arrows. If you would like to adjust all four settings at once, click the up/down arrows on the right. To remove all the borders, click the Set All to 0 option. To set the border back, click the Set All to 1 option. The last button, Outline, is used when more than one cell is selected. This option will only set a border on the outline of the selected cells. This eliminates the need to go to each cell individually and set the border to 0 or 1 just to create a border around the outskirts of the selected cells.

Using the Cell Borders Properties

With the Recipe form open, follow these steps to remove all the border entries from our example table:

1. Open the Table Properties InfoBox.

2. Click the Cell Borders tab.

3. Select all the cells in the table by placing the cursor in the upper left cell and swiping down to the lower right cell while holding the left mouse button.

4. Click the Set All to 0 button.

Now our table looks more like a form instead of a table (the users will never know).

The Table/Cell Background Properties

The Table/Cell Background tab allows you to set colors in various ways for both the entire table and individual cells. Once you select the tab, the window shown in Figure 19.21 appears.

FIGURE 19.21

The Table/Cell Background tab of the Table Properties InfoBox allows you to add color or images to the various rows and cells of a table.

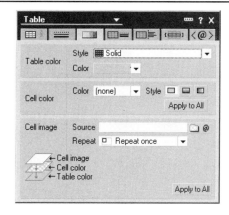

The first section, Table Color, is quite interesting. The Style drop-down list allows you to choose how to apply a color pattern to the entire table. There are eight different selections from which to choose: Solid, Alternating Rows, Alternating Columns, Left and Top, Left, Right and Top, Right, and Top. Select the color or colors for your pattern from the Color box. You also have the option of creating your own custom colors using the Color wheel in the upper right corner of the Color box. When you use this option for a Web application, make sure you only use colors from the Web color palette. Otherwise, everything but the color will render correctly.

NOTE When you are using the Table/Cell Background options, be aware that some options take precedence over others. A cell image overrides the cell color, and the cell color overrides the table color.

In the next section, Cell Color, you can set color for an individual table cell or a group of table cells. For an individual cell, just place the cursor within the cell and select the desired color from the Color box. For a group of cells, select the cells to which you want to apply the color and then select the desired color from the Color box. An added bonus for cells is the ability to apply gradient colors (a gradient color is a color that blends and fades into another color) by using one of three Style option buttons.

The first Style option button uses a solid color (the default). The second Style option button creates a gradient from bottom to top. The third Style option button creates a gradient from left to right.

When a gradient is used, a second color selection box will display as a To option. One limitation of using a gradient color is that they will not render correctly for a Web application.

 TIP If you would like to apply your cell color selection to the entire table, click the Apply to All button.

You can use the last section, Cell Image, to display an image in the background of one or more cells (like wallpaper). An image must be rendered from the image resources and therefore must already be a database image resource. Select the @ button to write a formula to evaluate to the name of an existing image resource. Select the folder button to select an existing image from the list of existing image resources. You can also decide how you would like the image to appear in the cell. From the Repeat drop-down list, you can choose Repeat Once, Repeat Vertically, Repeat Horizontally, Tile, Center, or Size to Fit.

 TIP If you would like to apply your cell image selection to all the cells of the table, click the Apply to All button.

 WARNING You cannot use the Cell Image property in a Web application. If you would like to set a background image for a cell in a Web application, you'll need to use the background HTML command and specify the name of the image resource, such as background=`"myimage.gif"`. This can be specified in the HTML tab of the Table Properties InfoBox.

Using the Table/Cell Background Properties

We are going to make a few changes to our sample application. Let's add a bit of color to the title of the form. With the Recipe form open, follow these steps:

1. Highlight the form title and press the Delete key (to remove the title).

2. Choose Create ➤ Table and select the basic table option with only one row and one column.

3. Display the Table Properties InfoBox for the new table. From the Table Layout tab, select Fit with Margins from the Width option in the Table section. Also select Center from the Vertically Align option in the Cell section.

4. Select the Cell Borders tab. In the Cell Border Style section, select Groove from the Style drop-down list box. Select a dark blue from the Color option. All four values for the Thickness option should be left at 1.

5. Select the Table/Cell Background tab. In the Cell Color section, select the left-to-right gradient option button (the button on the right) and choose white as the primary color and yellow as the secondary color.

6. With the cursor placed in your newly created table, type in the title for the form, **My Favorite Recipe**.

7. Highlight all of the title text inside the table. With the Properties InfoBox still visible, select Text from the Properties InfoBox drop-down list box. From the Font tab, select Arial as the font, 18 as the point size, and dark blue as the color.

We have now completed all the changes to the Recipe form using a basic table. When rendered in the Notes client, the completed form should look like Figure 19.22. To get a bit more practice, make the same changes to the Ingredient form so you will have a matched set. Just use the same naming convention you used for the Recipe form (that is, name the form Ingredient Using Basic Table | IngredientSTable). The remaining table properties will be discussed while we create the other table types.

PART

V

Beyond the Client: Uti-
lizing Domino Designer

FIGURE 19.22

The completed Recipe form using a basic table

My Favorite Recipe

Name of Recipe: Camping Scones

Recipe Instructions: Sift the flour and salt, rub butter into flour. Add sufficient milk to make a soft dough, put on floured board and knead very lightly. Roll dough out, about 3/4 inch thick. Cut into shapes. Garnish them with milk and place in hot camp oven for 7-10 minutes.

Comments: Make sure that the camp oven is hot enough. Very good and easy recipe.

Created By: Scot Haberman

Created On: 12/24/98 05:43 PM

Last Updated By: Scot Haberman

Last Updated On: 12/27/98 02:39 PM

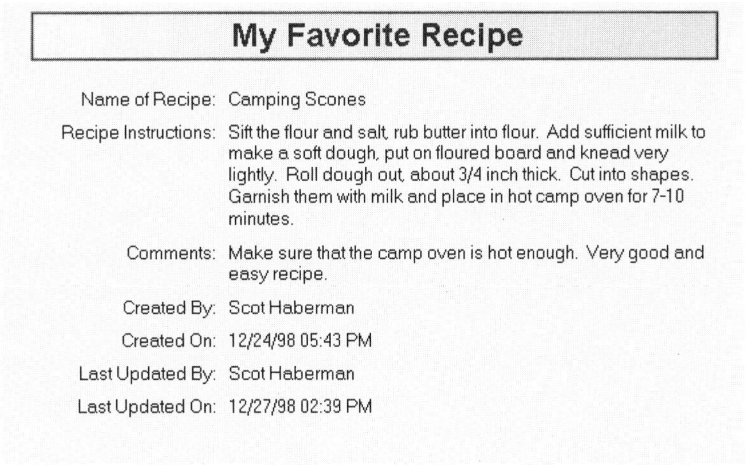

Creating a Tabbed Table

You've seen how you can use a table to improve a form's appearance. We've only covered some of the options, however. As we create the remaining table types, we'll use even more of the available options.

In this section, we'll create a tabbed table. This table type has a different user interface in Notes, but one that is very easy to understand. We are also going to use a nested table so we can build on our previous forms.

To add a tabbed table to the form, follow these steps:

1. Create a copy of the Recipe Using Basic Table and Ingredient Using Basic Table forms (these are the forms you just created).

2. Open the Recipe copy and change the name of the form to Recipe Using Tabbed Table | RecipeTTable. You can also update the comments in the Properties InfoBox to reflect the name change.

3. Place the cursor on the blank line in between the form title table and the table with the labels and fields.

4. Choose Create ➤ Table. Click the basic table button (yes, make sure it is the basic table) and make sure the table has two rows and two columns. Click the OK button and the table will be inserted on the form.

5. We are now going to nest a table within a table. Cut the first three rows from the original table containing the labels and fields and paste them into the first row. Cut the remaining four rows and then paste them into the second row of the new table. When you have finished, you should have a strange-looking form like the one in Figure 19.23.

We could have created a tabbed table from the Create Table dialog box, but we created a basic table first to avoid confusion when copying the fields from one table to another. As stated in the definition of a tabbed table, each tab represents one row in the table. In this example, we'll have a tabbed table with two tabs. To create a tabbed table, we'll use the Table Rows tab of the Table Properties InfoBox.

The Table Row Properties

Go ahead and open the Table Properties InfoBox for the new table. You must be very careful where you place the cursor. If you place the cursor inside the nested table, you will be using the incorrect Table Properties InfoBox. To be safe, place the cursor just above the nested table in the first row of the new table. Choose Table ➤ Table Properties to open the Properties InfoBox. To decide how to display the rows of your table, select the Table Row tab. Once you select the tab, the window shown in Figure 19.24 appears.

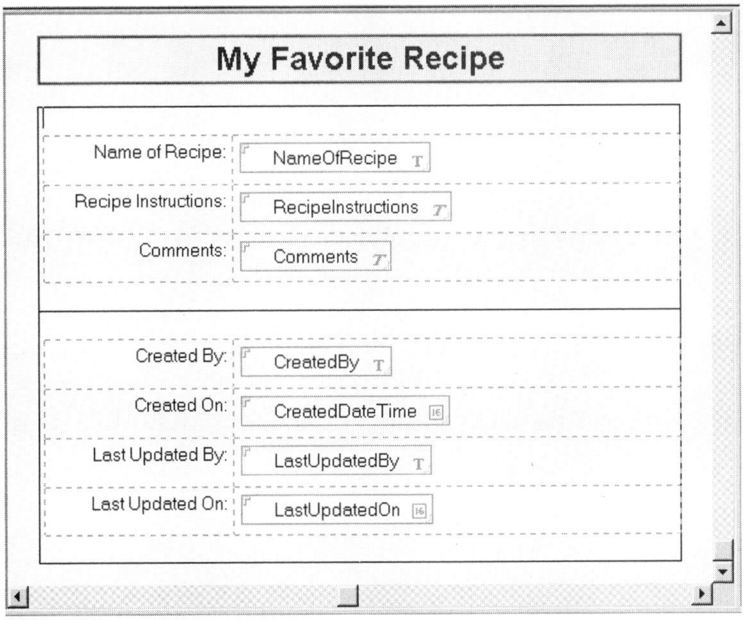

FIGURE 19.23

A nested table

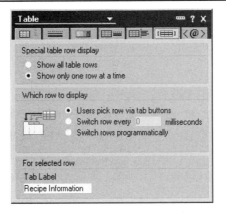

FIGURE 19.24

*The Table Row
properties for a
tabbed table*

When the dialog box is first displayed, there will be only two radio buttons and
the Show All Table Rows option will be selected. You need to select the Show Only
One Row at a Time option; when you do so, a new list of properties will be displayed.
By default, the Users Pick Row via Tab Button option is selected, which is what transformed the flat table into a tabbed table. Ignore the other two options for now (they
will be discussed for the other table types).

At the bottom of the dialog box is a For Selected Row section, which contains one field called Tab Label. Type in the text that you would like to see displayed on the individual tab. In our example, you have the first tab displayed, so type **Recipe Information**. Select the second tab of the table and type **Audit Trail** in the Tab Label field. Now you can start to see how the tabbed table is taking shape.

To make the tabbed table a bit easier to see, you can change each row to a different color. This is your choice. Any color will do. Just select the Table/Cell Background tab and change the cell color (don't forget to change the cell color for both rows). Your form should look similar to Figure 19.25.

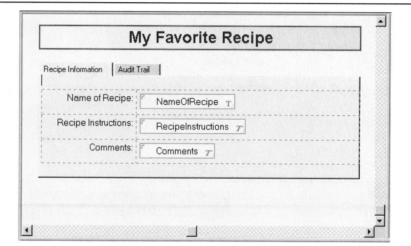

NOTE A Web application does not render the graphical tabbed pages in tabbed tables. There are still simulated pages that contain the same data displayed in the Notes client, but the look and feel is a bit different.

The Table Border Properties

To add a bit more pizzazz to your tabbed table, there are a few other formatting features that Notes can offer. When you select the Table Border tab, the window shown in Figure 19.26 appears. The options on this tab allow you to select the style, effect, and thickness of the border that surrounds your table.

FIGURE 19.26

The Table Border tab of the Table Properties InfoBox

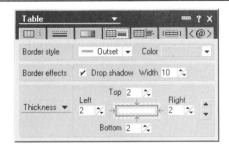

The Border Style section has options for the type of border for your table. Do not confuse this with the cell borders, although they are similar. The border style affects only the outer edge of the entire table. There are nine different styles to choose from: None, Solid, Double, Dotted, Dashed, Ridge, Groove, Inset, and Outset. Depending on the style you select, you can also select a color. For our example, select the Outset style with a light gray color. If nothing visible changes on your table, do not fret. There are a few other options you need to set.

The Border Effects section only has one option, which allows you to set a drop shadow around the table. For our table, enable the Drop Shadow option and set a width of 10—a very nice effect indeed.

In the last section, Thickness, you can determine the thickness of your border style and adjust each side of the border independently. These controls work in the same fashion that the controls for the Cell borders work. The drop-down list on the left side of the dialog box also allows you to select Inside and Outside as options. There are three parts to a table border, and you have full control over how thick each piece is. For our example, set the thickness to 2 all around. We are not going to fool with the dimensions for the Inside and Outside options.

NOTE Many of the table border options do not translate to a Web application. This is not so much a limitation of Notes but more a limitation of HTML.

The Table Margin Properties

The Table Margin tab allows you to set your table margins and how the text will wrap. Once you select the tab, the window shown in Figure 19.27 appears.

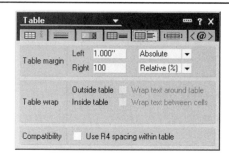

Now you have the option of setting the left and right margins for your table using an absolute position or a relative position. The Absolute option requires that you enter the number of inches to set the left or right margin, whereas the Relative option only requires a percentage. The percentage is based on the actual window size.

The Table Wrap section allows you to decide how text is wrapped both inside and outside a table. Text is only allowed to wrap around a fixed-width table. The Inside Table setting allows you to create a newspaper-style table by setting the height of a column; when the text fills one column, it will wrap into the beginning of the next column.

The last option, Compatibility, just resizes the table so it is equal to the size of tables in Notes Release 4.*x*. It seems that the tables in R5 are a bit smaller than they are in R4.*x*.

Now that you have created a tabbed table, make the same changes to the Ingredient form. Again, this will give you more practice and let you test what you just learned.

Creating an Animated Table

In this section, we'll create an animated table. It is an animated table because the table rows can be set to display for a specific amount of time. This table type is typically used for graphical animation, but it can also be adapted to other needs. The first thing to do is create a copy of the tabbed table forms (both Recipe and Ingredient) and then change the table properties to create an animated table. Follow these steps to get the forms copied and converted:

1. Create a copy of the Recipe Using Tabbed Table and Ingredient Using Tabbed Table forms (these are the forms you just created).

2. Open the Recipe copy and change the name of the form to Recipe Using Animated Table | RecipeITable. You can also update the comments in the Properties InfoBox to reflect this name change.

3. Let's add a table to the bottom of the Recipe Information tab. Place the cursor at the bottom of the tab (just below the existing table). Choose Create ➢ Table and click the button (the second button from the right). Enter **4** in the Rows field and **1** in the Columns field and click the OK button.

4. With the cursor in the first row of the table, choose Create ➤ Image Resource. Select JPG from the Image Type drop-down list box. By default, GIF is selected, which limits the display of images to only GIFs. We have already placed the images in the image resource library for you (you will learn how to do this later). Select the `Note1.jpg` file from the list and click OK. This will place the image into the first row of the table.

5. Insert images into rows 2 through 4 by selecting the appropriate image (`Note2.jpg`–`Note4.jpg`).

6. Open the Table Properties InfoBox, click the Table Layout tab, and click the Autosize button. This will shrink the width of the table to fit the size of the images. Also select Center from the Position drop-down list.

7. Select the Cell Borders tab and, for each cell of the table, remove the border by clicking Set All to 0.

8. Select the Table Row tab. Select the Switch Row Every X Milliseconds radio button and enter **100** in the milliseconds field.

9. Open the Picture Properties InfoBox by selecting a picture and choosing Picture ➤ Picture Properties (you can also right-click the picture and select Picture Properties). From the Picture Info tab, change the Text Wrap option to Wrap around Image for all four pictures. When you have completed all of these steps, your form should be similar to the form in Figure 19.28.

FIGURE 19.28

An animated table with graphics

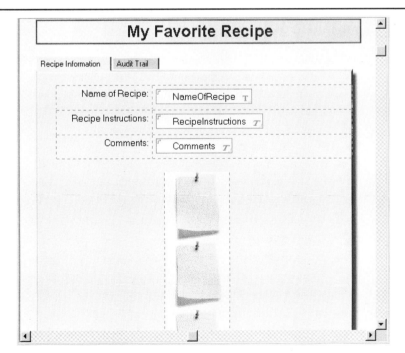

The animated table will display each row every 100 milliseconds, which will give the appearance of a moving image similar to an animated GIF file (we don't advise using this technique to animate graphics).

 WARNING The cycle for a continuous timed interval will stop once the document is placed into Edit mode.

There are some other options available for each row on the Table Rows tab of the Table Properties InfoBox. A new section, Transition When Switching Rows, is only displayed for an animated table. The Effect list allows you to select transitioning effects such as Wipe, Dissolve, Explode, and so on. With these options, you can create all types of effects for graphics. The Cycle through Rows list lets you decide how many times the cycle will take place. You can select Continuous (the default), Once When Opened, Advance on Click, or Once on Click. With this many options available, you can decide exactly how you would like your animated table to display to the end user.

 NOTE When using the animated table, keep in mind that the cycle options and effects will not work for a Web application.

Creating a Programmed Table

A programmed table is very similar to an animated table except the rows that are to be displayed are not based on a time interval or the click of the mouse button but rather on the contents of a special field, $table-name. Don't confuse this with the ability to create a table dynamically, because that is not possible. What is possible is the ability to programmatically determine which row to display. This ability is similar to using the Hide-When option.

A programmed table is set up through the Table Row tab in the Table Properties Info-Box. The first step is create a copy of the forms and then change the table properties to create a programmed table. Follow these steps to get the forms copied and converted:

1. Create a copy of the Recipe Using Tabbed Table and Ingredient Using Tabbed Table forms.

2. Open the Recipe copy and change the name of the form to Recipe Using Programmed Table | RecipeDTable. You can also update the comments in the Properties InfoBox to reflect this name change.

3. Display the Table Properties InfoBox and select the Table Rows tab. In the Which Row to Display section, select the last option, Switch Rows Programmatically. This sets up the mechanism for looking at the $Table-name field and causing the table to act dynamically.

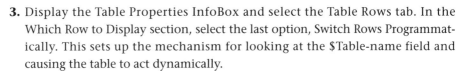

Now the table is programmed, but what about this special field? There is one final tab in the Table Properties InfoBox that allows you to define both a name for the table and a name for each row. The Table Programming tab displays the fields used for naming the table, rows, and cells for a table.

For our example, do the following:

1. Select the first tab on the table (the Recipe Information page). In the Table HTML Tags section, enter **RecipeTable** in the Name/ID field. This is the name of the entire table.

2. In the Row Tags section, enter **RecipeInfo** in the Name field. This is the name of the row that contains the recipe information data.

3. Select the second tab on the table (the Audit Trail page). Enter **AuditTrail** in the Name field in the Row Tags section. This is the name of the row that contains the audit trail information data.

What we just did was name all the elements that make up the table. We gave the overall table a name and also named each row in the table. We must name each row uniquely so we can programmatically access each individual row of the table.

Now we need to set up the $Table-name field. To do so, follow these steps:

1. Place the cursor in between the table and the page title. Type in the following text: **Please select which recipe you would like to see**.

2. Create a new field at the end of this text. Name the field $RecipeTable, which is our $Table-name (the $ followed by the actual name of the table).

3. Select Radio Button and Editable from the Type drop-down list boxes. Click the Control tab. Select Enter Choices (one per line), and in the Choices list box, enter the following entries on separate lines: **Recipe Information | RecipeInfo** and **Audit Trail | AuditTrail**. Note that the alias for each selection matches the name for each row in the table. This is how the table knows which row to display. The value of the $Table-name field determines which row to display based on the user's selection.

4. Select the Refresh Fields on Keyword Change option. This will ensure that the table is refreshed when a new choice is selected.

5. For the Default Value event for the field, enter **RecipeInfo**. This will ensure that the first row, RecipeInfo, will display when the form is first opened.

When you have completed all of these changes, you should end up with a form similar to the one shown in Figure 19.29. Go ahead and test the new form. By selecting a different value for the $RecipeTable field, either the recipe information or the audit trail data will display.

Automation Using Actions

Up to this point, everything has been accomplished by using the menu items (which is not a good idea if you plan to create a Web application because Web applications have no menu). Actions are typically used to emulate items from the Notes menu or to automate tasks such as creating a new document or running an Agent. When building an Action, you have the option of using a Simple action, a formula, LotusScript, or JavaScript.

Defining Action Buttons

An Action can be defined for both a view and a form. Action buttons are not stored as part of an individual document; they are stored as part of the design for the view or form. Once defined, all Action buttons are displayed in a special area of the Notes client called the Action bar. The Action bar is typically a horizontal button bar that is located at the top and runs the width of the design element. Usually, you create Action buttons that will speed up a task or tasks—such as saving and closing a document—for the end user. Even though some of the commands placed in an Action button may be accessible from the Notes client menu, you may want to create Action buttons for the more common tasks so the commands will also be available for a Web application.

Before creating an Action button, you need to determine if the Action to be performed is a one-time task or if the Action will be used in other forms or views in the same database. This is important because there are actually two types of Action buttons that can be created. One is called a Shared Action button and the other is just an Action button. Both have the same properties and are virtually identical in every aspect except where they are stored and created. The Shared Action button is stored in the design of the database, whereas the Action button is stored in an individual design element.

A Shared Action button can only be created from within the Actions work area of the Design workspace. To access this area, expand the Resources design element in the Design list. Once it is expanded, select Other and the Work pane will open. Select Actions from the Work pane and a complete list of all the shared Actions will be displayed in the work area of the programmer's pane (unless you have not created any yet). If this is your first shared Action, the Action Properties InfoBox will automatically display; otherwise, you can create a Shared Action button by choosing Create ➤ Shared Action. This will display the Action Properties InfoBox, which is shown in Figure 19.30.

FIGURE 19.30

The Action Properties InfoBox

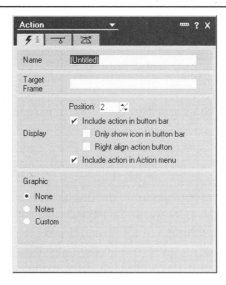

If you want to create a regular Action button, you must open the form or view and choose Create ➤ Action Button. This will also display the Action Properties InfoBox. If you don't want to create a new Action button but want to use an existing Shared Action button on your form or view, choose Create ➤ Insert Shared Action and a dialog box will appear allowing you to select the shared Action you would like to insert (assuming that at least one Action has been defined). When an Action button in placed on a form or view, you may notice that the Action pane automatically slides open. It lists all the current Actions defined for the element in the order they will appear to the end user on the Action bar.

 NOTE By default, there are always six predefined Actions for a form. They can be seen in the Action pane and are denoted by an asterisk. They are system commands and cannot be deleted, but you can change their properties.

 WARNING If you plan to use one of the system commands (such as Edit Document) for an Action button, be aware that these Actions will not be displayed for a Web Application. If you want to have an Action button that will allow a Web user to edit a document, you will have to create one.

 However you decide to create your Action button, the options on the Action Info tab are responsible for its look and feel. When the Action Properties InfoBox displays, this is the default tab. The most important field for an Action button is the Name field. This is where you enter the text that will be displayed for the Action button and give the user a clue as to what will happen when the button is clicked (unless you decide to use a graphic instead). The Target Frame field allows you to specify in which frame the action should take place (frames will be covered in more detail in Chapter 21). You can also change the relative position of the button using the Position field in the Display section. Every new button gets placed at the end of the list by default.

The other two options in the Display section let you determine if the Action button should only display on an Action bar, only display on the Action menu (the latter is only visible within a Notes client), or both. In some cases, you may want to place the less frequently used Actions on the Action menu so the Action bar won't be cluttered. But don't worry if you have too many Action buttons. The Action bar allows scrolling to all buttons that aren't visible. The Graphic section allows you to dress up the Action button. If you select either Notes Graphic or Custom, you can place a graphic along-side the Action button text to give your users another identifying characteristic.

 TIP To create an Action button with only a graphic, just delete the text in the Name field.

Once you set the look and feel for the Action button, you need to type in the actual Action to be performed. In the script area of the programmer's pane, you can use a formula, a Simple action, JavaScript, or LotusScript.

We are going to add a few Action buttons to make our form a bit easier to use. We'll add both Shared and regular Action buttons. To do so, just follow these steps:

1. Create a copy of the Recipe Using Tabbed Table and Ingredient Using Tabbed Table forms.

2. Open the Recipe copy and change the name of the form to Recipe with Actions | RecipeActions. You can also update the comments in the Properties InfoBox to reflect this name change.

3. The first Action button to create will be a Cancel button. Because this is common to all the forms, we will add a Shared Action button. Open the Work area in the programmer's pane for a shared Action. Choose Create ➢ Shared Action and type **Cancel** in the Name field. Select the Notes Graphic radio button and choose the big red *X* as the graphic. Click the Hide-When tab and select the Web Browsers, Previewed for Reading, Previewed for Editing, and Opened for Reading options. In the script area for the Shared Action button, select Formula and type in the following program code:

```
FIELD SaveOptions := "0";
@Command([FileCloseWindow])
```

4. Save the new Shared Action button.

5. Returning to the form, choose Create ➢ Insert Shared Action, and select Cancel from the Create Shared Action dialog box.

6. Next we'll create an Edit button. Choose Create ➢ Action and type **Edit** in the Name field. Select an appropriate Notes graphic (we use the red pencil). On the Hide-When tab, enable Opened for Editing because we don't want this option available once the document is in Edit mode. In the script area of the programmer's pane, select Formula and type in the following program code:

```
@Command([EditDocument])
```

7. The next button will be a Save and Close button. Choose Create ➢ Action and type **Save and Close** in the Name field. Select an appropriate Notes graphic

(we use the green check mark). On the Hide-When tab, enable all except Opened for Editing because we don't want this option available in Read mode. In the script area of the programmer's pane, select Formula and type in the following program code:

```
@Command([FileSave]);
@Command([FileCloseWindow])
```

8. Now we'll add a New\Recipe button. Choose Create ➤ Action and type **New\Recipe** in the Name field. Select the Custom Graphic radio button and, using the folder icon, select `recipe.jpg` from the Insert Image Resource dialog box. On the Hide-When tab, enable the Hide Action if Formula Is True option and enter the formula **@IsNewDoc**. In the script area, select Formula and type in the following program code:

```
@Command([Compose];"RecipeActions")
```

 TIP To cascade multiple Actions within one Action button, use the \ separator in the name of each Action. The text to the left of the separator should be the same, and the right side of the separator can contain any text (for example, *New\Recipe* and *New\Ingredient*). This will create a cascading Action button that will pop up a submenu.

---

9. Finally, we'll create a New\Ingredient button. Choose Create ➤ Action and type **New\Ingredient** in the Name field. Select the Custom Graphic radio button and, using the folder icon, select `recipe.jpg` from the image resources. On the Hide-When tab, enable the Hide Action if Formula Is True option and enter the formula **@IsNewDoc**. In the script area, select Formula and type in the following program code:

```
@Command([Compose];"IngredientActions")
```

 WARNING When you are using a custom graphic for an Action button, be aware that the image must be the correct height and width or it will not render correctly for a Web application. When run in the Notes client, the image is automatically sized.

Now that all the Actions have been defined, give them a try in the Notes client. Choose Design ➤ Preview in Notes and give the New\Ingredient Action button a try. If you look carefully, you will notice a graphical arrow on the button depicting that a submenu of options will be displayed when the Action button is clicked.

FIGURE 19.31

The Recipe form with
Actions

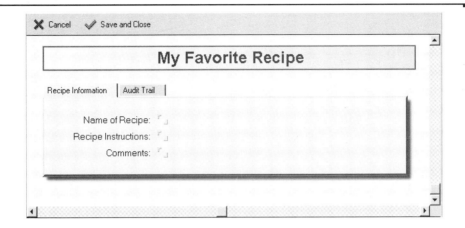

PART

V

Beyond the Client: Uti-
lizing Domino Designer

The Action Bar

You may not like how the Action buttons look on the Action bar, but there is a solution. There is a Properties InfoBox for the Action bar that will allow you to customize its look and feel.

NOTE The Action bar will automatically detect if there are more Action buttons than can physically fit on one line. If there are more Action buttons to display, graphical arrows will display on the right and left side, allowing the user to scroll from left to right and vice versa. Although this option exists, it is more intuitive to show all the Action buttons on one screen. If you have more buttons than can fit on one screen, try grouping common functions together by creating a cascading Action button.

To open the Properties InfoBox, select an Action from the Action pane and choose Design ➤ Action Bar Properties. There are five tabs that can be accessed and that address the look and feel for both the Notes client and Web application Action bar and buttons.

The Action Bar Info Tab   The Action Bar Info tab allows you to specify the alignment, background color, bottom border line, and Web access information for the Action bar. For the Alignment section, you have only two choices for the actual buttons to be displayed: Buttons Start at Left (the default) or Buttons Start at Right. The same holds true for the Background section. You can only select the background color for the Action bar. The Bottom Border option is a bit deceiving. This option does not allow you to place a border around the Action bar, only under it. You can think of this border as more of a separator bar distinguishing where the Action bar stops and the form starts. You can select from four options to position the border: None, Fit to

Window, Under Buttons Only, or Fixed Width. You can also specify the color and line style for the border. For our example, leave the position set to None. The Web Access section only applies to Web applications and allows the Action bar to be displayed either as HTML or with a Java applet. For our example form, select the Using the Java Applet option because it seems to be more intuitive and also offers a better look and feel for the end user.

 The Button Background Tab   We find the Button Background tab one of the more useful for creating a visual impact. In the Button Size section, you have the option of setting the height, width, and margin for each button that will be displayed on the Action bar. The Height drop-down list box allows you to select from four different options: Default, Minimum Size, Fixed Size, and Background Size. The default and minimum sizes were interchangeable at the time this book was written. They default to the typical size required for an Action button. The Fixed Size option allows you to specify the size in pixels for the Action button. When it is selected, another field will display, allowing you to enter the size for the height. The Background Size option will alter the height of the Action button to the size of the graphic you specify in the Background Button section, which will be discussed later.

The Width drop-down list box allows you to select from two different options: Default and Background Size. Both of these options work exactly the same as they do for the Height option (except this option changes the width of the Action button). The Margin drop-down list box allows you to also select from two options: Default and Fixed Size. Changing this option will change the size of the border that surrounds each button. For our example, leave both the Height and Width options set to Default. Change the Margin option to Fixed Size and set the number of pixels to 5. None of these settings affect the display for Action buttons for a Web application unless you use the Java applet. If you use the Java applet, the Action buttons work the same in both the client and the Web application.

The Button Border section allows you to change, via the Button drop-down list box, how the button border will be displayed to the user. There are three selection available: On Mouse Over, Always, and Never. It's nice to give the buttons a visual impact. If you select the On Mouse Over option, the button appears to change, giving a better presentation. For our application, set the Display option to On Mouse Over.

The last section on this tab, Button Background, allows you to change the background that will be displayed for each button. You have the option of using the Color drop-down list box to change the color, or you can specify a graphic. Selecting an image will override the Button Background Color option. The Image option can produce some fascinating button faces. Try experimenting with this option to see what combination works best for you. For our example, we will change the background color to a bright yellow to help it stand out against the pale yellow background of the Action bar. It is important that you choose colors that contrast so the user can visually detect that a button exists.

The Button Font Tab   The final tab, Button Font, allows you to change the font for the text displayed on the Action buttons. In our example, change the color to a dark blue and select the bold style. This will offset well with the yellow background.

After setting all the Action Bar properties, you should see a big difference in how your form looks. By using the Action buttons, you can "guide" your users through your forms, saving them from having to look for the commands.

Automating Using HotSpots

Another mechanism that you as a developer can use to automate tasks is the hotspot. You can program many different types of Actions to occur when the user clicks an area of the screen. You can associate a HotSpot Action with either text or an image. Most users will probably be quite familiar with hotspots if they frequently use a Web browser. Notes supports several types of hotspots:

- Text pop-up
- Formula pop-up
- Link hotspot
- Button hotspot
- Action hotspot

We're going to add quite a few hotspots to our example to demonstrate how they work (we'll add at least one of each type). Before we start, we need to create a new form on which to make our modifications. To do so, just follow these steps:

1. Create a copy of the Recipe Using Actions and Ingredient Using Actions forms.

2. Open the Recipe copy and change the name of the form to Recipe with HotSpot | RecipeHotSpot. You can also update the comments in the Properties InfoBox to reflect this name change.

Text Pop-Up

The Text Pop-Up HotSpot Action will display text information in a pop-up dialog box. This option is only available for the Notes client. Text pop-up hotspots will be ignored by a Web application. To create a text pop-up, follow these steps:

1. Open the Recipe with HotSpot form. On the Recipe Information tab, select the text *Name of Recipe:*.

2. Choose Create ➢ HotSpot ➢ Text Pop-Up, which will automatically display the HotSpot Pop-Up Properties InfoBox (see Figure 19.32).

FIGURE 19.32

The HotSpot Pop-Up Properties InfoBox

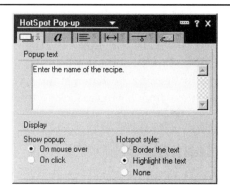

3. In the Popup Text field, type **Enter the name of the recipe.** This is the text that will be displayed in the pop-up dialog box.

4. For the Show Popup option, select the On Mouse Over radio button. When the user passes the mouse over the selected text, the dialog box will automatically appear.

5. For the HotSpot Style option, select the Highlight the Text radio button. This will highlight the text, giving a visual indication to the user that something will happen when the cursor is on the text.

6. Next, select the text *Recipe Instructions:* and create another text pop-up hotspot. In the Popup Text field, type **Enter step-by-step instructions for creating the recipe**.

7. For the Show Popup option, select the On Click radio button.

8. For the HotSpot Style option, select the None radio button.

9. Select the Font tab. Change the color of the text to a dark blue. Also select the underline style for the text. This will simulate a Web link and be quite intuitive to the user.

If you need to display the HotSpot Pop-Up Properties InfoBox, place the cursor in the hotspot and choose HotSpot ➤ HotSpot Properties.

 TIP You don't need to remove the text to remove a text hotspot. Instead, place the cursor in the hotspot and choose HotSpot ➤ Remove HotSpot.

Formula Pop-Up

The Formula Pop-Up HotSpot Action is similar to the Text Pop-Up HotSpot Action. The only difference is, with a formula pop-up hotspot, a task using formulas can be executed and the results will be displayed in a pop-up box. Be careful because the formula cannot execute formulas that take Actions such as @OpenView. Again, this option is only available for the Notes client; formula pop-up hotspots will be ignored by a Web application. To create a formula pop-up, follow these steps:

1. Open the Recipe with HotSpot form. On the Recipe Information tab, select the text *Comments:*.

2. Choose Create ➤ HotSpot ➤ Formula Pop-up, which will automatically display the HotSpot Pop-Up Properties InfoBox.

3. Deselect the Show Border around HotSpot option on the Basics tab.

4. Select the Font tab. Change the color of the text to a dark blue. Also select the underline style for the text.

5. To enter a formula for the pop-up, expand the HotSpot event from the Object tab in the programmer's pane and select the Click event (you can also place the cursor in the hotspot directly on the form). Type in the following formula:

```
@Name([CN];@UserName) + ", we look forward to your comments."
```

When the hotspot is displayed, the formula will be evaluated and display a message with the user's name. Although this example is not that practical, you could create a hotspot that displays the current date and time for the user.

Link HotSpot

The Link HotSpot Action will link to a URL, to a link (a database, view, document, or anchor), or to a named element (a page, form, frameset, view, folder, or Navigator). This option works in both the Notes client and a Web application.

In our example form, we'll create links to a URL, a link, and a named element. The HotSpot Resource Link Properties InfoBox is the key to setting different types of links. As shown in Figure 19.33, you can choose the type of link from the Contents section of the Info tab. This selection drives the remaining fields for the section.

PART

V

Beyond the Client: Uti-
lizing Domino Designer

FIGURE 19.33

The HotSpot Resource Link Properties InfoBox for the Link HotSpot Action

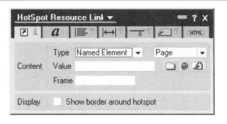

For a link to a URL, you only need to type **URL** in the Value field or use a formula to formulate the URL. For a link to a link, you must first use the Copy Link command to copy either a database, view, document, or anchor link to the Clipboard. Once the link is on the Clipboard, click the paste icon to place the link in the link hotspot and fill in the remaining Contents fields. For a link type to a named element, you have a few choices. You can select the element type from the list box and type in the name of the element. You can select the folder icon and, from the Locate Object dialog box, select the element type, the database, and the element name. You can also select the element type and type in a formula to evaluate to the correct element name.

For this example, we'll need to set up the form to allow the creation of the three various types of links. In the next series of steps, we'll guide you through both the form setup and the actual link hotspot creation. To get started, follow these steps:

1. Open the Recipe with HotSpot form. Place the cursor at the bottom of the Recipe Information tab (place it past the table). Choose Create ➣ Image Resource and select dotdomino.gif from the list.

2. Highlight the graphic and choose Create ➣ HotSpot ➣ Link HotSpot. Select URL from the Type drop-down list and enter **www.domino.com** in the Value field.

3. Place the cursor at the top of the form and type - **View Recipes Only** -. Highlight the text and choose Create ➣ HotSpot ➣ Link HotSpot. Select Named Element from the Type drop-down list and click the folder icon. Select View from the Kind of Object drop-down list. Leave the Database field on Current Database and for the View field, select (RecipesOnly). Notice that the text is already set to blue and underlined. Notes knows that it is going to be a link and sets it up for you accordingly.

4. Open the About document for the database by choosing Help ➣ About This Database. Once the About document is displayed, choose Edit ➣ Copy as Link ➣ Document Link. This will store the document on the Clipboard. Close the About document.

5. Place the cursor just above the table in the Recipe Information tab. Type **Need Help?** and then select the text. Choose Create ➣ HotSpot ➣ Link HotSpot. Because you already have a document on the Clipboard, Link and the correct values will be preselected in the Type option. Select the Font tab and set the color to red and the style to Underline.

Now you have completed all the links for the form. When you are finished, the form should look similar to Figure 19.34. All three links should work flawlessly in either the Notes client or a Web browser.

FIGURE 19.34

The completed form
with all three types of
link hotspots

- View Recipes Only -

My Favorite Recipe

Recipe Information | Audit Trail |

Need Help?

Name of Recipe: | NameOfRecipe T

Recipe Instructions: | RecipeInstructions T

Comments: | Comments T

.domino

Button HotSpot

The button hotspot is similar to an Action button. The main difference is that the button is placed within the contents of the form, whereas an Action button always displays on the Action bar. You would typically place a button hotspot next to a field where a process needs to occur. You can place a button anywhere you want, and you can also use a Simple action, a formula, LotusScript, or JavaScript to program the button to execute a specific task.

TIP To remove a button, simply highlight the button and press the Delete key. This type of hotspot is very different from all the others.

In the Button Properties InfoBox, you can type in text that will display in the button, which is the only real difference between the Button Properties InfoBox and the other Properties InfoBoxes. The button itself looks just like any other button and cannot be altered. The button's Action lies in the script area for the hotspot. You can have the button do anything you want, from setting field values to running Agents. To create a button hotspot, follow these steps:

1. Open the Recipe with HotSpot form. Select the Audit Trail tab. Place the cursor at the bottom of the tab underneath the table.

2. Choose Create ➤ HotSpot ➤ Button, which will automatically display the Button Properties InfoBox.

3. In the Button Label field, type **Save and Refresh Fields**.

4. Let's enter a formula for the hotspot. You will need to expand the Button event from the Object tab in the programmer's pane and select the Click event (you can also place the cursor in the hotspot directly on the form). Type in the following formula:

```
@Command([FileSave]);
@Command([ViewRefreshFields])
```

Now you can test the button hotspot. When the button is clicked, the document is saved and the audit trail fields are refreshed. Pay particular attention to the Last Updated On field because it will change to reflect the date and time.

If you need to redisplay the Button Properties InfoBox for a button hotspot, select the button on the form and choose Button ➤ Button Properties (or right-click the button and select Button Properties). To remove the button, just select it and delete it.

Action HotSpot

There is only one major difference between the Action hotspot and the button hotspot: how they look. Other than that, they are identical. An Action hotspot can be created on text or a graphic (similar to the other hotspots mentioned in this section). To create an Action hotspot, follow these steps:

1. Open the Recipe with HotSpot form. Select the Audit Trail tab and place the cursor to the right of the button. Press Enter to create a new line underneath the button.

2. Type **Save and Refresh Fields**. Highlight this text and choose Create ➤ HotSpot ➤ Action HotSpot, which will automatically display the Action HotSpot Properties InfoBox.

3. Enter the same formula you entered for the button hotspot.

We created equal hotspots to prove they both can accomplish the same tasks and also to point out how different from one another they look. When you have inserted these last two hotspots on the form, your form should be similar to Figure 19.35.

FIGURE 19.35

The completed form with the button and Action hotspots

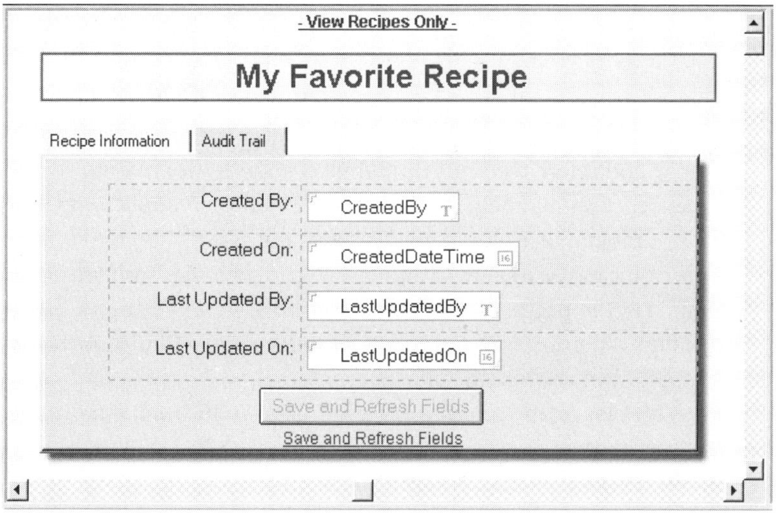

- View Recipes Only -

My Favorite Recipe

Recipe Information | Audit Trail |

Created By: | CreatedBy T |

Created On: | CreatedDateTime |

Last Updated By: | LastUpdatedBy T |

Last Updated On: | LastUpdatedOn |

Save and Refresh Fields

Save and Refresh Fields

Adding Graphics

Having graphics in applications is becoming more of a requirement than a nice touch, especially with the popularity of Web applications. In Notes, there are quite a few different ways graphics can be placed on a form. You can insert an image resource, import a graphic, create a picture, or paste a graphic (regular and special). Whichever method you choose, the end result on the form will be the same—a Picture element containing the image you selected.

 TIP Pasting a graphic is the least desirable of all the options. The main problem with this method is a loss of color clarity.

Image Resources

One of the main problems that has plagued developers is keeping track of images. In most cases, the images are scattered all over their local hard drives. If you're lucky, someone has had the forethought to create a Notes database and mandate everyone to place all images there. If you don't have some standard for storing images, this issue has been partially resolved in Notes R5 with a new design element call the Image Repository. We say "partially resolved" because images are stored in the Image Repository for each individual database instead of having some type of serverwide repository, and the databases will only store GIFs, JPEGs, and BMPs. It's not perfect, but it's a dramatic improvement over previous releases. An image can be stored once in the Image Repository and referenced multiple times throughout an application. This single point of reference should help developers maintain their applications and also help users avoid the problem of accidentally losing an image.

You can use images from the Image Repository for many different design elements, such as the pages, forms, tables, hotspots, Action buttons, and backgrounds, to name a few. Wherever you can insert an image, you will usually have the option of referencing it from the Image Repository.

It's easy to add an image to the Image Repository. First you must display the Work pane for the images. To access the images, expand the Resources design element in the Design list. Select Images from the list and the Work pane will list all the images currently saved for the database. To add a new image, click the New Image Resource Design Action button and the File Open dialog box will display. Just find the image to insert, highlight the filename, and click the Open button. You image will be saved with the original filename (you can change the name later).

Once an image has been added to the Image Repository, you can use the Image Resource Properties InfoBox to change its name, assign an alias, or change the number of images (see the sidebar "The Rollover Button Effect"). Select an image and choose Resource ➤ Resource Properties to open the Properties InfoBox (see Figure 19.36) for the image (you can also double-click the entry or right-click and select Resource Properties).

 TIP If you want to update an image, you do not have to remove the element from the Image Repository. Instead, highlight the Image element in the Work pane and choose Resource ➤ Refresh. The Open file dialog box will display and you can select the image.

FIGURE 19.36

The Image Resource Properties InfoBox

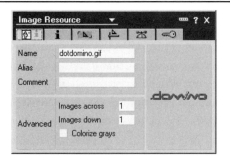

By default, the Name field contains the name of the original graphic file (including the extension). You can change it to anything you want, but you shouldn't delete the extension because it is used for filtering images in the Insert Image Resource dialog box that is displayed when an image is selected. You can also enter an alias and a comment for the image file. In the Advanced section, you can enter the number of images that are contained in the file (see the sidebar "The Rollover Button Effect").

 TIP Once an image has been inserted as an image resource, do not change its name because there is no easy way to determine which forms are using a copy of it. When an image resource is placed on a form, the source for the picture is the name of the image.

There are two ways to insert an image resource. If you want to insert an image where the cursor lies, choose Create ➤ Image Resource. The Insert Image Resource dialog box will then display (see Figure 19.37). You can select an image from this dialog box and it will be placed directly on the form, page, or whatever you happen to be editing at the time. The second method involves the properties of a specific design element. If you think back to the section on tables earlier in this chapter, you will recall a Table Property tab called Table/Cell Background. On this tab is a folder icon that displays the Insert Image Resource dialog box. If you select an image from this dialog box, a copy of it will be placed in the background for the selected table cell.

PART V — Beyond the Client: Utilizing Domino Designer

FIGURE 19.37

The Insert Image Resource dialog box

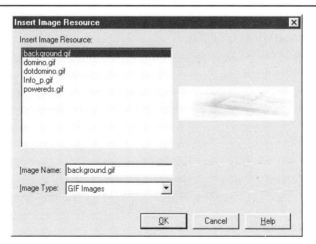

If you have inserted an image resource directly on the form, you may notice that the image is actually a Picture object. You can program the Picture object using JavaScript. The events that are available can be seen by selecting the Picture object and looking at the events listed in the Object tab window. JavaScript is outside the scope of this book, so we won't go into any more detail on this subject.

The Rollover Button Effect

One neat trick is to use an image resource to emulate a rollover button in an outline. To create this effect, you will need to create an image that actually contains two or more images, each separated by a one-pixel *image well*. For instance, in an outline, you can use up to three images; the first image is the normal state of the button, the second image is the state of the button when the mouse moves over it, and the third image is the state of the button when it is selected. Each entry in the image must be of the exact same height and width and *must* be separated by one pixel. For example, if you have a button that is 50 pixels wide and 25 pixels high, the image used as the image resource must be 152 pixels wide and 25 pixels high. Once the image has been inserted into the database as an image resource, you need to open up the Properties InfoBox and change the number of images to three. Give it a try.

Importing a Graphic

Another alternative to using an image resource is to directly import an image from the image file. This will place the image directly on the form (such an image is known as an inline image), but the only way to make changes to the image or to its position on the form would be to delete it and reimport the image again. This was typically the choice for versions of Notes previous to version 5. None of the image clarity is lost when importing.

To import an image onto a form, place the cursor where you would like the image to be positioned. Choose File ➤ Import, which will open the Import dialog box shown in Figure 19.38. Select the type of image you would like to import. You can choose from BMP, CGM, GIF, and JPEG. Once you have located the image file, highlight the filename and click the Import button. Once the file has been imported, you have the same capabilities for programming as you have for an image resource.

FIGURE 19.38

The Import dialog box

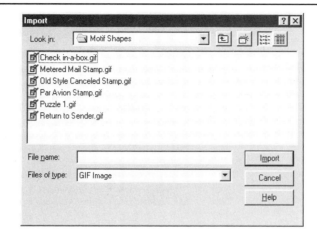

Creating a Picture

The last method for placing an image on a form is to create a picture. As the import option does, creating a picture will place the image directly on the form. To create a picture, place the cursor where you would like the image to be positioned and choose Create ➤ Picture, which will open the Import dialog box. Select the type of image you would like to import. You can choose from BMP, CGM, GIF, JPEG, Lotus PIC, PCS, and TIFF 5. Once you have located the image file, highlight the filename and click the Import button.

The Picture Properties InfoBox

Regardless of which method you use, placing a graphic directly on the form will result in the creation of a Picture element. If you would like to change any of the characteristics of the image, you'll need to open the Picture Properties InfoBox.

The Picture element has the usual assortment of property tabs, but the one that is of interest is the Picture Info tab.

The Source section has been mentioned briefly, but it deserves another look. If you have pasted, imported, or created a picture, the Source field for the image will not be editable; it will contain the text *[in-line image]*, as shown in Figure 19.39. Basically, unlike the image resource, the image is part of the form. If you used an image resource, the name of the resource, such as background.gif, will be displayed along with a formula icon (the @ symbol) and a folder icon. When the formula icon is clicked, a formula editor will be displayed in which you can write a formula to evaluate to the name of an existing image resource. If you click the folder icon, you can select an image from the image resources defined for the database.

FIGURE 19.39

The Picture Properties InfoBox for an imported graphic

The next section, Text Wrap, allows you to specify how the text should be formatted with the image. There are seven options to choose from; Don't Wrap, Align Baseline is the default. This option can be quite powerful and should not be overlooked.

The Scaling section allows you to resize the picture. If you click the Reset button, the image will return to its original size.

In the Alternate Text section, you can supply text along with the image. For a Web application, the text will be displayed in place of the graphic if the user has elected not to display graphics. The text will also be displayed while the Web page is loading. If you enable the Show Alternate Text as Caption option, the text will display underneath the image. This option only works in the Notes client and has no effect on a Web application.

 TIP You should always specify alternate text for an image.

The last section, HotSpots, allows you to add hotspots to the graphic. This is also a powerful option. You can insert a graphic and then create hotspots for specific areas on the graphic. When a hotspot is created, you can program an Action for the hotspot by using a Simple action, a formula, LotusScript, or JavaScript. This works in both the Notes client and a Web application. The Number field tells you the number of hotspots the graphic contains.

Embedded Elements

Embedded elements are objects that can be embedded on a form (and also on a document and a page). Table 19.1 shows a complete list of the elements that can be embedded and a brief description of each. To insert an embedded element on a form, choose Create ➤ Embedded Element and then select the element from the list.

TABLE 19.1: EMBEDDED ELEMENTS FOR A FORM

Element	Description
Outline	If you choose to embed an outline, you will be prompted to select from a list of outlines currently defined for the database. Once selected, the outline will be embedded on the form. If you want to be able to use an outline you have created, you *must* embed it. You have the option of embedding an outline in either a form or a page. An outline is typically used as a navigation menu for switching views, creating documents, or anything else you can think of. Because you, the developer, create the outline, you can decide how and where to use it. Once an outline is embedded, you can use the Outline Properties InfoBox to format it. You can embed more than one outline on a form or a page. Please refer to Chapter 21 for more information about outlines.
View	An embedded view will produce the same results in either the Notes client or a Web browser. Therefore, you won't have to worry about how the documents will display in either environment. To embed a view, select from a list of views currently defined for the database. You have the option of selecting a specific view or using a formula to evaluate to the name of the view to use. Once the view is embedded, you can use the Embedded View Properties InfoBox to change the look and feel of the display for both the Notes client and a Web browser. Only one view can be embedded on a form (once a view is selected, the option is no longer available on the menu).
Navigator	This option will prompt you to select from a list of Navigators currently defined for the database. You have the option of selecting a specific Navigator or using a formula to evaluate to the name of the Navigator to use. When using this type of Navigator, do not use the Hide-When property to hide the Navigator from Web browsers or the form will *not* display. You can embed a Navigator as many times as you like.
Import Navigator	This option will prompt you to select from a list of Navigators currently defined for the database. Once this option is selected, a "snapshot" of the Navigator will be taken and placed into a Picture object on the form. You can use the events and properties that are associated with a Picture object. You can import a Navigator as many times as you like.
Date Picker	If you embed a Date Picker, you can easily create a custom calendar application. The Date Picker displays a graphical monthly calendar in which a user can scroll from month to month and select a day. You can use it in conjunction with a frameset and place the Date Picker in one frame and a Calendar view in another. When the user clicks a day, a message is automatically broadcast. This message will be acknowledged by the Calendar view and that day will be displayed (this feature is only supported for a Notes client application).
Group Scheduler	The Group Scheduler control allows you to display the schedules of specific users. By default, the display is set to the one-day format, but it can be set to two-, five-, six-, and seven-day formats. When you design the form, the scheduling information will not be displayed. Only one Group Scheduler control can be embedded on a form (once a Group Scheduler control is embedded, the option is no longer available).

Continued ▶

TABLE 19.1: EMBEDDED ELEMENTS FOR A FORM (CONTINUED)

Element	Description
Folder Pane	In the Notes client, the database will display a default navigational pane that shows a list of all the views to which the user has access. The Folder pane is a control that displays the same list of views, but it's only used for a Web application. Instead of having to manually code a list of views to which the user has access, you only need to embed this element. Only one Folder pane can be embedded on a form (once it's embedded, the option is no longer available).
File Upload Control	If you want to attach a file to a document in the Notes client, you use the file attachment menu option. For a Web user, this menu option is not available and requires special handling. When embedded on a form and rendered on the Web, this control will display a field and a Browse button that will pop up a File Open dialog box on the end user's machine. When the user selects a file and submits the form, the file will automatically be sent over the Web and attached directly to the document. Only one File Upload control can be embedded on a form (once it's embedded, the option is no longer available).

The main reason for using an embedded element is to maintain a consistent look and feel across both the Notes client and the Web browser. As you have probably noticed by now, there are some significant differences in elements—the differences depend on the environment in which the elements are displayed. When you embed elements in a Web application, your application's functionality will more closely resemble what happens in the Notes client.

Summary

This chapter has dealt with quite a few advanced form features, including subforms, sections, layout regions, and tables. We also discussed how automation through Action buttons and hotspots can increase the functionality of an application. Finally, we showed you various ways to place images and graphics into your application so that forms are a bit easier to understand.

In the next chapter, we'll begin to see how all of the work you put on your forms can benefit the end user. What good is information if the user can't find what he is looking for? Using views to sort and display the contents of your data is an integral part of any well-planned application.

CHAPTER 20

Using Views and Folders

O ne of the biggest challenges facing workers today is *finding* information, not getting it. A view provides a mechanism for viewing the data in a document. A database can contain one or more views, each displaying the data in a slightly different way.

What Is a View?

In Notes, all data is stored in documents. A view can be thought of as a table of contents for those documents. In a book, a table of contents is used to navigate to a specific piece of information. You look through the table of contents for the information you want, find the page number, and turn to that page to see the information. A view is similar (except you don't have to turn pages). You select the view, look through the list of documents until you find what you want, and open the document. That's all there is to it.

One of the primary goals of a view is to help you find the information you need. Without views, finding information within each document would be extremely tedious. All the documents would be presented in some random layout that you would have to decipher. A view adds some structure to the process of finding your information, and it can display that information in a variety of ways. Unlike a static table of contents, a view can show documents alphabetically, grouped in categories, or in the order in which they were created. The ways you can display the documents within a view are practically endless.

Breakdown of a View

How does a document relate to a view? That's a good question, so let's take a look at a view and see. First, there are two styles you can use for views in Notes: the standard outline style and the calendar style. We bring these to your attention early because they are visually quite different, even though they are created in exactly the same way. A standard outline view is commonly referred to as a table view because the information is laid out in a row/column fashion. The calendar view, on the other hand, is laid out like a calendar, visually representing the days, weeks, and months. For the examples in this chapter, we'll use the example database Mastering R5 for Chapter 20. Go ahead and open the database in both Domino Designer and the Notes client because the screen shots in this chapter will be referencing both environments.

The Standard Outline View Style

The *standard outline view* can be thought of as a table of contents for the documents in the database and is depicted in Figure 20.1. From the Notes client, select Basic View from the Navigation pane. This is probably the most common style of view you will see for a Notes database. The contents of this view are grouped in rows and columns as they would be on a spreadsheet. Each row (depicted in alternating colors) is a representation of a document and displays selected pieces of information from that document. To be useful, each row should contain enough information for the user to easily identify the document. For example, look at the highlighted document (the document on the top) in Figure 20.1. The user would have difficulty identifying the document if we only showed the date the document was created instead of the recipe name. By using the recipe name as one of the row values, the user can easily identify each specific document.

PART

V

Beyond the Client: Utilizing Domino Designer

FIGURE 20.1

A standard outline view displayed in the Notes client

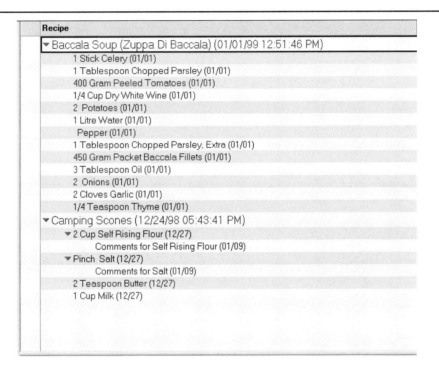

TIP What are those triangles to the left of some of the rows in Figure 20.1? In Notes-speak, they are known as *twisties*. The twistie indicates that there is more to the document, which can be seen by clicking the twistie to expand it. These are quite common in views that use the Response document hierarchy.

WARNING Do not confuse the standard outline view with a spreadsheet. A spreadsheet is a totally different concept because it is based on cells of data, but there are some similarities.

 NOTE Each database must have at least one view.

Not so obvious are the columns that make up a view. Each column displays a specific type of information about a document. The designer decides which element from a document should be displayed. One or more columns in the view are usually identified as organizing elements. In Figure 20.1, the documents are arranged alphabetically by the name of the recipe. The column containing the name of each recipe is then considered the organizing column. Columns can also be a bit deceiving. In our example view, it looks as if there is only one column labeled Recipe. There are actually two columns, but you cannot tell from looking at the view in the Notes client. To see both of the columns and the column definitions, you need to use Domino Designer to examine the view, as shown in Figure 20.2.

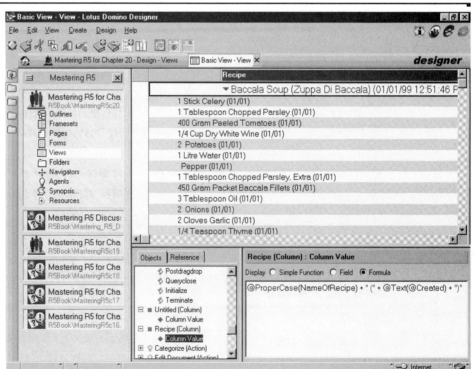

FIGURE 20.2

The standard outline view shown in Domino Designer

You can display information in a column by declaring some type of variable or formula for it. In most cases, the column will reference a field in the document. This doesn't mean that the column *must* reference a field. You can write a formula to display today's date if you so desire. You also have the option of using a simple function, referencing a document field, or writing a formula to display a column value. In our example, we used the field NameOfRecipe along with some @functions to create a formula that generates what is displayed in the column.

Using Simple Functions

A simple function is a shortcut to some of the more common functions used in a view column. There is nothing special about using a simple function; each selection has an @function counterpart, as shown in the following table:

Simple Function	@Function	Description
Attachment Lengths	@AttachmentLengths	Lengths of the attachments in the document
Attachment Names	@AttachmentLengths	Filenames of the attachments
Attachments	@Attachments	The number of attachments
Author(s) (Distinguished Name)	@Author	The name from the authors fields (Scot Haberman/Users/EDSTest)
Author(s) (Simple Name)	@Name([CN];@Author)	The name from the authors fields (Scot Haberman)
Collapse/Expand (+/-)	@IsExpandable	Returns a + if a row is expandable or a – if it is not
Creation Date	@Created	The date and time the document was created
Last Modified	@Modified	The date and time the document was last modified
Last Read or Edited	@Accessed	The date and time the document was last accessed
Size (bytes)	@DocLength	The size of the document in bytes
# in View (eg 2.1.2)	@DocNumber	A string representing the entry number of the document (2.3 represents the third entry below the second entry)
# of Responses (1 Level)	@DocChildren	The number of child documents for the current document
# of Responses (All Levels)	@DocDescendents	The total number of descendant documents for the current document

The Calendar View Style

The second style of view is called a *calendar view*. This view style is used to group documents by a defined date. Figure 20.3 shows an example of a calendar view style, called Create Date view, viewed from the Notes client. To see this view, select Create Date View from the Navigation pane in the Notes client. As you can see, the layout is quite different than the layout for the standard outline view. Instead of the typical row/column layout, the view looks more like a calendar (hence the calendar style). This view is used for grouping and displaying information that is based around some date/time information (for example, the date a document was created). One point to keep in mind when using this view style is that the first column in the view definition *must* be a field that evaluates to a date and time.

FIGURE 20.3

A 7-day calendar view displayed in the Notes client

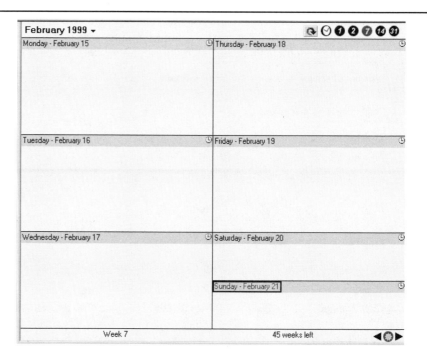

NOTE You cannot select the view style when you create a view. By default, all new views use the standard outline style. If you want to create a calendar-style view, first create the view and then change the style via the View Properties InfoBox.

TIP The first column of a calendar view must be sorted, must contain a time-date value, and should be hidden. You must also specify a second column that evaluates to the duration in minutes. If the duration does not apply, leave it set to 0. This column should be hidden as well.

If you look at the view from Domino Designer, you'll notice that it is almost identical to the Basic view. The only difference is that the first column is using the document creation date (and of course, the view is a calendar-style view) and the second column specifies the duration in minutes (because our example is not really an appointment, we set it to 0). The organization of the entire view is based on the first two columns so each entry can be associated with a specific date and time on the calendar. The calendar-style view can be quite functional when it is used in the correct application. For an excellent example, open your Notes mail and select the calendar view option.

Navigating Views: Client vs. Web

Before we get into the details of creating views and view properties, let's examine a view from both the Notes client and the Web perspective. It's important that you understand how a user navigates a view and how a view will display in each environment. This knowledge will be handy when you design views for your databases. For the examples, we'll use the Basic view and the Create Date view.

PART

V

Beyond the Client: Utilizing Domino Designer

Navigating the Standard Outline View

You've seen how a view is displayed in the Notes client. The default Notes database will have a Navigation pane (the pane on the left), which displays all the currently defined views and folders, and a View pane (the pane on the right), which shows the currently selected view. Figure 20.4 shows the standard outline view within the Notes client environment.

To navigate the view, the user can use the typical navigation keys: the up and down arrow keys, the Page Up and Page Down keys, and the like. To open a document, the user can double-click a row, highlight a row and press Enter, or right-click and select Open from the menu. Users can also select one or more documents for printing or deleting.

Figure 20.5 shows the same view Figure 20.4 shows, except it is shown in a Web browser. Nothing has been done to the view properties, so Notes is using the default navigational bar across the top and rendering the entire contents of the view as HTML. To open a document, the user just clicks a document link. To page forward or backward, the user must select either the Previous or Next link. One drawback of using the HTML view is that, every time the user wants to navigate or expand/collapse documents, a request must be made to the server and the results are returned to the browser. The Web browser is not as responsive as the Notes client. Another drawback is that you cannot select documents. You also cannot delete a document from a view listing. There is quite a large difference in using a view in the Notes client and using the HTML view in a Web browser.

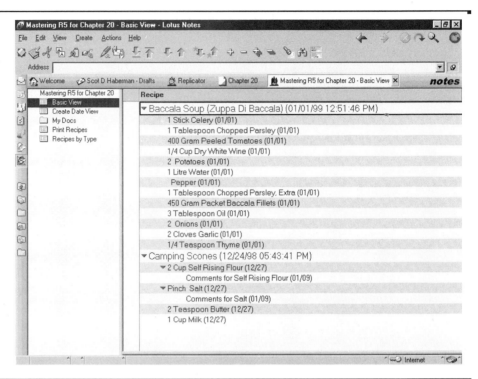

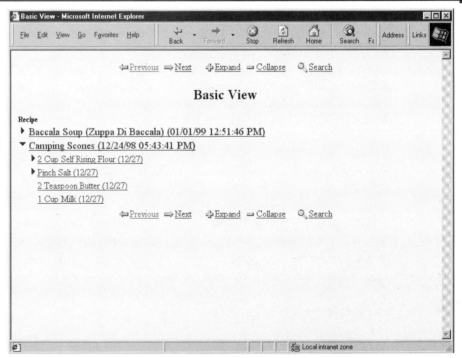

Luckily, there is an alternative to using the HTML view. New in Notes R5 is the view applet (see Figure 20.6). By selecting a property on the view, you can change the view so that it is a Java view applet instead of HTML (see "Setting the View Properties" later in this chapter). This view resembles the Notes client more closely, both in the way it looks and in the way it functions. A user can page up and down using the navigational keys just as they do in the Notes client. The only difference is that you cannot open a document by using the Enter key or by right-clicking on the document. To open a document, you only need to double-click one of the rows. You can select documents and also delete documents from the view applet. Because the view applet uses caching for the documents, navigating around the view and expanding/collapsing rows is just as quick as it is when you use the Notes client.

FIGURE 20.6

The standard view applet accessed via a Web browser

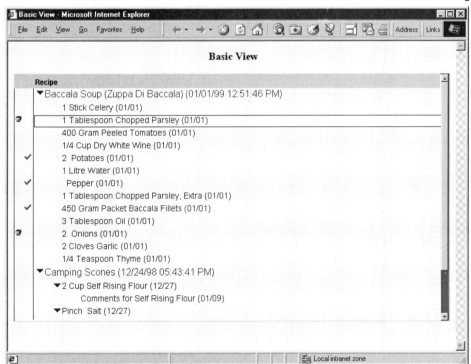

NOTE There are means other than the view applet that can be used to help "dress up" a Web interface for views. The intention of this section is not to show how to enhance a Web-based view but to show the differences between views displayed in a Notes client and a Web browser.

Navigating the Calendar View

Now let's compare the calendar view for the two environments (the Notes client and a Web browser). Figure 20.7 shows the calendar view within the Notes client environment. All of the usual navigational keys apply, and you can select to change the display to a 1-day, 2-day, 7-day, 14-day, or 31-day format. You can also display a yearly calendar. This is all automatically built in for a calendar view.

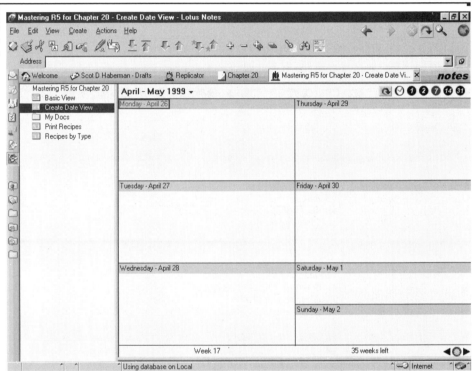

FIGURE 20.7

The calendar view accessed via a Notes client

Figure 20.8 shows the calendar view in the basic HTML form in a Web browser. There is not a view applet available for calendar views. You can still display the calendar in the various day formats and also display a yearly calendar, but the formatting of the view is quite different. You'll notice that the default navigation bar has been replaced with Previous and Next links. You can also select the link for the month (in this case, February), which will display the monthly view. Selecting the calendar icon will display the yearly view. Again, navigating the view in a Web browser is a bit different than it is in the Notes client, so keep that in mind when you create views for both environments.

FIGURE 20.8

The calendar HTML
view accessed via a
Web browser

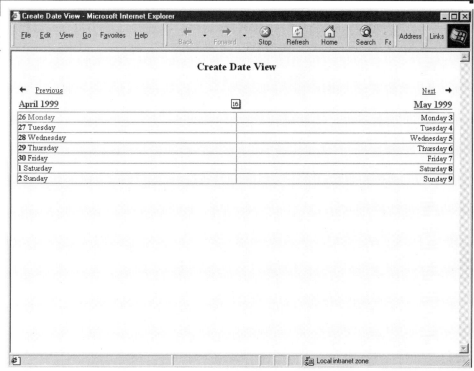

Creating a New View

Using the Mastering R5 for Chapter 20 database, let's create a new view that will categorize the recipes by type (whether it is an appetizer, a dessert, etc.). The database has
been set up with a new field called Categories (this field was not present on the Recipe
form in Chapter 19). To create the view, follow these steps:

1. Open the Mastering R5 for Chapter 20 database in Domino Designer.

2. Choose Create ➤ View. The Create View dialog box appears (see Figure 20.9).

   Now you need to make a few decisions. First, you need to give your view a
   name. By default, views will display in alphabetical order in both the Notes
   client and the Web browser. If you want a view list to display in a particular
   sequence, you must name the views accordingly. For example, you can precede
   each view name with a number or a letter—1 or A). Starting a view name with a
   hyphen will force the view to be at the top of the list.

FIGURE 20.9

The Create View dialog box

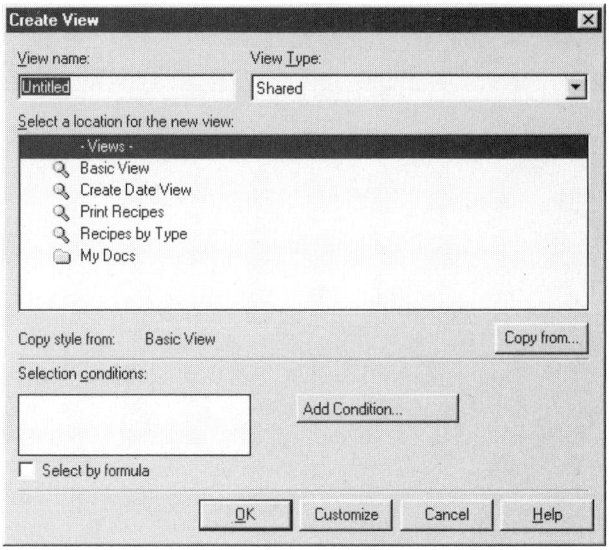

3. Type **Recipes by Type** in the View Name field.

TIP If you want to give the view an alias, enter the view name and the alias separated by a | in the View Name field. To create a "hidden" view, just place parentheses around the name. This will prevent the view from being displayed in the view Navigation pane. To create a cascaded view, use the backslash character (\) to separate the levels.

NOTE When a view name is enclosed in parentheses, it means that the view is hidden and used primarily for programming purposes. There are a few exceptions to this rule. There are four reserved view names that will not be hidden to the end user: ($All), ($Inbox), ($Trash), and ($Sent).

WARNING Be aware that a view that is hidden from the user can still be accessed by the user. You can press Ctrl+Shift while opening the database to display all the views (you can also press Ctrl+Shift, select View ➢ Go To, and select a hidden view from the list).

4. Select Shared from the View Type drop-down list (we'll discuss all six types in the next section).

5. Leave the Select a Location for the New View list box as it is. If you select a view from this list, the selected view becomes a parent and the new view will appear under it. In other words, it will create a cascaded view.

6. Click the Copy From button to display the Copy From dialog box (see Figure 20.10). The default is to use the default database view's layout when a new view is created. If you don't have a default view, a view will be selected at random from your list (usually starting at the bottom of the list). If you want to create a blank view, select Blank in the Copy Style From list box. (This feature is also a handy way to quickly create new views. If you're creating a new view that is similar to an existing view, copy from the existing view and save yourself a bit of work.) For our example, we'll create a blank view, so select Blank and click OK. The Copy From dialog box disappears, and you are taken back to the Create View dialog box (Figure 20.9).

 NOTE If you are unsure which view will be used or copied when you create your new view, look at the text next to Copy Style From in the Create View dialog box. If a view is specified, such as Basic View in Figure 20.9, that will be the view that is used as the starting point.

PART

V

Beyond the Client: Utilizing Domino Designer

FIGURE 20.10

The Copy From dialog box allows you to select a view on which to base your new view.

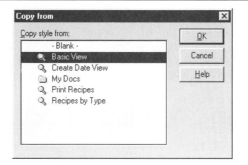

7. The last item to consider is the document selection criteria. The default is to select all the documents in the database. You can override this selection formula by enabling the Select by Formula option and entering a formula in the Selection Conditions text box. For our example, we'll use the default SELECT @All formula. The selection conditions can be easily changed after the view is created (see "Selecting Your Documents" later in this chapter).

 TIP If you leave the Selection Conditions text box empty, it will default to SELECT @All.

8. You have now entered all the criteria and are ready to generate the new view. If you click the OK button, the new view will be generated and displayed in the list of views. Another alternative is to click the Customize button. This will also create the view and open the new view in the Designer workspace to allow you to customize it (basically, this option opens the view for you so you don't have to open it yourself). In this case, click the OK button (we have a few more sections to cover before we actually design the contents of the view).

 NOTE When you create a Shared, Contains Documents Not in Any Folders view or a Shared, Contains Deleted Documents view, you don't need to enter a selection criteria because it is predetermined (the predetermined criteria for a Shared, Contains Documents Not in Any Folders view is, as its name implies, if a document is not in a folder, and the predetermined selection criteria for a Shared, Contains Deleted Documents view is if a document is deleted).

 NOTE You should always make sure that a database has a default view specified. Only one view can be set as the default and will be shown in the Work pane with a dark blue arrow (those with a light gray arrow are hidden views).

View Types

When we created the Recipes by Type view, we selected the Shared view type. There are six different types of views that fall under two main classifications:

- Shared
- Private

The only difference between these two main types is that a Shared view can be accessed by many different people, whereas a Private view can only be accessed by a single person.

Shared Views

A Shared view can be used by anyone who has at least Reader access to the database. Almost all the views that you will create will be Shared views because it is the most common type. There are five types of shared views that can be created for a Notes database.

Shared The Shared view is the generic and most common type of view. It is also the default for any new views that are created.

Shared, Contains Documents Not in Any Folders This is a special type of view in that it will only show those documents that are not in any folders.

Shared, Contains Deleted Documents   The Shared, Contains Deleted Documents view is another special type of view that will only show those documents that have been deleted. This view is only effective when the Allow Soft Deletions option in the Database Properties InfoBox has been activated.

Shared, Private on First Use   The Shared, Private on First Use view can be initially declared as shared to all the users. Once a user accesses the view, it immediately becomes a private view for that user. The actual private view is stored in the database.

Why Create Shared Views?

This is a good question with a simple answer. In many cases, you may get a request to create a view for a user. Instead of trying to tell the user how to create a view, you can easily create the Shared, Private on First Use view and let the user access it. This automatically creates the view for the user and makes you look like a hero.

Shared, Desktop Private on First Use   The Shared, Desktop Private on First Use view is exactly the same as the Shared, Private on First Use view with one exception: The view is not stored in the database but in the user's `Desktop.dsk` file.

 WARNING   Once the user has accessed the Shared, Private on First Use or Shared, Desktop Private on First Use view and the private copy has been saved, design changes you make will never be reflected in the user's private copy. The only way for a user to see new design changes is to remove the Private view and access the Shared view again (which will create a Private view once again).

Private Views

A Private view is no different than its counterpart, the Shared view, except that an individual user is responsible for creating it. There is only one type of Private view that can be created by a user.

Private   Just as the name suggests, the view is private and will only pertain to the person who actually creates it. No other person will ever see or have access to use this view. If the person creating the view has access rights to create a view or folder, the

Private view will be stored in the database. If the person does not have the access to create a view or folder, the Private view will be stored in the user's `Desktop.dsk` file.

 NOTE Private views and Shared views are visually the same. So you can tell them apart, a Private view will display a different icon than a Shared view icon in the Navigation pane in the Notes client. In Designer, a Private view will have a key icon. For a Shared, Private view, the icon will be the key with blue marking.

Selecting Your Documents

One of the main purposes of a view is to make sure the correct documents are being displayed. In the view we created earlier in the chapter, we did not change the default selection criteria (we left it blank). By default, a view will use the SELECT @All formula, which "selects" all the documents in the database. This may be fine for some views, but you may also want to restrict a view to a subset of documents.

When you create a view, you can determine the selection criteria that will be applied for the selection of documents. When we created the view earlier, you had the option of typing in a formula or using the Add Condition button (see Figure 20.9). For an existing view, you have the same two choices. You can enter the selection criteria before a view is created, or you can modify the criteria after the view is created.

Setting the Selection Criteria

To change the selection criteria after a view is created, you need to select the View Selection event. This is actually quite easy because this event is automatically displayed when a view is first opened. Let's go over the steps for displaying the View Selection event:

1. From Domino Designer, highlight the View element in the Design list. This will display all the views for the current database in the Work pane.

2. From the Work pane, double-click the Recipes by Type view (you can also right-click the view and select Edit). Now the View Selection event shows up in the script area of the programmer's pane, but it is not displayed in the Objects list.

3. Expand the Recipes by Type (View) entry in the objects list. By default, this entry will be highlighted.

4. Select the View Selection event and the programmer's pane will display as shown in Figure 20.11.

PART

V

Beyond the Client: Uti-
lizing Domino Designer

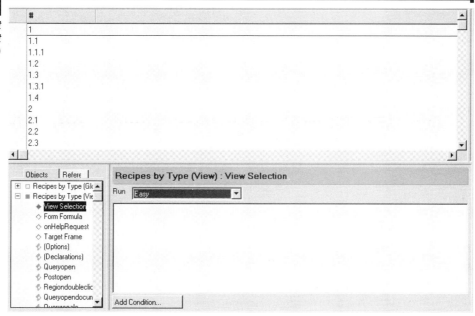

You'll notice that, in the script area, there is a drop-down list box with the entry Easy already selected. There are two possible selections: Easy and Formula.

Because the selection criteria uses a formula, you may be wondering what the Easy option is all about. When the Easy option is selected, the Add Condition button is displayed (refer to Figure 20.9 and you'll see that this button is also available when you are creating a view). The Add Condition button makes it *easy* to create the document selection criteria, hence the Easy option. You don't have to know how to program a formula, yet you can create the selection criteria.

So you don't have to manually code a formula for selecting records, the button will display a dialog box that will allow you to "point and click" to the selection criteria. When you click the Add Condition button, the dialog box shown in Figure 20.12 displays. Note that the title for the dialog box is Search Builder. In essence, using this mechanism will create the criteria to "search" for the documents. There are five choices in the condition drop-down box.

By Field　　The By Field option allows you to base the selection criteria on the values of a specific field. All you need to do is select a field from the Search for Documents Where Field drop-down list and type in the value of the field. For example, if you want to list only those recipes that contain the word *beef* in the title, just select the Recipe field, select the Contains condition, and type **beef** in the text box. Only documents that have *beef* in the Recipe field will be returned.

FIGURE 20.12

The Search Builder dialog box, which is used to select the criteria for searching for documents

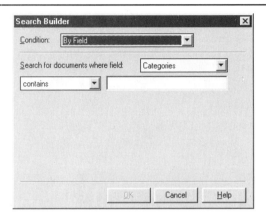

By Author   The By Author option is similar to the By Field option except Notes will search the authors fields on each document to find a match. The difference between this option and the By Field option is that *all* authors fields will be searched (you can have more than one on a document). This option is useful if a user wants to see a list of all the documents he created.

By Date   The By Date option allows you to select documents based on the creation or modification date of the document. It is important that you understand that the creation and modification dates are the only choices available with this option. One nice feature of using this criteria is the vast number of comparison operators. You can search between two date values, before a specified date, on a specified date, and so on.

By Form   The By Form option allows you to use an actual form to enter your selection criteria into the fields. As you can see in Figure 20.13, you can select one of the forms from the Form drop-down list and enter the search criteria into each field. If a document contains the information typed into any of the fields, it will be returned. This is an easy way to enter the selection criteria if you cannot remember the names of the fields.

FIGURE 20.13

Creating the view selection using the By Form feature

NOTE If one or more of your forms do not show up in the By Form list, make sure the Search Builder option on the Basics tab of each form's Properties InfoBox is enabled. This tells Notes that this form can be used in the Search Builder process.

By Form Used   The By Form Used option is probably the easiest and most widely used. You can select documents based on the form that was used to create them. For example, if we want to show recipes grouped by the food type and we only want the recipe documents that were created with the Recipe form, we would select the Recipe form from the form list (by placing a check mark next to it).

Setting the Selection Criteria with the Formula Option

It's a bit more difficult to create the view selection criteria with the Formula option. From the Run drop-down list in the script area (see Figure 20.11), select Formula. Notice that there is already a formula typed in for you. Look carefully and you will see that only those documents that have a value of Recipe in the field labeled Form will be selected. Doesn't that sound familiar?

That's correct. When you enter a Search Builder selection, Notes will automatically translate that selection to a formula. This is an excellent way to learn how to use selection formulas. You use the Add Condition button to add different scenarios and then switch to the formula to see how to write it.

We've covered most of the basic elements of a view that need to be defined (except for the data columns). As it is currently defined, our example view will select the correct documents, but it is still not perfect. Before deciding what data to actually display in the view, let's go over the view properties.

Setting the View Properties

A view also has a set of properties that control its look and feel; that is, they control how the view will behave when it is accessed by the user. One important factor to keep in mind when developing an application is how the data will be accessed by the user. Because views display various pieces of data contained within the documents, it's especially important to sketch out the different ways a user will want the data displayed. We cannot stress this point enough. Also, depending on the style of view (standard outline or calendar), the number of view option tabs will vary. With that in mind, let's go over the properties.

To open the Properties InfoBox for a view, just follow these steps:

1. Open the Mastering R5 for Chapter 20 database.

2. Open the Recipes by Type view.

TIP If you would like to see the current contents of the view, press the F9 key to refresh it.

3. Open the View Properties InfoBox by choosing Design ➤ View Properties (you can also right-click on the view and choose View Properties).

The View Properties InfoBox contains the following five tabs:

- View Info
- Options
- Style
- Advanced
- Security

The View Info Tab

The View Info tab (see Figure 20.14) allows you to specify four basic parameters for the view:

- Name
- Alias
- Comment
- Style

FIGURE 20.14

The View Info tab of the View Properties InfoBox

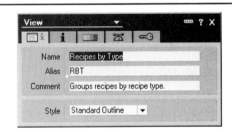

The Name field contains the name used when we originally created the view, Recipes by Type. The view is the only design element that has a separate Alias field. You have the option of typing the alias in the Alias field or using the vertical bar | and appending the alias to the view name. For this example, give the view an alias by typing **RBT** in the Alias field. The Comment field allows you to enter some comments about the view. A brief explanation of what the view is used for is typically enough. The comments will be displayed in the Work pane underneath the View element The last field determines the style of the view. As mentioned earlier in the chapter, a view can be either a standard outline or calendar view style. By default, all new views are standard outline. If you want to create a calendar view, you only need to change this parameter.

TIP Remember to always use an alias for a view design element and reference that element by its alias name. If the user does not like the actual name and you need to change it, you won't have to change any of your code because the alias name stays the same.

The Options Tab

The Options tab, shown in Figure 20.15, allows you to specify the overall behavior of the view. There are seven different options that can be selected.

FIGURE 20.15

*The View Options
Properties tab*

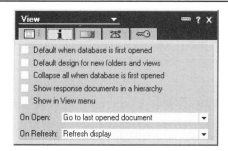

PART

V

Beyond the Client: Utilizing Domino Designer

Default When Database Is First Opened   Default When Database Is First Opened allows you to decide which view will automatically display the first time the database is opened. You can only specify this option for one view (Designer will automatically disable any other view when you enable this option and save the view). For our example, deselect this option if it is enabled. This option has no effect on a Web application.

Default Design for New Folders and Views   Default Design for New Folders and Views allows you to select which folder or view should be used as the default when a new folder or view is created. You may remember that, when we initially created this view, you could specify which view to copy (using the Copy From button). Using this option, you can specify that all new views automatically inherit the design from a specific view. For our example, deselect this option if it is enabled.

NOTE When creating a new view, it's sometimes hard to determine the design on which a view was based. If no view has been selected as the default view and no view has been selected as the default design, the view will use the default design view, which shows a single column displaying the document number and selects all the documents in a database. If a default view has been selected but no view has been selected as the default design, the new view will inherit the design from the default view. If a view has been selected as the default design, the new view will inherit the design from the default design view.

Collapse All When Database Is First Opened   The Collapse All When Database Is First Opened option only applies to views that have expandable rows. When it is selected, all of the rows will be collapsed. There is an exception, however, and it applies only to the Notes client. If the user is positioned on a specific document, the expandable category will not be collapsed. This option is helpful for large views with many categories. It's not available for calendar-style views. For our example, deselect this option if it is enabled. This option also applies to Web applications.

Show Response Documents in a Hierarchy   If your database contains forms for both a Main document and Response documents, the Show Response Documents in a Hierarchy option is important for maintaining and displaying the document relationships. Enabling this option will allow the view to automatically maintain the parent-child document relationship. You don't need to worry about how to include Response documents in the view. It is automatically done by Notes. We'll discuss this in detail in a later section. This option is not available for calendar-style views. For our example, deselect this option if it is enabled. This option also applies to Web applications.

Show in View Menu   When the Show in View Menu option is selected, the view displays as an option in the View menu of the Notes client (because there is no menu for the Web, this only applies to the Notes client). This option can be useful when you are not using the default view Navigator and wish to give the users another way to access the view. For our example, deselect this option if it is enabled.

On Open   The On Open option allows you to specify which document to highlight when the view is first opened. There are three choices in the drop-down list. Go to Last Opened Document takes the user to the same document they were viewing when they left the database. This is the most common option to use because it lets users keep their position within the view. Go to Top Row and Go to Bottom Row will position the user either on the first row of the view or the last row of the view. For our example, select Go to Last Opened Document. This option is not available for calendar-style views and also has no effect on a Web application.

On Refresh   The last option, On Refresh, determines how the user will see changes to a view. There are four choices in the drop-down list. Display Indicator will not show view changes automatically but displays the refresh indicator in the left corner of the view. The user must click the icon to see the changes. Refresh Display will automatically refresh the view before displaying it to the users. Refresh Display from Top Row updates the view from the top down. This is handy for reversed chronological views so the user will see the most recent changes first. Refresh Display from Bottom Row updates the view from the bottom up. This is handy when the user expects to see changes at the bottom of the view. For our example, select Refresh Display. This option has no effect on a Web application.

The Style Tab: Standard Outline

The Style tab for the standard outline view, shown in Figure 20.16, allows you to control how the view will look to the end user. You can control the colors for the view and also how each row in the view will be displayed. Color parameters are on the left side and column/row parameters are on the right side. There are a few other options for column/rows at the bottom of the dialog box as well.

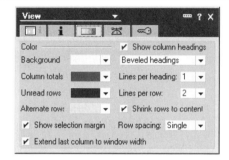

PART

V

Beyond the Client: Uti-lizing Domino Designer

Color is one of the most important aspects of the view. Too much color can turn the user off, but too little color can have the same effect. You should give the user just enough color to make information easily identifiable. Try to use subtle colors; a bright red background color can be distracting and make the information on the page hard to read.

You have the ability to control the color for the view background, column totals, unread rows, and alternate rows. For our example, set the background color to white, the column totals to red, the unread rows to blue, and the alternate row color to a light gray. This will help offset each row, making it much easier to see what information pertains to which document. This is extremely helpful when a document spans more than one row. The Unread Rows and Alternate Rows options have no effect when used in a Web application.

You can also control how each column heading and row will display. You have two choices for column headings: Beveled Headings and Simple Headings. The default is Beveled Headings (which we think looks best). If you have a long heading, you can select to have it span more than one line. You can also select to display multiple lines in the rows, which is useful if you have a large amount of information to display. And if some rows have less information, you can select the Shrink Rows to Content option, which will automatically compress each row to fit the size of the text being displayed. For our example, keep the column headings and set them to beveled. Set the Lines per Heading option to 1, set the Lines per Row option to 2, and enable the Shrink Rows to Content option. The Beveled Headings option does not have any effect on a Web application.

The last few options allow you to show the selection margin, set the row spacing, and extend the last column to fit the width of the window. The selection margin is a good visual indicator of which documents are deleted and selected. For our example, enable both options and set the row spacing to Single.

The Style Tab: Calendar

The Style tab for the calendar-style view, shown in Figure 20.17, allows you to control how the view will look to the end user. Many of the options are the same as the style options for the standard outline view.

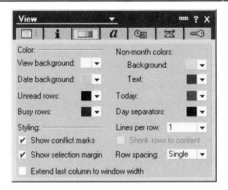

This dialog box has six options that aren't in the Style tab for a standard outline view. They all deal with entries that are specific to a calendar. Although our example is not a calendar-style view, we'll quickly review the options on this tab.

The options in the Color area are for the current month. The Date Background option sets the color to use for the header for each day in the calendar where the date is specified. When two or more calendar entries are scheduled for the same time period, you can use the Busy Rows option to set a color to mark conflicting rows.

There are two color options for months other than the current month in the Non-Month Colors area (these colors only take effect when displaying the view in month mode, which is the 31-day format). The Background option specifies a color for the current header for each day in the calendar where the date is specified. You can also specify that the text for these months be in a different color as well.

The two other color options, Today and Day Separators, allow you to specify the current header for today's date and the color used to separate the daily entries.

Under the Styling area, the Show Conflict Marks option will display an indicator visually warning the user if two entries are specified for the same date and time.

The Advanced Tab

The Advanced tab, shown in Figure 20.18, contains a set of the more complex view options. Two of the options, Refresh Index and Discard Index, have a direct impact on the speed of your database. There are four selections available for refreshing the index:

Auto, after First Use   Updates the view every time a user opens it after the first time it is opened (slow).

Automatic   Updates the view whether or not the user opens it (faster).

Manual   The view is not updated unless the user indexes it manually (fastest).

Auto, at Most Every   Updates the view index at a specified hourly interval (good for large databases).

When trying to determine which option to select, keep in mind how volatile the data is and also how quickly it changes. There are many options that need to be considered, and each situation is a bit different. For our example, set the Refresh Index option to Automatic.

FIGURE 20.18

*The Advanced
Properties tab for
a view*

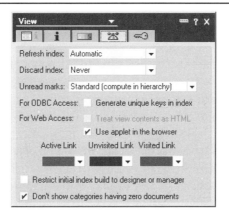

The Discard Index option also has a direct impact on speed. There are three options available:

Never   The view index is always retained, using more disk space but speeding up access time for opening a view.

After Each Use   Saves a lot of disk space but may cause long delays because the view index needs to be rebuilt each time the user opens the view.

If Inactive For   Removes the view index only when the index has not been accessed after a selected number of days.

The trade-offs with these Discard Index properties is either speed or disk space. If you always discard the index, the user will need to wait every time the view is opened and the index is rebuilding. If you always keep the index, you take up disk space. For our example, set the Discard Index option to Never.

The Unread Marks property is only useful within the Notes client (it doesn't work on the Web). Don't overlook how important this option is to many users. Unread marks allow users to open a database and quickly see which documents they have not read (or documents they have read that have been modified). This is one of the more useful options within a Notes database. There are three options available for unread marks:

None   Does not track unread marks.

Unread Documents Only   Displays an asterisk next to unread documents.

Standard (Compute in Hierarchy)   Displays an asterisk next to unread documents and any collapsed category containing unread documents.

For our example, set the Unread Marks option to Standard (Compute in Hierarchy).

 NOTE If you set the Unread Marks option to Unread Documents Only or Standard (Compute in Hierarchy) and unread marks are still not showing up, remember that there is a database property that can be enabled that prevents maintaining unread marks.

You should also be aware of the Use Applet in Browser and Don't Show Categories Having Zero Documents options. You now have the option of using the regular HTML view or the Java view applet when displaying documents on the Web. We prefer the new Java applet because it displays the data a bit more cleanly and provides functionality not available in the HTML version (such as the selection margin). The Don't Show Categories Having Zero Documents option prevents categories from being displayed in a view if there aren't any documents to be displayed for that category. This may sound silly. How can a category display with no documents? Simple. The documents may have a readers field (which prevents some users from seeing the document), yet the category for the document will still display. This was a huge annoyance in previous versions, but now it has been fixed.

 WARNING Setting the Don't Show Categories Having Zero Documents has an impact on performance.

The Security Tab

 The Security tab, shown in Figure 20.19, should already be familiar to you. You can select who has access to use the view and who does not. For our example, select All Readers and Above.

FIGURE 20.19

The Security Properties tab

The Font Tab: Calendar

The Font tab, shown in Figure 20.20, is only used for the calendar-style view. There is really nothing special about the font selection boxes, but you can select which elements of the calendar view to change from the drop-down list at the top. Your choices are as follows:

- **Time/Slots Grouping**   The time slots displayed for a calendar day
- **Header**   The month, day, and weeks/days remaining displayed in the header and footer for the entire calendar
- **Day and Date**   The date and day of the week displayed in the header for a calendar day

FIGURE 20.20

The Font Properties tab for a calendar-style view

The Date and Time Format Tab: Calendar

The Date and Time Format tab, shown in Figure 20.21, includes options for formatting the display of a calendar-style view. There are quite a number of options that allow you to have complete control over the display for this type of view. You can enable daily time slots, specifying the start time, end time, and duration increments (from as little as 1 minute to as much as 2 hours).

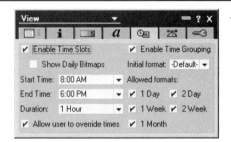

FIGURE 20.21

The Date and Time Properties tab for a calendar-style view

You can also set the default display when the view is initially opened to either 1 day, 2 days, 1 week, 2 weeks, or 1 month. The reverse is also true. You can limit the number of different display types to which the user is allowed to switch. For example, you may wish to allow the user to only display the calendar in 1- or 2-day displays.

NOTE Enabling the Show Daily Bitmaps option will display a small clock icon in the window for a daily entry. This option allows the user to turn time slots on or off on a daily basis instead of either having all time slots on or having all time slots off.

Defining the View Column Data

The next step is to actually put data into a view. As mentioned earlier in this chapter, each row in a view is actually a small representation of the contents of an actual document. Without this information, a view is meaningless. These columns of data allow a user to identify which document is actually being represented.

By default, when a new view is created (assuming that you did not create the view based on an existing view definition), only one column of data is created, as shown in Figure 20.22. This column is represented with a # as the column title and displays the document number for each document. As you can see, this is meaningless to an end user. A user is not going to be able to identify a specific document using 1, 2, and so on as the only identifier. To remedy this situation, we are going to add a few columns to identify a document uniquely.

FIGURE 20.22

*The default definition
for a new view*

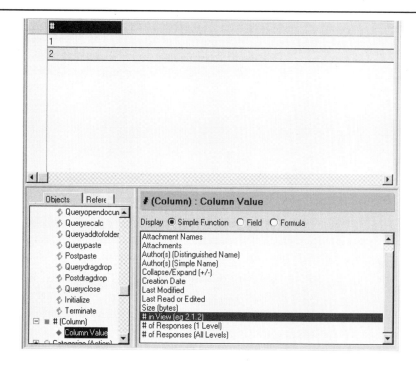

The Column Value and Properties

In our example, we want to change the value that the column is going to display.
To do so, just click the column header. This will display the value or formula for the
column selected in the script area of the programmer's pane. The selected column's
value is a Simple action of # in View (eg 2.1.2) (see Figure 20.22). If you select the
Formula radio button in the script area, you'll see that the Simple action is actually
using the @formula @DocNumber, which in turn displays the number for each document in the view.

For our view to be a bit more meaningful, we want to change the value of this column so that the type of recipe will be displayed (this value is contained in the Categories field). You have two options for setting this value. One would be to just type
Categories (the name of the field) over the formula @DocNumber. In some cases, you
may find this quicker. The second option is a bit easier in that you don't have to worry
about making a typographical error because you can select the field from a list.

To display a list of fields, select the Field radio button in the script area (see Figure 20.23). Just click the name of the field you want to use. In this case, select Categories. That is all there is to it. Now the column will show the contents of the Categories
field for each document in the view.

Selecting a column value from a list of defined fields for the database

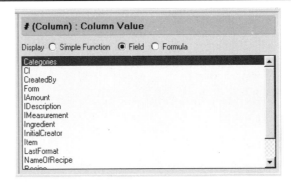

The next step in the process of setting up a column in a view is to change the column title or header. This requires you to open the Properties InfoBox for the column. To open the Properties InfoBox, follow these steps:

1. Select the column for which you want to display the properties by clicking the column heading.

2. Open the Column Properties InfoBox by choosing Design ➤ Column Properties (you can also right-click the column header and choose Column Properties or just double-click the heading).

The Column Properties InfoBox contains the following seven tabs:

- Column Info
- Sorting
- Font
- Numbers
- Date and Time Format
- Title
- Advanced

The Column InfoTab

The Column Info tab, shown in Figure 20.24, allows you to specify the following:

Title   This value is the title displayed in the column heading. For our example, enter **Type** (because we'll be displaying the types of recipes).

Width   This number is used to determine the actual width for the column. If you make it too short, values in the column will be cut off. If you make it too long, you'll waste valuable screen real estate. For our example, enter a value of 3. (You may think that this value is too low, but when we get to the Sorting tab, you'll see that this column is actually going to be categorized, and a categorized column is handled a bit differently.)

Multi-Value Separator   If a field contains multiple values, this option allows you to set how the values will be separated (None, Space, Comma, Semicolon, or New Line).

Resizable   Enabling this option will allow the user to change the width of the column.

Show Responses Only   Determines whether or not this column will display values for Response documents only. This will be explained in more detail in "Understanding the Response Hierarchy" later in this chapter.

Hide Column   Allows you to hide a column from the user. This option is handy for sorting the documents in a view without having to show the actual data for the column. For example, you may want to sort the view based on the 32-character document universal identifier (UNID), but you don't want to display this value to the end user.

Display Values as Icons   One handy feature of a view is that you can display an icon. If you select this option, make sure the column width is set to 1 (you're only going to display a small icon). Also, the value for the column must evaluate to an integer ranging in value from 1 to 172 (use 0 to signify no icon or blank). Each number represents an icon. For example, if you wanted to show the paper-clip icon to represent a document that contains an attachment, use the formula @If(@Attachment;5;0). A list of all the possible graphics is shown in Figure 20.25 (this table is also contained in the Help database).

FIGURE 20.24

*The Column Info tab
for the column*

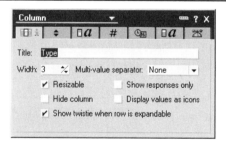

   TIP   Although Notes Help states that you cannot add to the list of view icons, that is not entirely true. The list of view icons is located in the Domino\Icons directory (look under the Notes root data directory). A view icon is named vnicnXXX.gif, where XXX is a number such as 001 or 125. This number matches the value for the icon. If you want to add a specific icon and it's not listed, or if you want to change an existing icon, you can do so by manipulating these graphic files.

FIGURE 20.25

The column icons and their respective numbers

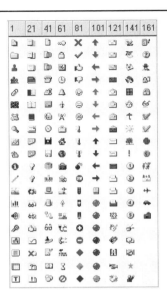

1	21	41	61	81	101	121	141	161

Show Twistie When Row Is Expandable   This option is used for a categorized row (see the following section, "The Sorting Tab") and also for Response documents (see "Understanding the Response Hierarchy" later in this chapter). A categorized row eliminates duplication of the value on every row of the view. Instead, the value is shown next to a twistie (an arrowhead), and when it's clicked, all the rows are either expanded (all the rows are shown for the value) or collapsed (none of the rows are shown for the value). Think of a categorized value as a "header" for all the "like" rows. For our example, enable this option.

The Sorting Tab

The Sorting tab, shown in Figure 20.26, allows you to control whether or not the data in the view should appear in a specific sorted order.

FIGURE 20.26

The Sorting tab for a column

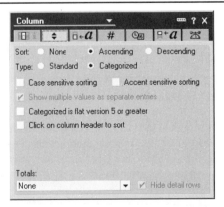

The following options appear on this tab:

Sort   This option sets the sorting rule (or sort order) for the column. You have the choice of None, Ascending, or Descending. For our example select Ascending.

Type   You can choose either a standard or categorized sorting type. If you select Categorized, you must specify a sorting rule (however, if you forget, the Ascending sort rule will automatically be selected for you). For a group of documents to be grouped under one category, the documents need to be sorted by that same value. For our example, select the Categorized option.

Case Sensitive Sorting and Accent Sensitive Sorting   These options allow you to decide if the case and accents should be taken into account when the data is sorted.

Show Multiple Values as Separate Entries   By default, a categorized column will display a multivalue field as a separate entry. This can be a major factor when you create documents because it allows a single document to be classified under many different categories.

Categorized Is Flat Version 5 or Greater   This option is typically used for hidden categorized views. It creates one entry for each category; it doesn't look good, but because the view is hidden, how it looks should not matter. Use this type of view for a performance improvement when accessing categorized views using features such as @DBColumn and @Dblookup.

Click on Column Header to Sort   You can specify that the column header can be used for altering the sort. The column can be sorted in ascending order, descending order, or both. This will appear to the user as up or down arrows in the column header. When an arrow is clicked, the sorting order for the column will change. Another handy feature is the ability to switch views when the user clicks the column header. Instead of actually changing the sort for the view, the user is quickly transferred to another view.

PART

V

Beyond the Client: Uti-
lizing Domino Designer

 WARNING If you allow the user to change the sorting order for views that contain categorized columns, the results may not be what you would expect. If a sorting order is changed, the documents won't be grouped together by the categorized column, hence the category is no longer valid. Because the categorized column is not really displaying the data for each document, it will just disappear. If the category is an important piece of information for distinguishing different documents, the results may confuse the user.

Totals This may be a bit of a stretch, but you do have the ability to add some statistics about the documents within the view.

The Font, Number, and Date and Time Format Tabs

The Font tab, Number tab, and Date and Time Format tab allow you to control how the values for the column are actually formatted. The Font tab allows you to control the size, color, and justification for text values. The Number tab allows you to control the display format for numeric data. You can select General, Fixed, Scientific, or Currency. You also have the option of selecting the number of decimal places, percentage values, negative numbers, or punctuation for numbers over 1,000. The Date and Time Format tab allows you to control how date and time values should be displayed. You have the option of displaying both date and time, date only, or time only. You also have various options available to format each of these types. For our example, the value is always text. Select the Font tab and change the size to 12, the style to bold, and the text color to navy.

 TIP One handy feature for time values is the built-in ability to adjust the value for local time zones. You can have the time automatically adjust to the user's local time zone, always show the time zone, and show the time zone only if it is not local.

The Title tab

The Title tab is used for formatting the title in the header column. The options are exactly the same as the options on the Font tab. The only difference is that this tab will only apply the formatting to the title of the column. For our example, just keep the default values.

The Advanced tab

The Advanced tab does not have many values to choose from. The Name property is used internally, and our advice is to never change this value. The only other parameter is for views that will be used on the Web. Selecting the Show Values in This Column as Links option allows you to select which column should be a link to the document when viewed in a Web browser. By default, the first column of a view is automatically the Web link. In some cases, this may not be your choice, so you have the ability to change it. You can also select more than one column to be used as a document link. Also, this option is only meaningful for views that will be rendered as HTML (remember that a view can also be displayed using a Java applet).

TIP If you don't want any of the columns to be links to documents (such as when you are generating an online report), the solution is a bit tricky. First, select any column and enable the Show Values in This Column as Links option. Close and save the view. Now open the view and disable the option on the column. Close and save the view again. Now none of the columns will contain a document link.

Adding Columns

Now that you understand the principles for defining the contents of a view, let's go ahead and create the remaining columns for our view. We'll add two new columns. To do so, follow these steps:

1. Choose Create ➢ Append New Column to append a new column to the existing view (you can also right-click the view and select Append New Column).

2. If the new column is not selected, click the column header to select it. From the script area of the programmer's pane, select the Field radio button and click the NameOfRecipe field (you can also select the Formula radio button and type in the name of the field).

3. Choose Design ➢ Column Properties to display the Properties InfoBox for the column (you can also right-click the column header and select Column Properties).

4. On the Column Info tab, type **Name of Recipe** in the Title field and set the width to 30. On the Sorting tab, select the Ascending sort option. On the Font tab, change the color of the font to navy.

5. Append another column to the view. For the column value, select the Simple Function radio button and select Creation Date.

6. Display the Column Properties InfoBox. On the Column Info tab, type **Date Created** in the Title field and set the width to 8. On the Font tab, change the color to navy. On the Date and Time Format tab, show the date only with the month/year format.

7. Close and save the view.

You have now created a view. If you open the database in the Notes client, your view should look like Figure 20.27. You'll notice that only the Recipe documents are being displayed, not the actual ingredients for the recipe. Remember that the view selection limits the document selection to only those documents that were created using the Recipe form.

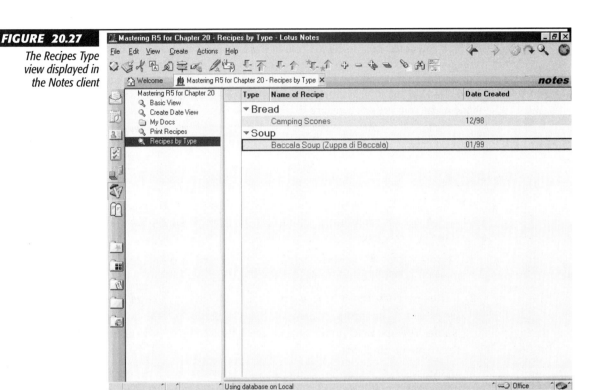

FIGURE 20.27

The Recipes Type view displayed in the Notes client

Creating a Lookup View

Another type of view that is typically used by Notes designers is a lookup view. This is not an actual view type but a name for a hidden view that is used "behind the scenes" to look up various pieces of data for documents. These types of views are used quite a bit in Notes, especially in the Name and Address Book (names.nsf). A lookup view is quite handy for use with either the @DBColumn or @DBLookup functions. You can call a hidden view anything you want, but surrounding its name with parentheses will keep it hidden from the users eyes. So let's create a quick example that we'll need to use later in the chapter. We'll create a hidden view that categorizes all the recipe ingredients by recipe name. To create this view, just follow these steps:

1. Select the View option from the Design list for the database.

2. Choose the New View Design Action button from the programmer's pane (you can also skip steps 1 and 2 and just choose Create ➤ View).

3. When the Create View dialog box appears, type **(IngredientList)** for the view name. Type **SELECT (Form = "Ingredient")** in the Selection Conditions

field. Click the Copy From button and select the Blank view option. Click the Customize button to create and open your new blank view.

4. Highlight the first column in the view (this column should have the title #). For the column value, select the field Recipe.

5. Open the Column Properties InfoBox. Leave the Title field blank and the set the width to 1 on the Column Info tab.

6. On the Sorting tab, select Categorized (this will also set the sort order to ascending).

7. Append a new column to the view. For the value, enter the formula **IAmount +
" " + IDescription + " " + Imeasurement**.

8. Open the Column Properties InfoBox. Leave the Title field blank and set the width to 30.

9. On the Font tab, set the color to navy.

10. Open the View Properties InfoBox. On the View tab, type **IList** in the Alias field and enter a brief comment.

11. On the Options tab, deselect all the options. On the Style tab, deselect the Show Column Headings option.

12. Close and save the view.

When you finish, the view should look similar to Figure 20.28. The purpose of this view is to give the user the ability to extract all the ingredients for a specific recipe (remember that we are only displaying the ingredients documents based on the selection criteria for the view). By categorizing the ingredients documents by recipe name, you now have a complete list of ingredients for each recipe. The reasoning behind this view will become more clear in the next few sections. For now, you just need to understand how the view was created and which options were used.

Using View Form Formulas

One very handy feature of views is that they give you the ability to change which form is used to display the document. In Chapter 18, we mentioned how Notes determines which form to use. Within a view, you can actually change this process by using a view property called a Form formula. When a document is opened from a view that has a Form formula defined, the Form formula will be evaluated, and the data will be presented based on the result; that is, it will be presented in the form the Form formula returned. Remember that the default form to use when displaying a document is usually saved within the document in the Form field. Using a Form formula does not alter this value; the data is just temporarily displayed using another form.

FIGURE 20.28

A list of ingredients for each recipe

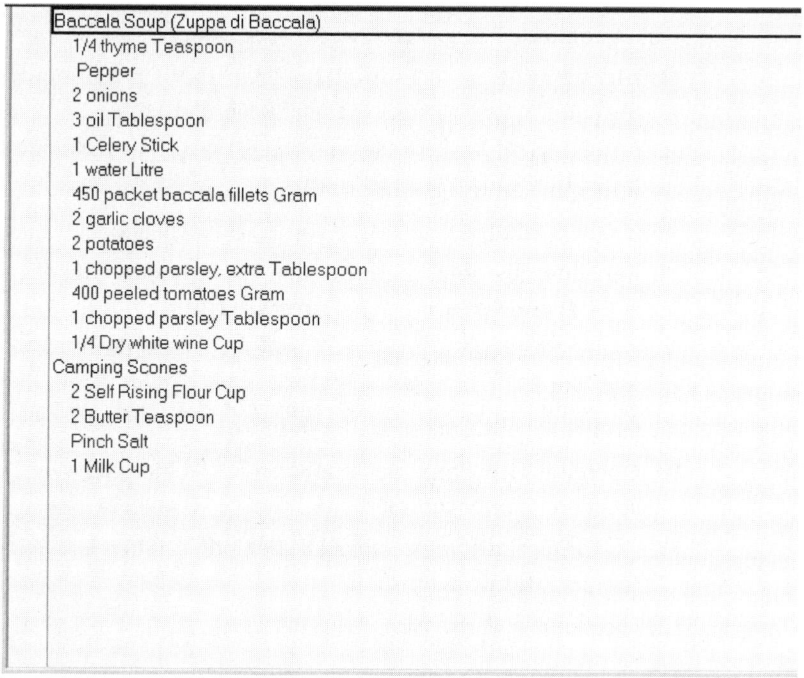

```
Baccala Soup (Zuppa di Baccala)
  1/4 thyme Teaspoon
  Pepper
  2 onions
  3 oil Tablespoon
  1 Celery Stick
  1 water Litre
  450 packet baccala fillets Gram
  2 garlic cloves
  2 potatoes
  1 chopped parsley, extra Tablespoon
  400 peeled tomatoes Gram
  1 chopped parsley Tablespoon
  1/4 Dry white wine Cup
Camping Scones
  2 Self Rising Flour Cup
  2 Butter Teaspoon
  Pinch Salt
  1 Milk Cup
```

Now at first glance, it may not be readily apparent how this property may prove useful, so here's an example. Open up the view called Print Recipes (this view has already been provided for you). In the programmer's pane, select the Form Formula event. You'll notice that the script area contains the text *"Recipes To Print"*, as shown in Figure 20.29 (this form has been supplied for you as well). Although this is not really a formula, the result is the same: the name of a form. You could use an intricate formula as well to calculate which form to use.

Because the name of the form Recipes To Print is in the Form Formula event in the Print Recipes view, whenever a document is opened using the Print Recipes view, the Recipes To Print form will be used. One reason for having this type of view is to provide a graphic-free form used primarily for printing. If you look at the Recipe form, you'll see that there are a lot of colors, graphics, and so on that really do not need to be there if all you want to do is print the recipe.

To try out the Form formula, open the Mastering R5 for Chapter 20 database in the Notes client and select the Print Recipes view. This view will display the documents categorized by type (just as the Recipes by Type view does). At first glance, these two views look identical, but go ahead and open one of the documents. You'll see that the form looks completely different, as shown in Figure 20.30. The form that is being used is the Recipes To Print form and not the Recipe form. If you look at the Document Properties InfoBox for the current document, you'll see that the contents of the Form field is still Recipe. The document has not been altered in any way except in how it is displayed to the user. This form displays all the recipe information, including the ingredients (we'll show you how the ingredients are displayed in the next section on embedded views).

FIGURE 20.29

Using the Form Formula event inside a view to display a document with an alternate form

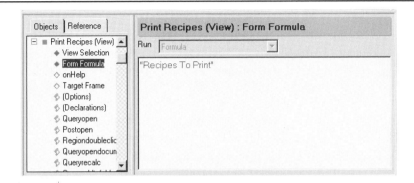

FIGURE 20.30

Displaying the contents of a recipe with an alternate form that shows all the recipe information and the ingredients listing

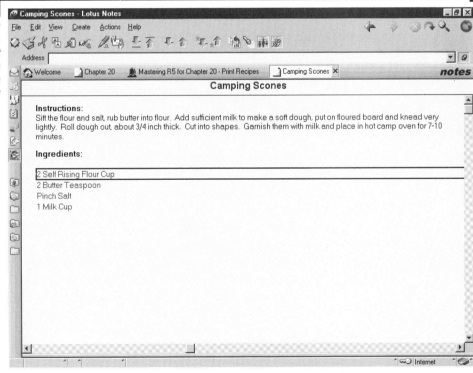

Using this technique, you have now given the users a quick way to print out all the information about a recipe. The user could have just opened the Basic view and printed the contents of the view. This would have given them the name of the recipe and the ingredients, but it would not give them both the instructions and comments. Using an alternate form, you can give the user the best of both worlds.

Embedding Views

You may recall from our form design that the contents for a recipe and the actual ingredients are stored in two different forms. In the preceding example, the contents of both of these forms were combined and displayed using one form. Although it may seem quite complicated to do something like this, it is actually quite simple if you use an embedded view.

Earlier, you created a lookup view that displayed all of the ingredients for a given recipe (remember that you categorized the ingredients by the recipe name). We can embed the lookup view into the form and show the list of ingredients. The categories from the lookup view are not being displayed because we are using a technique called a single category view. This option is only available for an embedded view and allows you to specify a key for a category to display. In our example, because all the ingredients are categorized by the recipe name, we'll set the key to the name of the recipe and only those ingredients will be displayed.

To set up a single category view, we must go back and look at the Recipes To Print form. Open up this form. You will see that the list of ingredients is showing up on it. Click the list of ingredients in the form and a box will be displayed around the list of ingredients, as shown in Figure 20.31. This list of ingredients is actually an embedded view. Looking at the Objects tab, you will notice that there are two events for the embedded view: Embedded Selection (the view to embed) and Show Single Category. We are interested in the latter. The formula for the Show Single Category event is the field NameOfRecipe. This field is actually used as the title for the form as well. Because the contents of this field contain the name of the recipe and the embedded view is categorized by the recipe name, the embedded view is smart enough to only display those documents for the selected recipe.

This type of embedded view can be extremely powerful. It allows you to limit the scope of a view to only those records pertinent to the record being displayed. This could be useful in situations such as when you only want to show items for a particular order in an invoice application. The implementation of this type of view is endless. Although the view is not really dynamic (a dynamic view would only select those records using the selection formula), it is pretty close. Notes programmers have been screaming for this type of programmability for a long time.

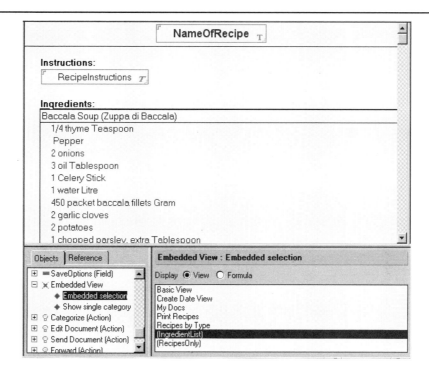

FIGURE 20.31

Using the Show Single Category event to limit the scope of an embedded view

PART

V

Beyond the Client: Utilizing Domino Designer

Understanding the Response Hierarchy

One of the more confusing aspects of creating views is understanding how Notes interprets the document response hierarchy. In the preceding section, you were shown how to display documents in a view, but we didn't go into detail about how Response documents are displayed.

Displaying a Response Document

As you may recall from the chapter on forms, there are three types of documents that can be created in Notes. The Main document (or parent), the Response document (or child), and the Response to Response document (child of the child). When you use these special document types, Notes automatically displays the documents in a view using a document response hierarchy. Although Notes understands the document response hierarchy, it doesn't display these types of documents automatically; you must understand how to set up a view so that responses will be indented properly.

As shown in Figure 20.32, it is useful to indent Response documents beneath the Main document when a user wants to see the progression of a discussion. The indentation scheme for responses is limited to 32 levels, and each response is indented three spaces beneath its predecessor. To set up a view that supports this type of structure, you must first make sure that you have designed the database to use Response and Response to Response documents. You must also make sure the Show Response Documents in a Hierarchy option is enabled in the View Properties Options tab. Otherwise, you may end up with a column in the view that displays Response documents only, which is what we'll cover next.

The Response Only Column

You can tell there is a response column defined in the view in Figure 20.32 because the Response documents are displaying. For a Notes view to display this hierarchy, you need to define a column specifically designed for Response documents (enable this option from the Column Info tab of the Column Properties InfoBox). If you open the Basic view in Designer, you'll see that there are only two columns defined for the view. The first column is the Response Only column and the second column displays the recipe name.

FIGURE 20.32

An example of the document hierarchy in a view

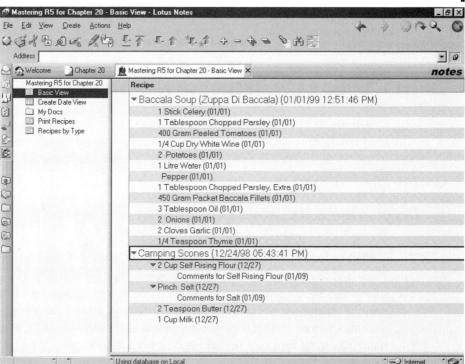

Although it doesn't make much sense, the Response Only column must be placed to the left of the column under which the responses are to be indented. You should also leave the Title field blank and set the width to 1. The most important factor is to enable the Show Responses Only option. If it is not enabled, the Response Only column will not work correctly.

Once you have set up the column properties, you must also specify a value for the column. Whatever value you decide to place in this column will be shown for every Response document in the hierarchy; it doesn't matter how many other columns are defined for the view. In most cases, a Response Only column shows the subject, author, and creation time (a good example of this can be found in the discussion database template included with Notes).

In the Recipe example, the formula for the response column is as follows:

```
@If(Form = "CI";
"Comments for " + Item + " (" + @Text(@Created;"D2S0") + ")";
IAmount + " " + @ProperCase(IMeasurement) + " " +
@ProperCase(IDescription) + " (" + @Text(@Created;"D2S0") + ")")
```

This column is only used for Response documents, so the formula checks the value from the Form field to determine which response form is being displayed. Because there is only one column in which to display the value for all Response documents, we had to determine if the document was a Comment or an Ingredient form so the appropriate field value would be displayed.

 TIP If you are creating a view that will show documents in a response hierarchy, make sure the View Selection formula does not exclude the Response documents.

Using Folders

A folder can be thought of as another type of a view. It has the same design elements as a view and is created in a similar manner: by choosing Create ➤ Folder (instead of Create ➤ View). The only real difference between a folder and a view is that a folder does *not* have a selection formula. Remember, for documents to show up in a view, the selection formula determines the criteria to collect the documents. A folder remains empty until a user adds documents to it (you can also add documents to a folder programmatically).

So how can a user add documents to folder? Very simply. All a user needs to do is drag a document from a view and place it on top of a folder. The document is not actually copied to the folder; instead, the folder references the document like a pointer. You can distinguish folders from views by the different icon used in the Navigation pane of the Notes client. A view folder is represented by a file folder icon, whereas a view is represented by a magnifying glass icon.

 WARNING When you remove documents from a view, remember that you are actually seeing a pointer to the document. If you decide to remove the document from the folder, do not use the Delete key. Doing so will remove the document permanently from the database. To remove a document from the folder, use the Remove from Folder option within the Actions menu.

 NOTE When moving Response documents to a folder, you must also move the parent document. The same is true when removing Response documents *from* a folder. In other words, the parent and child documents must all move around in unison.

 NOTE Web users cannot drag documents into folders.

Creating and Using Navigators

A Navigator is a graphical element that can be used to allow users easy access to views, documents, or other Notes applications. Using a Navigator is similar to using a Web application in that you can create a home page or a sidebar navigational element that helps users get around your site. Most Navigators contain some type of graphical background along with buttons and hotspots that perform some type of action when clicked.

 NOTE With Release 5, there are three new design elements that can be used in combination with one another (instead of using Navigators) to achieve a more flexible and dynamic environment. These new elements—pages, outlines, and framesets—are covered in more detail in Chapter 21.

A Navigator is not just one object but a combination of many different types of objects. By combining these objects, you can create a myriad of dazzling designs. Most Navigators begin with a background image, and then various types of buttons, hotspots, and text are added. In this chapter, we'll briefly cover how to create and use Navigators, but we feel that they are not the best selection for a graphical interface, mainly because of their lack of flexibility and security (Hide-When formulas for each object).

Creating a Navigator

In this section, we'll show you how to create a simple Navigator. We have already created some of the Navigators for you. This will eliminate the need for you to create the graphics; you can just copy an existing Navigator (you will, however, need to do some of the work). Although you can create a full-screen Navigator, we are going to create a Navigator that will be used in conjunction with the views. This is known as a split-screen Navigator because the left side of the screen will be the Navigator and the right side will contain the view.

To create a Navigator, follow these steps:

1. Open the Mastering R5 for Chapter 20 database in Designer and select Navigators from the Design list.

2. Normally, you would choose Create ➢ Design ➢ Navigator (you can also just select the New Navigator button), which will display a new blank Navigator. But we have already provided a blank Navigator that contains the background graphic. Right-click the Navigator called Blank and select Copy from the pop-up menu. Now right-click again and select Paste.

3. Open the newly copied Navigator called Copy of Blank. The Navigator should look like the one in Figure 20.33. If you want to create your own background, there are two options. The first is to copy the background graphic to the Clipboard and then choose Create ➢ Graphic Background to automatically paste the graphic to the background. The second way is to choose File ➢ Import and then select the file to use as the graphic background.

TIP Always try to use the File Import method to create a background because better color fidelity will be retained when the graphic is displayed.

NOTE You can only have one background graphic for a Navigator. The background graphic cannot be moved once it has been pasted. Keep this in mind when you create the graphic; the size really does matter.

FIGURE 20.33

The starting point for our Navigator for the database

The Navigator Properties

The next step is to set the properties for the Navigator. Choose Design ➤ Navigator Properties to display the Navigator Properties InfoBox (shown in Figure 20.34). Change the name to All Recipes because this Navigator will be used to display the All Recipes view. You can type in comments about this Navigator as well.

FIGURE 20.34

The Navigator Properties InfoBox

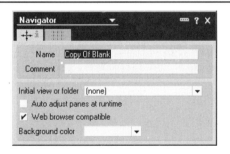

The Initial View or Folder option is very important. We were going to create a split-screen Navigator, which will display along with the view. You can use the Initial View or Folder option to have a view or folder automatically open along with the All Recipes Navigator. For this example, select Basic View from the drop-down list box. This will cause Notes to automatically display the Basic view (which displays all the recipes) when the Navigator is opened. Also enable the Auto Adjust Panes at Runtime option.

This option will automatically adjust the split-screen bar, which separates the Navigator and the view so that only the minimum amount of the screen will be used for the Navigator.

Adding Action to the Navigator Objects

Now you have a Navigator that, when opened, will automatically display a view containing a list of all the recipes. The only problem is that the user does not have any other options available for navigating to the rest of the views in the database. To alleviate this problem, we'll add some options to the Navigator that will allow the user to do so.

You have the option of adding text, buttons, graphical buttons, and other types of hotspots. For our example, we'll keep it simple and just add some buttons. To add buttons to the Navigator, follow these steps:

1. Choose Create ➢ Button. This will change the cursor to a plus sign. Hold down the left mouse button and draw the button. Once you have the correct size and placement, let go of the mouse button.

2. The Button Properties InfoBox displays automatically. Type **All Recipes** in the Caption field.

3. Select the Font tab and change the size to 14 and the text color to maroon.

4. Follow steps 1 through 3 three more times, but this time, type **Print Recipes** in the Caption field for the first button, **By Type** for the second, and **By Date** for the third. Don't change the color of the text, but set the size to 14.

5. When you have finished, your Navigator should look similar to the one in Figure 20.35.

FIGURE 20.35

*The All Recipes
Navigator*

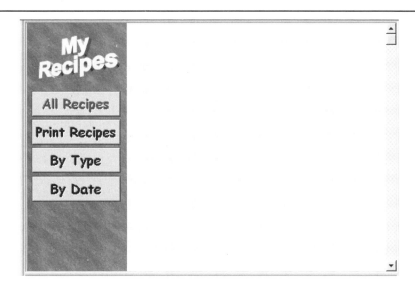

You have created your Navigator, but there is still one more step you need to perform. You created some nifty buttons, but nothing happens when you click them. We need to add some type of Action to each button.

To add an Action to a button, you first need to select the button object. Click the All Recipes button. In the script area of the programmer's pane, you'll notice that there are some options available for the Click event of the button. By default, the Simple Action option is selected. You can also code either a formula or LotusScript, but for our example, the Simple action will do.

In the Action drop-down box, select the Open Another Navigator option (you will notice that there are quite a few other options available). When this option is enabled, a second list box appears. From this second list box, you can select which Navigator you want to open when the button is selected. Because you are adding an Action for the All Recipes button, select the All Recipes Navigator. The script area should now look similar to the script area in Figure 20.36.

The action selection criteria for a Navigator object

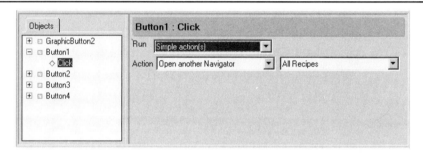

Now do the same thing for the remaining three buttons, making sure you select the correct Navigator to open for each button. As mentioned earlier, we have already created the remaining Navigators for you.

Let's recap what you have just done. You have added an Action that will open a specific Navigator when each button is selected. You have also specified that, when each Navigator is opened, its respective view will also open.

There is one last step that needs to be performed. How does the Navigator get displayed in the first place? Using the Database Launch option, you can tell the database to open a specific Navigator whenever the database is opened. We'll set this option to open the All Recipes Navigator.

Open the Database Properties InfoBox and select the Launch tab. From the Launch tab, select Open Designated Navigator from the On Database Open option. From the Type of Navigator option, select Standard Navigator. This will display a third list box from which you should select All Recipes. Now we are ready to give your Navigator a try.

Open the database in the Notes client. When the database is opened, the All Recipes Navigator and the Basic view should be automatically launched and look like Figure 20.37.

PART

V

Beyond the Client: Uti-
lizing Domino Designer

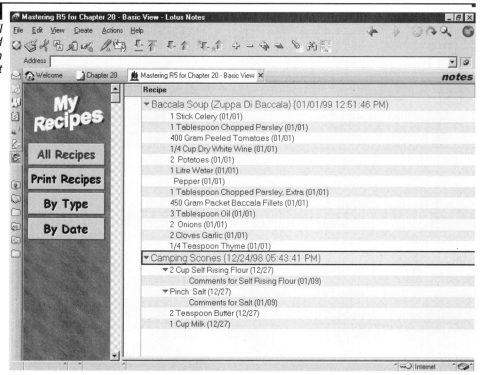

FIGURE 20.37

*Displaying our All
Recipes view and
the Basic view in
the Notes client*

Now go ahead and click any of the other buttons. When the button opens the Navigator, the view also opens.

Summary

By now, you've learned the majority of the basics. This chapter showed you how to give users access to the documents they create while also giving them a graphical interface in which to navigate. Views are an important aspect in Notes. Using a view, you can display documents in various ways that allow users quick access to the information they need. Using sorting techniques and the built-in response document hierarchy, you can display the data in an easy-to-use format similar to a table of contents for a book.

In the next chapter, we'll look at some new techniques for creating a visually appealing application for both the Notes client and the Web. Although pages, outlines, and framesets sound like purely Web techniques, the changes that have been made in Notes give you the ability to create an application that looks and works the same in both environments.

CHAPTER **21**

Outlines, Pages, and Framesets

All of the design elements discussed in this chapter—outlines, pages, and framesets—are new to Notes R5. You might think that these elements can only be used for Web applications, but that is far from the truth. These new design elements have been engineered so they can be used in both the Notes client and Web applications. The best part about them is that they virtually look and perform the same way in both environments.

Outline, pages, and framesets have been designed to give your applications a more cohesive look and feel. In fact, if you've been using your R5 mail database, you've already been exposed to them without even knowing it.

All of the examples in this chapter are in the Mastering R5 for Chapter 21 example database.

Each one of these design elements builds upon everything you have learned thus far. After reading this chapter, you should have a good understanding of how each one can enhance the quality of your application and when to use them.

What Is an Outline?

By now, you should be quite familiar with the Navigation pane (also known as the Folder pane), shown in Figure 21.1. This is the default navigation structure for a database. There's not much you can do to customize the look and feel of the default Navigation pane. The only option is to create a Navigator. Navigators are useful, but they lack some of the features you might need (such as the ability to hide specific elements based on a user's security). In Chapter 20, you created a Navigator and found out how time-consuming it can be.

FIGURE 21.1

The default Navigation pane for a database

This is where outlines come into play. An outline is also a navigational element, but it is completely customizable. With outlines, you are no longer limited to displaying just views and folders. Think of the outline as a hierarchical tree structure of all the links and elements for your database. You can place links to views, pages, forms, Web sites, or anything else you need for your application. The outline design element can be thought of as a high-level site map for your database. If you are familiar with Web programming, this concept should be quite familiar to you. The outline will help you structure your entire database, which in turn becomes the navigational structure for your application.

One major advantage to using an outline is that this design element is completely customizable. You can choose how the items will appear. With the Folder pane, you have to rename each view or folder if you want them to show up in a particular order (by default, the Folder pane displays the views and folders in alphabetical order). An outline is not limited to just views and folders. You can create an entry that links directly to any Notes element (such as a page or a form) and to elements not contained within your application (such as a Web site). You also have control over the outline's look. You can change the fonts and colors and add graphics for the entries.

 TIP   You can use an outline to lay out and plan your application. You can create an outline entry prior to creating each design element. This will allow you to create a blueprint of your entire application.

Another major advantage is the ability to program each outline entry individually. As you will see later in the chapter, there is a wide range a features available in the Outline Entry Properties InfoBox. You can use one set of features to display an outline in the Notes client and another to display it in a Web application. In addition, you're not limited to one outline per application. You can create as many outlines as you need. Because an outline can be embedded on just about any design element, you have enough freedom and flexibility to create quite a powerful application.

 NOTE   Keep in mind that an outline cannot be used by itself. It must be embedded within some other type of element, such as a page or form. Outlines can even be embedded in tables.

Using the Outline Designer

Before we create a new outline for our Mastering R5 for Chapter 21 example database, let's first go over the components of the Outline Designer. To display the Outline Designer, follow these steps:

1. Open the Mastering R5 for Chapter 21 database in Domino Designer.

2. Highlight the Outlines element in the Design list. All the outlines for the current database will be displayed in the Work pane.

3. To display the Outline Designer (see Figure 21.2), choose Create ➤ Design ➤ Outline (you can also right-click in the Work pane and select New or click the New Outline Design Action button).

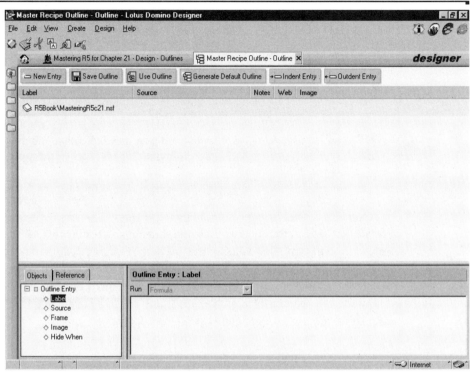

FIGURE 21.2

A new outline as it appears in the Outline Designer

The Outline Designer consists of three main areas:

- Design Action buttons
- The Outline pane (work area)
- The programmer's pane

Outline Design Action Buttons

Across the top of the work area are six Action buttons, which can significantly increase your productivity when you are creating a new outline.

New Entry   Use the New Entry button to create a new entry for your outline (you can also choose Create ➤ Outline Entry). When you click it, a new entry named Untitled will be created within the outline, and the Outline Entry Properties InfoBox will automatically display (see Figure 21.3).

FIGURE 21.3

The Outline Entry Properties InfoBox automatically displays when a new outline entry is created.

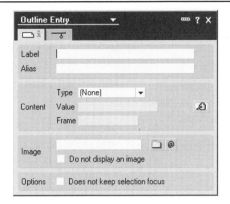

Save Outline   The Save Outline button saves the current outline. You can also choose File ➤ Save.

Use Outline   The Use Outline button automatically creates a new page and embeds your outline in it. Outlines are typically embedded in pages (although they can also be placed on forms), so this button can save you from having to create a new page and embed the outline yourself.

Generate Default Outline   The Generate Default Outline button automatically generates a default outline based on the contents of the current database. The outline will contain an entry for all the views and folders that are currently defined. This option also creates entries for all of your hidden views and four additional outline entries labeled Other Views, Other Folders, Other Private Views, and Other Private Folders (the last four entries are primarily placeholders for additional entries). By default, these are all hidden from both the Notes client and Web applications.

TIP   The Generate Default Outline button is a great time-saver when you are creating a new outline. If you select it, you won't have to add each view and folder to the outline manually.

Indent Entry   Use the Indent Entry button to indent the current outline entry. This feature is used to create a hierarchy of top-level and sublevel entries. You can indent more than one entry at a time by highlighting all the entries you wish to indent and clicking the Indent Entry button (you can also use the Tab key as a shortcut for indenting entries). This is a great feature for an outline that contains long lists of entries. You can also group logical entries under a heading.

Outdent Entry   The Outdent Entry button reverses the indented entry, or "outdents" it. Again, this is used to create a hierarchy for your outline. You can outdent more than one entry at a time by highlighting all the entries you wish to outdent and clicking the Outdent Entry button (you can also use the Shift+Tab key combination as a shortcut for outdenting entries).

The Outline Pane

The Outline pane is where you can modify your actual outline. You can use the drag-and-drop technique to change the sequence of the entries. To move an entry higher or lower in the hierarchy, click and hold down the mouse button on the entry you wish to move, drag the entry to its new location in the outline, and drop it (let go of the mouse button). When you use this technique, Designer will display a thick black bar showing you where the entry will be placed in the outline as you move the mouse along. From the Outline pane, you can open either the Outline Properties InfoBox or the Outline Entry Properties InfoBox (these will be discussed in more detail later in this chapter).

The Programmer's Pane

The programmer's pane for the outline is similar to the programmer's pane for other design elements in Designer. The Objects tab will only display one object at a time, which is always the outline entry (whereas all the objects for other design elements are shown). The events for the outline entry are always Label, Source, Frame, Image, and Hide When; they contain the values you typed into the Outline Entry Properties InfoBox.

Creating an Outline

You now have a basic understanding of outlines, so let's create a new outline for the example database. The goal of our outline is twofold: to create a layout or site map for the application and to give the users an easy and intuitive interface to interact with. To create a new outline, follow these steps:

1. Open the Mastering R5 for Chapter 21 database in Domino Designer.

2. Highlight the Outlines element in the Design list. This will display all the outlines for the current database in the Work pane.

3. Choose Create ≻ Design ≻ Outline (you can also right-click in the Work pane and select New or click the New Outline Design Action button). The Outline Designer displays (refer back to Figure 21.2).

4. Click the Generate Default Outline Design Action button.

You are now looking at a new outline that contains all the views and folders for the Mastering R5 for Chapter 21 database, as shown in Figure 21.4. By default, a new outline is always called Untitled, which is not very descriptive, so the first thing we'll do is change the name.

FIGURE 21.4

The default outline for the example database

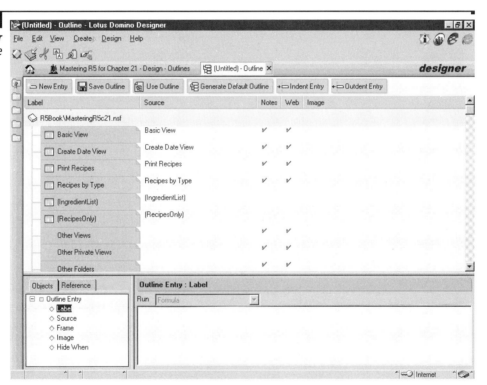

PART

V

Beyond the Client: Utilizing Domino Designer

The Outline Properties InfoBox

To change the name of the outline, you need to open the InfoBox for the outline properties. Choose Design ≻ Outline Properties (you can also right-click in the Work pane and select Outline Properties) and the InfoBox will display (see Figure 21.5). As you can see, there are not many properties for an outline. You can specify the name of the outline in the Name field and give the outline as alias in the Alias field. There is also a Comment field in which you can add a description for the outline. The last option, Available to Public Access Users, allows users with no access (except public access) to use the outline as well (public access was described in more detail in Chapter 16).

FIGURE 21.5

The Outline Properties InfoBox

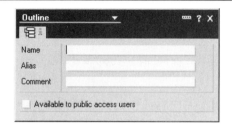

For our example, let's go ahead and fill in the fields and save the outline by following these steps:

1. Enter **Master Recipe Outline** in the Name field.

2. In the Alias field, enter **RecipeOutline**.

3. In the Comment field, enter a short yet descriptive title for the outline, such as **The recipe database navigation outline**.

4. Leave Available to Public Access Users unchecked.

5. Choose File ➣ Save to save your outline.

That's all there is to it. You have created a basic navigational outline for the database. If you would like to take a quick peek at what the outline would look like, click the Use Outline Design Action button. A new untitled page containing your outline will be generated; it's shown in Figure 21.6. When you've finished looking at your outline, just close the page. When you're prompted to save the page, click the No button (remember that the Use Outline option actually creates a new page with your outline embedded on it; we don't want to save it yet because we're not finished with the outline).

FIGURE 21.6

Click the Use Outline Design Action button to display your outline on a page.

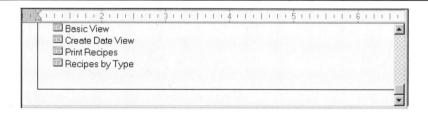

Removing Outline Entries

The default outline may or may not contain the entries you wish to use in your application. As stated earlier, the default outline contains an entry for all the hidden views and also inserts four other entries (or placeholders). The first thing we'll do is remove all the unwanted entries. In our example, we'll remove the hidden views, which are (IngredientList), (RecipesOnly), Other Views, Other Folders, Other Private Views, and Other Private Folders. The nice thing about using the generated outline is that all of these entries are grouped together.

To remove these six entries, follows these steps:

1. Open the Master Recipe Outline example outline in the Domino Designer.
2. Highlight the first hidden view, (IngredientList), by clicking on the entry.
3. Hold down the Shift key and highlight the last outline entry, Other Private Folders.
4. Press the Delete key.
5. When prompted to confirm that you really want to delete all of the selected entries, click the Yes button.

Now all the unwanted entries are gone. You should be left with only these four entries: Basic View, Create Date View, Print Recipes, and Recipes by Type. If you recall from Chapter 20, these are the four views that were displayed in your Navigator when the database was initially opened. We want to keep these views but change how they are displayed to the end user. To do so, we'll need to look at each entry's Outline Entry Properties InfoBox.

Changing the Outline Entry Properties

As with any design element, the outline entry has its own Properties InfoBox. If you want to change the text or an image, you must open the Outline Entry Properties InfoBox and modify the properties for each entry (unless you want to reorder or indent/outdent the entries).

The Outline Entry Properties InfoBox

The first entry in the outline is the Basic View. To open the InfoBox for the entry, highlight Basic View and choose Design ➤ Outline Entry Properties (you can also just double-click the entry). The Outline Entry Properties InfoBox only contains two tabs: Basics and Hide-When.

The Outline Entry Info Tab   The Outline Entry Info tab, shown in Figure 21.7, allows you to specify the characteristics for your outline entry. Both the Label and Alias fields are used for naming your entry. The purpose of the Label field is twofold. It contains the name of your entry, which is also the text the end user will see when viewing your outline. Basic View is not a very descriptive name, so type **All My Recipes** in the Label field. Then type **BasicView** in the Alias field.

FIGURE 21.7

The Outline Entry Info tab of the Outline Entry Properties InfoBox

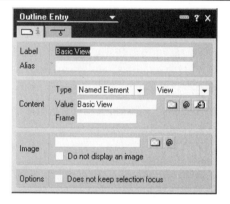

The Content section is the brains behind the entry. Your selections here allow you to specify what will happen when the user selects the outline entry All My Recipes. This section is quite dynamic in that your selection for the Type field will determine what other options are available for the remaining Content fields. The Type drop-down list box has five selections:

(None)   Specifies that the outline entry does nothing. The label is nothing more than that, a text label. When you create an outline for a database that does not yet contain any design elements, leave the Type field set to this option. This is the default selection for a new entry. No other field is available in the Content section when you select this option.

Action   Specifies a formula or Action to be performed when the outline entry is selected. Selecting the function icon will display the Edit Formula dialog box, where you can enter the formula for the Action.

Link   Specifies a database, view, or document link to open. You can also specify the target frame where the link should be opened by entering the name of the frame in the Frame field. If you select the link icon, the database, view, or document link currently on the Clipboard will be automatically populated in the second Type drop-down list box and the Value field. Remember that you must first copy the link to the Clipboard; if you don't, clicking the link icon may yield incorrect results. Once the link is pasted, the second Type drop-down list box will display the type of link (database, view, or document) and the Value field will display the source of the link.

Named Element   This is the most powerful of all outline entry types. When you select Named Element, you can select the type of named element you wish to use from the second drop-down list box. You can select Page (the default), Form, Frameset, View, Folder, or Navigator. Once you have selected from this field, the Value field will contain the actual name (or alias) of the named element. If you don't remember the named element's name, you can click the Design list icon to display the Locate Object dialog box, from which you can select the kind of object, the database, and the actual design element you wish to use. After making your selection, click the OK button and all the fields in the Content section for the outline entry will be populated for you. If you want to dynamically determine which design element to use, you can select the formula icon and write a formula to return the name of the design element. As with the Link selection, you can also specify the target frame in which the link should be opened by entering the name of the frame in the Frame field.

URL   Specifies a URL to link to when the outline entry is selected. You can either type in the URL or paste it in by clicking the link icon. You can also specify the target frame in which the link should be opened by entering the name of the frame in the Frame field.

In our example, Named Element was chosen for the Type field because the outline entry is based on a view. You don't need to change any of these options except for the Frame field. Although we have not covered framesets yet (they will be covered later in this chapter), go ahead and type **NotesView** into the Frame field.

The Image section allows you to specify whether or not to use an image for each of your outline entries. By default, the View icon will be used for each view and the file folder icons will be used for each folder. These are the same images that are used on the default Folder pane. You also have two other options available. You can select the Do Not Display an Image option, which will prevent an image from being displayed next to the text, or you can specify a custom image of your own. To specify a custom image, you must place the images to use in the Image Repository for the database. For your convenience, we have already included an image for you. To select it, click the folder icon to display the Insert Image Resource dialog box and select balls.gif from the list. This image is actually three images in one and is explained in more detail in the sidebar "Rollover Images for Outlines."

The Options section only has one selection available. You can enable Does Not Keep Selection Focus to prevent an outline entry from being highlighted when selected. By default, when an outline is selected, it will also retain the focus.

 The Hide-When Tab You've seen the Hide-When tab for other design elements, but this one is slightly different. You only have three options available for hiding an outline entry. In the Hide Outline Entry From section, you can select to hide an entry from a Notes client, a Web application, or both. You can also specify a formula for hiding the outline entry by enabling the Hide Outline Entry if Formula Is True option and entering a formula for evaluation. This is an extremely powerful tool. You have the ability to hide entries from a user based on anything that can be evaluated in a formula. If you want to hide an entry based on the user's security level, you can do so here.

Updating the Outline Entries

We have edited the properties for the Basic View outline entry. Now we need to update the remaining entries so they have the same look. To change the remaining entries, follow these steps:

1. Highlight the Recipes by Type outline entry in the Work pane. Choose Design ➤ Outline Entry Properties (you can also right-click the highlighted entry and choose Outline Entry Properties or just double-click the outline entry).

2. With the Outline Entry Properties InfoBox open to the Outline Entry Info tab, change the Label field to **By Food Type** and the Alias field to **RecipesByType**. In the Frame field of the Contents section, type **NotesView**. In the Image section, select the balls.gif image file (you can also type the name of the image in the field).

3. Highlight the Create Date View outline entry. If the InfoBox is still displayed, it will display the properties for the newly selected entry (if you closed the InfoBox, open it again for this entry).

4. On the Outline Entry Info tab, enter **By Date Created** in the Label field, **Create-DateView** in the Alias field, **NotesView** in the Frame field, and **balls.gif** in the Image field.

5. Highlight the Print Recipes outline entry and display the InfoBox.

6. On the Outline Entry Info tab, enter **Print My Recipes** in the Label field, **PrintRecipes** in the Alias field, **NotesView** in the Frame field, and **balls.gif** in the Image field.

7. Now save the changes to the outline by clicking the Save Outline Design Action button.

When you have completed all your changes, the outline should look like the outline in Figure 21.8.

FIGURE 21.8

The Master Recipe Outline example

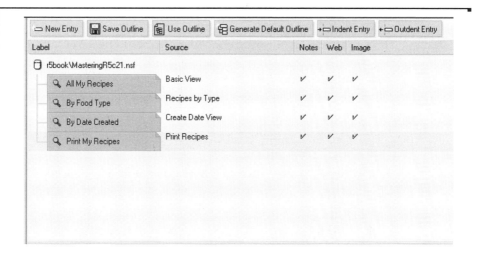

Rollover Images for Outlines

You can create rollover button effects in an outline by creating an image resource that contains three images. The images need to be separated from each other by one pixel, which creates what is called an *image well*. An outline needs to have three images. The first image is the normal state, the second image is the mouseover state, and the third image is the selected state. In the balls.gif image, the blue ball is the normal state, the red ball is the mouseover state, and the green ball is the selected state. When you use a rollover image in an outline, the entries will seem dynamic in nature, yet you really don't have to do much to create this effect.

To set up an image to be used as a rollover, you must follow a specific format. First, each image must be the same exact height and width. Second, you need to place all three images onto one image and separate them by one pixel (the image well). For the balls.gif example, we started with three individual images, which were each 16x16 pixels. We created a blank 50x16 image (16 + 1 + 16 + 1 + 16). Next, we placed a copy of the individual images into the blank image, ensuring each was separated by an image well (1 pixel). Then we just saved the image.

Next we created a new image resource and imported the balls.gif image. In the Image Resource Properties InfoBox, we specified in the Advanced section that the image consists of three images arranged next to each other. This tells Designer how to split up the image when it is used in the outline.

This technique has been popularized in applications used on the Web. With Designer, this process works well in the Notes client. To see the rollover image in action, open the Notes client and test the outline that you created in the Mastering R5 for Chapter 21 example database.

Adding a New Outline Entry

To show off some of the other functions of outline entries, we'll add some entries to the outline. First, let's set up a grouping (or hierarchy) to separate the views used for looking at and printing the Recipe documents.

We need to add a new entry to use as a parent or top level. Once the new entry is added, we'll need to indent the outline entries to create a hierarchical tree for the outline. To add a new entry, follow these steps:

1. Open the Master Recipe Outline example in Designer.

2. Choose Create ➤ Outline Entry (you can also just click the New Entry Design Action button). This will automatically display the Outline Entry Properties InfoBox for the new entry called Untitled.

3. In the Label field, type **Recipe Views**. You can also enter **RecipeView** in the Alias field.

4. In the Content section, leave Type set to (None); we don't want this entry to do anything except be the top-level outline entry.

5. Close the InfoBox. Next, depending on where your cursor was positioned when you created the outline entry, you may need to move the outline entry so it is positioned at the top of the list. To do so, click the Recipe Views outline entry and drag it to the top of the outline. We want this to be the first entry in the list.

We also want to arrange the remaining outline entries in a specific order (if they aren't already). Drag and drop the remaining outline entries one at a time so they are in the following order:

- Recipe Views
- All My Recipes
- By Food Type
- By Date Created
- Print My Recipes

Once the entries are rearranged, we'll indent them to create the hierarchy for the outline. All My Recipes, By Food Type, and By Date Created will be indented under Recipe Views. To accomplish this, highlight the All My Recipes outline entry (click on it). Hold the Shift key down and highlight By Date Created (click on it) so that all three outline entries are selected. Now click the Indent Design Action button (you can also just press the Tab key), and all three entries will be cascaded underneath the Recipe Views entry, as shown in Figure 21.9.

TIP You can cut and paste outline entries from other outlines.

FIGURE 21.9

Creating a hierarchical
outline

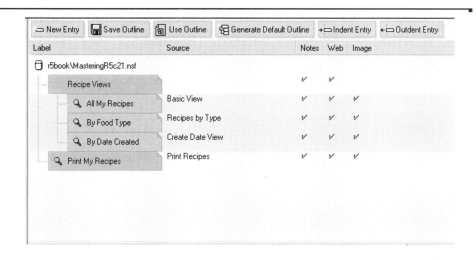

You've seen how an outline entry can link to views. Let's add three new outline entries that will allow the user to create Recipe and Ingredient documents. To do so, follow these steps:

1. Open the Master Recipes Outline example.

2. Append a new outline entry by highlighting the Print My Recipes outline entry and clicking the New Entry Design Action button.

3. This new entry will be used as a spacer. To leave the label blank, press the space-bar once. Select the Do Not Display an Image option in the Image section and the Does Not Keep the Focus option in the Options section.

4. Click the New Entry Design Action button again. Enter **Create Recipe** in the Label field and **CreateRecipe** in the Alias field. In the Type drop-down list box, select Named Element and click the folder icon to display the Locate Object dialog box.

5. In the Locate Object dialog box, select Form from the Kind of Object drop-down list box and Recipe from the Form drop-down list box (this will be the last drop-down list box whose name changes based on the kind of object you select). Click the OK button.

6. Enter **_blank** in the Frame field. Click the folder icon in the Image section and select the NewRecipe.gif image.

7. Append another blank outline entry as shown in step 3.

8. Add one last outline entry. Enter **Lotus Website** in the Label field and **LotusWebsite** in the Alias field. From the Type drop-down list box, select URL and type **www.lotus.com** in the Value field. Enter **NotesView** in the Frame field. For the image, select web.gif.

9. Save your outline by clicking the Save Outline Design Action button.

PART

V

Beyond the Client: Uti-
lizing Domino Designer

When you have finished, the outline should look similar to Figure 21.10. Now that you have an outline, you need to create a page in which to display it.

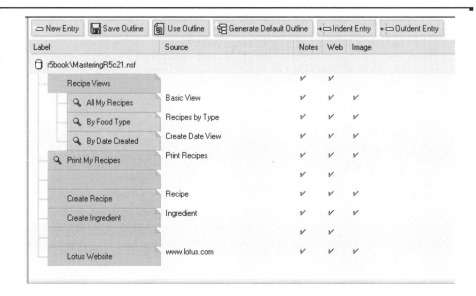

What Is a Page?

A page is a hybrid design element in that it is a cross between a standard form and the special Help About and Help Using forms. A page acts like a form (it can have Action buttons and events), but it cannot have any fields. Most of the capabilities of a form (images, hotspots, and attachments) are fully functional. Pages are stored as a separate design element too. You can refer to a page either by its name or by its alias.

If pages are so much like a form, why not just use a form? The main reason is that a form is used for gathering information, whereas a page is used for *displaying* information. This is a big difference for developers who want to control the layout of Web pages on Domino sites. Using a page eliminates the need to create forms and store documents that need to be displayed to the end user. This does not mean that pages are only for Web applications. That is far from the truth. Pages can be used for Help screens, home pages, splash screens—the list goes on. The major point to keep in mind when you're trying to decide between a form and a page is whether or not you need to gather information from the end user. If you do, don't use a page.

Another major reason for using pages is to replace the $$ViewTemplate field typically used in early versions of Notes for displaying embedded views. You can also launch a specific page when a database is opened so you don't have to use the About This Database form (in earlier releases of Notes, one of the database launch options was to display the About This Database form). Because pages have more options than the About This Database form has, you as a designer have more flexibility in designing your application.

A page is another type of design element that can be used anywhere in your application, and it can in turn contain the following types of design elements:

- Text
- Computed text
- Horizontal rules
- Tables
- Sections
- Links
- Graphics
- Imagemaps
- Attachments
- Actions
- Applets
- Embedded views, folders, Navigators, outlines, and Date Picker controls
- HTML
- OLE objects

A page cannot contain the following design elements:

- Fields
- Layout regions
- Subforms
- Embedded group schedules and File Upload controls

As you can see, a page is quite powerful. Now that you have a basic understanding of this design element, let's go ahead and create one.

Creating a Page

The process for creating a page is similar to the process for creating a form. We'll start with something simple. On the Recipes form, there is a hotspot labeled Need Help?; we'll create a page that will be displayed when the user clicks on it. The page won't have anything on it except text and some graphics. To create the new page, follow these steps:

1. Open the Mastering R5 for Chapter 21 database in Domino Designer.

2. Highlight the Pages element in the Design list. This will display all the pages for the current database in the Work pane.

3. Choose Create ➣ Design ➣ Page (you can also right-click in the Work pane and select New or click the New Page Design Action button).

You won't see much difference between the new page and a new form. The only major difference is in the Create menu. If you choose Create, you'll notice that some of the menu options that are available for a form are not present for a page.

The first thing we need to do is give the page a name. To open the InfoBox for the page, choose Design ➣ Page Properties. On the Page Info tab, type **HelpRecipe** in the Name field and **Help page for the recipe form** in the Comment field. The remaining tabs in the InfoBox are similar to those that have been covered for previous design elements, so we won't spend any time reviewing them here.

For the Recipe Help page, you can type in anything you wish. We have included a sample Help page named SampleHelp. To save time, you can copy and paste the contents of this page into the new page. Once you have copied the text and graphics to the new page, feel free to add anything else that you want. Once you are finished, just save and close the page.

Embedding an Outline on a Page

You've created a page, now let's get back to the outline. As we stated earlier, you must place an outline on some other design element in order to use it. A page is the perfect place because it is only used to display information to the user (as opposed to having the user enter information).

NOTE You can embed more than one outline on a page.

We need to create another page to hold the outline. Following the steps in the preceding section, create a new page and enter **dspOutline** for the name. Starting with a blank page, choose Create ➣ Embedded Element ➣ Outline. The Insert Embedded Outline dialog box will automatically display (see Figure 21.11). We only have one outline for the database, so select the only one in the list, Master Recipe Outline (if you had more than one, all of them would show up in the list). The outline will be automatically placed on the page, and the default properties will be set. Don't be alarmed if some of the outline entries you entered do not automatically display. They are actually there, but they're hidden from view based on the properties for the embedded view. To rectify this problem, we need to change some of the properties, so we'll review the Embedded Outline Properties InfoBox.

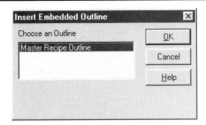

FIGURE 21.11

The Insert Embedded Outline dialog box

TIP Once an outline is embedded on a page, you don't need to worry about reinserting or modifying the current page if you make any modifications to the outline. This is handled by Notes and is a real time-saver.

The Embedded Outline Properties InfoBox

You may recall that, when you were creating your outline, there were not a lot of properties to choose from for the outline or the outline entries. Most of the options for the outline are actually contained in the Embedded Outline Properties InfoBox. There are many different combinations you can use to create various effects. The Embedded Outline Properties InfoBox has seven tabs:

- Info
- Font
- Background
- Layout
- Paragraph Alignment
- Paragraph Margins
- Paragraph Hide-When

To open the InfoBox, first select the embedded outline and choose Element ➤ Outline Properties (you can also right-click on the embedded outline and choose Outline Properties). By default, the first tab to display is the Info tab.

The Info Tab   The Info tab, shown in Figure 21.12, allows you to identify your outline and set the properties that control how the outline will be displayed to the user. The Info tab is made up of many different properties:

Name   This option allows you to identify your outline by name. It is a good habit to name all of your outlines because you can embed more than one on any given design element. For our example, type in **MainOutline**.

Type   This drop-down list box has only two options—Tree Style and Flat Style. The Tree Style option should be used for outlines (such as ours) that contain a hierarchical view. When this option is selected, the Show Twisties option is also displayed. You can use it to display the triangular icon that allows a user to expand and collapse the view. The Flat Style option is used to show only one level at a time. It should be used in conjunction with the Title Style Simple option. When Flat Style is selected, another drop-down list displays, allowing you to choose whether the outline entries should be listed horizontally or vertically. You can use this option to create a horizontal menu bar across the top or bottom of a page. For our example, select both the Tree Style option and the Show Twisties option.

Title Style   This drop-down list has only two options—Hide and Simple. Use the Simple option in conjunction with the Flat Style option to display the parent of the current hierarchical level so the user can navigate to upper levels. The Hide option will prevent the database title from displaying. For our example, select the Hide option.

Target Frame   This option allows you to specify the frame for the results of an action in the outline entry. (For example, you may have an outline that contains a link to a specific page on a Web site. This option allows you to specify the frame in which the Web page should appear when the link is clicked.) When you created the outline entries, you specified a target frame for each one in the Outline Entry Properties InfoBox. That target frame takes precedence over the target frame specified here. For our example, leave this field blank.

Root Entry   This is another handy feature for hierarchical outlines. You can place the alias of an outline entry in this field, and only the sublevels of that entry will initially be displayed in the outline (if no sublevels exist, the outline will be blank). You can use this in combination with the Title field's Simple Title option and your users will have a way to navigate to upper levels of the outline. For our example, leave this field blank.

Display As   This option doesn't have a label, but the drop-down list box is just to the right of the Root Entry field. There are four options—Expand All, Expand First, Display as Saved, and Collapse All (note that if you have selected Flat Style from the Type option, there is only one option available, Collapse All). This setting is extremely useful for hierarchical outlines because you can force the outline to display a certain way the first time it is displayed. For our example, set this option to Expand All.

Outline Size   The Outline Size section allows you to specify both the horizontal and vertical dimensions for your outline. Fit to Content is available for both dimensions and will automatically size your outline to fit its contents. The Fixed option is also available for both dimensions, and when selected, it will open a field in which you can specify the exact size of each dimension in inches. The Fit to Window(%) option is only available for the horizontal dimension; it allows you to specify the size based on a percentage of the actual window size. The Show Scroll Bar option will automatically display a scroll bar within the confines of the embedded outline. If you have quite a number of outline entries that extend beyond the height of the page, you should enable this option. This will allow the user to use the scroll bar to see the options that aren't currently visible. Also, you can deselect this option because we don't have many outline entries. Also, select Fit to Content for both dimensions.

Web Access   As the name applies, this option only applies to Web applications. It allows you to specify whether to use the Java applet or HTML. It is best to select the Use Java Applet option because many of the options won't work in a Web application unless you use the applet. So our page will look similar in both the Web application and the Notes client, select the Use Java Applet option.

FIGURE 21.12

The Info tab of the Embedded Outline Properties InfoBox

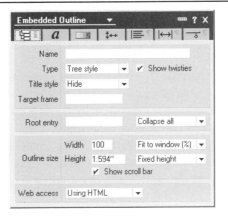

The Font Tab   The Font tab, shown in Figure 21.13, is similar to the Font tabs for other design elements. The major difference is the addition of a few drop-down list boxes in the upper left corner and along the bottom. The first drop-down list box allows you to select either Top-Level Font or Sub-Level Font. This selection determines whether the remaining font selections apply to the top-level outline entries or the sublevel outline entries. The Normal, On Select, and On Mouse drop-down list boxes allow you to change the color of the outline entry based on its state. Normal means no action has been taken yet. On Select means the entry has been selected. On Mouse means the mouse is hovering over the entry. For our example, select the Top-Level Font option and make the font bold. We are using a graphic icon for the various states, so there is no need to change the color of the text.

FIGURE 21.13

*The Font tab on the
Embedded Outline
Properties InfoBox*

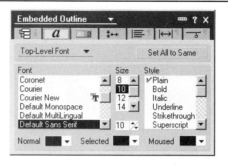

 The Background Tab   The Background tab, shown in Figure 21.14, allows you to
control the background colors not only for the entire outline, but also for each individual top-level and sublevel entry. In the upper left corner, there is a drop-down list
box that allows you to choose between three options: Control Background, Top-
Level Background, and Sub-Level Background. The selected option determines the
effect of the remaining options. Control Background determines the background
color of the overall outline. You can select a specific color from the Background
Color section, or you can use an image. If you use an image, you can use the Repeat
option to determine how it will be displayed. You can select Repeat Once, Repeat
Vertically, Repeat Horizontally, Repeat Both Ways, or Size to Fit (the Repeat option
does not work on the Web). The Top-Level Background and Sub-Level Background
options give you additional background color options. As you can on the Font tab,
you can elect to have a different color based on state (Normal, On Select, or On
Mouse). We're not going to use colors in our example because we already have icons
that change based on the state of the entry.

FIGURE 21.14

*The Background tab on
the Embedded Outline
Properties InfoBox*

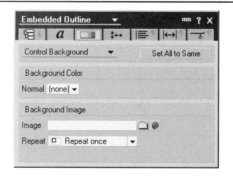

 The Layout Tab   The Layout tab, shown if Figure 21.15, allows you to control the
offsets for each entry in the outline. From the drop-down list box, you can select
either Top-Level Layout or Sub-Level Layout. Your selection determines which entries

are affected by the options displayed. There are three sections to this tab: Entry, Entry Label, and Entry Image. The Entry section allows you to specify the vertical or horizontal offset for the overall entry. Think of it as margin settings for an entry. The Entry Label section allows you to specify the vertical and horizontal offsets for the text label. If you don't specify an offset and you are using images, the text will overlay the image. For this reason, by default, an entry with an image is automatically offset horizontally. The Entry Image section allows you to specify the vertical and horizontal offsets for just the image. In both the Entry Label and Entry Image sections, you can also specify an Alignment option. You can choose from Top-Left, Top-Center, Top-Right, Middle-Left, Middle-Center, Middle-Right, Bottom-Left, Bottom-Center, or Bottom-Right. Using this option along with the offsets, you can create a wide array of visual effects, such as placing the entry image above the text label or to the right of the text label. For our example, just use the defaults that have been preset by Notes.

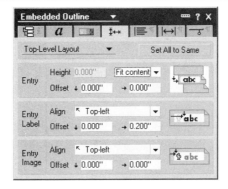

FIGURE 21.15

The Layout tab for the Embedded Outline Properties InfoBox

The Hide-When Tab   The Hide-When tab is no different than it is for any other design element. You can hide various outline entries by entering a formula. You could, for example, enter a formula that would hide an entry from users who have the letter *t* in their name.

Other Uses for Pages

You've seen just two uses for pages. We created a page to use as a Help page and one to use as an outline for our Recipe example database. There are plenty of other ways you can use pages; your choices are only limited by your imagination. To give you some ideas, we've defined some other pages in the example database for you.

The Welcome Page

As you have been working with pages, you may have noticed that there are a few other pages that begin with *dsp*. One of them is the dspWelcome page. It is designed to be used as an opening page (sometimes called a splash page) for the database; it displays when the user first opens the database. Because the text is only for display, a page is a better choice than a form. The Welcome page tells the user what the database's primary purpose is. It's not really necessary to have a Welcome page, but when we get to the section of frames and framesets, you will begin to see how it all ties together.

The Title Page

The dspTitle page does not contain much information except a brief one-word description of the database title. In this case, it says nothing more than Recipes. This will be used as a visual cue to help users quickly identify the database.

The Database Page

The dspDatabase page is similar to the dspTitle page except it displays the actual title users see when they open the database from the Notes client's Database Open dialog box. The Database page helps users become familiar with the database title so they can quickly identify the database.

What Is a Frameset?

Now that we have all of these pages and the outline, we can start tying them all together. This is where framesets come into play.

Framesets originated in Web applications. You can use them to divide the screen into blocks known as *frames*. If you are familiar with the Web, you know what a frameset looks like. In previous releases of Notes, a pseudo frameset design was possible with the Navigator pane, the View pane, and the Preview pane. The major stumbling block with the earlier design was that the programmer didn't really have any control over what displayed in each frame.

That has all changed with Notes R5. By default, a Notes database still uses the original three-pane design if a frameset has not been established. But it's a good idea to use a frameset when you are designing a database so you can control the behavior of the application. Each frame is an independent design element and thus can be controlled independently. You can also create frames that are scrollable. With the Internet becoming more and more popular, the use of frames is becoming a standard technique for presenting a multiple-pane interface to the user. You can associate any design element with each frame.

Creating a Frameset

Domino Designer has really taken the drudgery out of creating frames. Hand-coding a frameset can be tedious and prone to errors because you can't view the results. Framesets have their own special design components, which we will show you shortly. To create a new frameset, follow these steps:

1. Open the Mastering R5 for Chapter 21 database in Domino Designer.

2. Highlight the Frameset element in the Design list. This will display all the framesets for the current database in the Work pane.

3. Choose Create ➤ Design ➤ Frameset (you can also right-click in the Work pane and select New or click the New Frameset Design Action button). The Create New Frameset dialog box will display (see Figure 21.16).

FIGURE 21.16

The Create New Frameset dialog box

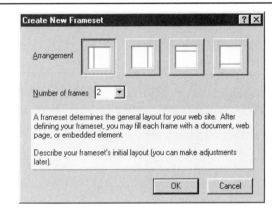

The first thing that you must consider when creating a frameset is how many frames you want to use. There are many schools of thought on this subject, but not many surefire answers. It boils down to what information you need to display to the user. Once you've decided how many frames to use, you must decide how to arrange them.

Frameset Arrangement and Frames

When the Create New Frameset dialog box appears, two frames are selected in the Number of Frames drop-down list by default. You can choose between two, three, or four frames. This does not mean that you cannot have more than four frames; it just means that you will start with only two, three, or four. Once in the Frameset Designer, you can add and remove frames at will. This is just a starting point; there is really no limit to the number of frames you can use.

Using the number of frames you've selected, the Arrangement option will display four different (or standard) scenarios. Figure 21.16 shows the possible arrangements for two frames, and Figures 21.17 and 21.18 show the possible arrangements for three and four frames. Once you have decided on the number of frames, just select the arrangement that best fits your needs by clicking the button. Then click the OK button and your new frameset will be displayed.

FIGURE 21.17

*Possible arrangement
for three frames*

FIGURE 21.18

*Possible arrangements
for four frames*

For our example database, we need to use four frames. To generate the frameset we need, follow these steps:

1. From the Number of Frames drop-down list box, select 4.

2. In the Arrangement section, select the icon on the right.

3. After selecting the arrangement, click the OK button and the frameset will be automatically displayed in the Frameset Designer, as shown in Figure 21.19.

FIGURE 21.19

*The generated
frameset with four
frames in the Frameset
Designer*

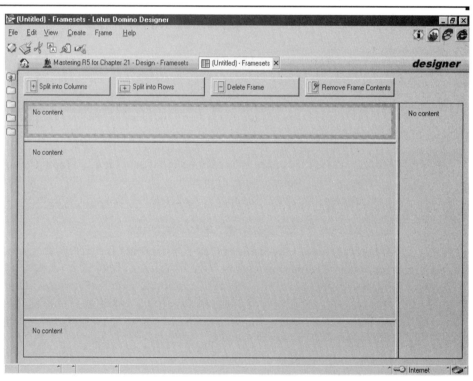

 NOTE The options that are available in the Create New Frameset dialog box are not the only options available for frames. You can make any number of adjustments once the frameset has been generated.

Now that the general structure for the frameset has been generated, let's manipulate the structure to fit the needs of the example database.

Using the Frameset Designer

Once the frameset is generated, you can add, remove, and manipulate the existing frames to further refine the interface. The layout shown in Figure 21.19 is close to what we need, but not exactly. We don't need to add or remove any of the frames; we'll just resize what we have. But first we need to name the frameset. And to do that, we need to display the InfoBox for the frameset.

 NOTE Do not confuse the frameset with the frame. Each frame is a unit of the frameset. The frameset defines the entire page; all frames are defined in the frameset. Think of the frameset as the outside walls of a house and each frame as a room.

The Frameset Properties InfoBox

The Frameset Properties InfoBox is used to refine some of the options for the frameset and frames. This InfoBox has two tabs, Basics and HTML, but we are only concerned with the first one. To name the frameset, type **MasterFrameset** in both the Name and Alias fields. You can also type a comment in the Comments field. The frameset title is the name that will appear in the title bar of your application in the Notes client and the Web browser. For our example application, type **"My Recipe Application"**.

Modifying Your Frames

The Frameset Designer has four Action buttons to help you design your frames:

- Split into Columns
- Split into Rows
- Delete Frame
- Remove Frame Contents

You can select the frame to modify and click one of the Action buttons. Depending on which button you clicked, the frame will break into two columns or two rows, it will disappear, or the contents will be removed. In our example, we don't need to add or remove any columns or rows because we already have the overall design (four frames) we want to use.

There are two options for resizing frames. One option is to place your cursor over one of the frame split bars and resize each frame by holding the mouse button and dragging the bar. This is a good way to get an idea of what you want, but it is better to actually size your frames individually using the Frame Properties InfoBox.

The Frame Properties InfoBox

The Frame Properties InfoBox is important because it determines the characteristics of each individual frame. It contains the following tabs:

- Basics
- Frame Size
- Frame Border
- Advanced
- Additional HTML

For our example, we are only concerned with the first three tabs because they contain the name, content, and border information.

The Basics Tab   The Basics tab contains two sections: Name and Content. With frames, the Name section is important. In the other Properties InfoBoxes we discussed in this chapter, there was a field called Target Frame. The name you placed in the Target Frame field must match one of names in the frameset. You can tell your application which frame to *target* when information is to be displayed (such as a specific frame to display a view). This is how the various pieces of your application can communicate in a framed environment. For example, if you have a Navigation frame that includes only links, you don't want the linked documents to appear in the Navigation frame when a user clicks the link; you want the document to appear in the document frame. In this example, the document frame would be the target frame of the Navigator frame.

NOTE   When you name a frame, it is important that the name matches the contents of any target frame field previously defined for other elements.

The other important part of the InfoBox is the Content section. You can choose what is to be displayed initially in each frame (remember that you can use the Target Frame field to change the contents of a frame). Selecting what to display in a frame is similar to selecting what to display in an outline. Just select what you want from the drop-down list boxes. The remaining option in the Content section is the Default Target for Links in This Frame option. You can set this field at a frame level, thereby eliminating the need for specifying it on components that make up the frame.

TIP   If a frame is specified as the target frame for a lower component, and another frame is specified as the target frame in the Properties InfoBox for the lower component, the properties for the lower component are used. For example, the contents of the Target Frame field for an outline overrides the contents of the Default Target for Links in This Frame field for the frame.

So let's start modifying the frames by setting the fields on the Basics tab. You should still have the new, blank frameset displayed in Designer. To change the values for each frame, follow these steps:

1. Open the InfoBox for the upper left frame by first selecting the frame and then choosing Frame ➤ Frame Properties (you can also right-click on the frame and choose Frame Properties).

2. Enter **topLeft** in the Name field. For the Type fields in the Content section, select Named Element from the first drop-down list box and Page from the second drop-down list box. Type **dspTitle** in the Value field (this page has already been created for you).

3. Next, select the middle, left frame with the InfoBox still showing. Type **left** in the Name field. In the Content section, select Named Element and Page. Type **dspOutline** in the Value field (this is the outline you created earlier in the chapter). Also type **NotesView** in the Default Target for Links in This Frame field. This will ensure that, if we forgot to place a target frame on any elements contained in the outline, they will automatically be displayed in the NotesView frame.

4. Now select the lower left frame. Type **leftBottom** in the Name field and in the Content section, select Named Element and Page. Type **dspDatabase** in the Value field (this page has already been created for you).

5. Select the last remaining frame. Type **NotesView** in the Name field, and in the Content section, select Named Element and Page. Type **dspWelcome** in the Value field (this page has already been created for you).

6. Save the frameset, and we'll continue with the next tab.

The Frame Size Tab   As its name implies, the Frame Size tab allows you to resize each frame. You can resize each frame manually by dragging the frame borders around. We prefer to use the Frame Size tab because it is more exact.

When sizing the frame, you have a few variations for the Height and Width fields. You can size a field based on a percentage, by the number of pixels, or relative to the other frames. You also have the option of setting a frame as scrollable and choosing whether or not the end users can resize the frame.

To adjust the sizing for our example database frameset, follow these steps:

1. With the InfoBox still open, select the Frame Size tab.

2. Select the topLeft frame and set Width to 200 Pixels and Height to 38 Pixels. We're using pixels in this frame because we don't want the size to change. When a view is displayed, the bottom border for this frame needs to match the border for the Action buttons in the NotesView frame exactly. Also set Scrolling to Off and Allow Resizing to On.

3. Select the left frame and set Width to 200 Pixels (this should already be set for you because all three left frames have to be the same width) and Height to 100 Relative. Set Scrolling to Off and Allow Resizing to On.

4. Select the bottomLeft frame and set Width to 200 Pixels and Height to 25 Pixels. Set Scrolling to Off and Allow Resizing to On.

5. Select the NotesView frame and set both Width and Height to 100 Relative. Set Scrolling to Default and Allow Resizing to On. Because this frame will contain various types of information that may extend beyond the bottom of the frame, we will allow scrolling if necessary.

6. Save the frameset, and we'll continue with the next tab.

The Frame Border Tab In the Frame Border tab, you can determine just how the frame borders should be displayed. By default, the borders are set to On, have a width of 7 pixels, and use the system color. We want to keep the borders but change them slightly so they have less of a 3D look. Change the properties in each frame as follows and then save the frameset:

- Set the Border field to On.
- Make sure the Border Width Default option is not selected and the size is set to 3 pixels.
- Set the Border Color option to Black

The Finished Product

There is one last change you need to make before testing the application. Open the Database Properties InfoBox and select the Launch tab. Because you have spent so much time setting up the application to use a frameset, we'll set the database launch option so the new frameset will be used when the database is opened. When the InfoBox is displayed, set the options that are set in Figure 21.20.

FIGURE 21.20

Setting the database launch options to use the frameset when the database is opened

To test the application, open the database in the Notes client. When the database is first displayed, it should look like Figure 21.21. Figure 21.22 shows the application in a Web browser.

You can see how the frames have separated the various parts of the application. The upper left frame displays a reference title, and the lower left frame displays the title for the database. The middle, left frame is where the user will perform all the navigation, and the right frame will display the application data.

Select All My Recipes. Notice how the ball icons change color to give the user a visual cue to what is happening. Also, the All My Recipes view is automatically displayed in the right frame. This is accomplished through the use of the Target Frame field in the outline (remember that, on the outline entry, you specified that the target frame would be NotesView; the right frame is named NotesView). Go ahead and navigate around the application and try viewing and adding new documents.

FIGURE 21.21

*The finished
application using the
Notes client*

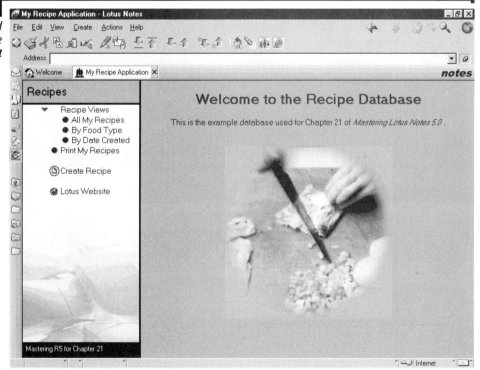

FIGURE 21.22

The finished application using a Web browser

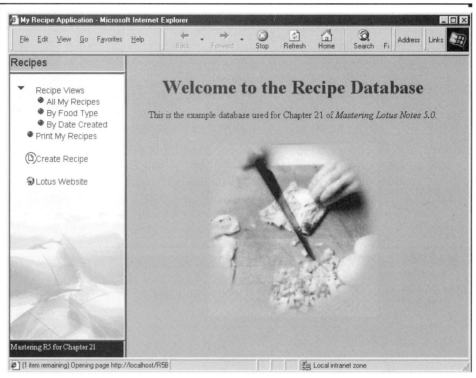

Summary

In this chapter, you were introduced to some features that add new functionality to Notes. But we only just scratched the surface. There are many different combinations you can use with an outline to create quite a fascinating navigational tool for your users. Using pages, you can combine the various elements Designer has to offer to create a dazzling array of text and graphics. The frameset is the glue that ties all of the design element pieces together. Using a combination of outlines, pages, and framesets, you are well on your way to creating some interesting applications.

In the next chapter, we'll look at Agents, which can be used to automate some of the tasks in a Notes application. Agents can limit the amount of manual effort required for routine tasks.

CHAPTER **22**

Using Agents to Automate Processes

You've already seen how you can perform a wide range of operations on documents and document fields with Simple actions and formulas. So far, you've had to make those actions happen in two ways:

- By using hotspots in forms, adding Actions to views and forms, and otherwise constructing buttons to press
- By using formulas in Form, Field, and View events, which are executed when a user opens a form, leaves a field, or performs an operation on a specific document or field, usually in a specific context

The limitation of those devices is that the user has to take action to make them happen. The formulas or Simple actions will execute every time a user presses the button, exits the field, and so on. But what if, for example, you want to send out daily summaries listing the documents that have been approved in a particular database? You could build the necessary formulas into a button somewhere, but someone would have to remember to press that button every day, and the summary might not go out if the person whose job it is to press the button didn't come in one day or left for another job. You could also put it into a Field, Form, or View event, but then the summary would be sent out every time someone performed the action that triggers the formula. That could potentially mean that your "daily" summary could go out many, many times every day if several people take the appropriate action, or not at all if nobody happens to take the appropriate action. This is where Agents come in. With Agents, many actions can be completely automated, running themselves so that you don't have to lift a finger.

An Agent is a database object that will perform actions for you. Like an Action button, it holds anything from a set of Simple actions to a complex LotusScript program. What makes Agents so powerful, however, is the control you have over when and how they run. An Agent can be set to run periodically (every day, every hour, etc.) to perform regular housekeeping or informative tasks, at certain events (when mail arrives, when documents are created) to automatically process data, or even manually, just like an Action hotspot or button. Agents act on documents, or at least in relation to them. Although they can sometimes use folders and views as organizational devices, they ultimately operate by gathering a collection of documents and performing actions either on them or based on the data in them. This chapter is about how to create, configure, and schedule Agents.

Why Use an Agent?

Before you dive into Agents, it might be a good idea to know what they're good for and how you can use them in your applications. Like form Actions and Action hotspots, Agents can perform complex tasks for you. However, Agents give you more flexibility when those actions are performed. The circumstances under which Agents run can be divided into four large categories:

- Manual operation
- Document events
- Scheduled operation
- Web access

Manual Operation

You can set an Agent to run when you select it from a menu or press a button. The manual operation options are most useful when you want to make the Agent's function widely available through your database. If an Agent is always available from a menu, you can use it anywhere in the database at any time, saving you the trouble of putting an Action button with the same set of instructions on every form, view, and folder. For example, if you have a database in which employees are supposed to note which documents they have read, you can use an Agent to let users mark each document with their name in a hidden People Who Have Read This Document field. Because Notes 5 lets you create shared Actions, the various manual operation options may not be used as widely as they have in earlier versions, but they're still the only way to get an Agent on a menu. You can also exert tighter control over the documents an Agent will run on than you can over those on which a shared Action will run.

There are a few different ways to run an Agent manually. Some Agents can be run from a menu (see "Manually from the Actions Menu" later in this chapter). However, you can make any Agent run with an Action button or hotspot. If you want to use a Simple action, the Run Agent option lets you select the Agent to run. You can also run a macro with the function @Command([ToolsRunMacro]). The syntax is @Command([ToolsRunMacro]; "*agentname*").

Macro? What's a Macro?

Don't worry, you don't need to learn about yet another programming tool or database design element. The word *macro* isn't used in Notes except to refer to Agents. In fact, it isn't really used for Agents very much either. The only reasons for *macro* to be used at all are historical. Way back in version 3, automation "programs" were called macros. Since then, Notes has become much more complex, macros have been supplanted by Agents, and the name *macro* has fallen by the wayside. However, a few commands in the formula language using the word *macro* survive for reasons of backward compatibility.

Document Events

Document events are *not* the same thing as the Form and View events discussed in Chapter 20. Rather, it's possible to make Agents run when certain document-related events take place. For example, you can make an Agent run automatically when new mail arrives or when documents are created. The power of these Agents lies in the fact that they will run without a user having to make them run. Instead, they run themselves. Using an event-related Agent gives you tremendous possibilities for automatic document processing. For example, an Agent in a mail-in order database could dismantle an original document sent from another database or submitted through the Web, sending order and shipping information on to a warehouse and credit and payment information off to sales personnel for processing. More important, it could perform the task as soon as the document comes in rather than waiting for a user to act on the new order.

Scheduled Operation

Like the document event–related Agents, scheduled Agents run themselves (that is, the user does not have to choose a menu item or press a button). However, scheduled Agents run not after certain events, but at set intervals. Unlike event Agents, which require a user or another automatic process to perform an action with a document, a scheduled Agent depends on nothing but time. Scheduled Agents can run as frequently as every five minutes or as infrequently as once a month. Like the document event Agents, scheduled Agents can be used for automatic document processing. However, because they operate at specific intervals, they will process documents in batches rather than one at a time, and there will always be a delay before the Agent runs rather than the Agent running more or less immediately.

Scheduled Agents are usually used to perform tasks that can or should wait to be performed at regular intervals. A scheduled Agent could be used to send out daily reminders to perform regular tasks (say, fill out a time card) or distribute weekly summaries of documents in a database. With a scheduled Agent, you could automatically send reminder messages to users of a workflow database, providing them with the titles of documents they need to approve. Or you could send out a weekly list of changes in a documentation database, informing users of documents that have been added or modified since last week.

If you're working in an environment with remote users or multiple Notes servers using scheduled replication, you can set the Agent schedules close to the replication schedule to centralize document processing. You can have documents that have been replicated to a central, powerful server processed at a time shortly after replication is finished and use your server to regularize the documents (for example, you might use it to assign unique, sequential numbers to the documents) rather than depend on the lesser processing power of individual workstations.

Scheduled Agents (the more frequently scheduled ones, at least) and document event Agents should be used with some caution. Users and designers see manually triggered Agents operate, so they quickly come to appreciate how long they take to run, and manually triggered Agents tend to use the client's "brainpower," so they have little impact on the server. Scheduled Agents, however, usually run on the server. A large, complex Agent can use a lot of the server's memory and processor time, slowing down server access for everyone. The same is true of Agents that operate on a large number of documents. In general, the more complex an Agent and the more documents it runs on, the less frequently it should run on a server.

Web Access

Finally, if you're designing a Notes application with an eye toward using it over a Web browser instead of through a Notes client, you can invoke Agents through a Web browser in several ways. You can run an Agent on a Notes document on the Web by using a Tools-RunMacro command in the WebQueryOpen form event (for opening the document) or the WebQuerySave event (for submitting the document). The Agent will automatically run on the document. If you're using LotusScript (which is discussed in the next chapter), use the DocumentContext property of the Agent's CurrentDatabase object to get the document.

You can also run an Agent directly without going through a document. The syntax to run an Agent is this:

```
http://servername/pathtodatabase/dbname.nsf/agentname?OpenAgent
```

Many formula commands can't be used over the Web (they're all listed in Designer Help), so be careful of which ones you use on your Web-enabled Agents.

Creating an Agent

Like other database elements, Agents have their own view in Designer, as shown in Figure 22.1. The Agents view lists all Agents in the database sorted first by whether they're shared or private (some Agents are only visible to and can only be used by their creator; we'll come back to this), then in alphabetical order by the Agent's name. Private Agents are listed with their creator's name.

Agents that operate on a schedule or on document events are listed with a check box. If the box is checked, the Agent is active and will run on the appropriate schedule or event. Such Agents can be deactivated simply by unchecking the box.

To create an Agent, select Create ➢ Agent in any database or click the New Agent button in the Agents view in Designer. This gives you a nearly blank canvas on which to create your Agent, illustrated in Figure 22.2.

FIGURE 22.1

The Agents view. The Agents are, in order, a shared, scheduled Agent; a shared menu Agent with a comment and an alias; a deactivated, shared, scheduled Agent; and a personal menu Agent.

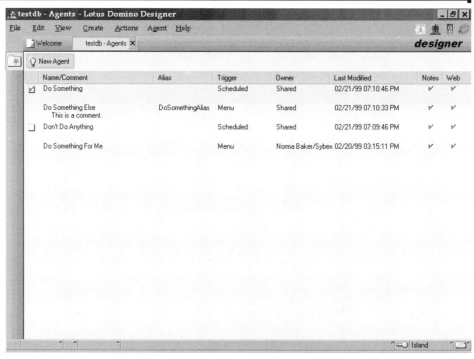

FIGURE 22.2

A new Agent

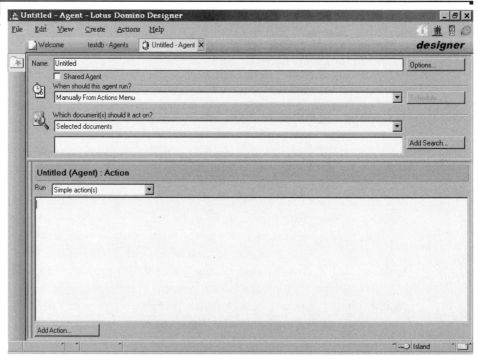

Once you have created the new Agent, there are four big things you'll need to decide:

- What it's called (and who can use it)
- When it runs
- What documents it runs on
- What it does

We'll start at the top, with naming the Agent, and work our way down.

Name and Options

The easiest part of creating an Agent is naming it. You can name an Agent just as you would a form, a view, or any other database design element. If you want to give the Agent an alias, put the alias name after a vertical bar character (|).

You also need to decide whether the Agent should be shared or personal. If you check the box to make it a shared Agent, other users can see it, run it, and if they have sufficient permissions in the database, edit it. If you don't check the box, the Agent is saved as a personal Agent, which only you will be able to use and edit. Others can see your personal Agents only if they have Manager access to the database.

You must decide whether you want the Agent to be shared or not before you save it for the first time. Once you save it, you cannot change this option. Fortunately, this is the only option that can't be changed. You may be prohibited from creating personal Agents, so check with your Domino administrator first. It's easy to distinguish personal from shared Agents in the Agents view. Shared Agents have *Shared* in the Owner column, whereas personal Agents have their owner's name. You may also not have permission to create shared Agents (see "Permissions and Security" later in this chapter); if you don't, you won't have the option to make it a shared Agent.

If you press the Options button, Notes will bring up the Options dialog box. The most important aspect of this dialog box is that it allows you to make comments about the Agent. For example, this is a great place to make notes about the purpose of the Agent, why it was written, the kinds of documents on which it's supposed to run, and anything else somebody else wanting to work with it should know. Any comments you make will appear in the Agents view under the Agent's name.

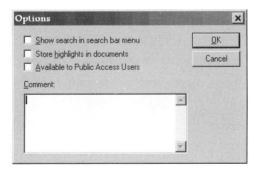

Schedule

The next big option to set is when the Agent runs (which is set in the Agents view in Designer). It can be run manually, on an event, or on a timed schedule. Each schedule option (discussed in the following sections) gives you another set of choices for the documents on which the Agent acts.

Manually from the Actions Menu

Choosing the Manually from the Actions Menu option puts the Agent on the Actions menu. Using the backslash character (\ ) puts the Agent on a submenu. For example, suppose you named an Agent My Actions\First. The item My Actions would appear on the Actions menu along with an arrow for a submenu. The submenu would contain the item First. If you created another Agent in the same database named My Actions\Second, you'd still see My Actions once on the Actions menu with an arrow for a submenu, but the submenu would contain two items: First and Second. You can see an example of this on the Actions menu of your mail database. The entries under Add Recipients, shown in the following graphic, are actually two Agents: Add Recipients\To New Group Calendar Entry and Add Recipients\To New Group in Address Book.

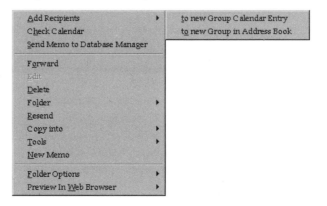

When you select this option, as when you select any scheduling option, you need to determine the documents on which the Agent will run. You have a number of options, ranging from a single document to every document in the database, and you can refine those choices further by adding search conditions. For the Manually from Actions Menu option, these are your search options:

All Documents in Database   This search condition is self-explanatory.

All New and Modified Documents since Last Run   The first time an Agent with this search condition runs, it runs on all documents. The Agent has never run on them, so it considers them new. It will also run on all documents the first time it is run after you change the Agent in any way.

All Unread Documents in View   With this search condition, you must run the Agent in a view. If you don't, the Agent will fail to run.

All Documents in View   An Agent with this search condition must also be run in a view.

All Selected Documents   This option is self-explanatory.

Run Once (@Commands May Be Used)   This is the only condition with which @commands may be used. They need a separate condition because some @commands (for example, `@Command([ToolsRefreshAllDocs]` or `@Command([Tools-RefreshSelectedDocs])`) already run on multiple documents. If you use this option with regular @functions instead of multidocument @commands, the Agent will run once on the current document.

Manually from Agent List

The Manually from Agent List option, inherited from earlier versions of Notes, doesn't run an Agent so much as it hides it. When the Agent is saved, Notes puts parentheses around its name. You'll probably recognize that as the way Notes hides a database object. In Notes 4.6 and earlier, Designer wasn't a separate client. Instead, there was a special view that showed all the Agents in the database: the Agent list. Users could go to the Agent list just as they could go to any other view and run Agents manually from there. This option is retained in Notes 5, although it is much less useful if the user doesn't have the Designer client. An Agent that is run from the Agent list can be run by right-clicking to bring up a menu and selecting Run. This is also a good place to put Agents you want to use with `@Command([ToolRunMacro])`, but be sure to include the parentheses around the Agent name if you do.

The Manually from Agent List option has the same list of options for documents to run on as the Manually from the Actions Menu option does.

Before New Mail Arrives

Before New Mail Arrives is the first truly automatic Agent option. This Agent runs as mail is delivered to a database. The most obvious use of this option is to create mail processing Agents for your mail database. Rules, presented back in Chapter 5, can shuffle documents between folders, but if you use an Agent, you can use far more powerful and flexible tools, such as the @formula language or LotusScript. You can, for example, use an Agent to automatically respond to incoming mail or change the values of fields (such as, for example, the subject line) in incoming mail to make the affected documents easier to spot and sort. It can also be used in applications that share data by mailing documents to one another. For example, you could have a set of databases mail documents to a central data "reservoir." Using a new mail Agent, the central database could give documents produced with different forms a set of standard fields, modifying the documents to fit into its own organizational scheme.

Your choice of documents on which to run the Agent is far more limited. A "Before New Mail Arrives" Agent can run only on arriving mail. It will not run on other documents.

After New Mail Arrives

An Agent with the After New Mail Arrives option, another holdover from earlier versions of Notes, runs once mail is delivered and appears in a database. There is usually a brief delay, usually a minute or two, between the time a new document appears and the time the Agent runs. This option is also good for automatically processing documents coming into your mailbox. As with the Before New Mail Arrives option, this kind of Agent only runs only on newly delivered documents.

If Documents Have Been Created or Modified

An Agent with the If Documents Have Been Created or Modified option runs when any new or existing document is saved. As with the After New Mail Arrives option, there may be a delay between when you save a document and when the Agent actually runs. You might use such an Agent to edit the document's contents, making sure that its fields have values that fall into an acceptable range.

As it is with the new mail Agents, your choice of documents on which to run is strictly limited. A "Created or Modified" Agent will only run on new and modified documents.

If you choose this option, you'll notice that the Schedule button, which has been grayed out for the previous Agent settings, is now available. This does not mean that "Created or Modified" Agents run on a schedule. It *does* mean that you can choose where the Agent runs. You could, for example, tell it to run on a specific server rather than on your workstation. However, this gets complex, so we'll hold off on a full explanation until we discuss the On Schedule More than Once a Day option.

If Documents Have Been Pasted

If you choose the If Documents Have Been Pasted option, the Agent will run when documents are pasted into the database. An Agent with this option can be an excellent tool for ensuring that all documents in your database follow the rules you set down for them. Because documents that are copied and pasted in from another database are not mailed in, nor are they created with a Save operation that would trigger a "Created or Modified" Agent, pasting would otherwise be a hole in the rules governing documents in your database. You could use an "If Documents Have Been Pasted" Agent to add or modify important fields, marking the documents as having been pasted in for later review. If you want to be draconian about it, you could even delete them immediately.

By this time, it should come as no surprise that a document of this kind will only operate on newly pasted documents.

On Schedule More Than Once a Day

If you choose On Schedule More than Once a Day, the Agent, as well as all of the remaining Agents, runs not when a user tells it to or when an event triggers it, but on a timer. This particular kind of Agent can be set to run several times a day. When you select this option, the Schedule button to the right of the schedule selection will no longer be grayed out. Clicking it will bring up the Schedule dialog box, which is shown in Figure 22.3. You'll use this dialog box to give Notes the additional information necessary to make the Agent run.

FIGURE 22.3

The Schedule dialog box for "More than Once a Day" Agents

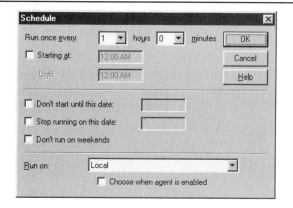

The top section holds information on the interval at which the Agent should run. For "More than Once a Day" Agents, you can choose a number of hours and a number of minutes. This kind of Agent defaults to running once every hour (that is, every 1 hour and 0 minutes), but you can choose anything from every 5 minutes to every 11 hours and 55 minutes. If you check the Starting At box, you can restrict the Agent so that it runs at particular times during the day. For example, you might have an Agent you use to send alerts run only during regular business hours because there's no point in having it run when nobody is likely to be around. Conversely, you might have the Agent run outside of business hours so it won't slow down other processes on the server when people are likely to be using it.

The second section lets you set day and date parameters. If you check the Don't Start until This Date check box, you can give the Agent a date before which it will not run. Then you can write and set up the Agent well in advance of the time you'll need it but not have it run before other objects or documents are ready. If you check the Stop Running on This Date check box, you can give it a date after which it will not run. You can use this to set up an Agent that will run for a while and then shut itself off. Finally, you can tell the Agent not to run on weekends.

The bottom section tells the Agent where to run. You can choose between Local and any server your Designer client knows about. There are a number of permissions and settings issues related to where you tell an Agent to run.

If you choose Local, a Notes client or a Domino server must be running on your computer and the Agent must be in a database on your computer in order for it to run. You can set an Agent to run locally, but if the Agent isn't on your computer, it can't run there. Likewise, if Notes isn't running when the Agent is scheduled to run, the Agent won't run either. Scheduled Agents must also be enabled. To let your Notes client run scheduled Agents locally, select File ➤ Preferences ➤ User Preferences. In the Startup Options section of the Basics tab, make sure Enable Scheduled Local Agents is checked.

There's a more subtle permissions issue here as well. You should be aware that, for scheduled Agents, the Local option doesn't really mean the local machine (that is, the computer on which you're currently working). What it really means in this context is the local *identity*. A local scheduled Agent has to run on a computer with a Notes client running, but the Notes client must be running under your ID. If someone switches to another ID, the Agent won't have permission to run (see "Permissions and Security" later in this chapter).

If you choose to make the Agent run on a server, be sure that you have permission. Your Domino administrator can assign various levels of permission to Notes users. You can be prohibited from running certain types of Agents or from running Agents altogether. By checking the Choose when Agent Is Enabled check box at the very bottom of the Schedule dialog box, you can leave the choice up to the person who activates the Agent. When the Agent is activated, Notes will bring up a dialog box in which the user can choose between servers and local operation.

You have two choices for documents on which to run this kind of Agent:

- All Documents in Database
- All New and Modified Documents since Last Run

Scheduled LotusScript Agents

The other major permissions issue for Agents has to do with Agents using LotusScript, Notes's most powerful built-in programming language (discussed at length in the next chapter). Domino servers distinguish between *restricted* and *unrestricted* Agents. Unrestricted Agents can use every command in the LotusScript language. Restricted Agents can use most of the language but are prohibited from using some of the commands that are most susceptible to abuse. Among the commands that restricted Agents cannot use are those related to manipulating external files. An unrestricted LotusScript Agent could, theoretically, navigate through folders, read text files, and mail documents as attachments; a restricted LotusScript Agent could not. Before you start writing Lotus-Script Agents, check with your Domino administrator to see whether or not you can write unrestricted Agents. You can also be prohibited from writing LotusScript Agents on a database-by-database basis.

On Schedule Daily

An Agent for which you've chosen the On Schedule Daily option is in all ways identical to a "More than Once a Day" Agent except for its scheduling. Instead of selecting an interval, you give the Agent a time during the day to run. It will run once a day at that time.

On Schedule Weekly

If you choose the On Schedule Weekly option, the Agent is also identical to a "More than Once a Day" Agent except for scheduling. A "Weekly" Agent takes both a day of the week (Sunday through Saturday) and a time of day. Also, the Don't Run on Weekends check box is permanently grayed out. After all, if you choose a day from Monday through Friday, it will never run on a weekend, and if you were to choose Saturday or Sunday and not let it run on weekends, it would never run at all.

On Schedule Monthly

A "Monthly" Agent is identical to a "Weekly" Agent except that it takes a day of the month (1 through 31) instead of a day of the week. Like the "Weekly" Agent, it cannot be turned off for weekends.

On Schedule Never

An "On Schedule Never" Agent will never run. At least, it won't run on a schedule or on any other behind-the-scenes event. The purpose of having an Agent like this is to allow a designer to temporarily disable a scheduled Agent without losing the All Documents/All New and Modified Documents since Last Run setting. Like all other Agents, it can still be run through @Command([ToolsRunMacro]) and all the other methods of running an Agent manually.

Add Search

Because you have the option with all Agents to add a search to the documents on which they are set to run, the subject is worth a separate discussion. The choices of documents you're presented with are very coarse. It is quite likely that you'll want to run an Agent on all documents created with a particular form or all documents that fit a specific category instead of on, for example, all documents. You can refine the set of documents on which any Agent runs by adding search conditions. To add conditions, click on the Add Search button in the Agents view in Designer.

Does the following dialog box look familiar? It should. It's the same Search Builder you probably remember from running database searches and building views. The conditions do not determine the set of documents on which an Agent runs; they only refine the set. For example, if you have an Agent that runs on selected documents and you add a condition such as Created after 7/4/99, the Agent would only run on those selected documents that were created after July 4, 1999.

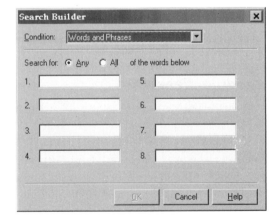

You may think of the Search Builder as a tool for refining the search conditions for scheduled and other "hands-off" Agents, but you can also use it as a tool to make sure your manually triggered Agents don't run on documents you don't want them to.

Actions

Finally, you'll need to tell your Agent to do something. You can give your Agent instructions in the programmer's pane at the bottom of the Agent window. When you create an Agent, you have a choice of four "languages," which you can select from the menu:

- Simple Action(s)
- Formula
- LotusScript
- Imported Java
- Java

The selected language defaults to Simple Action(s). Selecting a language modifies the programmer's pane appropriately, giving you access to Help files, field lists, and so on.

If you select Simple Action(s), you can use the Add Action button at the bottom of the window to give the Agent a series of Actions.

Selecting Formula gives you the same formula programmer's pane you recognize from working with Actions and Action hotspots.

The Action you provide, whether it's a Simple action or a formula, is performed on each document the Agent runs on. Simple actions and formulas can't "remember" data between documents, and they can't perform a single aggregate Action using the sum total of the documents on which the Agent runs. For example, suppose you wanted to report on the number of documents in a view on demand. To do so, you use formulas like this to set up an Agent run from the Actions menu that runs on all documents in the view:

```
ListOfItems := @DBColumn("":"";"":"MyDB.nsf";"ReportingView";1);
Listcount := @Elements(ListOfItems);
Messagetext := "There are " + @Text(Listcount) + " documents in
ReportingView."
@mailsend("MailingGroup";"";"";"ReportingView Contents";Messagetext;
"")
```

This code uses the @DBColumn formula to get a list of everything in the first column of the view and @Elements to count the elements in the list. If ReportingView is uncategorized, the number of elements returned by @Elements is the same as the number of documents in the view. That number gets tossed into a string that is sent out with @Mailsend. Mission accomplished? Yes, but only too well. Because a formula Agent acts on every document, you'll send out this message once *for every document in the view*. If there are a hundred documents in the view, that's a hundred separate but identical mail messages. Usually, you'll actually want to do the same thing 10 or 100 times, but this isn't one of those times.

LotusScript and Java (the Imported Java option lets you import entire Java programs written outside Notes), discussed in the next chapter, give you more power and flexibility, but they also break some of the rules you've learned for formulas and Simple actions. When a LotusScript or Java Agent runs, the language's own rules take over, making single operations on a mass of documents possible. If you want a LotusScript Agent to perform an action on a currently open document, read the next chapter, then look in the Domino Designer Help for the `NotesUIDocument` class. To run a LotusScript Agent on the set of documents retrieved by the Agent's search conditions, use the UnprocessedDocuments property of the NotesDatabase object.

Permissions and Security

Because Agents are so powerful and versatile, there are inevitably some security concerns. Agents themselves don't cause holes in your database's security, but they can act on large number of documents and can potentially do so without you or anybody else being aware of it, so they can point up inadequacies in security. A poorly written Agent or even an excessive number of well-behaved Agents can slow a server or workstation to the point of uselessness, and a very badly written Agent in an unsecured environment can cause enormous damage to your data. Imagine, for example, somebody with Editor access to a discussion database writing an Agent that changes the subject line of the documents on which it runs to "New Topic," but instead of having it run on selected documents in a view, he inadvertently sets it to run on *all* documents.

It is, therefore, useful to know how Agents fit into the greater scheme of things. Agents act like either the person running them or the last person to modify them (see the next section for more on this). However, to keep databases uncluttered, a database designer might want to restrict permission to create Agents. Although most security concerns presented by Agents are more the concerns of a Domino administrator than a database developer—and are therefore not covered in this book—there are some things the developer should be aware of.

Agents and You

An Agent doesn't just perform actions on your behalf. It performs actions as though it *were* you. That has implications for what the Agent can do and how it will make things appear.

If you run an Agent manually (that is, manually from the Agent list, from the Actions menu, or through `@Command([ToolsRunMacro])`), it has the same permissions that you do. In other words, it operates just like an Action button. If you don't have permission to read a set of documents, any Agent you run will be unable to read them as well. If you don't have at least Author permission to documents, your Agent can't edit them, and if you don't have Delete permission to the database, your Agent can't delete them.

Scheduled Agents also share permissions. However, because scheduled Agents don't actually have anybody running them, they behave a bit differently. When you save an Agent, you sign it as well. Notes uses that digital signature to determine permissions. If the Agent has a valid signature, it runs with the same permissions the person who signed it has. That usually means that an Agent runs with the permissions of the last person who saved it. Of course, if you don't have permission to run Agents on the server, your scheduled Agents won't run at all regardless of the permissions you may have in individual databases and documents.

A scheduled Agent also operates under the name of the person who signed it. This means that, if you create a scheduled Agent that sends mail, it will have your name in the From field. If your Agent modifies data, it will add your name to the $ModifiedBy field.

Agents and ACLs

Several Access Control List settings will affect Agents and how they run. Broad permission levels, of course, put severe limits on what a user can do with an Agent. Someone with Reader permission can't use Agents to modify documents, and a user without permission to delete documents can't use an Agent to delete documents either.

There are also several ACL settings that govern the creation of Agents. By default, a user can create Agents with as little as Reader access to a database. Just as they can create personal folders, users with Reader access or better can create personal Agents. Shared Agents, of course, require Designer access.

ACLs contain additional settings governing Agent creation, all of which are visible in Figure 22.4. One option a designer might strongly consider is preventing users from creating personal Agents. Personal Agent creation can only be disabled for users with Reader, Author, and Editor access. Those with Designer and Manager access have that permission automatically and it cannot be taken away.

Part of the reason to prevent the creation of personal Agents is simply to keep databases clean. If users create lots of Agents, your database will unnecessarily become a bit larger, which makes it harder for designers and managers to find the Agents they need to work with. More important, if users create lots of their own scheduled or document event–triggered Agents, a heavier load is put on the server. Preventing the creation of personal Agents also keeps enthusiastic but unskilled users from making poorly written Agents that will delete documents, alter important data, or otherwise interfere with the proper workings of your nicely designed database. However, if your users are predominantly nonprogrammers, it's probably not worth worrying about.

PART

V

Beyond the Client: Utilizing Domino Designer

FIGURE 22.4

An ACL: The settings governing Agents are on the right side.

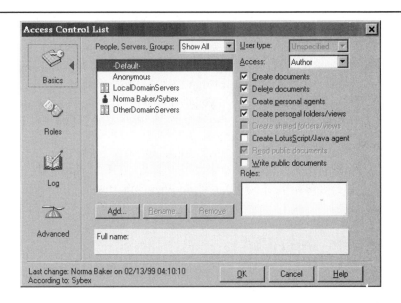

The other Agent-related setting controls users' ability to use LotusScript and Java to create Agents. The power and potential dangers of LotusScript were mentioned earlier in the chapter. With the extensive integration of Java into Notes 5, the same goes for that language as well. A manager can prevent users from using both LotusScript and Java to create Agents, and unlike the control you have over personal Agents, you can prevent designers from creating Agents that use LotusScript and Java. Agents using LotusScript and Java are an even greater risk in the hands of undisciplined users than other kinds of Agents, but because they require an uncommonly high level of skill to begin with, it's a setting you probably won't have to worry about unless you're developing applications for an audience of programmers.

To completely stop processor-eating Agents, you'll need to go to another place altogether. If you've spent any time at all examining databases, you'll be familiar with Figure 22.5, the Basics tab of the Database Properties InfoBox. By default, a database can run background Agents; that is, Agents running on the server without the user's intervention. However, if you check Disable Background Agents for This Database, no background Agents will run. If you've already prevented the creation of personal Agents, this probably won't be an issue, but it's worth checking if you want to be absolutely certain that the database will use as little of your server's processor time as possible. It's also a good idea to schedule Agents, if possible, during "off-peak" hours. If you need to run big, slow Agents that operate on huge batches of documents, you can usually get away with it if they run outside of regular business hours. After all, if the servers are slow when none of your users are trying to get their mail or access any other databases, nobody will know or care.

PART

V

Beyond the Client: Uti-
lizing Domino Designer

FIGURE 22.5

*The Basics tab of the
Database Properties
InfoBox*

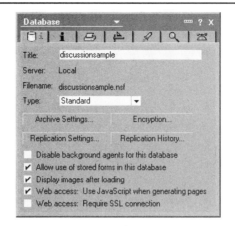

Summary

Agents are a means of automating Actions in Notes databases. They can be run manually as menu items or through Action buttons, but they are most powerful when they run on their own: on certain document-related events or on a schedule. Depending on the conditions under which an Agent runs, it may run on a particular set of documents, which can be refined further with the Search Builder. Agents run under the name of their author or the user running them, but the database designer may want to disable scheduled Agents or prevent users from creating Agents, saving memory and processor time.

In the next chapter, we'll discuss advanced language extensions in Notes: LotusScript, Java, and JavaScript. You'll learn how to write programs in LotusScript and how to integrate Java and JavaScript into your Notes applications.

CHAPTER 23

Language Extensions

One of the most powerful features of Notes and Domino is one that most users and even some developers will never see: LotusScript. LotusScript is a complete object-oriented programming language and an nth generation descendent of BASIC, one of the first programming languages (and still one of the most influential) developed for entry-level programmers. LotusScript is used by several Lotus programs, such as the spreadsheet program 1-2-3. It can also be used across platforms. As long as your script doesn't deal with certain system-specific features such as directory structures, it will run whether your database happens to be on a Unix box, a Mac, or a Windows computer.

LotusScript programs, known informally as *scripts*, lurk behind Agents, buttons, and events that happen invisibly when a user does things with documents, views, databases, and even individual fields. In fact, scripts run every time you open or close a document in your mailbox. With LotusScript, you can create applications that give the programmer tremendous control over databases, documents, and even external files, including:

- Extremely complex manipulation of and access to documents. For example, you can use LotusScript to move large groups of documents into and out of folders and views with just a few instructions or to base workflow on the number and attributes of documents already awaiting a user's approval.

- Access to and control over database properties. You can write your own maintenance utility programs to keep track of database size and utilization or even control Access Control Lists (ACLs).

- Access to external files. With the ability to manipulate text files and Open Database Connectivity (ODBC) data sets, you can integrate your Notes databases with your relational databases and with applications that can output structured text files.

Because LotusScript is powerful, it is also complex and has the potential to be dangerous if used carelessly. It is also a very different tool from what you've seen so far. With fields, forms, views, and folders, you've been seeing a visual development environment, and you've never been very far away from the objects in question. With scripts, you'll be writing a lot of instructions, without much in the way of ready-made lists of fields or forms to help you.

Nevertheless, LotusScript is relatively easy to learn as programming languages go. If you already know another scripting language, such as perl or Visual Basic for Applications (VBA), you're already well on your way to understanding LotusScript. If you haven't done any programming before, hang tight. You'll need to pick up some very different new techniques early on, but when you get to the section on Notes object classes, things will start to look familiar again.

But LotusScript isn't the only programming tool you can add to your arsenal. Notes allows you to use JavaScript to help "Web-enable" your databases. Notes 5 also has a range of new features for Java programmers. In this release, the entire Notes object model has been opened up for use in Java and JavaScript, providing a set of Notes-specific classes.

This chapter discusses where and how to use scripts, the basic rules of LotusScript syntax, and how to use some of the fundamental LotusScript object classes. Although Java and JavaScript are part of the Notes programming environment as well, this is *not* the place to learn them. For more in-depth coverage, you might be interested in *Mastering Java 2*, by John Zukowski (Sybex, 1998), and *Mastering JavaScript*, by James Jaworski (Sybex, 1997). This chapter concentrates on LotusScript, but it will point out how the Java and JavaScript classes can be accessed and used.

Why, When, and How to Use Scripts

If you've mastered formulas, you may wonder why you would want to bother with another, completely different and far more complex language. The answer is that scripts are much more powerful. You can do things with a script that simply can't be done with formulas. For example, the Out of Office Agent cycles through new messages, compares the senders' addresses to several different lists (addresses to receive a special reply, addresses to receive no reply, and addresses to which a reply has already been sent), composes appropriate messages from several different parts, sends them on their way, and modifies lists as appropriate. The Out of Office Agent's tasks would be difficult if not impossible to do with formulas. Scripts give you the following benefits:

- Fine control over complex data types that formulas have no access to. For example, you can use LotusScript to manipulate ACLs and ODBC data sets.

- The ability to read and write external files.

- The ability to deal with errors that would cause formulas to stop dead in their tracks.

- Superior access to other database objects. Although you can make a formula agent run on a set of documents, the formula itself can only affect the database object on which it is running at the moment.

- The capacity to write extremely intelligent programs that can make complex choices and remember what they've already done.

Of course, just because you can use a script doesn't mean you have to. There are often instances where you can do the same things with a script and a formula. For example, here's a script (don't worry about what it means; you'll find out later) for a button:

```
Dim ws As NotesUIWorkspace
Dim uidoc As NotesUIDocument
Set ws = new NotesUIWorkspace
```

```
Set uidoc = ws.UIDocument
Call uidoc.Print
```

This formula does the same thing:

```
@Command([FilePrint])
```

For a very simple task like this, it's clearly a better idea to use the formula. Formulas and Simple actions also run slightly faster than scripts of comparable size. Given the choice, if a script and a formula can perform exactly the same function and the formula isn't terribly hard to write, you'll probably want to go with the formula.

In some cases, the choice is made for you. For example, a field's Input Validation and Input Translation events will only take a formula, whereas the field's Entering and Exiting events can only take script (rich text fields don't have Validation and Translation, so if you want to validate them, you'll have to use script and the Exiting event).

Beyond that, it's your choice. If you're a novice programmer, you're less comfortable with script, and you can make formulas work, use them. If you're a more experienced programmer, use script. Some professional developers reach the point where they don't use formulas at all.

And where, exactly, do scripts go? Agents, buttons, view and form Actions, form and view events, and just about anything else that can take a formula can take script instead.

So What Is a Script, Anyway?

You've dealt with formulas (you have done that, haven't you?), so you've already gotten close to what you'll be doing with scripts. Like a complex formula, a script consists of a batch of instructions the computer executes when you press the related button, when the Agent triggers, when you enter or leave a field, and so on. A script, however, can have a far more complex structure.

A script consists of one or more subroutines, which are blocks of instructions (usually called code) meant to perform particular tasks. This has a number of advantages. First, it's much easier to organize and modify large programs if you can write smaller blocks of code (each with its own special function) and arrange them into a larger structure. Second, you can reuse code by going back to specific subroutines as many times as necessary. Formulas always execute from the top down, but you can write a script that repeats code or decides whether or not to use parts of itself while it runs. Imagine a program that, at various times, needs to calculate the sales tax on an item depending on the state in which it's being sold. Using formulas, you'll need to rewrite (or at least copy and paste) a huge formula every time you need to calculate the tax, resulting in a much larger block of formulas and making it very difficult to update if a state's sales tax ever changes. With LotusScript, you write the code once and, when you need it, refer to the subroutine by name. If something changes, you only have to modify it once.

You also know, more or less, where to write scripts. Scripts are written in the same programmer's pane where you write formulas, although a script editor will look a little different than a formula editor. Create an Agent, name it, and tell it to run LotusScript instead of a Simple action. Figure 23.1 shows what you'll get. Instead of the diamond you've seen in the lower left pane, there's a list of items marked with scrolls. If it were JavaScript, you would see circles. If there's code in any of those places, the scroll will be shaded. In addition to the familiar Design pane features, a LotusScript programmer's pane has a number of other features, visible and otherwise, to help you write scripts. The interface you use to write scripts has enough going on in it that it has a name of its own: the *integrated development environment*, more commonly called the IDE. The IDE gives you a place to write scripts and helps you debug them.

FIGURE 23.1

An Agent using LotusScript

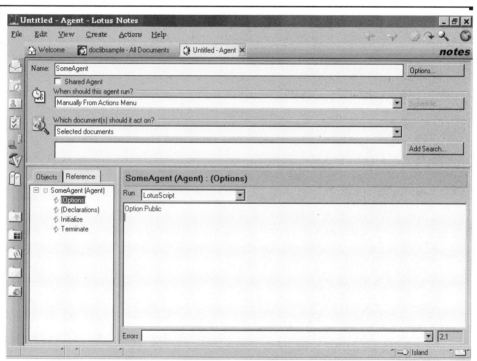

PART

V

Beyond the Client: Utilizing Domino Designer

The left pane displays a list of objects, events, and LotusScript (or Java) subroutines associated with them. The right pane, where you've already written Simple actions and formulas, is where you'll write the script. An additional feature of the script editor is the Error bar across the bottom of the screen. If you make an illegal statement in your script, Notes will flag the error and define it in the bottom bar. Finally, in the field at the bottom right, Notes displays the current position of the cursor in the format *line number, position*. For example, if it says 23, 12, the cursor will be 12 characters into the 23rd line of the script.

As you write your script, the script editor will help you keep track of what the words mean by coloring them. By default, identifiers (the names of variables and other user-defined objects) are black, keywords (commands, operators, and other words reserved by LotusScript) are blue, comments are green, errors are red, and other blocks of text are purple. However, you can change the colors from the Properties Info Box for the programmer's pane. Unlike form design, which gives you 256 colors to chose from, you can only choose from 16 colors for your scripts.

Commenting

You can insert a comment into a script by typing a single quote (') or the word *REM* (short for *remark*, a holdover from ancient versions of BASIC). A comment can start anywhere in a line, and everything after the comment marker is part of the comment. You can't start a comment part way into a line and then end it and enter more commands on the same line. After the comment marker, you can write anything you want: a description of what the following code will do, a warning about possible errors, a history of changes, or even snide comments about the script's development process. When the script runs, Notes will completely ignore comments, even if they happen to contain legal commands.

"Why," you may ask, "would anybody want to write something in a script that the program will ignore?" The answer is that comments aren't for the computer. They're for you and anybody else who might have to look at the script. Try as you may to indent lines properly and give your variables names that make immediate sense, you'll still write scripts that are long, convoluted, and incomprehensible on first glance. Even if your scripts are short and to the point, it won't be immediately obvious what they're supposed to do or, more important, why they were written to begin with. It's a good idea to insert header information in your scripts before the executable code starts; the header information can describe the script's purpose and perhaps contain other useful information such as the programmer's name (so you'll know who to contact in an emergency, or at least who to hold accountable) or a list of modifications. A typical header might look like this:

```
' Script name:  PeaceAndLove
'
' Author:  Marion Morrison
'
' Last Modified:  2/3/99
'
' Description:  Spread peace, love, and understanding
' among all mankind, using a Domino server.
```

In addition to any "header" comments, you should put internal comments into your script to keep the reader posted on what's going on. Even if you can keep track of what a large script does while you're writing it, you won't remember in six months, and if somebody else has to look at your script, they won't have any idea how it works. Eventually, you may be able to read through the script and figure out how it works, but you'll save a lot of time if you just write a few brief comments describing what's going on. Comment lavishly. It will take an extra few minutes while you're writing, but it will save you hours later on.

Subroutines

Go back to the list of scrolls on the left side of the LotusScript programmer's pane in the agent you created and click Initialize. Each item on the list represents a subroutine. Clicking the Initialize subroutine brings up a few lines of code. The Sub Initialize and End Sub are what make the subroutine exist. The (Button as Source) bit in the Sub line is declaring a variable in a way that makes it easy for the script to refer back to the button. Certain form events come with other variables built in. For example, events related to opening and closing a form, such as PostOpen and QueryClose, have built-in variables that make it easy to refer to the document being opened. That's not important right now, but it can be a useful tool, and we'll get back to it later in the section on scope.

To create a subroutine, just add another Sub statement *after* the End Sub line. In the example from the preceding paragraph, go to the End Sub line in the Initialize subroutine, press Enter to go to the next line, type in **Sub Main**, and press Enter again. That will create an empty subroutine named Main (the End Sub line is created automatically) and put you in it. Those subroutines form the structure in which programs are written.

To use a subroutine in a program, just type in the name. When a subroutine finishes running, the script will return to where it started. For example, the following script runs three subroutines (Firstroutine, Secondroutine, and Lastscript) in order; then it runs Firstroutine a second time:

```
Sub Initialize
' This calls a series of other routines
    Firstroutine
    Secondroutine
    Lastscript
    Firstroutine
End Sub
```

Now you should be able to construct the skeleton of a LotusScript program. However, a batch of subroutines won't do you any good if they don't do anything individually. Now it's time to start learning the LotusScript language.

PART

V

Beyond the Client: Utilizing Domino Designer

Basic LotusScript Programming

This section addresses basic programming terms and techniques. If you're a programmer, you might want to skim this section or just skip ahead to the section on using the Notes object model. If you're not a programmer, or you've never programmed in a BASIC-compatible language before, read on.

Variables and Data Types

If you've dealt with Notes formulas or just taken algebra, you know what a variable is: an expression that stands for a value. However, unlike in an algebraic expression, a variable in LotusScript doesn't just stand for a number. It can stand for a string (that is, text), numbers (both integers and floating-point numbers), dates and times, and Notes-native objects such as databases, documents, views, and fields.

Declaring Variables

It's a good idea, if not always necessary, to declare a variable before you use it. When you declare a variable, you're telling Notes what its name will be and what type of data it will hold. Variables are declared with the Dim statement, like this:

```
Dim variablename as type
```

In the early days of programming, *dim* was short for *dimension*, setting up a space in memory for the variable's value. The old terminology is long gone, but the function stays the same. When you declare a variable, Notes sets up a space in memory large enough to hold the information for the type of variable you declare.

You can declare several data types, each of which can have values that fall into a given range (see Table 23.1).

TABLE 23.1: LOTUSSCRIPT DATA TYPES

Type	Values
Integer	Integers (whole numbers) from −32,768 to 32,767.
Long	Integers from −2,147,483,648 to 2,147,483,647.
Single	Any number from −3.402823E+38 to 3.402823E+38.
Double	Any number from −1.7976931348623158E+308 to 1.7976931348623158E+308.
Currency	Any number from −922,337,203,685,411.5807 to 922,337,203,685,411.5807. Currency variables may have at most four decimal places.
String	Any plain text value.
Variant	Any value.

The data types listed in Table 23.1 are all for *scalar* variables, simple variables that hold a single value of a simple type. You may also declare a variable as an array (a set of values of the same type, discussed in "Lists and Arrays" later in this chapter), as a Notes object class, or as a Java class, but those follow slightly different rules (we'll get to that later). Although you might be tempted to declare everything as an easy-to-handle variant, don't. A variant takes up from two to eight times as much space in memory as any other kind of variable. Any one variable will take up a nearly trivial amount of space, but a big script that juggles a lot of variables can be slowed down if it takes up too much room.

A variable name must start with a letter and can contain any combination of numbers, letters, and underscores up to 40 characters. These are valid:

```
Dim MyText As String
Dim time1 As Double
Dim some_money As Currency
Dim anunreasonablylongbutlegalvariablename As Long
```

These are not:

```
Dim 1variable As Integer
Dim my text As String
Dim avariablenamesoamazinglylongthatititisntalegealnameanymore As Long
```

It's also tempting to give your variables simple, one-letter names like we all remember from high school algebra (x, y, a, b, etc.), but don't do that either. Near-meaningless variable names are OK for counters (that is, variables you use to count the number of times a process has happened, the number of times through a loop, etc.) and other "throwaway" variables that are used once or twice and ignored for the rest of the script, but it's a good idea to give your variables meaningful names. For example, *docA* and *docB* for a pair of documents that you want to compare or *fullprice* for an undiscounted price would be good variable names. You'll notice that, in the examples later dealing with Notes objects, a fairly regular set of variable names is being used: *vw* for a view, *doc* for a Notes document, *db* for a Notes database, and so on. LotusScript reserves a number of words, mostly commands and statements, which should not be used as variable names. It might be tempting to use *notesdocument* as the name of a variable representing a Notes document, but *notesdocument* happens to have a meaning. You should avoid using the names of objects, properties, and variables to avoid confusing both yourself and Notes.

Setting Values

Once a variable has been declared, you can assign a value to it with an equation, like this:

```
Dim x As Integer
x = 2
```

This sets the value of the variable *x* to 2. Notice that you just use the = sign, not :=
like you would in a formula. In LotusScript, = is used for both comparison and assignment. The variable you want to assign the value to goes on the left side of the equal
sign, and the value you want to assign goes on the right. You can put any valid expression on the right side. This code sets *x* equal to four:

```
y = 2
x = y*2
```

If you want to concatenate strings, use the + or & sign, and be sure everything you
want to concatenate is a string.

This code sets *thirdstring* equal to "Hello world!":

```
firststring = "Hello "
secondstring = "world!"
thirdstring = firststring + secondstring
```

If you concatenate a string with a number or some other non-text variable, use the
Cstr() command to turn the variable into a string. For example:

```
x = 4
thestring = "There are " + Cstr(x) + " lights!"
```

After this code, the value of the variable *thestring* is "There are 4 lights!"

Lists and Arrays

In addition to scalar variables, LotusScript provides for some more complex data
types: lists and arrays, variables that hold sets of values of the same type. A list is
declared by adding the List operator to the Dim statement. For example, a Currency
list, which might be used to hold a list of prices, would be declared like this:

```
Dim priceList List As Currency
```

Members of a list are named. You can use a string or a string variable. The following code creates two entries (named "Apples" and "Oranges") for the Currency list
and assigns values to them, using a string to name the first item and a string variable
to name the second:

```
Dim priceList List As Currency
Dim itemName As String
PriceList("Apples") = 1.05
ItemName = "Oranges"
PriceList(itemname) = 0.85
```

Notice that variable names aren't case sensitive. Both *ItemName* and *Itemname* work
to name the variable. You can create as many list items as desired.

Like a list, an array can hold a number of values, but it can be far more complex. An array is declared with a range (defining the number of values it can have) in parentheses, thus:

```
Dim valArray (5) As Integer
```

Because arrays start counting at zero, the preceding array can hold up to six values, and those values can be referred to using the numbers 1 to 5 as indices. You can also name the lower bound of the array. This defines an array identical to valArray:

```
Dim otherArray (0 to 5) As Integer
```

Any given item in the array is addressed by using the variable name and the appropriate index number in parentheses. A value could be assigned to the last member of the array like this:

```
valArray(5) = 2
```

You can, of course, use any values you want to assign the upper and lower bounds. The array defined by Dim valArray(10 to 15) as Integer also holds six values, but the last member of the array would be valArray(15).

So far, an array is hardly different from a list. But one of the advantages of an array is that, because the "names" of the items in the array are numbers, the values of an array are arranged in a meaningful order. You can speak of the first member of an array, the second member, and so on, which you can't do with a list. For example, it's easy to set up a loop (see "Forall" in the section on looping later in this chapter) to cycle through the list of values. One of the other advantages is that an array can be multidimensional. You can think of valArray as a table with one row and six columns. However, we could create a table of multiple rows with multiple columns by giving the array a second range:

```
Dim twoDArray(1 to 5, 1 to 4) As Integer
```

In this code, twoDArray has two dimensions, not just one. It could be considered a table with five columns and four rows. The value of the second column, third row would be set like this:

```
twoDArray(2,3) = 1
```

In LotusScript, an array can have as many as eight dimensions.

You may have thought it strange that arrays start counting at zero instead of one. The reason is that arrays can be multidimensional. Think back to high school algebra and geometry again. All of those grids you graphed parabolas on had an origin point at 0 on the x-axis and 0 on the y-axis. That kind of geometric thinking has carried over into programming, so the first value of an array is not at one, but at ground zero, both virtually and literally. This makes particular sense when you consider that arrays are built to deal with multidimensional grids, where starting from a zero point is essential. LotusScript does hide its heritage a bit by letting you declare both the upper and lower bounds of arrays that you create, but unless you tell it otherwise, it uses 0 as the default lower bound.

Option Base

If your brain can comfortably change gears to start counting at zero rather than at one when it comes to arrays, it shouldn't be a problem to refer to arrayname(0) whenever you want to retrieve a value. But if it annoys you, you can take steps to change the way LotusScript acts. If you go to the (Options) routine, you can add the line Option Base n, where *n* is the default lower boundary of an array. Adding Option Base 1 will make the default lower bound 1, which would make arrayname(1) the first member of an array. However, be careful using Option Base if you're going to use multidimensional arrays. Option Base 1 would move the "center" of a three-dimensional array from (0,0,0) to (1,1,1), which can lead to some exciting math.

LotusScript gives you the ability to resize arrays, so you can declare an array even if you have no idea how big it needs to be when the script begins. Use the ReDim command to resize the array like this:

```
Dim valArray(2) As Integer
ReDim valArray(4) As Integer
```

valArray has gone from having three members (0 through 2) to five (0 through 4). In this particular case, valArray was declared with members, but it would be possible to declare an array with no members at all (Dim valArray () as Integer) and use the ReDim command later. If you already have values in an array and want to keep them, use the PRESERVE keyword to keep the values from being erased when you resize the array. Here's an example:

```
Dim valArray(1) As Integer
valArray (0) = 1
valArray (1) = 5
ReDim Preserve valArray (2) As Integer
```

After this code, valArray has three members, the last of which, valArray(2), is null.

Two invaluable functions for dealing with arrays are Ubound and Lbound. These functions return the upper and lower boundaries of an array. You might use them like this:

```
' assume that valArray has been declared as an integer and has had
' values set elsewhere
x = Ubound (valArray)
ReDim Preserve valArray (x + 1) As Integer
valArray (x+1) = 1
```

This code finds out the upper bound of valArray and uses it to add another member to the array.

When and Where to Declare

In certain cases, you must declare variables before you use them. Arrays must be declared, although you can reset their bounds. If you put Option Declare in the Options section of a script, you must declare all variables no matter what kind they are. Notes developers who have worked with earlier versions of LotusScript will be interested to know that they no longer have to declare Notes objects. In earlier versions of Notes, you had to declare variables for documents, databases, and so on, but improvements in the LotusScript compiler make that unnecessary.

If you don't use Option Declare, you can create variables implicitly, which is to say, without declaring them first. Just use a name that has not previously been used as a variable and Notes will create it with a null value. For example, if x and y haven't previously been declared, the following statement will return the value 0 for x and 2 (2+0) for y:

```
y = x + 2
```

The use of Option Declare (Option Explicit, the syntax that some other dialects of BASIC use, will also work) is worth a little attention here. Often, LotusScript programmers will go to the Options section of their scripts and put in the line Option Declare. This option prohibits creating variables implicitly, forcing programmers to declare any variables they intend to use. The advantage of not using Option Declare is that it's a little faster for the experienced programmer to create variables at will. Not having the Dim statements makes the script a bit shorter, and more important, a programmer who knows exactly what she's doing can write operational code without having to type in an extra line for every single variable.

However, there is a downside—several downsides, actually. First, if you don't declare a variable, Notes won't know what kind of data you're about to drop into it. Therefore, it creates a variant, which takes up more room in memory than other data types.

Second, if you have complete freedom to create new variables on the fly, you have complete freedom to get them wrong. Consider this code:

```
Firstvar = 1
Secondvar = 2
Thirdvar = Fristvar + Secondvar
```

The inattentive programmer might expect *Thirdvar* to equal 3, not realizing that he's suddenly creating the variable *Fristvar* instead of using the variable *Firstvar*. If Option Declare is used, Notes will let the programmer know about any misspelled variable names immediately. It may not sound like much on the surface, but half of debugging is cleaning up punctuation and spelling errors. Using Option Declare can save a lot of time and hair-pulling trying to find a well-hidden mystery variable.

Scope

It's not enough just to declare your variables. You've also got to know where to declare them. Where a variable is declared determines what parts of a script can know about it;

in techno-speak, its *scope*. A variable's scope is the range of subroutines in which it can be used. If you declare a variable within a subroutine, it can only be used within that subroutine. If your script moves to another subroutine, that variable (and its value) will go away. If you're not declaring variables before you use them, your script will lose them as well.

LotusScript gives you several methods to give variables a wider scope. You can build variables into the definition of the subroutine or into a function by declaring it with parameters. In addition to the built-in LotusScript functions (type conversion variables that perform much the same tasks as @functions such as **@text**, mathematical functions such as tangents and cosines, etc.), LotusScript allows you to write your own special-purpose functions. For example, you might want to create a convenient means for calculating sales tax for different states or for computing the check digit for a UPC code.

You create a function much like you create a subroutine, but functions require a more complex syntax. Use the FUNCTION keyword rather than Sub, give the function a name, provide parameters, and give the function a data type. For example, this line creates a function named volume that requires three parameters and returns a single-precision floating-point number:

```
Function volume (height,width,length) As Single
```

At some point in the function, you must set the function name equal to some value. This will be the value returned by the function. Our `volume` function might look something like this:

```
Function volume (height,width,length) As Single
    volume = height * width * length
End Function
```

To use a function you wrote yourself, simply use it as you would any of LotusScript's built-in functions, plugging in values as necessary. The line below sets x equal to the value of the `volume` function with a height of 2 and width and length equal to the variables *firstnumber* and *secondnumber*.

```
x = volume (2, firstnumber, secondnumber)
```

The values you plug into the function will become the values of the variable names you use in the parameters you used to create the function.

Just as you can define parameters for a function, you can define them for a subroutine. For example, if you created a subroutine with the line `Sub myroutine (myvar as String)`, you would invoke it not just by using the name of the subroutine, but with a line like this:

```
myroutine(some_string_value)
```

By plugging a value into the subroutine call, you can pass the value of a variable from one subroutine to another.

Most of the time, that isn't good enough. You may need to pass a great many values from one subroutine to another, making it tedious to create the whole list of parameters, or you may not be able to fill in all of the parameters with values. Fortunately, you can also give variables a broader scope by declaring them in a special place. Most objects and events that can take LotusScript have a special subroutine named (Declarations). The Declarations subroutine can only take Dim statements, but any variable declared there has a scope of the entire script. You can use the variable in any subroutine, and it will keep its value as you move from one subroutine to another. Although the Declarations subroutine is probably the best place to declare your variables, don't try to instantiate them with As New (if you don't know what instantiation is, don't worry; we'll come back to that later). You'll have to put `Dim objectname as objecttype` in the Declarations subroutine and put `Set objectname = New objecttype` in the subroutine where you actually start using it. Forms have a Globals section with a Declarations subroutine that may be used to declare variables valid in any script used in the form.

Looping and Branching

Two vitally important tasks that a full programming language needs to perform are *looping* and *branching*, also called iteration and flow control. Looping is when a program repeats a block of instructions, usually until a particular condition is met. Branching is when a program is presented with a set of choices, selects one, and executes a related set of instructions. Lack of looping and branching is what keeps Notes's @formula language from being a fully featured programming language. The @if function provides only limited branching, and there is no looping at all. LotusScript, on the other hand, provides a number of methods for both.

Conditions

Looping and branching techniques depend on *conditions*, expressions that will allow them to determine what they should do. A condition can be any function or equation that will return a Boolean value (that is to say, any statement the computer can evaluate as being true or false). For example, a line of code might have the condition $(x > 1)$. If x is 1 or less, the expression is false. If x is greater than 1, it is true. Although equations may be more familiar, Notes also has a number of functions that will return Boolean values. For example, the `IsNumeric` function examines a string variable. If the string can be converted to a number, the function is true. If not, it is false. The expression `IsNumeric(mystring)` is true if *mystring* is, say, `"123"`, but false if it is `"onetwothree"`.

A condition can even be an expression that can be evaluated as a number. If the expression evaluates to 0, the condition is false, otherwise it is taken as true. For example, $(x + 1)$ is a valid condition. If $x = -1$, the expression becomes $(-1 + 1)$, which becomes 0, and is therefore false. Any other value would make the condition true.

Complex conditions can be built by connecting them with Boolean operators, usually the keywords AND, OR, and NOT. For example, `((x > 1) and IsNumeric(mystring))` is true so long as *x* is greater than one or *mystring* can be converted into a number.

Conditional expressions should always involve variables. It's certainly possible to have (2+2=4) as a condition, but unless something goes terribly wrong with your computer, it will always be true.

Branching

Branching, though a standard term, may not be the best word to describe what it does. It implies that the program goes down one path or another, never rejoining the main "trunk." Nothing could be further from the truth. Most "branches" are of the character "if some condition is true, set this value and continue; if not, just continue" or at most "if this is true, perform these instructions, then come back here and go on to the next line." The two important branching methods in LotusScript are the If...Then statement and the Select Case statement.

If...Then   The most straightforward and commonly used branching method is the If...Then block. It checks a condition and, if it's true, executes the code. The end of the block is marked by an End If, thus:

```
x = Inputbox("Type in a number")
y = Cdbl(x)
If y < 1 Then
    Msgbox("The number is less than 1")
End If
```

The preceding code brings up a dialog box asking for a number (the input is a string, so we convert it to a double-precision floating-point number with the `Cdbl()` function). If the number is less than one, it brings up a message saying so. Otherwise, it does nothing. With the Else statement, you can set up two different bits of code. If the condition is true, the code after the If statement is true. If not, the code after the Else statement runs. This code does almost the same thing as the preceding code, but it will also put up a message if the number is one or more:

```
x = Inputbox("Type in a number")
y = Cdbl(x)
If y < 1 Then
    Msgbox("The number is less than 1")
Else
    Msgbox("The number is greater than or equal to 1")
End If
```

An If...Then block can actually get much more complex, turning into an If...Then...ElseIf...Else block. In this kind of block, each ElseIf gets its own condition, setting up as many different possibilities as the programmer wants. The program will run through the conditions until it finds one that is true and executes the associated instructions. Once that code is executed, the program will skip down to the next line after the End If. Consider this example:

```
x = Inputbox("Type in a number")
y = Cdbl(x)
If y < 1 Then
    Msgbox("The number is less than 1")
Elseif (y >= 1) Then
    Msgbox("The number is greater than or equal to 1")
Elseif (y >= 2) Then
    Msgbox("The number is greater than or equal to 2")
End If
```

If someone were to type in a 2, the resulting message box would say "Y is greater than or equal to 1" because the first condition that is true is y >= 1.

There are several methods you can use if you want to fill multiple conditions. For example, you can check the values of two variables in a single If statement like this:

```
If x > 1 And y = "a" Then
' …some instructions here
End If
```

Or you can check them by nesting two statements, putting one inside the other, like this:

```
If x > 1 Then
    If y = "a" Then
' …some instructions here
    End If
End If
```

If the first instruction is true, Notes will look at the second If statement. If it's not true, Notes will skip over it.

You may have noticed that statements within the If…Then block are indented. That's no accident. Another nice thing the script editor does for you is automatically indent the contents of conditional statements and loops. That makes it a lot easier to tell where a block of instructions begins and ends. It's purely for display; you can add and remove spaces all you want without affecting the operation of the script.

Select Case   A Select block is like an If…Then…ElseIf block. The block starts with a Select Case *variablename* statement, which tells the block which variable to examine. It is followed by a number of Case statements. Each Case statement takes a possible value of the variable. If the variable *Chosen* in the Select Case line is equal to the value in the Case line, Notes will execute the block of code associated with that value. The block can also take a Case Else statement for code to execute if none of the other conditions are true, and it always ends with an End Select statement. Select Case statements are usually used when the programmer expects a limited range of input, like this:

```
x = Inputbox("Type in the number 1, 2, or 3")
Select Case x
Case 1
  Msgbox("You chose 1")
Case 2
  Msgbox("You chose 2")
Case 3
  Msgbox("You chose 3")
Case Else
  Msgbox("You chose something not on the list")
End Select
```

If you type in 1, 2, or 3, you'll get a message box telling you the number. In this example, the Case Else block will tell you that you typed in something not on the list. However, if you want nothing to happen if the variable isn't one of the choices, simply omit the Case Else statement and go directly to End Select.

Select Case statements are best used when you know that you'll have a limited range of inputs. For example, a routine like this might be used to translate an abbreviation (stateabbr) into the name of a state (statename):

```
Select Case stateabbr
Case "AL"
  Statename = "Alabama"
Case "AK"
  Statename = "Alaska"
Case "AR"
  Statename = "Arkansas"
' ...and so on, forty seven more times.
Case Else
  Statename = "(no state)"
End Select
```

Looping

Branching may not be the best word to describe what branching does, but *looping* is the best possible word for what it is used to describe. A loop goes around and around, running the same code repeatedly until it decides or is told when to stop. However, rather than doing the exact same thing over and over again, loops can be smart enough to do slightly different things on each loop. A loop might perform the same set of actions on a different document each time through or perform a calculation with a different number.

Among the most commonly used looping commands are For...Next, Do...Loop, and Forall.

For...Next   A For...Next loop executes a block of code a set number of times. It needs a variable to act as the counter, a beginning value, and a final value, and the block ends with a Next statement. For example, this code will print the numbers from 1 to 10:

```
For x = 1 to 10
   Print x
Next
```

You can, of course, begin and end with any value. This code prints the numbers from 18 to 34:

```
For x = 18 to 34
   Print x
Next
```

You can also control the pace and direction of a For...Next loop by qualifying the For line with a Step statement. This code counts down from 10 to 0:

```
For x = 10 to 0 Step -1
   Print x
Next
```

This counts from 0 to 10 by twos. It will print 0, 2, 4, 6, 8, and 10:

```
For x = 0 to 10 Step 2
   Print x
Next
```

Do...While/Until...Loop   Unlike a For...Next loop, which runs its code a given number of times, a Do...Loop repeats the code while a condition is true (for a Do...While...Loop) or until it becomes true (for a Do...Until...Loop). This code comes up with a random number and asks the user to guess what it is until he guesses right:

```
' This line uses the rnd() statement to come up with
' a random number between 0 and .999…, multiplies it
' by ten to turn it into a number between 0 and
' 9.999…, turns it into an integer (rounding down) and
' adds one, ending up with a random number between 1
' and 10
X = cint(rnd()*10)+1
Guess = Inputbox("Guess a number from 1 to 10")
Do Until X = Guess
   Guess = Inputbox("Guess a number from 1 to 10")
Loop
Msgbox("Right!")
```

A useful feature of Do...Loops is that you can put the condition either at the beginning (right after the Do statement) or at the end (right before the Loop statement), as illustrated in the following code. This makes a difference in the number of times the code will execute:

```
Do While X > 1
' ...some code goes here
Loop
Do
' ...more code here
Loop While X > 1
```

The difference between these two examples is that in the first loop, if *x* is less than or equal to 1, the code in the loop won't execute. Putting the condition in the Do line tells the script to run the code if the condition is met. In the second example, the code will run at least once. The Do statement is unqualified, so the following code gets executed. Putting the condition in the Loop line tells the code go back and do it *again* if the condition is met.

When you use Do...Loops, you'll need to keep an eye out for infinite loops. An infinite loop is a set of instructions that will repeat over and over again because the condition under which the loop ends never comes true. Often, a loop becomes infinite when the programmer forgets to write instructions that affect the condition. Do not try this one at home:

```
x = 1
Do While x < 2
   ' The Beep statement tells the computer to make a
   ' single beep sound.
   Beep
Loop
x = x + 1
```

If the x = x + 1 statement were before the Loop statement, the script would beep once, *x* would go from 1 to 2, and you'd be on your way. Here, however, there's nothing inside the loop to change the value of *x*. The loop will repeat over and over, beeping incessantly until you do violence to the computer.

Forall   Forall is a looping command that can be used with lists, arrays, and object collections. The Forall statement takes the name of a variable to stand for values and the name of a container (Forall *variablename* in *containername*) and ends with an End Forall statement. In the loop, the variable name stands for the value of the object in the collection. For example, this script sets all of the values in the array to 1:

```
Dim shortarray(1 to 5) As Integer
Forall x In shortarray
```

```
      x = 1
  End Forall
```

Forall is particularly useful when you want to perform an operation on every document in a collection.

LotusScript Notes Object Classes

This is where the experienced programmers should come back into the room. The techniques we've been discussing are fairly standard, but getting into Notes objects requires specific commands not found in other languages and BASIC dialects. It takes a little more code to deal with Notes objects than it does to deal with other variables, but with a few extra lines of code, you can manipulate entire Notes databases and their contents.

LotusScript and Object-Oriented Languages

Java and LotusScript are object-oriented languages. With the rise in popularity of Java and mass-market, application-conscious languages like LotusScript and VBA, *object-oriented* is one of buzzwords of the day. If you're new to the game, you may wonder just what it means. In addition to doing all of the other things you'd expect a programming language to do (count, do math, look for files, beep, throw messages on the screen…), an object-oriented language has *objects*, complex data constructs that have specific attributes and on which specific operations can be performed.

All explanations of object-oriented languages include an extended metaphor using a real-world object, so here is one. Consider, for example, a book. Every book has a number of characteristics that other objects (say, an ice cream cone) won't necessarily have: number of pages, binding (hardcover vs. paperback), Library of Congress number, and so on. Likewise, there are a number of operations you might perform on a book that you might not perform on other objects (if you do any of these to the ice cream cone, we don't want to know about it): take book off shelf, flip through pages, put in bookmark, smash annoying bug, put back on shelf. In an object-oriented language, the type of object is called a *class*. Bits of data contained by the object (number of pages) are called *properties*, and the things you can do to or with the object (flip through pages) are called *methods*.

Another powerful aspect of object-oriented languages is that many properties are actually objects themselves. To return to the metaphor, the pages of the book are themselves objects, with properties such as page number and the text each page contains. Likewise, a set of books may be contained by another object, such as a book bag or a bookshelf, and bookshelves might be contained by a library "object."

The way this plays out in Notes is that just about every object you're used to dealing with in a Notes database has a programming counterpart you can use in a script. For example, a Database object has (as properties) views and documents, and many common Notes actions (such as printing documents or changing ACL entries) can be performed by using methods with LotusScript and Java classes. You can count the number of items in a multi-item field, mail a document, or change the font in a rich text field with a single line of code. The capacity for using familiar Notes objects along with conventional programming techniques makes LotusScript and Java programming within a Notes database an extremely powerful tool, so mastery of the Notes object model is essential for the Notes developer.

Strictly speaking, an object-oriented language must also give you the ability to create new classes with their own properties and methods, and where necessary, new classes must be capable of inheriting properties and methods from existing classes. Java programmers create new classes left and right, and LotusScript programmers can create new classes as well, but they probably won't need to. Creating new classes with LotusScript is an advanced and special-purpose task that won't be discussed here.

Something you'll be seeing a lot in this section is references to objects and their methods and properties. Any property of any object can be referred to by using the name of the object, a period, and the name of the property. For example, every Notes database has a title, which means that a Notes database object has a Title property. If a script has a variable *db* representing a database, the expression that would return the database's title would be `db.Title`.

Object methods can be invoked in a similar way. Use the keyword SET or CALL, then the variable name, a period, and the method. CALL is used for methods that perform an action, and SET is used as part of an equation with methods that return another object. For example, a document represented by the variable *doc* could be sent as an e-mail message with the line `Call doc.Send`. Getting the first document in a view represented by the variable *vw* might be performed with the line `Set doc = vw.GetFirstDocument`. The big, complex classes like databases and documents have a lot of useful properties. It's well worth the time to look up the classes in the Designer Help files and read about the possibilities.

Fundamental Classes

LotusScript allows you to read and manipulate just about any Notes object or Notes-native property, from ACLs to time zones. However, most of your programming will be done with an eye toward dealing with documents and their contents. Therefore, we'll be concentrating most of our attention on the classes that you'll use to get to documents and fields.

You probably already think of Notes objects as existing in a hierarchy. For example, a database holds documents, documents hold fields, and fields may, in the case of multivalue fields, hold a set of values. Databases also contain views and folders, which in turn hold documents. LotusScript thinks the same way. You'll need to start at the top of the hierarchy to get to the specific parts, but depending on what you're trying to accomplish, you can use different hierarchies. If your script works on the currently open database or document, you'll be starting with the front-end classes, but scripts that deal with databases and documents that aren't open will work with back-end classes.

Things get a little weird here, so hang on. When you write code that acts on an open document or an open database, you're actually dealing with two different versions of it. First, there's what appears on your screen. That's what is called the *front end*. The Lotus-Script classes are called, not surprisingly, front-end classes. The front-end classes all have *ui*, short for *user interface*, at the beginning. The most important front-end classes are NotesUIWorkspace, which refers to the currently open Notes workspace window; Notes-UIDatabase, which refers to the currently open database; and NotesUIDocument, which refers to the currently open document. NotesUIWorkspace is the big container here. The NotesUIWorkspace contains all of the other ui classes, so you must address it first to get to the other front-end classes.

Back-end classes, on the other hand, refer to a copy of a database or document that is held in memory and not necessarily displayed on screen. NotesUIDatabase and Notes-UIDocument are directly related to two back-end classes, NotesDatabase and Notes-Document. NotesUIWorkspace doesn't have a direct correspondent among the back-end classes, but there's an equally important back-end class: NotesSession. Just as Notes-UIWorkspace contains all of the other front-end objects, a NotesSession contains all back-end objects.

Using Front-End Classes

Let's return to the short programming example we used at the beginning of the chapter. Remember this? Now we can explain how it works:

```
Dim ws As NotesUIWorkspace
Dim uidoc As NotesUIDocument
Set ws = new NotesUIWorkspace
Set uidoc = ws.CurrentDocument
Call uidoc.Print
```

First, we set up some variables. Objects are a little trickier than scalar variables. Although, unlike in earlier versions of LotusScript, it is no longer absolutely necessary to initialize an object variable with a Dim statement, you do have to *instantiate* some classes with the NEW keyword before you can use them. Instantiation is object-oriented language–speak for getting down to cases. The Dim statement just sets up a space in memory big enough to hold the object. However, objects have properties that need to be filled in (for example, creation date). That's what the Set statement is for. It takes the memory space you've set aside and tells Notes to fill in all of the properties neces-sary to make it an object of the desired type. Remember the book metaphor we used earlier to explain objects? Dim clears a space on the bookshelf; Set fills the space with a cover and some (possibly blank) pages.

We could save a line with the `NotesUIWorkspace` by declaring and instantiating it at the same time. `Dim ws as New NotesUIWorkspace` would do the same thing as the Dim and Set lines together, and for this script, it might be a good idea just for compactness. However, be aware that you can't use `Dim variablename as New type` in the (Declara-tions) routine. The `as New` makes the line an executed instruction, not just a Dim state-ment, and thereby a line you can't use in (Declarations).

The lines used to set up `uidoc` do something similar. A `NotesUIWorkspace` has a num-ber of properties (that is, objects and attributes associated with it), including the docu-ment that happens to be open at the moment. First, the Dim statement sets up a space for the `NotesUIDocument`, then the Set statement goes into the hierarchy of the `NotesUI-Workspace` to get the currently open document, a *property* of the `NotesUIWorkspace`. Finally, the Call line calls a *method* that can be performed on a `NotesUIDocument`, namely, telling it to print out on a printer. Essentially, what this script does is tell Notes, "Look at the copy of Notes I'm running, get the document that's open in front, and act like I selected File ➢ Print."

Code to Remember

Bookmark this page or type the code in somewhere to copy and paste. Almost every script you write that deals with front-end objects will use this code or something very much like it. These six lines give your script access to the workspace and the current document:

```
Dim ws As NotesUIWorkspace

Dim uidoc As NotesUIDocument

Dim doc As NotesDocument

Set ws = new NotesUIWorkspace

Set uidoc = ws.CurrentDocument

Set doc = uidoc.Document
```

What's the `NotesDocument` for? Read on....

Using Back-End Classes

If you're writing scripts for your own personal use, you may tend to think in terms of using the front-end classes. After all, you'll probably be working with the objects that happen to be open at the moment. However, sooner or later you'll need to go into the back-end classes. The front-end classes can't be used on databases, views, and documents that *aren't* currently open and at the front of the Notes Workspace. This means, among other things, that scheduled Agents and Agents that you want to run on a server can't use front-end classes. Although they may select and act on Notes objects, those objects aren't actually open. Also, there are some important properties in the back-end classes that the front-end classes don't have. It's much easier to retrieve and manipulate document data on the back end than with the front-end classes.

The first thing to create when you're using back-end classes is a new `NotesSession`. The `NotesSession` is the environment the script is running in, giving the script access to a broad range of data, including information about the current user, the version of Notes being used, and environment variables and access to address books. It's also the first step in getting to objects in the database running the script or even other databases on the same computer or on a connected Domino server.

There are two commonly used ways to get from the `NotesSession` to a database. First, there's the GetDatabase method. GetDatabase takes as parameters the name of the server the desired database is on and the path to it. For example, to get the database `mydb.nsf` on the server Sales, you might use the line `Set db = session.GetDatabase ("Sales", "mydb.nsf")`. More often, however, a script will want to address the database from which it's running. To get the database the script is in, use the `CurrentDatabase` property, which needs no parameters, thus: `Set db = session.CurrentDatabase`.

Getting from database to individual documents can be trickier. If you want to jump directly to documents, you can use the Search method on a database object to collect a batch of documents. The Search method takes three parameters: a formula, a date, and a maximum number of documents. The formula can be any valid formula that could be used to provide conditions for a view. The date, in a *NotesDateTime* variable, provides a creation date after which the document was created (if you want to search through all the documents in the database, provide a date before the database was created). The search will return no more than the maximum number you provide unless you use 0, which imposes no maximum number. Using the Search method creates a document collection object, so you'll need to declare a *DocumentCollection* variable and, to create the collection, use a line like this:

```
Set dc = db.Search("Duedate > @Now", SomeDateVariable, 0)
```

This line will populate a document collection named dc with all the documents where the value of the Duedate field is later than the current time and the document was created after the date provided in the variable *SomeDateVariable*.

However, you might find it easier to let existing database objects do some of the work for you. If you have an agent that you want to run on some or all documents in a view or folder that already exists, you can get the view to gain easy access to the documents. All you need to do to use the GetView method and the name of the view or folder. For example, to get the "To Process" view, you'll use a line like `Set vw = db .GetView("To Process")`.

Once you have the view or document collection, you can navigate through the documents. You can use the GetFirstDocument and GetLastDocument methods to get the first and last documents (particularly useful if you're dealing with the contents of a sorted view) and GetNextDocument and GetPrevDocument to move from one document to the next. For GetNextDocument and GetPrevDocument, you must refer to a Notes document you have set elsewhere. The following script gets the contents of a view, loops through its documents, and counts the number of documents that were created before January 1, 1999:

```
' Get the declarations out of the way

Dim s As NotesSession
Dim db As NotesDatabase
Dim vw As NotesView
Dim doc As NotesDocument
Dim CreateTime As Variant
Dim doccount As Integer

' Create a Notes session and drill down to the view MyView

Set s = New NotesSession
Set db = s.CurrentDatabase
Set vw = db.GetView("MyView")
' Get the first document in the view
Set doc = vw.GetFirstDocument

' Perform the loop until there are no documents left
' and get the creation date of each

Do Until doc Is Nothing
   CreateTime = doc.Created

' If the creation date is after 1/1/99, add one to
' the counter

   If (CreateTime > datenumber(1999,1,1)) Then
      doccount = doccount + 1
   End If

   ' Make the document that the variable doc refers to equal
   ' to the next document relative to the current one
```

```
    Set doc = vw.GetNextDocument(doc)
Loop

' Show us the count

Messagebox(Cstr(doccount) + " documents were created before 1/1/99.")
```

Now that you've gotten the Notes document, you can finally manipulate field values. Just as there are many ways to get Notes documents, there are several ways to get to field values. The easiest way to get to most values in a Notes document is by treating the field in question like an array. Consider the following code:

```
Dim s As NotesSesson
Dim db As NotesDatabase
Dim vw As NotesView
Dim doc As NotesDocument
Dim price As Double
Set s = new NotesSession
Set db = s.OpenDatabase("MyDB")
Set vw = db.OpenView("MyView")
Set doc = vw.GetFirstDocument
price = doc.Price(0)
```

This code goes to the database MyDB, opens the view MyView, takes the first document, and sets the value of the variable *Price* to the first item in the Price field. Fields are treated as properties of documents, so they can be referred to with the *object.property* notation, but if they're referred to that way, they are themselves arrays, so they need an index. Although most fields have single values, you can refer to the different values of multivalue fields by changing the index. If *Price* were a multivalue field, the second value (if any) would be `doc.Price(1)`, the third would be `doc.Price(2)`, and so on.

 TIP Remember that, if you use `Option Base 1`, the first value in a field is `document-.fieldname(1)`.

You can set values just as you would any other array value. To set the value of *Price*, you might use a line like this:

```
doc.Price(0) = 49.95
```

If you want to save a changed value, you must use the Save method on the document. Up to that point, changes are made on a copy of the document held in memory. Changes are only saved to disk if you actively save the document. For example, in the following script, Notes gets the first document in the MyView view, doubles the price, and saves the document:

```
Dim s As NotesSesson
Dim db As NotesDatabase
Dim vw As NotesView
Dim doc As NotesDocument
Dim price As Double
Set s = new NotesSession
Set db = s.OpenDatabase("MyDB")
Set vw = db.OpenView("MyView")
Set doc = vw.GetFirstDocument
price = doc.Price(0)
price = price * 2
doc.Price(0) = price
' Up to this point, everthing is happening in memory.
' If the script stopped at this point, the changes would
' not be saved.
Call doc.Save
' Now the changes are saved.
```

More Code to Remember

Just as most of your front-end scripts will start with the code given in the preceding sidebar (see "Code to Remember"), most of your back-end scripts will start out with a standard bit of code. Here's something to drop into any script that will use back-end objects:

```
Dim s As NotesSesson
Dim db As NotesDatabase
Dim dc As NotesDocumentCollection
Dim vw As NotesView
Dim doc As NotesDocument
Set s = New NotesSession
```

Colorless Green Ideas Sleep Furiously: Debugging

When you start writing scripts, rest assured that you *will* get things wrong. The Notes programming environment provides some help as you write your script. When you save a script, it gets compiled; that is, it gets translated from the more-or-less English language commands of LotusScript into fast-running machine code. If you type in a flatly impossible or nonexistent command (say, you try to declare a variable but type in *Din* instead of *Dim*, or you leave the second set of quotation marks off of a string), the compiler will catch the error. Notes will stop and flag the error in the Error bar at the bottom of the LotusScript programmer's pane. Notes won't be able to tell you exactly what you should have written. After all, it doesn't really know what you're trying to do. However, it can give you some idea of what's missing.

But more often, you'll make errors that are far more subtle. The instant error checking provided by the compiler only ensures that individual lines of code are legally structured. The most common cause of errors, however, is that you will write a script with instructions that are each perfectly legal individually but, once assembled and run, don't work. For example, a line like myarray(10) = 1 is fine by itself. It simply sets an element of an array to a particular value. The script editor won't flag it as an error, but when you actually run the script, you will get an error if you haven't defined the array myarray() as having enough elements or if you have defined it as a string rather than as a numeric value. There are many other ways for your script to go wrong. You may try to compare string variables with integers, call subroutines that don't exist, forget to increment counters, add instead of subtract, or make an expression true when you want it to be false. You won't know that you did anything wrong until you run a script that does nothing or does something but does it very, very wrong. Sometimes, the only way to tell why your script doesn't work is to follow it through every step of the way to see where it goes wrong. Fortunately, Notes lets you do just that.

If your scripts aren't working, you can turn on the debugger. The debugger will allow you to run through a script line by line or jump through or over chunks of functional code to get to problematic areas while monitoring the values of variables and the contents of Notes objects. If you write scripts, you'll be using it a lot, so it's a good idea to familiarize yourself with it early.

To turn on debugging, select File ➤ Tools ➤ Debug LotusScript. While that option is checked, the debugger will appear whenever a script runs. The upper pane of the debugging window displays the script being run. It starts with the first line in the first subroutine that contains instructions. For most scripts, it starts at the first line of the Initialize subroutine, although it will start with the appropriately named subroutine for the event-related scripts. Statements in the (Options) and (Declarations) subroutines will be executed, but the debugger will not put them on screen.

The debugging window appears in Figure 23.2. The buttons across the top of the upper pane allow you to move through the script, processing it in chunks, going through it one line at a time, or even skipping over parts of it. The buttons you'll probably be using most are Step Into and Continue. Step Into runs the program one line at a time. When you click it, Notes will execute the line of code and move on to the next, stopping there without executing it. Don't confuse the Step Into button with the Step Over button, which will execute the next line of code but not take you into any subroutines or functions called by that line.

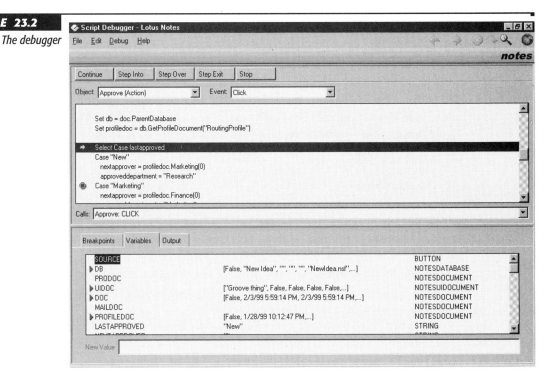

FIGURE 23.2

The debugger

The Continue button tells the script to continue running as it would normally unless it hits a breakpoint. A *breakpoint* is a line in the script at which the debugger will pause until told to continue. To set a breakpoint, simply double-click a line in the script. A red "stop sign" will appear next to the line, alerting you to the fact that there's a breakpoint there. Double-clicking again will put a yellow slash next to the breakpoint. The breakpoint is still marked for you, but it has been disabled; the debugger won't stop there, but it does show you where you set the breakpoint earlier. Double-clicking one more time will remove the breakpoint. You can set as many breakpoints in a script as you want.

The debugger will stop at each one before executing it, and you can use Continue, Step Into, or any of the other buttons.

The upper pane of the debugging window shows you the program, but it's the lower pane that will show you what you actually get out of it. There are three tabs on the lower pane: Breakpoints, Variables, and Output. All are useful, but you'll probably be spending most of your time looking at the Variables tab. This tab shows the values of all variables the script knows about in a three-column format: variable name, value, and type (string, variant, notesdocument, etc.). Complex data types, such as arrays and documents, don't have a single value. Instead, they are displayed with a twistie next to them. You can expand them to see what's in them. Figure 23.2 shows a Variables tab displaying the values of the array `Myarray`. The values in the Variables tab change as the variables themselves change during the execution of the script. When you step through a script with the Variables tab selected, you can see exactly what your script is up to.

Debugging, by the way, is one of the big, big advantages LotusScript has over formulas. If your script doesn't work, you can walk through it in the debugger and find out fairly quickly where it's going wrong. Formulas either execute or they don't. If they don't do exactly what you want them to, it's much harder to find out where they go wrong.

Doing Something with It All

So far, you've learned basic LotusScript programming techniques and some important object classes. The next step is to make them do something useful. This section will show you how some scripts can be used to perform some important tasks, integrate with other database elements, and fulfill a business purpose.

The scripts in this section are designed to work within a workflow database. A New Product Idea document is created by users in the research department, using the NewIdea form shown in Figure 23.3. The head of research approves the idea, which alerts the head of marketing (by sending him an e-mail message) that he needs to approve the idea. When marketing approves the idea, the head of finance is alerted to give final approval. Anybody can make a change in an idea at any time in the process. However, if any change is made, the idea goes back to the beginning so that every department head gets the chance to approve the altered idea.

To perform the necessary tasks, we'll need two scripts. One is a script in an Action button. When the button is clicked, the script will check to see who approved the document last and then change the document's status to move it on to the next person. There will also be a button to reject the idea and send it back to the original department. Both actions will put a date stamp on the document so users can tell how long it has been since action was last taken on it. The second script is for the form's QuerySave event.

FIGURE 23.3

The NewIdea form

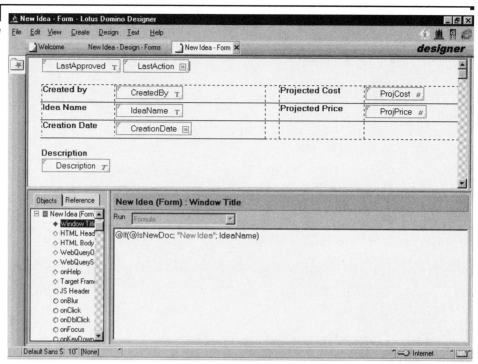

The Approve Button

This script lurks behind the Approve Action. It marks the document with the stage and time of approval and sends a mail message to the next person who needs to look at it. As the value of the LastApproved field changes, the document will appear in different views:

```
Sub Click(Source As Button)

    ' This script marks the document as being approved by the appropriate
    ' person and informs the next approver of the approval.

    ' First, declare the variables.

    Dim db As notesdatabase
    Dim prodoc As notesdocument
    Dim uidoc As notesuidocument
    Dim doc As notesdocument
    Dim maildoc As notesdocument
    Dim profiledoc As notesdocument
    Dim lastapproved As String
    Dim nextapprover As String
```

```
Dim bodytext As String
Dim approveddepartment As String

' Next, drill down from the workspace to the
' back-end document

Dim w As New notesuiworkspace
Set uidoc = w.currentdocument
Set doc = uidoc.document

' Get the last approver and figure out from that
' who the next approver should be. This operation
' refers to a profile document.  To get that, the
' script has to go through the database object;
' profile documents are properties of databases,
' and can be obtained with the GetProfileDocument
' method.

lastapproved = doc.LastApproved(0)

Set db = doc.ParentDatabase
Set profiledoc = db.GetProfileDocument("RoutingProfile")

Select Case lastapproved
Case "New"
     nextapprover = profiledoc.Marketing(0)
     approveddepartment = "Research"
Case "Marketing"
     nextapprover = profiledoc.Finance(0)
     approveddepartment = "Marketing"
Case "Finance"
     nextapprover = "Complete"
     approveddepartment = "Approved"
End Select

' Mark the document status and the time it
' was approved.

doc.LastApproved(0) = approveddepartment
doc.LastAction(0) = Now

' Create a document in memory, assign it a
' mail-to address, a subject, and a body field.
' Then use the Send method to mail it to the
' next person who needs to see it, but only if it
' isn't Finance's final approval.
```

```
        If Not(nextapprover = "Complete") Then
            Set maildoc = New notesdocument(db)
            maildoc.SendTo = nextapprover
            maildoc.Subject = "New Idea: " + doc.IdeaName(0)
            bodytext = approveddepartment + " has just approved "
            bodytext = bodytext + "a new product idea. Please consult "
            bodytext = bodytext + "the appropriate view."
            Call maildoc.send
        End If

        Call doc.save(False,False)
        Call uidoc.close
    End Sub
```

This script depends on a profile document to get mail sent to the right people. The RoutingProfile form is shown in Figure 23.4. It would be less work in the short term to write the names into the code itself, but in the long run, it's better to put them into an easily maintained profile document. That way, when an old department head leaves the company and a new one takes the position, an administrator with a regular Notes client can make the change, not a programmer with a Designer client.

FIGURE 23.4

The RoutingProfile form

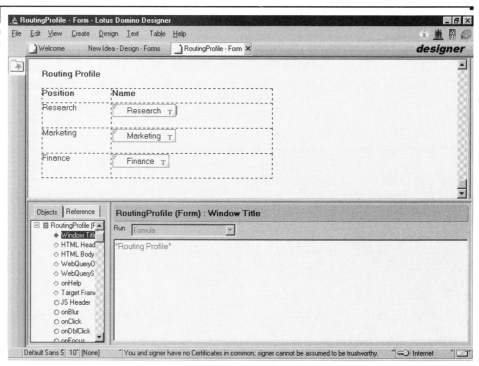

The Deny Button

This is code behind the Deny button:

```
@Command([FileSave]);
@Command([FileCloseWindow])
```

Yes, that's right. It's not a script. This is a case where it's just as easy to use formulas. You'll also notice that the Deny button doesn't appear to have anything to alter the status of the document. Saving the document actually does alter its status, but in a hidden way. Unlike the Approve script, which uses LotusScript, the use of @Command([File-Save]) triggers the QuerySave event. That event runs the script in the following section, and it does change the document's status.

The QuerySave Event Script

This is a script that runs when the user saves the document by using any method other than the Approve button:

```
Sub Querysave(Source As Notesuidocument, Continue As Variant)

    ' This script runs if changes to the document are
    ' save by any method other than pressing the
    ' approve button.  It removes prior approvals and
    ' moves the document back to the New view.

    ' First, declare the variables.

    Dim db As notesdatabase
    Dim prodoc As notesdocument
    Dim uidoc As notesuidocument
    Dim doc As notesdocument
    Dim maildoc As notesdocument
    Dim profiledoc As notesdocument
    Dim lastapproved As String
    Dim nextapprover As String
    Dim bodytext As String
    Dim approveddepartment As String

    ' Next, drill down from the workspace to the
    ' back-end document

    Dim w As New notesuiworkspace
    Set uidoc = w.currentdocument
    Set doc = uidoc.document
```

```
' Get the last approver and figure out from that
' who the next approver should be. This operation
' refers to a profile document.  To get that, the
' script has to go through the database object;
' profile documents are properties of databases,
' and can be obtained with the GetProfileDocument
' method.

doc.lastapproved = "New"
Call doc.Save(False,False)

End Sub
```

Where to Go from Here

The preceding scripts illustrate a flexible but bare-bones workflow setup. Here are some things you might consider developing if you use the scripts as the basis for a more complex database:

- Use authors and readers fields instead of just text fields to give the document some security.

- Take advantage of multivalue fields to keep track of the entire history of approval, not just the most recent approval.

- Use the AppendDocLink method to give the informative e-mail an immediate link to the idea document.

- Use Agents to remind approvers if there are documents that have been awaiting their approval for more than a few days.

JavaScript and Java

In addition to LotusScript and the @formula language, Notes allows you to use two languages that are used widely outside of Notes: JavaScript and Java. Experienced programmers can use those languages in limited ways in their Notes applications.

JavaScript

In earlier versions of Notes, programmers could use JavaScript in a very limited fashion, putting JavaScript routines in the $$HTMLHead field and adding a few small instructions to field or button HTML attributes. Use of JavaScript was limited to Web applications. Notes 5 expands the use of JavaScript considerably. JavaScript programs can be built directly into button and field events.

More important, you can now use JavaScript in Notes as well as on the Web. Still, JavaScript within Notes faces several restrictions:

- JavaScript can only be used with some objects (form fields, Actions, and buttons). It cannot be used in form and view events or in Agents.
- For JavaScript to run on a Notes client, the user must first enable JavaScript in the User Preferences (under Advanced Preferences). If JavaScript is not enabled on the client, objects that run JavaScript will simply do nothing.
- JavaScript on a Notes client runs a limited set of commands. You can, for example, use the form object hierarchy to retrieve and set the values of fields, but you can't use the form Submit method to save a Notes document. You may need to create duplicate buttons for some operations (for example, save and submit buttons), using JavaScript for one and hiding it from Notes clients and using formulas or LotusScript for the other and hiding it from Web browsers.

With those limitations in mind, you can use JavaScript to write some very portable commands into buttons and Actions. For example, the following code takes the values of the fields First and Second, adds them together, puts up an alert box informing you of the new value, and sets the field Third to that value. This code will work equally well on the Web and in a Notes client:

```
var firstvar = this.form.First.value
var secondvar = this.form.Second.value
var thirdvar = firstvar + secondvar

alert ("The field will be set to " & thirdvar)
this.form.Third.value = thirdvar
history.go(0)
```

Java

Whereas JavaScript works best on the front end, Java works on the back end. Java has an even more restricted range than JavaScript. It can only be used in Agents and applets.

To use Notes classes in a Java program, the Agent or applet must import the lotus-.domino package (`import lotus.domino.*;`). Notes objects in Java look a lot like the objects in LotusScript, although an intermediate object, a property of the Session object, has to be retrieved in order to get to databases and other objects. From the Session, you'll need to use an AppletContext or AgentContext object. From there, things will start to look familiar.

One of the nice things about the Java programmer's pane is that Notes creates some obligatory pieces of code for you. In the following example, all of the code for this Agent up through "Your code goes here" and everything after the `doc.save();` line was automatically generated.

The following example shows how some of the basic Notes object classes are used in Java. The Agent script gets a view in the database MyDB, finds the number of documents (that is, the number of rows in the view), and saves that number in a new document:

```
import lotus.domino.*;

public class JavaAgent extends AgentBase {

  public void NotesMain() {

        try {
                Session session = getSession();
                AgentContext agentContext = session.getAgentContext();

                // (Your code goes here)
      Database db = session.getDatabase ("", "MyDB");
      View view = db.getView("All Documents");
      int vwcount =  view.getRowLines();
       Document doc = db.createDocument();
      doc.replaceItemValue("Form", "Doc Counter");
      doc.replaceItemValue("DocCount", vwcount  + " documents");
      doc.save();

        } catch(Exception e) {
                e.printStackTrace();
        }
    }
}
```

Summary

This chapter dealt with the basic elements of LotusScript and included brief examples of other languages you can use with Notes. LotusScript programs consist of a series of subroutines containing instructions. You can use looping and branching techniques to repeat a block of instructions or have your program choose between different options. With the LotusScript object classes, you can manipulate familiar Notes objects with your code. You can also use JavaScript and Java with your Notes databases. JavaScript can be used with buttons and Actions both on the Web and in Notes clients. Java can be used in Agents and applets. Java also has a set of Notes object classes, which are almost identical to LotusScript object classes.

PART **VI**

Developing Databases

CHAPTER 24

Developing Applications

The previous chapters of this book have outlined the basic use and architecture of Notes: the core databases, the anatomy of databases and database objects, and the rudiments of Notes's various languages. The following chapters are about what to do with all of that; in short, on how to build applications with Domino Designer for use with the Notes client and other applications, and even with other hardware platforms.

This chapter is less about the actual code and database element design (although there is a certain amount of that, as well) and more about the "best practices" to use when designing applications in Notes, as well as the range of approaches available to plan and design applications. Among the issues dealt with in this chapter are

- Appropriate applications for Notes and Domino

- Procedures and conventions to use while building databases

- Different environments in which you might deploy the applications you build with Domino Designer

- Making your application secure and easy to maintain

- Building resilient and easy-to-use applications, including user help and code that can recover from errors

This chapter also discusses certain aspects of system administration. Although the skills of a Notes developer and a Domino administrator are largely separate, a developer does need to have some knowledge of how Domino systems work and what they are capable of.

 NOTE The terms *application* and *database* are used more or less interchangably in this and the following chapters. Usually, there isn't a difference. Each Notes database will be self-contained, performing all the functions of a specific business task. However, an application may sometimes overflow the bounds of a single database. Your application may integrate two or more Notes databases (the example application in Chapter 28 does this) or may integrate Notes databases with other databases and external files.

Why *Not* to Use Notes

You might be surprised to see a book about Notes questioning the use of Notes, but this is worth thinking hard about. You may like Notes. You may even *love* Notes. After all, Notes is a powerful, versatile tool, and Notes databases can do a great deal. Nevertheless, it's still a good idea to think about all the tools that might be available to you.

Don't forget the old adage: "If all you have is a hammer, everything starts to look like a nail." Notes does a lot of things well and a lot more things adequately; it even does some things that other programs don't do at all. But it doesn't do everything perfectly. The first few pages of Chapter 3 briefly discussed some of the things that Notes does and does not do well, but we'll go into a little more detail here. Notes is an excellent choice if your application involves one of these:

Process tracking   Notes can track workflow, serial approval, and other processes where a set of information moves from one person or one stage to another. Even left to its own devices, Notes keeps track of who has edited a document and when. It's also easy to build Notes applications that route data and keep track of a document's history in more detail. This capability is excellent for approving expense reports, time cards, and drafts of documents.

Content searching   Notes has an extremely powerful search engine that allows you to search a large body of distinct documents quickly and find very specific results. This makes Notes a great platform for product catalogs, FAQ databases, policy and instruction manuals, dictionaries, encyclopedias, and other reference works. With R5's new Domain Search feature, you can even use Notes to search non-Notes data on the server, such as static HTML pages and text documents.

Personalizing data   Notes provides you with quick and easy tools to show and display data and set a broad range of permissions on editing data for individuals and groups. You can also use profile documents and environment variables to set default values for applications. For example, you can create buttons that create documents based on different forms depending on who presses the button.

Partially distributing data   Suppose that you've got an enormous database, but not everybody needs all of the data. Perhaps you have a central office that needs to see all potential data, but other users who only need to see the data relating to their own geographical region, their department, or only recent data. Between its personalizing features and controls on replication, Notes can quickly and easily separate out data relevant to specific sites and users, making potentially large applications compact and portable. For example, an organization might use separate replicas of a Help Desk application. It could be set up so that the East Coast office will see only documents for the East Coast, the West Coast office will see only West Coast documents, and the home office will see *all* the documents.

Filling in forms   Notes is well suited to applications that require a user to fill in a form: registration, applications, polls and surveys, proposals, and the

PART

VI

Developing Databases

like. Notes forms are an excellent means of presenting users with something that tells them "This is the information I need."

Cross-platform distribution   Multiple versions of Notes clients will allow you to deploy applications to users who run the Mac OS, various flavors of Unix, OS/2 (for Domino servers), and 32-bit varieties of Windows (that is, Windows 95, 98, and NT). Domino also allows you to take your applications directly to the Web, sometimes with little or no extra effort on the developer's part. Notes is already capable of communicating with the popular PalmPilot PDA and synchronizing address books, appointments, and so on. With a bit of work, it's also quite possible to design Notes applications that can interact with Pilots.

Scheduled tasks   With scheduled Agents, it's very easy to get a Notes application to perform tasks on a predictable, regular basis. For example, you may need to send out periodic notifications or import regularly generated new data from an external source into a more widely distributed form.

Secure communications   Notes provides you with a number of powerful security options. For communication over the Internet, Notes supports both S/MIME (for encrypted e-mail) and SSL (for secure Web traffic and other communications). Internally, it supports its own powerful 128-bit encryption. Between encryption and Notes's own security schemes, it's easy not only to show users what they need to see, but also to hide what you don't want them to see. The CIA and NSA have both deployed large Notes installations. Need we say more?

 NOTE   Notes on a PalmPilot? There's no Notes client as such for the Pilot. But, straight out of the box, the Notes mailbox and Personal Address Book can synchronize messages, appointments, and contact information with the Pilot's built-in similar features. We'll be showing you an example of how to share even more information between Notes and PDAs in Chapter 29.

Those are things that Notes does well. This list contains things that Notes isn't so well suited for:

Concurrency   Notes isn't so good at managing concurrent changes to data by multiple users or at making changes happen instantly. Remote replicas of databases are only updated as often as the user or server responsible for them initiates replication, not as soon as changes are made in any one database or document. (Although clustered servers make replication so fast as to be nearly instant.) The Administrative Process doesn't make immediate changes, nor do many Agents. There can also be problems if more than one user tries to update a document at the same time. If you have an absolute need for concurrent and immediate access to data throughout your organization, you might consider using a different platform for your application. This is the sort of task that large relational databases are better at, although they don't provide many of Notes's more esoteric functions. Also, providing concurrency between different sites requires more than just the right application platform; it also requires a heavy-duty network to push large quantities of data at high speeds.

Large masses of very structured data   While it's possible to build views and folders that will present tabular data (that is, data appearing in rows and columns), treating data in such a structure isn't what Notes does best. For those of you familiar with relational databases, Notes also doesn't do unique key values or table joins particularly well. It can produce unique values with the @Unique function, but you can't designate your own values as unique keys. For example, if you want to build an application where people are listed by their Social Security Number, you can't be sure that there will be one and only one document containing a given Social Security Number. If your application is just rows and columns of simple data rather than complex data types (like lists and rich text) and semi-structured documents, you might consider a relational database or even a spreadsheet instead of Notes.

Precise text formatting and automation of text formatting   R5's Print Preview feature and improved LotusScript classes for handling rich text make this version of Notes a better platform for fancy text applications and printed documents than earlier versions. However, Notes is not a word processor or a page layout program. If you need to automate the way your application deals with text (such as automatically imposing standardized spellings, search-and-replace across documents, expanding acronyms, or intelligently applying style conventions or user-configurable defaults) or precisely lays out pages, you may want to look at another program. Depending on your needs, you may want a dedicated desktop publishing program (say, Quark or Framemaker) or, quite possibly, a recent-model word processor.

Extremely simple applications   Notes can certainly perform tasks that require little or no automation or structure, but it may not be worth the effort it takes to get them running as Notes applications. For example, if you're compiling a list of addresses to send form letters to and never, ever intend to use those addresses for any other purpose, you could use a Notes address book, perhaps even customizing it a bit. Nevertheless, it might be quicker and easier

PART

VI

Developing
Databases

to perform the task as a mail merge in a word processor. Likewise, you could set up a Web site consisting of nothing but a few static pages on a Domino server. But if you don't already have Domino up and running as a Web server with all of the specialized security concerns that entails, and you have no plans to do anything more elaborate, you might look into cheaper solutions. (For example, if you've got moderately skilled personnel, getting an Apache Web server running under Linux can literally cost you nothing.) If you're not going to take advantage of Notes's unique capabilities, perhaps you shouldn't be using it.

Do note that none of these tasks are things that Notes *can't* do. You can, for example, mock up some very elaborate printed pages with careful use of forms and hand-tooled rich text and use multiple forms to subtly reformat documents for printing. Large masses of JavaScript, @formulas, or LotusScript could be used to turn a form full of editable fields into a small spreadsheet. If you really need the functionality, you can even embed a spreadsheet in a document. It's possible to build views whose rows and columns mimic relational database tables in order to provide data sources for @DBLookup commands and drop-down lists. Indeed, some of the topics in later chapters will recommend building these views. However, these are things that other programs may be able to do better. If your application will involve one or more items on the second list and none on the first, Notes probably isn't the way to go.

There are, of course, large gray areas. Consider a purchase order system. Picking a vendor, an item, and item options off of successive pull-down lists is a task that a relational database would do handsomely. On the other hand, once the purchase order is filled out, sending it around the organization for approval is exactly the kind of task Notes was built for. The platform you ultimately choose will depend on the specifics of the task you're building your application for and the kind of expertise you can draw on, both during the development process and after deployment, to keep the system running smoothly.

The Development Environment

When you set out to develop an application, you'll need a lot of tools to build it. Of course, you'll need the Domino Designer client, but you'll want more than that if you can get it: Notes clients, Web browsers, and even your own Domino servers. You may also want to follow a set of regular practices to make it easier for you and others to find your way around the application later and to upgrade and distribute it.

Many organizations and instructors recommend sets of *best practices*, which are conventions for design and programming that are aimed at making applications consistent, easy to use, and easy to maintain. If you always structure your programs and scripts in the same way, apply the same testing standards to each application you develop, use the same principles to design your user interface, and otherwise follow a consistent set of procedures when building your application, your applications will be easier for you and others to maintain and extend, and easier for your users to learn about and use. It is often more work to follow these practices, sometimes a lot more work, but it's a very, very good idea to do so. The easier it is to figure out your database, the easier it'll be to fix things when they go wrong. Also, the more closely you adhere to a specific set of standards, no matter what those standards are, the easier it is to figure out your applications.

The term *best practices* is one we're not going to use much here, since we're not trying to convince you that what is being presented here is the absolute and definitive best methods to use. Rather, this section presents a framework for developing your own best practices. Many experienced developers and large organizations already have well-established guidelines for application development. The suggestions here can be used to help integrate those practices with Notes techniques. They can also be used as a core for less experienced developers to develop their own best practices by trial and error and by discussion with other Notes professionals. At the moment, there aren't any industry-wide best practices, but as Notes continues to mature, they may develop.

Configuring the Development Environment

While it's certainly possible to develop applications on a client machine with only Domino Designer, it's very inefficient. Indeed, it's next to impossible to develop an application well without having Domino servers to work on. You may also need a wide battery of other programs to test your application. Setting up a development environment requires some knowledge of Domino administration. The specifics of setting up a server are beyond the scope of this book, but the Administration Help (one of three Help files that is installed with Notes) is good. Also, don't overlook the many fine online resources for Notes and Domino, such as Lotus's own support Web site at support.lotus.com.

If at all possible, you should work in three different environments:

- Development
- Testing
- Production

The *development* environment is where you do all of your design and construction work. This is where you build databases, write scripts, and try new Agents. This is also the first place to try out upgrades, install new software, and try new methods of dealing with external files. Only developers need access to your development servers.

The *testing* environment is somewhat more pristine. This is where you perform full-blown operational tests on your databases and where you first show your databases to the users. In order to provide the best results during testing, this environment should be a scaled-down model of your production environment: similar servers, similar clients, similar network topologies, and similar patterns of use. As a result of that last item, at least a few regular users will need access to your testing environment.

Finally, there's the *production* environment. This is the environment where users actually do work. Ideally, all the developer will do to the production environment is look at it. By the time an application gets to the development server (or, for a distributed application, servers), all design work should be complete, except for, perhaps, the final steps that will be performed by system administrators. All the work that should remain is to set database permissions and distribute database links or replicas to the users.

You probably have limited control over your organization's computing environments. In a small organization, you may be lucky to have so much as a single workstation devoted to application development. However, if at all possible, you should try to separate the three environments as much as possible. In the best of all possible worlds, each environment should have at least its own server. How you arrange those servers may depend on your own hardware resources. However, even if you can't set up different physical servers (that is, servers on different computers), Domino allows you to set up *partitioned servers*, multiple servers on the same physical machine. Having multiple servers on the same machine can be a strain on the hardware, but it makes simulating a network or even building a network in parallel to the production servers very easy. It also makes moving files around a near-trivial task. You may also have different client machines for each environment and server, or at least configure the machines differently depending on how you want to test each environment.

Whether you put your different servers on the same or different client machines, it's a good idea to make your servers members of different domains. Each Domino domain has a different certifier ID to identify users and ID files belonging to that domain. More importantly, each Domino domain has its own main address book. The nature of groupware and the kinds of applications you are likely to develop with Notes means that you must have considerable control over the server environment during the development process, including the full range of security features. You may also need to do a great deal of work in the server address book. You'll also send out a lot of what amounts to junk e-mail during the development and testing process.

If you use separate domains in your development, testing, and production environments, you can send all the mail you need to and experiment with security to your heart's content in one environment without hurting anything in the others. You also will not worry network administrators by having access to sensitive data. In a less resource-rich organization, you might also look into building a special Notes Domain for development. See the Administration Help for more on hierarchies and hierarchical IDs.

As with any other computer task, backing up your work is important and can be a particular concern in the development environment. You may want to invest in automatic backup software for both servers and development clients. If your servers run constantly, you'll need software capable of backing up open files. (The server address book, `names.nsf`, and several other less obvious files including the server log and the free-time schedule are essentially always open.) If something goes very wrong, there are also products like PartitionMagic and ImageCast that will allow you to take "snapshots" of your computer so that you can quickly and easily replace the entire contents of your hard drives, down to the operating system and partitions. Such software may not be appropriate for regular backups, but it's good for recording important stages of development.

You should configure your environments based on your production environment. For example, if the users' client machines all have Lotus 1-2-3, Microsoft Word, and Adobe Photoshop, so should the clients you test on. If your network's servers have Domino on both Solaris and NT, so should your development servers. You'll also need to make sure that all of the same services are running: HTTP, IMAP, automatic cataloging, and so on. Of course, you should also be using the same versions of Domino servers and Notes clients as in the production environment. Designing with the R5 Designer client for a 4.*x* environment won't make anybody happy.

Configuring your environment for the Web is more difficult. If you're working with a company intranet, you may only have to work with one or two approved browsers and not have to worry about others. However, if you're building a publicly available Web site, you may want to test things with a broader range of browsers. At the very least, you should use Netscape Navigator 4, Navigator 4.51, and Microsoft Internet Explorer versions 4 and 5. (Navigator 4.6, the latest version as of this writing, apparently has some issues with Domino applets and JavaScript. You might check to see if there are known problems when you start developing.) To ensure maximum coverage, you may also want to test your Web applications with Navigator and Explorer 3, and perhaps minority browsers like Opera and Lynx. Many minority and no-longer-current versions of more popular Web browsers are available from `www.download.com`.

PART

VI

Developing
Databases

One Computer, Many Environments

Just because you use different servers doesn't mean that you have to use different Notes clients. You can use a single Notes client to talk to all the different Domino servers your computer is capable of communicating with. All you have to do is create different Connection documents and perhaps different Location documents for each server in your Personal Address Book. The Connection documents will determine how you connect to your servers, while the Location documents can be used to help you act like different users even though you're using a single machine. Be sure to have all the relevant ID files as well. You'll also probably need to add a number of mail databases to your bookmarks.

Using Templates to Control and Distribute Versions

As an application goes through its life cycle, it will inevitably need alterations. It may be a small fix, such as repairs to an Action button that doesn't quite do what it's supposed to. Or, it may be a major revision, such as adding a set of new views and actions to give the application a whole new function. When those changes need to be made, you'll have to decide exactly when to implement your changes and how to make sure that those changes get to all of your users in a timely fashion.

It is certainly possible to make changes directly to an application in the production environment. If it's a quick fix that absolutely must be made right now (say, removing a single line of code from an Agent or adding a Close button to a form where you forgot to place one), you may be tempted to go into the .nsf file and hack away. If you work at the same site where the application is used, there's only a single copy of it in use and nobody else is doing anything with it. In this case, it's probably even safe to make your change in the production environment.

Nevertheless, it's not a habit you should get into. Making changes to an application in active use is a little like trying to make repairs on a car with the engine running: unwise at best, and usually foolhardy. If you inadvertently change something you didn't intend to, users will start using the altered version immediately. If that happens, once you realize your mistake, you'll have to go back and repair your repairs and perhaps put data, as well as design elements, back in order. It is an even bigger mistake to make more extensive changes directly to a production database. Users would see incomplete stages of changes as you work and, not knowing any better, might try to use incomplete new features, with all the confusion and potential damage that that implies.

It would be far better if you could make your changes in one place, test them, and then make those changes happen all at once in the production environment. Fortunately (you saw this coming, didn't you?), Notes provides you with facilities for doing exactly that.

While Notes R5 does not have widely used tools for formal version control in the way that some other development tools do, there are features of Domino design that allow you to control deployed versions of your databases very nicely on your own. The main tool you'll use to control application designs is the database template. When you're ready to deploy your application in the production environment, you should make sure that the file that you've developed is a template. (See Chapter 16 for how to make templates.) As you may recall, you can use templates to store a database design and transmit changes to that design to databases in use. When you've created a template, you should use it to create a new database for actual use as the application. When the time comes to make changes to the application, you can make a copy of the template (keeping the same template name), make changes to the copy, and test them on a new database made from the revised template. Better still, you might get a copy of the production database moved to your testing environment and update the design of the production database copy with your revised template so that you can run your test using real data. That way, you can test your changes before committing yourself in the production environment. Once you're ready, you can move your revised template to the production environment to update the production database's design.

In addition to not disturbing the production environment with alterations of dubious reliability, using templates for design control gives you a number of other advantages:

> **Ease and rapid deployment of changes**   When you use a template, Notes's own automatic processes handle the work of doing the updates for you. Any design changes you make, no matter how obscure or complex, will be made automatically and instantly (at least, as close to instantly as Notes can manage) across all servers where you can deploy a copy of your revised template.

> **Rollback**   Sooner or later, it will be decided that a recent round of changes in an application was a bad idea, and that all the changes that were made should be undone. If you work with successive copies of templates rather than making changes in a single template, you can keep a library of designs for your applications. If you need to turn back the clock to the previous version or, indeed, any version, all you need to do is deploy the appropriate template, and the application's design will change back to an earlier version just as easily as it was upgraded.

PART

VI

Developing
Databases

Self-repair Inheriting a design from a template keeps you and others from making permanent, arbitrary changes to an application's design. For a critical application, that's exactly what you want. Any changes anyone makes directly to an application based on a template, rather than to the template itself, will be wiped out overnight (or on whatever schedule your servers use to refresh designs). In this way, any damage sustained by somebody making ill-advised changes in an application can be minimized. If somebody manages to damage the template, you can replace it with a backup copy, returning the database's design to its undamaged state.

For ease of identification, you should use regular numbering or naming schemes to indicate which version of an application a given template is. You may decide to use a date (for example, MyApp110499 for a version deployed on November 11, 1999), a version number (MyApp 2.0 for the second release, MyApp 2.1 for the first significant modification to the second release), or both. Version numbers work well in filenames, but you should certainly also record a version number and a date in the design's About document. That way, if there's a problem, users can check the About documentation and immediately identify the version of the application they're having a problem with.

 NOTE While Lotus doesn't provide formal versioning tools, there are third-party tools that can help. Ives Development produces products for versioning that you may want to investigate.

The User Environment

In their recent evolution, Notes and Domino have become more and more devoted to serving a broader variety of platforms. That means that you, as a Notes and Domino developer, need to be familiar with those platforms so that you can take full advantage of Notes's capabilities. There are a number of factors that you'll have to take into account when building an application relating to where the application runs: the number of users, the operating system, the type of client, and whether it's a client-based or server-based operation.

The Operating System

Notes R5 clients are, as of this writing, only available for Windows systems (95, 98, and NT) and the Mac OS. Domino R5 servers are available for Windows NT (Intel and

Alpha), Solaris (Sparc and Intel), IBM AIX, IBM AS/400, and IBM OS/390, and Linux. Most Notes features operate perfectly well across all platforms, but there are a few subtle cross-platform differences that you'll need to be aware of, primarily as they apply to scripts.

Of course, to take advantage of platform differences, you will often have to determine what platform you're dealing with when using Notes's programming languages, such as LotusScript or @formulas. In LotusScript, the Platform property of the Notes-Session will tell you the platform that a script is running on. You'll want to use two different bits of syntax depending on what language you're using: one for @formulas and one for LotusScript. The Domino Designer Help spells out most of the differences in detail (search for "Platform Differences"), but there are further implications you should think about.

The Directory Structure

Unix systems use a / to separate directory names (for example, /bin/lotus/domino/data/names.nsf), while Windows systems use a \ (C:\lotus\domino\data\names .nsf), and the Mac OS uses a colon (as in Hard Drive:Lotus:Notes:Names.nsf). An implication that you should be aware of is that the Mac directory structure makes it much harder to write scripts that look for external files. For example, while you can fairly reliably find Windows 95 and 98 system files in C:\Windows, you can't reliably find system files on a Mac. System files will be in the System Folder. But the current startup device, the Mac equivalent of the root C:\ directory, can be (and often is) renamed by the user. Scripts dealing with external files on Macs may need to warn the user that they want a specific name on the hard drive.

Unix file and directory names are case sensitive. For example, */usr/bin* is not the same as */Usr/Bin*. If you're working with Linux or any other Unix-flavored system, be sure you've got upper and lowercase names in order.

A number of file system commands are written specifically to deal with versions of Windows. They work differently or not at all on other systems, so it's particularly important that you research Notes's directory-related commands before you attempt to use them on other operating systems.

Line Breaks

Different operating systems end paragraphs in different ways. The @Newline @function will insert appropriate characters for the operating system it operates under. To insert appropriate characters to produce a new paragraph with LotusScript, you need to name specific ASCII characters using the Chr$() function, as detailed in Table 24.1.

PART

VI

Developing
Databases

TABLE 24.1: RETURN CHARACTERS

Operating System	LotusScript Expression
Unix systems	Chr$(10)
Mac OS	Chr$(13)
Windows	Chr$(10) + Chr$(13)

Other Differences

There are technologies available to, or used by, some platforms but not others. For example, OLE automation is available only on Windows platforms, while Mac OS implementations of Notes can't use Environment variables.

Another initially confusing difference between the Mac OS platform and other platforms is the more complex Mac file structure. If a file is attached to a mail message on a Mac and you attempt to open it on another operating system, Notes may ask you if you want to detach the data fork or the resource fork. A resource fork is one part of the Mac file structure, containing certain kinds of identifying information, such as the file's icon and various other bits of information. However, the actual data in the file is in the data fork, which is what you should detach.

Earlier Versions of Notes

While you may have the full range of Domino R5 design tools, the organization you build applications for may not be up to the current version of Notes. Most likely, they have not yet had the available manpower to undertake the process of upgrading users from 4.x clients to R5. This isn't an insurmountable problem. You can still build applications with the R5 Domino Designer that can be used by earlier clients, and an R5 Domino server can serve out databases from earlier clients, as well. However, you'll have to be careful in designing databases that may be used with pre-R5 clients. Version 4.x clients cannot use the following design elements:

- Outlines
- Framesets
- Pages
- Image Resources
- Shared Actions
- Applets

If you use any of these features in an application that you will run with pre-R5 clients, they will, at best, fail to appear. For example, consider the illustration in Figure 24.1, which is an R5 mailbox opened in Notes 4.6. Compare it with the mailbox you'd expect to see, as shown in Figure 4.4. You'll see that the Outline listing the default set of views and folders; the Navigator letting you switch between mail, calendar, and to-do functions; and the Frameset holding them don't appear. They may also cause errors that will keep users out of your application. The same is true when any of those objects are embedded in forms.

FIGURE 24.1

This is an R5 mailbox opened in a Notes 4.6 client, after eight error messages were cleared out. The same errors and more occur every time a button is pressed. Don't do this at home, kids.

A number of @functions, LotusScript commands, and constants can't be used with earlier versions of Notes. (For a fairly comprehensive list, search the Designer Help for the words new with Release 5.) If you build a cross-version application, it is a good idea to build separate forms or, perhaps, subforms that collect all of the R5-specific features in one place so that you can leave them out if the document is opened on a lower-version client. You can use the @Version formula to determine which version of Notes the client is using. Also, a number of objects have a "Hide from version 4.6 or later" box in their hiding conditions.

PART

VI

Developing
Databases

The Web

One of Domino's big claims to fame is the ability to translate Notes documents into HTML on the fly. This allows you to put your databases onto the Web with a minimum of effort. That's only approximately true. Domino's document-centric approach is well suited to the Web's page-centric orientation. Domino does a good job of rendering document content, views, and most other design elements into HTML equivalents. But, to make a complex application work, you'll probably need to do some careful work with Agents for processing submitted documents, with JavaScript to perform tasks on the page itself in order to take some of the load off the server, and perhaps some hand-tooled HTML on the documents themselves. There are enough differences between basic Domino design and additional modifications for the Web that the subject is discussed separately in Chapter 26. What you need to be aware of here is that on the Web, you're dealing with a broad variety of clients: a range of different versions of Netscape Navigator, Microsoft's IE, and even minority browsers such as Opera and Lynx. Before you add Java applets and JavaScript functions, you should consider how these functions will impact and limit your audience.

Server-Based vs. Client-Based Applications

Something that Notes allows you to do fairly easily is to create applications that can be run in a distributed fashion. You can create an application where documents are manipulated on a server through a client, or entirely on a client, perhaps using replication through a central server to coordinate the contents of local databases. Domino servers and Notes clients are different environments in many different respects, particularly in how they deal with security.

Security in client-based applications must be approached very carefully. Unless specific steps are taken, databases accessed locally essentially have Manager access, no matter what is listed in the ACL. For some databases, like a user's own mailbox, that's not a problem since they should have Manager access anyway. But, for just about any multi-user application, it's a large concern.

One way of getting around the problem is by checking the Enforce Consistent ACL Across All Replicas option in the ACL. This option is available on the Advanced tab of the ACL dialog box. If the option is checked, ACL settings will be enforced within the database even on copies of the database accessed locally rather than through a server. This setting does not provide absolute security since a user with a sufficiently high level of permission who is accessing the database locally can circumvent the option, allowing them to take back full control. Once it is unchecked, the local user regains full control. However, a database with the Enforce Consistent ACLs option unchecked will fail to replicate to a database where this option is checked. In short, the ACL can be set so that any damage a user does to documents won't be replicated to a server or to other users.

One of the other large security-related differences between a completely client-based environment versus accessing a server through a client is the lack of connection with certain important resources, particularly the server's main address book. This causes another security problem, albeit one granting too little access rather than too much. Without access to the main address book or to a local address book with appropriately named groups, a local database can't determine group memberships. It's possible to circumvent the lack of appropriately named groups by creating them in the local address book. However, local group contents can supercede groups in the main address book when the remote machine connects to the server. To make security work properly, it's usually best to have the appropriate server address books replicated to the client machines. You'll also have to be careful using roles (see the "Security" section) since roles don't function on locally accessed databases under some circumstances.

Preventing Replication and Save Conflicts

Two types of problems you're likely to encounter on any Notes system where you have a number of users working on the same documents are Replication and Save Conflicts. Replication and Save Conflicts happen in the following situations:

- When two users have a document open for editing at the same time and the document is saved at the same time, this causes a Save Conflict.

- When an Agent and a user, or two Agents, try to modify the same document at the same, or two very close, times, this also causes a Save Conflict.

- When users save changes to the same document on different replicas of a database, this causes a Replication Conflict.

Notes compares what it is saving with the current version of the document (that is, the most recently saved version) and realizes that there are more differences between the current document and what it is trying to save than there should be. Instead of overwriting the current document, Notes saves the document as a sort of response, as shown in Figure 24.2. A user with appropriate permissions can examine the documents later, decide what the proper data for the document should actually be, make appropriate changes, and delete the conflicting document. Replication Conflicts, which happen when different replicas hold different data, can be reduced by selecting the Merge Replication Conflicts option. However, this only eliminates conflicts when different fields are changed. If a given field has changes made to it in separate database replicas, a Replication Conflict will still result.

PART

VI

Developing
Databases

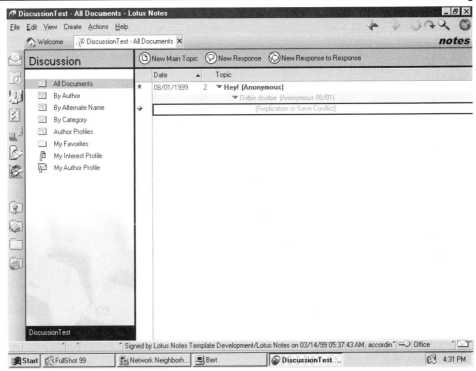

FIGURE 24.2

A Replication or Save Conflict message in a view

While you can recover from Replication and Save Conflicts, they are very annoying, particularly in multi-user databases where they can proliferate tremendously. Manually fixing a conflict requires human intervention and the examination of every field in both documents to make absolutely certain that all possible conflicts are reconciled. Depending on the form fields, nature of the data, and number of conflicts, the task can become overwhelming.

In some applications, particularly applications distributing editorial power over the same document equally across several replicas, this is unavoidable. However, the danger of conflicts can be minimized through careful use of security, replication settings, and the appropriate code.

Security and Replication Settings

Part of preventing Replication and Save Conflicts is in enforcing sensible security. If users don't have permission to edit a document, they can't create a Save Conflict with it. You should strongly consider the use of Author fields. (See the section on security at the end of this chapter.)

For distributed applications replicated over multiple locations, you might consider working with your database's replication settings. (Review the "Replication Settings" section in Chapter 9.) If you can, you might consider using the replication settings to limit the documents that a user can replicate to only those documents that are relevant to the person or location. Not only will this reduce Replication Conflicts, it will also save replication time over a slow network or modem connection. For example, imagine a workflow database where documents pass through the hands of certain individual users. Each user has a local replica of the database. To save time and reduce conflicts, each user could go to the Advanced tab of Replication Settings for their copy and tell the replica to replicate by a formula. The formula might be something like SELECT CurrentReviewer = *My Name*, where *My Name* is the user's name. When a user replicates, Notes will only replicate those documents that the user is associated with. If there are a lot of users, this can save each individual user a lot of disk space and a lot of time on-line replicating because only a small fraction of the documents will be replicated.

Example Technique: Checking Forms In and Out

Out of the box, Notes does nothing to prevent you from attempting to edit a document that is already being edited by somebody else. In part, this is impossible. To do so, Notes would have to keep track of every document and be constantly in touch with all replica databases, and each Domino server would have to keep extremely close tabs on all clients and databases. The former can't be done since the whole point of replicas is to have independently functioning copies of a database, and the latter would increase the server's overhead tremendously.

It's possible to set a form property that tells Notes to automatically merge Replication Conflicts. (Review the "What Are Replication and Save Conflicts" sidebar in Chapter 18.) But this is only a partial solution since Domino can't resolve Replication Conflicts under many circumstances. Instead, it is better to keep conflicts from happening in the first place, but how? One approach is to borrow a concept from a different kind of database. Most relational databases allow you to implement *record locking*, which marks a row or several rows of data as "in use" so that nobody else can use them until the first user is done. Strict record locking goes beyond the capability of Notes, but you can use Notes's tools to partially emulate record locking's function.

To implement a pseudo-record-locking capability, you need to be able to mark a document as being "in use" and to clear that setting once a user is done with the document. While the document is in use, only the designated user can make changes to it, although other users can read the document.

Our first step is marking the document as being in use. For that, we'll use a pair of form Actions. One Action will *check out* documents, marking them as in use, or potentially in use, by a specific user. The other Action will check them back in. Both

PART

VI

Developing
Databases

Actions operate by looping through documents that are selected in the view and changing the value of the CheckedOutBy field, depending upon whether the document is in use or not.

 NOTE In the following chapters, we will use the continuation arrow (➡) to indicate code that is on the same line. The code is printed on a new line here due to space constraints.

Here's the checking-out code:

```
Sub Click(Source As Button)
    On Error Resume Next
    Dim session As New NotesSession
    Dim db As NotesDatabase
    Dim collection As NotesDocumentCollection
    Dim doc As NotesDocument
    Dim CurrentCheck As String
    Set db = session.CurrentDatabase
    Set collection = db.UnprocessedDocuments
    For i = 1 To collection.Count
        Set doc = collection.GetNthDocument( i )
        CurrentCheck = doc.CheckedOutBy(0)
        If CurrentCheck =  session.UserName Then
            doc.CheckedOutBy = ""
            Call doc.Save( False, True )
        Else
            Msgbox ("Could not check out document with the title " +
➡   doc.CheckedOutBy (0))
        End If
    Next
End Sub
```

And here's the checking-in code:

```
Sub Click(Source As Button)
    On Error Resume Next
    Dim session As New NotesSession
    Dim db As NotesDatabase
    Dim collection As NotesDocumentCollection
    Dim doc As NotesDocument
    Dim CurrentCheck As String
    Set db = session.CurrentDatabase
```

```
Set collection = db.UnprocessedDocuments
For i = 1 To collection.Count
   Set doc = collection.GetNthDocument( i )
   CurrentCheck = doc.CheckedOutBy(0)
   If CurrentCheck =  session.UserName Then
      doc.CheckedOutBy = ""
      Call doc.Save( False, True )
   Else
      Msgbox ("Could not check out document with the title " +
   doc.CheckedOutBy (0))
   End If
Next
End Sub
```

This code, which goes into the QueryModeChange event of a form, is the key to making the check-out process work in the UI. When a user attempts to put the document into editing mode, the QueryModeChange code is executed. This script checks to see if the current user is named in CheckedOutBy. If not, it refuses to put the document into editing mode and alerts the user to the fact that somebody else is using it.

```
Sub Querymodechange (Source As Notesuidocument, Continue As Variant)
Dim doc As NotesDocument
Dim s As New notessession
Dim x As Integer
If Not isnewdoc Then
   Set doc = source.document
   If doc.HasItem("CheckedOutBy") Then
      If Not (doc.CheckedOutBy(0) = s.UserName)Then
         Msgbox("This document is currently in use by " & doc.
      CheckedOutBy(0) & ". You may only edit it after it has been
      checked in.")
         Continue = False
      End If
   End If
End If
End Sub
```

NOTE The check-in and check-out code can be adapted for use in form Actions, letting you work on one document at a time. For Web use, you can also use some Agent-based methods, which we'll discuss in Chapter 26.

PART

VI

Developing Databases

This code will prevent users from attempting to edit a document at the same time. This will prevent the bulk of your problems with Save Conflicts, but it isn't a 100% solution. It prevents multiple users from making changes through the user interface, but it won't in itself prevent Agents and Actions that use scripts from making changes to the back-end document. However, you can modify Agent code and search conditions to test for the CheckedOutBy field.

Also, as a safety precaution, you might consider making a scheduled Agent that will sweep through the database and clear out the CheckedOutBy field at intervals. Careless users might forget to check documents back in once they're done with them, keeping others from doing necessary work.

 NOTE Want to automate the check-in and check-out process further? You could adapt the check-out code for use in a form's QueryOpen event and the check-in code for use in QueryClose, but be careful. Checking a document back in requires making a change to the document and saving it, so you could run into a problem if somebody closes an edited document without wanting to save changes.

Creating Programming Standards

Any organization that uses Notes extensively, or any developer that works in Notes frequently, is eventually going to end up with a lot of program code—be it @formulas, JavaScript, LotusScript, or Java—distributed across a number of databases. Some of it will be easy to understand. (If you can't figure out what an Action button labeled Close and containing only the line `@PostedCommand([FileCloseWindow])` is supposed to do, you may be in the wrong business.) Most of it will not. Chapter 23 had some suggestions for making individual scripts easier for the programmer to understand, but if you develop more than a few databases, or if you develop databases collaboratively with other developers, you may need to do more.

Many organizations adopt conventions to make it easier to read and understand code. These conventions may involve obligatory comments in code, common practices for naming variables, and even ways of structuring programs. These practices are collectively called *programming standards*. Make no mistake: Using programming standards will make it take longer to write code. You may have to think more about what you name variables. You may have to build programs with more and shorter subroutines than you'd like. However, the extra time you spend making your code conform to standards will pay off many times over when it comes time to modify your code, or when somebody else has to do maintenance on it.

At the moment, there aren't any dominant programming standards for programming with LotusScript or @formulas. In fact, if you look at the templates that come with the Notes client, you'll see that Lotus's own programmers don't use any apparent programming standards. It is not necessary to use programming standards to write good code; nevertheless, it is a good idea. Many other programming languages and platforms (including C, Java, and VBA) have at least one, and often several, competing sets of standards. If the suggested standards that we will discuss next don't appear to suit your needs, you might look into standards for other languages and adapt them. Standards are merely an aid to making your programs easily understood. The standard you use is probably less important than picking a standard and using it consistently.

Code Headers and Formula Comments

Chapter 23 mentioned code headers for LotusScript programs. You might also consider code headers for elaborate @functions. The REM statement gives you a way not only to comment on lines of code within your @functions, but also to describe their purpose. To save some room, the scripts in this book won't include the header comments, but here are some bits of information you might want to consider including in your headers:

- Purpose of the script
- History of changes
- Script author
- Parent object name (If your code is one subroutine of a large, complex Agent or other script, it can be useful to remind yourself what it is a part of.)
- Explanation of parameters (Try as you may to come up with descriptive names for your variables, it may not be immediately obvious where they come from, what they're supposed to represent, and why they're named the way they are.)
- Calling object names (This can be more difficult to maintain, but extremely useful. If you record within a function or shared subroutine the names of scripts that use it, you'll be better able to anticipate what impact changes on the routine will have throughout your database.)

As an example, here's a possible script header for the state-abbreviation-translation routine (shown in the "Select Case" section of Chapter 23) after a few rounds of changes:

```
Function FullStateName (ST As String, Ctry As String) As String
 ' Name: FullStateName
 '
```

PART

VI

Developing
Databases

```
' Purpose: Given a two-letter abbreviation and a country, returns
' the full name of the state or province.
'
'Changes: 1/1/99: Converted from a subroutine in an agent to a
' function in a script library so that it could be used through
' the database.
'  4/1/99: Canadian provinces added; to support possible future
' expansion, country parameter added.
'
' Parameters: ST (string, standard postal abbreviation for state
' or province), Ctry (string, abbreviation for country name)

Select Case Ctry
Case "US"
 Select Case ST
 Case "AK"
   FullStateName = "Alaska"
 Case "AL"
   FullStateName = "Alabama"
 Case "AR"
   FullStateName = "Arkansas"
   ' This goes on for fifty states.
 End Select
Case "CA"
 Select Case ST
  Case "AB"
  FullStateName = "Alberta"
   ' And so on for more provinces
 End Select
Case Else
 FullStateName = "(no state/province)"
End Select

End Function
```

Naming Conventions for Variables

Another way to make your code easier to work with, particularly when it comes to debugging and avoiding data type mismatch errors, is to adopt naming conventions for variables. It is common practice (or, at least, commonly encouraged if not actually done) to attach a descriptive prefix or suffix to the name of a variable to tell the programmer the variable's data type. For example, consider a variable counting the number of documents in a view, which you would want to call DocCount. If DocCount was declared as an integer, you might want to call it iDocCount, intDocCount, or int_DocCount. If you declared it as a long integer, you might use lDocCount, lngDocCount, or lng_DocCount. Descriptively named variables are sometimes called *self-documenting variables*. The variable name carries information about the kind of data it holds, essentially documenting itself. Table 24.2 lists one possible scheme for variable naming.

TABLE 24.2: SUGGESTED VARIABLE NAME PREFIXES FOR COMMONLY USED DATA TYPES

Data Type	Variable Prefix
Integer	int_
Long	lng_
String	str_
Single	sng_
Double	dbl_
Currency	cur_
Variant	var_
Notes Document	doc_
Notes Database	db_
Notes View	vw_
Notes Document Collection	dc_
Notes Date/Time	dat_
Notes Session	s_
Notes UI Document	uidoc_
Notes UI Workspace	uiws_
Notes Item	itm_
Notes Rich Text Item	rtitm_
Array (Since arrays have another data type, this should be appended along with another prefix to denote the full data type; for example, a_int_ for an integer array.)	a_
List (Like an array, lists are complex and should use a compound prefix.)	lst_

In short scripts, where there's only a single instance of an object, you may save yourself some typing by just using the short prefix. For example, if you only have one NotesSession in a script, do you really need to call it s_thissession or the like? Most of the scripts that follow will use this convention, but some will not in order to allow you to judge how useful the convention is in reading and modifying scripts.

Creating Friendly Applications

The greatest challenge a developer faces is not getting a database to work, but rather, getting it to work for the intended users. All of your elegant code, your rigorously defined processes, and your pretty pictures on buttons and navigators won't do any good if users can't figure out how to use the database, or if using it is so difficult that they try to circumvent your database instead of using it.

When building Notes applications, you might consider looking at books on Web design. The organizational aspects of Notes application design are a lot like Web design: organizing data input and display in a document-centric medium. Indeed, a lot of your Notes design might *be* Web design, since Domino can throw your application directly onto the Web, and the Web is an increasingly important medium for Domino design. In that spirit, we recommend *Web Pages That Suck* (Vincent Flanders and Michael Willis, Sybex, 1998). While their concerns about bandwidth are slowly becoming outdated as average modem speeds increase (and may even be irrelevant, since many potential users of Notes applications will access them through high-speed internal corporate networks), the basic principles of building easily understood documents are the same. However, since a Notes application tends to perform more tasks than the more static Web sites most Web design books address, you'll also have to consider how to present the results of Agents and other automated processes. Your application must be easy to navigate, it must be able to guide lost and confused users, and it must be able to recover from errors. It's also a good idea to consider shortcuts for smart and experienced users. A slow, step-by-step approach to navigating an application is useful for casual users, but power users will get bored and try to make shortcuts. If there are to be shortcuts, it's best that you make them.

Using a Consistent Interface

Making it easy to find things in your database goes beyond making individually readable forms. (Review the sections on designing a form in Chapter 18.) One of the best things you can do to help your users find their way around your database is to make your forms look as similar to one another as possible. This is not to say that you should go through contortions to make all your forms identical. However, you should establish a look and feel for your database through your form design. For example, if you divide a large form into parts, only a few of which will be visible at any time, you should decide early on to use either collapsible sections or tabbed tables across all of your forms. Likewise, it's generally a good idea to use a single font and as few font sizes and styles as possible across your forms and to use them as consistently as possible. It will help your users find things on your forms if section headings are all, say, twelve point and bold, while field labels are all ten point and plain. Also, adopt a single label and button icon for common Actions. By the time you've built two or three databases, you'll probably have the necessary code for things like Save and Close, Create Document, and Close Document. You should also have picked out favorite icons to use for each of them. And don't forget that you can use templates to store and control your frequently-used design elements.

Shared Actions can be an extremely useful tool. You can create nearly ubiquitous buttons like Save, Save and Close, Send, and Edit Document once and use the same code, the same hide-when conditions, and the same easily identifiable graphic throughout your application. Since you're using code from a single source, you can change the code and have that change take effect immediately throughout your application rather than having to update the code in a number of different forms. A drawback to Shared Actions is that you can't re-label them as you put them into individual forms. For example, you may have different Close buttons for Notes and Web use: one using @Command([FileCloseWindow]) and the other using a JavaScript function. They'll both be labeled Close, making it difficult for you, the designer, to tell them apart. However, you could create an Action without a formula, named Web Actions or Web Only, and put your Web versions under that (Web Actions\Close, for example). Then, you can make a Notes Actions Action and put the Notes versions under that (Notes Actions\Close).

However, for any application, you need to worry about more than just the forms themselves. You need to consider how that information is presented in views and folders, and how access to those objects is granted through outlines and navigators.

Something that you've read before in this book bears repeating: *Get your users involved as early as possible*. Ultimately, it is their database, and they are the ones who will have to use it to get their work done. Make them sketch out the views they need in detail: columns, categorization, and Actions.

Consistency counts in views and folders just as much as it does in forms. Like form Actions, view and folder Actions should have consistent icons. The other shared resources are obvious tools to use to give an overall look and feel not just to your forms but to your whole database. Subforms will let you drop large clusters of fields and hotspots into documents easily, even dynamically. Shared images and applets let you recycle all kinds of content in a number of different design elements. Unfortunately, as convenient as they may be for you, shared resources may not be so friendly to your users. Shared resources can slow your forms down, particularly over the Web. If you use shared resources, you may want to keep an eye on the performance of other objects you use them in. If they're too slow, consider removing them.

For simple applications, you may decide that Notes's default appearance is sufficient. The default has a Navigation pane on the left, which displays views and folders, and a view-listing Document pane on the right, (or perhaps a split View folder and Document Preview pane). If your users are used to Notes 4.*x* applications, which often offered little else, this may be particularly true. However, the more complex your

PART

VI

Developing Databases

application and the more varied its functions, the more you'll need larger organizational devices.

The ultimate destinations in your applications will be views, folders, and documents. But, in order to get there, you'll need to use Navigators, Pages, and Outlines. As already observed, Navigators are quickly built and have their own special areas of flexibility (in particular, the ability to place text and graphics exactly where you want to). However, since they lack the ability to embed other objects and have no provisions for security, you'll probably be using Pages and Outlines to do most of your navigation. But don't dismiss Navigators out of hand. You can do things very easily with Navigators that you'd be hard pressed to do with Pages. For example, the Navigation Control Panel in Figure 24.3, which was constructed quickly and easily as a Navigator, could be mocked up with an arrangement of tables in a Page, but only with much more effort.

FIGURE 24.3

A peculiar Navigator

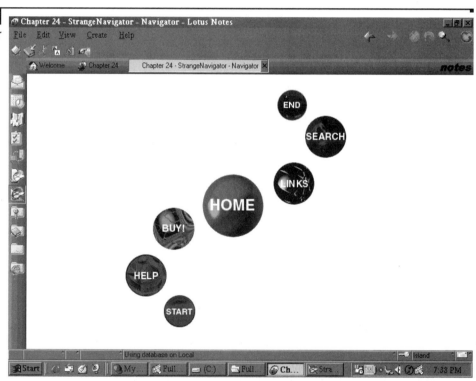

Framesets can be a powerful tool for organizing and navigating through the database. You can use different frames for different levels of navigation. The Personal Address book shown in Figure 24.4 is a good example of the use of frames. The small frame in the lower left provides a top level of navigation, allowing the user to switch between the address book's data and administrative tasks. The tall, narrow frame on the left provides a finer, second level of navigation, displaying a list of items related to the area selected in the small frame. Finally, the main data frame provides a place to actually work or display data. The mailbox follows the same theme with a small frame that can switch between mail, calendar, and to-do areas; a larger frame with views and folders; and a large frame for content. Two-pane and three-pane schemes are the most common on the Web and in Notes applications. There are a few four-pane schemes, but framesets more complex than that run the risk of becoming too complex and tend to subdivide valuable space on the monitor screen so much that none of the frames is big enough to display a useful amount of data.

FIGURE 24.4

Frames in the Personal Address Book

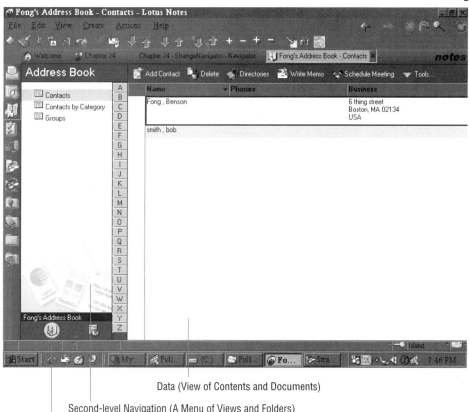

Data (View of Contents and Documents)

Second-level Navigation (A Menu of Views and Folders)

Top-level Navigation (View of Address Book or Settings)

The conventional wisdom is that you should provide five to eight choices in any given set of buttons or list of menu items. If you can manage that in your design, be happy. If not, don't worry about it and don't unnecessarily complicate your design to make your database conform to some kind of mathematical ideal. Notes's eminently navigable mailbox template has examples where a frame provides more than the ideal number of choices. The default Mail navigator contains nine items and can acquire more if you create more views and folders of your own.

Good and bad use of framesets can be learned from the many Web sites that use frames. Users will probably be most familiar with, and therefore most comfortable with, two-pane or three-pane schemes, where small panes are used to control navigation and large panes are used to display content. As with forms, the important thing with frames is to be consistent. For example, if you have a narrow frame across the top that navigates between user, manager, and administrative functions and a side or bottom frame that switches between Outlines, you shouldn't have buttons elsewhere that put Outlines in the top pane and move the user, manager, and administrative page to a different frame. Make sure that your users have to do as little looking around and as little scrolling as possible.

 NOTE The sample applications in Chapters 27 and 28 use some simple two-frame framesets. Both have one frame on the left for navigation and one on the right for data. And, speaking of consistencies between applications, you might want to keep an eye on the Close, Save and Close, and Edit Document buttons.

Providing Help for Users

While you should, if at all possible, train users in how to use your application, you can't be there to hold their hand every time they use it. An elaborate application is always better off if it has some kind of online help features built into it. In R5, Notes gives you a dazzling array of options for providing users with instructions while they're using the database.

For a general overview of the database, Notes provides you with About Database and Using Database documents, mentioned in "The Other Elements" section of Chapter 15. You can put text, links, buttons, and pop-ups on these documents to explain its use and purpose. While there are no restrictions on actual content, it's a good idea to explain the database's purpose on the About Database document and give an over-view of its use and function on the Using Database document. If you need more than one or two screens full of text to explain the database, you should strongly consider some of the other possibilities outlined next. The About Database document might also hold contact information for the database's administrators and help personnel. You may even want to add a panic button that the users can press to send mail to administrators or support people.

For simple instructions, text pop-ups can be extremely useful. The Personal Address Book (see Figure 24.5) is a good example of the use of text pop-ups. Most forms accessible through the Settings views have clickable text pop-ups. Clicking a field label brings up a brief description of the field. Unfortunately, they're inappropriate for descriptions of process, and text pop-ups don't translate to the Web.

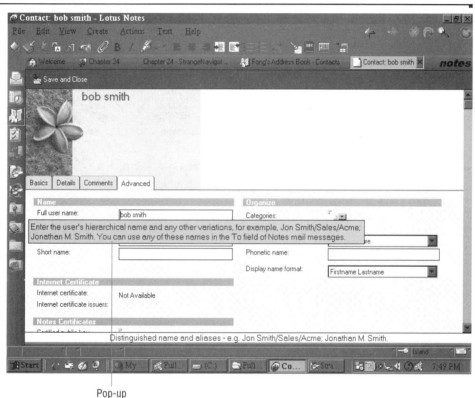

FIGURE 24.5

A helpful pop-up in a Personal Address Book

Pop-up

If you use pop-ups, you'll have to figure out how to mark the items that have pop-ups associated with them so that users will know to click labels, roll the mouse over pictures, and so on. The outlining style of pointing out text hotspots provided by Notes may not be appropriate for your application, particularly if you're dealing with one section of closely set text. If you don't highlight your pop-ups, you will need to educate your users that they are there. Rollover pop-ups may become apparent sooner or later, but pop-ups won't appear unless a user thinks to click a caption or label. Because most users are familiar with Web-browser conventions, assigning an underline style for the hotspot text is a legible and easily understood compromise between highlighting and not highlighting. Using a special color is also a useful marker. If that

Developing
Databases

appears too disruptive or isn't sufficient to inform your users, you might just enter **"Clicking field labels will tell you their use"** at the top of your forms.

Link hotspots can be a very useful tool for providing help. You can insert three different types of links:

- Document links in your forms to provide help on specific issues
- View links to provide help for large related areas
- Web links to connect users to relevant Web pages

This is an extremely versatile way of providing help, since it can provide information inside or outside of Notes, and it can also function in applications accessed through a Web browser.

The drawback of link hotspots is that, unlike pop-ups, they require more navigation. Calling up a linked document will, at the very least, put a new document in the user's way that they must close or otherwise move in order to get back to work. If only a sentence or two of help is needed, pop-ups are a superior solution. Linked documents are a better solution for extensive help.

A new feature in R5 is the HelpRequest event. In many Windows programs, pressing the F1 key brings up some kind of Help file. In previous releases, pressing F1 in Notes would open up the Notes Help database. However, it now triggers an event that allows you to bring up your own documents using @formulas, which is a very useful feature for large, complex applications. There's also a new @command to use in conjunction with the event: @Command([OpenHelpDocument]).

The @Command([OpenHelpDocument]) command always requires the name of a view and a key value, much like the @DBLookup command. Provided with only that information, the command will open a document in the named view from the appropriate Help database (for example, Administration Help if you're in the Administration client). However, if you designate a server and database, you can bring up a document from the database of your choice. This means that if you build a documentation database for your applications, you can call up relevant documents with a single keystroke or the press of a button. Here's an example:

```
@Command([OpenHelpDocument]; ""; "CompanyHelp.nsf"; "(HelpCategories)";
Form)
```

This formula finds a database named CompanyHelp.nsf, goes to the hidden Help-Categories view, and opens the first document in the view that has the calling document's form name in the first sorted column.

Like document links, the @Command([OpenHelpDocument]) command will bring another document to the foreground. But, since you can designate a document programmatically, you can just write a formula and won't have to copy and paste document links. While the HelpRequest event only exists in the Notes client and not on Web browsers, the @Command([OpenHelpDocument]) command works perfectly well in buttons on both the Web and in Notes clients. If you use your own Help databases, be sure that all users have permission to read them!

 TIP Just because it's called the `@Command([OpenHelpDocument])` command doesn't mean that it has to open documents that describe how to use the database. You can potentially use it to open any document from any database as long as you have appropriately structured views and can come up with formulas to find them.

Error Handling

All kinds of things can go wrong with a script when it gets used in the production environment. You may use the wrong data type, an object may not be instantiated at the right time, an Agent might run without the proper permissions, and so on. When this happens, Notes will usually produce a message box containing a sometimes-enigmatic error message and will then stop running the code. If the code is in an object event, such as QuerySave, the event won't take place. If the code is part of a scheduled or triggered Agent, you won't even get the message box, although you may be able to get some problems with Agents reported to you through the server's log.

However, one of the features of LotusScript (indeed, one of the important features of any good programming language) is *error handling*, sometimes also called *error trapping*. When an error occurs, rather than suffering through your script bailing out at some poorly defined point, you can have Notes tell you more explicitly what is going on and where. More importantly, you can have Notes tell *anybody* what went wrong. While "object variable not set" may mean something to a Notes developer, it almost certainly won't mean anything to the average user. If you use error handling, you can have Notes provide the user with a detailed message about the error the script encountered, as well as instructions to record the error message and to contact the system administrator or the database developer.

It's also possible to recover from script errors. With error handling, you can have a script recover from the error and keep running. Full recovery may not be possible, but you can at least exit from the script gracefully.

The first step in error handling is to put an On Error statement at the beginning of your script. The On Error statement must be followed by a GoTo or Resume statement, which tells Notes where to go.

The simplest error handling is to use the line On Error Resume Next. With that instruction at the beginning of a script, Notes will react to an error in the script by going to the next line as if nothing happened. Using a Resume Next statement ensures that a script will complete. However, it won't complete successfully, and it won't inform anybody of the error.

Using a GoTo statement allows you to do far more sophisticated error handling. Using GoTo, you can jump to another section of code specifically built to deal with errors. To use GoTo, you have to use a label to mark the section of code within the procedure where you'll insert the On Error statement. A label can simply be a line containing a name, followed by a colon (:). When an error occurs, Notes will jump from the line where the error occurs to the label. Notes will then continue executing the code from that point. For example, the code here would cause a message box to pop up immediately after the attempt to access the document.

```
On Error GoTo ErrorRoutine
Dim s_thesession as NotesSession
Dim db_testdata as NotesDatabase
Dim doc_firstdoc as NotesDocument

Set s_thesession = NotesSession
' Since we haven't set the value of db_testdata, this next line will
➡   cause an error
Set doc_firstdoc = New NotesDocument(db_testdata)
' This line won't execute
Msgbox("This would appear if the error handler had said Resume Next.")

ErrorRoutine:
Msgbox("Object variable not set.  The database variable db_testdata
➡   hasn't been given a value.")
Exit Sub
```

At the end of the error-handling routine, you'll also need an instruction telling the routine where to go once it's done. The most commonly used commands are Exit Sub or Exit Function, which ends the current routine just as though the routine had hit an End Sub, or End Function, and Resume Next statement. Using Resume Next in an error-handling routine moves the program to the line after the one where the error occurred. If you want to get fancy, you can try variations on the Resume statement. Resume *label* moves to another labeled section of code, just like a GoTo statement does.

The Problem with GoTo

There's a joke in some circles to the effect that a computer scientist is someone who, on being told to go to Hell, regards the verb rather than the noun as the objectionable part

Continued

CONTINUED

of the sentence. GoTo, and its cousin GoSub, have a very bad reputation in programming languages. If you're new to programming, you might wonder why. On the surface, GoTo and GoSub may appear quite useful. GoTo and GoSub aren't limited to use in error handling. You can use them at any time to move around within a subroutine. If you put a Return statement at the end of a labeled section of code, the execution of code will jump back to the line after the last GoTo or GoSub, picking up where it left off. So why are old programming hands so leery of it?

The reasons for the general disdain for GoTo and GoSub are largely historical. Moreover, they don't apply to LotusScript. In earlier programming languages, like Pascal and the original BASIC, GoTo and GoSub could be used to bounce out of subroutines at any time, sometimes with no way back to where the original GoTo was. This could result in some very poorly structured programs. However, GoTo is far better behaved in Lotus-Script. GoTo and GoSub only work within a subroutine and, though you do have to remember to put it in, Return will put you back where you began after the GoTo's code is finished. Essentially, using GoTo is a slightly less efficient way of structuring a script, but it is by no means dangerous programming. If an old hand sneers at your use of GoTo and GoSub, tell him that things have changed since the old days.

There are some special functions you'll probably want to use to help you build your own error statements: `Err`, `Error`, and `Erl`. `Err` and `Error` give identifying information about the error that has just occurred. The `Err` function returns a number identifying the error, while `Error` returns a text message. `Erl` provides information about *where* the error occurred, returning the line number of the instruction that caused the error. You can combine these three functions to create a generic error message like this:

```
On Error GoTo MyError

' Some code goes here, and then...

MyError:
Magbox "Error in line " + Cstr(Erl) + ": " + Error + " Please inform
➥   the database administrator that this error has occurred.",,
➥   "Error #" + Cstr(Err)
Resume Next
```

When an error occurs, an error message appears that details what the error is and where it happened, and urges the user to transmit the information to people who might be able to do something about it (see Figure 24.6).

FIGURE 24.6

*The custom error
message*

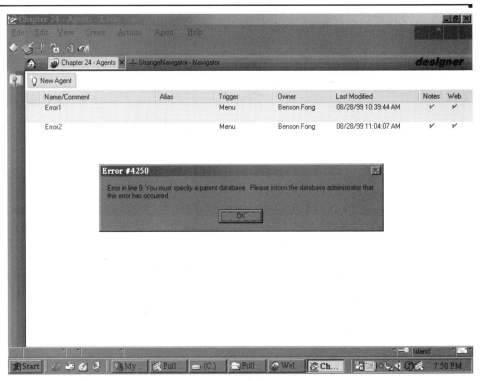

Now the code is all well and good for producing a meaningful error message, but it will only be effective if somebody is looking at it. It won't help at all if an error occurs in a scheduled or triggered Agent, where there's no convenient user interface in which to show the error, nor much of a chance of there being a user there to see it. However, because your error handler is part of a LotusScript program, you have pretty much the whole of LotusScript in which to incorporate your error handling. One approach you might take is, rather than using dialog boxes, have the error handler send an e-mail message containing the error message. In the code shown next, an error causes a message to be sent to the database's managers.

```
MyError:
Set doc_ErrorDoc = New NotesDocument(db_ThisDB)
doc_ErrorDoc.Subject =  "Error #" + Cstr(Err) + " in database " +
➥   db_ThisDB.Title
doc_ErrorDoc.Body = "Error in line " + Cstr(Erl) + ": " + Error
doc_ErrorDoc.SendTo = db_ThisDB.Managers
Call doc_ErrorDoc.Send(false, false)
Resume Next
```

If you run a large system, you may want to keep a centralized set of records to keep track of errors in all of your Notes databases. If you follow that strategy, you can have your error handler create a document in an error-tracking database, like this:

```
Dim agent as NotesAgent
Set agent = s_thesession.CurrentAgent
 FirstErrorTime = Now


' More code causing an error here


ErrorHandle:
Set db_errors = s.GetDatabase( "",
"D:\Lotus\Domino\data\LotusScriptErrors.nsf" )
Set doc_error = New notesdocument(db_errors)
doc_error.Form = "ErrorReport"
doc_error.AgentName = agent.Name
doc_error.ErrorCode = Err
doc_error.ErrorMsg = Error
doc_error.ErrorLine = Erl
doc_error.RunTime = FirstErrorTime


Call doc_error.save(True, True)
Resume Next
```

This Agent assumes that a number of declarations have been made up front (for example, doc_error as a document). As you can see, this routine creates a document in a database (LotusScriptErrors.nsf) that records the error information (both the error number and the corresponding error messages), the name of the database, and the name of the Agent where the error is being generated. This routine takes advantage of the CurrentAgent property of the NotesSession class to identify which Agent is triggering the error; the same error could be modified to identify a specific document if the error-handling routine is in a document event. The *FirstErrorTime* variable is intended as aid in tracing the error. By being set the first time through the error-handling routine and not changing thereafter, the *FirstErrorTime* marks the first time an error occurs within the current run of the Agent. This can be an aid to administrators investigating the error later, helping group together errors that took place during different runs of the same Agent. An Agent-generated error report document might look something like Figure 24.7.

Developing
Databases

 TIP   In a way, the *FirstErrorTime* solution is the hard way to do it, but it's useful to know that you've got complete freedom to create new documents. However, there's also a NotesLog class that you can use to capture information on a running Agent.

FIGURE 24.7

*An automatically
generated Error
document*

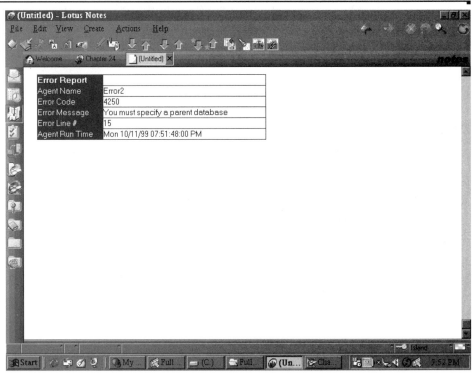

While the most common use of error handling is to create generic error messages, you can also use error handling to give users very specific feedback about problems that may arise at runtime. As you've seen with the Err function, Notes generates an error code every time an error occurs. If you anticipate a particular type of error (say, a type mismatch error when dealing with values in document fields), you can set up very specific responses when those errors occur.

One way of using that is to incorporate the error codes into your code using some kind of branching, like an If...Then or Select Case block. However, a better way of dealing with specific errors is to make your initial error-handling instructions more explicit. The On Error statement can take an error code as an argument. You can use multiple On Error statements, each of them directing the script to a different error-handling routine. Here's an example:

```
On Error GoTo GenericError
On Error 13 GoTo TypeMismatchError
On Error 53 GoTo NotFoundError
```

If the routine running this code encountered a type mismatch (Error #13), it would go to the code labeled TypeMismatchError. If it couldn't find an external file (Error #53), it would go to the code labeled NotFoundError. With any other error, it would go to the code labeled GenericError. Fortunately, you don't need to know error numbers to make this work. If you include appropriate .lss libraries in your code (put a line reading %Include "*libraryname*.lss" in the (Options) section of the Agent or the Globals section of a form), you can replace the code numbers with somewhat easier to understand text constants. The previous code could be written more meaningfully like this:

```
(Options)

%Include "lserr.lss"

Sub Initialize

On Error GoTo GenericError
On Error ErrTypeMismatch GoTo TypeMismatchError
On Error ErrFileNotFound GoTo NotFoundError
```

You can search the Domino Designer help for "Handling run-time errors" and check the details for a full list of libraries, error codes, and their corresponding constants.

Constants

A type of declaration statement glossed over in Chapter 23 is the constant. You can set up "variables" that have a constant value throughout a routine. Constants may be public (can be used outside the subroutine where they are created) or private (may only be used in the subroutine where they are created). For constants, you don't control the data type; Notes selects the appropriate one: string, double-precision number, integer, or long integer, depending on the type of data you put into the constant. If you had the line Public Const Data_Path = "d:\lotus\domino\data\" in the (Declarations) section of an Agent, you could use the expression Data_Path anywhere in the rest of the Agent to stand for the path to your Domino data directory.

Properly used, constants can make your code very portable and easy to modify. Imagine an Agent that runs through every database in the data directory and reports back to the databases' managers a list of databases above a particular size. The Data_Path constant, as used here, could be used in conjunction with a Size_Threshold constant to define the size of database to look for. Those constants could be set to one value (say, d:\lotus\domino\data and 200MB) for one location. If the Agent is run on another server, where there's a different server configuration and disk space is more critical, they could be set to different values (say, e:\lotus\domino\data and 150MB). If the Constant statements are all conveniently placed in the (Declarations) section of the Agent, a remote administrator with little experience in LotusScript could be walked through the process of resetting the values with little fear of hurting something important.

Continued

CONTINUED

So why use constants rather than just declaring a variable and setting the value? First, constants are a little faster. It takes one line to set a constant, and two to declare and populate a variable. Second, and more importantly, constants are just that: constant. If it's important that the value never change, you should use a constant. Finally, even if you don't use constants, it's important to understand them because there are some powerful nuts-and-bolts operations in LotusScript (as you've seen with error handling) that take advantage of them.

One of the implications of being able to identify specific errors is that it may be possible not just to report on them, but to actually fix them. For example, the code here looks up a document in a view and sets the field Date to the current date and time. If the GetDocumentByKey method doesn't return a document, the next line (doc_RecordDate = Now) will return an Object Variable Not Set error. However, because of the error-handling routine, a new document will be created, fixing the problem and letting the Agent complete its run as usual.

```
On Error ErrObjectVariableNotSet GoTo NoDocErr

' Declare and set values for vw_lookup, str_Creator
' Declare doc_Record as a Notesdocument and db as a Notesdatabase

Set doc_Record = vw_lookup.GetDocumentByKey(str_Creator, True)
doc_Record.Date = Now

' More code to process the document.

NoDocErr:
   Set doc_Record = New Notesdocument(db)
   doc_Record.Date = Now
   Resume Next
```

As useful as "self-repairing" code can be, it has a very special purpose. In the previous example, the error-handling routine works fine if the preceding code hasn't found an appropriate document, but what if there was a failure obtaining appropriate values for other objects like db or vw_lookup? The error-handling code, which was designed specifically to note a failure in document lookup, would be an inappropriate response but would be triggered by those errors. If you're going to use error-handling code that fixes errors, use it with caution.

Alternative Error-Handling Methods

In LotusScript, formal error trapping is the best way of generically handling problems in code and execution. However, there are alternative methods of dealing with errors in LotusScript, as well as ways of dealing with errors in @formulas. For short scripts and routine operations, some of these methods may be faster to write and just as effective as generic error-handling methods.

LotusScript Method Results

If you look through the Domino Designer help, you may notice that formal error handling isn't used in many of the scripts. However, you may see a lot of lines that look like If *variable = object.method* Then, but the variable is never used again. The reason for this is that many methods return a Boolean value. If the method succeeds, it can be used to return a True value. If it fails, it can return a False value. If you use the method to set a variable value, it won't cause an error. Instead, you can use the value or even the method itself in an If...Then block in order to take care of errors that may occur with that specific command. Here's an example:

```
If Not (doc.Save(True, True)) Then
  Msgbox("The document was not saved!")
End If
```

This code attempts to save a document. If it isn't saved, a message box pops up and the script continues.

The advantage of this method of error handling is that it makes your scripts somewhat easier to write and follow. Rather than jumping around through the script as a result of GoTo and Resume statements, your error handling is far more linear, following the structure of the conditional statements you use. The drawback is that the error handling it provides couldn't be less generic. You trap errors for one and only one operation at a time. If an error happens anywhere else, your script won't be able to respond to it.

@IsError

As has already been observed, one of the problems with @formulas is that they're much harder to debug. They are even harder to equip with generic error handling. With LotusScript, you can insert error-handling code to deal with potential problems. On the other hand, @functions either work or they don't. At best, they give the user a message about the nature of the problem, but don't tell exactly where in the function they happened. As a result of their rigid top-down execution, there is no way that @functions can do generic error handling.

However, with the `@IsError` function, you can perform something like the one-statement-at-a-time error handling that is possible in LotusScript. You can have Notes itself test for errors at specific points within a larger function and take steps to deal with the problem. Running `@IsError` on another function will return a True value if the function fails or produces some kind of error. For example, `@IsError(@Command-([FileSave]))` will attempt to save a document and return a True value if the operation fails. If you use `@IsError` in an `@If` statement, you can insert lines in larger functions that will ensure that you will get some kind of valid result.

Consider this @formula:

```
@DbLookup("";"";"LookupView"; Keyfield; 2)
```

The formula goes to the view LookupView and returns the values in the second column for all lines in the view where the first sorted column is equal to the value of `Keyfield`, be it a field on a form or a variable created within an Action or Agent. If the value `Keyfield` doesn't appear in LookupView, the function will return an error value, which can cause all kinds of problems later on, including preventing you from opening the document. However, the next statement will return the appropriate lookup value if there is one, or a zero if there isn't.

```
@If(@IsError(@DbLookup("";"";"LookupView"; Keyfield; 2)); 0;
➥    @DbLookup("";"";"LookupView"; Keyfield; 2))
```

Exactly what value is appropriate as an error response is, like in LotusScript error-fixing routines, entirely dependent on the intent of the formula.

There is certainly no need to put `@IsError` statements in every @formula you use, but there are places where they can be particularly useful. Errors are particularly likely in @DBLookups, where you can't guarantee that a corresponding lookup document will exist. Also, type mismatch errors can frequently crop up in formulas that manipulate the contents of automatically generated documents.

Security

While maintaining security in an application is an administrative task, setting up security is a task that falls to the designer. Part of the purpose of security is to keep sensitive information hidden. A more practical part of security, though, is keeping people from inadvertently altering data incorrectly. In addition to keeping your data safe from general tampering, Notes and Domino security features can be incorporated into your application design to help personalize its appearance, influence workflow, and present specialized options to users.

You have three major tools to use in setting up database security:

- ACL
- Roles
- Author and Reader fields

To control access to, and privileges in, your application, you will often end up using all three in conjunction with each other.

 WARNING   Using views and folders to hide and display documents does *not* constitute security. Users can build their own private views that bypass any view formulas you use, and they can build Agents that may act on documents they don't even know about. If your security depends on users not stumbling over documents they're not supposed to deal with, it's not really secure.

The ACL

The most fundamental control on a user's permissions in a database is the Access Control List, which you saw in the "Access Control Lists" section of Chapter 12 and in more detail in the "Protecting the Data Using the ACL" section of Chapter 16. When someone starts using a database, Notes generally grants them the most "permissive" level of permission available to them, but can be limited by explicit naming. For example, if a database has No Access as its default and a user is a member of a group that has been granted Reader access to a database and he is a member of another group with Editor access, that user is granted Editor access to the database. However, if the user is explicitly named in the ACL, that permission will override any group memberships. For example, if a user is a member of a group that has been granted Reader access to a database, is explicitly listed in the ACL as having Editor access, and is a member of a group with Manager access, that user is granted Editor access to the database.

Whenever possible, you should grant permissions to access a database to groups. Doing so will make life much easier for the administrators who have to deal with your applications on a day-to-day basis, since groups can be centrally administered in the organization's NAB. It's easier to grant access to a few groups and add and delete people from them than to add individuals to databases as they come and go, recreating entire sets of permissions as you go. People may come and go, but DepartmentManagers and BasicUsers groups are likely to be part of an organization forever.

The ACL sets an upper limit on the level of access a user can have. Users with Reader access to a database cannot create or edit documents, even if they are granted a role that would otherwise allow them to do so, or if they are listed in documents' Author fields. The ACL listing grants a theoretical maximum level of permission, which may be modified by other conditions.

In general, the highest level of access you should grant to any regular user of an application is Editor. Editor access will allow users more or less complete control over data and documents (except as modified by roles and Author and Reader fields, which we discuss next). Designer and Manager permissions should be reserved for people doing general administration of the server or construction work on the database's design elements.

The additional access privileges (the check boxes to the right of the basic ACL) can be very useful in refining group and individual permissions. As you can see in Figure 24.8, some privileges are inherent in a permission level. For example, Create Documents permission cannot be taken away from Editors. You've already seen in Chapter 22 why you may want to prevent the creation of Agents. You may also strongly consider preventing the creation, and especially the deletion of, documents for some applications. For example, consider a workflow database that sends an expense account around for approval. While a number of people may have Author or even Editor permission in order to approve or deny the expense report, they should not be allowed to delete the expense report out of hand.

FIGURE 24.8

Default access privileges for Reader, Author, Editor, and Manager access

a)

b)

c)

d)

Roles

Roles can be thought of as modifications to ACL permissions or as groups that only exist within a database, whose membership can include only members of the ACL. Roles should be used to differentiate small distinctions in status between database users at a given general level of permission. For example, perhaps all members of a department can create and edit documents in a database, but only a few can mark them as approved. If that's the case, a role should probably be created for those few users.

Roles do not themselves appear in the basic ACL. Rather, once you've created a role, you can assign it to people and groups in the ACL. To do so, simply select the entry in the ACL that you want to assign roles to and select the appropriate roles, as shown in Figure 24.9.

FIGURE 24.9

An entry in an ACL with several roles selected

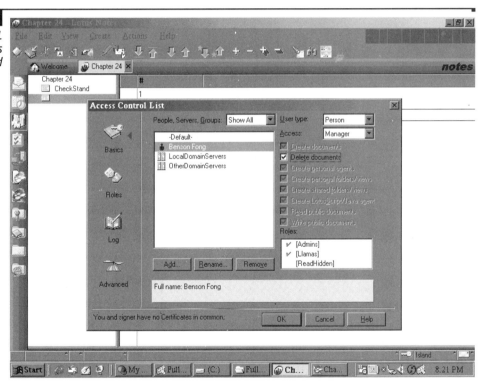

You can use roles in several ways. First and probably most obviously, you can use the names of roles in forms and fields just as you can use the names of individuals and groups. You can name roles as authors and readers of documents. (For more details, see the next section, "Authors and Readers Fields.") You can also use roles just as you would use group or individual names in a form's security properties, as shown in Figure 24.10. The Main Address Book template uses this function of roles extensively, restricting the creation and modification of documents, such as Server documents and Person documents, to members of specific roles.

FIGURE 24.10

A Form Security tab with roles

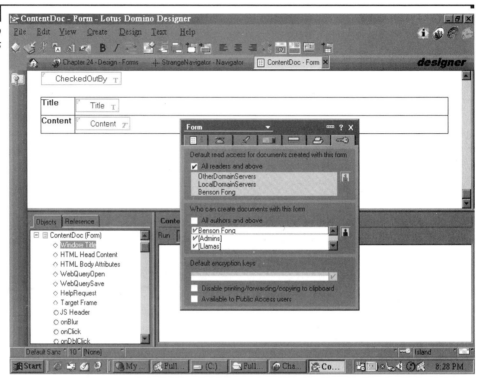

However, the major advantage of roles is that they're immediately accessible to @formula language. Although it is possible, generally through the use of LotusScript, to search through the Main Address Book and compile a list of all the groups an individual is a member of (it's possible but harder to do it with @formulas), this is a very time-consuming, inefficient method. On the other hand, the roles a given user has can be retrieved with @UserRoles. This command produces a list of all the roles the current user has (including roles assigned to any groups the user is a member of), or " " if the user has not been assigned to any roles. Therefore, roles can be used in hide-when formulas.

The way to use @UserRoles in a hide-when or other conditional formula is usually @Contains(@UserRoles, "[*rolename*]"). (Remember, always use square brackets around role names.) This statement will return whether or not the current user has been assigned a given role. In a hide-when formula, this statement can quickly hide or show items as appropriate. For example, you may use this formula to display a button that opens up a profile document only to an [AppAdmins] role. To have an Approval button appear to different people in the course of a workflow application, you might even use a formula like `@Contains(@UserRoles, fieldname)`, where *fieldname* is the name of a field containing the name of a role.

Roles also have limited application in distributed applications. If `@UserRoles` is executed on a server copy of a database or on a local replica, it returns a list of roles when "Enforce a consistent ACL across all replicas" is checked. If that option is unchecked on a local replica, `@UserRoles` will return "". Be very, very careful about your use of roles in a database that will be used as a local replica.

Some of what can be done with roles can be done with references to Profile documents, as well. For example, consider a hide-when formula that uses the condition `@Contains(@GetProfileField( "AdminProfile"; "Administrators"); @UserName)` to retrieve a list of names and see if the current user's name is in that list. Using the Profile document will let you achieve much the same result as `@Contains(@UserRoles, "[rolename]")`. Moreover, if you use a Profile document, you can hand day-to-day administration of the database over to somebody without Manager access to the database. However, using roles gives you finer control over the creation of forms. Also, since Profile documents don't replicate, roles gives you blanket security over multiple server replicas.

Authors and Readers Fields

As observed in Chapter 18, it is important not to confuse Authors and Readers fields. Author fields essentially refine only the Author permission. In order to edit a given document, a user with Author access must be in an Authors field or be a member of a group within the Authors field.

On the other hand, Readers fields are universal. If a document has a Readers field, only individuals or members of groups named in the field can read the document, regardless of their permission in the ACL. Of course, a user who doesn't have Reader access in the ACL won't be able to read a document even if his name is in a Readers field.

It is generally a good idea to make Authors fields multi-value fields. It is almost vital that Readers fields be multi-value, since you'll always want your Administrators group (or the name of the person or group you grant blanket administrative powers to) to have access, as well as at least one user or group of users.

It is possible, although sometimes confusing, to have multiple Authors and Readers fields. If you make extensive use of Readers fields, you might get into the practice of putting a "universal" Readers field on all of your forms. This would be a Readers field including your administrative group and probably LocalDomainServers, as well.

PART

VI

Developing
Databases

This would be an excellent use for a Shared field. You might also use a role in the field, which you can assign to as few or as many individuals or groups as you desire.

Maximum Internet Access

There's one other setting in the ACL that is important for Web applications. Toward the middle of the Advanced tab of the ACL, shown in Figure 24.11, there is a Maximum Internet Name And Password setting. This setting imposes a maximum level of access on any kind of Internet access, so it applies to POP and IMAP access to mailboxes, as well as Web access. Anyone who accesses a database through an Internet protocol is limited to the given level of access. For example, if a database has its maximum Internet access set to Author, users with Author, Editor, Designer, and Manager access will only have Author access. Like roles, the maximum Internet access level won't increase access; in the example, users with Reader access will still have Reader access. Editor is the default maximum level, so be sure to reduce it unless you want to grant people Internet access to your databases.

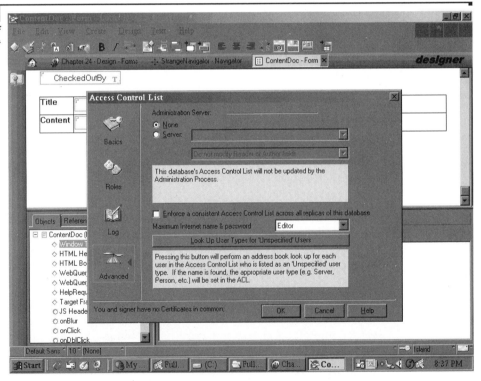

FIGURE 24.11

The Advanced tab of the Access Control List

Summary

This chapter discussed some general guidelines and cautions for developing applications in Notes. When developing applications in Notes, the best of all possible worlds is to have a development environment to use as a proving ground before moving to the production environment, where the application will actually be used. Once you do move on, it's best to move your application in the form of a template.

There are a number of measures you can take to make your application easier to use and maintain, both for you and for your users, including building an navigable interface, following programming standards, and adding Help features. Finally, Notes comes with a broad range of security features in addition to the ACL, letting you refine security on a document-by-document level.

The next chapter deals with tools and procedures you might use to get common tasks done in a database, such as structuring workflow, dealing with external data sources, modifying existing templates, and using some of the more obscure Lotus-Script classes.

PART

VI

Developing
Databases

CHAPTER 25

Tips, Tricks, and Good Ideas

Notes is an enormously complex tool that can be used to perform a broad range of tasks. It is so complex, in fact, that it can sometimes be hard to know where to begin when you need to perform a particular task. This chapter provides some direction for performing some of the more complex, powerful tasks that you may want a Notes application to perform.

This chapter is more technical than the last one, getting into specific bits of code and sample designs. It deals with ways of using Notes tools to perform a number of desirable tasks, such as

- Routing documents through a workflow process

- Communicating with other databases and data formats, including text, ODBC, DECS, and OLE automation

- Extracting useful objects from other databases and customizing templates

This chapter also uses a great deal of LotusScript, so if you're not comfortable with the language yet, you might want to review Chapter 23.

Workflow and Approval

Although it does many other things, Notes is probably best known for its ability to do workflow and approval and to pass responsibility for, and control over, data from person to person. Ironically, workflow tools aren't directly built into Notes. However, between Notes's security and messaging features, it's very easy to construct these tools if you keep a few simple principles in mind.

Of course, before you start building, you'll need to map out your workflow process. There are a number of questions you'll need to answer, such as:

- Do all documents go through the same number of people?

- Does a document go through a fixed cycle (always passing from one specific person to another), or does it vary depending on who originated the document or on the contents?

- What kind of control over a document should users have as it goes through the cycle?

- What kind of control should users have over the document routing?

- Can one user substitute for another or "force" approval?

- What should users know about documents being routed, and when should they know it?

Most workflow applications, both in and outside Notes, are built around serial workflow. In a serial-workflow Notes application, responsibility for a document or set of documents is passed from one person to another until the process is finished. Only one person at a time holds responsibility for a document. You can see a very simple serial workflow process (see Figure 25.1) in the sample database presented in Chapter 23. Responsibility for the document goes from one department head to the next in a fixed order with no exceptions or alternate routing possibilities.

FIGURE 25.1

A simple serial-workflow process

Submitted ⟶ Research ⟶ Marketing ⟶ Finance ⟶ Approved

Another (usually) simple and potentially more flexible approach to structuring workflow is to create a routing list within the document itself. Notes's capability for multi-value fields makes this relatively easy. You can prepare a form for workflow by giving it two fields: a list of future users (a multi-value field) and a field for the current user. Although it isn't strictly necessary, it's often desirable to maintain a list of past users (another multi-value field), as well, to indicate who has already dealt with the document, and perhaps even a list of approval times.

To start the document through the workflow process, you'll populate the future user's field with a list of people who need to see the document in the order that they'll need to see it in. This might be done manually, picking a number of users out of an Address dialog box, or automatically with @formulas, LotusScript, or JavaScript. Sending the document through the process is simply a matter of appending the name in the current user field to the past user field (if you're tracking past users) and moving the name at the top of the future user list to the current user field.

The form in Figure 25.2 is equipped for this kind of workflow. The user populates the FutureUsers field with a number of names and then presses the Send For Review button, which has this formula:

```
REM "Make sure the document is in edit mode if it isn't already.";
REM "If it isn't, the changes won't stick.";
@Command( [EditDocument] ; "1");
REM "Read a subset of future users into a temporary variable.";
REM "This has to be done before another value is written into the field.";
ftrusrs := @if(@Elements(FutureReviewers) > 0; @Subset(FutureUsers;
➥   1-(@Elements(FutureUsers))); "");
REM "Set field values as appropriate.  ReviewedBy gets CurrentUser
➥   added to it,
REM "CurrentUser gets the top item on the FutureUsers list, and
➥   FutureUsers gets the first item removed.";
FIELD ReviewedBy := ReviewedBy: CurrentUser;
```

```
FIELD CurrentUser := @Subset(FutureReviewers; 1);
FIELD FutureReviewers:= ftrusrs;
FIELD ApprovedDates := ApprovedDates; @Now;
REM "Send mail and close the document.";
@MailSend(CurrentUser;"";"";"Please review this document";"Please
➡    review the document and pass it on at your earliest
➡    convenience"; ""; [IncludeDoclink]);
@PostedCommand([FileSave]);
@PostedCommand([FileCloseWindow])
```

In addition to keeping track of the list of past users, this code also keeps a list of when each user passed on the document in the ApprovedDates field, a multi-value date/time field. This Action should probably have a hide-when formula that hides it when FutureUsers becomes "", or perhaps marks the document status as "Done" or "Approved" when the last user is done with it. If everybody likely to access this document has Editor access or better to the database, the Action should be given hide-when conditions that compare the user's name to the value of CurrentUser so that only the right user can approve the document and send it on its way.

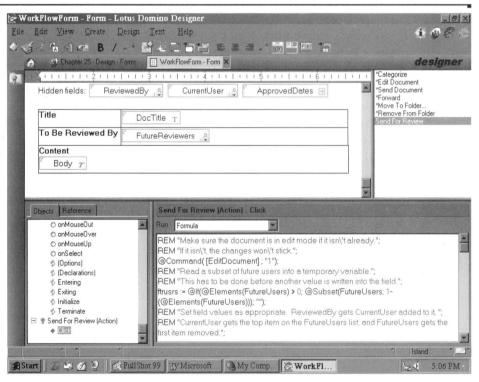

FIGURE 25.2

A serial workflow form

One of the benefits of keeping track of past users is that it becomes possible to "roll back" the workflow process, allowing the current user to send the document back to the beginning of the process or at least back to the previous user.

This Action script reverses the scheme of the previous Action, taking care to remove the last approval date, as well:

```
@Command( [EditDocument] ; "1");
revby := @if(@Elements(ReviewedBy) > 0; @Subset(ReviewedBy; 1-
➥    (@Elements(ReviewedBy))); "");
FIELD FutureUsers:= CurrentUser:FutureUsers;
FIELD CurrentUser := @Subset(ReviewedBy; 1);
FIELD ReviewedBy := revby;
appdates := @if(@Elements(ApprovedDates) > 0; @Subset(ApprovedDates;
➥    1-(@Elements(ApprovedDates))); "");
FIELD ApprovedDates := appdates;
@MailSend(CurrentUser;"";"";"Please review this document
➥    again";"Please review the document in light of my comments and
➥    pass it on again at your earliest convenience"; "";
➥    [IncludeDoclink]);
@PostedCommand([FileSave]);
@PostedCommand([FileCloseWindow])
```

The scripts creates a workflow scheme with short @formulas rather than slightly longer LotusScript programs, so they're a trifle faster than the workflow script presented in Chapter 23, although probably not so much as to make a noticeable difference. What makes this workflow scheme flexible is the lack of programmatic control over the people it goes to. For example, if you trust the users, or at least the user who starts the document through the process, you can drop the field on the form as a visible, editable field. The initial user can construct the list as appropriate, perhaps using buttons to call up the contents of fields in Profile documents to initially produce a list that can be customized. The user building the list can delete approvers if an abbreviated path is needed, or she can add names for a document that needs extra care.

The main drawback to this kind of workflow, however, is that it's not sensitive to changes in organization. While the Chapter 23 workflow machinery calls up approver names on the fly, this process gathers all its names at the beginning. If someone leaves the organization, or if somebody in the workflow path is replaced by somebody else, that person's name is not automatically replaced. Of course, it can be done fairly easily with an Agent using the @Replace function, but it doesn't maintain itself as well as the programmatic workflow mechanism.

Another concern is security. Since the list of future users is stored in the document rather than imposed from outside, a user can theoretically alter the path of a document, changing its routing mid-stream. This is both a strength and a weakness. Again, the lack of outside control makes it flexible. If a user can manually change the routing list, it is possible for the routing list to recover from the lack of automatic updating. On the other hand, this makes it far less desirable for applications requiring high security, such as those containing sensitive information or that result in large sums of money being spent (say, purchase orders or expense account tracking). A serial workflow mechanism is more appropriate when information sharing is required or, at least, acceptable.

Sooner or later, you'll be tempted to use a workflow mechanism like this with group names rather than individual names. For some organizations, it makes eminent sense. For example, *any* manager might be able to approve a proposal, or *any* member of a given department might be able to indicate that they have seen a document. More frequently, an upper-tier manager might be allowed to approve anything that a lower-tier manager can. You might also attempt parallel rather than serial workflow (see Figure 25.3), constructing a list of document approvers or reviewers and sending documents to all of them simultaneously. Like in a serial workflow process, a specific set of people work on a document, but they can do so independently of one another, unlike in a serial workflow process where they must do so one at a time.

FIGURE 25.3

Serial vs. parallel workflow

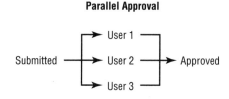

For a number of workflow applications, this might seem like the natural way to structure your workflow, but there's a significant drawback to a parallel approval scheme: Save Conflicts. Let's say that you've got a document that everybody in a department needs to read, comment on, and mark as being done with. Notifications with doclinks (for a Notes-only application) or hypertext links (for a Web application) are sent to everyone in the department simultaneously. If members of the group are paying attention to their e-mail (and, if they've got Notes Minder running, they probably are), a number of them will open the document simultaneously, or so close to simultaneously as to make no difference. They will then work on and save the document one after another, creating a sudden storm of Save Conflicts.

One way of dealing with the problem is to incorporate parallel elements into what is essentially serial workflow. You could make everybody aware of the document simultaneously, but use Author fields to pass the power to actually make changes from one person to another in a serial fashion. Of course, there are a few drawbacks to this. One of them is that it could be a bit confusing. Users might have trouble distinguishing between being told that a document is available and being told that it's their turn to edit it. It also only works if users have Author permission to the database, which may not be the case for the application in question.

You might also adopt a check-in–check-out scheme like the one presented in the previous chapter. Only one person has the power to work on any given document at a time, but that power can pass quickly between people. If the workflow process only involves approval or denial of the document, acknowledgment of having read it, or similarly simple input, you might also try tracking workflow elsewhere. You could provide users with a button that would send a message to a mail-in database or keep a corresponding Approvals List document that is written to with Agents, using the CodeLock functions so that no more than one person at a time can edit it (see Chapter 26 for more on code locking).

No matter how you structure the regular workflow, it would be wise for the designer to consider the possibility of needing to circumvent the workflow model. After all, real-world business processes are rarely as clean as theoretical models. For example, an urgent document might need the approval of a manager who happens to be out on vacation that week or just out sick for the day. You may want to provide additional tools to database administrators so that they can help documents through the process under the direction of senior managers if the need arises. For form Actions like the ones presented in this chapter, which do not themselves pay attention to who is performing them, all it should take is the creation of a new role for administrators that gives them access to the regular workflow tools at any time. More complex workflow tools, where the code involves checks to make sure that it is being run by the right person, may require more sophisticated solutions that allow some users to bypass the usual restrictions.

Notifying Users

Something that you'll need to consider when setting up your workflow is notification. There are several methods you can use to alert users to tasks they need to perform and documents they need to review. Most of them involve Notes's ability to send programmatically composed e-mail messages.

Since Notes can potentially mail *any* document (create a SendTo field, populate it, and use the Send method in LotusScript or use the @Mailsend formula without parameters), it is possible to notify users of documents that they need to review simply by sending the documents directly to their mailboxes. Meeting Invitations, which can be regarded as a kind of workflow application, work this way. One user creates a special document and sends it to others, who use specialized controls to respond to or modify it. You can do something similar with serial workflow applications, as well, routing a document among users, then mailing it back to a mail-in database that holds finished documents.

This kind of notification has the advantage of making data and tools for manipulating it immediately available to users, who need to look no further than their mailboxes. However, the speed and flexibility comes with a number of drawbacks:

- This scheme only works if your users have Notes mail. If you use Notes only for applications (rare in organizations using Notes clients, but not so rare if Notes is used primarily for Web applications), you'll have to find other methods of notification.

- As you create customized workflow forms, you'll have to find a way to get those forms into the users' mail databases. You will have to add the form to the mail database template, which may cause system administrators to balk. Or, the document must be created with the Store Form In Document option checked, which will increase the size of the messages. This option can cause problems if you later change your design.

- If you mail documents directly to users, you lose significant control over them. Without additional elaborate code that communicates with a central database, you can't tell whose hands the document is in at any given time, nor can you force the document along if the current user has taken too long to deal with it. Perhaps worst of all, if it's in a user's mailbox, it can be inadvertently deleted.

Mailing the document itself rather than notification can be very convenient and effective, but should be used carefully.

The workflow schemes demonstrated here use far less elaborate e-mail notifications. Instead, they use doclinks to provide immediate access to the document in question. If the mail message has a suitably descriptive subject line and body text, this is a very effective form of notification. It lets the user know what he needs to do and points directly to the document that needs attention.

Of course, doclinked e-mail has certain drawbacks. For the doclink to function, the user must be using a Notes client for mail rather than a plain POP or IMAP mail client. And, the target document must be in a database that the Notes client has access to, making it unsuitable for applications where users often operate detached from the Domino server.

The limitation of doclinks to Notes mail is a point in favor of Web-based applications. If you construct your application to work over the Web, you can have it send out automatically constructed URLs rather than doclinks. Many mail programs, including Notes itself, automatically treat anything starting with *http://* as a hyperlink, which means that you can extend the power of direct linking to your Domino application to a variety of mail packages, as well.

Notification may also be a problem if your users are already deluged with e-mail. As e-mail becomes a more and more common tool, busy people may be snowed in by a blizzard of easily sent electronic messages. People in your organization may decide that they don't want to take advantage of Notes's capacity to automatically generate meaningful mail messages on the grounds that they get too much mail already, and more messages would just cause clutter.

If you're not going to send mail notifications, you will need to organize your database so that it is very easy for users to find the documents that are relevant to them. Categorized views are one possibility. You could create a view of pending documents that are sorted and categorized by the name of the current approver, and that open with all categories collapsed by default. Users can go down the list until they find their own names, expand that category, and take appropriate actions. If there is a small pool of approvers, you may be able to educate the users to check the view regularly to find the documents that they should deal with. But, as Figure 25.4 illustrates, if there are more than a few potential approvers, that quickly becomes an unwieldy solution.

You could also use a view that shows users only their own documents. A view using a selection formula like SELECT *fieldname* = @UserName should do the trick, but there are limitations here, as well. Because @Username behaves strangely in public view selection formulas (search the Designer Help for "@UserName" for more detail, but not much more), you'll need to make it either Shared, Private On First Use; Shared, Desktop Private On First Use; or Private. The problem there is that views that become Private aren't maintainable. Once a user has accessed a Public view that becomes Private, you can't make changes to their view, which can become a problem if you ever need to change the view's design.

However, there is an intermediate step. Using LotusScript rather than @formulas, you can create a mail message that contains doclinks for a number of documents. Instead of sending four or five messages, each with one doclink, you can send one document containing a comprehensive slate of doclinks. To do this, you'll need to learn two new classes: the document collection and the newsletter.

A *document collection* is just that, a collection of documents within a database. You can think of it as sort of a temporary virtual view. It is similar to a view in that it is created according to conditions that may be expressed in @formulas. However, those conditions are provided in the course of the operation of a script. So far, the scripts that you have seen have depended on the existence of a view. Document collections can free you of that, letting you call up large sets of documents on the fly.

FIGURE 25.4

A very large categorized view

A document collection is created by using one of the various search methods that are available for a Notes database object. This is analogous to searching a database with the Search Bar, either indexed or not. The next example uses the Search method, although there are several other methods. One of the methods, FTIndex, uses full-text indexing with all the speed boost that that implies. However, it should be used with caution. If the database's full-text index is not set for immediate updating, the search could fail to find appropriate documents. Every method for producing a document collection must be provided with search conditions that should be expressed as @formulas that are appropriate for selecting documents for a view. The example here, appropriate for use in a scheduled Agent, was built to implement a corporate e-mail policy that deletes messages from the database that have been there for six months or more.

```
Dim s as New NotesSession
Dim db_MyMail as NotesDatabase
Dim dc_OldDocs as NotesDocumentCollection
```

```
Dim str_Conditions as String
Dim dat_SixMonthsAgo as NotesDateTime

' This assumes that the code is being run within a database.  If it were
'being run from outside, we'd use the Open method on a New database.
Set db_MyMail = s.CurrentDatabase

' The NotesDateTime is a complex date/time object, and one worth
➡    looking up in the Help.  We're creating a time value of "now"
➡    and decrementing it by six months.
Set dat_SixMonthsAgo = New NotesDateTime(Now)
Call dat_SixMonthsAgo.AdjustMonth(-6)

' This starts to assemble the selection criteria.  We only want to delete
'mail messages, which means we're deleting documents made with certain
'forms or, for documents coming on through the Internet, no form at all.
str_Conditions = "((Form = ""Memo"") | (Form = ""Reply"") | (Form =
➡    ""ReplyWithHistory""))"
str_Conditions = str_Conditions + " & (@Created <= ([" +
➡    dat_SixMonthsAgo.DateOnly + "]))"

'Now assemble the collection.  The Search method wants a condition,
'a date (if there is a date, it only includes documents created or modified
'on or after that date), and a maximum number of documents to return
'(0 means all documents that apply.
Set dc_OldDocs = db_MyMail.Search(str_Conditions, Nothing, 0)

'This line deletes the documents.
Call dc_OldDocs.Remove
```

A *newsletter* is a special Notes object summarizing a document collection. Much like a Reply With History inherits a mail message into the message body, a newsletter can be rendered into a document containing either links to documents or the entire contents of the documents themselves. So, to take the previous example, what if instead of deleting the old documents we wanted to do something less draconian? The users would prefer that a list of documents over six months old be mailed to them. Instead of the last line with the Remove method, we might have something more complex. We could create a newsletter, turn it into a document with a bunch of links, and send that as a notification to the user. If you send a newsletter, the user can review the documents and delete them more selectively. The code might look like this:

```
' Dim the additional objects, of course
```

PART

VI

Developing
Databases

```
Dim doc_Newsletter as NotesDocument
Dim nlttr as NotesNewsletter

' Make a newsletter out of the document collection
Set nlttr = new NotesNewsletter(dc_OldDocs)
' When we turn this into a list of doclinks, the SubjectItemName will attach
'a subject line to each link using the document field we name.
nlttr.SubjectItemName = "Subject"
'Turn the newsletter into a document
Set doc_Newsletter = nlttr.FormatMsgWithDoclinks(db_MyMail)
'Assign some other mail items and send.
doc_Newsletter.Subject = "Six-month-old messages"
doc_Newsletter.SendTo = s.CommonUserName
doc_Newsletter.Form = "Memo"
Call doc_Newsletter.Send(False)
```

Once received, the document will look something like Figure 25.5. The set of links allows the user to check all of her old documents and deal with them herself.

FIGURE 25.5

A newsletter sent as mail

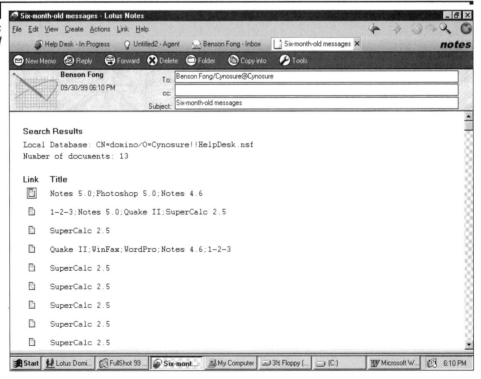

Using External Data in Notes

As the discussion on whether or not to use Notes indicated, there are tasks that you may not want to perform with Notes. You may want the flexible number crunching of a spreadsheet program, the elaborate manipulation of structured data provided by a relational database, or the near-universal portability of plain text. You may also have to develop in an environment where other databases and applications are already well established. However, that doesn't mean that you can't use Notes. Using some advanced techniques, mostly LotusScript, you can read data from a wide variety of external files and even write data back to them. Properly used, you can integrate your Notes applications with other kinds of data, giving your organization not just a single application, but an integrated system for sharing and using all kinds of data.

Notes and Text

Plain ASCII text is, without a doubt, the single most portable format for electronic information. Plain text can be dealt with by just about any computer platform and a huge range of software from spreadsheets, to databases, to just about every programming language worth speaking of. In Chapter 11, you've already seen that you can do a lot by importing text directly into Notes fields and views. As you might expect, Notes also provides you with programmatic ways of dealing with external text files.

Dealing with files is a little different from most of the rest of LotusScript programming. From seeing how Notes deals with it's own internal documents and other database objects, you might expect to create some sort of "external file" object and perform methods on that. However, that's not the case. Dealing directly with external files is about the only place in LotusScript where you will work mainly with statements rather than objects, methods, and properties.

To open a file, use the Open statement with a path to a file and a number to identify it. External files opened with the Open statement aren't identified by object variables (unlike a document, which can be identified by the variable *doc_responsedocument*). Instead, they need to be given a number as a "handle." For example, the line Open "C:\sample.txt" As #1 will prepare the C:\sample.txt file to be read and written to. When operations are performed on it, the instructions will incorporate *#1*. Usually, you can just pick an arbitrary number, but you may want to use the FreeFile() function to pick a number for you. FreeFile will return an integer not currently being used to identify an open file. Using FreeFile is a very, very good idea if you can't tell in advance exactly how many files a script is going to open.

NOTE The path to open a file doesn't have to be an absolute file path from the computer's root directory. You can use a file path from the root of the drive (for example, `d:\lotus\domino\data\file.txt`) or relative to the Notes or Domino directory (`data/file.txt`).

The Open command can take a number of parameters to limit what can be done with the file it opens. These options can be confusing because they overlap somewhat. And it's quite easy to write a legal command that will always produce an error. An Open command can take three types of parameters:

For   This parameter determines how you can work with the file. The choices are Output (writing to the file), Input (reading from the file), Random (both reading from and writing to the file), Append (writing to the file but adding items on rather than replacing the current contents), and Binary. (In Binary mode, you can, theoretically, open any file, like a `.gif` image or a 1-2-3 spreadsheet with the Open command, but this requires an intimate knowledge of specific internal file structures, so we won't be getting into its use.) If you don't specify a For parameter, Notes will attempt to use Random. If the file you're trying to open doesn't exist, Random, Append, Output, and Binary will create a file of the specified name. (Be careful; anything but Append will replace an existing document!) And trying to open a nonexistent file with Input selected as the For parameter will cause an error.

Access   This is where it gets a bit confusing. The options are Read, Read Write, and Write. If you choose Read, you'll only be able to read from the file. If you choose Write, you'll only be able to write to it. And if you choose Read Write, you can do both. Notes will default to an Access mode appropriate to the For condition (Read for Input, Write for Output or Append, Read Write for Random and Binary). However, you can construct a contradictory command like `Open "C:\textfile.txt" For Output Access Read As #1`, and the debugger won't notice the contradiction because it is actually a legally structured command. But you will get an error when you try to run the code. If for some reason you do decide to use Access parameters, be very careful about them.

Lock   Here, we return to sensibility. This parameter controls the access of other programs and other computers to the file while your program is using it. The choices are Shared, Lock Read, Lock Write, and Lock Read Write. Shared, the default option, allows others to read or write to the file while your script is working with it. The other lock options prevent the named operation. Lock options probably don't matter if the Agent will run on computers disconnected from a network. But if other people can potentially work with the same files as your script, you may want to use at least Lock Write.

Once you have opened the file, the general technique is to work through it line by line, processing the contents or adding data to it one line at a time. However, it's also possible to jump around the document, reading and writing to specific positions in the text.

To write data to a file, use the Write, Print, or Put statements. Print and Write should only be used on files used for Output or Append. While Put should be used on files used for Random. Write and Print statements take the file number and a series of variables or string or numeric values. Each statement writes that information to the file in its own line. The difference between Write and Print is that Write puts each "entry" in the line in quotes and separated by commas, while Print does not. So these lines:

```
Write #1, "First Statement", "Second Statement"
Print #1, "Third Statement", "Fourth Statement"
```

would create text that looks like this:

```
"First Statement", "Second Statement"
Third Statement Fourth Statement
```

If you want to create easily human-readable text, Print is probably the way to go. While Write creates neatly delimited text for programmatic use. The Put statement requires a file number, a line, and a single variable or value. The value is written to the file at the designated line.

To read data, use the Get or Input statements. Like Write and Print, Input requires a file number and a string of variables. The statement will fill values directly into the variables you provide according to a specific scheme. Notes takes it upon itself to divide the data into individual values, using spaces and commas as value separators and ignoring quotation marks around strings. The first piece of data is filled into the first variable you provide, the second piece into the second variable, and so on. For example, this line:

```
"Bob Smith", 500 Green 298-28-3872,4/27/56
```

read by this line:

```
Input #1, str_name, int_DeptCode, str_color, str_SSN
```

would return these values:

```
str_name = Bob Smith
int_DeptCode = 500
str_color = Green
str_SSN = 298-28-3872
```

The final value (4/27/56) is discarded because there's no variable to put it in.

PART

VI

Developing
Databases

This works reasonably well for comma-delimited files or files where the values are separated by spaces, but not so well for other delimiters. For example, you may have to deal with files where values are separated by tabs or the pipe character (|). In these cases, you'll need to get into the text value and separate it into individual values yourself. To do that, you'll need a variant of the Input command: *Line Input*. Line Input takes a file number and a variable name, but rather than bringing in data and dividing it up according to its own scheme, it reads an entire line and lets you process the text as you want to.

The next example does just that in order to create a batch of Contact documents for a personal address book. The data comes in a tab-delimited file, with one "record" on each line. Each record holds name, address, and phone number data. Normally, bringing regularly formatted text of this kind into a Notes database would be accomplished by importing into a view using a .col file. However, in this particular case, that won't be sufficient to the task. The source from which the data was exported had different records for individuals' home and office addresses. Notes can hold both personal and business information in the same Contact document. But to join personal and business information into the same document, the data has to be processed through LotusScript.

The text files follow this format:

```
Home/Office  Firstaname  Lastname  Address  City  State  Zip  Phone
```

The first "field" in each line is the word *Home* or *Office*, indicating what kind of address it is. The code, suitable for a Run Once From Actions Menu Agent, opens a text file named `addresses.txt`, reads through it one line at a time, and divides it into individual entries, putting the values into an array. Chr$(9) is the tab character, so this script expects tab-delimited text.

This script takes advantage of three functions we haven't dealt with before, but they're very useful when dealing with text: `Instr`, `Right`, and `Left`. `Instr` returns a number giving the position of a given character within a string. `Right` and `Left` are much like the @Right and @Left functions. They return a batch of characters from a string counting from either the right or left end of the string.

The following script opens a text document and reads from it line-by-line. It takes each line and chops it up into its tab-delimited components. Then it takes those components and creates documents using the data from the text file to populate fields.

```
(Declarations)

Dim s as NotesSession
Dim db_MyAddresses as NotesDatabase
Dim vw_MyContacts as NotesView
Dim doc_Contact as NotesDocument
```

```
Dim str_theline as String
Dim rightpart as String
Dim leftpart as String
Dim newtop As Integer
Dim fullname As String
Dim Wordparts as Variant

Sub Initialize

On Error Resume Next

Set s = New Notessession

' Get our hands on the Contacts view.

Set db_MyAddresses = s.CurrentDatabase
Set vw_MyContacts = db_MyAddresses.GetView("Contacts")

' Define an array to hold the parts of the string

Redim Wordparts (0) As String

' Open the file and start reading, a line at a time

   Open "addresses.txt" For Input As #1

   Do Until Eof(1)
      Line Input #1, str_theline

' Go through the line, breaking off one tab-delimited segment at a time.
' Each segment gets put into an array, which expands to fit the data

      Do While Instr(str_theline, Chr$(9)) > 0
         limitpoint = Instr(str_theline, Chr$(9))
         newtop = Ubound(Wordparts) + 1
         Redim Preserve Wordparts (0 To newtop) As String
         leftpart = Left(str_theline, limitpoint - 1)
         rightpart = Right(str_theline, Len(str_theline) - limitpoint)
         Wordparts(Ubound(wordparts)-1) = leftpart
         str_theline = rightpart
```

```
      Loop
      wordparts(Ubound(wordparts)) = str_theline

       ' Once the array is full, search for a matching Contact document.

fullname = wordparts(2) + ", " + wordparts(1)
doc_Contact = vw_MyContacts.GetDocumentByKey(fullname, True)

      If doc_Contact Is Nothing Then

 ' If there's no document, create one and fill in the "key" values of
➥    first and last name.

set doc_Contact = new Notesdocument(db_MyAddresses)

doc_Contact.FirstName = wordparts(1)
doc_Contact.LastName = wordparts(2)

 ' After the "key" values are set, the rest is identical to what
 ' we'd have to do to an existing document, so rather than writing
 ' the routine twice, we'll use a subroutine.

SetDocVals

Else

 ' Otherwise, just fill in the values.

SetDocVals

End If

 ' Clear out the array for the next loop

      Redim wordparts(0)
   Loop
   Close #1
   Msgbox("Done!")
End Sub
```

```
Sub SetDocVals

   If Wordparts(0) = "Home" Then

' If it's a "home" record, set the appropriate values.

      doc_Contact.StreetAddress = wordparts(3)
      doc_Contact.City = wordparts(4)
      doc_Contact.State = wordparts(5)
      doc_Contact.Zip = wordparts(6)
      doc_Contact.HomePhone = wordparts(7)

   Else

' Otherwise, set values for the office fields.

      doc_Contact.OfficeStreetAddress = wordparts(3)
      doc_Contact.OfficeCity = wordparts(4)
      doc_Contact.OfficeState = wordparts(5)
      doc_Contact.OfficeZip = wordparts(6)
      doc_Contact.Phone = wordparts(7)

   End If

' No matter what changes have been made, save them.

   Call doc_Contact.Save(false, false)
End Sub
```

Notes and ODBC

Notes is a peculiarity in the world of databases. Its document-centered approach, which allows it to deal quickly and flexibly with unstructured batches of data, is a far cry from the heavily structured table-based world of relational databases. Nevertheless, you may be able to use Notes to get into your organization's structured data from databases like Oracle, DB2, Microsoft Access, and SQL Server via an ODBC (Open Database Connectivity, a standard for communication between databases and across platforms) connection, and use that highly structured data along with less structured Notes data. With ODBC, you can use data that is more structured and easier to navigate than what you'll find in text files. With ODBC in LotusScript, you also return to a more object-oriented approach to doing things.

PART

VI

Developing
Databases

Before going into specifics, we'll briefly address what you need to do outside of Notes to make it work. To use a database through ODBC, you must create a DSN (Data Source Name), which is a handle by which your computer identifies the database. At the very least, creating a DSN requires a name by which to identify the database and the file location. You may also be able to provide a default username and password and other information specific to the connection or the type of database. The specifics of how to set up a DSN and what information it requires vary considerably from platform to platform and from file type to file type, so you'll have to consult the documentation for the platform in question. However, once the DSN is set up, *any* ODBC-compliant program can draw data from that database using SQL (structured Query Language), an industry standard language for drawing information from structured data sources.

ODBC and @Formulas

Three @formulas can take advantage of an ODBC connection: @DBLookup, @DBColumn, and @DBCommand. You may already be familiar with @DBLookup and @DBColumn from working with formulas. Within a Notes database, @DBLookup and @DBColumn can retrieve either a single value appearing in a view or folder (or, under some circumstances, a list of values), or a whole column of values. However, with somewhat different syntax, these commands can return values from a query or table from any database that you can reach through an ODBC connection. @DBCommand goes a step farther, retrieving not just a value or column, but the contents of an entire table or query.

As an example of how you might use one of these @functions, imagine a company that has a relational database holding frequently updated stock price data. The company also has a Notes database containing documents detailing a number of corporations. Each document contains a history of one corporation, including contact information. A periodic Agent could be used to update each corporation's document with stock price data. The relational database has a table named StockData, with the corporation's ticker symbol as its key (the field in the table is named Symbol), and a field named CurrentPrice, which holds the most recent stock price. The Notes database's corporation documents have a field named CorpSymb, which contains the ticker symbol. The formula to retrieve the current stock price from an ODBC connection named Stockprices would look like this:

```
@DBLookup("ODBC": "NoCache"; "Stockprices"; "username"; "password";
➡   "StockData"; "CurrentPrice"; "Symbol"; CorpSymb)
```

This assumes that "username" and "password" are valid identifying information for the ODBC database. External databases aren't handled by Notes security, so you'll have to take care of that separately. The database that lies behind the DSN Stockprices happens to be an Access database. If another type of database is being used, the @DBLookup might look slightly different.

ODBC and LotusScript

The @functions are limited in a number of ways. First, since they're @functions, they can't be used inside any kind of looping or branching. Second, they can only retrieve values. You can use the @functions to read ODBC data sources, but not to delete, edit, or alter records. However, LotusScript has none of those limitations. LotusScript has a wide range of properties and methods allowing you to create, navigate, and edit ODBC data sets and data sources.

To use ODBC in script, you'll need to put the line `UseLSX "*LSXODBC"` in the (Options) section of the object your script appears in. This loads certain libraries necessary to run ODBC queries in LotusScript, which are not loaded otherwise. If you don't load these libraries, LotusScript's ODBC classes won't work.

You'll also use the three ODBC-related classes: `ODBCConnection`, `ODBCQuery`, and `ODBCRecordSet`. You'll use these classes in that order. *ODBCConnection* represents a connection from Notes to a DSN, including security information such as username and password. *ODBCQuery* represents a query definition, including both the SQL code for the query and the name of the connection to use. *ODBCRecordSet* represents the results of the query once it has been run. You'll create each of them as you would any other new Notes object (`Dim` *objectname* `as` *objecttype* and `Set` *objectname* `= New` *objecttype*, or `Dim` *objectname* `as New` *objecttype*) and use them to run a query. First, use the `ODBCConnection`'s ConnectTo method to pick an ODBC DSN. Next, make the `ODBCQuery`'s SQL property equal to a string containing a valid SQL query and set its Connection property equal to the `ODBCConnection` object. Finally, set the `ODBCResultSet`'s Query property to the `ODBCQuery` and call the Execute method to run the query.

Once you do that, assuming that you have constructed a valid connection and query, you'll be able to use various `ODBCResultSet` methods and properties to navigate through the query results and use the values it holds in your Notes application. If you've dealt programmatically with data sets in VBA, the methods of the `ODBCResultSet` class will be hauntingly familiar, although not identical. Use the FirstRow, LastRow, NextRow, and PrevRow methods to do most of your navigation. If, for example, you wanted to loop through the query results and process the information one row at a time, you'd use `Call` *variablename*`.FirstRow` and set up a Do loop with *variablename*`.NextRow` as the last command in the loop. The condition ending the Do loop should be `Until` *variablename*`.IsEndOfData`. Or, if you wanted to go through the data, you could replace the FirstRow and NextRow methods and the IsEndOfData condition with LastRow, PrevRow, and IsBeginOfData.

Once you've designated a row (and you must use at least one of the row navigation methods before you can retrieve values), you may take data from that row. You can retrieve values using the GetValue method by providing either a field name or column number. For example, x = *variablename*.GetValue(1) sets the variable *x* equal to the value in the first column of the current row. The equation x = *variablename*.Get-Value("Address") sets *x* equal to whatever is in the Address field of the current row.

The previous four methods allow either fast and crude navigation (with FirstRow and LastRow) or slow and precise navigation (with NextRow and PrevRow) between rows of your result set. Usually, that's not a problem, but you may want to jump around the result set a bit more in search of specific data. To do this, you can use the LocateRow method. LocateRow allows you to jump to the next row in the record set that fits up to three conditions. Simply provide it with column names or numbers and desired values. For example, Call *variablename*.LocateRow(1, "Green", "Size", "Large") moves to the first row after the current position where the value in the first column is Green, and the value in the Size field is Large. (As you can see, column number and column name can be used simultaneously.) With careful use of the LocateRow method, you can effectively perform a selection query on the result set that is returned by the query.

Consider the following code:

```
resultset.FirstRow
Do Until resultset.IsEndOfData
Call resultset.LocateRow("SomeColumn", "SomeValue")
' Some processing code might go here.
Loop
```

Each pass through the loop moves from one row, where the value of SomeColumn is SomeValue, to the next. Therefore, the code used to process the "current" row will only operate on those rows, not on every row in the result set. However, LocateRow only moves forward, not backward. For example, if the previous code began with resultset.LastRow rather than resultset.FirstRow, it would immediately exit the loop and process no rows. There would be no subsequent rows fitting the conditions primarily by virtue of there being no subsequent rows.

Quick and Dirty ODBC

Here's more code to tuck away somewhere. This is the bare minimum that you'll need to get to the first record of the first row of a record set drawn from an ODBC connection. It declares the bare minimum of objects, substantiates them, opens a connection, and moves to the first row of a data set.

```
(Options)


Uselsx "*LSXODBC"
```

Continued

CONTINUED

```
(Declarations)


Dim con_thedata As odbcconnection
Dim qry_thequery As ODBCQuery
Dim rs_results As ODBCResultSet
Dim res_results As ODBCResultSet
Dim var_value As Variant
' var_value is being declared as a variant for demonstration only.
' It could be any simple data type, depending on the value of the
' data type of the "key" column in your database query.



Sub Initialize


Set con_thedata = New odbcconnection
Set qry_thequery = New ODBCQuery
Set rs_results = New ODBCResultSet
con_thedata.ConnectTo("Your DSN Here")


' If you need a username and password for your ODBC data source,
' the previous line would look like this:
' Call con_thedata.ConnectTo("Your DSN Here", "username", "password")


Set qry_thequery.Connection = con_thedata
```

(In the next line, *Your SQL Here* should be replaced by an actual SQL statement.)

```
qry_thequery.SQL = "Your SQL Here"
Set res_results.Query = qry_thequery
res_results.Execute
res_results.FirstRow
var_value = res_results.GetValue(1)
```

Unless you're working in an exceptional environment, it's a good idea to limit your use of ODBC-related commands to Agents running on a server or on a few reliable client computers, and to let them run on off-peak hours. To function successfully, ODBC formulas and Agents need to rely on resources that cannot be controlled from within Notes. ODBC commands must refer to a named DSN, which may not be configured on the client machine, and expect to communicate with a specific database, which the client machine may not have access to. You should, at least, have control over the server's configuration. Also, you will almost certainly want to make sure that the DSNs you use are system DSNs, not user DSNs.

Error Handling and ODBC

You learned basic error handling in Chapter 24. When working with ODBC classes, standard error-handling techniques still apply. However, the ODBC classes have some additional error-related methods of their own. The ODBC process itself may return error messages. Those messages aren't available through the `Err` and `Error` functions, but they are available through the objects themselves.

With `ODBCConnection`, `ODBCQuery`, and `ODBCRecordSet`, you can use the *GetError*, *GetErrorMessage*, and *GetExtendedErrorMessage* methods to retrieve error information. GetError retrieves an integer value that also corresponds to a string constant. (Check the Designer Help for a full list.) GetErrorMessage retrieves a corresponding brief description. GetExtendedErrorMessage retrieves a longer, more detailed message. But, be cautious. These methods produce a value even if there is no error. If an ODBC method is successfully performed, the GetError message will return a value of 500. You can test for that value or the corresponding constant DBstsSUCCESS. However, all other values are actual errors.

Since an ODBC error is just as much an error as any other, you can combine the ODBC classes' native errors with the generic LotusScript error functions. If you use error handling in a script with ODBC classes, you might try an error-handling routine like this:

```
If Not (connectionvariable.GetError = 500) then
    Msgbox connectionvariable.GetErrormessage & " " &
➡    connectionvariable.GetExtendedErrorMessage, , "ODBC Error on
➡    line " & Cstr(Erl)
If Not (queryvariable.GetError = DBstsSUCCESS) then
    Msgbox queryvariable.GetErrormessage & " " &
➡    queryvariable.GetExtendedErrorMessage, , "ODBC Error on line "
➡    & Cstr(Erl)
If Not (resultsetvariable.GetError = 500) then
    Msgbox resultsetvariable.GetErrormessage & " " &
➡    resultsetvariable.GetExtendedErrorMessage, , "ODBC Error on
➡    line " & Cstr(Erl)
```

```
Else
    Msgbox "Error #" & Cstr(Err) &   ": " & Error, , "Error on line " & Cstr(Erl)
End If
```

Simulating Relational Tables in Notes

The main drawback of ODBC is that its versatility comes at the price of performance. ODBC connections are not known for being high-speed. It takes time to open a connection, run the query, move through the data set, and so on. Therefore, for performance reasons, you might want to limit your use of ODBC formulas to occasional Agents rather than computed and computed-for-display fields.

But don't let the performance factor discourage you from bringing relational database data into your Notes applications. Probably the best strategy for getting relational data into a Notes database is to get it and convert it into Notes documents. If you can populate a view with Notes documents containing relational database data, you'll have a central reservoir of data that you can reference with @DBLookups and all the other methods of getting data from one part of a Notes database to another.

To make the view-as-table strategy work, you'll need three things: a view, an Agent, and an SQL query. You should model the view as closely as possible after the intended results of the SQL query. Each field returned in the query should have a corresponding column in the view. Although Notes doesn't have primary keys like relational databases do, you should have a column in your view that you would be using as a key if it were a relational database table. Sort the view by that field. For convenience, you should probably make your "key" the first column. Since @DBLookups and @DBColumns don't have to pay attention to column headings, you don't, strictly speaking, need to label them. However, it's a very good idea to give columns a good descriptive heading anyway since this will make it easier for you to find the appropriate columns later when you write your @formulas. It's also a good idea to number the columns so that you don't have to count through them to figure out that, say, price is column 11. The view selection conditions can be anything appropriate to uniquely identify documents that your Agent will create. For example, you may create a field (say, AppearInLookupView) that marks the document's inclusion in the view, or you might rely on the form used to create the field as the selection condition for the view.

The Stock Prices view, illustrated in Figure 25.6, is an example of a view structured for lookups. The view will hold documents with stock price information. The view will display the ticker symbol, the corporation name, the day's starting price, the day's high, the day's low, the current price, and the volume traded that day. The company's ticker symbol and the corporation name are both unique (that is, not shared by any other company), so they'd both make good keys. However, the ticker symbol is shorter, so it will get used for this example. The view's selection formula looks for the form a document was created with: SELECT Form = "RelationalDBData".

PART

VI

Developing
Databases

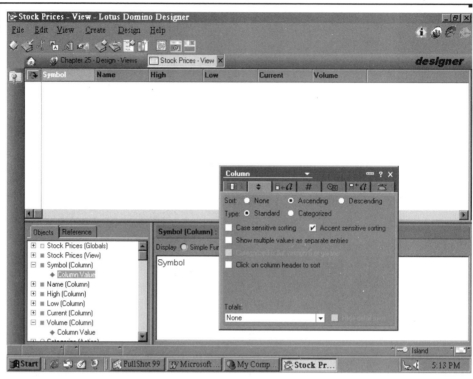

FIGURE 25.6

The Stock Prices view

The Agent is more complex. In order to synchronize the contents of the view with the contents of the table, it must accomplish these tasks in more or less this order:

- Open an ODBC connection and run a query to get the necessary data.

- Go through the record set, one row at a time.

- For each record, check for documents in the mock table view. If there's a record with the appropriate key value, update the data fields in the document. If not, create a new document, filling fields with data from the row.

- If any existing documents aren't updated, they must represent records that no longer exist in the relational database query. Therefore, after going through the entire record set, remove any documents that weren't updated on this run-through. Since the update process in the previous step only updates one document with a given key value, this ensures that inadvertently created duplicates are removed, keeping key values unique. Notes does not inherently support unique key values in the way that relational databases do, but this script at least approximates that capability.

An Agent to populate the Stock Prices view might look like the following example. You should recognize elements of the first section as being adapted from the quick and dirty ODBC code presented earlier. Once the script fetches a data set from the ODBC data source, it starts to cycle through it, one row at a time. Using the GetDocumentByKey method, it searches for a Notes document matching the current row in the data set. If a document exists, a set of fields is updated. If not, the script creates a new document and sets values accordingly. Finally, after the data set is finished, any documents not updated this time around (which is to say, any documents for which there were no records in the record set) are deleted.

```
(Options)


Option Public
Option Explicit


Uselsx "*LSXODBC"


(Declarations)


Dim con_thedata As ODBCConnection
Dim qry_thequery As ODBCQuery
Dim rs_results As ODBCResultSet
Dim s_currentsession As NotesSession
Dim db_thisDatabase As Notesdatabase
Dim res_results As ODBCResultSet
Dim doc_RecordDoc As Notesdocument
Dim vw_dataview As Notesview
Dim str_stocksymbol As String
Dim str_runtime As String
Dim int_doccount As Long
Dim int_currentdoc As Long


Sub Initialize

    ' Create new objects where necessary and point to the correct view.

    Set con_thedata = New ODBCConnection
    Set qry_thequery = New ODBCQuery
    Set res_results = New ODBCResultSet
    Set s_currentsession = New NotesSession
```

PART

VI

Developing
Databases

```
       ' Get the time the agent starts running and feed it into a
➡      variable.  We'll use this later to indicate the
       ' time individual documents were updated.

    str_runtime = Now

       ' Connect to the database, create a query, and execute it.

    Set db_thisDatabase = s_currentsession.CurrentDatabase
    Set vw_dataview = db_thisDatabase.GetView("StockPrices")
    con_thedata.ConnectTo("StockPrices")
    Set qry_thequery.Connection = con_thedata
    qry_thequery.SQL = "SELECT * FROM StockPrices;"
    Set res_results.Query = qry_thequery
    res_results.Execute

 ' Start with the first row and start looping

    Call res_results.FirstRow

    Do Until res_results.IsEndOfData

          ' Get the key value from the current row and look for a
➡      related document.

        str_stocksymbol = res_results.GetValue(1)
        Set doc_RecordDoc=vw_dataview.GetDocumentByKey(str_stocksymbol, True)

          ' If there isn't a document with the key value, create one
➡      and fill in all the fields using the
          ' current row's data.

        If doc_RecordDoc Is Nothing Then
            Set doc_RecordDoc = New NotesDocument(db_thisDatabase)
            With doc_RecordDoc
               .Form = "RelationalDBData"
               .Symbol = res_results.GetValue(1)
               .CorporationName = res_results.GetValue(2)
               .Start = res_results.GetValue(3)
```

```
                    .High = res_results.GetValue(4)
                    .Low = res_results.GetValue(5)
                    .Current = res_results.GetValue(6)
                    .Volume = res_results.GetValue(7)
                    .LastUpdated =  str_runtime
                End With


            ' If there is a document, update all the values and note
➡    when it was last updated.

        Else
            doc_RecordDoc.CorporationName = res_results.GetValue(2)
            doc_RecordDoc.Start = res_results.GetValue(3)
            doc_RecordDoc.High = res_results.GetValue(4)
            doc_RecordDoc.Low = res_results.GetValue(5)
            doc_RecordDoc.Current = res_results.GetValue(6)
            doc_RecordDoc.Volume = res_results.GetValue(7)
            doc_RecordDoc.LastUpdated = str_runtime
        End If
        Call doc_RecordDoc.Save(True,True)


        ' This is where the loop ends.  We have to be sure to move on
➡    to the next row or else we'll have an
        ' infinite loop on our hands.

        res_results.NextRow
    Loop


    ' The Close method "puts away" the result set, letting you use the
➡    variable for a different result set later,
    ' if you so desire.

    res_results.Close


    ' Now it's time to clean up the view by getting rid of the
➡    documents that weren't updated in the
    ' current run.  Loop through the view and count the documents.

    Set doc_RecordDoc = vw_dataview.GetFirstDocument
    While Not ( doc_RecordDoc Is Nothing )
```

```
        int_doccount = int_doccount + 1
        Set doc_RecordDoc = vw_dataview.GetNextDocument(doc_RecordDoc)
    Wend


    ' Now loop through the view again, removing the ones which don't
➥   have the right date stamp.

    For int_currentdoc = int_doccount To 1 Step -1
        Set doc_RecordDoc = vw_dataview.GetNthDocument(int_currentdoc)
        If Not (doc_RecordDoc.Lastupdated(0) = str_runtime) Then
            Call doc_RecordDoc.remove(True)
        End If
    Next


End Sub
```

The first time you run this Agent, it will take several minutes. As slow as ODBC access is, processes that require writing to the computer's hard disk are slower. Since the first run will have to create a document for every record returned by the query, it will be writing to the disk with a vengeance. However, once you have initially populated the view, subsequent runs will go much faster.

What the astute reader may have noticed missing from this scheme is a form. We haven't recommended a form because, strictly speaking, it isn't necessary. If you'd like to create a form (like the one in Figure 25.7), you may do so to make examining individual fields a little easier. If you want to make changes to the data manually rather than automatically, a form is absolutely necessary. However, if you've structured your view to display all the data in the document, opening the document with the form won't show you anything you can't see in the view. It's a good reminder of the difference between forms and documents. Forms are great for displaying data and providing you with tools for manipulating it. But, if you can see all the data in a view or through @DBLookups and the Agent already takes care of all the data manipulation, why bother building the form?

Notes as a Data Source for Relational Databases

Updating can go the opposite direction, using Notes data to alter the contents of the ODBC database. You'll use the same classes to establish the connection, but you may use an Action query (for example, using the DELETE keyword) or the connection to query as you would for selecting data. Then use a different set of methods on row data to make changes and save them back to the source database.

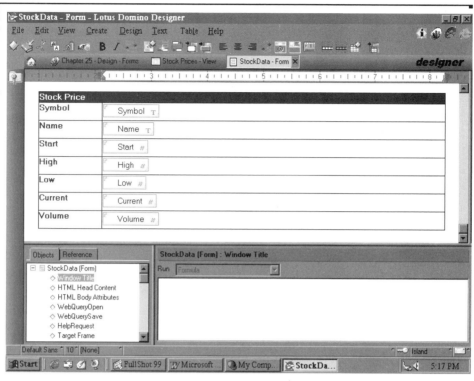

The easiest method of manipulating relational database data is by running Action queries. The code here would delete all records from a table named TempTable in the database defined by the ODBCConnection object.

```
qry_thequery.SQL = "Delete * from TempTable"
Set res_results.Query = qry_thequery
res_results.Execute
```

While you may use Action queries from time to time if you use Notes with ODBC data sources, you'll probably get most of your work done by manipulating individual rows and row data. For that, you'll need four methods for the ODBCRecordSet class: *DeleteRow*, *AddRow*, *SetValue*, and *UpdateRow*.

The DeleteRow method deletes the current row. It takes a table name as a parameter so that there's no confusion about which table the record should be deleted from. For example, if you were to go row by row, you'd reproduce the function of the previous delete query with code that looks something like this:

```
qry_thequery.SQL = "Select * from TempTable"
Set res_results.Query = qry_thequery
```

```
res_results.Execute
res_results.FirstRow
Do Until res_results.IsEndOfData
res_results.DeleteRow("TempTable")
res_results.UpdateRow
Loop
```

Of course, if you just wanted to delete the table's contents, the delete query would get it done faster. We'll come back to what UpdateRow is for shortly.

The AddRow method creates a blank new row, to which you can add new data. AddRow puts you in a strange place in the result set. Using AddRow puts you in the new row, but the added row is not actually part of the result set when you create it. If you create a row and use, for example, the PrevRow or NextRow methods, you'll move to the row before or after the row you were on *before* you created the new row. However, if you navigate around the result set after you create the new row, it won't vanish. Instead, it is kept in a special place in memory. You can return to the new row by setting the result set's CurrentRow property to the special constant DB_AddRow (*resultsetvariable*.CurrentRow = DB_AddRow).

SetValue is the simplest method to use and understand. It takes a column name or number and a value, and sets the value of the designated column in the current row to the value provided. For example, *resultsetvariable*.SetValue(1, "First") sets the value of the first column in the current row to First.

This is where UpdateRow comes in. The first three methods manipulate rows and individual values. UpdateRow commits your changes to the source database. You must invoke the UpdateRow method before you move away from a deleted row or from a row you have set values for, or before you close a result set where you have added a row.

To demonstrate the use of these methods, here's an Agent that will populate a table in an external database with a bare minimum of information from the People view in an address book, this allows you to use Notes data in your relational database applications:

```
(Options)

Option Public
Option Explicit

Uselsx "*LSXODBC"

(Declarations)
```

```
Dim con_thedata As ODBCConnection
Dim qry_thequery As ODBCQuery
Dim rs_results As ODBCResultSet
Dim s_currentsession As NotesSession
Dim db_thisDatabase As Notesdatabase
Dim res_results As ODBCResultSet
Dim doc_RecordDoc As Notesdocument
Dim vw_dataview As Notesview
Dim str_stocksymbol As String
Dim str_runtime As String
Dim int_doccount As Long
Dim int_currentdoc As Long


Sub Initialize

    ' Create new objects where necessary and point to the correct view.

    Set con_thedata = New ODBCConnection
    Set qry_thequery = New ODBCQuery
    Set res_results = New ODBCResultSet
    Set s_currentsession = New NotesSession

    ' Connect to the database, create a query to delete data, and execute it.

    Set db_thisDatabase = s_currentsession.CurrentDatabase
    Set vw_dataview = db_thisDatabase.GetView("People")
    con_thedata.ConnectTo("Addresses")
    Set qry_thequery.Connection = con_thedata
    qry_thequery.SQL = "DELETE * FROM AddressTable;"
    Set res_results.Query = qry_thequery
    res_results.Execute
    res_results.Close

    ' Now create a new query so we can put some data back into the table

    qry_thequery.SQL = "SELECT * FROM AddressTable;"
    Set res_results.Query = qry_thequery
    res_results.Execute
```

```
' Start with the first document in the view and start looping, creating a
➡    new row for each document

Set doc_RecordDoc = vw_dataview.GetFirstDocument
While Not ( doc_RecordDoc Is Nothing )
 res_results.AddRow
 Call res_results.SetValue("Fullname", doc_RecordDoc.FullName(0))
 Call res_results.SetValue("Firstname", doc_RecordDoc.FirstName(0))
 Call res_results.SetValue("Lastname", doc_RecordDoc.LastName(0))
 Call res_results.SetValue("EMail", doc_RecordDoc.ShortName(0))
 Call res_results.SetValue("Phone", doc_RecordDoc.OfficePhoneNumber(0))
 res_results.UpdateRow
 Set doc_RecordDoc = vw_dataview.GetNextDocument(doc_RecordDoc)
Wend

End Sub
```

This Agent takes a rather brutal approach to the data in the target table. It wipes out the data completely and repopulates it from scratch. This means that it's essentially futile to enter data from any other source. This is fine if you're using the Domino address book as your ultimate source of data. But it will require modification if you want to use both Notes data and data from other sources.

Using Notes from Outside Applications

If you install the appropriate drivers (available for free download from Lotus), you can also use Notes itself as a data source from within other applications. The ODBC driver will allow you to use views and folders in Notes databases as a data source. This allows you to use Notes data in queries within other databases or as the basis of reports with ODBC-compliant reporting tools, such as Crystal Reports. Since Notes uses views and folders as data sources rather than documents, you won't be able to bring rich text fields through the connection. But, since rich text isn't accommodated by the ODBC standard, you're not losing any functionality if you use Notes as your data source.

You can also open Notes sessions from other applications using OLE automation. This allows you to use external applications to manipulate Notes objects, not just data. For more details, search the Designer Help for "OLE and Using Domino Designer classes in Visual Basic."

Notes and OLE Automation

One of the most powerful, but in some ways most limited, methods for dealing with non-Notes data is through OLE object automation. Programs with appropriate programming interfaces can be opened, created, manipulated, and saved using (approximately) their own programming languages, but within a LotusScript program. Many common programs (including Lotus 1-2-3, Visio, and the Microsoft Office suite) provide you with this capability. Unfortunately, it only works on Windows platforms (Windows 95, 98, and NT; presumably, it will work in Windows 2000, as well). OLE automation won't work on the Mac OS, any of the many flavors of Unix, or other operating systems. It also won't work on a Web browser since LotusScript Agents don't run on the browser. It can be made to work in a Web Agent running on a Domino server. But be very cautious about an application that will allow outsiders to create files on a server.

To deal with another application through LotusScript, you must start by creating an application object. The object represents another application running invisibly in the background (or, if you desire, visibly in the foreground). To manipulate the object, you'll use the OLE object's own classes and methods. If you're not very familiar with OLE objects, don't worry too much about having to learn another language if you want to take advantage of this feature. LotusScript can do most of the work. And, OLE commands, classes, and methods are very similar to an application's native commands. You'll have to consult the documentation for specific applications in order to determine how to use them as OLE objects, but if you know Notes and the target application, you shouldn't have any trouble.

To create an OLE application object, declare a variable as a variant and set its value with either `CreateObject` or `GetObject`. The syntax you use depends on where you want to create it. To create an independent object that you can later save as an external file, `CreateObject` requires the name of a class. The class name is usually "*applicationname*.application." (Check your documentation to be sure.) For example, to create a Microsoft Word object, you'd use a line like this:

```
Set obj_word = CreateObject("Word.Application").
```

`GetObject`, provided with a file path and an application class, opens an existing document, although many applications can open a document once you've created the OLE object. While `CreateObject` and `GetObject` both work as functions, they can also be used as methods of the `NotesUIDocument` class. CreateObject creates a file attached to the document, while GetObject opens a file already attached to the document.

Once you have created the object, what you do with it depends on what the application in question can do. Here is a small example of LotusScript interacting with Microsoft Excel 97.

PART

VI

Developing
Databases

WARNING Be careful using this script if you've got an earlier version of Excel installed. Among other things, early versions of Excel will object to a filename longer than eight characters.

This script, designed to be an Agent in a mail database, invisibly creates an Excel object and a new worksheet and then goes through the documents in the user's Inbox. For each document, it creates a new record in the spreadsheet, including the sender's name and the message's subject line, as well as a small calculation that indicates how old messages are. The script also performs some minor formatting, which categorizes the list and puts in a title row.

```
(Options)
Option Public
Option Explicit

(Declarations)
Dim s As notessession
Dim db_mail As NotesDatabase
Dim vw_inbox As NotesView
Dim doc_message As NotesDocument
Dim int_line As Integer
Dim str_lastdate As String
Dim dat_currentdate As NotesDateTime
Dim str_currentdate As String
Dim ole_excel As Variant
Dim str_cellname1 As String
Dim str_cellname2 As String
Dim str_cellname3 As String
Dim str_cellname4 As String

Sub Initialize

    ' Set up some initial values.  str_lastdate a string holding the
➡    creation date of the last document
    ' the agent examined.  There hasn't been a document examined yet,
➡    so we'll set it to a null
    ' string.  int_line represents the line of the spreadsheet we're
➡    on.  We'll start with one.
```

```
str_lastdate = ""
int_line = 0
UpdateCells


' Create an Excel object and add an actual worksheet do work on.
➥    Setting the visible property
' to false makes it all happen without screen updating, which will
➥    let it move a little faster.

Set ole_excel = createobject("excel.application")
ole_excel.visible = False
ole_excel.workbooks.add


' Now we move on to some Notes stuff.  This gets us to the first
➥    document in the Inbox.

Set s = New notessession
Set db_mail = s.CurrentDatabase
Set vw_inbox = db_mail.GetView("($Inbox)")
Set doc_message = vw_inbox.GetFirstDocument

' Take a moment to set up some "header" information in the spreadsheet
ole_excel.range(str_cellname1).font.bold = True
ole_excel.range(str_cellname1).value = "Inbox contents report for
➥    " + s.CommonUserName
UpdateCells


' This is where the real work of looping through the documents and
➥    writing the spreadsheet begins.

Do Until doc_message Is Nothing


    ' To categorize the documents by date (not just sort them), we
➥    need to compare the creation date
    ' of the current document to the last one.  When dates change,
➥    create a header row.

    Set dat_currentdate = New notesdatetime(doc_message.Created)
    str_currentdate = dat_currentdate.DateOnly
```

```
    If str_currentdate <> str_lastdate Then
        ole_excel.range(str_cellname1).font.bold = True
        ole_excel.range(str_cellname1).value = str_currentdate
        ole_excel.range(str_cellname4).font.bold = True
        ole_excel.range(str_cellname4).value = "=(round(Now() - " +
➡  str_cellname1 + ",0)) & "" Days Old"""
        str_lastdate = str_currentdate
        UpdateCells
    End If

    ' In any case, create a row showing the document's sender and subject.

    ole_excel.range(str_cellname2).value = doc_message.From(0)
    ole_excel.range(str_cellname3).value = doc_message.Subject(0)
    UpdateCells
    Set doc_message = vw_inbox.GetNextDocument(doc_message)
Loop

' Save and close the spreadsheet and announce that it's done.

ole_excel.workbooks(1).saveas("C:\InboxReport.xls")
ole_excel.workbooks(1).close
Msgbox("Done")

End Sub


Sub UpdateCells

    ' This subroutine updates cell references. When it is called, the
➡  line counter, int_line, is
    ' incremented, and string variables are calculated for use as
➡  pointers to cells.

    int_line = int_line + 1
    str_cellname1 = "A" + Cstr(int_line)
    str_cellname2 = "B" + Cstr(int_line)
    str_cellname3 = "C" + Cstr(int_line)
    str_cellname4 = "D" + Cstr(int_line)


End Sub
```

The script produces a report something like the spreadsheet shown in Figure 25.8.

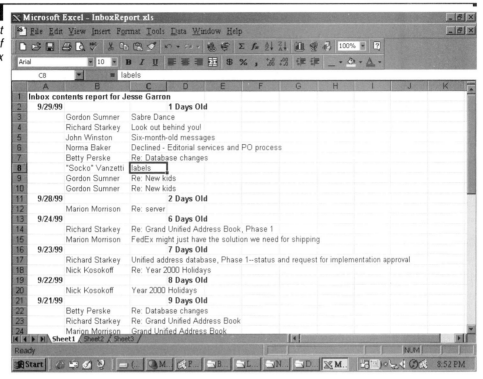

Of course, you're not limited to just creating new objects. You can interact with existing objects, as well. Consider this code:

```
Dim theval as String
Set ole_excel = createobject("excel.application")
ole_excel.workbooks.open("C:\InboxReport.xls")
theval = ole_excel.range("A1").value
ole_excel.range("A1").value = ""
ole_excel.range("B1").value = theval
ole_excel.workbooks(1).Save
ole_excel.workbooks(1).close
```

When dropped into an appropriate context (say, an Agent with the same declarations as the previous one), this code will open the spreadsheet created earlier, move the value from cell A1 to cell B1, save the spreadsheet, and close it. Pretty useless by itself, but consider the implications: You can create an elaborate spreadsheet as a template, plug values from a Notes document or documents into it, and save it under another name. You could open a word processor document, read data from book-marked sections, and incorporate that data into fields in Notes documents. With some careful construction, you can have your Notes databases interacting with a broad range of other applications. It isn't a live connection, but it gives you a lot of possibilities for creative imports and exports.

If you've worked with VBA, you may notice some similarities between VBA code and the commands being given to the previous spreadsheet object. You should, since that's almost exactly what the code would look like in a VBA code module in Excel. That should also tell you how easy it is to use OLE to coordinate two programs, assuming that you know both of them reasonably well.

If you're a little shaky on the kinds of methods and objects you can use with any given OLE object, there's a reference within Notes. In any LotusScript programmer's pane, click the Reference tab, click the arrow to bring up the drop-down menu, and scroll down from LotusScript Language to OLE Classes. The reference pane will show you a list of applications that you can potentially use with OLE automation, as shown in Figure 25.9. Most of them are Microsoft applications, including the full range of Office 97 applications. (They're listed in the reference list as being version 8, an obscure, but technically accurate, way of referring to the Office 97 applications.) Each application can be expanded into lists of objects, classes, methods, properties, and other entities appropriate to the application. While it is not a full help feature because it does not explain the use of any of the objects and methods or for their parameters, it is a complete listing of the objects, properties, and methods that you can use in OLE automation with the listed applications.

FIGURE 25.9

OLE reference in Notes

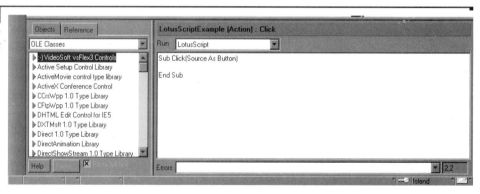

DECS

Domino R5 comes with a built-in feature for keeping Notes databases coordinated with relational databases. *DECS* (Domino Enterprise Connection Services) allows you to set up a connection to an external database on a Domino server and build documents that share values with records in the database.

To make DECS work, you'll need several elements:

- At least one Connection document on the Domino server

- At least one Activity document on the server

- A form in the Notes database where you want to keep the data

In addition, the DECS service must be installed and started on the server (check with your Domino administrator), and you'll probably want a view to hold the documents that the data is in.

Before you start configuring DECS Connections and Activities, you should build a form in a Notes database that holds the same data, or at least some of the same data, as the external data source. You should build the form much as you would a form to hold ODBC data, keeping names and data types similar. The form will be used to represent individual records from the external data source, one document per record.

DECS is a server-based task, so to set up Connections and Activities, you'll need to launch the Administrative client. If DECS is installed on the Domino server, there should be a DECS entry in the outline under the Server tab that gives you two views: Connections and Activities. The first view to visit is Connections. A Connection document prepares a single table from an external data source. To create one, click the New Connection button and select a data source type. While you can get native (which is to say faster) access to only a few databases, you can use ODBC data sources, as well. This allows you to get into just about every database worth speaking of. The Connection document (see Figure 25.10) lets you enter identifying and security information for the database and pick a table from the database.

 NOTE If these screenshots look different from what's in the documentation, it's because the screenshots there were taken in a 4.6x client. The tools are the same in 4.6x and R5, but they appear in a slightly different context.

Once you have created a Connection document, you can create an Activity document (see Figure 25.11). An Activity is an association between an external data source and a form in a Notes database. Because everything in the Connection document is

PART

VI

Developing
Databases

configurable, Notes runs a setup wizard when you create the document that will walk you through the steps.

FIGURE 25.10

*Configuring the
Connection document*

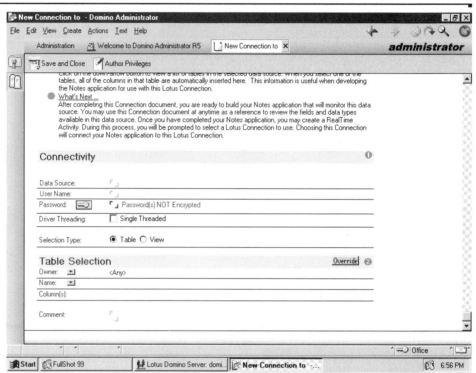

The wizard will ask you to pick a Notes database on the server, a form in that database (don't be thrown by the grandiose term "specific metadata"), a Connection picked from a list of existing Connections, and field mapping instructions (see Figure 25.12). This is perhaps the trickiest and most important part of setting up a DECS connection. DECS divides form fields into two types: key fields and data fields. The DECS service will use the fields you designate as key fields to identify the document and the record in the external table that it matches. If the Connection's external table has only one key field, you should designate only one key field. If the table has two key fields, designate two Notes form fields as keys, and so on. To map fields to one another, click the field name in the list of available Notes form fields, then click the corresponding field in the list of external data source fields. Not all fields need to be mapped. The example in Figure 25.12 is mapping fields in a Notes form to an Orders table. (If you have Microsoft Access, you may recognize the fields as being from the Northwind database.)

FIGURE 25.11

An Activity document

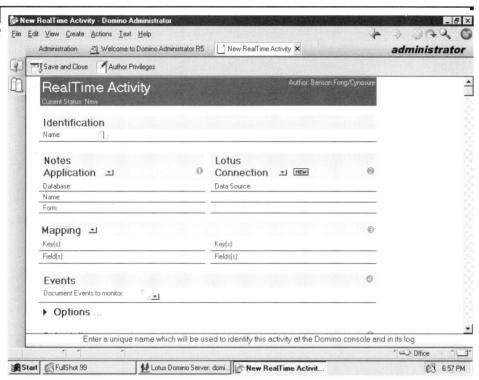

FIGURE 25.12

DECS field mapping

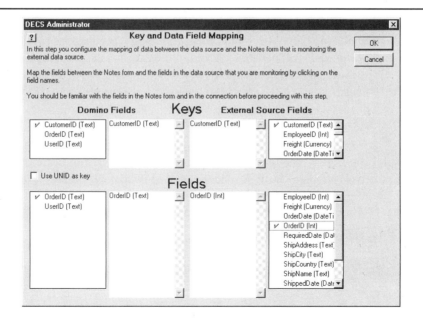

Once the fields are mapped, Notes will ask you what kind of events to monitor for changes to the external database. (For example, if you select Delete, deleting a document in Notes will delete the corresponding record in the external data source.) Then Notes will prompt you for a name. Once the Activity is complete, it can be activated.

When the Activity has been activated, Notes will start monitoring documents in the designated Notes database that are made with the designated form. If a change is made in the document, that change is transmitted in real time to the database, and vice versa. The DECS service pays attention only to the form, not to folders and views. However, even if the computer doesn't care, you probably should. Although a view selecting all documents made with the form named in the Activity document is not necessary, it's a very good idea.

While DECS performance is reasonably good if there aren't a great many connections, or if there is not a lot of activity in the back-end database, greater activity puts a greater burden on the server. Also, DECS requires a Domino server. DECS is a good solution for a server-based application, such as a Web site, but it is not so good for distributed applications where users don't have constant access to the Domino server that handles the DECS task.

One of the hidden drawbacks of DECS is that the data transfer is not entirely symmetrical. If you make a change in a record in one data source, either Notes or the external database, that change will be transmitted to the other. If you delete a record on one, the record will be deleted in the other. If you add a document in Notes, a record will be created in the external database. Unfortunately, adding a record in the external database won't trigger creation of a new document in Notes. DECS only operates where there are Notes documents with appropriate key values to match to values in the external data source. If a new record is created in the external database, there is no corresponding document in Notes. If your application is designed so that new records will never be created in the external database, that won't be a problem. However, if both Notes and the external data source are used for data entry, you will need to occasionally check the external data source for new records and create new documents as necessary. This would be a good use for a scheduled Agent using ODBC. Existing data also won't cause new documents to be created when DECS is started. Therefore, if you're incorporating an already-existing data source into your Notes application, you may also have to run another Agent to initially populate the database with documents that correspond to the data in the external data source.

Recycling a Template

Along with the Notes and Domino software, Lotus provides you with templates for a number of different databases, including threaded discussions and document storage.

These templates provide perfectly functional databases out of the box. But, as designed, they may not be entirely appropriate to your needs. You may also want one or two features from a database template but not all of the features that are included. Since there is no particular security or other protection on the templates, it's quite possible to break them up for parts, taking what you need, modifying it as you desire, and leaving the rest behind. In fact, Lotus distributes the templates in an unprotected form precisely so that you can alter them as you desire. However, to repurpose parts of a database, you need to understand the database's entire structure. Some of the templates are very complex, and it's easy to break something if you don't get all the parts working together properly.

When you start to tinker with a template, it's a very good idea to create a new copy of the template to work with. For any database that you're borrowing template design elements for, make sure that your new database or template does not inherit its design from the original template. If it does, your modifications may be lost, overwritten by the update process that keeps database designs in synch with templates. Instead base your new database or template on the copy of the original template that you created.

After you have a completely independent copy of the template that you want to modify, it's time to go exploring. As an example of how to go through a template, we'll investigate some aspects of one of the most complex templates that Notes provides: the mailbox. To demonstrate the investigation, we'll create the Company Calendar application that is found on the CD (look for the `CompanyCalendar.nsf` file). The Company Calendar was built when the managers of an organization, intrigued by meeting invitations in the Notes calendar, decided that they wanted a common calendar that would hold the dates of company holidays, company-wide events, important conferences, industry conventions, and other events of general interest. For these events, they also wanted to be able to send out invitations, ready-made calendar documents that people could put in their calendars with the ease of meeting invitations.

The Notes calendar, as it stands, is clearly not up to the task. First, the Company Calendar application needs to send out all-day events, not meeting invitations. Second, the calendar needs to be viewed through the organization so that people who have decided not to add entries to their own calendars can still see all the events that their colleagues and key people in other departments might be concerned with. Since the basic functions (Calendar view, all-day events, and automated invitations) are all to be found in the basic Notes calendar, this seems the obvious candidate for modification.

Be warned: We're heading into the heart of darkness here. The Notes calendar does a lot of different things, and all of the versatility and automation it provides requires a huge array of design elements and program code. There is a lot to keep in mind here, but once it's over, you'll have a solid grasp of how the mailbox template is put together.

PART

VI

Developing
Databases

To find out what needs to be modified, we'll start by looking for the appropriate form. Examining the properties of any calendar entry or invitation reveals that they are all built with a form named Appointment. A look through the Forms view of the mailbox template doesn't show any Appointment form, but Appointment is the alias of the form _Calendar Entry, shown in Figure 25.13. Clearly, that's the place to start.

FIGURE 25.13

The Calendar Entry form

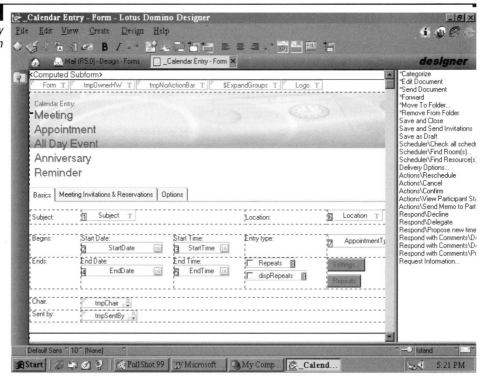

The first thing we'll do is to see what makes the versatile Calendar Entry form look like an all-day event or a meeting invitation, and how to combine features of both into a less flexible form that only shows us the features that we'll need for this application. If you've used calendar entries much, you've seen how they change shape quickly when you change the selection in the Entry Type combo box (the AppointmentType field on the form). Quick changes of appearance on a form usually indicate the use of computed subforms or hide-when formulas.

On this form, there is only one computed subform. (The subform (vCSItems) will appear at the top of the form in Web clients.) Sure enough, examining the text properties of the appointment type titles (Meeting, Appointment, and so on at the top of the form) and the Meeting Invitations & Reservations tab reveals hide-when conditions based on the value of AppointmentType. Checking the values available for AppointmentType, we discover that the names are actually just aliases: The actual value of Meeting is 3 (remember, values of combo box, list box, and other list fields are always text), and the value of All Day Event is 2. Since we only want a single type of event available in this form, we'll change this field to a computed-when-composed text field with a value of 2. Except for the other changes that we'll make, elements of the form will be treated as though they are All Day Events. We'll have the AppointmentType field hide under all conditions and remove all the other choices, as well, since we'll never want it to be different.

However, we'll need to make some further changes so that we can get the invitation fields that we'll need to mail out invitations to the event. We'll turn our attention to the Meeting Invitations & Reservations tab. The tab and the text in its nested tables all have hide-when formulas that include `AppointmentType != "3"`, which hides the tab and its contents when the document isn't an invitation. We could either change that hiding condition to `AppointmentType != "2"` (or any number other than 3) or eliminate it altogether. It doesn't really matter, but to reduce the chance of typos, we'll just remove it altogether. However, *don't* remove the other hide-when conditions. While AppointmentType is no longer an issue, other fields might be. We'll also remove the reservations fields, since we do not want to reserve resources with this form, we only want to send out notices.

Another item we'll need to modify is the Save and Save Invitations Action button. Like the Meeting Invitations & Reservations tab, the Action is hidden if AppointmentType is 3, so we'll remove the condition there, as well.

This is where things get difficult. We've got a form that looks like an All Day Event that also has an Invitations tab and a Save and Send Invitations button. However, if you test it, you'll see that it doesn't send invitations out.

Look at the code behind the Save and Send Invitations:

```
FIELD tmpAction ="6";
@If(@PostedCommand([FileSave]); @PostedCommand([FileCloseWindow]); "")
```

The button code itself does very little. The @commands here simply set a field value; attempt to save the document; and, if successful, close the document. However, in saving and closing the document, these @commands trigger three form events: QuerySave, PostSave, and QueryClose (see Chapter 18 to review form events).

Checking the code for those three events shows that they appear to be calling a method of a class. For example, from QuerySave:

```
Call uicsdoc.QuerySave(Continue)
```
And from QueryClose:
```
If(uicsdoc.WasSaved) Then Call uicsdoc.QueryClose(Continue)
```

But what is `uicsdoc`? Where is it declared, and where is it instantiated? The answer is in two places. If you search through the various scripts attached to the form (use

Developing
Databases

Ctrl+F to find), you'll find three instances of the word. One of them is the PostOpen event, where another method is called. The other two are QueryOpen, where it is set (`Set uicsdoc = CSUIDocOpen(1, source, mode, isnewdoc, continue)`), and the Global (Declarations) routine (`Dim uicsdoc As UIEventDocument`). It appears that `uicsdoc` is a `UIEventDocument`, created by the `CSUIDocOpen` function operating on the UI document ("`source`" in the function). Marvelous, you say, but it's not in the Designer Help. It's not in the Notes Help or the Administration Help either. So far as the documentation is concerned, it doesn't exist. So where can you look now?

The clue here is in the (Options) section, in particular the line `Use "CSUIDocClass"`. Here, we come to a type of shared resource that we haven't dealt with yet: the *code library*. Code libraries are places to keep code that you may want to share between LotusScript or Java Agents, Actions, and event scripts. You've already seen the Use statement used to call up the necessary extra program elements to run ODBC operations. The same construction is also used to include functions and subroutines from script libraries. `Use "libraryname"` makes the code from a library available within a script. Sure enough, the mailbox design has a script library named `CSUIDocClass`. It's worth noting at this point that `CSUIDocClass` has in its (Options) section the line `Use "CSEventClass"`, and, in turn, the `CSEventClass` library uses the Common library.

This means that we've got three large and unfamiliar chunks of code to look through in order to find some code relevant to what we're after (which, lest we forget, is code which sends invitations out). However, we've got some things to look for. First, there's the `UIEventDocument` to investigate. Second, what we're ultimately looking for is something that sends a document. In short, we're looking for a .Send method.

First, we'll look for the `UIEventDocument` in the script libraries. Fortunately, that's pretty easy to find. At the very top of the `CSUIDocClass` (Declarations) section, below a handful of constant declarations, there is the line `Class UIEventDocument`. Chapter 23 mentioned that it was possible to create new classes; this is how it's done. If you scroll down to the end of (Declarations), you'll see an `End Class`, just like you'd contain a function between `Function` and `End Function` or a subroutine between `Sub` and `End Sub`. The routines within it define the class's properties and methods.

One of those routines holds the method that we're looking for. Near the end of the definition of the `UIEventDocument` class is the SendPrimaryRequest routine. This is the only routine in any of the libraries in question which uses the .Send method:

```
Sub SendPrimaryRequest()
  ' callback routine from backend to send the primary notice
  Call m_uidoc.reload()
  Call m_uidoc.send()
End Sub
```

Classes vs. Design Elements

Most of the classes that we've dealt with so far have been very closely tied to Notes design elements. The NotesDocument class is a document, a NotesDatabase is a database, and so on. If you save an object of the NotesDocument class, you'll end up with a document in your database, with all that that implies. With user-defined classes, you can create virtual objects that don't resemble Notes design elements so closely. However, what you create is likely to be, ultimately, a bundle of familiar data types and routines performed using familiar LotusScript methods. Moreover, if you save something you create with your own class, you'll have to save it in familiar Notes terms. Specifically, you'll have to save objects as documents or individual field values.

For example, you could create a Color object, representing an RGB value for use on the Web. You could give the object Blue, Red, and Green properties that represent the intensity of each color, and give the methods properties like MakeMoreBlue, MakeLessRed, and so on to adjust the values of each color. However, if you want to save an RGB value, you'd have to save it as a text or number value (for example, as text using a standard Web color value like FFFFFF for white, or as a multi-value field containing 255, 255, 255). For a fuller explanation of building your own classes, check the Designer Help for "User-defined classes."

Even if other routines contained the .Send method, it would be a good bet that this was the one to pay attention to. It calls the .Send method on the object m_uidoc, which is declared early on as a property of the UIEventDocument.

We've found out where the document is sent, so now we need to backtrack through the program to find the connection between SendPrimaryRequest and the UIEventDocument's QuerySave or QueryClose routines. Searching the three code libraries, we find that SendPrimaryRequest is only called in a routine in the Common library. This routine is called CSDocSendPrimaryNotice. These are the relevant sections of code:

```
Sub CSDocSendPrimaryNotice(vBEObject As Variant, vCallBackObject As
    Variant, vContinue As Variant)
  Dim fSendOptions As Integer
  If Not(vBEObject.IsWorkflowEnabled) Then Exit Sub
  fSendOptions = vBEObject.PrimarySendOptions
  If (fSendOptions And 1) Then
     Call vCallBackObject.SendPrimaryRequest()
```

PART

VI

Developing
Databases

If the IsWorkflowEnabled property of the vBEObject isn't true (that is, if its value is zero or null), the subroutine ends. If fSendOptions isn't zero or null, the SendPrimary-Request Action is called. The value of fSendOptions comes, like IsWorkflowEnabled, from a property of the vBEObject, which is called PrimarySendOptions. At this point, we've got *two* things to look for: CSDocSendPrimaryNotice, the routine that calls the method that sends the document; and the vBEObject object, which is used in the same routine. We'll have to back up at least one more level to figure out where this all comes from.

Doing another search, we find that the routine CSDocSendPrimaryNotice is only called in one place, the CSDocSave routine in the Common script library. Here's the line:

```
If (dAction And ACTION_SEND) Then Call
    CSDocSendPrimaryNotice(vBEObject, vCallBackObject, vContinue)
```

There's good news and bad news here. The good news is that the two things we were looking for so far are still related. We were looking for both CSDocSendPrimaryRequest and vBEObject. CSDocSave calls CSDocSendPrimaryRequest, so now we have to look for a routine calling CSDocSave. However, here's the line that sets up CSDocSave:

```
Sub CSDocSave(vBEObject As Variant, vCallBackObject As Variant, Byval
    dAction As Long, Byval dOptions As Long, vContinue As Variant)
```

As you can see, vBEObject is a parameter called by the subroutine and is passed directly to CSDocSendPrimaryRequest. So, in looking for CSDocSave, we're also looking for vBEObject.

On the down side, we're looking for two more variables: *dAction* and *ACTION_SEND*. We'll search for those later.

So to return to CSDocSave: This routine is called in only one place, and it's an encouraging sign. CSDocSave is called in the QuerySave event of the UIEventDocument definition in the CSUIDocClass script library. Remember the line in the QuerySave event of the _Calendar Entry form (Call uicsdoc.QuerySave(Continue))? We've found it. To sum up, here's the sequence of events:

1. Pressing the Save and Send Invitations button sets a field value and saves the document.

2. Saving the document triggers the QuerySave event of the form.

3. The QuerySave event of the main form triggers the QuerySave event of the UIEventDocument class.

4. The UIEventDocument's QuerySave routine calls the CSDocSave routine.

5. Under certain conditions, CSDocSave calls CSDocSendPrimaryNotice.

6. Under certain conditions, CSDocSendPrimaryNotice calls the SendPrimary-Request routine.

7. Finally, SendPrimaryRequest sends the document.

Now that we've got the basic series of events mapped out, we can look at those certain conditions to figure out what it is about the all-day event that prevents invitations from being sent out.

As a result of our investigation, we have discovered that there are four values that could prevent the message from being sent:

- dAction
- ACTION_SEND
- fSendOptions (vBEObject.PrimarySendOptions)
- vBEObject.IsWorkflowEnabled

The structure of the If...Then statements in which these values appear simply checks for a value. If any one of the values is zero or null, the invitations won't be sent. At this point, we could start backtracking through the code for each of the variables, just as we did for all the events. However, that might be more work than it's worth. We can narrow down the field by testing for values. If we can determine which one or ones are null or zero, we can take Action on those values and ignore the rest.

Typically, you would check the values of the variables in the debugger. But, as we've already observed, the debugger won't help us here. The code in the code libraries won't appear there. Still, the values can be coaxed out of the scripts in a number of ways. In this case, we'll use the Msgbox command. Go to the CSDocSend-PrimaryNotice routine and insert a few lines of code:

```
Sub CSDocSendPrimaryNotice(vBEObject As Variant, vCallBackObject As Variant,
➥    vContinue As Variant)
    Dim fSendOptions As Integer

    On Error Resume Next

    ' This is where the new code starts.
    Msgbox("dAction: " + dAction)
    Msgbox("ACTION_SEND: " + ACTION_SEND)
    Msgbox("PrimarySendOptions: " + vBEObject.PrimarySendOptions)
    Msgbox("IsWorkflowEnabled: " + vBEObject.IsWorkflowEnabled)
    ' And this is where it ends

    If Not(vBEObject.IsWorkflowEnabled) Then Exit Sub

    fSendOptions = vBEObject.PrimarySendOptions
```

The new lines of code will flash the relevant values on the screen when you attempt to send invitations. As it turns out, everything but vBEObject.IsWorkflowEnabled has

PART

VI

Developing
Databases

a value that evaluates as true. `vBEObject.IsWorkflowEnabled`, on the other hand, is false, plain and simple. We've found the obstacle.

So what do we do about it? This decision is more art than science, but there is a guideline to follow. We're only trying to make one small change in function. Therefore, rather than tracing IsWorkflowEnabled back to its source or changing it's value globally, it's a good idea to start by making a small, local change. There is a great deal of code we haven't looked at. IsWorkflowEnabled may be used elsewhere, and we don't want to break anything. All we have to do is to keep IsWorkflowEnabled from getting in the way in CSDocSendPrimaryNotice. The easiest way of doing that is to delete the line. However, a better idea is to comment it out, so that the line looks like this:

```
'  If Not(vBEObject.IsWorkflowEnabled) Then Exit Sub
```

Adding the single quote turns the line into a comment, which is ignored when the script runs. IsWorkflowEnabled is out of the equation, and invitations will be sent.

Now that the desired function has been added, the rest is just housekeeping. You'll want to keep the following elements:

- The _Calendar Entry form
- The ($Calendar) view
- The Common, CSUIDocClass, and CSUIEventClass script libraries

We can also clean some things up to make the _Calendar Entry form less cluttered and adapt it to our purposes. First, we can delete a number of items: all the text showing what kind of document the form is because, in this database, they're all All Day Events. We won't be using the Options tab at all, so we can change its hide-when conditions to hide it at all times. Finally, we can remove just about all the Actions. At this point, the form should look something like Figure 25.14.

We should also remove a number of items from the ($Calendar) view: most of the Actions and the Start and End columns. The resulting view will look like Figure 25.15.

Finally, the database's About and Using documents should be changed, and the database icon should be redone. When opened, the resulting database will look like Figure 25.16.

Authorized users can create a new calendar entry, like the one in Figure 25.17. Note that there is no way to change the appointment type, and there are no fields for adding rooms or resources. There is no special security on the database on the CD. But, if you create a database like this, you'll probably want to limit the power to create new documents to a small group of people.

Once invitations are sent off, they will appear in users' mailboxes much like meeting invitations. Each user who receives an invitation can add it to their Notes calendar with the push of a button.

FIGURE 25.14

The modified
Calendar Entry form

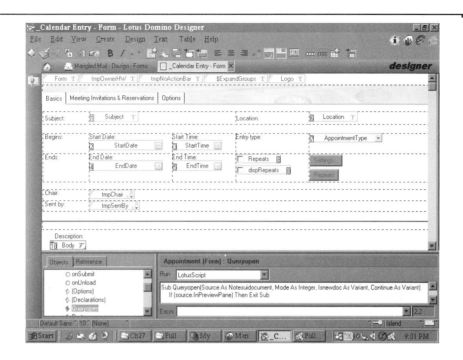

FIGURE 25.15

The modified
($Calendar) view

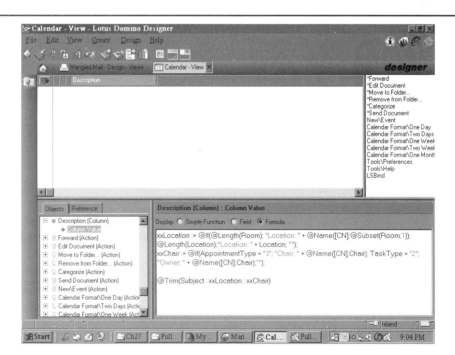

FIGURE 25.16

The Company Calendar

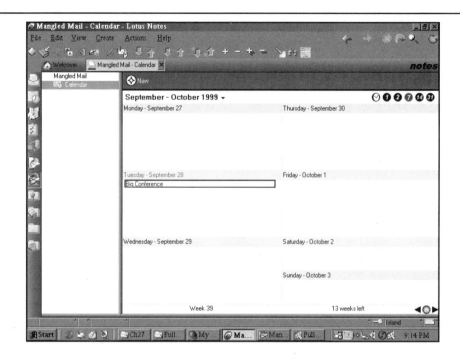

FIGURE 25.17

A company calendar entry

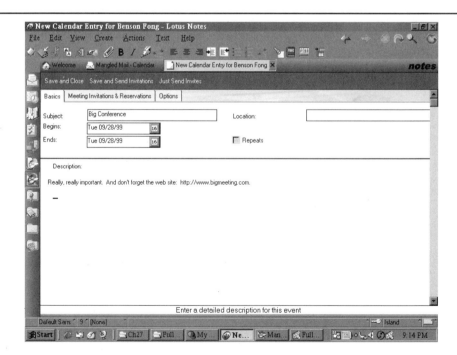

Summary

This chapter dealt with a number of more advanced programming topics. There are a number of ways to build workflow into an application. Each method is a trade-off between ease of use, ease of programming, and security. There are a number of methods for using Notes to communicate with data from other programs and file formats. Text is very portable but requires a great deal of processing using syntax that doesn't resemble much of the rest of LotusScript. ODBC is a standard for communicating with relational databases that can give you extensive access to external databases but requires both extensive programming and external-to-Notes configuration of the computer using it.

DECS gives you access to external databases without having to rely on programming, but it requires a server to mediate the connection. Also, the data flows more easily in one direction than the other, so it may need to be supplemented by some other means of getting data. OLE automation lets you manipulate files associated with many popular word processor, spreadsheet, and other programs. The templates provided with Notes are an ample source of design elements and program code. And, their design is completely accessible so that you can modify them as you please. But you may need to exert considerable effort to map out how the template works.

The next chapter explores the use of Notes and Domino as a programming and development platform for the Web.

PART

VI

**Developing
Databases**

CHAPTER **26**

Web-Enabling Your Applications

Domino enthusiasts may tell you that you can take any Notes database to the Web instantly through a Domino server. The server will translate your documents into HTML on the fly, letting you pull them up and work on them anywhere in the world where you can get a Web connection to your server. Surprisingly, this is largely true. Domino will render documents, doclinks, views, framesets, and other design elements on the fly as appropriate bits of HTML and will send them off to you anywhere your Web browser can connect to the Domino server. Views, folders, and framesets appear as tables of links to documents, along with navigation tools. Search functions provide you with forms to submit to Domino's powerful search engine, which will give you results just as comprehensive as what you'd get using a Notes client.

Still, the enthusiasm needs to be taken with some caution. There are limits to what Domino can do to turn elaborate code into something that can be executed through a Web interface. And, the Notes client provides Notes databases with resources and control that Web browsers simply don't have. Certainly, you can view any Notes database on the Web, but making an application work over the Web is a different matter. It requires a somewhat different approach and an understanding of how the Web environment is different.

The topics this chapter addresses include:

- Navigating Notes databases on the Web

- Web-specific form features

- Web Agents

- Web searching

- Applet configuration and behavior

This chapter assumes a basic knowledge of HTML and Web protocols. There are many good books on the subject. (You could do worse than *Mastering HTML 4.0*, by Deborah S. Ray and Eric J. Ray, Sybex, 1997.) There are also any number of perfectly adequate primers and references available on the Web for free. This chapter also assumes a very basic knowledge of JavaScript and Java, as well as such LotusScript as has already been presented.

What Doesn't Work on the Web

A number of Notes features don't work on the Web at all. You should familiarize yourself with these before you start building specifically for the Web. For example, security on the Web is a very different matter. Your *connection* over the Web can be made secure through SSL (Secure Sockets Layer), so somebody eavesdropping on your connection wouldn't be able to read your data. However, Web browsers don't have access to Notes ID files, so Notes digital signatures and encryption are impossible. For other reasons, pop-up hotspots and layout regions can't be translated into HTML. For a full listing, check the Designer Help for "Overview of features to avoid using in Web applications." We'll be discussing some of these features and what you can do to replace them, but that document will provide you with pointers to the features that you should not use.

Navigating Notes Databases on the Web

Before you can see Notes databases on the Web, the Domino server has to be willing to show them to you. This means that the Domino server must be running the HTTP service. The HTTP service is a special process that can be run on a Domino server, allowing it to translate Notes database objects into HTML. It also allows the server to act as a more mundane Web server, serving out plain HTML pages. The HTTP service is easy to install, but it is *optional* and may not be running on every Domino server, so check with your system administrator to make sure that it is running before you start doing Web work.

As with any other object on the Web, the basic tool for communicating data and giving commands to a Domino server over the Web is the URL. A Domino server follows orthodox URL syntax for opening files through the HTTP protocol. For example, if your server's fully qualified name is www.domino.org, the URL http://www.domino.org/index.html will open the HTML file index.html. (Exactly where on the server index.html resides can vary. By default, Domino looks for HTML documents in the /domino/html subdirectory of the /data directory, and for Notes databases in the /data directory itself. But that's really an administration issue.) It should come as no surprise that a URL like http://www.domino.org/frontpage.nsf will open the database frontpage.nsf by using the On Web Launch setting in the Database Properties. However, because Notes databases are more elaborate than simple files, the URL syntax to get into and manipulate them is also more complex.

When you start using Notes databases on the Web, you'll see URLs that look something like this:

```
http://www.domino.org/notesdb.nsf/78ced56jr893o78v729vh362sd109rf9/
eaa47bcc39cde55gp94ks107vc876de1?OpenDocument
```

Hideous, isn't it? Let's handle the last element first. Almost every URL that is used to access a Notes database ends in a command, which is separated from the rest of the URL by a question mark or an exclamation point. By default, Notes uses a question mark, but you can use a URL instead.

In most cases, what comes after the question mark is simply `Openelementname`. For example, in opening a form, the URL would end with ?OpenForm. (This command essentially creates a new document using the form.) In opening a view, the URL would end with ?OpenView, and so on.

There are a few commands that work a little differently. The ?OpenAgent command causes the named Agent to run and return any output it may have to the browser. For opening individual documents, ?OpenDocument opens a document in read-only mode, while ?EditDocument opens a document in editing mode. (That is, it opens the page as an HTML form whose editable fields are available for editing.) Under certain circumstances, other data can come after the question mark, such as parameters for searching. (We'll be discussing that later.) A database's About document can be opened with the URL `database.nsf/$about?Open`, while the Using document is opened with the URL `database.nsf/$help?Open`.

The harder part to deal with is the long strings of apparent gibberish that make up the bulk of the URL. Left to its own devices (for example, when preparing doclinks or view entries for the Web), Notes uses 32-digit alphanumeric strings to uniquely identify documents and design elements in a database. In this case, the URL indicates that we're opening a document with a unique ID of eaa47bcc39cde55gp94ks107vc876de1 through a view with a unique ID of 78ced56jr893o78v729vh362sd109rf9, in the `notesdb.nsf` database on the server www.domino.org. You can uncover the unique ID numbers of design elements by going to the list of elements and checking the Document IDs tab of the Design Document Properties InfoBox, as shown in Figure 26.1. For individual documents, the unique ID can be found on the Document IDs tab of the Document Properties InfoBox or through the @DocumentUniqueID formula. Through careful hand-coding and use of formulas, you could address every document and design element in the database.

Fortunately, you won't have to. In fact, while you might, on rare occasions, consider using the unique IDs as diagnostic tools, you'll probably never have to use a document or design element ID to call up a page or hand-code a URL. When it generates its own URLs, Domino will use the unique ID numbers, but you can just use names. For example, the URL http://www.domino.org/notesdb.nsf/MainView?OpenView will open the view MainView in the database `notesdb.nsf`.

A design element's
unique ID

Finding documents is a little more difficult because they aren't named like design elements are. But there are some relatively easy ways to get to them. You can use a URL to essentially look up a text value in a view. Consider this URL:

```
http://www.domino.org/notesdb.nsf/MainView/Notification?OpenDocument
```

This URL tells the Domino server to go to the view named MainView and return the first document that has the value "Notification" in the first sorted column. This gives you a relatively easy way of finding documents in the database, although it does depend on having unique values in a column. This may often be the case, but it cannot be absolutely guaranteed.

It's also possible to perform searches on Notes databases using specially constructed URLs. They are very flexible; they are also very elaborate. See the "Searches" section for more information.

Designing Forms

When a user accesses a Notes database through the Web, she may go through navigational features such as views, outlines, and pages. But, if you've used Notes properly, most of what she'll be looking at will be documents; and, as you realize by now, looking at documents means looking at forms. Here, you'll get into the specifics of how to make forms that look and act the way you want them to on the Web.

Designing Forms for Web vs. Notes Use

There are differences between the ways Notes clients perform operations and how the corresponding operations are performed on the Web. Therefore, you will have to design differently for the Web than for Notes clients. But what if you have a multi-platform application and want to use the same objects on Notes and on the Web? There are three main strategies you can take:

- Hide-when formulas
- View form formulas
- Shared-alias forms

PART

VI

Developing
Databases

With @ClientType, you can determine whether an object is being viewed on the Web or through a Notes client. You can incorporate this information into hide-when formulas and make text, fields, Actions, and so on appear or disappear as necessary. If the only difference between the Web and Notes versions of your objects is a few lines of text or a field or two, this is a reasonably quick and efficient strategy. If you make changes to a form, those changes take effect for both the Web and Notes versions simultaneously. This keeps maintenance low. However, if there are significant differences between the Web and Notes versions, it can make your forms large, unwieldy, and a bit slower to load as Notes processes all of the hide-when formulas. And, if there are LotusScript Actions on the form, you'll have to rewrite them completely.

Option "one and a half" is to use subforms. You can use a computed subform to drop Web-only fields into a document, buttons to replace form Actions, or extra text to give additional instructions to Web users. You can even provide additional JavaScript functions for Web use only by putting the JavaScript in the subform, wrapping it in <Script> tags, and making it all pass-thru HTML (see the next section for details on making pass-thru HTML). If you can isolate most or all of your Web-only elements and put them all in one place, you can put them all on a subform and add a computed subform to the main form using @ClientType in the formula. Putting all the Web content in one spot makes the form easy to maintain. Like the hide-when option, the use of subforms can lead to performance problems, but it is a viable option. You may notice that the Notes mailbox template uses hide-when formulas and subforms for a number of dual-purpose forms.

A second option is to use form formulas in a view. It's possible to go through a view in order to show documents on the Web (for example, http://server/viewname/document?OpenDocument). If you use separate views for Web and Notes access, you can govern which version appears in Notes or on a browser. However, this approach is fraught with problems. It only works with forms, not with views, pages, or other objects. It's also very slow.

Your best option is to take advantage of aliases. Any design element, be it a form, a view, an outline, or what have you, can be given an alias. If you create two objects of the same type and with the same alias, make one visible only in Notes and the other visible only on the Web. Domino will choose the appropriate one for the context. This means that you can, for the most part, create navigation objects and links once and have them work in both Web and Notes client contexts.

To make an object available only on the Web or in Notes, go to the appropriate design view (see Figure 26.2), right-click the element in question (but do *not* open it), and select Design Properties. Go to the Design tab and check the appropriate Hide Design Element From tab.

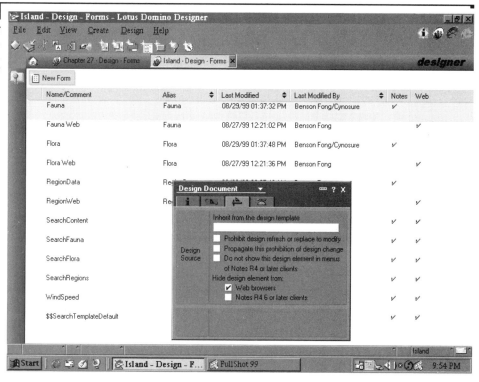

FIGURE 26.2

*A set of forms:
some for Notes use,
some for Web use,
some for both*

Once you've got the aliases sorted out, Notes will select the appropriate item to open. For example, say you have two forms, WebDoc and NotesDoc. Both forms are aliased to MainDoc. You also have a view with the command @Command([Compose]; "MainDoc"). WebDoc is hidden from Notes clients, while NotesDoc is hidden from Web browsers. If you use the view Action while on the Web, it will actually create the document using WebDoc. However, if you save the document and open it later in Notes, it will be opened with the NotesDoc form. The only significant drawback is that it makes form maintenance harder. Any modifications in the form's look or function will have to be made twice, once on each version.

Special Design Features

You can make a perfectly functional form for Web use without knowing HTML because Domino does all the HTML translation work for you. However, if you know HTML, you can (and, in some cases, probably should) incorporate it directly into your forms for use on the Web. You already saw in Chapter 18 how you can add HTML attributes to individual fields. You can also add the contents of fields or text directly to the form by using pass-thru HTML.

PART

VI

Developing
Databases

Pass-thru HTML is text that the Domino server sends to the Web browser as is rather than trying to convert it into HTML. Essentially, it stops the process of rendering a passage of text into HTML, which the server usually does to make the text appear in the Web browser as it does in Notes. Confused? Here's how it works:

Let's say you have "Word!" on a form. If you call up the form in a Web browser, Notes will render it into HTML so that it will look like it does on the Notes form. In other words, if you have "Word!" on the form, you'll see "Word!" in the Web browser. However, if you make it pass-thru HTML, the Domino server won't try to turn the batch of text into something that approximates what appears on the form. Instead, it will pass the text along to the browser without trying to do anything special to it. If the text involved happens to contain HTML tags, those tags will be treated appropriately. If "Word!" is marked as pass-thru HTML, you'll see **WORD!**, in boldface text, in the Web browser.

There are several ways of making text pass-thru HTML. One of the best methods is to select the text (including document fields) that you would like sent through as HTML. Then, from the Text menu, select Text ➤ Pass-Thru HTML. However, you may also create a style named HTML and apply it to the selected text. The first method has the advantage of being highlighted in the form, as illustrated in Figure 26.3. You'll also be able to apply another style to it if you need to.

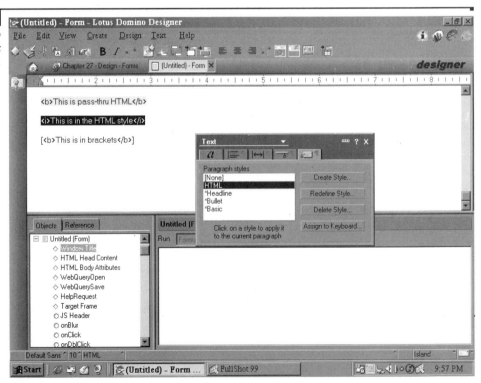

FIGURE 26.3

A form design showing various styles of pass-thru HTML

Developers coming to R5 from 4.*x* versions know that putting text in brackets (that is, square rather than curly brackets: [ ]) in a form or in documents still makes the text pass-thru HTML. While the pass-thru HTML method from the Text menu is probably the best way of handling HTML, the square-brackets method is a trick we'll be using in many other cases. Figure 26.4 shows how all of those formats are interpreted as HTML in a Web browser.

FIGURE 26.4

The same form shown in a Web browser

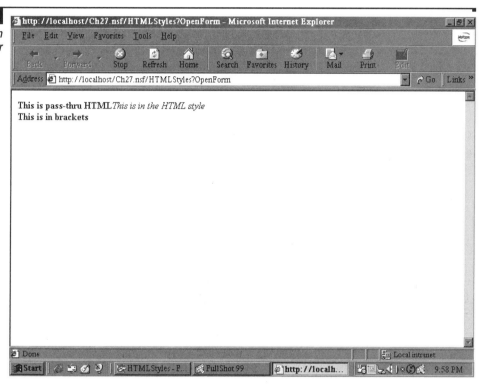

There is a fourth way of creating pass-thru HTML, but it's not one for the faint of heart. In the Defaults tab of the Form Properties Infobox, there is a On Web Access section. The first check box is Treat Document Contents As HTML. If you check this box, *all* of the contents of a document viewed through that form will be treated as HTML. Essentially, the Domino server will strip out the plain text content of the form and send it along rather than trying to convert the content into HTML on its own. Any text styling in the form will be lost when the form is viewed on the Web. Tables will vanish, Actions won't appear, embedded objects will go away, and anything that can't be converted into ASCII text will not be sent to the Web browser. Figure 26.5 demonstrates how some features don't come through at all.

PART

VI

Developing
Databases

FIGURE 26.5

This is a form design with the Treat Document Contents as HTML check box selected, a document using the form viewed in Notes, and a document using the form viewed on the Web. (Don't select this check box if you want people to enter data over the Web.)

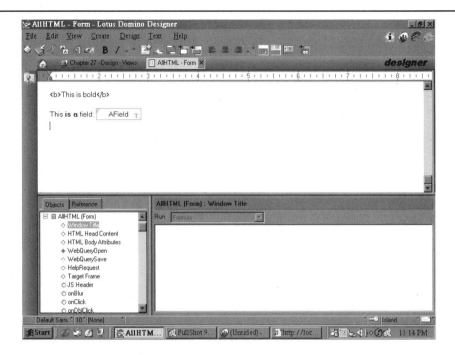

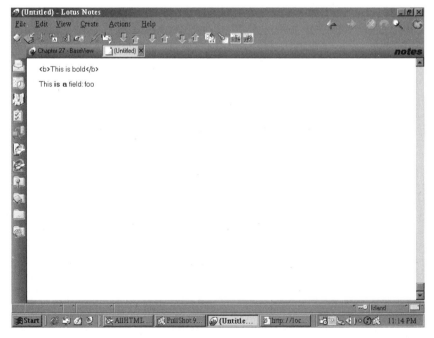

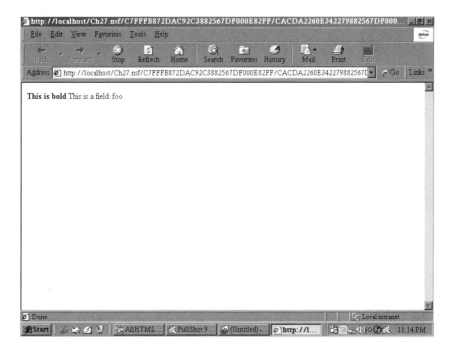

One of the most important implications of treating document contents as HTML is that field contents come through as uneditable text, not as editable fields. Indeed, Domino won't even let you try to edit a treat-documents-as-HTML form. Attempting to use the OpenForm method of the form or the EditDocument method of a document will return a Type 500 error. Using the Treat document contents as HTML option is OK if you want pinpoint control over your HTML (for example, if you want to import an elaborate HTML document produced with a WYSIWYG Web page creator) or if you want to set up forms for use by CGI applications. But, if you want inter-Action with the Notes database itself, you're much better off using a combination of Notes features and other kinds of pass-thru HTML.

The most obvious advantage of using pass-thru HTML is that it allows you precise native control of the appearance of your documents on the Web because it allows you to hand-tool HTML to your heart's content. You can replace embedded images with <Img> tags. This improves performance by keeping the caching down for both the Notes database and for the Domino server. You can create hypertext links in a conventional, easily read format rather than hiding the link behind a URL hotspot. (Of course, this is a relative advantage. If you're coming from the Notes world, you'll probably be more comfortable with hotspots. But, if you're coming from straight HTML design, you may want your design more "exposed.")

More importantly, though, if you use pass-thru HTML in conjunction with fields and computed text, you can dynamically structure links and content over the Web or use easily built and configured Notes controls as part of building a Web page. If you mark a field as pass-thru HTML using any of the methods described, its contents will be treated as HTML, just as static text on the form is. For example, consider a Web site that has home pages for all of the people who worked on individual documents. Each home page is named `lastname.html`. The forms used to display the documents could have a computed-for-display field with this formula:

```
AuthorName := @Subset(@Author; 1);
ExplodedName := @Explode(AuthorName; " ");
LastName := @Subset(ExplodedName; -1);
"<a href = \"http://www.website.com/" + LastName + "\">" + AuthorName
➥   + "'s Web Page</a>"
```

As plain text, this field would yield an ugly jumble of text and punctuation. However, if marked as pass-thru HTML and viewed through a Web browser, it becomes a neat, clean hypertext link to the author's Web page, as shown in Figure 26.6. The link doesn't have to be hard-coded into the form design, nor does a URL link hotspot have to be created in each new document. Instead, Notes computes the link as it would compute any other text field.

FIGURE 26.6

A form with pass-thru HTML on a field and the corresponding Web page

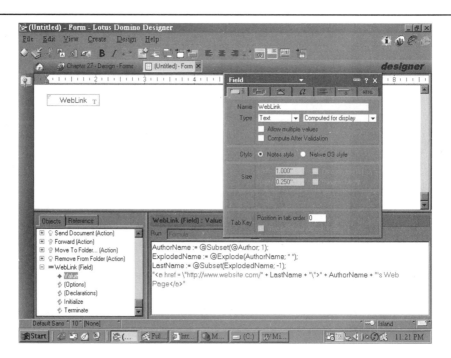

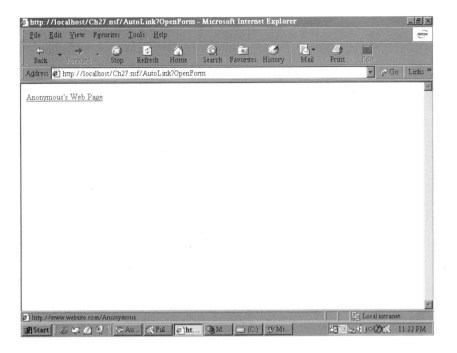

Another reason to use pass-thru HTML is to use new HTML features. The HTML that Domino generates does not use CSS (Cascading Style Sheets) and other new features of the HTML 4 standard. While some Notes objects give you some hooks to use HTML 4, Domino doesn't generate these on its own. For example, if you use a named style in your Domino form, Notes will emulate the text with ad-hoc HTML tags (<Font>, <B>, <I>, and so on) rather than trying to create a style on its own. This can be regarded as a positive feature. By sticking with an earlier HTML standard, you can be sure that earlier browsers will be able to interpret the Web pages that Domino produces for you on the fly. However, you may want to use HTML features not supported by Domino's HTML translation capabilities. pass-thru HTML allows you to do just that. Domino doesn't understand HTML 4, but it doesn't have to. All it has to do is to pass the text along to a browser that can.

Customizing Responses

Form submission is the most obvious example of the fact that Domino's translation of documents into HTML is technically functional but not everything the user might desire. If you build a simple Form Submission button into a form, the result of submitting the form looks like Figure 26.7. The form has been submitted, but the act of submitting it takes you to a dead end. To get to some place useful, the user will have to use the Web browser's Back button at least twice: The first time to pass over the page that was just submitted. This is about as bad as Web design can get.

FIGURE 26.7

The default result of submitting a form page

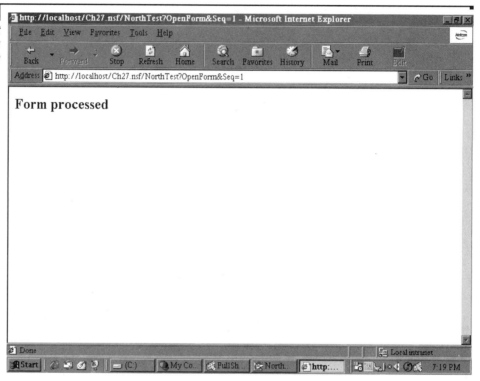

But, as you may imagine, Notes provides you with several ways of customizing the response form.

It's quite easy to build a response directly into a form meant for Web use. One of the most useful fields you'll use on a Web-enabled document is $$Return. $$Return is a name reserved by Notes for use in Web forms. When you build a field named $$Return, it should be a text field, but can be editable, computed, computed for display, or computed when composed. When you submit a Domino form, the contents $$Return will be returned to your browser. If you make $$Return a computed field, Domino will calculate the contents of the field after you submit it and return that to the browser. For example, a $$Return field with the formula here will return a page like the one shown in Figure 26.8.

```
"<center><H2>" + @Name([CN]; @UserName) + ", your form has been
➡   submitted.  Click <a href=\"thisdb.nsf\">here</a> to return to
➡   the front page."
```

FIGURE 26.8

After you submit the
form, you get a
customized message.

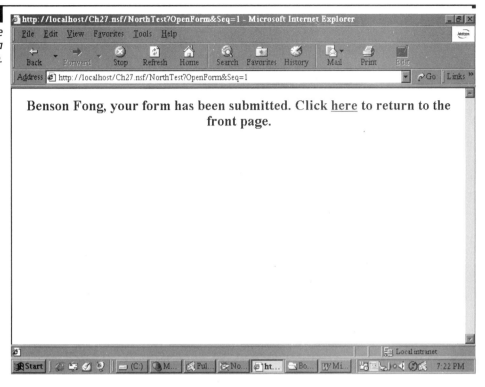

Potentially, you could create an entire Web page with links, image tags, and so on in the $$Return field. But if you want a more sophisticated response to form submission, there's an easier way to go about it. If the $$Return field computes to a URL in brackets, Domino will send you to that URL when the form is submitted. For example, if a form's $$Return field contains "[http://www.lotus.com]", submitting the form will send the user straight to Lotus's home page. There wouldn't be much point in that. But you could just as easily send a user to the front page of your Web site; to an external HTML page indicating that the form has been submitted; to a page or frameset in the database; or, if you use a computed $$Return field, to a specific external HTML page or to a document within a Notes database, depending on the contents of the form that the user fills in.

Now, we can deal with a little bit of unfinished business. Remember the workflow form used at the beginning of Chapter 25? With a little renovation, we can make that form work on the Web. There are two things we really need to change to Web-enable it. First, we need to alter the Send For Review Action to make it a little more Internet-friendly. If everyone using the application uses Notes mail either through a Notes client or through the Web via a Domino server, the strategy of using a doclink

PART

VI

Developing
Databases

in the informational e-mail message will still work. However, if your users are using POP, IMAP, or other mail clients, the link is lost. Instead, if your application is supposed to be accessed on the Web, you can simply provide a URL, like this:

```
ftrusrs := @If(@Elements(FutureUsers) > 0; @Subset(FutureUsers; 1-
➥   (@Elements(FutureUsers))); "");
FIELD ReviewedBy := ReviewedBy: CurrentUser;
FIELD CurrentUser := @Subset(FutureUsers; 1);
FIELD FutureUsers:= ftrusrs;
FIELD ApprovedDates := ApprovedDates; @Now;
Bodytxt := "Please review the linked document and pass it on at your
➥   earliest convenience:
➥   http://www.servername.domain/database.nsf/" + @DocumentUniqueID
➥   + "?OpenDocument";
@MailSend(CurrentUser;"";"";"Please review this document";Bodytxt; "");
@PostedCommand([FileSave]);
@PostedCommand([FileCloseWindow])
```

Notice that instead of sending a message with an appended doclink, the body text of the message includes a URL that incorporates @DocumentUniqueID and points directly to the document in the database. An increasing number of mail clients are Web savvy and will turn anything starting with *http://* into a clickable hypertext link. This provides you with the same functionality as a Notes doclink, but on a non-Notes platform.

The other thing we'll need to do is to provide the Web browser with a place to go once the document is submitted. That can be accomplished by adding a $$Return field. We can use fields from the document in a computed text field. This results in an informative message that assures the user that the document has been submitted and also gives him somewhere else to go. You might use a formula like the one here in your $$Return field:

```
"This document has gone on its merry way to " + CurrentUser + ".
➥   Click <a href://www.servername.domain/database.nsf>here</a> to
➥   return to the front page of this application."
```

Validating Fields

The $$Return field is a versatile tool for creating responses that notify the user that a form has been successfully submitted. But sometimes users don't fill in forms the way they should. Just like regular Notes forms, you'll often want to validate the content of Web forms. And just as there are several ways to customize form responses, there are a number of ways to validate form input.

Field input validation works within forms submitted over the Web, although it has many of the same problems that were presented by form submission. If a form is submitted with a field that fails validation, the text to be returned by @Failure messages is presented in the browser, as illustrated in Figure 26.9.

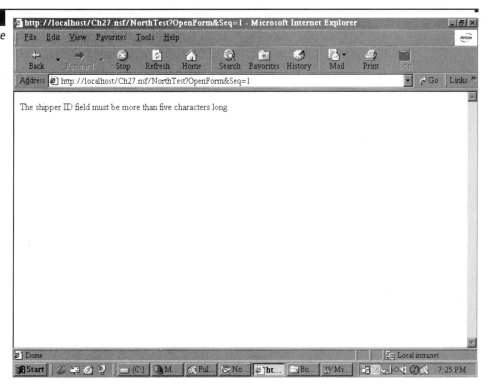

It is possible to improve the appearance of the response for the Web. This is another place where placing text between square brackets will pass it along to the response as HTML. Domino will set up appropriate <Body> tags, so any pass-thru HTML you insert in the validation formula will be interpreted properly, as demonstrated in Figure 26.10.

Since you can put a hand-tooled HTML page into your validation response, you can get very sophisticated. Not only can you tell the user what she did wrong, you can also include hyperlinks to pages containing more information on the subject and use <Meta> refresh tags to send the user to another page automatically. The validation formula here produces a page that points out a problem in the user's submission; provides a link to a page with more information; and, if the user does nothing, automatically sends her that information page.

```
@If(TestScore > 100 | TestScore < 0; "<Head><Title>Form
➥   Submitted</Title><Meta http-equiv=refresh content = \"10;
➥   url = http://homepage.corporation.com/testscores.html\">
➥   <\Head> <Body>Score problem:  test scores cannot be over 100
➥   or under 0.  Follow the <a href = \"
➥   http://homepage.corporation.com/testscores.html\">link on the
➥   homepage</a> for more details.</Body>"; @Success)
```

FIGURE 26.10

An HTML-ized response with HTML tags

The page that is produced will look something like the one in Figure 26.11.

Still, performing validation through Domino and using HTML tricks to navigate and display information is a bit limiting. The obvious drawback is that pure HTML can't return a user to the page that he just visited in order to correct what is probably a minor error. At the very least, he will have to navigate back to the page he submitted in order to try submitting it again. A more hidden, but equally important, concern is server load. If you rely on regular Notes field validation, the Domino server does all the work, which can be a problem if it has to perform a lot of validation. However, with JavaScript, you can make the client machine do all of the work and do it before the user submits the form to the server. This greatly simplifies the navigation and puts less strain on a busy server, thereby increasing overall performance.

FIGURE 26.11

A fancier validation message

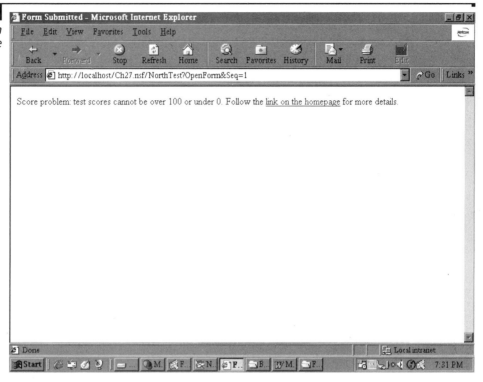

There are a few different places you might want to put JavaScript validation formulas. The best places to invoke validation formulas is probably the onBlur event for individual fields so that you can validate fields as users exit them (that is, when the field loses focus).

For example, consider a field used to collect the number of employees working at a company. Clearly, that number must be a number, not text. If text is put in, the user should be informed. Let's call this field EmpCount. You might put a function like this in the JS Header:

```
function emptext(){
var emps = document.forms(0).EmpCount.value;
if(isNaN(emps)){
alert("Number of employees must be a number, not text.");
}
}
```

PART
VI

Developing
Databases

Also, the EmpCount field should have `emptext()` in its onBlur event. When the user exits the field, the JavaScript routine will read the value of the field (form fields on the Web have the same names that they do on the Notes forms) and see if it's a number. If it isn't, it throws up an alert.

Duplicating field validation when you save a document is just a bit trickier. You need to combine your validation functions in such a way that your Web browser knows if there is a problem with any of the fields. If there are problems, the user should see alert messages. If not, the form can be submitted. What you may want to do is to have your individual validation functions return a value, then use that value to tell another function what to do. Here's an example:

```
function emptext(){
var emps = document.forms(0).EmpCount.value;
if(isNaN(emps)){
alert("Number of employees must be a number, not text.");
return 1;
}else{
return 0;
}
}

function checksubmit(){
var isproblem = 0;
isproblem = isproblem + emptext();
if(isproblem == 0){
document.forms(0).submit()
}
}
```

The form should be given a button with `checksubmit()` on its onClick event.

The CheckSubmit performs a number of steps to validate form input. First, a slight modification of the `emptext()` function returns a value. When used by itself in a field's onBlur event, the value returned by the function doesn't matter. When used within the `checksubmit()` function, the value returned by `emptext()` determines whether or not the form gets submitted.

 WARNING Be aware that all of the JavaScript code in this book was written for Internet Explorer. Because different Web browsers can deal with JavaScript differently (and some can't handle it at all), you may encounter some problems if you use the JavaScript in this book exactly as it is presented in your applications.

> ⚠️ **TIP** One of the useful side effects of using JavaScript field validation (as well as JavaScript input translation, discussed next) is that it works within Notes, as well as in a Web browser. You may not be able to incorporate JavaScript field validation into saving a document in Notes. But if you just check field values, you can write the code once and use it in both Web and Notes clients.

Input Translation and Computing Fields

Input translation and computed fields also work on the Web. Unfortunately, like input validation formulas, input translation formulas only operate on form submission, while computed fields are only calculated when calling up the page and after the form is submitted. A pure Domino-generated form on the Web won't update computed fields automatically like it will in Notes. But this is yet another limitation that you can get around by using JavaScript.

To make translation work, just put a function in the onBlur event of a field, and perhaps in the onSubmit event of the form (or, of course, incorporate the translation function into another onSubmit function), and in the appropriate functions in the JS Header. For example, consider a field used to collect the number of employees working at a company. Clearly, that number must be a whole number. Some input translation that automatically rounds the number off to an integer might be in order. Let's call the field EmpCount. You might put a function like this in the JS Header:

```
function roundemp(){
var emps = document.forms(0).EmpCount.value;
var empsround = Math.round(emps);
document.forms(0).EmpCount.value = empsround;
}
```

You'd also put roundemp() in EmpCount's onBlur event. When the user exits the field, the function will round it off.

However, because input validation and input translation JavaScript routines will often need to share the onBlur event, you may need to write somewhat more complex formulas in order to duplicate Notes Input Validation and Input Translation formulas. A more realistic version of the previous formula would incorporate both validation and translation, like this:

```
function roundemp(){
var emps = document.forms(0).EmpCount.value;
if(isNaN(emps)){
alert("Number of employees must be a number, not text.");
document.forms(0).EmpCount.value = "";
```

PART

VI

Developing
Databases

```
}else{
var empsround = Math.round(emps);
document.forms(0).EmpCount.value = empsround;
}
}
```

This function checks to see whether or not the value in the field is a number rather than text (say, *10* rather than *ten*). If it's text, it gives a warning and clears out the field. If not, it rounds the number. If the functions were more elaborate, it might be best to split the validation and translation into different functions.

Reproducing the functionality of computed fields that refresh automatically is a little trickier. The first thing to be aware of is that if you want a field to update automatically, it must be an editable field. Computed fields appear on the form as just plain text, and are no more editable on the Domino-rendered Web page than a heading or a table boundary.

The second aspect of fields that are set up to compute automatically is that they make heavy use of the onBlur event. This makes things a little more crowded unless you program carefully. To completely emulate automatic field refreshes, every field on which a computed field is based must have a JavaScript formula in its onBlur event. This means that you could ultimately have four functions attached to a single change in the field:

- A function to update the "computed" field after input translation

- A function to translate input after field validation

- A function to validate input

- An overall function that calls all of the above when the user exits the field

As an example, we'll go with something a little less elaborate. Imagine a form with three fields: Price, TaxRate, and AdjustedPrice. Price is the price of an item, TaxRate is a percentage sales tax rate. And AdjustedPrice is the full price of the item, including the tax. In Notes, we'd make AdjustedPrice a computed field with a value of `Price * (1 + (TaxRate/100))`. Assuming the form was set to automatically refresh fields, any change in either Price or TaxRate would trigger a recalculation. In a Web browser, we'll need some code like this:

```
function TaxCalc(){
var theprice = document.forms(0).Price.value;
var therate = document.forms(0).TaxRate.value;
var thetax = theprice * (1 + (therate/100));
var adjprice = theprice + thetax;
document.forms(0).AdjustedPrice.value = adjprice;
}
```

Both Price and TaxRate should have `TaxCalc()` in their onBlur event. When either field changes, AdjustedPrice is updated.

While it's a good idea to incorporate input validation and input translation functions within functions that will potentially submit a form, it's all but necessary in forms that compute fields. If a field value is set immediately before the form is submitted, the user can't change it, inadvertently or otherwise, and the proper value will be saved. However, if the proper value is not set, an incorrect value could potentially be sent to the server. If you use this method for documents that are to be used on both the Web and in Notes, you may also need to use either separate Web and Notes forms, or at least separate Web and Notes subforms.

Web Agents

One of the major limitations on building Notes databases for Web use is that a limited set of @formulas and no LotusScript Actions or buttons can be taken directly to the Web. JavaScript can fill in some of the holes. For some uses, such as validation, it's quite superior. But for other uses, it is not very effective, particularly when it comes to affecting other documents. However, while you can't take LotusScript directly to the Web browser, you can do the next best thing: Have certain form events trigger Agents on the server. Using Web Agents is absolutely necessary if you want opening or submitting a document to kick off an operation that requires the unique properties of Java and LotusScript, such as iteration or processing other documents. For example, imagine a form where you fill in a value. When you submit the form, all documents containing that value are stamped with the current date. To do that, you'll have to rely on a Web Agent.

To have an Agent run automatically when a form is opened over the Web or when the document is saved, go to the form's QueryWebOpen and QueryWebSave events. You should always find the relevant @Command (`@Command([ToolsRunMacro])`), already in the code for both events. Just fill in the name of the Agent you want to run. Agents that you want to run over the Web should probably be designated as Manually From Agent List or On Schedule Never. If you run a Manually From Agent List Agent, be sure to include parentheses in the @Command (for example, `@Command([ToolsRunMacro]; "(SaveAgent)")`).

Getting the Document

To use Agents on the Web, you'll also have to write them differently. To perform Actions on the current document in a Notes client, you can use the UI classes. Unfortunately, you can't use those classes in a Web browser. The UI classes only work on elements currently open in a Notes client. Because you are on the Web, there is no Notes client, so there can't be anything currently open.

Instead, you'll have to rely on a new class: `DocumentContext`. `DocumentContext` is a property of a `NotesSession`. Getting the `DocumentContext` property returns a Notes-Document object, containing all the fields and other properties of the document you created or opened on the Web. To get to the document in LotusScript, you'll use code like this early in the Agent to instantiate the Web equivalent of the current document:

```
Dim s as New NotesSession
Dim doc_web as NotesDocument
Set doc_web = s.DocumentContext
```

A great deal of code in the previous chapters was written with external files in mind or was embedded in objects within documents. Neither of these situations is particularly well suited to using Java. However, document-oriented Agents are a great place to put Java. If you've been working with Java in Notes, you may already have been dealing with the `DocumentContext` property. In case you haven't, here's how to get there:

```
Document_doc = agentContext.getDocumentContext();
```

Actually, you need to create a Session and an AgentContext object. Since those objects are already created when you create a Java Agent, you only need to write a single extra line of code.

You can think of the code you put in the QueryWebOpen Agent as substituting for the QueryOpen event, and the code for the QueryWebSave Agent as substituting for both the QuerySave and QueryClose events, except with only a NotesDocument object to work with, not a UINotesDocument. The name QueryWebSave is slightly misleading from a Notes point of view but makes eminent sense on the Web. The Agent in QueryWebSave is triggered when the form is submitted, regardless of whether or not the document was saved.

 WARNING Be sure Web Agents have been signed by somebody with permission to run Agents on the server. If they aren't, they won't run, and the forms they're attached to will return errors when the documents are opened or saved.

Agents for QueryWebOpen might be used to update data in the document before it is sent to the user, to test for certain attributes of the user, and perhaps to deny access or to send out messages elsewhere in the database. As an example of an Agent appropriate to QueryWebOpen, the code here is a simple access counter. Every time the document is opened on the Web, the Agent takes the value of the TimesAccessed field, increases it by one, and saves the new value.

```
Sub Initialize
  Dim s As New notessession
  Dim db As notesdatabase
  Dim doc As notesdocument
  Dim timesaccessed As Integer

  Set doc = s.DocumentContext

  timesaccessed = doc.timesaccessed(0)
  timesaccessed = timesaccessed + 1
  doc.timesaccessed = timesaccessed
  Call doc.save(False, False)

End Sub
```

And here's how to do it in Java:

```java
import lotus.domino.*;

public class JavaAgent extends AgentBase {

  public void NotesMain() {

    try {
      Session session = getSession();
      AgentContext agentContext = session.getAgentContext();

      // (Your code goes here)

    Document doc = agentContext.getDocumentContext();
    int timesacc = doc.getItemValueInteger("TimesAccessed");
    int newcount = timesacc++;
    Integer replacecount = new Integer(newcount);
    doc.replaceItemValue("TimesAccessed", replacecount);
    doc.save();
```

```
    } catch(Exception e) {
      e.printStackTrace();
    }
   }
  }
```

Of course, this all assumes that there's a numeric field called TimesAccessed on the form.

You'll probably find more use for QueryWebSave Agents. This is what you'll use to process the contents of documents, pass around workflow documents, and trigger other processes in the database. To make it work well, though, you will need to be able to pass data back to the browser once you've submitted the document.

Returning Results

Getting data into and out of the document is just part of what you can do with Web Agents. You can also run Agents that return very specific results. Indeed, in some cases, you will have to.

The key here for LotusScript Agents is the Print statement. In an Agent run on a Notes client, the Print statement would make a line of text appear in the status bar at the bottom of the client. It's great for flashing unobtrusive status messages for a user, but not particularly useful for more than that.

However, for Agents run over the Web, the Print statement can be a powerful tool. Instead of going to a status bar somewhere, the results of a Print statement are sent to the user's Web browser, overriding any instructions that may be in a $$Return field. If your Print statements return HTML, the browser will interpret it accordingly. This means that you can construct an entire Web page on the fly. For example, here's a simple registration form (see Figure 26.12) and a LotusScript Agent that will produce a customized HTML response. The form is designed to register employee preferences for the location of this year's company Christmas party. The form contains two fields (employee ID and location choice) and a button that submits the document. The form triggers the Agent OnSave when it is submitted, which saves the document and constructs an HTML response using the form's contents (see Figure 26.13). The Christmas party committee can review the saved documents later to count up votes and decide where to hold the party. Here's the Agent code:

```
Sub Initialize   Dim s As New notessession
    Dim doc As notesdocument
    Set doc = s.DocumentContext
```

```
    Call doc.save(False, False)
    Print "<title>Vote Registered</title>"
    Print Chr(10) + Chr(13)
    Print "<body>"
    Print Chr(10) + Chr(13)
    Print "Your vote for the " + doc.VoteOptions(0) + " has been registered."
    Print Chr(10) + Chr(13)
    Print "<br><br>"
    Print Chr(10) + Chr(13)
    Print "Click <a href=""http://company.homepage.com"">here</a> to
➡    return to the intranet home page."
End Sub
```

FIGURE 26.12

The Vote form

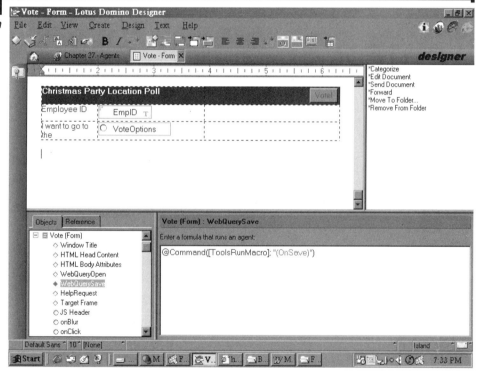

For Java Agents, you'll need something a little more complex: a PrintWriter object. To send output to the Web browser, start by pulling in the appropriate classes with the line `import java.io.PrintWriter;` at the beginning of the program, just as Notes automatically imports the `lotus.domino` classes. Next, create a PrintWriter object with the getAgentOutput() method. The PrintWriter object is instantiated by setting a variable equal to getAgentOutput(). Finally, to send text to the browser, use the println method of the PrintWriter object that you just created. This code does in Java what the previous code does in LotusScript:

```
import lotus.domino.*;
import java.io.PrintWriter;
public class JavaAgent extends AgentBase {

  public void NotesMain() {

    try {
      Session session = getSession();
      AgentContext agentContext = session.getAgentContext();
```

```
    // (Your code goes here)

  Document doc = agentContext.getDocumentContext();
  String MyVote = doc.getItemValueString("VoteOptions");
  doc.save();
  PrintWriter pw = getAgentOutput();
  pw.println("<Title>Vote Registered</Title>");
  pw.println("<Body>");
  pw.println("Your vote for the ");
  pw.println(MyVote);
  pw.println(" has been registered. ");
  pw.println("<br><br>");
  pw.println("Click <a href=\"http://company.homepage.com\">here</a>");
  pw.println(" to return to the intranet home page.");

  } catch(Exception e) {
    e.printStackTrace();
  }
  }
}
```

There's another extremely important reason to use the Print/println method in Web Agents in preference to $$Return fields: debugging. Notes gives you the Lotus-Script debugger, allowing you to step through an Agent, pause anywhere you want, examine the value of every variable, and even make changes midstream. On the Web, you don't have that. You simply can't test Web Agents in a Notes environment. In fact, the only debugging tools you have for Web Agents are the ones you build yourself. The way to build those tools is by using error-handling routines and the Print method. Enable error handling in your Web Agents just as you would for a Notes Agent (that is, through the use of On Error statements; review Chapter 24 for how to do this). For your error-handling code, write some instructions that use the Print statement to send information to the browser instead of, for example, to a message box. This code returns reports for errors taking place in a Web Agent:

```
WebError:
Print "<b>Error in line " + Cstr(Erl) + "</b>"
Print "<br>"
Print "Error #" + Cstr(Err)
Print "<br>"
Print Error
Print "<br>"
Print "<br>"
Resume Next
```

This routine will print out information on every error that takes place when the Agent runs, as illustrated in Figure 26.14.

FIGURE 26.14

Output from an error-handling routine on the Web

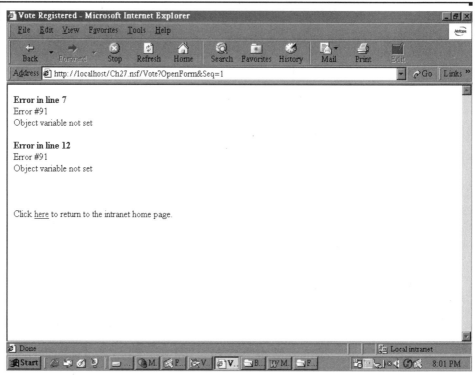

In addition to the usual error items, you will almost certainly want to track the values of individual variables. You should add Print statements for the value of the variables you want to track with appropriate informational labels.

Very Elaborate Responses

Using the Print method, you can generate as elaborate of a Web page response as you want. However, if you're building a response page for an elaborately designed Web site, that could mean a lot of typing and careful punctuation. JavaScript headers, image tags, nested tables, and so on may require elaborate dodges to build them into Print statements and can make your code next to unreadable. However, there's an easy way around that. Using the Open statement presented in the previous chapter, you can open a standard HTML file and feed it line by line to a Web browser through Print statements.

Continued ▐▶

CONTINUED

Let's say you have a standard look that involves a banner across the top of the page, navigation buttons down the side, and content in the middle of the page. You can create an HTML file that holds all the common elements and puts in a special line to indicate where custom content should go. With the code snippet here, Notes will open the file and go through it line by line, sending the current line to the Web browser. However, if the line reads "<CustomContent>" (it could be anything, but it would be obvious to anybody reading the HTML file that that line isn't an actual HTML tag), it executes some code that will print customized HTML. For example, it might provide a link to another page or print out an HTML-formatted message that thanks the user for submitting a form.

```
Open filename for Input as #1
Do Until EOF(1)
Line Input #1, str_outputline
If str_outputline = "<CustomContent>"
   ' Custom content code goes here
Else
   Print str_outputline
End If
Loop
```

In addition to easily allowing you to incorporate elaborately formatted HTML in your Web Agent responses, it also makes maintenance easier. If you desire, you can seed the HTML file with a number of different flags for different purposes and call the same page from different Agents. This gives all of your responses the same look. When you want to change the look of the responses, you can simply change the HTML file.

Code Locking

The Web is not immune to Save Conflicts. If two users try to save changes to the same document at the same time, it will naturally result in a Save Conflict. However, using LotusScript Agents, it is possible to minimize the possibility of Save Conflicts. The key here is code locking. LotusScript 4 has a feature that allows you to make a script wait to run until other scripts have stopped running. The application of code locking on the Web should be clear: If you use Agents to save and process your Web documents, you can use code locking to have the Agents politely queue up and run one at a time rather than all at once. If the Agents aren't running at the same time, they can't try to save the same documents at the same time, *ergo* there are fewer Save Conflicts.

Locks are a little tricky at first, but once you get the idea, they become quite easy to use. There are four steps to using code locking:

- Attempting to create a lock
- Getting the lock
- Releasing the lock
- Attempting to destroy the lock

A *lock* is really just a flag for LotusScript to keep an eye on, a named object that any script can check for the existence of. In fact, you could even have a script that created a lock but didn't use it. A lock is created with the `CreateLock()` function. This is the confusing part: To create a lock, you provide the `CreateLock()` function with a name (that is, a text value). However, the `CreateLock()` function returns an integer value, which is what the other code locking functions use. Let's say you want to create a lock with the identifying name MyLock. You'd create the lock like this:

```
Dim str_LockName as String
Dim int_LockID as Integer
str_LockName = "MyLock"
int_LockID = CreateLock(str_LockName)
```

Lock-related functions will use `int_LockID` rather than `str_LockName` to identify the lock. You can create a lock anywhere in a script. You may want to do it at the beginning of a script, just to get the task out of the way, or you may want to wait until you're ready to use it. The only important thing is that you create the lock before you use it.

`CreateLock()` doesn't necessarily create a lock. Rather, it attempts to create the lock using the name you have provided. Either way, it returns an integer value. If you use it with a name that has been used to create an existing lock, it will return the same ID number that was returned when the lock was first created. So, in the previous example, if another script ran the same code as the previous script a moment later, it would get the same value for `int_LockID`. And if you later used that ID number in the other locking functions, you'd be using the same lock you created earlier. You might think of it this way: `CreateLock` translates between a name, which *you* use to identify a lock, and an ID number, which *Notes* uses to identify a lock.

The ID number gets used in the other locking functions: `CodeLock`, `CodeUnlock`, and `DestroyLock`. These functions, which all take an integer as a parameter (presumably, the integer you got when creating a lock), will return a true value if they work, or a false value if they don't. You'll use `CodeLock` in a line like this:

```
Call CodeLock(int_LockID)
```

If the code lock is successful, Domino will check to see if any other scripts are using the lock. If so, it will wait until the lock becomes free. Once the lock is released, the Agent gets to run its own code and make any other Agents trying to use the same lock wait until it is released.

Once you're done with the lock, be sure to clean up after yourself and put everything away. First, use the CodeUnlock command to release the lock you obtained earlier. For the code we've used so far, the command would simply be CodeUnlock-(int_LockID). If you don't release the lock, other scripts attempting to use the same lock won't be able to get it. This means that they'll never run.

Likewise, always use the DestroyLock command at the end of the script. Continuing the code we've used so far, the command would be DestroyLock(int_LockID). If a lock isn't going to be in active use, it shouldn't exist.

How it should look in practice is something like the code here. You might recognize it as the Web document saving Agent in the "Returning Results" section, modified to incorporate code locking.

```
Sub Initialize
    Dim s As New notessession
    Dim doc As notesdocument
    Dim thelock as Integer
    Dim DocID as String
    Dim x as Integer
    Set doc = s.DocumentContext
    DocID = doc.UniversalID
    thelock = CreateLock(DocID)
    x = CodeLock(thelock)
    Call doc.save(False, False)
    X = CodeUnlock(thelock)
    X = DestroyLock(thelock)
    Print "<title>Vote Registered</title>"
    Print Chr(10) + Chr(13)
    Print "<body>"
    Print Chr(10) + Chr(13)
    Print "Your vote for the " + doc.VoteOptions(0) + " has been registered."
    Print Chr(10) + Chr(13)
    Print "<br><br>"
    Print Chr(10) + Chr(13)
    Print "Click <a href = ""http://company.homepage.com"">here</a> to
➥    return to the intranet home page."
End Sub
```

This Agent takes advantage of the UniversalID property of the `NotesDocument` class. Remember those big, ugly, 32-digit alphanumeric strings in Domino-generated URLs? That's what the UniversalID is. If you use the document's ID number, you create a separate lock for each document. Multiple instances of the same document use the same lock. If we set `DocID` to the same value every time the Agent runs (say, `DocID = "TheCodeLock"`), *every* attempt to save a document would use the same lock. On a high-volume Web site, every single attempt to save a document would queue up one after another, killing performance. However, this version will only cause the Agent to pause if two Web documents share the same ID. This gives you good performance, as well as preventing Save Conflicts.

Searching

Users of Notes databases on the Web can take advantage of Domino's powerful searching capabilities just as users of Notes clients can. Some additional work will be necessary to give Web users access to the search machinery. After all, on a Web browser, you can't just turn on a Search bar. However, if you build just a few extra forms to collect and display data, you can give users the ability to search not only a view or a database, but also your entire Web site, including Notes databases *and* other documents, static HTML Web pages, and plain text documents.

To search a database over the Web, the database must be full-text indexed, and additional steps must be taken to include databases and other documents in broader searches. (These are mostly administrative tasks, but we'll cover the basics). Once the database is indexed, you can pass URL commands or form results to the Domino server and get back search results. There are a number of ways to refine your search, from customizing input to search a specific view, to generically searching your entire Web site.

Creating Search Forms

The key to searching over the Web is to create a form to gather search information, then pass it to the server with a special URL. There are three kinds of searches that you can perform over the Web:

- View search
- Site search
- Domain search

The technology behind site searches isn't quite up to the standards of the other searches and appears to be on its way out (it's still supported for backward-compatibility), so we'll be concentrating on view and domain searching.

The first part of conducting a search is collecting search criteria. Notes provides you with powerful tools for searching in the Notes client, such as the Search bar and search builders, that allow you to search by author, field, form, and so on. The Web doesn't have those tools. You'll have to construct them yourself by building specialized forms.

The most important thing to collect is a search value. This would be equivalent to text typed into a Search bar. Without the search value, you can't perform a search. To collect the search value, use a text field.

In addition to the search value, you can collect a number of parameters to modify the search and the way the results are displayed. For example, you can control the number of results returned by the search, sort the results, and find word variants. Where the search value is text, the other controls are numbers or Boolean values. Here are some commonly used parameters and the kinds of values they take:

Maximum number of documents returned This control takes any integer as its value.

Sort order This control takes 1, 2, or 3 as its value. A value of 1 means a sort by relevance, 2 is an ascending date sort, and 3 is an ascending date sort. It's very easy to make this easily comprehensible to users by using a keywords field that uses aliases for the actual values. For example: "Sort by Relevance | 1."

Search for word variants This control takes a value of True or False. If you provide a true value, Domino will search for variants. For example, a search for *burger* would return documents holding both *hamburger* and *cheeseburger*. This is another good place for a keyword field.

There are several other possible parameters to use for searching views. Check the Designer Help for "URL commands for searching for text."

Once you have a way to collect the data, you can assemble it to actually conduct a search and get some results on the screen. To do that, you'll need to construct a $$Return field that constructs a URL with a format something like this:

```
http://server/pathtodatabase.nsf/viewname?Searchview&Query=texttosearchfor&-
otherparameters
```

You've already seen how to call up forms, views, documents, and so on, so most of this format should come as no surprise. However, unlike other Domino URLs, search URLs require a set of parameters.

The only absolutely necessary parameter for a search URL is Query. After all, you can't conduct a search without something to search for. All the other parameters have default values, either inherent in them or set by the Domino administrator. The default parameters can be overridden if you provide other values. For example, the parameter to search for word variants is SearchWV, while the parameter to set the maximum number of documents returned is SearchMax. With the Search form presented in Figure 26.15, the formula for the $$Return field should be something like this:

```
"[http://server/pathtodatabase.nsf/viewname?SearchView&Query=" +
➡   QueryString + "&SearchMax=" + MaxRecords + "&SearchVW=" +
➡   SearchVariants + "]"
```

?SearchView must come directly after the view name, but the order of the other parameters doesn't matter. And, of course, don't forget to add a button or Action to the form that will submit it.

FIGURE 26.15

A simple Search form

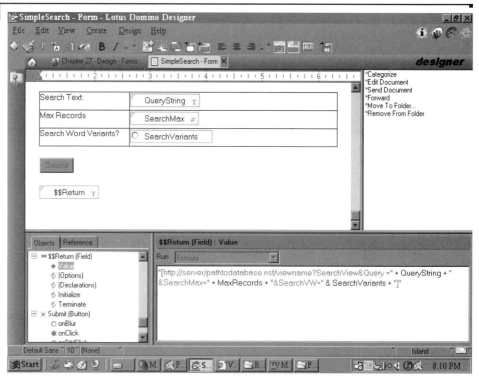

By default, the search results page will look something like Figure 26.16. The little square gray icons are there to emulate the shaded relevance indicators of search results in the Notes client.

FIGURE 26.16

A search results page

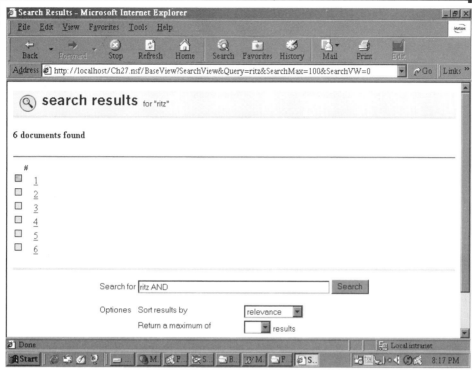

Passing Parameters: A Crash Course

This is a little beyond a basic working knowledge of HTML, so we'll discuss this briefly for those of you who aren't familiar with CGI programming and URL parameters. To pass parameters along with a URL, you put a question mark after the URL for the "page," then add a series of parameter names and values. You've already seen how this is done to pass commands to the Domino server (to run Agents, open documents, and so on). But you can pass data, as well. Parameters follow the format *parameter-name=value* and are joined by ampersands (&).

While most searches will be performed through custom Search forms, you don't absolutely need to collect data from a form to perform a search. All you really need is the search URL. For example, you could have a Keyword field in a form that holds

PART

VI

Developing
Databases

important categorizing words to identify the document, and a computed field that generates URLs to search for those words. Consider a field named Keywords and another field that is marked as pass-thru HTML and computed for display with this formula:

```
"<a href=\"http://www.domino.org/testdb.nsf/AllContents?SearchView&Query=" +
➥    Keywords + "\">" + Keywords + "</a>"
```

When viewed through the Web browser, the field will be filled with clickable links, each of which will search for a given keyword.

Customizing Results

Building custom search tools doesn't stop with data collection. You can also exert considerable control over how the results are displayed. This process uses techniques left over from 4.x that aren't covered in the Designer Help, but they still work in R5. Indeed, the Domain Search forms take advantage of them, so you may as well be able to use them also.

You've already seen how you can embed views in pages. Views can also be embedded in forms that are viewed over the Web. A form that holds a view must be named some variation of $$ViewTemplate. For example, the "$$ViewTemplate for *viewname*" form can be used to display the named view. However, the form must also have a text field named $$ViewBody, which must hold the name of the view to be displayed. When you call up the view, Domino will display the named view that is embedded in the form. This only works for Web clients. And the view can only be displayed as HTML, not rendered as an applet.

There's a special variation on this for searching. A Search Results form should be named $$SearchTemplateDefault. It should have a $$ViewBody field with the value `"$$Return"`. Be careful here: The value of the field should calculate to the string $$Return, *not* to the contents of a $$Return field on the form. If you have a $$SearchTemplateDefault form in your database, the Domino server will return that form with the search results embedded in it in the $$ViewBody field. Figures 26.17 and 26.18 show a custom Search Results form and how search results might appear with it.

Note that, since it's a form, you can have a JavaScript header, Actions, buttons, and other fields. In the case here, there's a line showing the current date and time. However, the full range of data collection fields from the Search form illustrated in Figure 26.15 could be reproduced at the bottom of the Search Results form, as well. With those added in, a user can perform repeated searches, viewing one set of search results after another if an individual search's results are unsatisfying.

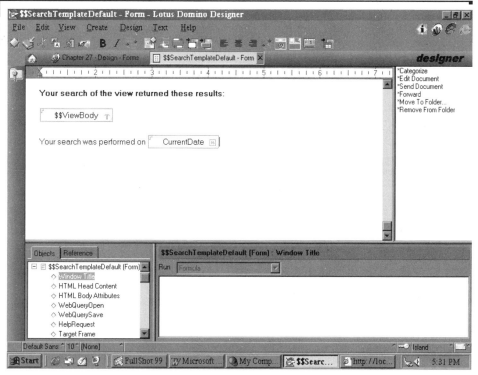

FIGURE 26.17

A custom Search Results form

Another thing you can do if you use a Notes form for your results is to take advantage of some special field values. When you do a search, you can get a long list of values that you can use to populate fields in a Notes form. You can get the query expression (that is, the text being searched for), the number of documents returned by the search, the search parameters (maximum number of documents, whether or not to use word variants, and so on), and more. A full list of values can be found in the Designer Help (search for "Customizing Search Forms"). We'll show you how to use some of them with a heavily customized Search Results form, shown in Figure 26.19.

The first thing you'll notice on this form is a table filled with query information. Each of the fields is one of the special values returned by a search, with one exception: Path_Info. In addition to letting you use some special values in searches, any page called up through the Web from a Notes database gives you access to a number of standard CGI variables. Path_Info is the path to the page being opened relative to the server's root directory. This page also expects to be passed a Count variable, which indicates the maximum number of hits to return per page.

PART

VI

Developing
Databases

FIGURE 26.18

*Search results
displayed in the form*

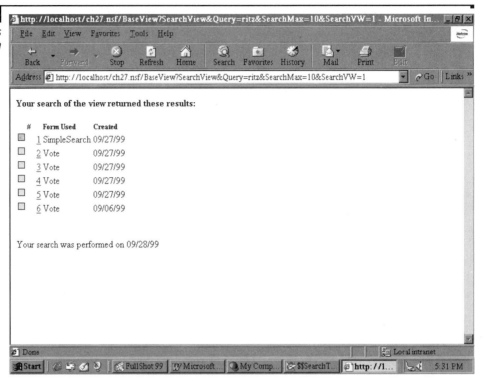

The CurrentTitle field takes some advantage of this information, showing the user where in the search results she is. However, the form doesn't really take advantage of all of these apparently extra fields until they appear in a pair of Action hotspots at the bottom of the page. Note where the form says "Previous Page of Search Results" and "Next Page of Search Results." Both of those hotspots use the command @URLOpen to pass a complex URL. The URL used in the Next Page Of Search Results field is shown here:

```
REM "Get the path info";
startPath := @Left(Path_Info;"?SearchView");
@URLOpen(startPath + "?SearchView&Query="
+@ReplaceSubstring(Query;" ";"+")
+ "&SearchOrder=" + @Text(SearchOrder)
+ "&SearchMax=" + @Text(SearchMax)
+ "&Start=" + @Text(Start+Hits)
+ "&Count=" + @Text(Count)
+ "&SearchWV=" + @Text(SearchWV)
+ "&SearchFuzzy=" + @Text(SearchFuzzy))
```

FIGURE 26.19

A more complex
Search Results form

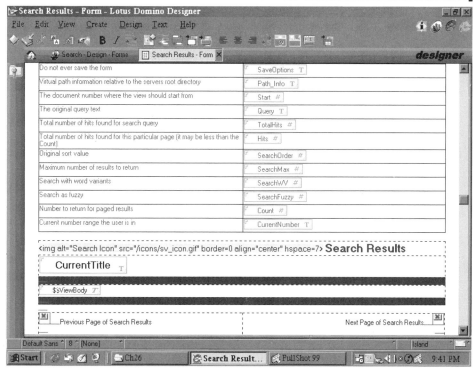

Clicking the hotspot opens a URL very similar to the one that was opened when you clicked the search results page. The expression using Path_Info gives you the path to the database, the database itself, and the view being searched. Query is the text being searched for, SearchOrder is the order of sorting, SearchMax is the maximum number of hits to return, and so on. However, this formula will call up a page that shows a set of results a little farther down the list from the current page of results. The important variables to pay attention to here are *Start*, the number of hits into the search where the current page starts to display results, and *Hits*, the number of search hits displayed on the page.

For example, if you performed a search that returned ten hits per page, the first page of results would start with the first hit and show the first ten. The previous formula would also show ten hits, but it would start at the starting place of the previous page (one) plus the number of hits per page (ten), which is to say that it would start at the eleventh hit. In short, this formula allows you to page forward through the search results, viewing them one convenient screen at a time. The previous results hotspot does the same thing, only using Start - Hits as the formula to determine where to start. This means that it points backwards rather than forward. Both the previous and next hotspots have hiding conditions that make them vanish when there aren't more search results in their respective directions. In use, the results look something like Figure 26.20. Notice how the results fit neatly on the screen at 800 × 600 resolution.

FIGURE 26.20

Search results page

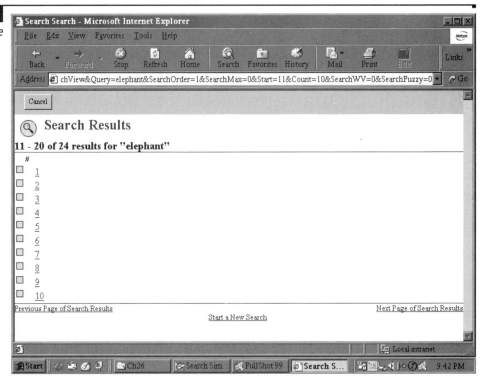

One last aspect of this page is the Start A New Search hotspot at the very bottom of the page. This link calls up the database's default search page. You could make this page even more complex and versatile by reproducing the query and condition fields to make it a compound results-and-search page. However, to make it work, you'd have to be extremely careful about naming fields and constructing search URLs.

Creating Generic Search Forms

Following the instructions for building search URLs that you've seen so far, you can perform highly customized searches with very specific results. For example, you could have simple Search forms for each different regular view in a database, perhaps collecting just a search expression, a maximum number of documents, and a detailed Search form for a hidden All Documents view that would give you the full range of options. However, those instructions are for one-view-at-a-time searching. It's possible to customize a Search form for every view search you perform on the site. However, to do so, we'll have to duck outside Notes and Domino for a moment.

You can search any view using a URL built like this:

`http://server/database.nsf/viewname/$SearchForm?SearchView`

This URL will call up a Search form that looks like Figure 26.21. The search will return something like Figure 26.22.

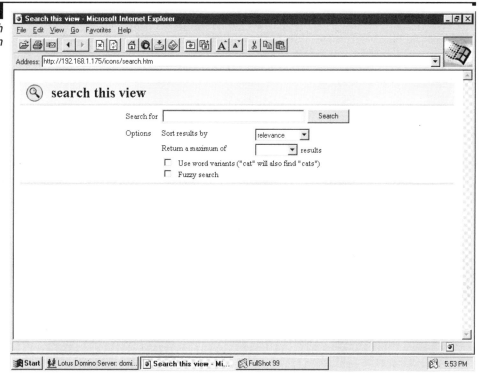

You might be surprised to discover that the Search form and Search Results form don't exist inside Notes. Rather, they're plain HTML files: `search.htm` and `srchbar.htm`, respectively. Both files reside in the Domino server's `/domino/icons` directory.

The `$SearchForm?SearchView` URL operates in one of a number of ways, depending on the kinds of data submitted with it. By itself, with no parameters, it tells Domino to open up the appropriate HTML file. If you open the file and examine the HTML, you'll notice some familiar names on the fields: Query, SearchMax, SearchOrder, and so on.

PART

VI

Developing
Databases

FIGURE 26.22

The generic Search
Results form

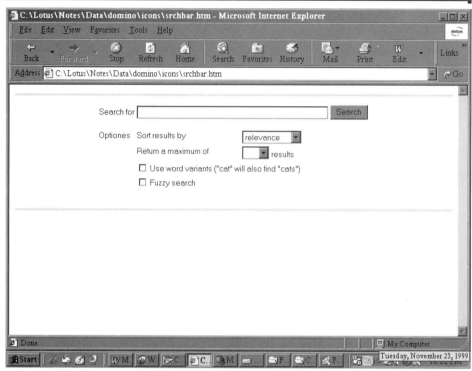

Clearly, this form can collect all the necessary fields for a Web search. But how does that data get sent to the server? The answer isn't in the HTML file itself, but in the processing. The opening <Form> tag of search.htm goes like this:

```
<form method = "POST" action="">
```

However, when called up on the Web, the generic Search form's opening <Form> tag looks like this:

```
<FORM METHOD="POST" ACTION="/databse.nsf/uniqueID?SearchView">
```

Here, the HTML file hasn't been sent directly to the browser. Rather, it has been processed by the Domino server, which prepares the form to be submitted to a particular view and operation. Submitting the form through a Post operation sends data along just as if the data were attached to the URL, as we did when we started building search URLs in the $$Return field. When the search is performed, Domino will return the results using the default search results page, srchbar.htm.

Because the basic Search forms are just HTML, you can customize them easily by editing the files. You can change the labels, add backgrounds, add JavaScript field validation, and otherwise tweak them to fit the look and feel of your Web site. You could even create a series of external HTML files to perform searches on specific views, giving them <Form> tags along these lines:

```
<Form Method="Post" Action="/database.nsf/viewname?OpenView">
```

Because the external file isn't generated through a $SearchForm/SearchView URL, it won't be prepared in advance to search a specific database. You will have to specify one in the Action parameter of the tag.

If you customize search.htm and srchbar.htm for your Web site, be aware that the change will affect *every* form search for which you don't create a specific Search form. While you can change certain aspects of the forms (for example, SearchMax, which is presented in the HTML file as a drop-down list, could be turned into a text input field), be sure not to change the field names.

Domain Search

One of the most powerful new features of R5 is the *domain search*. Domain searching extends Domino's search engine across any number of databases and even into the file system, letting users perform searches not only of database content, but also of external files, as well.

To perform domain searches, Domain Searching must be enabled on the server. This is fairly easy, but falls into the realm of administrative tasks, so check the Administrative Help for instructions. Enabling Domain Searching will create a domain catalog database, called catalog.nsf, by default. This database is a central repository of data for databases and other files across the Domino domain. You will use this database to perform domain searches.

In addition to being full-text indexed, a database must be marked for inclusion in multi-database searches. The setting may be found in the Database Properties InfoBox (see Figure 26.23). You might also want to check with your Domino administrator to make sure that the Catalog process is running on the server. Once those steps are completed, domain searches will return documents from the database.

The Catalog database comes with some very elaborate forms to enable domain searching. The basic form is the Domain Search form, shown in Figure 26.24. As you can see, this form is very large. (We had to break it into four separate screen shots to get a picture of it!) Part of the reason this form is so complex is that it is for both Notes and Web use. It works very hard at duplicating the look and feel of the Notes form on the Web.

PART

VI

Developing
Databases

FIGURE 26.23

The Include In Multi-Database Indexing property is enabled.

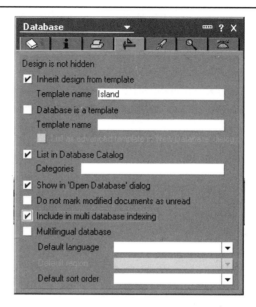

FIGURE 26.24

The Domain Search form

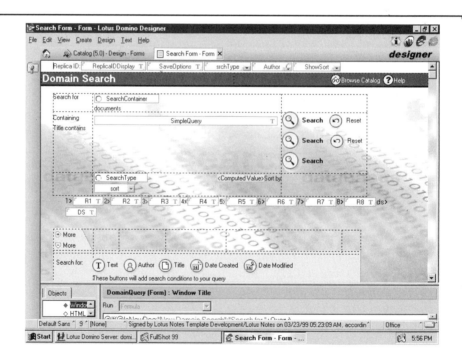

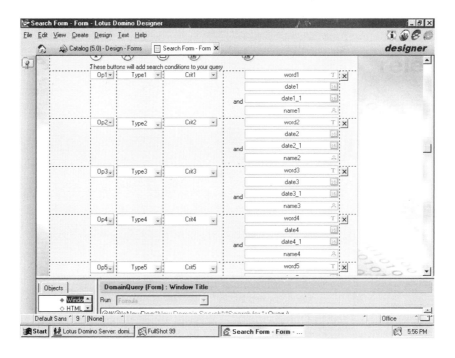

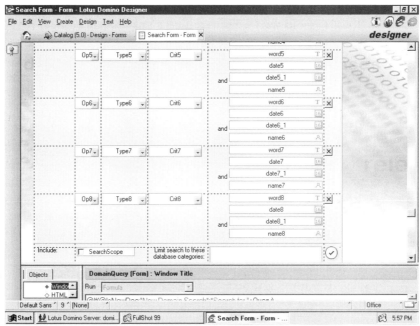

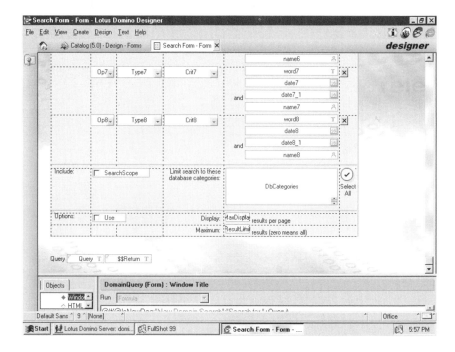

Search results are displayed by three forms working in conjunction with one another: (SearchResults), shown in Figure 26.25; and (ResultEntry) and (DetailedResultEntry), shown in Figure 26.26. When you run a domain search, Notes prepares a sort of mock view, using documents rendered into a rich-text Body field if viewed in Notes, or an actual view rendered as HTML and embedded into a form using a $$ViewBody field if viewed over the Web.

Like search.htm and srchbar.htm, you can customize the look of the forms in order to make it fit with your site by substituting your own graphics, changing font sizes and styles, and so on. However, you should be extremely careful not to change the names of fields, field formulas, Agents, and so on unless you know exactly what you're doing. You can also make several copies of the forms and customize each of them as you see fit. This will give you a number of different search possibilities.

The typical way to start a domain search is by opening the Search form (http://server/catalog.nsf/DomainQuery?OpenForm). You can rename copies to anything you like. To call a customized results page, you need to change the way the form is submitted. If you glance back at Figure 26.24, you'll see that there are three identical magnifying-glass icons near the top of the page. The second one down is the one that Notes uses to submit the form for domain searches over the Web. It's a formula Action hotspot. To change the form used for results, get into the hotspot's properties and scroll down to the bottom, where you will find a line beginning with this:

```
@URLOpen("/" + DBName + "/SearchResults?SearchDomain&Query="
```

Replace SearchResults with the name of the Results form you want to use instead.

FIGURE 26.25

The (SearchResults) form

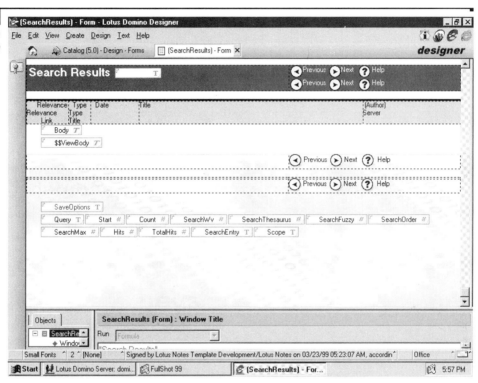

Much like view searches, you can perform domain searches by using a customized URL, which you can hard-code or construct with a customized Search form, just as you can use a customized URL to search views. However, you have a broader latitude for customization and for making changes. As you can probably guess, the URL should use ?SearchDomain instead of ?SearchView. The ?SearchDomain command should be proceeded by the name of the Search Results form you want to use. The ?SearchDomain command takes the same parameters as ?SearchView and absolutely requires a Query parameter, but it can take some special parameters of its own. It can also take a very complex Query parameter. Instead of searching for a single text expression, you can search for text in documents, titles, authors, and dates. Table 26.1 outlines the possibilities and how to search for them.

PART

VI

Developing Databases

FIGURE 26.26

*The (ResultEntry) and
(DetailedResultEntry)
forms*

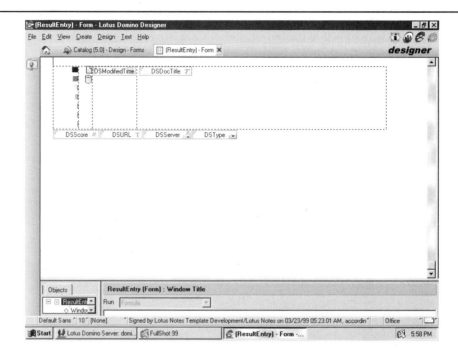

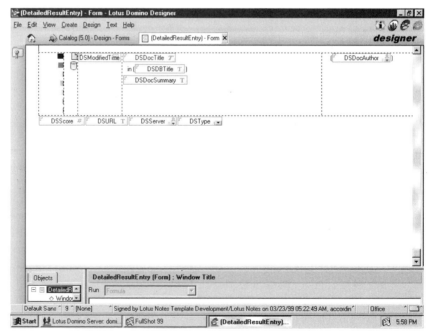

TABLE 26.1: FIELDS FOR DOMAIN SEARCHES

Data	Syntax
Authors/editors	Use (`[$UpdateBy] Contains` *name*) to search for the name of people who have modified the document.
Title	Use (`[_Title] Contains` *text*) to search for text in document titles.
Date Created	Use (`[_CreationDate]` *operator date*) to search for a creation date. For example, (`[_CreationDate] = 1/2/1998`) will search for documents created on January 2, 1998. While (`[_CreationDate] < 4/6/2000`) searches for documents created before April 6, 2000. Use the operators >, <, =, and !=.
Date Modified	Use (`[_RevisionDate]` *operator date*) to search for a modification date. Use operators as you would for the date created search.
Text	No additional expressions are necessary, but the text to search for should be put in parentheses.

You can also combine search conditions. To join search conditions, put each individual condition in parentheses and join them together with And, And Not, or Accrue. And and And Not are for the logical And operations, while Accrue is a logical Or operator. For example, the Query expression for searching for documents that contain both *football* and *baseball* would look like this:

```
(football) And (baseball)
```

The Query expression for searching for document containing either *football* or *baseball* would look like this:

```
(football) Accrue (baseball)
```

Once you have collected everything in your search expression, you can use it to set the value of the Query part of a ?SearchDomain URL. However, before you do, you should process the search expression through the @function, @URLEncode. To go out over the Web for a URL, a lot of characters have to be specially encoded. For example, spaces become "%20." Many other characters used in a domain search have to be encoded, as well. While you could get the job done with repeated uses of @Replace-Substring, you'd have to know all the coding conventions. The (sadly undocumented) @URLEncode does it all for you. @URLEncode returns a string formatted for use in a URL by a particular type of server. To incorporate it into a domain search URL, you might use an expression like the following:

```
"http://server/catalog.nsf/SearchResults?SearchDomain&Query=" +
➡    @URLEncode("Domino"; searchexpression)
```

Two other special parameters for ?SearchDomain deserve special attention. One of them is SearchEntry. SearchEntry takes as its value the name of the form you want to use to display individual search result entries. With an unmodified Catalog database, the two possible values are SearchEntry and DetailedSearchEntry (see Figures 26.25 and 26.26). If you modify copies of those forms, you can use the new form names, as well.

The other special parameter is Scope. Scope determines what kinds of files the search will return. There are three values. This means that it is a good candidate for a drop-down menu. The values are shown in Table 26.2. If you don't use this parameter in your URL, the default is zero.

TABLE 26.2: VALUES FOR THE SCOPE PARAMETER

Scope **Value**	**Files Searched**
0	Notes databases and external files
1	Notes databases only
2	External files only

Applets and Embedded Objects

Notes allows you to render various objects as Java applets. This allows you to reproduce large parts of the Notes objects' functionality. This is particularly useful on the Web. But before you decide to render everything as Java applets, it's best that you know the limitations of applets, as well as their capabilities. Using Java applets gives embedded objects increased functionality, but also significantly increases the download time over slower dial-up connections. Also, be aware that old browsers may not be able to run Java applets. Know your audience before you start using applets.

Rich Text Fields

As you saw in Chapter 18, a rich text field can be rendered on the Web as a Java applet. The Rich Text Field applet allows some of the same capabilities as a rich text field within a Notes document, but not all of them. The applet is structured to provide about as much rich text functionality as something on the Web can. For example, it provides three "pseudo-fonts": monospaced, serif, and sans serif. While font names may change between platforms, almost every computer is likely to have a serif font (like Times New Roman), a sans serif font (like Arial or Helvetica), and a monospaced font. Using these three types of font, it strikes a balance between diversity in style and portability across platforms. It also provides a much wider range of colors by using the whole Web palette.

However, what is more important to know is the functions the Rich Text applet can't reproduce. Like fonts, text styles are limited to bold, italic, and underline. Tables of any kind cannot be created. Like any other Notes object on the Web, a Rich Text applet can't be encrypted. Finally, external files can't be brought into a Rich Text applet in any way. They cannot be imported, embedded, or attached.

There is one other drawback to the Rich Text applet: If you set a rich text field to be rendered as a Java applet rather than HTML, it will be rendered as a Java applet even when the document is viewed for reading instead of for editing. This means that the field will take significantly longer to load over slow dial-up connections even if the applet's special properties won't be used.

Uploading Files

While the Rich Text applet can't give you file attaching capabilities, the File Upload applet can. You can insert a File Upload applet into a form by selecting Create ➣ Embedded Element ➣ File Upload Control. The applet will provide you with a control like the one illustrated here.

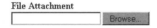

Clicking the Browse button brings up a standard file navigation dialog, which allows you to pick the file you want to upload.

The File Upload applet is a Web-only feature. In a Notes client, the applet appears as a featureless box, as shown here. If you use a File Upload applet in a form and you choose to use that form both on the Web and in a Notes client, you should probably hide the applet from Notes clients.

File Attachment
File Upload

When you upload a file through this control, the file is attached to the document itself. It is not embedded in a specific rich text field or uploaded as a separate file on your Web server.

Views

Views can be rendered as applets, as well. To render a view as an applet, embed a view in a page or form, get the embedded object's properties, and select the "Render as Java applet" check box. You can also adjust the applet's size in the Object Properties dialog box.

The View applet, shown in Figure 26.27, performs most of the important functions of a Notes view. You can sort the view by clicking a column header (assuming, of course, that the view the column is based on is sortable), select multiple documents, mark multiple documents for deletion, and double-click documents to open them.

PART

VI

Developing
Databases

FIGURE 26.27

A View applet

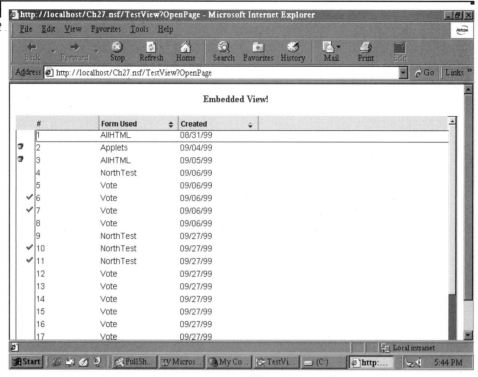

Unfortunately, that's about all you can do with the View applet. Objects outside of the View applet, including view Actions, don't know what is selected inside the applet. Therefore, you cannot run script Actions and Agents that are intended to run on a batch of selected documents, or create responses to documents.

Outlines

Like views, outlines can be rendered as applets. Again, embed the outline, get its properties, and check the appropriate box.

Because outlines are generally composed of what are, ultimately, links—be it to views, pages, documents, or other places on the Web—their functionality translates very well to the Web. However, there are a few differences between the way outlines behave in Notes and how they behave on the Web.

If you use the multi-image rollover outline trick shown in Chapter 21, you must set the outline to be viewed as a Java applet. If you set it to render as HTML, the outline will display all parts of the image simultaneously, side by side, instead of setting up a rollover routine, as shown in Figure 26.28.

FIGURE 26.28

A rollover outline
rendered as HTML
versus one rendered
as an applet

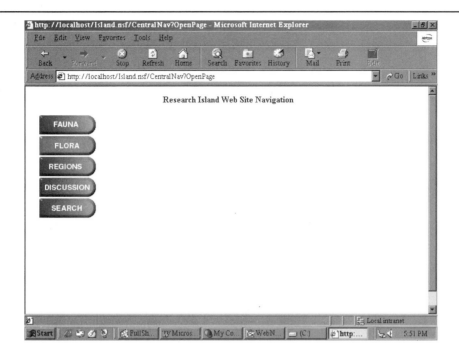

You must also be careful when setting the size of the outline if you are going to embed the outline in another design element. While a Notes client will be responsive to the Fit To Content setting in the Outline properties, the Java applet will not. The size that the Domino server passes to your Web browser may not be appropriate to your screen resolution. Therefore, you may need to pick an outline height appropriate for a number of screen resolutions. You can do so in the Outline Size Height text box of the Embedded Outline Properties window, shown here.

Summary

While Domino can render Notes documents and many Notes functions into HTML and JavaScript, the Web is a fundamentally different programming platform from a Notes network. There are several strategies for optimizing Notes forms for use on the Web, including using separate forms for the Web and for Notes forms, or using pass-thru HTML to incorporate features that cannot be easily built with traditional Notes objects. Writing code for the Web is also different from writing it for Notes clients and may use different methods and structures. It is possible to run extensive searches over the Web, using specialized URL commands. Finally, Notes provides you with a number of Java applets to reproduce the functionality of Notes objects on the Web.

The next chapter shows you how to build a simple application. It is a Help Desk application, which demonstrates how various features of Notes can interact with one another to perform a task.

CHAPTER 27

An Example Notes Application: Help Desk

This database demonstrates some fairly conventional Notes workflow functions and also some fairly simple forms. This database is for an organization's computer support personnel to use to record users' computer problems and track the progress of efforts to solve those problems. It holds identifying information about users and the computers on which the problems occurred, detailed information about the problem itself, and provides tools to analyze that information and move it around to the appropriate personnel.

The Scenario

HotShot Software, an up-and-coming software publishing company, has abruptly grown from a start-up in a garage to a large company with offices in three different locations across the West Coast. There are enough people using computers that the Technical Support department has had to adopt a formal system of tracking user problems. This system needs to meet specific needs for technical support personnel, for managers, and for users. Technical support personnel need to record as much detail as possible about user problems. They also need to either indicate how the problem was solved or refer more difficult problems to second-tier technical support specialists. Managers will use this tracking information to determine what software is causing the most problems and if user problems are being solved in a timely fashion.

While many of the summary functions that management wanted could be supported by a relational database, Notes was chosen as the platform for the application because of the absolute need for flexible workflow and detailed narrative content.

The database must support several different sets of functions.

- Users should be allowed to report problems directly to the database rather than having to call technical support personnel at the help desk. They can create incident reports, but they cannot alter them once they have been saved. While they will be given access to enter identifying information and a description of their problem, they cannot enter any workflow information.

- First-tier help desk analysts can create incident reports and have full powers to edit existing documents. Help desk analysts, on taking charge of an incident (either creating a document or reviewing a user-created document), can mark the problem as resolved or pass it on to anyone else in the Technical Support department until the incident is finally marked as resolved.

- Managers aren't directly involved in workflow, but they do want to be able to analyze the data to see what the biggest problems are and how effectively they are being dealt with. The questions they want answered include: How long does it take for Technical Support to get to a user-created incident report? How long does it take to resolve a problem? What software causes the most problems and the most difficult problems?

The Forms

The main function of this application centers around a form that collects data on a single user problem and moves from help desk person to help desk person until it is finally marked as resolved. However, there are a number of considerations with its design, such as security and the specific shape that workflow will take.

One of the first concerns is workflow. Workflow in this database might be described as freeform, following the path illustrated in Figure 27.1. Computer problems are likely to be so complex and interrelated that the designers decided that there was no point in trying to program a given progression or routing path into a document or into the database as a whole. Instead, the process works like this:

1. A Web user or first-tier help desk analyst creates an Incident document that describes the problem. Then, the analyst collects information on the user and the user's system.

2. A first-tier help desk analyst works with the person who has a complaint and attempts to solve the problem in the Incident document. If the problem is resolved, the incident is marked as closed.

3. If the incident is not resolved, the first-tier help desk analyst selects someone else in the department to refer the problem to. That analyst is informed by e-mail.

4. If the second analyst can't resolve the problem, it can be referred to a third analyst. The third analyst can refer it to a fourth, and so on until the problem in the Incident document is finally marked as resolved.

FIGURE 27.1

Workflow for the Help Desk application

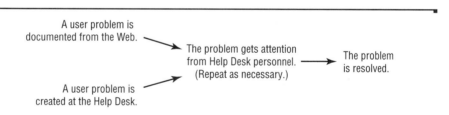

It is expected that an incident might go through several people before it is marked as resolved. It may even go back and forth through the same people repeatedly as they support one another.

Another concern is tracking. After the fact, managers will want to evaluate the performance of the help desk staff. They'll want to see how long it took to solve problems, both individually and on average. They'll want to know what the problem areas seem to be, who gets the most calls, and how many help desk personnel a problem runs through until it gets solved.

PART

VI

Developing
Databases

Once the database's purpose and functions were mapped out, the designer created forms to address each of these concerns.

The Incident Form

The main data collection tool is the Incident form, shown in Figure 27.2. The Incident form has "Incident" as both its name and its alias.

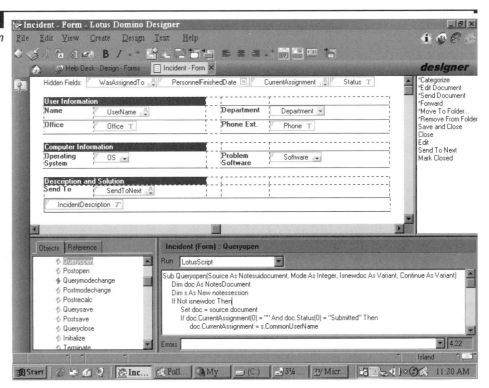

FIGURE 27.2

The Incident form

The form starts with four hidden fields:

WasAssignedTo   This is a multi-value Names field. This field will hold the names of people assigned to work on the incident once they have passed it on to somebody else.

PersonnelFinishedDate   This is a multi-value Date/Time field. This field will record the time when each person assigned to work on the incident finished with it and either passed it on or marked it as complete.

CurrentAssignment   This is a single-value Names field. This field holds the name of the person currently assigned to work on the incident. Since Incident forms are only created by help desk personnel, this field defaults to the current user's name.

Status   This is a single-value text field. This field indicates where in the process the incident is: Submitted (newly submitted from the Web), In Progress (being worked on by help desk personnel), or Complete (problem resolved or regarded as unsolvable due to lack of information or other problems). This field's default value is In Progress.

The values of hidden fields will be manipulated by Actions and code related to the form. The remaining fields can be edited by the user as necessary. For readability, the form is divided into several sections (That is, it is divided into tables on the form, not actual Notes sections. The designer decided that there wasn't enough discrete information on the form to require collapsible sections or tabbed tables).

The first section holds data about the user:

UserName   This is a single-value Names field using the Address dialog for data. This field holds the name of the user who is having a problem. This field has the input validation formula @If(UserName = ""; @Failure("There must be a user name."); @Success). The formula ensures that a username has been entered.

Department   This is a single-value combo box that indicates which department the user belongs to. The names of departments (Engineering, Executive, Finance, Marketing, etc.) are written into the field definition. This field has an input validation formula much like the one for UserName. This formula ensures that there is a department.

Office   This is a single-value text field that holds the user's office number. Again, there's a validation formula that ensures that the field is not null.

Phone   This is a single-value text field that holds the user's phone number extension. All phone extensions in the organization are numeric and contain only digits from 0 to 9, but since they may be "zero padded" (that is, 042 instead of just 42), the field must be a text field. Because the phone numbers fall into a predictable range, there's an input validation formula. It checks to make sure that the value of the field is a number and no more or less than three characters long:

```
IsANumber := @TextToNumber(Phone);
ExtSize := @Length(Phone);
@If(!IsANumber | ExtSize != 3; @Failure("Phone extensions must be
➡     three digit numbers."); @Success)
```

The tab-like effect of the User Information section label was obtained by merging the first two cells of the table's first row, then giving the merged cell a different background color and text color.

The next section identifies information about the computer and the software that is causing problems:

OS This is a single-value dialog list field that uses the Operating System view as its source. This field holds a description of the user's computer.

Software This is a multi-value dialog list field that uses the Software view as its source. This field holds a list of programs and operating systems that are believed to be causing the problem.

The Description and Solution section contains two fields:

SendToNext This is a single-value Names field that draws from the Personnel view. This field is used to designate the person a document should go to next if the current user can't resolve the problem.

IncidentDescription This is a rich text field. This field is used to describe the problem and keep track of attempts to solve it.

In addition to some standard Save and Close, Close, and Edit Document buttons, this form has two Actions to support the application's workflow features. Send to Next alerts another user that the document needs his attention. The hide-when conditions keep it from appearing if there is no name in the SendToNext field. The Send-ToNext field is blanked out when the Action runs, so a user has to consciously designate the next recipient before the Action can take place. Send to Next contains the following code:

```
FIELD WasAssignedTo := WasAssignedTo: CurrentAssignment;
FIELD CurrentAssignment:= SendToNext;
FIELD PersonnelFinishedDate := PersonnelFinishedDate: @Text(@Now);
FIELD Status := "In Progress";
SendTo := SendToNext;
FIELD SendToNext := "";
@MailSend(SendTo;"";"";"Please review this document";"Please review
➥    the document and pass it on at your earliest convenience"; "";
➥    [IncludeDoclink]);
@PostedCommand([FileSave]);
@PostedCommand([FileCloseWindow])
```

The name of the help desk analyst who is currently assigned to the incident is added to the list of past personnel, the person designated to get the document next gets e-mail notification, and the document is saved and closed. This gets the document out of the current user's way. The line that sets the status to In Progress is there to make sure that the status is correct when action is taken on a document from the Web.

The second Action, Mark Closed, is a bit simpler:

```
FIELD WasAssignedTo := WasAssignedTo: CurrentAssignment;
FIELD PersonnelFinishedDate := PersonnelFinishedDate: @Text(@Now);
FIELD Status := "Complete";
@PostedCommand([FileSave]);
@PostedCommand([FileCloseWindow])
```

The current help desk analyst's name is added to the list of past personnel, the Status field is marked as complete, and, again, the document is saved and closed.

There is also some code in the form's events. To prevent multiple people from working on the same documents, there are provisions to limit editing. This code, in the form's QueryModeChange event, keeps anybody but the person currently assigned to the document from editing it:

```
Sub Querymodechange(Source As Notesuidocument, Continue As Variant)
Dim doc As NotesDocument
Dim s As New notessession
Dim x As Integer
If Not isnewdoc Then
    Set doc = source.document
      If Not (doc.CurrentAssignment(0) = s.UserName) and Not
➡   (doc.Status(0) = "Complete") Then
           Msgbox("This document is currently assigned to " &
➡   doc.CurrentAssignment(0) & ". Contact the help desk
➡   supervisor if you need to take it over.")
           Continue = False
    End If
End If
End Sub
```

This code only stops the change to editing mode if the document's status is In Progress or Submitted. Since Completed documents will rarely, if ever, be edited, the designer decided that there was little point in burdening the computer by trying to prevent editing documents with this status.

There is also code to immediately assign a document with Submitted status to the first person who opens it:

```
Sub Queryopen(Source As Notesuidocument, Mode As Integer, Isnewdoc As
➡   Variant, Continue As Variant)

Dim doc As NotesDocument
```

PART

VI

Developing Databases

```
Dim s As New notessession
If Not isnewdoc Then
   Set doc = source.document
   If doc.CurrentAssignment(0) = "" and doc.Status(0) = "Submitted" Then
      doc.CurrentAssignment = s.UserName
      doc.Save(False,False)
   End If
End If
End Sub
```

You may ask, "Why all the code? Wouldn't it be simpler to make CurrentAssignment an Author field?" As with everything else in database design, the answer is "It depends." In this case, the way CurrentAssignment works depends on the structure of the organization's administrative hierarchy. In some organizations, where there is a clear distinction between help desk analysts who would deal with requests and help desk administrators who manage content, CurrentAssignment could be an Author field. Analysts would pass information along through regular channels, administrators would maintain data documents, and their functions would never overlap. However, in this organization, some of the people who will be dealing with Incident documents are also administrators, who need Editor access because they might need to deal with documents regardless of who is assigned to them. Their Editor access would override any protection granted by Author fields. Therefore, something else is in order. However, for added protection, you could make CurrentAssignment an Author field anyway. That way, you could give the regular help desk analysts Author, rather than Editor, access. Help desk administrators should have Editor access. This allows them access to any necessary document, while keeping the various reference documents (Personnel, Operating System, and Software, as detailed next) safe from accidental tampering by anybody but the supervisors.

WebIncident Form

For Web users, there is a WebIncident form, shown in Figure 27.3. When Web users enter the database, they'll create a WebIncident form (a URL with either Incident?OpenForm or WebIncident?OpenForm will work equally well). WebIncident is aliased to Incident, so when a user creates an Incident document from the Web, that document appears using the Incident form when it is opened in a Notes client.

It has only one of the hidden fields from the Incident form: Status. The Status field on this form defaults to Submitted rather than In Progress. This is a flag to make the document appear in a view for documents that help desk personnel have not dealt with yet.

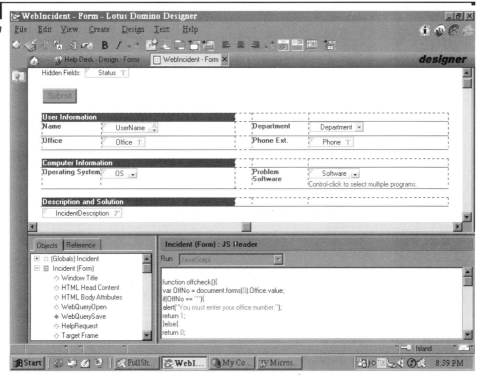

FIGURE 27.3

The WebIncident form

The WebIncident form shares these user-editable fields with the Incident form:

- Department
- Office
- Phone
- OS
- Software
- IncidentDescription

IncidentDescription is set to be rendered as a Java applet in the Web browser. On this form, the User Name field is a computed-when-created field, which automatically captures the user's name. For this to work, users need to log into the server, have an Internet password set up in the main address book, and not be logged in anonymously.

Keyword fields viewed over the Web can't use View dialogs as their data source. So, we'll have to do something different to get data into the OS and Software keyword fields, which WebIncident shares with Incident. Rather than using a View dialog, both Software and OS keyword fields use a formula. Here's the formula for the Software field:

```
@DbColumn(""; ""; "Software"; 1)
```

The OS field uses the same formula but draws from the Operating System view.

Department, like OS and Software, is a field that uses a pick list. But unlike OS and Software, it doesn't need to draw its possible values from a source outside the form itself. Instead, it has its possible values built into the field, so there's no need to change its design from the version in the Incident form.

The WebIncident form uses the following JavaScript routine in its JS Header to handle field validation:

```
function offcheck(){
var OffNo = document.forms(0).Office.value;
if(OffNo == ""){
alert("You must enter your office number.");
return 1;
}else{
return 0;
}
}


function phonecheck(){
var phoneno = document.forms(0).Phone.value;
if((isNaN(phoneno)) | (phoneno == "")){
alert("You must enter a three digit phone number.");
return 1;
}else{
return 0;
}
}


function checksubmit(){
var isproblem = 0;
isproblem = isproblem + offcheck() + phonecheck();
if(isproblem == 0){
document.forms(0).submit()
}
}
```

The offcheck() function checks to make sure that there's a value in the Office field, while phonecheck() checks to make sure that there's a value in the Phone field. Of course, the Phone and Office fields have the appropriate functions in their onBlur events.

The other fields don't need validation. The User Name field is computed and is beyond the user's control. The OS and Department fields have values by default, although the user must make sure to select the proper value. The Software field can be blank because problems can arise with the computer itself before any applications are launched. The IncidentDescription field is a rich text Java applet that can't take field validation.

The form has no $$Return field because responses are created by the Agent called by WebQuerySave: WebIncidentSubmit. Finally, there are no Actions on the form. Rather, there's a Submit button that has `checksubmit()` on the onClick event. The JavaScript functions run both of the validation formulas and, if there aren't any problems, they submit the form.

The Software and OS Forms

This database keeps lists of software and operating systems supported by the help desk in the SoftwareForm form. The operating system and software forms are very simple, holding only the name of a single software package or operating system platform. The SoftwareForm form, shown in Figure 27.4, has a single field. It has three Actions: Save and Close, Close, and Edit. The corresponding OSForm form is identical, except that it has a slightly different name and label.

FIGURE 27.4

The SoftwareForm form

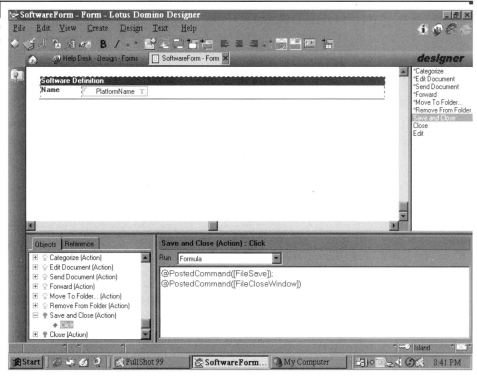

PART

VI

Developing Databases

The PersonnelForm Form

The database holds a list of help desk personnel in the PersonnelForm form. This form provides the help desk personnel with a list of people to whom problems can be referred. PersonnelForm, shown in Figure 27.5, has three fields:

Person   This is a single-value Names field that draws values from the organization's address book by using the Address dialog.

OS   This is a multi-value text field that draws values from the Operating System view. A person can have expertise with more than one operating system.

Software   Another multi-value text field, this one draws values from the Software view. A person can also have expertise with more than one software package.

Like the operating system and software forms, PersonnelForm also has Save and Close, Close, and Edit Actions.

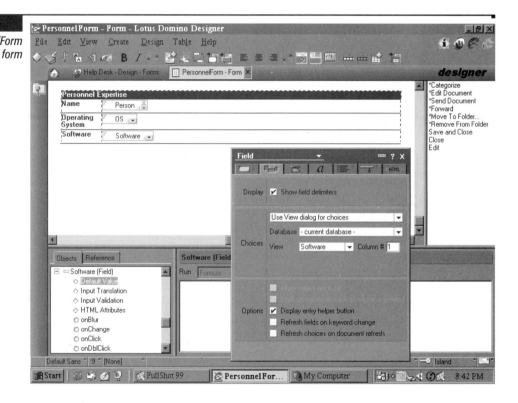

FIGURE 27.5

The PersonnelForm form

The Views

Although important data is held in documents, its arrangement in views is equally important for this database. The views can be loosely divided into two categories: work views and administrative views. The *administrative views* hold background data documents on the operating system, software, and people. The *work views* hold Incident documents, indicating how long documents have been in the process and where they stand.

The Administrative Views

The OSForm and SoftwareForm documents have their own views (see Figure 27.6), which are essentially identical to one another. Each has rows of alternating colors to make it more readable. Each view also has a Create Document button that creates a new document using the appropriate form.

FIGURE 27.6

The Operating System view

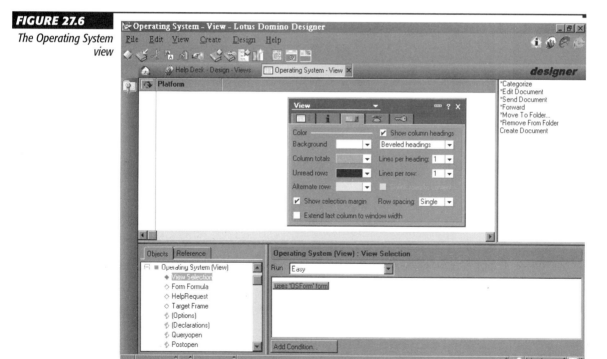

PART

VI

Developing
Databases

The Personnel view, shown in Figure 27.7, shows all PersonnelForm documents. Unlike the other views in the database, this one is set to display multiple lines. Each document in the view can show up to five lines of data, but will shrink to fit so a document won't take up more lines than it has to. This view's Create Document button creates a PersonnelForm document.

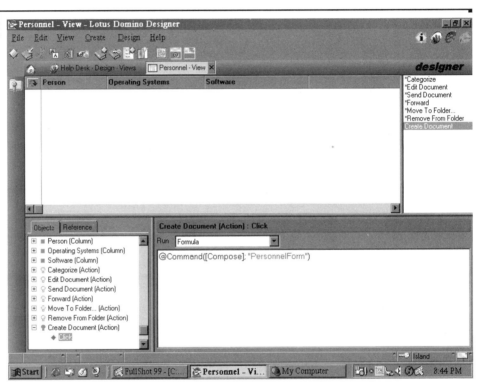

FIGURE 27.7

The Personnel view

The Work Views

The Submitted From Web view, shown in Figure 27.8, holds all documents where the Status is Submitted. The only documents that can have a Status value of Submitted are documents submitted from the Web. Notes-created Incident documents start out with the In Progress status, and other documents don't have a Status field. So, the documents appearing in this view are reliably only those submitted from the Web. The Person, Date Submitted, OS, and Software fields are fairly self-explanatory. The view is sorted by Date Submitted in ascending order, so the oldest documents are always at the top.

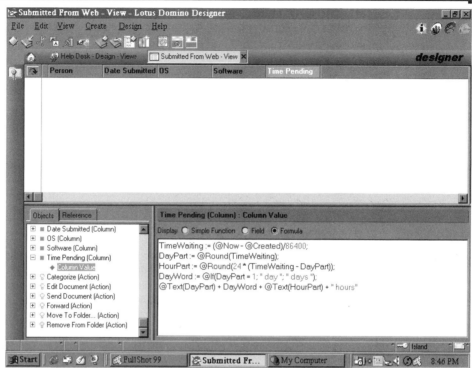

FIGURE 27.8

Submitted From Web view

The Time Pending column has this formula:

```
TimeWaiting := (@Now - @Created)/86400;
DayPart := @Round(TimeWaiting);
HourPart := @Round(24 * (TimeWaiting - DayPart));
DayWord := @If(DayPart = 1; " day "; " days ");
@Text(DayPart) + DayWord + @Text(HourPart) + " hours"
```

Here's how the formula creates a display of the amount of time that a document has been waiting for attention: If you subtract one date from another, you get the time difference in seconds. If you divide by 86,400, you get the time difference in days (60 seconds × 60 minutes × 24 hours). *DayPart* is the number of full days that the document has been waiting. *HourPart*, which multiplies the fractional day by 24, is the number of hours that the document has been waiting. The process could be repeated, taking the whole number of hours and multiplying the fractional hour by 60 to get the number of minutes, or even taking the fractional part of minutes and multiplying by 60 to get seconds. But, for readability, the designer decided to round the number of hours off at two decimal places and leave it at that.

PART

VI

Developing
Databases

The first column, which is unlabeled and a mere one character wide, has this formula:

```
TimeWaiting := (@Now - @Created)/86400;
@If(TimeWaiting > 1; 115; TimeWaiting > .5; 120; 114)
```

What makes this at all notable is that this column has also been instructed to make its value appear as an icon. If a document has been pending for more than a day, a red ball will appear. If the document is half a day old, the ball is yellow. For younger documents, the ball is green. This means that the column will give a quick visual indication of how old a document is.

The In Progress view, shown in Figure 27.9, shows all Incident documents with a status of In Progress. The view has six columns:

Assigned To   Is the first column. This column is sorted and categorized. It shows twisties where the category is collapsible.

Unnamed   Is an unnamed second column. It uses the same formula as the visual-cue icon column from the Submitted From Web view.

Created   Is a hidden column that holds the document's creation date. It is sorted in ascending order. This ensures that older documents are near the top where they can receive more attention.

FIGURE 27.9

In Progress view

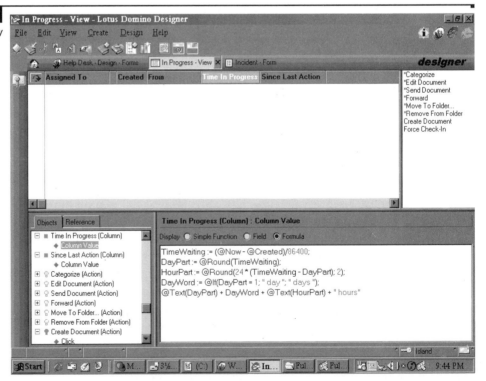

From   Is the fourth column. It shows the contents of the UserName field. It is not sorted.

Time In Progress   Is the fifth column. It uses the same formula as the Time Pending column of the Submitted From Web view.

Since Last Action   Is the sixth column. It uses the same formula as Time In Progress, except it uses @Modified rather than @Created. With this column, the view will show not only how long it has been since the incident was reported, but also how long it has been since somebody did something about it.

This view also has two Actions: Create Document and Force Check-In. Create Document creates an Incident document. Force Check-In reassigns all selected documents to the current user. The Action is hidden from everyone except users with the [Help-Admin] role. It is intended to be used by administrators, who can use it to take control of documents that are in the care of help desk personnel who are unable to deal with incidents by themselves (for example, people out sick or on vacation) and then assign them to others. The Force Check-In code, presented here, loops through the selected documents and changes its assignment to the current user. The administrator can then reassign the documents individually as desired.

```
Sub Initialize
    ' Checking Out
  On Error Resume Next
  Dim session As New NotesSession
  Dim db As NotesDatabase
  Dim collection As NotesDocumentCollection
  Dim doc As NotesDocument
  Dim CurrentCheck As String
  Set db = session.CurrentDatabase
  Set collection = db.UnprocessedDocuments
  For i = 1 To collection.Count -1
    Set doc = collection.GetNthDocument( i )
doc.CurrentAssignment = session.UserName
      Call doc.Save( False, True )
  Next
  End Sub
```

There is a corresponding My Incidents view, shown in Figure 27.10. The selection formula is as follows:

```
SELECT (@Contains(Status; "In Progress") & (CurrentAssignment = @UserName))
```

Because it is a view incorporating @UserName, the designer made it a Shared, Private On First Use view in order to appropriately capture the username. It has all the same columns as the In Progress view, except for Assigned To, which is no longer necessary.

FIGURE 27.10

The My Incidents view

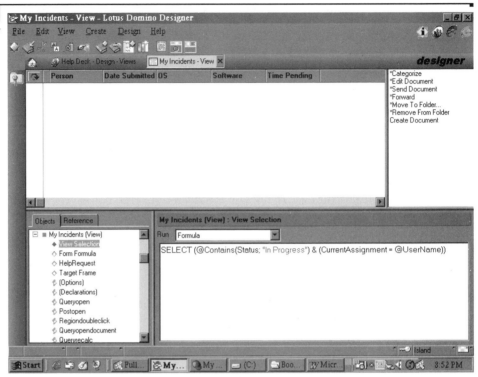

While this view has a Create Document button, it does not have the Force Check-In Action. After all, if the document appears in this view, the user already has control over it.

From the My Incidents view, we move to another non-personalized view. The Completed view, shown in Figure 27.11, shows all Incident documents with a Completed status. The columns for this view are as follows:

Person   Is the User Name field. It is sortable.

Date Submitted   Uses the formula @Created. It is sorted in ascending order and is sortable.

Date Finished   Uses the formula @Subset (PersonnelFinishedDate; -1). By getting the last date in that field, it shows the date the incident was marked as closed. It is sortable.

Time In Progress   Uses the same formula as Time Pending in the Submitted From Web view. But instead of using @Now, it uses the same date as Date Finished.

Closed By   Uses the formula @Subset (WasAssignedTo; -1), which uses much of the same logic as Date Finished to show the person who marked the document as Completed.

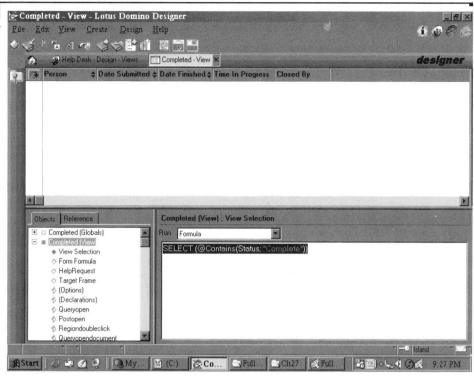

The Completed view has one Action: Export For Analysis. The individual documents hold complete histories of who has dealt with them, as well as an accounting of the problematic software involved. However, that information isn't in a form amenable to intense statistical analysis. However, this Action takes that information and breaks it down into individual records in a spreadsheet.

The user selects a number of documents and presses the button. The Action takes each document and cycles through the lists of people who have worked with it and the dates that they worked with it. Each item in the WasAssignedTo list is written to the spreadsheet, along with the name of the user who had the problem, the name of the OS, the name of the software involved, the date that each user got the incident (more or less, the first person has to make do with the date the Incident document was created), and the date that each user finished with the document. Here's the code:

```
(Declarations)
Dim s As notessession
Dim db As NotesDatabase
Dim doc_current As NotesDocument
Dim dc_Selected As NotesDocumentCollection
Dim int_line As Integer
```

PART

VI

Developing
Databases

```
Dim str_lastdate As String
Dim dat_currentdate As NotesDateTime
Dim str_currentdate As String
Dim ole_excel As Variant
Dim str_cellname1 As String
Dim str_cellname2 As String
Dim str_cellname3 As String
Dim str_cellname4 As String
Dim str_cellname5 As String
Dim str_cellname6 As String
Dim ar_str_names As Variant
Dim arr_dat_dates As Variant
Dim maxapproved As Integer
Dim x As Integer

Sub Click(Source As Button)

  int_line = 0
  UpdateCells

  Set ole_excel = createobject("excel.application")
  ole_excel.visible = False
  ole_excel.workbooks.add

  Set s = New notessession
  Set db = s.CurrentDatabase
  Set dc_Selected = db.unprocesseddocuments
  Set doc_Current = dc_Selected.GetFirstDocument

  Do Until doc_Current Is Nothing

    Set dat_currentdate = New notesdatetime(doc_Current.Created)
    str_currentdate = dat_currentdate.DateOnly
    ar_str_names = doc_Current.WasAssignedTo
    arr_dat_dates = doc_Current.PersonnelFinishedDate
    maxapproved = Ubound(ar_str_names)-1
    For x = 0 To maxapproved
      ole_excel.range(str_cellname1).value = doc_Current.UserName(0)
      ole_excel.range(str_cellname2).value = doc_Current.WasAssignedTo(x)
```

```
        ole_excel.range(str_cellname3).value = str_currentdate
        ole_excel.range(str_cellname4).value =
doc_Current.PersonnelFinishedDate(x)
        ole_excel.range(str_cellname5).value = doc_Current.OS(0)
        ole_excel.range(str_cellname6).value = doc_Current.Software(0)
        If x <maxapproved Then
         Set dat_currentdate = New
notesdatetime(doc_Current.PersonnelFinishedDate(x+1))
          str_currentdate = dat_currentdate.DateOnly
        End If
        UpdateCells
      Next

      Set doc_Current = dc_Selected.GetNextDocument(doc_Current)
    Loop

    ole_excel.workbooks(1).saveas("C:\AnalysisList.xls")
    ole_excel.workbooks(1).close
    Msgbox("Done")
End Sub

Sub UpdateCells

    int_line = int_line + 1
    str_cellname1 = "A" + Cstr(int_line)
    str_cellname2 = "B" + Cstr(int_line)
    str_cellname3 = "C" + Cstr(int_line)
    str_cellname4 = "D" + Cstr(int_line)
    str_cellname5 = "E" + Cstr(int_line)
    str_cellname6 = "F" + Cstr(int_line)

End Sub
```

The Other Organizing Elements

In addition to the forms and views, there are a few elements to keep everything organized. One is an outline named HelpOutline, shown in Figure 27.12. There are regular
entries for the work views (that is, Submitted From Web and the other views containing

PART

VI

Developing
Databases

Incident documents). There are also some nested entries for the administrative views: Personnel, Operating Systems, and Software.

FIGURE 27.12

HelpOutline

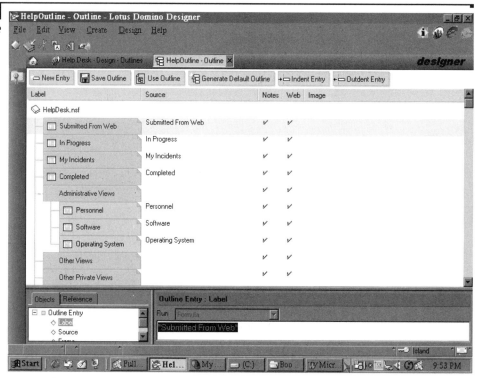

To be displayed, the outline has to be embedded into something. In this case, it is embedded in a page named OutlinePage, shown in Figure 27.13.

Finally, all of these elements are arranged into a frameset, named HelpFrames, shown in Figure 27.14. The page OutlinePage appears in the left frame (Navigation), while everything else appears in the right pane (Contents). The Contents frame defaults to showing the Submitted From Web view, so when a user first opens the database, they are presented with a list of documents that nobody has worked with yet.

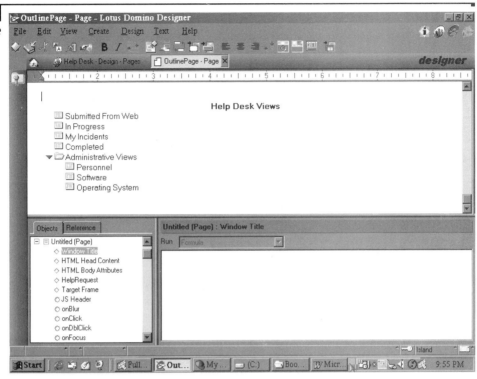

FIGURE 27.13

OutlinePage

The WebIncidentSubmit Agent

The database contains a single Agent: WebIncidentSubmit. WebIncidentSubmit is an Agent set to run once from the Agent list. However, its real purpose is to run when a WebIncident form is submitted from the Web. To assure users that their problems will be addressed, the Agent performs a sort of double-notification. First, the user gets a message in the Web browser confirming that the incident has been recorded and that it will be dealt with. Second, a mail message is sent confirming that the problem is being dealt with. This gives the user both an ephemeral but instant notification (the Web page) and a somewhat later but permanent notification (the mail message) that she can refer to later. This may be more notification that is absolutely necessary, but it will make users feel much more confident that their concerns are being heard and that they will be addressed.

FIGURE 27.14

HelpFrames

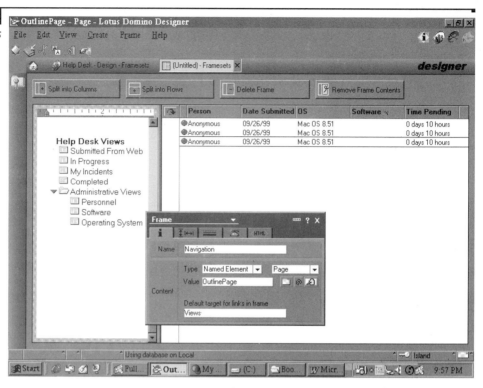

Here's the code:

```
Sub Initialize

    On Error GoTo WebError

    Dim s As New Notessession
    Dim db As Notesdatabase
    Dim doc As Notesdocument
    Dim maildoc as Notesdocument
    Dim bodytext as String

    ' Get the submitted document and current database
    ' The first action to take is to save the document; if that
    doesn't work, nothing else should happen.

    Set doc = s.DocumentContext
    Call doc.save(False, False)
```

```
      Set db = s.CurrentDatabase

      ' Set up and mail a message to the guy submitting the document

      Set maildoc = New Notesdocument(db)
      maildoc.SendTo = doc.UserName(0)
      maildoc.Subject = "Problem Reported"
      bodytext = "Your probem has been received by the help desk.  If
➥     you do not receive a response within a day, call the help desk
➥        supervisor at extention 049."
      maildoc.Body = bodytext
      Call maildoc.Send (false, false)

      ' Now print a response on the screen.

      Print "<head><title>Problem Registered</title></head>"
      Print "<body>"
      Print " Your probem has been received by the help desk.  If you do
➥     not receive a response within a day, call the help desk
➥        supervisor at extention 049.</body>"

EndTheSub:
   Exit Sub


WebError:
Print "An error occurred while trying to record your problem. Please
➥     report this information to the help desk:"
Print "<br>"
Print "<br>"
Print "Error in line " + Cstr(Erl)
Print "<br>"
Print "Error #" + Cstr(Err)
Print "<br>"
Print Error
Print "<br>"
Print "<br>"
Resume EndTheSub

End Sub
```

Deploying the Application

There are a few tasks that need to be performed before the database is deployed. The tasks range from creating a database to configuring underlying data documents.

First, a new database should be created based on the template file `HelpDesk.ntf`. The name doesn't matter, but `HelpDesk.nsf` would be a good one.

Second, help desk personnel should be given permission to the database, using either group names or individual names. As the database is constructed, help desk personnel should be given Editor access. Supervisors should be given the [Help-Admin] role.

Third, help desk supervisors should create Software and Operating System documents to populate the Software and Operating System views.

Fourth, help desk supervisors should create Personnel documents for all help desk personnel.

Finally, the last permissions should be set. Anonymous and default access should have no access to the database. Also, a group or groups of users should be granted Depositor access. In fact, maximum Web access can be set to Depositor because only remote users will be accessing the database from the Web.

Using the Database

Everything in the application begins with the creation of an Incident Report form. For users creating their own reports, the company intranet home page provides a link with this URL:

```
http://server/HelpDesk.nsf/Incident?OpenForm
```

Clicking the link creates a WebIncident form, shown in Figure 27.15. Users will be presented with a dialog box asking for their username and Internet password if they haven't already logged into the Domino server. The Web interface allows a user to enter information on his problem from his own computer or, if the problem has made his computer lock up or crash, from a colleague's computer. Note that the OS field is a drop-down menu and the Software field is a multiple select box. This is a consequence of the former being marked as a single-value field in Notes and the latter being multi-valued.

Once the form has been submitted, it returns the confirmation message shown in Figure 27.16. A mail message is also sent to the user's mailbox. If an error occurs, a different message is returned.

FIGURE 27.15

A new WebIncident document in progress

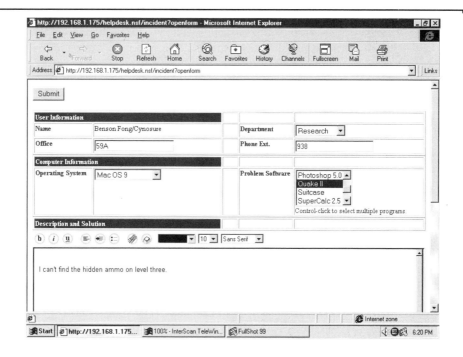

FIGURE 27.16

The confirmation message that appears after the Incident document is submitted

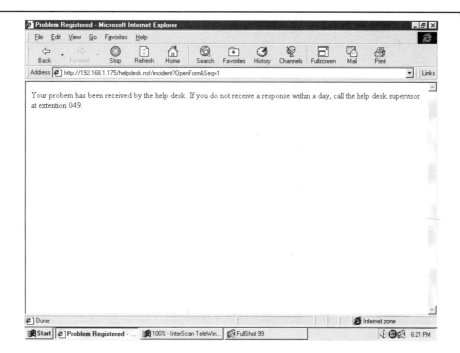

Developing Databases

When a help desk user opens the database, they see the HelpFrames frameset, shown in Figure 27.17, which prominently displays the Submitted From Web view. This arrangement gives the help desk user immediate access to the Web-submitted documents, as well as reminding her that there are documents that need attention. The color icons give users a visual cue about how long the document has been waiting for attention.

FIGURE 27.17

The Submitted From Web view

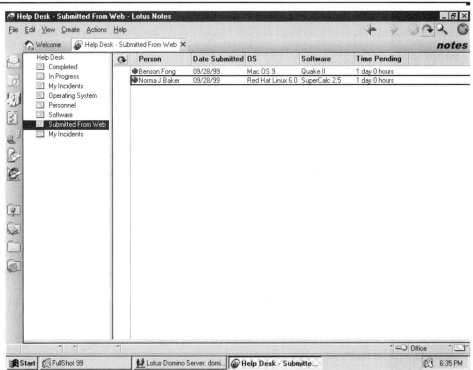

A number of help desk personnel are assigned to go through the Submitted From Web view during the day in order to field help requests submitted from the Web in a timely fashion. This could easily lead to a barrage of Save Conflicts if users can simultaneously open documents, edit them, and save them. But the code on the Incident form's QueryOpen event assigns the document to the first user who opens it, and the code on the QueryModeChange event keeps anybody but the person assigned from bringing the document into editing mode. All of this code forestalls the possibility of Save Conflicts.

You may have noticed the Refresh button in the upper left corner of the Submitted From Web view. If you deploy the database on your own server, you'll see it on your own computer. The reason the Refresh button is always visible has to do with the presence of the @Now function. The time functions @Now and @Date return the current time. But, as the Rolling Stones pointed out, time waits for no one. @Now is a moving target, and Notes realizes that fact. Whatever the value of the current time Notes used to compute the contents of a view was, it won't be the same as the time the user sees the view. Even if the contents of the view don't change from moment to moment, the data underlying the view does. Therefore, any view using @Now or @Date will always show the Refresh button, even if nothing has visibly changed.

Other personnel are assigned to field calls directly from users. When a user calls the help desk, the help desk personnel go to the In Progress view (see Figure 27.18) and create a new Incident document (see Figure 27.19).

FIGURE 27.18

The In Progress view

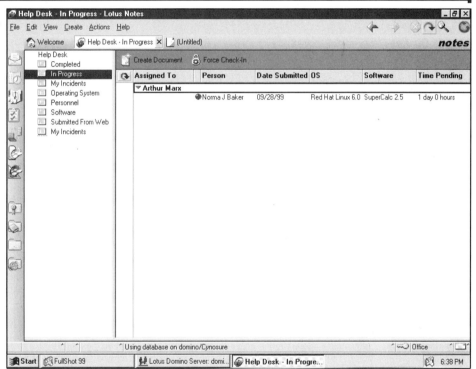

The new Incident document, created by a help desk person, has no visible fields filled in with default values. Rather, everything is completely editable. The Operating System, Software, and next-person fields use view dialog boxes, making it easy to find appropriate items. The Personnel dialog, shown in Figure 27.20, shows not only the people available to work on Incident documents, but also the hardware and software that those people are qualified to work with. This information makes it easy for new employees (who don't know everybody's specialties) and old employees (who don't remember them) to find the right people to send problems to.

PART

VI

Developing
Databases

FIGURE 27.19

A new Incident
document

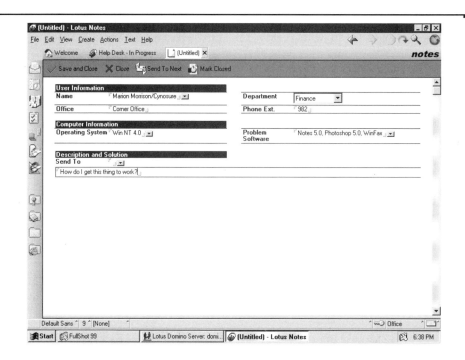

FIGURE 27.20

The Personnel view
dialog

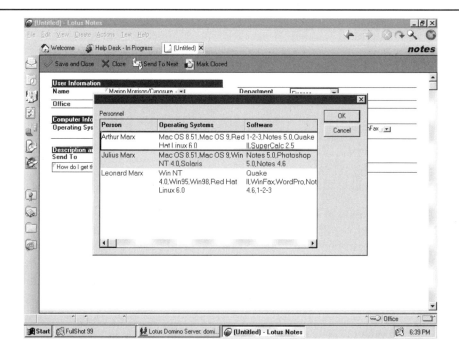

Eventually, every Incident document will end up in the Completed view, shown in Figure 27.21. This view can be sorted by several important single-value criteria: date of incident, date closed, user, and help desk person responsible for closing the incident. It also has the Export For Analysis Action, making it possible for the user to extract more detailed information for use in spreadsheets and other tools that are more suitable for serious statistical analysis.

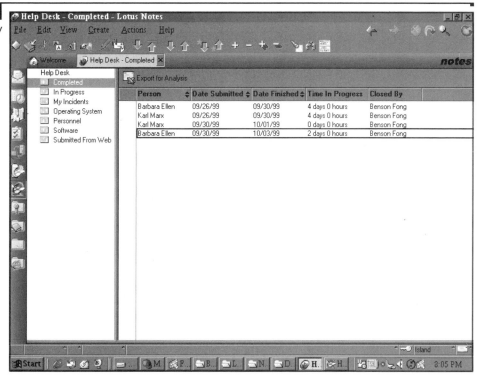

FIGURE 27.21

The Completed view

In addition to the work views, there are a few administrative views that hold reference documents containing information about software packages supported by the help desk, operating systems, and personnel. The Software view, shown in Figure 27.22, is typical in these kinds of views. It lists all documents made with the Software form. Administrators will create Software documents to indicate which programs the help desk will provide assistance with and make it easier for analysts to indicate which programs users are having trouble with.

FIGURE 27.22

The Software view

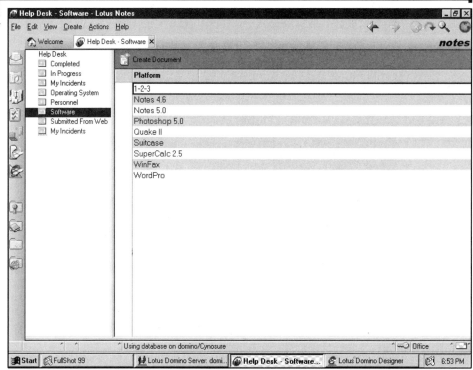

Summary

This chapter presented a simple Notes application. With it

- Help desk personnel can create documents to describe user problems.
- Users can register their own problems through the Web if they are unable to reach the help desk.
- Help desk personnel can pass the documents between themselves and route them to the appropriate personnel at will until the incident is declared resolved.

The next chapter contains a more complex application. It presents a pair of databases that constitute an encyclopedic description of a research project and a geographical region. One database provides read-only information, while the other allows outside users to provide comments and ask questions.

CHAPTER **28**

Another Example Notes Application: The Research Island Web Site

This application demonstrates a little bit of what Notes can do as a platform for Web development. It provides a framework for an encyclopedia-like guide to a region with self-maintaining current information from a relational database. It also provides an area for threaded discussions, which allows users to ask questions of the people running the site. Finally, on a properly configured server, this application takes advantage of Domino's Domain Search, letting users search both within and across databases.

 NOTE   For those of you who want to sing along, there are four databases on the CD that you might want to look at: Island.nsf (a database with a few documents in it), Island.ntf (the template that Island.nsf is based on), IslandTalk.nsf (a special discussion database with a few documents), and IslandTalk.ntf (its corresponding template).

The Scenario

For the past several years, Gigantic State University has been sponsoring a research project by a group of naturalists who are visiting a remote island. The scientists have placed small, automated weather stations that constantly feed weather information to computers at the university at locations across the island. There is a small but constant presence of researchers on the island, who are communicating with the mainland and the university computers through a satellite link.

To publicize the project and educate the public on its findings, the research team has decided to create a Web site. They want the site to describe the island's various ecological zones, as well as its native plants and animals. They also want visitors to be able to interact with the Web site, search for data that interests them, and ask questions of the researchers working on the project. Finally, if at all possible, they'd like to present some of the weather data that their expensive automated weather stations are gathering.

The solution is a Notes database. Or rather, two databases:

Island.nsf   Is a database that holds researcher-generated documents for Web visitors to read.

Islandtalk.nsf   Is an interactive database for Web site visitors to study the project and interact with the researchers.

Working in Notes, the researchers create Region documents, one for each region that has a weather station. The database has an Agent that builds a body of documents that have weather information. The database uses a connection to a relational database via ODBC to build and maintain the weather information. The Region documents look up the appropriate weather information when they're opened. The researchers also create documents that describe plants and animals found on the island and link them to the Region documents. Finally, there is a second database with a set of forms and views that support threaded discussions. Visitors are allowed to create documents to ask questions that on-site authorities can respond to. They can also search the Web site for information on topics that interest them.

Island.nsf

The first part of the Research Island application is a read-only database (from the Web visitor's point of view) that allows researchers to enter and maintain data about their project and make it available to users on the Web.

The Forms

Like the HelpDesk.nsf database in Chapter 27, Island.nsf is largely defined by a set of forms and views. However, Island.nsf takes greater advantage of Notes's ability to display the same data through different forms. To display data more effectively, basic data is input in one Notes form and shown through another via a separate Web form. The forms in the Island.nsf database are

- RegionData
- RegionWeb
- Flora
- Fauna
- Flora Web
- Fauna Web
- WindSpeed
- SearchRegions
- SearchFlora
- SearchFauna
- SearchContent

PART

VI

Developing
Databases

The RegionData Form

The basic data entry form for this database is the RegionData form, shown in Figure 28.1. Researchers can enter data for a region by completing fields that contain the following data:

Region name   This is a free-form, plain text field.

Latitude and longitude (in degrees, minutes, and seconds)   Because the island is small and approximately centered at 14 degrees south latitude and 155 degrees west longitude, no part of the island is north of 13 degrees south or much beyond 14 degrees south. Likewise, no part of the island will be outside of the 154 to 155 degrees west range. Therefore, the programmer decided to incorporate this fact into validation formulas on the latitude and longitude degree fields (LatDeg and LonDeg). If a user inadvertently tries to put in an inappropriate number, Notes will prevent it. The validation on the minutes and seconds fields (LatMin, LatSec, LonMin, and LonSec) is less sophisticated, simply ensuring that the value falls into a 0 to 60 range.

Terrain type   This is chosen from a list of three terrain types that the researchers composed at the beginning of the project.

Typical flora   Flora is a multi-value field whose values are chosen from a list of important plants that were found during the project. This field draws its list from a view that contains documents that describe the island's flora.

Typical fauna   Fauna is another multi-value field, whose values are chosen from a list of important animals found on the island. Like the flora list, this field draws its values from another view within the database.

The RegionData form also has a rich text field (Description) to enter a narrative description of the region. With a minimum of training, a project researcher can take advantage of the rich text fields' ability to insert pictures, create links, arrange information in tables, and so on.

On rollover, each of the field labels has a text pop-up that outlines the purpose and limitations of the fields. For example, rolling the mouse over the words Latitude and Longitude in an open document would bring up a pop-up that points out the field limitations. The roll-over help message for the Flora and Fauna lists reminds the user that documents must be created in the Flora and Fauna views before organisms will be included in those fields. You should also be aware that rollover messages don't appear when you move the mouse over hotspots while the document is in Edit mode. In Edit mode, you must click the hotspot to bring up the text pop-up.

Finally, the form has Edit Document, Save and Close, and Close buttons, much like documents in the HelpDesk.nsf database. These buttons are hidden from Web browsers. The assumption is that researchers will be working with their documents at Notes clients and won't need editing machinery on the Web.

FIGURE 28.1

The RegionData form

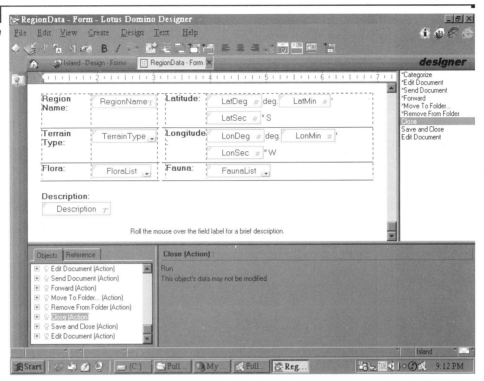

One of the things that might strike an observer about the RegionData form is that it is amazingly drab. The brief information fields are arranged in a table at the top of the form, followed by a long expanse of empty space for the Description field. This is because the RegionData form was made as simple as possible to allow quick and easy data entry. There are no extraneous pictures, distracting headers, or anything else to get in the way of data entry. It wouldn't be very interesting for readers visiting the Web site, but visitors to the site will never see that form.

The RegionWeb Form

Web site visitors will see the RegionWeb form. The RegionWeb and RegionData forms share the alias RegionData. But RegionWeb is only visible from the Web, while RegionData is only visible in a Notes client. Therefore, just like the Incident and WebIncident forms in HelpDesk.nsf, the appropriate form will be used depending on the client type.

RegionWeb itself is even more drab than RegionData. It contains no Actions, no buttons, no fields, and no text. Its sole content is a single computed subform, keyed to the TerrainType field. There are three subforms: Littoral, Slope, and Caldera. (Caldera is shown in Figure 28.2.) The three subforms differ only in color scheme and a brief description of the terrain type. They display much the same data as in Region-Data, but with a different arrangement, and some hyperlinks calculated on the fly.

FIGURE 28.2

The Caldera subform

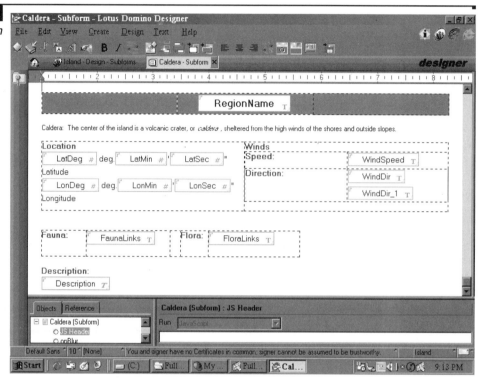

This peculiar arrangement is the result of the researchers deciding that they wanted a distinctive look for each type of ecological zone. These three subforms are a more elaborate demonstration of Notes's ability to show the same document in a number of different guises. Not only is a Region document shown differently depending on whether it is viewed over the Web or on a Notes client, the Web display is further dependent on the content of the document.

NOTE   Could we have replaced the three separate subforms with a single document and a batch of hide-when formulas? Yes, certainly. The database designer decided not to go that route despite the potential performance hit of having three separate subforms because it would have produced an extremely cluttered form design that might be more difficult to maintain.

Although they have a somewhat different look, all three subforms have the same fields and calculations as one another. Many of the fields on the subforms have the same name as fields on RegionData, so they'll display the same data. However, there are a number of computed fields, as well.

The wind speed and wind direction fields (that is, the WindSpeed and WindDir fields) are fairly straightforward computed-for-display text fields, depending on @dblookups, that use the region name as a key to look up data in the Winds view. Here are the formulas:

```
@If(@IsError(@DBLookup("";"";"Winds"; "RegionName"; 2)); "";
➥     @DBLookup("";"";"Winds"; "RegionName"; 2))
@If(@IsError(@DBLookup("";"";"Winds"; "RegionName"; 3)); "";
➥     @DBLookup("";"";"Winds"; "RegionName"; 3))
```

Note the @IsError statements used to avoid problems if something goes wrong with the wind speed data documents.

The formulas for displaying the Flora and Fauna lists are complex in a different way. They take advantage of pass-thru HTML. The formulas for the FloraLinks and FaunaLinks fields produce appropriate text for hyperlinks to the documents for the named plants and animals, accessing those documents through the FloraWeb and FaunaWeb views. This is the formula for the Fauna list:

```
"<a href = \"/Island.nsf/FaunaWeb/" + FaunaList + "?OpenDocument\">"
➥     + FaunaList + "</a><br>"
```

And this is the formula for the Flora list:

```
"<a href = \"/Island.nsf/FloraWeb/" + FloraList + "?OpenDocument\">"
➥     + FloraList + "</a><br>"
```

This code will generate a separate link for each entry in the list. Because the fields are marked as pass-thru HTML, they're active links to the related descriptive pages. The <BR> tag at the end of each line of code is inserted because, while the multi-value fields are set to put a new line between every record, that new line is just a return character. Because the fields are pass-thru HTML, that doesn't translate into a new line in the HTML display.

The WindDir_1 field is also a computed-for-display field set as pass-thru HTML. Instead of a hyperlink, the resulting text is an image tag, pulling up a small .jpg image of an arrow pointing in an appropriate direction. Here's the formula for that:

```
"[<img src = \"/icons/" + WindDir + ".jpg\" alt=\"\">]"
```

As you can see, the formula creates an <Img> tag incorporating the name of the latest wind direction (NNE.jpg, SW.jpg, etc.). Since the field has been marked as pass-thru HTML, the graphic image itself, which resides in the Domino server's icons directory, will appear in that table cell and point to the latest wind direction. If there is no

PART

VI

Developing
Databases

data for the region, it will call up a blank image (named, appropriately, `blank.jpg`). Since the fields are all computed for display, the server will call up the latest data whenever the document is accessed.

Note that there are no Actions or buttons of any kind on the RegionWeb form or on its associated subforms. This is because the Web forms are meant for read-only access. Users who see this form are Web users. They are intended to use links and some search functions, but they will not be doing any kind of data entry or manipulation.

The Other Data Entry Forms

There are two other data entry forms: one for data on plants, named Flora, and the other for data on animals, named Fauna (see Figures 28.3 and 28.4). Like the Region-Data form, they are extremely simple, with fields for the plant or animal name, the scientific or Latin name, a picture, and a description. The Picture and Description fields are both rich text fields. The intention is for the scientist who is entering data to import a graphic image into the Picture field and put any formatted text that is desired into the Description field. Both forms have the standard Close, Save and Close, and Edit Document Actions. Because there are no clear boundaries on any of the information on these forms, there are no field validation or translation formulas.

FIGURE 28.3

The Flora form

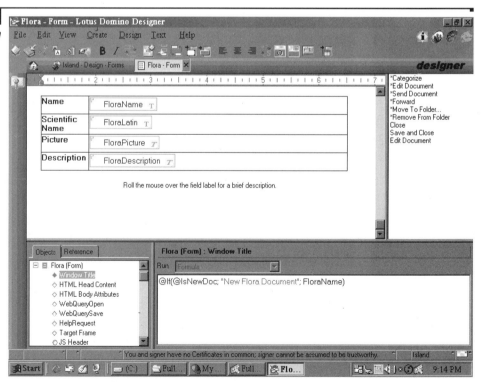

FIGURE 28.4

The Fauna form

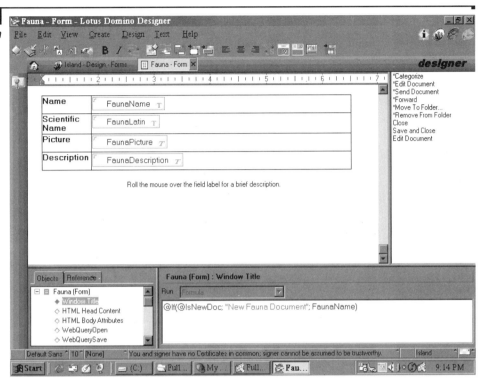

Like the RegionData form, these forms have their own display forms for the Web, shown in Figures 28.5 and 28.6. Like the related data entry forms, they're relatively simple, with no computed fields. And like the other for-display forms, they have no Actions that would be of any use in editing. Also like RegionData, the field labels have text pop-ups to remind the researchers what they should be doing.

Now, you might wonder why the researchers entering data are expected to import an image directly into the document for Flora and Fauna forms, while graphics are pulled up through standard <Img> tags for many other images. Couldn't the researchers filling out the form just type in the name of an image stored on the server and, like with the wind direction pointers, call them up from outside the document? This would save room in the database and improve performance. Well, it is certainly theoretically possible, but very undesirable in this case.

The fundamental problem is that for this scheme to work, the people responsible for the site would have to be granted access to the Web server in order to put the graphic files on the server. In part, this is a security issue. Of all security measures in any kind of network environment, one of the most important is limiting access to your servers. Remember that in Notes, local access equals Manager-level access. If the

PART

VI

Developing
Databases

end users (in this case, the research scientists who fill out the forms and select the images) are given access to the servers, they get access to the whole Notes system. Even if they aren't likely to do anything malicious, they might do something unwise, like inadvertently rename an important file or directory. The task of placing the files in appropriate directories might be handed off to a Notes system administrator, but it's far better to give as much responsibility for tasks related to a database to the actual user rather than to systems administrators. While network permission controls are generally sufficiently flexible to severely limit user permissions within the directory structure, it does put an additional burden on the system administrators to impose additional security restrictions on the system.

FIGURE 28.5

The Flora Web form

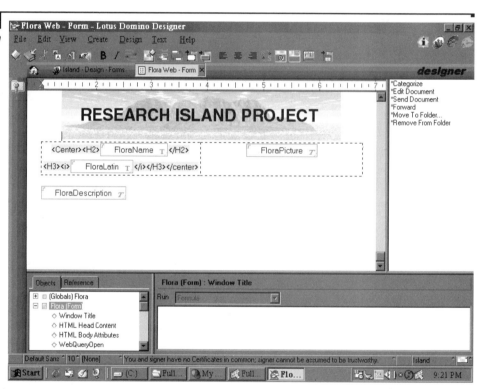

This scheme also assumes that the users have regular access to the server directories. That may not be the case. The research scientists may be filling in forms on the island and sending data to the mainland Web server using replication over a low-bandwidth connection. Navigating around remote server directories over a low-speed connection is more time-consuming for the user than importing the images into a document locally and, at a convenient time, starting replication. The amount of data transferred is more or less the same, but the user just presses one button rather than having to navigate.

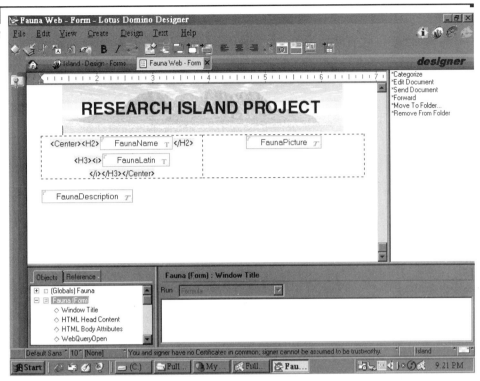

FIGURE 28.6

The Fauna Web form

Finally, there's the issue of education and reliability. If you use features like hyperlinks and image tags, it's vital that the spelling is absolutely correct. If a user has to type in the name of an image, there's a chance that they could type it in wrong and no image would appear. If the image is imported into the document, spelling is not an issue.

The Search Forms

SearchRegion, SearchFlora, SearchFauna, and SearchContent are customized search forms for Web use. The four forms are identical to one another (SearchContent is shown in Figure 28.7) except for the formula in the $$Return field. They have the following fields in common:

Query   This is an editable text field used for searches.

MaxResults   This is an editable text field for the maximum number of documents to be returned. This field results to All.

Fuzzy   This is a radio button with one entry: "Fuzzy."

PART

VI

Developing
Databases

As you can see, the designer decided to take advantage of only a few of the available parameters for Web searching. It was decided that most of the available options wouldn't make much sense to casual visitors to the site, so options like SearchOrder weren't included.

FIGURE 28.7

The SearchContent form

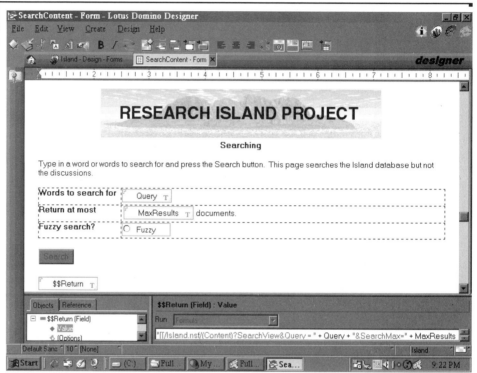

The forms use a bit of JavaScript in order to handle validation. The Search button has a single line of JavaScript in its OnSubmit event: ValAndSubmit(). The ValAndSubmit function, lurking in the form's JSHeader, does both input validation and some useful input translation. As you saw in Chapter 26, if you want no limit on the number of documents returned by a Web search, you pass a value of zero for SearchMax in the URL. That's all well and good, but it's not the most intuitive arrangement that Lotus could have come up with. As you can see on the form, the user is told to type in a number for the maximum number of documents returned, or to type All for no limit. The JavaScript routine checks first to see if the value in the field is a number. If it isn't, the script checks to see if the value is All. If the value is All, the script changes the value of the field to zero and immediately submits the form. The translated value is passed along in the URL, not the word *All*. If the value isn't All, the script shows the user an error message and doesn't submit the form. Finally, if the value is a number, the script submits the form. Here's the code:

```
function ValAndSubmit() {
var checkval = document.forms(0).MaxResults.value
if(isNaN(checkval)){
if (checkval=="All"){
document.forms(0).MaxResults.value = 0
document.forms(0).submit()
}else{
alert("The maximum documents returned must be 'All' or a number.")
}
}else{
document.forms(0).submit()
}
}
```

The $$Return fields are computed text fields that use this format:

```
"[[/Island.nsf/viewname?SearchView&Query=" + SearchText +
➡    "&SearchMax=" + @If(Fuzzy = "Fuzzy"; "&SearchFuzzy=TRUE"; "")
➡    + "]]"
```

The field generates a search query, gathers options from the page, and returns results from the view named in the field formula.

The WindSpeed Form

The WindSpeed form, shown in Figure 28.8, has no editing or other automation features. While it has several information fields, it is meant to be generated by an Agent and not meant to be edited or even read directly by a human user. Documents using WindSpeed will only be created by the Agent that draws information from the ODBC data source.

The Views

The documents in Island.nsf are displayed in eight views:

- Regions
- RegionsWeb
- Flora
- Flora Web

- Fauna
- Fauna Web
- (Content)
- Winds

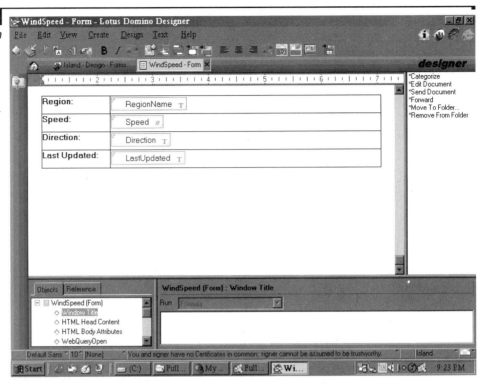

Like the forms, the views exist in Web and Notes versions using a pair of aliases. Regions and RegionsWeb share the alias Regions. Flora and Flora Web share the alias Flora. And Fauna and Fauna Web share the alias Fauna. The hidden (Content) view, used for database searches, has no alias. The Winds view isn't intended to be viewed anywhere, but since there are no links to it anywhere, whether it is shown on the Web or not is moot.

All of the views are fairly simple. The Regions view (shown in Figure 28.9) lists documents made with the Region form and shows the region name and terrain type, sorted by region name. The Flora view (shown in Figure 28.10) shows documents built with the Flora form. And the Fauna (shown in Figure 28.11) view shows documents built with the Fauna form. Both the Flora and Fauna views display the organism's common and scientific name, sorted by common name. All three views have a Create Document Action, which uses @Command([Compose]; "*formname*") to create a Region, Flora, or Fauna document as appropriate to the form.

FIGURE 28.9

The Regions view

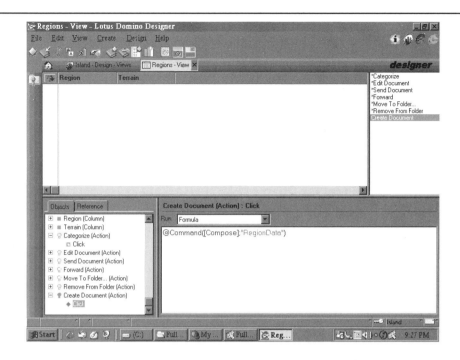

FIGURE 28.10

The Flora view

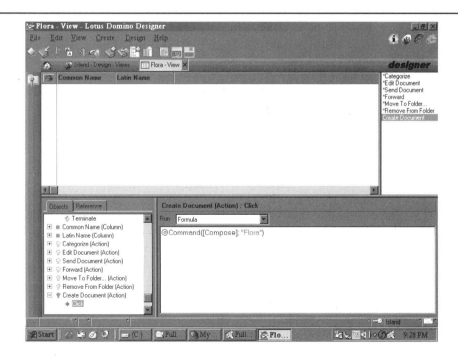

FIGURE 28.11

The Fauna view

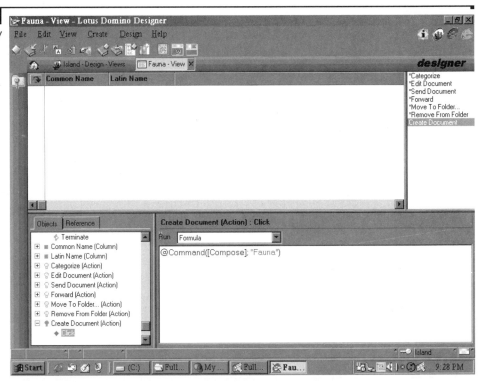

The Web versions of the views in Figures 28.9 through 28.11 are identical to the Notes versions, except that they lack the Create Document Actions.

The (Content) view, shown in Figure 28.12, shows all Flora, Fauna, and RegionData documents. This is a simpler version of the respective document forms that shows only the title of the document, using this formula for its single column:

```
@If(Form = "Fauna"; FaunaName; Form = "Flora"; FloraName; RegionName)
```

This view will be used to search the real content of the database; that is, it will be used for searches on documents with narrative content, excluding the WindSpeed data.

The Winds view, shown in Figure 28.13, is structured for lookups. It contains documents created with the WindSpeed form. It is sorted by the first column, which shows RegionName, with wind speed in the second column and direction in the third.

Other Design Elements

While the forms and views are the most important design elements, a few other elements are necessary to control navigation and move data.

FIGURE 28.12

The (Content) view

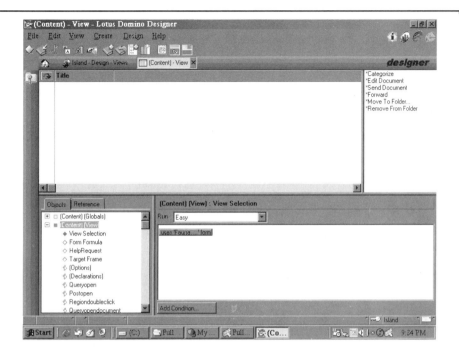

FIGURE 28.13

The Winds view

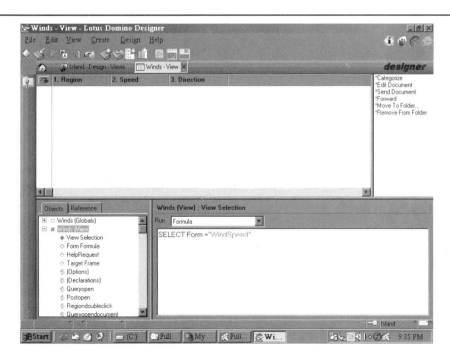

Outlines and Framesets

To easily navigate between views and get access to additional functions, the database has an outline and a single frameset. The frameset, named IslandFrames (see Figure 28.14), contains two frames in a configuration similar to that of the default Notes database. There is a narrow Navigation pane to the left, named Navigation, and a larger pane for views and documents, named Content. By default, the left pane contains the page with the NavigationOutline outline embedded in it. Depending on how the frameset is viewed, the page in question may be either CentralNav or WebNav. The right pane contains the SplashPage page. By default, links in Navigation have been set to target Content, so any view selected in the Navigation pane will call up the view in the Content pane to the right. The database is set to display this frameset when opened, so it's the first thing any user will see.

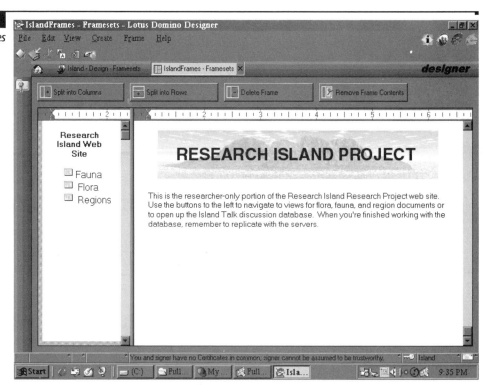

FIGURE 28.14

IslandFrames

The outline, named (in a burst of no creativity whatsoever) NavigationOutline (see Figure 28.15), has entries for all of the views and links in the discussion database, `IslandTalk.nsf`.

You'll notice that there's some apparent overlap in the outline entries: two fauna-related entries, two flora-related entries, and so on. One of each pair is visible on the

Web, while the other is visible in Notes. The Notes version of a given entry opens a view, while the Web version opens a page. Even though we'll use a single outline on both the Web and in Notes, it will appear completely different depending on its context.

FIGURE 28.15

NavigationOutline

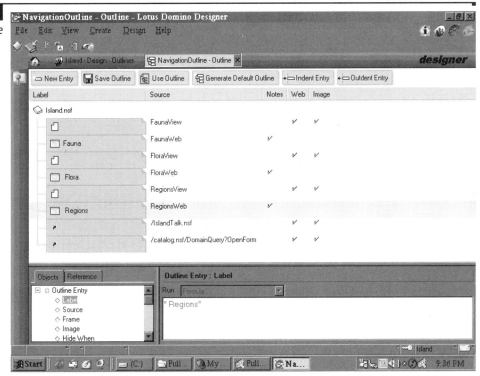

The Notes-only entries are links directly to views. Or, in the case of the discussion database link, the entry links directly to IslandTalk.nsf. However, the Web entries are links to pages that happen to have embedded views. In addition, there is a Search the Site URL link (/catalog.nsf/DomainSearch?SearchDomain) and a link to the discussion section, Ask the Scientists (/IslandTalk.nsf). The designer checked with the Domino server administrator to make sure that domain searching is enabled and that the names of the important forms haven't been changed.

The Web-only entries all take advantage of the image rollover trick presented in the "Rollover Images for Outlines" sidebar (see chapter 21), but take it a step further. Each of the entries has its own image resource. (For example, DiscussButton.gif is the image resource for the link to the discussion database.) Each image is quite large, about 108 pixels wide per individual graphic (check the shared images), which is about as big as you want a button to get on a monitor using 800 x 600 resolution, (in fact, it may already be a shade too big). On the other hand, each graphic image contains its own text, so a text label is unnecessary. Each entry in the outline is labeled with a blank space, leaving the image itself. By default, the image shows a blue button with white text, but the button turns green (still with white text) when the mouse rolls over it.

Pages

The database also contains several pages, primarily used to embed other database objects. The RegionsView, FaunaView, and FloraView pages are completely unremarkable. They consist of a title heading, an embedded view, and a link to a search page. RegionsView is shown in Figure 28.16. The views are set to be rendered as HTML, and each page has a link to an appropriate search form for the embedded view content (/Island.nsf/*searchform*?OpenForm), as well as a link to search the database (/Island.nsf/SearchContent?OpenForm).

FIGURE 28.16

The RegionsView page

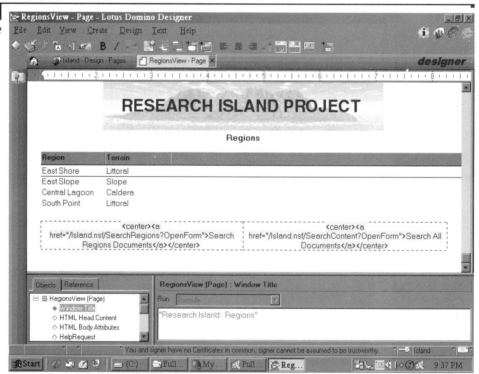

There are two different front pages for the database, shown in Figures 28.17 and 28.18. The front page for the Web (WebSplash) holds a pretty picture and a few links to other sites, but no other kinds of automation. NotesSplash is more akin to an About or Using document. It presents the Notes user with brief instructions for using the database and for entering data. Both of these front pages are aliased to Splash. One will be selected automatically on the Web, and the other will be automatically selected in Notes.

FIGURE 28.17

The Web splash page,
WebSplash

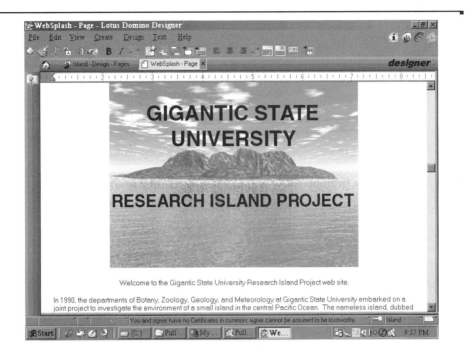

FIGURE 28.18

The Notes splash
page, NotesSplash

PART

VI

Developing
Databases

NavigationOutline is embedded in two pages: CentralNav (see Figure 28.19) and WebNav (see Figure 28.20). These are both fairly unremarkable pages, containing only an embedded outline and a little text. But check the properties of the embedded outline in WebNav. The text of the outline is twenty point. Why so big? Since there's no text in the Web navigator, text size isn't an issue. However, graphic size is an issue. When outlines use graphics, Notes will scale them to fit the height of the line of text if they're too tall. If they are left at the twelve-point default size, the graphics would be squashed into illegibility. (Try it yourself and see!) The embedded outline is also set to use a Java applet because the graphic roll-over trick won't work if the object is rendered as HTML. Although they look nearly identical when viewed in the Designer client (the Designer client displays the outline as it would appear in Notes and hides the Web-only content), it will look very different on the Web, as we'll see later.

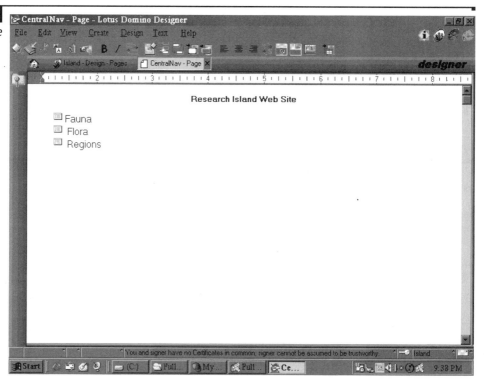

FIGURE 28.19

The CentralNav page

FIGURE 28.20

The WebNav page

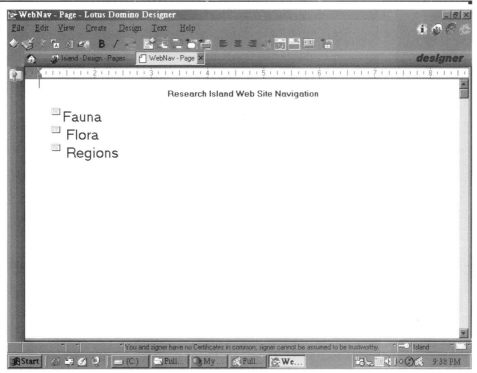

The Agents

To keep the wind speed data up to date, the database runs an Agent, UpdateWind-
Speed, hourly. Here is the code for the Agent:

```
(Option)
Option Public
Option Explicit

Uselsx "*LSXODBC"

(Declarations)

Dim con_thedata As ODBCConnection
Dim qry_thequery As ODBCQuery
Dim rs_results As ODBCResultSet
Dim s_currentsession As NotesSession
Dim db_thisDatabase As Notesdatabase
```

PART

VI

Developing
Databases

```
Dim res_results As ODBCResultSet
Dim doc_RecordDoc As Notesdocument
Dim vw_dataview As Notesview
Dim str_regionname As String
Dim int_currentdoc As Long

Sub Initialize

' This agent pulls data from the Research Island Weather Database
' through an ODBC connection, updating documents for existing
' regional weather stations and creating documents for new stations.

   On Error Resume Next

   Set con_thedata = New ODBCConnection
   Set qry_thequery = New ODBCQuery
   Set res_results = New ODBCResultSet
   Set s_currentsession = New NotesSession

   Set db_thisDatabase = s_currentsession.CurrentDatabase
   Set vw_dataview = db_thisDatabase.GetView("Winds")
   con_thedata.ConnectTo("ResearchIslandData")
   Set qry_thequery.Connection = con_thedata
   qry_thequery.SQL = "SELECT Region, WindSpeed, WindDir,
➡   LastRecorded FROM WeatherData;"
   Set res_results.Query = qry_thequery
   res_results.Execute
   Call res_results.FirstRow

   Do Until res_results.IsEndOfData
      str_regionname = res_results.GetValue("Region")
      Set doc_RecordDoc = vw_dataview.GetDocumentByKey(str_regionname, True)
      If doc_RecordDoc Is Nothing Then
         Set doc_RecordDoc = New NotesDocument(db_thisDatabase)
         With doc_RecordDoc
            .Form = "WindSpeed"
            .RegionName = res_results.GetValue("Region")
            .Speed = res_results.GetValue("WindSpeed")
            .Direction = res_results.GetValue("WindDir")
            .LastUpdated = res_results.GetValue("LastRecorded")
```

```
        End With
    Else
            .Speed = res_results.GetValue("WindSpeed")
            .Direction = res_results.GetValue("WindDir")
            .LastUpdated = res_results.GetValue("LastRecorded")
    End If
    Call doc_RecordDoc.Save(True,True)
    res_results.NextRow
Loop

res_results.Close

End Sub
```

This update Agent draws data from an ODBC data source (the DSN is ResearchIsland-
Data). The Agent updates and creates WindSpeed documents with data that is generated
by the island's automated weather stations and sent to a central relational database. The
designers thought it would be unnecessary to identify or destroy out-of-date weather
data documents, so no steps were taken to do so.

 NOTE We've provided an Access database on the CD, named `WeatherDB.mdb`, which
could be used as a data source.

The default access on `Island.nsf` should be set to Reader, so external users can
read all documents but can do no editing. The maximum Internet access should also
be set to Reader. However, members of the Researchers group, to which all the
researchers working on the island will belong, should have Editor access. For proper
searching, a full-text index must be created, and it should be marked for inclusion in
multi-database indexing.

IslandTalk.nsf

`Island.nsf` displays information to Web users. However, it doesn't provide for any
interaction between the scientists and Web users. For the question-and-answer section
of the application, the designer considered basing a database on the discussion database template that comes with Notes, Discussion–Notes & Web (R5.0). (The filename
is `discsw50.ntf`.) However, that database has more features than the researchers
thought were necessary, as well as some that the designer considered unnecessary and

PART

VI

Developing
Databases

possibly dangerous. The researchers didn't see any point in having elaborate personal information about themselves in Author and Interest profiles, which are elements of the discussion database. In addition, the designer was very dubious of the value of the file upload control. Although, attaching files to documents is fine for casual information sharing within an organization, where all kinds of policies can be enforced and individuals can be held responsible for uploading inappropriate files, that feature seemed inappropriate for an application available to anyone in the world. The basic features of the discussion database template are good, but the design is more elaborate than it needs to be, so a database built directly off the discussion database template was not the best option for this job.

Another possibility would be to start with the discussion database template and remove everything that the researchers don't want. However, the designer saw that he would have to spend a tremendous amount of time culling undesired features out of the design elements in the discussion database template. Therefore, he decided to build a new database from scratch and perhaps borrow elements from the discussion template where appropriate. Also, small, simple forms will replicate much faster over the slow data connection between the island and the servers.

The Forms

The discussion database template revolves around seven forms:

- Main Topic
- Response
- Response to Response
- Web Topic
- Web Response
- Web Response to Response
- TalkSearch

Like the RegionData, Flora, and Fauna forms, there are relationships between these forms. Main Topic and Web Topic both have the alias MainTopic. Response and Web Response both have the alias Response. And Response to Response and Web Response to Response both have the alias ResponseToResponse. Like most of the rest of the forms in the database, the Notes forms are very plain, and the forms for use on the Web have some additional formatting and a little extra pass-thru HTML for better performance. The Main Topic and Web Topic forms are shown in Figures 28.21 and 28.22. The Response and Web Response forms are in Figures 28.23 and 28.24. And the Response to Response and Web Response to Response are in Figures 28.25 and 28.26.

FIGURE 28.21

The Main Topic form

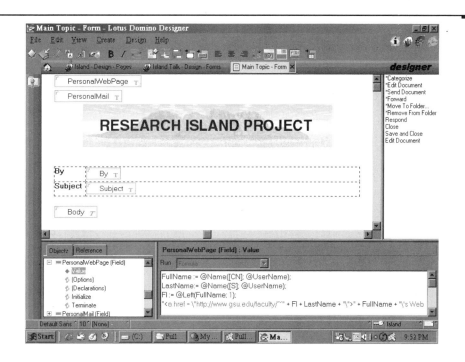

FIGURE 28.22

The Web Topic form

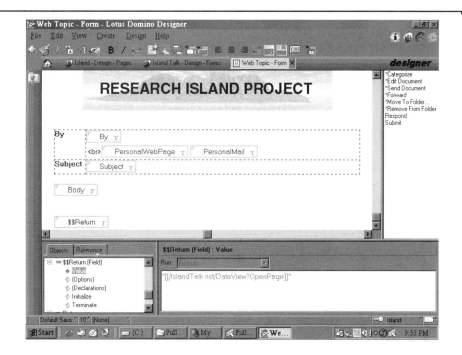

PART

VI

Developing
Databases

FIGURE 28.23

The Response form

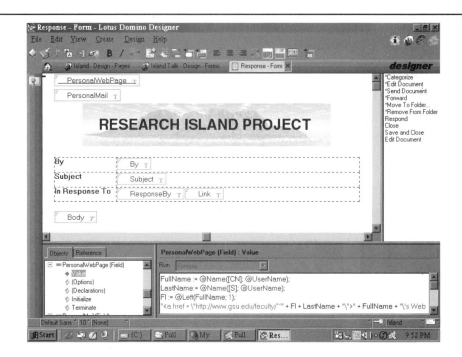

FIGURE 28.24

The Web Response form

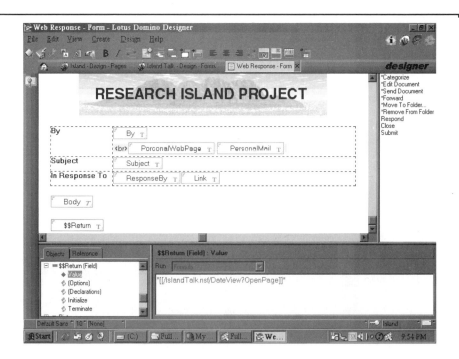

FIGURE 28.25

The Response to Response form

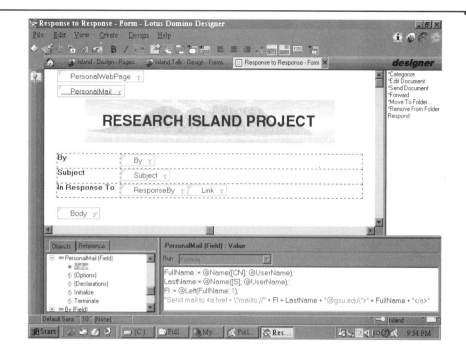

FIGURE 28.26

The Web Response to Response form

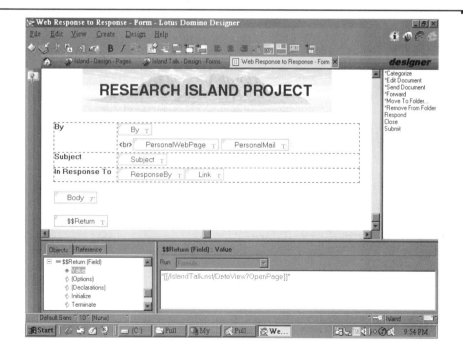

PART

VI

Developing
Databases

These forms all have a number of simply constituted fields in common:

Subject This is a freely editable text field, which the creator can use to give the document a subject.

By On a Notes client, this is a computed-when-composed text field that returns the user's name using this formula: @Name([CN]; @UserName). However, in the Web version, it's an editable text field. In other words, if the form is filled in on a Notes client, which is how the researchers will be accessing it, the user's name will fill in automatically. However, on the Web version, users can fill in their own name.

Body This is a rich text field that is used for content. The body field is set to be rendered as a Java applet, giving Web users the chance to use rich-text capabilities.

The Web forms also have a $$Return field. This field is a computed-when-composed text field with the value [/IslandTalk.nsf/DateView?OpenPage]. When a document is submitted, the user will be returned to the page with the By Date view embedded in it. The By Date view is sorted in descending order by date, so the newest document, presumably the one the user has just submitted, will be at the top.

As an added convenience, the Notes forms have some more elaborate computed-when-composed fields. The PersonalHomePage has the following formula:

```
FullName := @Name([CN]; @UserName);
LastName:= @Name([S]; @UserName);
FI := @Left(FullName; 1);
"<a href = \"http://www.gsu.edu/faculty/~" + FI + LastName + "\">" +
➡    FullName + "'s Web Page</a>"
```

The PersonalMail field has a similar formula:

```
FullName := @Name([CN]; @UserName);
LastName:= @Name([S]; @UserName);
FI := @Left(FullName; 1);
"Send mail to <a href = \"mailto://" + FI + LastName + "@gsu.edu\">"
➡    + FullName + "</a>"
```

These fields pre-generate complete HTML for mail and Web page links. The designer took advantage of the fact that Gigantic State University has predictable e-mail and Web addresses based on the individual's first initial and last name. For example, if Dr. Carol Smith were to create a document, the resulting HTML for PersonalHomePage would be

```
<a href = "http://www.gsu.edu/faculty/~CSmith/">Carol Smith's Web Page</a>
```

For PersonalMail it would be

```
Send mail to <a href = "mailto://csmith@gsu.edu">Carol Smith</a>
```

In Web versions, these are computed-when-composed text fields that are equal to themselves. This means that, for documents created on the Web, they'll be null. However, the Web versions are also marked as pass-thru HTML. This means that a document that a researcher posts in the discussion database automatically contains links to her own Web page and mail. While these fields could be made editable for forms created on the Web, the designer and researchers decided not to since there is no way they could be sure they were getting valid e-mail addresses and URLs.

A Possible Modification

The scheme described in this section for generating URLs and mail addresses is a little simplistic. Personnel from different departments might have Web pages in different directories (say, www.gsu.edu/geology/~CSmith/ versus www.gsu.edu/botany/~NCoward/), or researchers might come from other institutions whose URLs and e-mail addresses aren't so predictable. However, these complexities could be dealt with if the formula looked up values in the main address book. Person documents have a vast range of fields for Web pages, alternate e-mail addresses, department and supervisor assignments, and so on. While taking advantage of this information might require the construction of a new view in the main address book, this view can be accessed easily with a few @DBLookups.

The forms all have the standard Save and Close button. The Notes forms also have Edit Document buttons. For your convenience, the database on the CD gives Manager access by default. However, once you deploy it, the researchers should be granted Editor access, allowing them to edit the content of any document. They should also have permission to delete documents so that they can remove inappropriate postings. The default permission level should be set to Author, with permission granted to create documents.

If the ACL is set as described, anonymous users from outside the system can create new documents, but because there are no Authors fields on any of the forms, they may not edit the documents once they are created.

Each form has an Action for creating responses using the format @Command([Compose]; "*formname*"). The MainTopic form has an Action for creating Response documents, while Responses and Response to Responses have an Action for creating Response to Response documents. The Actions have a hide-when formula, @IsNewDoc, so responses to a document can't be created until the document itself has been saved.

Responses and Response to Responses also have a field named Doclink. Doclink is a computed-for-display text field with the formula @If(@IsNewDoc; ""; $Ref). The $Ref field is a hidden field inherent in any Response document containing the unique ID number of the document it is a response to. If used by itself in a text field, it becomes a doclink to that document. This formula, then, produces a link to previous documents once the document itself has been saved.

Like Island.nsf, IslandTalk.nsf is searchable and includes its own search form, shown in Figure 28.27. As you can see, the form is very similar in appearance and almost completely identical in design to Island.nsf's search forms. It even uses the same JavaScript confirmation function. Because all views in this database show the same documents, although they sort them differently, it makes little difference which view the TalkSearch form launches a search of, particularly considering that the search imposes its own sort order. It searches the By Subject view, but could search the By Author or By Date views equally well.

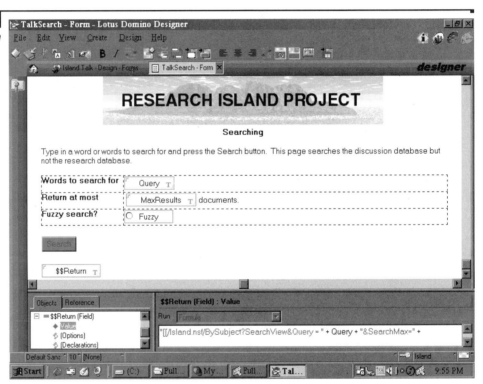

FIGURE 28.27

The TalkSearch form

The Views

The IslandTalk.nsf database has three views:

- By Subject

- By Author

- By Date

Each of the views displays all the documents in the database. Unlike `Island.nsf`, there's no real need for separate Web views because both Web and Notes users are performing essentially the same tasks. The By Subject view, shown in Figure 28.28, is a typical view. Note that the only Action button is a Start Topic button, which creates a new Main Topic document. Remember that reply documents can't be created from a view on the Web, even by using a view applet.

FIGURE 28.28

The By Subject view

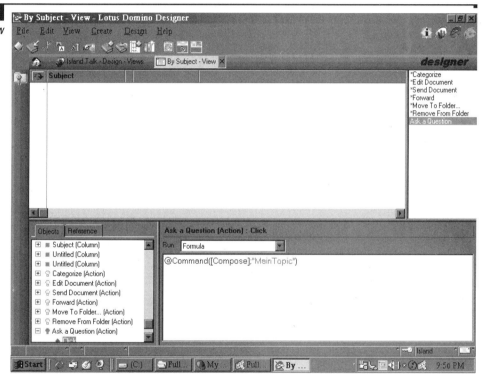

The first column in the view, either Subject, Author, or Creation Date, is sorted in and categorized (with twisties) in bold text. The By Subject and By Author views are sorted in ascending order. The By Date is sorted in descending order, with the newest documents at the top. The remaining two columns are a combination of whatever isn't in the first column (author and date in By Subject, subject and date in By Author, and author and subject in By Date). The second column is a responses-only column. The entries there will appear indented under the main topic documents in the third column.

PART

VI

Developing
Databases

The Other Objects

There are a number of pages in the IslandTalk.nsf database for displaying views. Like the view display pages in Island.nsf, these are also fairly simple, displaying a title, the view itself, a link to a search page, and a link to the home page. SubjectView, the page displaying the By Subject view (see Figure 28.29) is typical. There are also a pair of splash pages, named NotesSplash and WebSplash. They are both aliased to Splash, just as they are in Island.nsf. In fact, they are identical to the splash pages in Island.nsf, except for a few changes in the text.

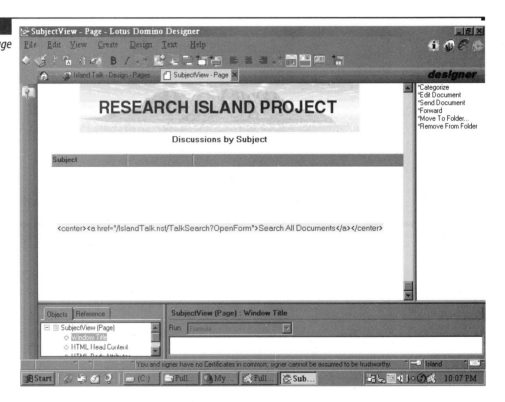

FIGURE 28.29

The SubjectView page

The database has a single outline, TalkOutline, shown in Figure 28.30. It is very similar in structure to the outline in Island.nsf, except that it opens the embedded-view pages in IslandTalk.nsf.

Finally, there's a frameset, TalkFrames (see Figure 28.31), for navigation in the discussion database. TalkFrames is built much like IslandFrames in Island.nsf. The frameset opens up to a page with TalkOutline in the left pane and SubjectView in the right pane. Again, links in the left pane target links in the right pane.

FIGURE 28.30

TalkOutline

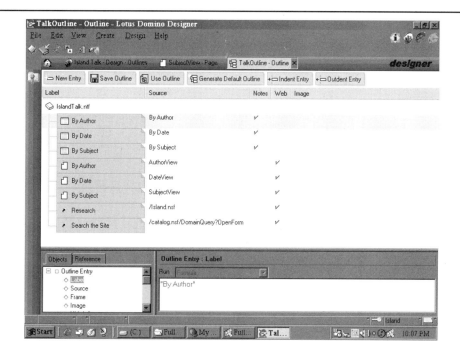

FIGURE 28.31

TalkFrames

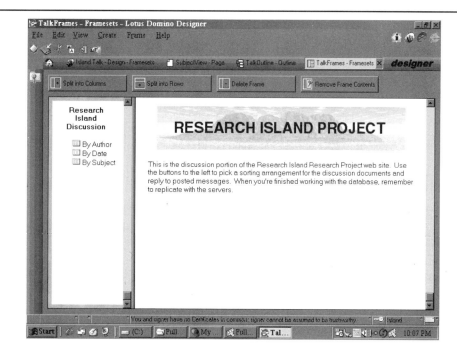

This database has no other automation or Agents of any kind. Its only purpose is to hold onto threaded discussions.

 NOTE   Could the functions of `Island.nsf` and `IslandTalk.nsf` have been combined into a single database? Certainly. The designer decided not to because it would have made security a little more difficult. Besides, using two databases is an excuse to show off Domino R5's new Domain Search capabilities.

Deploying the Application

Once the databases are fully tested and ready, a few tasks have to be performed in order to get the application up and running. For the purposes of this example, we'll assume that the stunningly obvious requirements have been met. Specifically, we'll assume that the HTTP task is running on the Domino server and that it can be accessed from the Internet. While you'll need to create the new databases first, the rest of the steps can be performed in more or less any order.

Create databases from the templates.   You'll find a pair of templates (`Island.ntf` and `IslandTalk.ntf`) on the CD, as well as a pair of databases created from them. Be sure to inherit the database design from the template. The discussion database should be named `IslandTalk.nsf` to ensure that the hyperlink in `Island.nsf`'s Web navigator will work. The researcher-only database must be named `Island.nsf` for the same reason.

Set security.   The Domino server administrator should make sure that there's a group named Researchers in the server's NAB, then add that group to the ACL of both new databases. The Researchers group should have Editor access to both databases. For `Island.nsf`, the default access should be set to Reader. For `IslandTalk.nsf`, the default access should be set to Author, with permission to create documents.

Set up for ODBC access.   Make sure the server has an appropriately named DSN (ResearchIslandData) pointing to the relational database that holds the weather data. (We've provided an Access 97 database on the CD, `WeatherDB.mdb`, which you can use as a data source if you have the appropriate drivers). It should be a system DSN rather than a user DSN. Open up the Agent UpdateWeatherData and make sure it is scheduled and has been signed by an ID that has appropriate permission to run on the server.

Create full-text indices for both databases.   This is a necessary step to enable searching in the individual databases.

Make sure both databases are set for inclusion in multi-database indexing and be sure that the server is configured for domain searches.   This is necessary to be able to search all databases at once.

Copy the external image files (the wind direction pointers) into the server's Icons directory.   These files are also provided on the CD.

Replicate copies of both databases to the researchers' computers. This step enables the researches to begin entering data. You'll also need to set up a replication schedule to make sure that data from the researchers' copies of the databases gets back to the Web server.

Once these steps are completed, the application is ready to use. The researchers can create documents in Island.nsf, probably starting with Flora and Fauna documents. Once they've got the Flora and Fauna documents populated, they can start creating RegionData documents with the Flora and Fauna fields filled out. Although they could start work on RegionData documents and come back and fill in the Flora and Fauna fields later. Finally, when the researchers have enough documents in Island .nsf, the site can be publicized and made public however its administrators see fit. You might wait until this point to grant access to outsiders. After all, there's no point in putting a database on the Web if there's no data in it.

Using the Application

The Research Island Project application has two distinctive looks depending on whether the user is a researcher entering data or somebody viewing the site through a Web browser.

Researchers Using the Application

Researchers are presented with as simple an interface as possible so that they can get to their data with as little fuss as possible. When they open the database, they see a frameset presenting an outline and the application's front page, as shown in Figure 28.32.

Clicking a button will bring up the appropriate view in the database. Like the bare form, a RegionData document is completely unremarkable but fairly efficient (see Figure 28.33). The Flora and Fauna forms are much the same. A Flora form is shown in Figure 28.34.

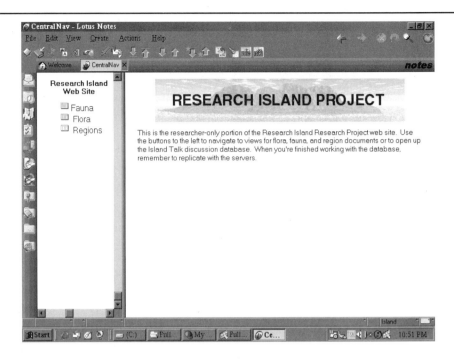

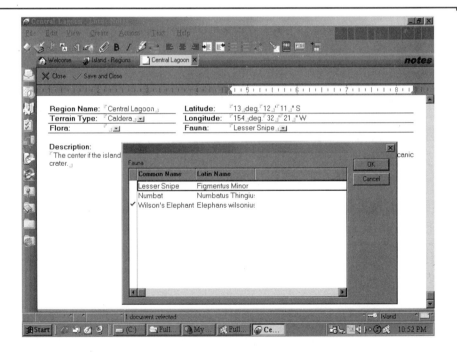

FIGURE 28.34

A Flora form is being edited in Notes. Note the text pop-up.

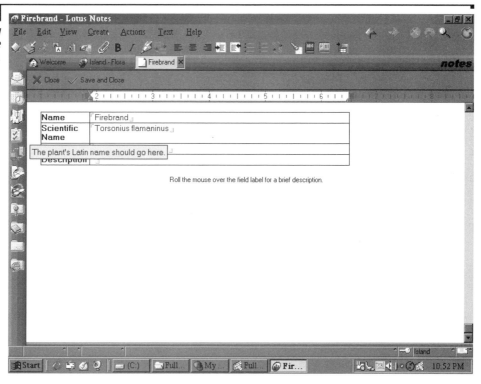

Although `IslandTalk.nsf` presents a similar front page to `Island.nsf`, its views differ slightly. `IslandTalk.nsf` has categorized views that display response hierarchies, as you can see in Figure 28.35.

Attention to unread marks is rather important in this database. The researchers will need to look through the discussion views and look for new documents. Somebody will also need to keep an eye out for inappropriate content, such as gratuitous offensive language, advertisements, and so on.

Web Users Using the Application

Web users are presented with a flashier front page than Notes users, as shown in Figure 28.36.

As promised, the navigator embedded in the left pane looks very different. Running the mouse over the buttons will make them change color. Clicking one of the buttons brings up a page with the appropriate view, rendered in HTML. Clicking a link opens a document.

Opening the document brings up a page that looks very different from the data entry form, as you can see in Figure 28.37. The computed fields have been replaced by text, hyperlinks, or an image indicating the direction of the wind.

PART

VI

Developing
Databases

FIGURE 28.35

The Regions view in `Island.nsf` *compared to the By Subject view in* `IslandTalk.nsf`

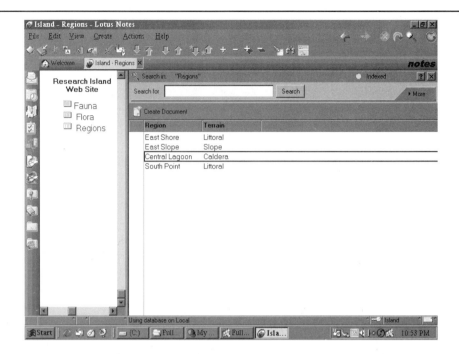

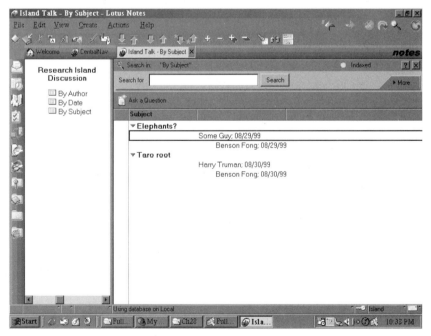

FIGURE 28.36

Island.nsf, *when first opened on the Web*

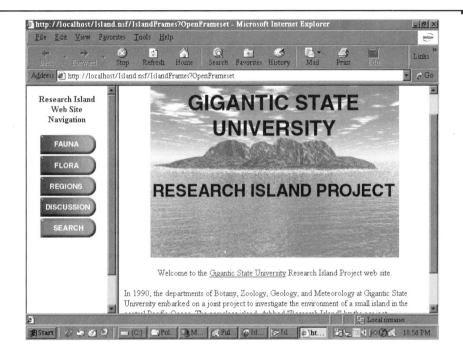

FIGURE 28.37

A Region document opened on the Web

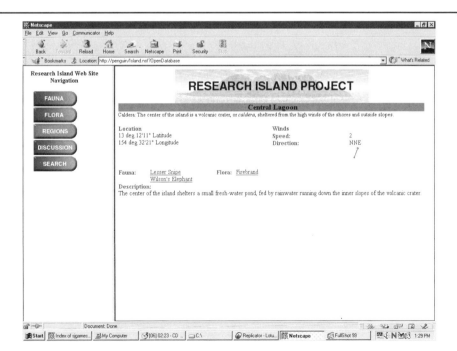

Clicking one of the Flora or Fauna links brings up the appropriate page in turn, as shown in Figure 28.38.

FIGURE 28.38

Wilson's elephant, as seen by Web users

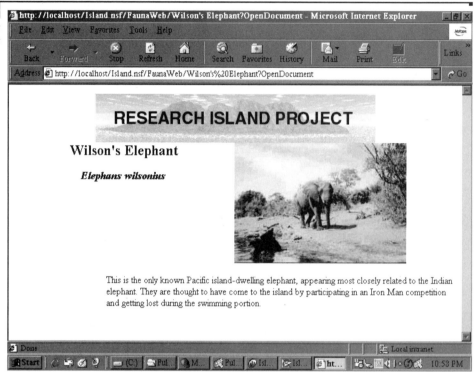

Clicking a view or database search link brings up a search page like the one in Figure 28.39. Because of the way the frames are targeted, when a Web user fills in and submits a search form, it returns the results inside the appropriate frame, as shown in Figure 28.40.

The Discussion Database

Web and Notes users can interact with each other by using the discussion database. When a Web user clicks the Discussion button, he is sent to a frameset that contains the outline and splash page for the discussion database. Clicking the By Author, By Date, or By Subject links brings up the appropriate view. Each view has a single Action button, Ask a Question, which creates a Main Topic document (see Figure 28.41).

Clicking the Submit button takes the Web user back to the By Date view, shown in Figure 28.42. Note the Search All Documents link at the bottom of the page.

FIGURE 28.39

A Search form

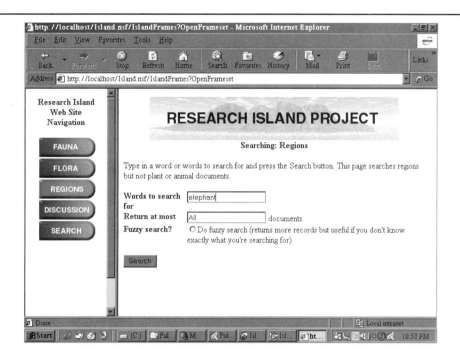

FIGURE 28.40

...and the search results

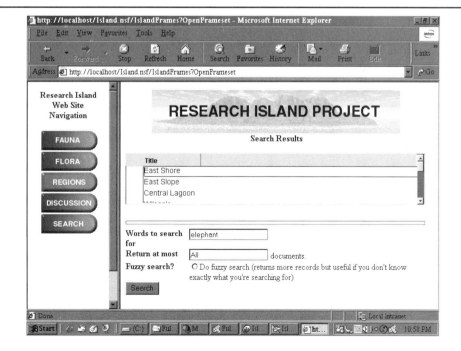

PART

VI

Developing
Databases

FIGURE 28.41

A Main Discussion document

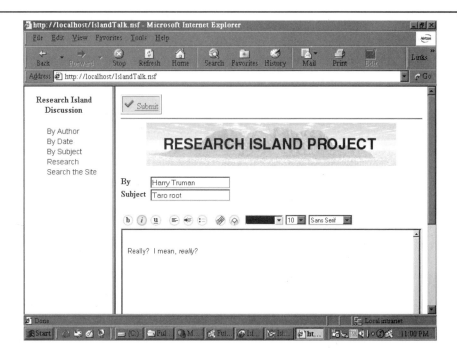

FIGURE 28.42

The By Date view, which is seen by the Web user after a document is submitted

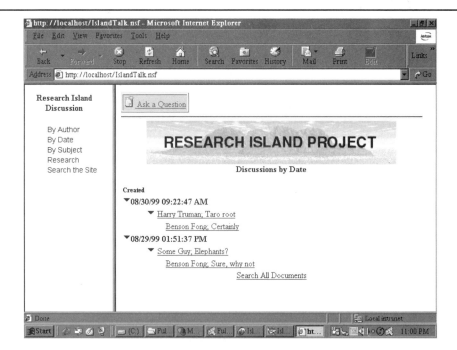

At this point, a Notes user might open the database and find the new document that was submitted by the Web user in any view. After opening the document, the Notes user can click the Respond button to create a Response document (see Figure 28.43). The Notes user's name is automatically filled in. When the Response document is viewed by the Web user, it will include a Web page, a mailto link, and a link to the previous document in the In Response To line (see Figure 28.44).

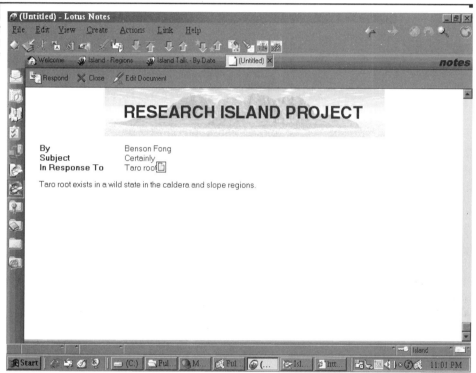

FIGURE 28.43

A Response document created by a Notes user

 WARNING When you try some of the hyperlinks to places outside the Island.nsf and IslandTalk.nsf databases, they may lead somewhere, but because everything in this application is fictional, don't expect the links to lead anywhere connected to this application. For example, the Web address for the fictional Gigantic State University, www.gsu.edu, is actually the home page for Georgia State University. They've got nothing to do with any of this, so if you have problems with any of this material, please don't bother them.

FIGURE 28.44

The same Response
document viewed by
the Web user

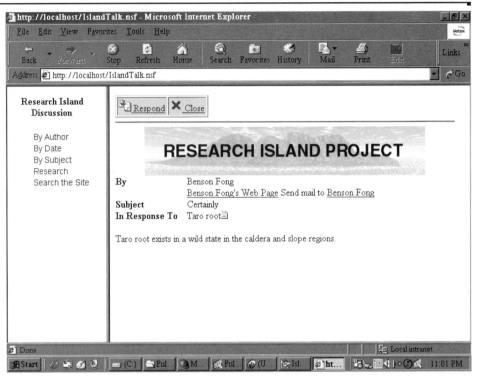

Summary

This chapter presented a simple Web application with two databases. Researchers working in Notes create content using simple forms, and the content is displayed in a more complex way on the Web. pass-thru HTML is used to combine Domino's ability to compute data on the fly with the power and simplicity of hyperlinks and image links. A variety of search pages allow users to search the contents of the Web site in several different levels of detail.

The next chapter takes Notes even farther afield. So far, you've seen how to build Notes applications for Notes clients and for the Web. The next chapter demonstrates how you can use Notes to communicate with the PalmPilot.

CHAPTER 29

Integrating Your PDA with Notes R5

Yes, it is true. You can put Notes databases on a Personal Data Assistant (PDA) and interact with them just like you would on your PC. Although this functionality is not native to the Lotus software, you can purchase a third party product called PylonPro, by the company Groupware Computing, which easily allows you to port a Notes database to the PDA and keep the data in-sync with your desktop or server. Currently, the software is only supported for either the 3Com PalmPilot or the IBM WorkPad.

NOTE PylonPro, which allows you to transform custom Notes databases into custom 3 Com PalmPilot applications, is included on the CD.

One of the nicest features of PylonPro is that you do not need to do any programming in order to put a database on your PDA. All that is required is for you to select a Notes database, a form, a view, and then HotSync to your PDA. That is all there is to it. Once your database is loaded onto the PDA, you can interact through a familiar interface, as shown in Figure 29.1.

FIGURE 29.1

A familiar database icon interface

Another added feature of PylonPro is that you can also use the Pylon Conduit software to HotSync your Notes mail file, address book, Personal Journal, calendar, and To Do list. This is the same functionality that is allowed using the Lotus product EasySync. But do not despair, if you like EasySync, you can use PylonPro just to HotSync your custom databases and not touch anything else. The product is quite flexible in the setup configuration, as you will soon see. For information on the advantages of PylonPro over EasySync or other software applications, see the PylonPro documentation.

Installing PylonPro and Pylon Conduit

We will not be going through each step involved in installing the Pylon products. There is a good help file that accompanies the software and gives a very detailed explanation of the steps that are required. We will go over a few points that we found to be a bit confusing or easily overlooked.

Whether you are installing the trial version or the full version of the Pylon software, you need to get a valid Pylon license number in order to use the software. The license number is based on your fully qualified Notes user ID. This is a very important step and cannot be skipped or misspelled. For example, my fully qualified name is Scot D. Haberman/xzck92/Employees/People/EDS/US. This is also known as the abbreviated format. Do not use your common Notes username (for example, Scot D. Haberman) or your username in canonical format (for example, CN=Scot D. Haberman/OU=xzck92/OU=Employees/OU=People/O=EDS/C=US). One typo and your license will not be valid, and PylonPro will not work.

 TIP   If you ever change your Notes name, you will need to re-register to obtain a new valid Pylon license. For example, if I changed my fully qualified name from Scot D. Haberman/xzck92/Employees/People/EDS/US to Scot D. Haberman/xzck92/Contractors/People/EDS/US, I would need to contact Globalware Computing with my new Notes name. They will issue a new valid Pylon license number.

After receiving your license number, the next step is to make sure that your Notes data and your PDA are in sync. To do this, make sure that you HotSync your data before beginning to use the PylonPro software. Skipping this step can create a bit more work, as you will most likely encounter quite a few Replication Conflicts for your existing documents.

Now, just follow the instructions for installing the PylonPro software. The installation process is pretty typical. The only stumbling block we encountered was during the selection of the Custom options. During the installation process, on the Setup Type screen, you can decide to select either the Typical, Compact, or Custom installation.

Being the overzealous developers that we are, we opted for the Custom installation. The Custom installation screen is not very difficult to understand, except that you can overlook some of the basic options. As shown in Figure 29.2, the default selections may not be exactly what you want. First of all, the PDA has only one address book, while Notes has one address book database with two types of addresses stored within one record: In Notes each address record allows both business and personal information to be stored. These two types of addresses are commonly known as the personal and the business entries. You need to select either your personal or business address information to be copied to your PDA. You cannot have both of your personal and business records automatically placed into the PDA's address book. Although, there are a few workarounds offered by PylonPro that allow you the same functionality. The help file that accompanies the software does a good job of showing you two alternatives to this dilemma. By default, your personal addresses will be synchronized to the PDA.

FIGURE 29.2

The default options for the Custom Installation screen

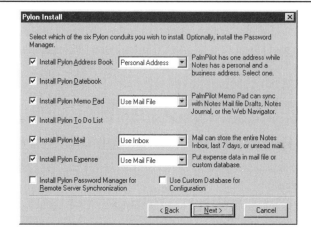

The next tricky part is the Memo Pad selection. The default selection is to pull all the documents from your Drafts folder in the mail database. Not that this is bad, it just may not be what you expect. We changed our selection to synchronize documents contained in our Personal Journal with the Memo Pad. You can also elect to synchronize the Web Navigator database, but the decision it up to you.

Another confusing default selection deals with the Expense database. Again, by default, all the entries will be placed into your Mail file. We opted to create and synchronize all the expense entries into a custom database that will be placed into our Notes root directory.

WARNING If you elect not to install using the Custom Install, certain data records may be placed into your Notes Mail file. Depending on your configuration, your mail file may reside locally on your hard drive or on a Domino server.

The last two options we will discuss are shown at the bottom of the Custom Installation screen. These are two check boxes that have significant meaning and can be overlooked. At first, the Install Pylon Password Manager For Remote Server Synchronization check box is a bit confusing. Selecting this option will remove the additional prompt for your password when you synchronize databases. This is a great convenience option and will allow your password to be submitted automatically when initiating a synchronization process to a Notes server. For more information about the possible configurations and risks, please refer to the PylonPro Help documentation.

The last check box, Use Custom Database For Configuration, is especially important and gave us the most grief. (We initially took the default setting and then tried to change it later. Don't do this because it takes a bit of work to clean it up). By default, all of the PylonPro configuration options will be saved into your current Location document at the time of installation. If this check box is selected, the installation process will create a new PylonPro Configuration database in the Notes Data directory. We personally do not like programs altering any of the default Notes databases and urge you to select this option. Selecting this check box will not tie your PylonPro configuration to any one Location document and will also allow you more flexibility in the long run.

Once you have completed selecting all of your options, press the Next button and complete the rest of the process. Once the installation is complete, you are ready to synchronize your Notes data with the PDA.

Your First Sync

When the installation is complete, do not jump into synchronizing your data just yet. The installation process has added the files shown in Table 29.1 to your Notes Data directory.

TABLE 29.1: LIST OF FILES INSTALLED FOR PYLONPRO

Filename	Description
Pylaunch.exe	This is used to help launch the PylonPro Configuration document. This Configuration document may be in a separate database or in your Location document depending on the installation selections.
Pyloncfg.nsf	This is a Configuration database that contains each user's configuration options. Depending on the installation options, the Configuration document may be in your Location document.
Pylonexp.nsf	This is the expense database that allows you to record expenses while traveling, etc.
Pylonpro.nsf	This is the sample database that shows how to use a lookup field for the PDA.
Pylonug.nsf	This is the PylonPro user guide database. It does not contain the documentation about the product. The documentation about the product is in the Pylondoc.pdf file.
Pyloncfg.ntf	This is the template database for the PylonPro Configuration database.
Pylonexp.ntf	This is the template database for the PylonPro expense database.
Pylondoc.pdf	This contains the PylonPro software documentation.

PART

VI

Developing
Databases

Assuming you decided to use the installation options mentioned in the previous section, start the Notes client and open the Pylon Configuration database using the File ➤ Database ➤ Open command. The Open Database screen appears, as shown in Figure 29.3. You can also open the Pylon Configuration document from the Windows start menu by selecting the Configure Pylon Program icon that is installed in the program folder. The default name for the program folder is PylonPro and Pylon Conduit, but you can override this name during the installation.

FIGURE 29.3

*Opening the Pylon
Configuration database*

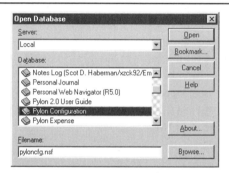

When the Configuration database is opened for the first time and you have not synchronized the data with your PDA, you should see the view shown in Figure 29.4. Open up the -setup- document. To ensure that you do not get any duplicate records during the first synchronization process, you need to mark all the databases so that Notes will overwrite the Palm data.

NOTE Before PylonPro can synchronize any data, it first must find a Configuration document. The software will determine who the user is and attempt to find a matching Configuration document in the following order: Palm username, current service name, -setup- document, and -default- document. This may seem quite silly if your Pylon Configuration database resides on your personal PC since you will be the only user. This flexibility will also allow a system administrator to place the Configuration database on a server and have it contain a document for each user, thus, simplifying maintenance.

To change the synchronization options, scroll down to the Pylon Conduit section of the Pylon Configuration's -setup- document, as shown in Figure 29.5. You can either select the drop down list for each of the six main databases (Date Book, Address Book, To Do List, Memo Pad, Mail, and Expense) or select the Arrow button, shown here, which will automatically change all of them for you. Once you have completed this task, you are ready to setup your first synchronization. Save and close the document. Once the document is saved, you can synchronize your PDA with your desktop.

FIGURE 29.4

The main Pylon
Configuration view

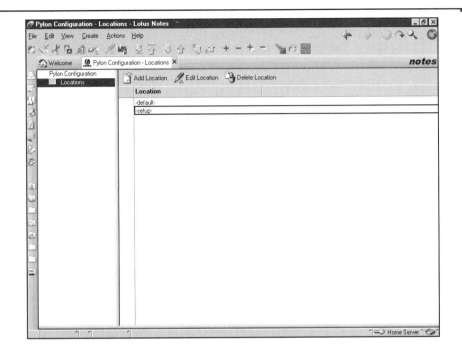

FIGURE 29.5

The Configuration
section for the Pylon
Conduit

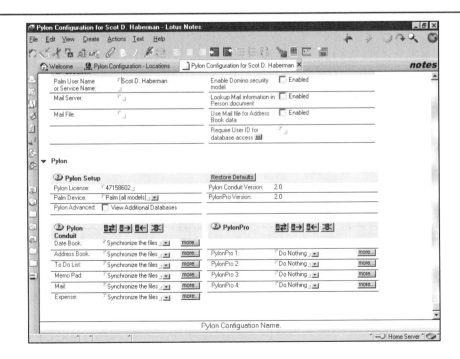

PART

VI

Developing
Databases

Depending on the amount of information that needs to be copied to your PDA, this first synchronization could take a while. Once the process is complete, you should have all six of the databases installed on your PDA. You should not have received any errors. If you did, refer to the PylonPro documentation, as it is quite extensive in listing the typical errors that are encountered. If an error occurred, more than likely, it is due to an invalid Pylon license number or a typo (commonly on either a filename or a server name).

If the synchronization executed cleanly, go back to the Pylon Configuration database. (You should still have this database open from the previous steps.) Refresh the Main view, and you should see that the -setup- record has now changed to reflect your Palm username, as shown in Figure 29.6. Open up the Configuration document and scroll down to the Pylon Configuration section once again. Before, you changed the database options so that your desktop would overwrite all the data residing on you PDA. Now, you need to change this option back so that whenever data has been changed, either on the desktop or the Palm, the documents will be synchronized. If you fail to do this, and changes on the PDA will always be overwritten by the data from the desktop. To change the selection, you can either select the Synchronize The Files option from the drop-down list box for each database or select the Two Arrow button, shown here, which will change this selection for all six databases. Once you have completed this task, save and close the document.

That takes care of the initial setup for synchronizing Notes and your PDA. To recap, you have installed both the PylonPro and the Pylon Conduit software. The Pylon Conduit is responsible for synchronizing the core Notes databases (mail, address book, etc). There are many other options available that show how the Pylon Conduit is an extremely powerful and flexible program (such as multiple address books), but that is beyond the scope of this chapter. The PylonPro software has been installed onto your desktop but not yet on the PDA. (This will occur when the first database is installed, which we will get into later.) Keep in mind that the help file that accompanies the Pylon software is an invaluable tool in showing you the power of the product. To find out more about the product, you can also visit the Globalware Discussion database online at http://www.globalware.com/discussion.

Designing a PDA Application

The PylonPro software is pretty sophisticated in that it translates the Notes database design using a technology called SmartDesign. This technology takes an existing Lotus Notes database and translates it into a format understood by the PylonPro Palm device. What this means to you is that you do not need to understand any programming for the Palm device, but only how to develop and design a Notes database. This technology will also retain the look and feel of your custom Notes database. So, before we get into how to setup the synchronization of your Notes database, let's first design an application and point out what should and should not be done. All of the examples we'll use for this section are in the Palm Enable Customer (PalmCust.nsf) and Palm Enabled TimeSheet (PalmTime.nsf) databases.

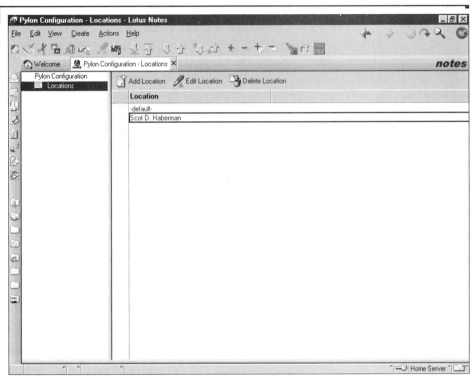

Creating a Palm-Enabled Database

As we mentioned before, you do not need to do any special programming in order to place a custom Notes database on the Palm device. However, there are a few things to keep in mind when designing the database to ensure that you take advantage of the Palm device's capabilities. Like most software, there are a few limitations that we will discuss in this section.

We are going to create a time entry database to illustrate how to design a database for the PalmPilot and how to dynamically pull data from one database to populate another. Like most people, you probably need to record or log your time when you work on a project. We are going to create a database that allows you to record your time. This database will be flexible enough to allow you to record time on both your PDA and also from a Notes client. The Palm Enabled TimeSheet (Time Entry–PalmTime.nsf) database will allow you to track and log the time that you spent with customers that are located in the Palm Enabled Customer (Customer–PalmCust.nsf) database. This tracking information can be used for billing a particular customer or for management reporting.

First of all, when designing your database, you need to keep in mind that the PylonPro software will require a form and a view when configuring the software. It is best that you create a separate form and a separate view that can be used specifically for this task. The reason is that the PDA has an extremely small screen. Most forms will look their best if they are designed to take advantage of the size of the screen that they will be viewed on. The same holds true for the view. You are limited in displaying only four columns in a view for the PDA. Also, there are some other limitations when using PylonPro, which are listed here:

- Layout regions are supported, but, since the data is ordered and stored differently in Notes than in native fields, it is best not to use them in order to control the field layout.

- Computed and hidden fields are not transferred from Notes to the PDA during synchronization.

- You are limited to only 128 editable fields per form.

- A view column value cannot use a formula. You must use a field name.

- You are limited to one rich text field per form.

Now this may seem like a lot of limitations, but, actually, it is not. The most cumbersome one is the lack of support for computed values in both forms and views. With all the bad news out of the way, some of the more notable features that are supported are listed next:

- You can add Notes-style field lookups into other databases or to the same database.

- You can change fields that are currently displayed in the PDA's view. Any field on the form can be selected to display.

- You can make on-the-fly adjustments to the column width.

- You can create dialogs for both Time and Date fields.

- There is support for most data types, such as numeric, text, keywords, check box, etc.

- You can use the built-in search capability to finding data.

- There is support for the Notes/Domino security model.

With these features in mind, let's get started with designing our database.

Creating the PDA Form

We are going to create a database that is usable in both the Notes client and on the PDA. To do this, we are going to need two separate Time Entry forms, one that is going to be used in the Notes client and one that is going to be used on the PDA. We will start by creating the form for the PDA since it is the smaller and easiest of the two.

The PDA form will contain the following four fields:

CustomerName   Allows you to select a customer name from the Customer database.

AccountNumber   This is the internal account number that is assigned to a customer based on the CustomerName. It is pulled directly from the Customer database.

TimeEntryDate   This is the date when the work actually occurred.

TotalHours   This is the total number of hours worked on the TimeEntryDate.

To add these fields to a new form, perform the following steps:

1. Start Domino Designer and open the Palm Enabled TimeSheet (`PalmTime.nsf`) database.

2. Choose Create ➢ Design ➢ Form.

3. Create a table with two columns and four rows, which will contain our field labels and fields.

4. In the first cell of the first row, type **Customer Name:**.

5. In the second cell of the first row, choose Create ➢ Design ➢ Field.

6. The Field Properties InfoBox will appear. In the Name field, type **Customer-Name**. Make sure that the Type is Dialog list and Editable. Also make sure that Allow Multiple Values is not selected. We only want to be able to select one entry.

7. In order to pull in the values from the Customer database, you will need to set the properties on the Control tab (see Figure 29.7). In the Display area, select the Show Field Delimiters check box.

8. Since PylonPro does not support the use of functions for Keyword fields (that is, @DBLookup), in the Choices area, select the Use View Dialog For Choices option from the drop-down list.

9. In the Database drop-down list, select the Palm Enabled Customer option.

10. In the View drop-down list, select the Customer Listing option.

11. In the Column # text box, type in the value **1** for the column number to use to display in the field.

PART

VI

Developing Databases

12. In the Options area, select both the Display Entry Helper Button and the Refresh Fields On Keyboard Change check boxes.

13. Close the Properties InfoBox.

You have finished all the mapping that is required for creating a Lookup field. But we want to accomplish a bit more.

 NOTE PylonPro allows you to do lookups from other databases. (You can also do a lookup within the same database.) But you cannot use the @DBColumn or @DBLookup functions like you can in a typical Notes application. In other words, you cannot use the Use Formulas For Choices option in the Choices drop-down list.

Let's finish creating our field labels and fields.

1. Select the Default Values event for the CustomerName field. For the default value, type in **"CustomerName,AccountNumber,CustomerName, Account-Number";""**. This syntax has special meaning for the PylonPro software. First, you need to specify which fields you want to populate. In this example, we are going to populate the CustomerName and AccountNumber fields of the current form. This accounts for the first two entries in the string. Next, you need to specify which fields you are going to pull this data from. In this example, the fields happen to be of the same name, CustomerName and AccountNumber, and will be pulled from the lookup database. This extended syntax is not required to do a lookup but allows you to retrieve and populate additional fields. If you were going to populate just the CustomerName field, the syntax would be "Customer-Name,CustomerName";"".

2. In the remaining first cells of the table, type in **Account Number:**, **Date:**, and **Hours:**.

3. In the remaining second cells of the table, create the following fields:

Name	Type
AccountNumber	Text and Editable (Even though this field is automatically populated via the CustomerName field and PylonPro, remember that every field must be editable or it will not show up on the PDA.)
TimeEntryDate	Date/Time and Editable
TotalHours	Number and Editable

4. Save the form by choosing File ➤ Save.

5. When prompted for a form name, type in **Time Entry for Palm | TimeEntryPalm**.

You have completed the first of the two forms for the database. Your form should look similar to Figure 29.8. You may notice that there is not much to the form. Keep in mind that the PDA will render the form in its own format, so glitz and glamour are not required. The main goal of this form is to lay out the fields in the order you want. Once rendered on the PDA, the fields and labels will be shown in a single-list format.

Creating the Notes Client Form

Now, let's get started on the second form.

1. Create a new form.

2. Create the tables and labels, as shown in Figure 29.9. (Do not worry about the fields yet; we will step through them one at a time.) Your copy of the form does not have to look exactly like that shown in Figure 29.9, as the tables and borders are used mainly for visual effect, just make sure that you have the proper number of columns and the proper labels.

3. Once you have completed the tables and labels, choose File ➤ Save.

4. When prompted for the form name, type in **Time Entry | TimeEntry**.

The first thing you may have noticed about this form is that there are more fields than on the PDA form that we designed. We have added the following three fields:

- Body
- Image
- Categories

FIGURE 29.8

The completed Time
Entry For Palm PDA
form

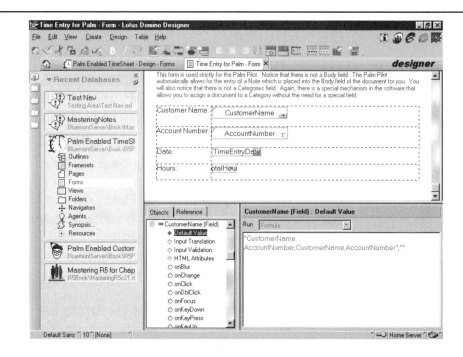

FIGURE 29.9

The completed Time
Entry Notes form

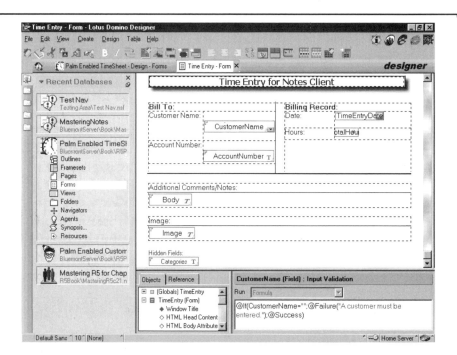

These fields are also used by the PDA form, but they are not actually on the form itself. These are special fields that are used by the PDA and are defined in the configuration options for the database. We will explain more on how to configure and use these fields when we start actually using the PDA form. For now, let's get back to the Notes client form.

Assuming that you have followed the layout show in Figure 29.9, let's begin adding the fields. To add these fields to a new form, perform the following steps:

1. In the cell next to the Customer Name label, choose Create ➢ Design ➢ Field. The Field Properties InfoBox appears.

2. In the Name field of the Field Properties InfoBox, type **CustomerName**. Make sure that the Type is Dialog list and Editable. Also, make sure that the Allow Multiple Values check box is not selected. (We only want to be able to select one entry.)

3. To pull in the values from the Customer database, set the properties for the Control tab to Use Formulas For Choices from the drop-down list in the Choices section of the Field Properties InfoBox.

4. For the formula, enter the following formula, which will dynamically display all the current customers:

```
ServerName := @Subset(@DbName;1);
DBName := @Subset(@DbName;-1);
NewDB := @If(@Contains(DBName;"\\");@LeftBack(DBName;"\\") +
➡    "\\" + "PalmCust.nsf";"PalmCust.nsf");
TempErr := @DbColumn("Notes":"NoCache";
➡    ServerName:NewDB;"Customer";1);
@If(@IsError(TempErr);"Error retreiving customer names";TempErr)
```

 NOTE We have used the continuation arrow (➡) in formulas to show that code is on the same line. It is only printed on different lines due to space constraints.

5. Also, in the Field Properties InfoBox, make sure that the Refresh Fields On Keyword Change option is enabled.

6. In the cell just below the CustomerName field, choose Create ➢ Design ➢ Field.

7. Type **AccountNumber** in the Name field. The Type should be Text and Computed. This value is associated to the selected CustomerName value so we need to put in a formula for the Value event. By default, when you create a Computed

PART

VI

Developing
Databases

field, the Value event is selected. Just type in the following formula in the Script Area of the screen:

```
@If(CustomerName="";@Return("");"");
ServerName := @Subset(@DbName;1);
TempDBName := @Subset(@DbName;-1);
DBName := @If(@Contains(TempDBName;"\\");
➡   @LeftBack(TempDBName;"\\") +
➡   "\\PalmCust.nsf";"PalmCust.nsf");
TempErr := @DbLookup("Notes":"NoCache";
➡   ServerName:DBName;"Customer";CustomerName;2);
@If(@IsError(TempErr);"Could not find the customer";TempErr)
```

This code will take the value of the CustomerName field and do a lookup in the Customer database to retrieve the account number.

8. In the table cells next to the Date and Hours label, add the two fields: TimeEntry-Date and TotalHours. The TimeEntryDate field should be defined as Date/Time and Editable. And the TotalHours field should be defined as Number and Editable. You do not have to worry about any default values since these should be supplied by the user when entering data.

9. The remaining three fields—Body, Image, and Categories—were not present on the PDA's version of this form. The first field, Body, should be defined as Rich Text and Editable. The second field, Image, should be defined as Rich Text and Computed.

10. Since Image is a computed field, you need to supply a value. Type in **Image** as the value, which will default to the contents of the Image field. (You may start to wonder why Image is defined as computed. If you cannot enter data directly into the Image field from the Notes client form and the Image field was not defined on the PDA form, just how are we going to get any data into that field? Do not worry, it will make more sense in a moment. As a hint, I will say that the PDA will allow you to enter data into this field, just not through a field defined on the form.)

11. Lastly, we need to create the Categories field. This field should be defined as Dialog List and Computed in the Field Properties InfoBox. Also, enable the Allow Multiple Values option and make sure that this field is marked as hidden. (We tend to highlight all hidden fields and text in red.)

12. Save the form by choosing File ➢ Save from the menu.

Now let's test the form. Assuming that your Customer database has at least one entry (the sample Customer database already has some data filled in), open up the form in the Notes client. The easiest way to do that is by clicking the Notes Preview icon in the upper right hand corner of Domino Designer. When the form is displayed, it should look similar to that in Figure 29.10.

NOTE In Notes, users can assign categories to a document without having to actually open up a document and change a field value. This can be accomplished using the Actions ≻ Categorize menu option when displaying a view. In order for this menu option to work, you must first have a Categories field defined on the form as a text list that allows multiple values. Next, you must also have a view whose leftmost column is either categorized or sorted on the Categories field. Using this view, the user can select one or more documents and enter one or more categories.

FIGURE 29.10

The completed Time Entry form as shown in the Notes client

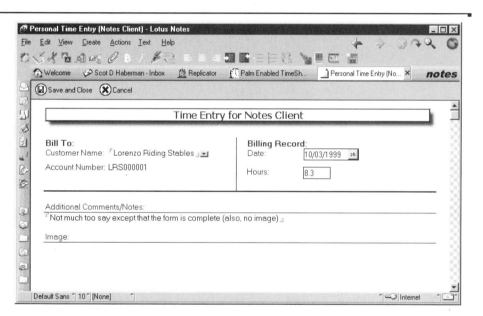

When you select a customer from the Customer Name drop-down list, the Account Number field is automatically filled in with the customer's account number as defined in the customer database. To test the form, select a date and type in some hours. You can also make some comments in the Additional Comments/Notes field, but you cannot type or enter an image in this field from the Notes client. This can only be done on the PDA. Now that the forms are complete, we will show you how to create the PDA view.

PART

VI

Developing
Databases

Creating the PDA View

If you have gotten this far into the book, you are probably already familiar with how to create a view, so we will not bore you with explaining how each view was created. The sample database gives you four example views that you can use, including the view for categorizing documents. We will discuss the view that is used on the PDA.

You do not need to create a separate view for the PDA. We chose to do this to simplify the example. As stated before, PylonPro will ignore any columns that use a formula for computing the column data. With this in mind, the PDA view is very simple. Each column can only display the contents of a field. In other words, the value for a column needs to be a field name. Also, PylonPro does not categorize documents like those in the Notes client. So, if you decide to use a view that contains a categorized column, it will not look like what you would expect. Instead of a twistie next to the categorized value, which expands to show all the documents for that category, the PDA will display the categorized value on each individual row of the view. Keeping these limitations in mind, the view for the PDA becomes even more simplistic.

One limitation of the PDA application is that a view can only show a maximum of four columns. Now this may seem like a problem, but remember that the screen on the PDA is extremely small and trying to display more than four columns gets to be a bit much. For our example, we opted to display three columns of data:

- TimeEntryDate (This is called DATE in the sample database.)
- CustomerName
- TotalHours (This is called HOURS in the sample database.)

To create this view, perform the following steps:

1. From the Design list of the Design pane, select the View entry.
2. Choose Create ➤ View. The Create View dialog box appears.
3. In the View Name field, type **(Palm View)|PalmView**.
4. Click the Copy From button and make sure that the -Blank- entry is highlighted in the Copy From dialog box.
5. Press the OK button. When the Create View dialog box reappears, click the Customize button. This will take you to the design for the newly created view.
6. Highlight the first column. (There should be only one–by default, it places a # as the column title.)
7. Choose Design ➤ Column Properties. The Column Properties InfoBox appears.
8. In the Title field, enter **Date**.
9. In the Script area of the Designer pane, select the Field radio button and highlight the TimeEntryDate field.

10. Append a new column to the view by choosing Create ➤ Append New Column.

11. In the Title field of the Column Properties InfoBox, enter **Customer Name**.

12. In the Script area of the Column Properties InfoBox, select the Field radio button and highlight the CustomerName field.

13. Append one last column named Hours. Make sure the TotalHours field is selected as the column value.

That is all there is to it. When you have completed all of the changes, save the view. To test the view, select the Notes Preview button and the contents of the view will be displayed in the Notes client. Your view should be similar to that shown in Figure 29.11.

FIGURE 29.11

The completed PDA view

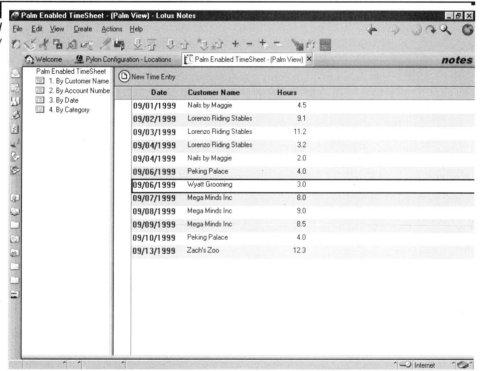

You have completed all the programming that is required for the PDA application. We told you that it would not be difficult. Now, let's move your application over to the PDA.

PART

VI

Developing
Databases

Syncing Your Custom Notes Applications

In the earlier section, we walked you through installing the Pylon Conduit and Pylon-Pro software, and got your basic databases synchronized with your PDA. Now, we show you how to synchronize your custom Notes applications with your PDA.

Configuring PylonPro

In order for you to be able to interact with a Notes database on the PDA, the PylonPro module needs to be loaded on the PDA. The .PRC file should be loaded for you automatically the first time a Notes database is synchronized, but there are a few issues with the Palm III that may require a second synchronization to get the module installed correctly. If all else fails, synchronize, and the issues will probably get fixed.

 NOTE If for any reason you remove the PylonPro application from the PDA, do not spend a lot of time looking for the PylonPro PRC file for installation. The PRC file does not exist as an installable application. Instead, the PylonPro software is automatically installed for you when you synchronize.

To install a Notes database on the PDA, you must first configure the software using the Pylon Configuration document, as shown back in Figure 29.5. Earlier, we concentrated on the Pylon Conduit section. To install Notes database applications, we will use the PylonPro section.

The PylonPro section is where you can add your custom Notes database applications for synchronization. For our example, we are going to install both the Customer and the TimeSheet databases. You will see that the Customization dialog box for adding the databases is very similar to the Pylon Conduit section.

 TIP With version 2 of the PylonPro software, you are allowed to transfer up to 16 additional databases (Pylon 1–Pylon 16) to the PDA. In the Configuration document, there are only four slots available for databases. To get the extra fields needed, just enable the View Additional Databases option in the Pylon Setup section of the Configuration document. These 16 databases are in addition to the 8 additional databases allowed in the Pylon Conduit section.

To add the TimeSheet database, follow these steps:

   1. Next to the Pylon 1 label, select the More button. ThePylonPro Conduit–Configure PylonPro 1 dialog box appears.

2. You can either type in the server name where the TimeSheet database resides, or you can select the ... button next to the Server dialog box. Use the default of Local or select the server where the database resides.

3. In the Database dialog box, enter the file path (relative to the Notes Data directory) for the TimeSheet database. If you are not sure of the exact file path and name, select the ... button, and all the databases that currently reside on that server will be displayed in the Database dialog box.

4. For the View or Formula dialog box, type in **(Palm View)** or select the ... button and highlight the view.

5. For the Form dialog box, type in **Time Entry for Palm** or select the ... button and highlight the form.

When you have finished, your Configuration form should look similar to Figure 29.12.

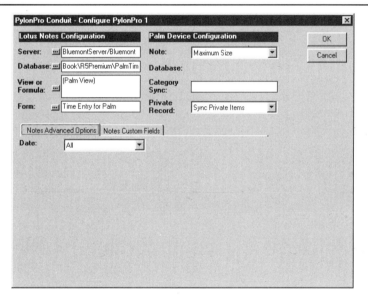

FIGURE 29.12

The completed custom Notes database Configuration dialog box

That is all that is actually required in order for the application to work properly on the PDA. We are going to delve further into some of the more advanced features and show you how to use some of the fields (specifically Categories, Body, and Image).

Select the Notes Custom Fields tab. Notice the three additional input fields for Category Field, Note, and Image. Type in **Categories**, **Body**, and **Image** for the three input fields respectively. You have told PylonPro that you would like to use the Categories field to categorize documents on the PDA, the Body field to contain comments data, and the Image field to contain your images. (Do not worry if this does not make sense yet, it will.) Click the OK button, and the information will be stored for the PylonPro 1 database.

PART

VI

Developing
Databases

Now, perform the same steps for the Customer database. This time, select the Customer database, the Customer Listing view, and the Customer Account form. Do not enter anything for the fields contained on the Notes Custom Fields tab because the sample database is not setup to take advantage of them. Click the OK button to save the information.

The last step in the configuration process is to setup the type of synchronization that should take place. The drop-down list next to each label (PylonPro 1, etc) tells the synchronization software what type of synchronization should take place. By default, the action is Do Nothing. We need to change this to Notes Overwrites Palm.

 WARNING The first time that you synchronize, the synchronization action needs to be Notes Overwrites Palm. If you do not select this option, your synchronization may have unpredictable results. Also, if you ever change the design of a database, you need to setup the Notes Overwrites Palm synchronization action, or the new design changes will not get updated to the PDA.

Now that you have set up your Configuration document, you are ready to synchronize your data to your PDA. Save the Configuration document, plug your PDA into either your cradle or synchronization cable, and initiate the synchronization process. Once the process is complete, your PDA should have an option for PylonPro, as shown in Figure 29.13. (The application will initially be placed in the Unfiled category.)

FIGURE 29.13

The PylonPro option as seen on the PDA

Working with the PDA

Now that you have your application installed on the PDA, it is time to see how it works. To display the databases that have been installed on the PDA, select the PylonPro application. This will display all of the currently installed Notes applications, as shown back in Figure 29.1. (Although your PDA should only display two databases: Customer and TimeEntry.) Notice that the icon used for the database is strikingly similar to the icons on the old Notes workspace.

The Database Icon

Let's open the TimeEntry database and see what it looks like. You may notice that on the Database icon, there is a drop-down arrow in the upper right hand corner. Selecting this arrow will display three choices:

- Info...
- Delete DB
- About PylonPro

The Info menu option will display the entire database title, your username, your PylonPro serial number, and the current size of the database. The Delete DB menu option does exactly that, it prompts you to see if you really want to delete the database from the PDA, as shown in Figure 29.14. The About PylonPro menu option displays the current version, release date, and copyright information for the software.

FIGURE 29.14

You are prompted to verify that you want to delete the database.

 NOTE   Selecting the Delete DB option from the Database icon will not remove any data from the actual database residing on your server or workstation. It only removes it from the PDA.

The Database View

If you select the Database icon, the view of the data will display, as shown in Figure 29.15. Let's go over a few things about the view before we move on to the actual document data.

PART

VI

Developing
Databases

FIGURE 29.15

The PDA view of
the data

When we were creating the view, we mentioned that a view on the PDA can only display a maximum of four columns of data. This is true, but there is a slick feature of PylonPro that makes this limitation not really a limitation at all. When we created the view (Palm View), we only had three columns of data (TimeEntryDate, Customer-Name, and TotalHours), which are displayed in Figure 29.15. Since you can only have one view displayed on the PDA, what can you do if there are some people who want to see the view display different columns of data? You could create different views for the various people, but that is not necessary. PylonPro allows you to change the columns of the view on the fly. Not only can you mix and match the column data you see on the view, but you can also select fields from the document. For example, some users may prefer to see the customer name in the first column of the data. This is easily accomplished by selecting the menu option on the PDA. This will display the PDA menu bar at the top of the screen. Select Options from the menu bar, and you should get the drop-down menu, as shown in Figure 29.16.

FIGURE 29.16

The PylonPro
Options menu

Selecting the Columns menu option will display the PylonPro Column dialog box, as shown in Figure 29.17. From here, you can decide how many columns of data you wish to see (from 1 to 4 columns). You can also decide which fields should display in which columns. For our example, if the user wants to see the customer name in the first column, they just need to select the CustomerName field from the Column 1 drop-down list, as shown in Figure 29.18. You can mix and match any of the four columns with any of the document fields to create an ad-hoc view. Also, the changes that you make remain in effect until the next time you download the design of the database, or until you press the Restore Defaults menu option.

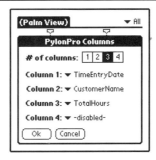

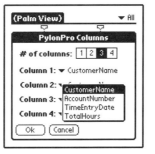

So, let's change the view around a bit. From the PylonPro Columns dialog box, select four columns to display. Let Column 1 show the CustomerName field, Column 2 show the AccountNumber field, Column 3 show the TimeEntryDate field, and Column 4 show the TotalHours field. Press the OK button, and your new view should look like Figure 29.19.

Now the view may seem a bit cramped, and you cannot see all of the text. You can also resize the columns of data as you can in the Notes client. Just tap and slide the Resize icon above any of the columns, and you can resize the column to any width you desire (limited by the screen, of course). Another handy feature is the Lookup field in the bottom right hand corner of the PDA screen. In this field, you can begin spelling out the entry you wish to locate, and the PDA will automatically find any

PART

VI

Developing
Databases

match in the first column of the view. For example, if you want to find the customer Wyatt Grooming, just write a *W*, and the first document beginning with a *W* in the first column will be highlighted, as shown in Figure 29.20.

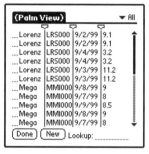

To open an existing document from the view, just select the row, and the document will display. If you want to create a new document, just select the New button at the bottom of the view. With that in mind, select the New button, and we will begin creating a new document.

The Database Document

Selecting the New button will create an empty document, as shown in Figure 29.21. By default, the cursor is automatically placed on the first field of the form. In this case, it is the Customer field. The labels that identify each field are limited in size, and sometimes the text may be cut off so that the entire label is illegible. (For example, look at the Account number field, which only displays *Account N.*) You can shorten the names of all your fields so that they fit neatly on the screen, but a better alternative is to enter detailed help information for each field. Entering a detailed explanation of each field will allow the user to get a better understanding of what should be entered. At the bottom of the form, there is the text "Select the customer which shou_." Again, the text is cutoff. If you tap the text, a dialog box will display showing the complete text, as shown in Figure 29.22. In the text, you can explain what and how to use the field.

FIGURE 29.21

The new Time Entry form on the PDA

FIGURE 29.22

The Help Text dialog box

To enter data into any of the fields, you only need to tap on the field. The first field on the form, Customer, is a bit different. When creating the form, we used a very special formula that would dynamically pull data from the Customer database and display a list to the user. Well, here it is in action. If you tap the field, the Customer Listing view appears, displaying a list of customers and their account numbers, as shown in Figure 29.23.

Select the Crazy Cars entry, and the Customer name, along with the correct account number, is automatically filled in with your selection, as shown in Figure 29.24.

Moving on to the Date field, placing the cursor on that field will automatically display the typical PDA date input selection. You can select Today, Tomorrow, One week later, No Date, or Choose Date (which brings up a calendar selection). For this example, select Tomorrow. Tap on the Hours field and enter **5 hours**. That completes the main fields for the document, but there are some special fields we have not mentioned that are unique to the PDA.

PART

VI

Developing
Databases

FIGURE 29.23

The Customer database data shown as a selection from the Time Entry form

FIGURE 29.24

The Time Entry form is automatically filled in with your customer selection.

Special PDA Options

If you look along the bottom of the screen, you will notice three buttons:

- Done
- Note
- Image

Done is quite obvious, but we are more interested in the Note and Image options. When configuring PylonPro, you were asked to add field names to three fields within the Notes Custom Fields tab on the form. They were Categories, Note, and Image. The field names you typed in were Categories, Body, and Image. This is where those configuration settings come into play. (At least, the Note and Image fields—we will get to Categories in a moment.)

Select the Note option. A free-form note is automatically displayed. You can type in any type of comments that you wish, as shown in Figure 29.25. Whatever you type into this field will automatically be saved into the Body field on the Notes document the next time you synchronize. Since the PDA screen is so limited in size, the software only allows you one free-form or rich text field per form. This is why the form we created for the PDA did not contain a viewable field for Body. Even if we made the rich text field viewable, it would not display properly. The Configuration document is what tells the PylonPro software which field to use in Notes for saving this free-from data.

Tap the Done button and select the Image option. This is a built-in graphics program that allows you limited capability for graphics, as shown in Figure 29.26. You can write on the screen, and the program will capture your keystrokes. You can use this for capturing signatures if you wish. Tap the Done button, and your image will be saved.

Now that you are back on your new note, tap the Done button to save your document data. It should appear at the top of the view since the new document contains the most recent date. (Remember, we selected Tomorrow as the entry date.)

 WARNING The PDA image field currently goes in only one direction. In other words, you can create images on the PDA, and they will be saved to the Notes document. But you cannot create an image in the Notes document and have it saved onto the PDA.

The last special field we will discuss is the Categories field. Again, we did not create a viewable field for the PDA form because there is a built-in function designed for this purpose. If you look in the upper right hand corner of the view, you will notice a down arrow with All next to it. Tap this area and a drop-down list showing the complete list of current categories will appear. (In this case, All, Unfiled, and Edit Categories is shown.) Let's create a new category by selecting the Edit Categories option. When this option is selected, a new dialog list will appear, as shown in Figure 29.27.

Tap the New button and enter the Category **Billable**. Tap OK and add another category called **Non-Billable**. You have created two new categories that you can use for categorizing your documents. Tap the OK button from the Edit Categories dialog box. You will go back to the view of all the documents.

The Edit Categories dialog box allows you to dynamically add and remove categories on your PDA.

To categorize a document using the PDA, you need to open the document in Edit mode. To do so, follow these steps:

1. Select the Crazy Cars document. The document will appear in Read mode.

2. Tap the Edit button.

3. In the upper right hand corner, you can select a category. Tap the category.

4. From the drop-down list box, highlight the Billable category option.

5. Tap the Done key. Your change will be saved.

To verify that your document has been categorized, from the view, tap the category in the upper right hand of the screen. Select Billable. The view, with only the Crazy Cars document visible, should appear. Since you have only categorized one document for Billable, it makes sense that you should only see that one document.

That covers the major functions of the PDA and the Notes documents. Now, let's make one final synchronization and make sure all of our edits took place.

The Final Sync

The final step in this entire process is to get the data from the PDA over to the Notes database. (We have already shown how to get the Notes data onto the PDA.) The synchronization process is quite similar to that of the Notes replication process. Connect your PDA to the HotSync cable (or put the PDA in the cradle) and start the HotSync process.

Once the synchronization process is complete, open the TimeEntry database. Select the By Category view (in the View pane, 4. By Category). Expand both the Billable category and the Crazy Cars category. Hopefully, your view will match the one shown in Figure 29.28. Looking at the view, you can see that assigning the document to the Billable category worked successfully. You can also see that the customer name of Crazy Cars is also correct. The hours should match, as well.

FIGURE 29.28

The view displayed in the Notes client

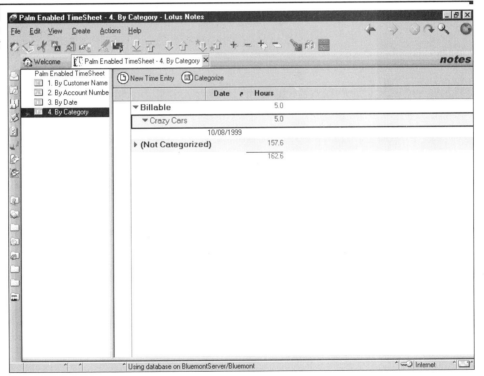

Now, let's open the document to check that all of the data got carried over. Double-click the document. You can see that the fields you input data for were saved correctly, as shown in Figure 29.29. You can also see that the data input for the Note option and the Image option have been carried over.

As you can see, the PylonPro software is very easy to use for a Notes programmer. There are many reasons to use a PDA and a Notes database. The TimeEntry database is just one small example of the versatility of the product. Now that you know the basics, go out and get creative!

PART

VI

Developing
Databases

FIGURE 29.29

The document created from the PDA

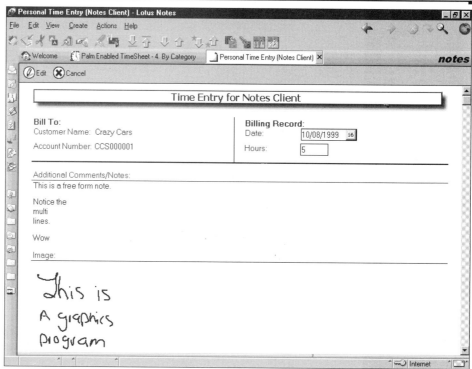

Summary

Setting up a Notes database that can be used in both the Notes client and the PDA is not difficult. There is not a lot of special coding required because the PylonPro software does all of the database translation for you. As a developer, you only need to decide what data to capture and how it should be displayed to the user. The PylonPro software does the rest.

In the following Appendices, we explain how to install Notes, both as a new installation and as an upgrade to your existing Notes 4.*x* implementation. We have also compiled a list of some of the more interesting yet overlooked internal and predefined fields that can be used on a Notes form.

APPENDICES

APPENDIX **A**

Installing Lotus Notes 5

O ne nice feature of Notes is that the installation process is fairly simple. We've installed Notes countless times, and we have yet to have a problem. This section will cover the installation process for the Notes client, the Domino Designer client, and the Administration client. We won't be going through the steps of installing a Domino server. Even though you may not have a need for the Administration client, all three programs are included in the same installation program, so we'll mention the Administration client when applicable.

There are two types of installations that can be performed: a new clean install (use this if you don't have Notes on your current machine) and an upgrade. The process for both types of installations is the same. There are a few minor differences, and we'll discuss them as they occur.

The Notes Installation Program

The Notes installation process has been completely redesigned. There are two components to the installation process. The first portion, the Notes startup and component selection process, is quite graphical in nature and allows you to select the software components that you want to install. The second portion is completely controlled by Install-Shield (a fantastic installation program), which is solely dependant on your selections from the first portion of the installation process. If you are familiar with installing previous Notes releases, this is a dramatic change from what you are used to.

To install any of the Notes software, place the Notes installation CD into your PC and the installation process will begin automatically. If for some reason the installation program does not automatically start, you can view the contents of the CD and run the setup.bat program, which will manually start the process for you. When the program starts, a short advertisement video (complete with music) will begin. After the short commercial, the installation screen, as shown in Figure A.1, will display.

There are five options to choose from (excluding the Exit button of course), which are as follows:

Install   Allows you to select which Lotus product to install

Getting Started   Displays the start.txt file, which is nothing more than a readme file

Explore This CD   Displays the file listing for the CD using Explorer

www.notes.net   Jumps to the Notes.net Web site using your browser

Contact Us   Displays the various ways to contact Lotus about their products

To install any of the three clients, select the Install option, which will display the product installation selection screen, shown in Figure A.2. There are three options available on the screen: Clients, Servers, and Other. You can hover your mouse over any of the three options for more information. The Servers option should only be selected if you intend to install a Domino server. Installing a Domino server is beyond the scope of this book; the remaining two options will be discussed in more detail.

FIGURE A.1

*The installation options
selection startup screen*

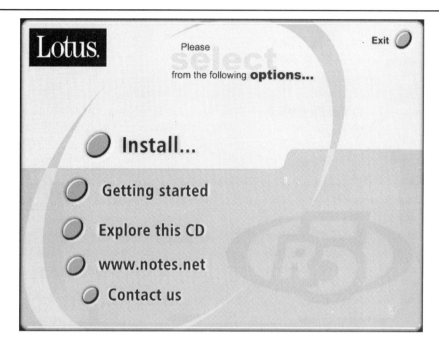

FIGURE A.2

*The product installation
selection screen*

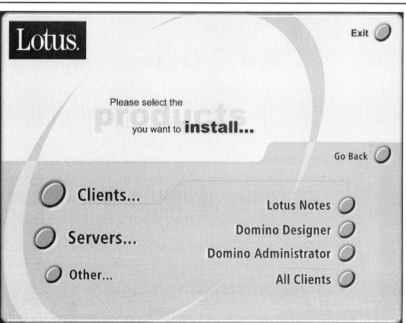

The Other Software Components

Included on the CD are some non-Lotus products that may complement your Notes installation. Selecting the Other option will display the subcomponents, as shown in Figure A.3.

FIGURE A.3

The expanded installation options for the Other selection option

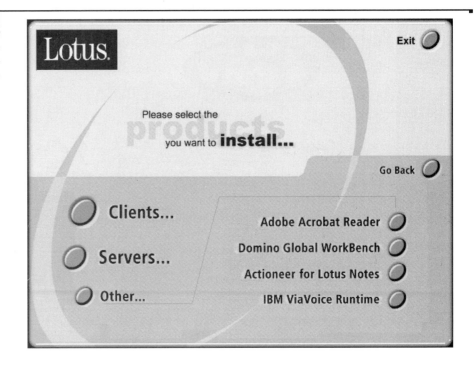

Selecting the first option, Adobe Acrobat Reader, will display the Acrobat Reader installation screen. To install the software, just select the Standard Install button and follow the prompts.

The second selection, Domino Global WorkBench, will display the Global Work-Bench installation screen. This software, along with Domino Designer, gives you a comprehensive set of tools to easily create, update, and manage Domino-based multi-lingual applications. To install the software, just select the Standard Install button and follow the prompts.

The third selection, Actioneer for Lotus Notes, will display the Actioneer installation screen. This software is a separate product that integrates seamlessly with the Lotus R5 client product and is designed to help you enter information into Notes quickly without having to run the Notes client. You can enter appointments, To Do items, and reference items into your calendar, To Do list, and journal using an intuitive, natural-language interface. The text that you enter into Actioneer is interpreted and placed into the appropriate destination (the calendar, To Do list, or journal). Actioneer is speech enabled for those of you who use speech recognition software in a future release, and it includes another product that allows you to use Actioneer on your palm device. To install the software, select the Standard Install button and follow the prompts.

The last option, IBM ViaVoice Runtime, is the runtime for ViaVoice (and Actioneer) and is provided for your convenience. To install this software, select the Standard Install button and follow the prompts.

The Client Software Components

When you select the Clients button, the expanded list of possible client installations will be displayed. You can choose to selectively install just the Lotus Notes client, the Domino Designer client, the Administrative client, or all three. The selection is quite important because the InstallShield portion of the installation process is based solely on your selection from this screen.

When you select which client you wish to install, a second screen will appear; it will be similar to the screen shown in Figure A.4 (the screen may look slightly different depending on your selection, but the process is exactly the same). You can choose from two options: Custom Install or Standard Install. Unlike the Standard Install option, the Custom Install option will give you the ability to selectively choose which additional components to install (all of the components are covered in "Client Customization" later in this appendix). It is important that you realize that the component selection is contained within the InstallShield portion of the installation process, and if you don't select the Custom Install option, you won't have the ability to pick and choose which subcomponents to install. Once you select either the Custom Install or Standard Install button, the InstallShield process will take over.

When the InstallShield install process begins, a dialog box with a progress bar will appear informing you that the installation program is loading. The time it takes will vary from machine to machine. Once the R5 logo appears, the start-up screen will display, welcoming you to the Notes setup program. If you've installed other programs, this screen will probably be familiar to you. Once you have finished reading the text on the screen, click the Next button to proceed with the installation or the Cancel button to exit the installation.

The next screen to appear is the license agreement. Read it carefully, and if you agree with the terms and conditions, click the Yes button; otherwise click the No button, which will terminate the installation process.

 NOTE You must accept the license agreement to continue installing the Notes client.

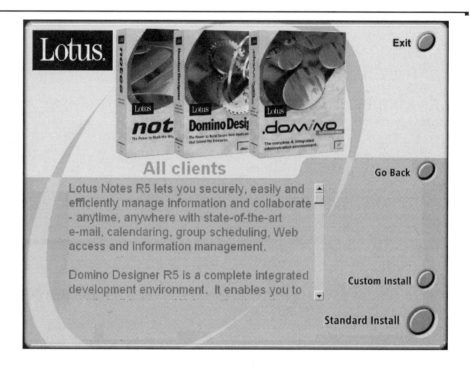

User Information

In the user information screen, enter your name and company name (if applicable) in the Name and Company fields. Make sure the Shared Installation option is not checked (unless you are a Notes administrator, you won't need this option enabled). Once you have filled out the appropriate fields, click the Next button.

The Installation Folder

The next screen, shown in Figure A.5, displays the folders where the installation program will install the Notes clients. There are two folders specified in the Destination Folder section of the dialog box. The Program Folder field shows the folder that will house all of the Notes program files. The Data Folder field shows the folder that will house all of the Notes databases and other data-related information. By default, the program folder will be installed into C:\Lotus\Notes, and the data folder will be installed into C:\Lotus\Notes\Data.

FIGURE A.5

The Notes program and data folder selection screen

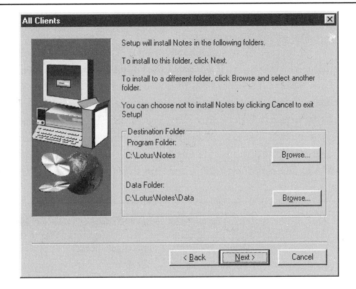

NOTE If you already have a copy of the Notes client software on your PC, the default folders in the dialog box will reflect where the current installation of Notes resides. Before overwriting your current installation of Notes, it is a good idea to make a backup of your current Data folder just in case something goes wrong.

If you want to install Notes in folders other than those listed, click the Browse button to the right of either the Program Folder or Data Folder field. This will display the Choose Folder dialog box, where you can select a current folder or type in the name of a folder that does not yet exist. If you type in the name of a folder that does not exist, a message box asking you if you would like it to be created will display. To create the folder, click the Yes button; otherwise, click the No button (the latter option will take you right back to the Choose Folder dialog box).

 TIP It is a good practice to always name the Notes data folder Data and to place it under the Notes folder containing the Notes program files.

Once you have finished selecting the folders in which to install the Notes client and data folders, click the Next button to continue with the installation.

Client Customization

If you elected to use the standard install during the first phase of the installation process, you can skip this section because the customization options will not appear. If you bravely decided to customize the options for the client (or clients), you should see the customization box as shown in Figure A.6. As you can see, there are quite a number of components that are available for the clients (in this example, we elected to install all the clients). Table A.1 displays all of the possible components, the applicable client type, and a brief description of each (note that this chart does not display the All Clients option).

FIGURE A.6

The All Client installation options selection

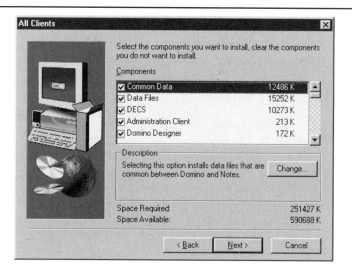

TABLE A.1: AVAILABLE COMPONENTS BY CLIENT TYPE

Component	Client Type			Description
	C	**D**	**A***	
Common Data	x	**x**	**x****	Files common to Notes and Domino.
Data Files	x	**x**	**x**	Standard set of Notes/Domino data files (always install these).
DECS	x	**x**	**x**	Domino Enterprise Connection Services used for connecting to external data sources.
Administration Client		x	**x**	Domino Administrator, the administration client for maintaining Domino servers.
Domino Designer		**x**	x	Domino Designer client for creating and maintaining Notes/Domino databases and applications.
Domino Web Services	x	**x**	x	Required if Domino Designer is installed for the client.
Help	**x**	**x**	**x**	Notes/Domino Help files. These are quite large. Help can also be accessed from the Domino server.
Migration Tools	x	x	x	Mail migration tools.
Notes Minder	**x**	**x**	**x**	Component that detects if new Notes mail has arrived and tells the user without the need for Notes to be up and running.
Notes Program Files	**x**	**x**	**x**	Core program files.
Spell Checker	**x**	**x**	**x**	Spell-checking engine for all languages.

* C– Notes client, D– Domino Designer, A– Domino Administrator

** A boldface entry indicates that the component is selected by default.

You may notice that the Change button becomes active when a component is highlighted in the customization screen. Some of the client components also have a set of subcomponents that can be selected for even further customization. If the Change button is active, clicking it will display the subcomponent customization screen, shown in Figure A.7. Table A.2 lists all of the components, the applicable client, and the available subcomponents.

FIGURE A.7

The Select Sub-Component screen

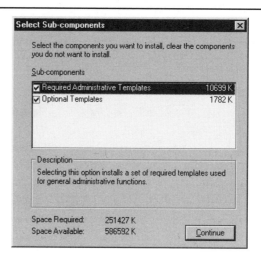

TABLE A.2: COMPONENTS AND SUBCOMPONENTS

Component	Client Type			Subcomponent
	C	**D**	**A***	
Common Data	x	x	x**	Required administrative templates
	x	**x**	**x**	Optional templates
Data Files	**x**	**x**	**x**	Required data files
	x	**x**	**x**	Modem script commands
	x	**x**	**x**	Optional data files
	x	**x**	**x**	Readme file
DECS	x	**x**	**x**	DECS documentation
	x	**x**	**x**	DECS programs
Administration Client				N/A
Domino Designer				N/A
Domino Web Services	x	**x**	x	Domino Web Services data
	x	**x**	x	Program files

Continued ▌▶

TABLE A.2: COMPONENTS AND SUBCOMPONENTS (CONTINUED)			
Component	**Client Type**		**Subcomponent**
Help	**x** **x** x		Administration guided tour
	x **x** x		Designer guided tour
	x x **x**		Administration Help
	x x x		Client Help
	x **x** x		Designer Help
Migration Tools	x x x		ccMail client migration tools
	x x x		Calendar client migration tools
	x x x		Eudora client migration tools
	x x x		Organizer migration tools
	x x x		Groupwise4 Admin Migration
Notes Minder			N/A
Notes Program Files	**x** **x** **x**		External viewers
	x **x** **x**		Program files
	x **x** **x**		Required program files
	x **x** **x**		Java support
	x **x** **x**		JIT debugger
Spell Checker	x x x		International dictionaries
	x x x		Chinese spell checker
	x **x** **x**		English dictionaries

* C– Notes client, D– Domino Designer, A– Domino Administrator

** A boldface entry indicates that the component is selected by default.

Once you have selected all of the components you wish to install, click the Next button to continue with the installation.

The Program Folder

In the next installation screen that displays, you can decide where to place the Notes application icons. By default, the installation program will create a program folder named Lotus Applications. To change the folder destination, just type a new folder name in the Program Folders field. You can also select an existing folder from the Existing Folders list box.

Once you have entered or selected the program folder, click the Next button to continue with the installation. Now the setup program will begin copying the Notes files onto your computer. This is the longest part of the installation process. A percentage status bar will reflect the installation's progress.

When all of the files have been copied over, the Lotus Product Registration screen will display. You can skip this part for now (you will be reminded later) by clicking the Exit button on the screen. If you decide to fill out the form, you'll have the option of submitting it via the Internet, printing it out and faxing it to Lotus, or registering by phone. Once you have finished processing all of the screens, a thank you screen will appear.

Starting Lotus Notes

The Notes product is now installed, but there is still one more step that needs to be performed. To complete the installation process, you need to start the Notes client. Start the program by selecting the Lotus Notes icon from the program group you specified during the installation.

Completing the Notes R5 Installation

When the Notes client starts, the program will recognize that a new version has been installed. This will kick off a series of screens and questions that will help you define your Notes environment. It doesn't matter whether you've upgraded or installed from scratch, you'll still need to go through the series of screens and answer the questions. It's a simple process, and if you don't know the answer to a question, just skip it (or answer No); you can come back to it later (you can also change your answers).

You'll go through a series of questions asking how you want to use the Notes client. Your answers to the questions will determine if further information needs to be entered. With that in mind, let's get started.

Connecting to a Domino Server

As shown in Figure A.8, the first question you'll need to answer is whether or not you are going to connect to a Domino server. There are only two options available: I Want to Connect to a Domino Server and I Don't Want to Connect to a Domino Server. This seems pretty straightforward, but to have the installation process set up your client correctly, you must have access to a server (if you intend to use a Domino server). If you have access to the Domino server, select the first option and click the Next button. If you don't, just select the second option and proceed with the installation by clicking the Next button. If you have no intention of connecting to a Domino server, select the second option and click the Next button. In either case, you can skip the remaining portion of this section and go directly to "Who Are You?"

FIGURE A.8

*Do you want access to
a Domino server
configuration?*

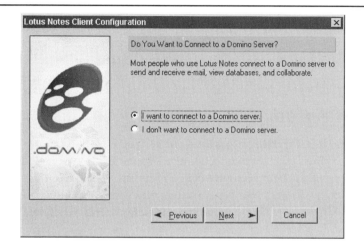

If you have access to a Domino server and selected the first option, the next screen to appear will be one in which you can choose the type of connection you want to install for accessing the Domino server. There are three options available, as shown in Figure A.9 (the third option is a combination of the first and the second). You can either connect to the server using a local area network (LAN) connection (the first option), a phone connection (the second option), or both (the third option).

FIGURE A.9

*How will you connect
to the domino server?*

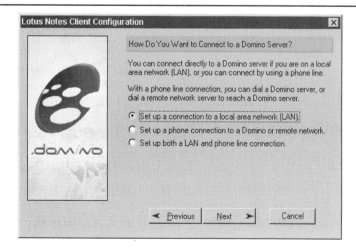

If you elected to connect to the server using a LAN connection, the next screen to appear will prompt you for the name of the Domino server. If you will be using a phone connection, a screen will appear asking for the type of phone connection (directly to the Domino server, through a network server, or both) and then prompting you for the name of the Domino server. If you are unsure of the name for the Domino server, ask your Domino administrator. If you enter an incorrect server name, another installation screen will appear telling you that the server could not be found. Again, your Domino administrator should supply you with this information. Once you've completed this step, the installation program will need to know who you are.

Who Are You?

In this step of the installation process, you'll need to supply either a Notes ID (or User ID) or enter your username. If you are upgrading from a previous version of Notes, you'll probably want to supply your current Notes ID. Just click the Browse button and select the location of your Notes ID (typically, your Notes ID is in the Notes Data folder or on a floppy disk). If you are installing a new version of Notes, type in your username. The first time you connect to the Domino server, you will be prompted to enter your Notes password, and your username will be used for verification. If you are using a Notes ID as your identity, you will be prompted to enter your Notes password when you click the Next button.

After you click the Next button, you will have completed the LAN portion of the Notes installation. If you elected to not connect to a Domino server, you'll see one more screen asking if you want to set up a remote connection to a remote network server. In either case, the Domino-related installation information is complete. The next section deals with setting up the Notes client for Internet access.

Installing Internet Access

As we said in the first few chapters of this book, the Notes client is not just for accessing Domino servers anymore. You can use the Notes client for Internet mail and newsgroup access as well. For the Notes client to send and retrieve mail and also allow you to browse Internet newsgroups, you'll need to supply some basic information.

Internet Mail

If you have an Internet mail account, you can use the Notes client for both your Domino (Notes) mail and your Internet mail. The next series of screens deal only with accessing your Internet mail account. To set up the Notes client properly, you need your e-mail address, your Internet mail provider's Simple Mail Transfer Protocol (SMTP) server name, your Internet mail provider's Post Office Protocol (POP) or Internet Message Access Protocol (IMAP) server name, and your Internet mail account username and password.

If you're not sure what the answers to these questions are, you can get them from your Internet Service Provider (ISP). Once you've entered the information on the Internet mail installation screens, you'll be asked if you would like to access newsgroups via a news server.

Newsgroups

If you decide that you would like to set up access to a newsgroup server, you will need to know the name of the server. You can get that information from either your ISP or, in some cases, your Domino administrator. You can also come back later and configure Notes to access newsgroups.

Internet Directory Server

Another option you can install will give you the ability to use the Lightweight Directory Access Protocol (LDAP) to search for people. The address book within the Notes client supports LDAP, which allows you to search other Internet directory services. By default, the Notes installation routine will add a few of the more common LDAP servers automatically, such as Bigfoot and Four11. You can get the LDAP server names from either your ISP or your Domino administrator.

Internet Connection

The final step is to let Notes know how you would like to access your Internet mail or newsgroup. You can elect to use your existing LAN connection or dial your ISP. If you decide to dial your ISP, a screen will prompt you to select the correct dial-up entry.

Congratulations

Finally, a Congratulations screen appears; you have finished answering all the questions the program needs to configure your Notes client correctly. Once you click the Finish button, Notes will begin the configuration process. When the process is complete, a message box telling you that the Notes setup has completed will display.

Upgrading Notes

For those of you who are upgrading from previous versions of Notes, we would like to mention what entries the installation process has affected. The most important impact is that your notes.ini file has now been moved from your Windows folder to the program folder in which Notes is installed. Your Windows Registry has also been altered (now there is an entry for Notes 5). The installation process also upgrades the Notes program executables in the Notes program folder and the Notes templates in the Notes Data folder.

When Notes is initially launched and you have completed answering all of the installation questions, the final portion of the upgrade takes place. Your desktop.dsk file has been copied to desktop5.dsk. The bookmarks.nsf and headlines.nsf files have also been automatically created. The bookmarks.nsf file is configured based on the contents of your desktop.dsk file, so you have not lost your desktop settings. The names.nsf design has been automatically updated for the new R5 template along with the perweb.nsf database (if you had one). Both the mail.box and smtp.box databases are also replaced. The upgrade process is quite seamless and occurs without the loss of any of your settings.

 WARNING Your mail database design is not automatically upgraded. This must be done manually.

The Dangers of Old Code

If you're one of those ambitious souls who played with the beta releases of Notes 5, you've already seen in-progress versions of many of the features we're discussing here. Your computer has seen it, too, and that can be a problem. Previous installations of Notes, including installations of the early R5 betas, can leave traces in your system. Usually, that's OK. In fact, it's usually exactly what you want. If you're upgrading an existing installation of Notes, you probably want your Notes client to talk to the same server, keep using the same ID file, and so on. Lotus's installers have historically been very good about keeping the settings you probably do want while getting rid of obsolete DLL files and executables, and if you're coming to version 5 from one of the flavors of version 4, you have nothing to worry about. However, if you're coming from a beta release of Notes 5, there may be problems in your notes.ini file, which isn't replaced when you upgrade.

For example, one feature available in some of the betas was an option to make deletions from your Sent folder easier. You could set your client so that Notes would immediately get rid of documents "marked" for deletion in your Sent folder without stopping for confirmation; once you pressed the Delete key or dragged documents into the trash, they were gone. If you selected that setting, it left a line in your notes.ini (DeleteFromSent=1). Although the released version of Notes 5 makes it very difficult to turn that setting on, it may still be there in your notes.ini file, possibly causing Notes to delete documents before you actually want them gone. If you're installing Notes 5 over a beta release, it's a good idea to completely uninstall the beta version and throw away the notes.ini file. If you've already installed Notes 5 over a beta version of Notes 5 and documents unexpectedly vanish from your Sent folder, you might want to hunt for that line and delete it.

APPENDIX B

Internal and Predefined Notes Fields

Some Notes documents contain internal and predefined fields that are not always obvious to the developer. Some of these fields may be the result of setting certain form properties (such as versioning), and others may be based on some action that occurs (such as creating a Response document or attaching a file). In either case, it is best that you have a good understanding of these fields and how Notes uses their values.

Internal Fields

Most internal fields that Notes generates automatically begin with $ (but not all of them). However, not every field that begins with $ is an internal field. Because many of these fields may be hidden, you may not even know that they exist in a document unless you view the document's properties. To view all the fields for a document, open a Notes database and select a document from a view. Choose File ➤ Document Properties to display the Document Properties InfoBox. The left side of the Fields tab (the second tab from the left), displays a list box containing all the fields on the document. When you select (or highlight) one of the fields, all of the information for the field (including its value) is displayed on the right. All of the fields that begin with $ are listed first. Table B.1 lists the most common internal fields that you'll come across when you develop Notes applications.

TABLE B.1: INTERNAL NOTES FIELDS	
Field Name	**Description**
Form	Contains the name of the form that was used to create the document or the most recent form used to save the document.
Posted Date	Displays the date and time the document was mailed.
$Anonymous	Indicates that the form has been set as an Anonymous form (the Anonymous Form property has been selected on the Basics tab of the Form Properties InfoBox). A value of 1 indicates that the form is anonymous and will not contain an $UpdatedBy field.
$File	Indicates that an attachment is contained in the document (each $File field represents one attachment).
$Links	Indicates that the document contains links (each link is stored as an individual entry in one $Links field).
$Readers	Contains a list of authorized readers. This field is typically created by setting security for authorized readers on the form.

Continued ▌▶

TABLE B.1: INTERNAL NOTES FIELDS (CONTINUED)	
Field Name	**Description**
$Revisions	Contains the date and time of each editing session.
$Title, $Info, $WindowTitle, $Body	Identify a document in which a form is stored. The form is stored in the document by setting the Store Form in Document property on the Basics tab of the Form Properties InfoBox.
$UpdatedBy	Contains the document authors and editors from each editing session.

 WARNING Be very careful when accessing internal fields. You can access the $ fields by using any one of the Notes programming languages, but if you change the value of an internal field, you could corrupt the document.

Predefined Fields

The predefined Notes fields are a bit different. These types of fields have inherent capabilities that do not require any programming. They are not automatically generated by Notes; instead, they are placed on the form by the developer. Notes recognizes that these special fields are for a specific purpose. Table B.2 lists the more common predefined Notes fields used by application developers.

TABLE B.2: PREDEFINED NOTES FIELDS	
Field Name	**Description**
$VersionOpt	Controls version tracking for the document. The field can contain the following values:
	0 No versioning.
	1 New versions become responses when saved with File ➤ Save as New Version.
	2 New versions automatically become responses when saved.

Continued ▌▶

TABLE B.2: PREDEFINED NOTES FIELDS (CONTINUED)

Field Name	Description
	3 Prior versions become responses when saved with File ➢ Save as New Version.
	4 Prior versions automatically become responses when saved.
	5 New versions become siblings when saved with File ➢ Save as New Version.
	6 New versions automatically become siblings when saved.
FolderOption	Puts new documents in a folder. A value of 1 prompts the user to select a folder; a value of 2 saves the document to the current folder.
BlindCopyTo	Sends a blind copy to those listed in the field, which can be a person, group, or mail-in database.
CopyTo	Sends a copy to those listed in the field, which can be a person, group, or mail-in database.
SendTo	Sends mail to those listed in the field, which can be a person, group, or mail-in database. This is required for all forms that mail documents.
MailOptions	Automatically mails the document when a value of 1 is specified.
$AutoSpell	Automatically spell-checks the document before it is mailed when a value of 1 is specified.
Encrypt	Encrypts mailed documents when a value of 1 is specified.
Sign	Adds an electronic signature of the creator to the document when a value of 1 is specified.
DeliveryPriority	Delivers mail as high (H), normal (N), or low (L) priority.
DeliveryReport	Returns a report when mail is delivered to the mail recipient.
ReturnReceipt	Returns a receipt when the user reads the mail message.
SaveOptions	Controls whether or not a document is saved. When a value of 1 is specified, the document is saved; when a value of 0 is specified, the document is not saved.
$$ViewBody	Contains the name of a view to embed (this is for backward compatibility); only applicable in Web applications.
$$ViewList	Displays a Folder pane (this is for backward compatibility); only applicable in Web applications.
$$NavigatorBody	Contains the name of a Navigator to embed (this is for backward compatibility); only applicable in Web applications.

Continued

	TABLE B.2: PREDEFINED NOTES FIELDS (CONTINUED)
Field Name	**Description**
$GroupScheduleRefreshMode	Contains a numeric value specifying the frequency for refreshing an embedded group scheduling control.
$GroupScheduleShowLegend	Displays the color legend for an embedded group scheduling control when a value of 1 is specified.
$ChargeRead	Creates a billing record whenever a user opens a document.
$ChargeWrite	Creates a billing record whenever a user creates, copies, edits, or saves a document.
Categories	Contains the list of categories for a document.
HTML	Passes HTML directly to the server.
$$HTMLHead	Passes HTML information that is to be placed between the <HTML> and </HTML> head tags.
$$Return	After a Web user submits a document, overrides the default confirmation when a customized confirmation is specified in this computed field.

Metadata Fields

One new feature in Notes R5 is the ability to include metadata about a document. Metadata is information that will allow people to find and sort documents in an efficient manner. To input metadata for a document, you must use the Notes client and access the Meta tab of the Document Properties InfoBox. You can enter the title, creator, keywords, description, and type for any document. The data is published to the Domino Catalog, where the metadata then becomes a link to the document. Metadata is also stored within the documents by using the metadata fields described in Table B.3.

	TABLE B.3: NOTES METADATA FIELDS
Field Name	**Description**
$Title	Contains the title of the document. This field may already be populated for you by Notes.
$Creator	Contains the name of the person who created the document. This field may already be populated for you by Notes.

Continued ▶

TABLE B.3: NOTES METADATA FIELDS (CONTINUED)

Field Name	Description
$Categories	Contains the keywords specified on the Meta tab; the keywords help in categorizing the documents.
$Description	Contains additional information about the document.
$Type	Contains the type of document.

 NOTE If your organization uses a Domain Catalog, you can post the metadata to it.

INDEX

Note to the Reader: Throughout this index **boldfaced** page numbers indicate primary discussions of a topic. *Italicized* page numbers indicate illustrations.